In this compelling study of international aluminium cartels, Dr Bertilorenzi deploys his fine grained analysis of a wide coverage of the key sources to explore the political economy of cartelization. The International Aluminium Cartel makes a significant contribution to discussions of varieties of capitalism. It will be read with equal profit by academics and students in humanities and social science faculties, as well as business and management schools alike. Policymakers and regulators will also profit from it.

Andrew Perchard, *Associate Professor, University of Strathclyde, UK*

Scholars have for long regarded the aluminium industry as the prime evidence of cartelization in the 20th century. Bertilorenzi offers a new insight and new information about the inducement, the modus operandi and the disintegration of the various cartels with a well-structured and accessible style. I strongly recommend it.

Hans Otto Frøland, *Professor, The Norwegian University of Science and Technology, Norway*

T0384233

# The International Aluminium Cartel, 1886–1978

The Business and Politics of a Cooperative Industrial Institution

Aluminium was one of the most cartelised industries in the international economic panorama of the twentieth century. Born following the discovery of electrolytic smelting process in 1886, this industry, even in its infancy, established a cartel which characterised its history until nearly 1980. Managers of the aluminium industry from various historical eras and countries shared the same vision about the development of their industry: to keep prices as stable as possible in order to encourage expansions and to provide return on investments. Price instability, which characterised the trade of other commodities, was unknown to the aluminium industry.

This book neither argues that cartels are fundamentally evil, nor attempts to demonstrate that cartels are optimal business organisations. It instead provides an in-depth and frank analysis of the internal working of these industrial organisations and of the interplay between cartels and political powers and institutions. *The International Aluminium Cartel* offers explanations for the construction and collapse of cartels, descriptions of their operations and an historical interpretation of their experiences.

Incorporating information gleaned from a unique collection of private and public archives from several countries, this unique study will appeal to a wide variety of readers, including academics interested in industrial and business history.

**Marco Bertilorenzi** is a Researcher at the Institut d'histoire moderne et contemporaine (Equipe d'histoire des techniques), Université Paris I Panthéon-Sorbonne.

# Routledge International Studies in Business History

Series editors: Jeffrey Fear
and
Christina Lubinski

# The International Aluminium Cartel, 1886–1978

The Business and Politics of a Cooperative Industrial Institution

Marco Bertilorenzi

Routledge
Taylor & Francis Group

LONDON AND NEW YORK

First published 2016 by Routledge

2 Park Square, Milton Park, Abingdon, Oxfordshire OX14 4RN
711 Third Avenue, New York, NY 10017

*Routledge is an imprint of the Taylor & Francis Group, an informa business*

First issued in paperback 2018

*British Library Cataloguing in Publication Data*
A catalogue record for this book is available from the British Library

*Library of Congress Cataloging-in-Publication Data*
Bertilorenzi, Marco, author.
The international aluminium cartel, 1886-1978 : the business and politics
of a cooperative industrial institution / Marco Bertilorenzi.
  pages cm. – (Routledge international studies in business history)
  Includes bibliographical references and index.
  1. Aluminum industry and trade–History. 2. Cartels–History. I. Title.
  HD9539.A62B47 2016
  338.8'876697220904–dc23                                    2015013235

ISBN: 978-0-415-74254-2 (hbk)
ISBN: 978-1-138-34020-6 (pbk)

Typeset in Bembo
by Wearset Ltd, Boldon, Tyne and Wear

To Patricia, Gemma, and Fifi

# Contents

xii   *Contents*

# Figures

# Tables

# Acknowledgements

This book is the outcome of many years of research. Started in 2006 as a PhD 'co-tutelle' project about the international aluminium cartels from 1886 to 1945 at the Università degli Studi di Firenze and at the Université Paris Sorbonne,[1] it benefited afterwards from two post-doctoral positions held at Université Paris-Sorbonne and at Aix-Marseille Université between 2010 and 2013, granted by the French National Research Agency (ANR) 'CréAlu – Creation and Aluminium'. During this period, my research benefited from the unique intellectual environments of these institutions and of the frequency of contact with the scholars who directed and supervised my works, to whom I would like to address my warmest acknowledgements. Luciano Segreto, at Università degli Studi di Firenze, was my mentor during my PhD and he continued to follow and comment on my research with constant but friendly criticisms also afterwards. Dominique Barjot, in his double role of PhD mentor at Paris-Sorbonne and of supervisor during a first post-doctoral position, has always been generous in providing advice and comment that allowed me to successfully advance in this research. Philippe Mioche, at Aix-Marseille Université, proved to be a kind of 'third' mentor for me, who showed a real interest towards my research and helped in improving it reading through this manuscript and commenting on significant parts of my arguments in his twofold expertise of business historian and of expert in European construction history. A special thanks is also for Gian Carlo Falco, of the Università of Pisa, who was my MB supervisor before starting my PhD project: he taught me not only economic history for the first time, but he also initiated me to the research.

During this period, several lucky encounters contributed to craft my research and to reshape the heuristic approaches of my study. Hoping not to forget anybody, I would like to thank here the several scholars that, reading my papers or attending the presentations of my research, provided me with valuable insights: Adoracion Alvaro-Moya, Franco Amatori, Wolfram Bayer, Bram Bouwens, David Burigana, Erik Bussière, Ludovic Cailluet, Valerio Cerretano, Andrea Colli, Alain Cortat, Joost Dankers, Olivier Dard, Pierre-Yves Donzé, Nadine Dubruc, Clotilde Druelle-Korn, Richard Emptoz, Susanna Fellmann, Jeffrey Fear, Hans Otto Frøland, Carlo Fumian, Anne-Françoise Garçon, Sébastian Goex, Margaret Graham, Florence Hachez-Leroy, Leslie Hannah, Adrian Knoepfli, Niklas Jensen-Eriksen, Pierre Lanthier, Margaret Levenstein, Michel Margairaz, Margrit Müller,

Carmine Nappi, Andrew Perchard, Philippe Petitpas, Anne Pezet, Thierry Renaux, Christophe Reveillard, Neill Rollings, David and Kerrie Round, Pal Sandvik, Harm Schröter, Martin Shanahan, Jonathan Silberstein-Loeb, Giuseppe Telesca, Paul Thomes, Laurent Tissot, Xiang Wang, and Laurent Warlouzet. This study would never be published without the direct implication and the encouragement of Ray Stokes and Matthias Kipping, the former editors of Routledge's series 'International Studies in Business History', who supported my proposal since a very early stage, helping me in crafting the general construction of this study and showed me a real interest. I acknowledge also Taylor & Francis for the permission to republish here some parts of the article of mine 'Business, Finance, and Politics: The Rise and Fall of the International Aluminium Cartels, 1914–1945', already published in *Business History*, and to Routledge's editorial board members who worked with me during the preparation of this manuscript: Brianna Ascher, Jabari Legendre, Sally Quinn, Laura Stearns, David Varley, and Lauren Verity. Carlotta Montefiori, who I would like to thank here, has helped me during the revision of my writing and helping me with some translations.

The Institut pour l'Histoire de l'Aluminium deserves a special mention in these acknowledgements. This institution has never ceased to materially and immaterially support my research about an unconventional, and perhaps uncomfortable, subject. Not only has the IHA generously supported my research with grants and funds during and after my PhD, IHA's documents represented for me a real goldmine, even though it has not been the sole source of this research. The liberal way in which I was provided access to them allowed me to come across conventional beliefs about the history of aluminium cartelisation and to explore this history until very recent periods. The locals of IHA have been a kind of second home for a long period, during which I did not only learn a lot of things about aluminium, but I also started lasting and valuable friendships. In particular, I would like to thank Maurice Laparra, IHA's president, Ivan Grinberg, IHA's general secretary, Jenny Piquet, IHA's archivist, Patricia Helie, IHA's assistant, and the researchers that served as scientific secretaries of this institution during my research (in chronological order): Mauve Carbonell, Claire Leymonerie, and Yves Tesson. My thanks are also to Simon Fieschi who was one of my best encounters at IHA. My sincere acknowledgments are also to the various archivists from about 35 institutions who stoically disclosed key documents at my request. In particular, a special thanks is for Andrea Gernich, at the Mannheim Technoseum, Bartolomeo Lucido, at Zurich Rio-Tinto ALCAN holding, David Grinnel and Alexis Maclin at the Pittsburgh Heinz History Center, Matthias Wiessmann at the Basel Schweizerische Wirtschaftarchiv, Ute Mayer at the Darmstadt Hessisches Wirtschaftsarchiv, Laura Gilmore Stoner at the Virginia Historical Society in Richmond, VA, and Jan-Anno Schuur at OECD archives in Paris. I would like to thank also Patrick de Schrynmakers, the former general secretary of the European Aluminium Association, who provided me a free and very liberal access to the historical archives of the association. A special thanks is also for Lee Bray, mineral commodity specialist of the US Geological Survey.

A special acknowledgement also goes to my parents, Antonella and Michele, to my brother Enrico, and to my grandmother Anna, for always supporting me in my choices and believing in my capacities. I am sure that they will be proud of this big achievement.

Finally, my warmest and heartfelt thanks goes to the person who shared her life with me and who supported me during the difficulties of beginning an academic life, Patricia. She gifted me of a true love, which I hope to have refilled even during the busy period that characterised the long years of archive research and the last period of preparation of this manuscript. Thanks to her, I built up not only – I hope so – solid research, but also a splendid family that was recently gifted of a wonderful daughter, Gemma, and of a lunatic but loyal dog, Fifi. To Gemma, Patricia, and also to Fifi is dedicated this volume. As usual, I am solely responsible for all mistakes or imprecisions.

## Note

1 Marco Bertilorenzi, *Il controllo della sovrapproduzione. I cartelli internazionali nell'industria dell'alluminio in prospettiva storica (1886–1945): Le contrôle de la surproduction. Les cartels internationaux dans l'industrie de l'aluminium en perspective historique (1886–1945).* PhD thesis, Università degli Studi di Firenze & Université Paris-Sorbonne, 2010.

# Note on archive sources

This research was possible thanks to thorough archival research in many countries. Roughly, around 30 archives were explored (see list of abbreviations), which belong to four different types of sources.

First, taken together, several producers' corporate archives provided full access to internal cartel records during the whole period. In particular, documents about the period 1890s to 1945 are very substantial, and provided a basis for a comprehensive study of the inner working of cartels, the interplay of firms, and their links with other actors. These sources show how cartels were a dominant factor in the establishment of firms' strategies: to reach a good position within the cartel framework was a decisive entrepreneurial action. Furthermore, the cartels produced also their own materials, thanks to ad hoc structures, which firms used constantly to run their strategies: statistic surveys, joint R&D committees, guidelines for expansions, and financial devices for international trade. This documentation includes also minutes of meetings, cartel working notes, correspondence, and documents related to joint R&D agencies. For the period from the late 1920s to the end of the 1930s, complete verbatim transcripts of speeches during cartel meetings were also found, allowing a more explicit study of each firm's positions in the interplay. Documents for the following period (1945–1978) allow the reconstruction of an impressive number of meetings and conferences dedicated to discussing common policies or to setting up agreements. In this case, minutes of meetings, notes on agreements, and correspondence were also used. Also the documents coming from the trade association of aluminium industry (both in Europe and in the United States) were decisive to understand the nature of the interplay of the producers and of their international model of governance.

Second, public archives provided information in particular on aluminium industry regulations. In many cases, governments either endorsed or tolerated international cartel schemes and national participation in these international schemes. Yet, governmental actions challenged the authority of the international cartel as soon as aluminium was recognised as a key war-related material, leading to the clash of different visions for the regulation of this industry. Antitrust agencies' documents, in many cases, made up for things missing from private archives. Legal authorities not only explored the working of cartels and thought about economic solutions for cartelisation; they also collected in many cases a lot of evidence of cartel activities and behaviour from firms' archives during their trials and investigations.

Third, archives of banks and financial backers also represent an important source for this study. This is because cartels in the aluminium industry were reshaped during the 1930s and the 1970s because of financial considerations, which were in turn linked to the establishment of new tools for financing the excessive accumulation of inventories. In these cases, firms received substantial financial facilities from banking consortia, whose vision shaped the strategies undertaken by producers.

Fourth, aluminium often represented a model for the broader cartel move-ment and for regulatory issues carried out by international institutions. That is reflected in the availability of an important quantity of documentary evidence in the archives of international institutions such as the United Nations, OECD, European Commission, and International Chamber of Commerce. These other sources not only completed the institutional side of this study; they allow also comparisons of solutions adopted in the aluminium industry with those adopted in other industries during the same periods.

# Abbreviations

## Archives and centres of documentation

| | |
|---|---|
| ABI | Brookings Institution Archive – Washington DC, United States of America, Louis Marlio Personal Papers |
| ACL | Archives du Crédit Agricole, Crédit Lyonnais Documents – Paris, France |
| AEMC | Archivio Edison-Montecatini – Milan, Italy |
| AEPAA | Archives of the European Primary Aluminium Association – Brussels, Belgium |
| AGR2 | Archives Générales du Royaume, Depot Joseph Cuvelier – Brussels, Belgium. Documents of Tracionnels and Société Générale de Belgique |
| AHCE | Archives Historiques de la Commission Européenne – Brussels, Belgium |
| AHMAE | Archives historiques du Ministrère des affaires etrangères – Paris, France |
| AHSG | Archives historiques de la Société Générale – Paris, France |
| ALSE | Archives of the London School of Economics – London, United Kingdom. Documents Siegmund W. Warburg |
| AN | Archives Nationales – Paris, France |
| AOECD | Archives Organisation for Economic Cooperation and Development – Paris, France. Documents of OECD and OEEC |
| ASBCI | Archivio Storico Banca Intesa San-Paolo, Documents Banca Commerciale Italiana – Milan, Italy |
| ASBI | Archivio Storico Banca d'Italia – Rome, Italy |
| ASIRI | Archivio Storico Istituto per la Ricostruzione Industriale – Rome, Italy |
| ATR | Archivio Thaon de Revel, Fondazione Luigi Einaudi, Turin, Italy |
| BCM | Bibliothèque Cujas, Manuscript Division – Paris, France. Documents of UN and UNCTAD |
| BEA | Bank of England Archives – London, United Kingdom. |
| CLH | Commons and Lords Hansard – available at http://hansard.millbanksystems.com/ |
| HHC | Heinz History Center – Pittsburgh, United States of America. Documents of ALCOA |

| HWA | Hessische Wirtschaftsarchiv – Darmstadt, Germany. Documents of Metallgesellschaft |
| IHA | Institut pour l'histoire de l'aluminium – Paris, France. Documents of Pechiney and its forerunners |
| JTA | Jersey Trust Archive – Saint-Helier, Jersey Islands |
| NARA | National Archives and Records Administration – College Park, United States of America |
| NARA I | National Archives and Records Administration, Legislative Papers – Washington DC, United States of America |
| OCA | Oberlin College Archives – Oberlin, United States of America. Documents of Charles Martin Hall |
| RPA | Rio Tinto, ex-Pechiney Archives – Paris, France. Documents of Pechiney, of its forerunners, and of the Aluminium-Association (1901–1930), of Alliance Aluminium Compagnie (1931–1955) and of the 'Club' (1953–1969) |
| RZA | Rio Tinto Holding, ex-Alusuisse Archives – Zurich, Switzerland. Documents of SMG, AIAG and Alusuisse |
| SWA | Schweizerische Wirtschaftsarchiv – Basel, Switzerland |
| TMA | Technoseum Mannheim Archives – Mannheim, Germany. Documents of AIAG (1887–1915) and of Aluminium-Association (1901–1921) |
| TNA | The National Archives, Kew Garden – London, United Kingdom |
| UGD | University of Glasgow Documents – Glasgow, United Kingdom. Documents of BACO |
| UNA | United Nations Archives – Geneva, Switzerland. Documents UN and League of Nations |
| VHS | Virginia Historical Society – Richmond, United States of America. Documents of Reynolds Metals Company |
| ZBW | Zentral Bibliothek für Wirtschaftswissenschaften – Kiel, Germany. Statistical yearbooks of Metallgesellschaft and other printed documents of the international metal traders, including Metal Bulletin |

## Enterprises and organisations

| AA | Aluminium-Association |
| AAA | American Aluminum Association |
| AAC | Alliance Aluminium Compagnie |
| AAH | Alliance Aluminium Holding |
| AE | Aluminio Espagnol |
| AEF | Afrique Equatoriale Française |
| AEG | Allgemeine Elektrizität Gesellschaft |
| AF | Aluminium français |
| AFC | Compagnie des produits chimiques et électrométallurgiques d'Alais, Froges et Camargue |
| AFCO | Aluminium Foils Conference |

| | |
|---|---|
| AFRAL | Société Européenne pour l'Etude de l'Industrie de l'Aluminium en Afrique |
| AIAB | Association Internationale de l'Aluminium Brut |
| AIAG | Aluminium Industrie Aktiengesellschaft |
| AIC | Aluminium International Company |
| ALCAN | Aluminium Company of Canada |
| ALCOA | Aluminum Company of America |
| ALCOR | Aluminium Corporation Ltd. |
| ALEUR | Aluminium Européen |
| ALTED | Aluminium Limited |
| ALUCOR | Aluminium Corporation Ltd. |
| ALUGUI | Aluminium Guinée |
| ANCO | Anglo-Norwegian Aluminium Corporation Ltd. |
| AOF | Afrique Occidentale Française |
| APAIC | Aluminium Producers Industry Advisory Committee |
| ASA | Alluminio Società Anomina |
| ASCO | Auminium Supply Company Ltd. |
| ASO | Aluminium du Sud-Ouest |
| AVG | Aluminium-Verkaufs Gesellschaft |
| AWC | Aluminium World Council |
| AZ | Aluminium Zentrale |
| BACO | British Aluminium Company |
| BAW | Bayerische Aluminium Werke |
| BEW | Board of Economic Warfare |
| BIA | Bureau International de l'Aluminium |
| BIEP | Bureau International de Propaganda et Reinsignements |
| BMTC | Bausch Machine Tool Co. |
| BT | Bauxit Trust |
| CECA | European Coal and Steel Community |
| CET | Common External Tariff |
| CFGE | Chemische Fabrik Griesheim Elektron |
| CIDA | Centre pour le developpement de l'industrie de l'aluminium |
| COBEAL | Compagnie Belge de l'Aluminium |
| DG IV | Direction of the Concurrenece, of the European Economic Commission |
| DNN | Det Norsk Nitrid |
| DPC | Defense Plant Corporation |
| EAF | European Aluminium Federation |
| EC | Société d'Electrochimie |
| ECSC | European Coal and Steel Community |
| EEC | European Economic Community |
| EIA | Entente Internationale de l'Acier |
| EMSE | Société Electrométallurgique du Sud-Est |
| EPAA | European Primary Aluminium Association |
| EURAL | Association Européenne de l'Aluminium Brut |
| EWAA | European Wrought Aluminium Association |

| | |
|---|---|
| FAAD | Fabrika Aluminiuma A.D. |
| FTC | Federal Trade Commission |
| GATT | General Agreement on Trade and Tariffs |
| GIRA | Groupement d'Importation et de Repartition de l'Aluminium |
| IAMB | Inter-Allied Munitions Board |
| IBA | International Bauxite Association |
| IBRD | International Bank for Reconstruction and Development |
| IFTRA | International Fair Trade Practice Rules Administration for Primary Aluminium |
| INA | Industria Nazionale Alluminio |
| IPAI | International Primary Aluminium Institute |
| ISC | International Steel Cartel |
| ISCO | International Selling Corporation |
| ITO | International Trade Organisation |
| KMAG | Kriegsmetall AG |
| KRA | Kriegsrohstoffabteilung |
| LLL | Lavorazione Leghe Leggere |
| LME | London Metal Exchange |
| LoN | League of Nations |
| MAP | Ministry of Air Production |
| MG | Metallgesellschaft |
| NACO | Northern Aluminium Company |
| NCPC | North Carolina Power Company |
| OEA | Organisation Européenne des Affineurs |
| OECD | Organisation for Economic Co-operation and Development |
| OEEC | Organisation for the European Economic Cooperation |
| PCAC | Produits Chimiques d'Alais et de la Camargue |
| PRC | Pittsburgh Reduction Company |
| PTL | Pittsburgh Testing Laboratory |
| PYR | Société des Produits Electrochimiques et Electrométallurgiques des Pyrénées |
| RFC | Reconstruction Finance Corporation |
| RMC | Reynolds Metals Company |
| RTZ | Riotinto Zinc Pillar LTD |
| RWE | Rheinisch-Westfälisches Elektrizitätswerk AG |
| SACO | Southern Aluminum Company |
| SARV | Société des Forces Motrices de l'Avre |
| SAVA | Società Anonima Veneta Alluminio |
| SBA | Syndicat Belge de l'Aluminium |
| SEMF | Société Electrométallurgique Française |
| SFFA | Syndicat des Fabricants Français d'Aluminium |
| SFIA | Société Française pour l'Industrie de l'Aluminium |
| SGB | Société Générale de Belgique |
| SGN | Société Générale des Nitrures |
| SGW | Siegmund George Warburg & Co. Ltd. |
| SIA | Società Italiana Allumina |

| | |
|---|---|
| SIAAM | Société Industrielle de l'Aluminium et des Alliages Métalliques |
| SIAP | Société Industrielle de l'Alumine Pure |
| SIC | Società Idroelettrica del Cismon |
| SIDA | Società dell'Alluminio Italiano |
| SIFA | Società Italiana per la Fabbricazione e la Lavorazione dell'Alluminio |
| SMG | Schweizerische Metallurgische Gesellschaft |
| SNAL | Società Nazionale Alluminio |
| SNN | Société norvégienne des nitrures. |
| SSW | Siemens Schuckert Werke |
| SWACO | South-Walsh Aluminium Co. Ltd. |
| TNEC | Temporary National Economic Committee |
| USAMC | United States Aluminium Metal Company |
| VAW | Vereinigte Aluminium Werke |
| VIAG | Vereinigte Industrieunternehmungen Aktiengesellschaft |
| VLW | Vereinigte Leichtmetall Werke |
| VMR | Vereinigte Metallwerke Ranshofen-Berndorf |
| WMB | War Munitions Board |

# Introduction

At the annual round-table of the American Metal Market Forum of 1978, the audience of journalists asked Ian Forster, the chairman of the London Metal Exchange (LME) committee, if any link existed between the legal action of the European Commission and the concomitant launching of a futures market for aluminium at LME. This question rose from the news about a forthcoming contract for aluminium, which provoked much surprise amongst the market analysts. Actually, this operation was announced a few days after the delivery of the dossier of objections that the European antitrust authorities formulated against all the European aluminium producers, accusing them of cartel behaviour. A great change was predicted because LME and other commodity exchanges tried to start a futures market for this metal several times during the previous decades, enticing the strong opposition of the majors of this industry, of many governments, and also of users' associations. Until then, it was believed that aluminium was different from other non-ferrous metals, which were historically traded through the LME device, because its long-lasting price stability made the hedging operations of a futures market needless. Behind the official announcement of the LME aluminium contracts, many observers thought that the intervention of the European Commission was the main cause of this change, which helped to curb the resistance both of governments and, above all, of producers in the transition of aluminium to the new model of trade. However Forster deluded the curiosity of his audience and, baffling the question, quickly replied: 'Pure coincidence. If you want any more information, please chat with the EEC Commission lawyers'.[1]

Three decades later, no historical study was carried out to explain either the path of this transformation or the governance issues that lie behind this change, even though almost every observer agreed on the importance of LME in reshaping the global aluminium industry. Many studies have tried to seize or explain the efficiency of LME in regulating the international aluminium market, but without taking into account the transition of this commodity from a stable prices system to a volatile one and without looking into the historical causes of this long-lasting model of industrial governance.[2] Some observers described it also as the outcome of the decisive changing industrial situation that lies behind the history of the aluminium industry in the long run, which meant a decisive transformation in the general market regulation of this metal. It is always advocated that the achievement of the 'maturity' of the aluminium market and the increasing competition of new actors, which eroded the market shares of the majors, were the key factors that pushed LME to successfully start a trade on aluminium.[3] In particular, Carmine Nappi rightly showed that the decreasing control that the 'big-six' (the six leading aluminium producers) had over international aluminium output dramatically decreased during the 1970s and the 1980s, while new producer countries, with different strategic positions and producing structures, emerged in the aluminium industry. As Nappi epitomised, while before LME this industry was 'regulated by the volumes [*régulée par les volumes*]', meaning that output volumes changed while prices lasted as stable, afterwards aluminium became 'regulated by the prices [*régulé par les prix*]', i.e. their fluctuations shaped global production.[4] However, neither the studies about LME's efficiency in regulating the international aluminium market, nor explorations about the introduction of this commodity at LME, clarified the links that existed between the governance methods of the aluminium industry and its long-lasting cartelisation, which characterised aluminium historical price stability.

This study does not want only to 'chat with the EEC Commission lawyers'; its scope is broader. Its aims are to provide a far-reaching description and explanation of the international cartelisation of this industry in the long run, searching for the causes that made aluminium live as a different commodity for almost a century. It would like to serve as a case study to consider the industrial development and the firms' strategies and structures from a standpoint that takes into account cartels as an institution, which provided governance tools to this industry as a whole. Aluminium price stability was a direct outcome of its long-lasting cartelisation that, since the inception of this industry, has lasted for almost a century. After being adopted during the 1890s, this pricing choice was then crystallised in the first official cartel, the Aluminium-Association of 1901 (see the group portrait in Figure I.1) and became the common shared background of the aluminium producers. Even when the old-fashioned cartels were dismantled after the Second World War, both firms and governments continued to share the 'credo' of price stability that was achieved through new means of cooperation. In a certain way, the introduction of aluminium at LME meant the end of an industrial cooperative model for international governance, which dominated this industry until then. Aluminium was very different from other non-ferrous metals, even though they knew a deep cartelisation over their history as well, because the specific feature of the aluminium cartel was its coincidence with a long-run strategy of price stability that bridged pre-1945 and post-1945 periods and with a unique record of growth.

This is not the first time that the aluminium cartels have drawn the attention of scholars. It is already known to the scholarship that from 1901 to 1939 four main cartel agreements succeed in controlling this industry and that these cartels were reasonably 'global', including in theory the totality of the world producers. From an early stage, some publications have sketched the evolution of cartels. Except for a few studies already published before the Great War,[5] and Donald Wallace's influential study of 1937,[6] a bulk of publications proliferated during the 1940s. Some of these last studies were linked to the US Federal Trade Commission examinations of ALCOA, which at that time owned the national monopoly

*Figure I.1* First meeting of the Aluminium Association, 1 November 1901 (source: ©
Institut pour l'histoire de l'aluminium, Paris).

Note
From the top: Martin Schindler and Gustav Naville (AIAG); Manuel (AIAG), Emile Collin (PCAC),
unknown (PRC); Jules Dreyfuss (SEMF), Emmanuel Ristori (BACO), Arthur V. Davis (PRC), Adrien
Badin (PCAC); Charles F. Jones (BACO), Gustav de Munerel (SEMF), Emil Huber-Werdmüller
(AIAG), Alfred R. Pechiney (PCAC), Emile Vielhomme (SEMF). On table, Huber – the president of
the Association – is holding the Agreement of the Association.

of aluminium production, and they exploited the documents about the cartel
gathered by the US antitrust authorities during a long-lasting inspection that the
US firm had endured throughout the 1930s. As a consequence, these studies,
which for a long time were the only available sources about aluminium cartelisation, were actively implicated in the debate about ALCOA monopoly at the end
of the Second World War and about its links with the international cartelisation.[7]
Also a couple of insider visions about the aluminium cartelisation before 1945
have been provided by Louis Marlio, the president of the French firm Pechiney
and chairman of the international cartel during the 1920s and 1930s, and by Ernst
Rauch, a German delegate of the international cartels during the 1920s and part
of the 1930s.[8]

More recent studies have tried to provide a more objective description of the
international cartelisation. However, in many cases they rely only on partial
archive documentation and either provide a limited temporal dimension of

aluminium cartelisation[9] or a limited geographical approach to it.[10] In all these cases, they focus only on the strategy of firms, misunderstanding the importance of price stability as a governance model and of the nexus that linked the cartels to governmental actions in the international governance of this industry. Both of these facts, we believe, are indeed the key specificity of aluminium in the panorama of non-ferrous metals or, broadly speaking, of commodities. They should be explained and explored in detail, covering the gap of the former studies, for a twofold reason. First, price stability continued after the end of the formal cartelisation at the aftermath of the Second World War, representing a bridge that linked pre-1945 to post-1945 aluminium economy. The achievement of price stability made aluminium diverge from other commodities that, being intrinsically more volatile, were interested in various intergovernmental programmes. Second, not only firms, but also governments collaborated with this strategy and served in some cases as allies, in some others as competitors, of the international governance of the aluminium industry. The international cartelisation of the aluminium industry was not a mere outcome of firms' strategies, but it lived as a complex nexus between national and international economic and political actors. The search for the reasons and the methods in which industrial cooperation was reshaped by its actors in the long run is one of the key research questions of this volume. While the institutional change from the pre-1945 period, when official cartels with quotas and written agreements existed, to the post-1945 era is huge, the long-run achievement of a relative price stability bridged these two periods and represented a unique historical model of international business organisation.

Past studies about the aluminium industry often believed that cartels existed only before the Second World War. In a former article of mine, published in *Business History*, I also argued that the 1930s cartel was not resumed after the Second World War because the strategic policies of the US administration hampered its resumption.[11] While it is true that official cartels were stopped after 1945, we will show in this study that formal pre-1945 cartelisation has been followed by other forms of industrial cooperation, engaging also in cartel-like behaviour, but that excluded the re-casting of an organisation such as the ones that existed before 1945. About the post-1945 period, only few studies are available and no consensus about the periodisation exists. In a seminal study about this topic, John Stuckey argued that the proliferation of joint ventures helped dialogue amongst firms to a certain extent. According to Stuckey's study, which was published in 1983 when, even though LME futures contracts already existed, they had not won yet the resistance of the majors, the interlocking directorships of aluminium firms and a strong vertical integration helped an informal understanding about the regulation of the aluminium market. Stuckey's key suggestion is that pricing behaviours were coordinated in the previous decades somewhere and he indicated joint ventures as the place of this coordination.[12] In another study, Steven Holloway suggested that this coordination could have been effectively carried out during the post-1945 period also by the trade associations of this industry, which were created on both the national and international levels.[13] Neither Stuckey nor Holloway have taken into account the great institutional change that is linked to LME's futures trades and to the concomitant EEC Commission's action. Moreover, not having access to private or public archives to support their studies, these studies did not describe the actual working of the industrial governance that, as we will see, mixed formal and informal phases of cartelisation with institutionalisation of inter-firm cooperation through associations, gentlemen's agreements, and official political places.

This study aims to describe for the first time and with consistent and as large as possible archive documentation the actual working of the aluminium cartel from the birth of this industry in 1886 to the introduction of aluminium at LME in 1978. The history of the aluminium cartel perfectly matches Jeffrey Fears' insight according to which

> cartels boomed in the 1920s, peaked in the 1930s, reappeared strongly after 1945 before they gradually faded away, especially after the 1970s [...] The general narrative about cartels may not be a story of rise and fall, but rise, boom, collapse, revitalization, gradual decline, and then criminalization.[14]

Actually, the first international cartel was established in 1901, arising after the partial agreements on patent licensing and market shares at the end of the nineteenth century proved not to be effective to control this industry. This cartel represented a laboratory leading to the perfect type of agreement and, apart from a passing crisis between 1909 and 1911, it lasted until the First World War and served as a model for the following cartelisation. In the interwar period, cartelisation boomed: cartels were the producers' answers to international economic and political issues. During the 1920s, a first cartel was employed to drive business back to normality following the shock of the war and to coordinate investments and growth. During the 1930s, a new agreement sought to cope with the global economic crisis and the slowdown of sales. The Second World War led to the collapse of this last cartel; yet already in the 1950s links amongst producers were revitalised. Even though a formal cartel was not re-established, the framework of producers was henceforth able to control international markets and to set an agreed price list. From this informal framework of producers, a European trade association was formed in the late 1960s and a worldwide one at the beginning of the 1970s. In 1978, a few months after the notification of accusation by the European Commission that 'criminalised' the cartel experience, the first futures trade of aluminium was started at LME overcoming the long lasting resistance of producers against these commercial methods. By the mid 1980s, the European antitrust charged the producers and the last resistance to the 'price list' was removed as well; the long-lasting history of the aluminium cartel, characterised by relatively stable prices, was over.

Despite the actual existence of a dozen of separate cartels and other agreements, we have chosen to call this book 'the international aluminium cartel', not only to provide a quick reference to John Hillman's work on tin,[15] but also because we believe that this history has one leading thread that merges the multiplicity of agreements and of actors that were implicated in them: price stability.

Thus, the key question of this study is to explore the reasons that led aluminium to choose price stability and to explain how firms and other actors fulfilled this goal. The case of aluminium seems very similar to the one of oil, which, like aluminium, lived as a stable priced commodity for almost a century before entering a new unstable and speculative phase, which made it converge to a new market model.[16] In the aluminium industry, the cartel was the kernel of this long-lasting market governance, which made aluminium essentially different from other commodities. Without taking into account this leading background, it would be impossible to seize the real nature of aluminium cartelisation and to describe the continuity that bridged pre-war and post-war experiences in the aluminium industry's international governance. For that reason, 1978 was chosen as the end of this study: once the LME took control over the formation of prices, the long-lasting producers' strategy and their cooperative structures were driven to an end. As a matter of fact, the resilience to LME lasted until 1984, when the publication of price lists was definitively concluded. In other words, while the introduction of aluminium in LME meant the end of the former long-lasting cartelisation, this change was helped by a specific legal situation opened by the action of the European antitrust authorities in the late 1970s, which profoundly changed the perception of the cartel problem, starting to consider it as a per se evil. These two concomitant facts merged into one of the most impressive historical modifications of a global industry, which in less than a decade converged to the model of all the other commodities.

Aluminium is nowadays a key commodity for our civilisation. Its uses are very eclectic, going from drink can to planes, passing through architecture structures, luxury cars, computers, electrical equipment, and food wrappings.[17] For a long time, aluminium has been also a key strategic material, which drew the attention of governments in the administration of its production and trade.[18] As we will show in the following chapters, its strategic importance was perceived only lately during the Great War and the changing relationships between producers and political powers also had a direct impact on cartelisation, affecting its specific interplay. In spite of its present diffusion and of the utmost military importance of this metal, aluminium is relatively young because its industrial production only started after the discovery of electrolysis by Paul Toussaint Héroult and Charles Martin Hall in 1886. Before 1886, aluminium was a rare metal, whose price was next to the luxury metals. New electrolytic technologies opened the door to a new industry, which started to develop at the end of the 1880s when the leading international firms were incorporated. Since its inception, this industry has known a continuous series of cartel agreements that have come one after the other for almost a century. Until the late 1970s, aluminium had known a unique record of growth, that led this metal from being almost a mere curiosity to become the first amongst the non-ferrous metals for production and consumption, second only to steel in the broader groups of industrial metals. Aluminium came to the fore as an essential material of our society and it progressively overcame the older non-ferrous metals for its global production and consumption, reaching a yearly average growth of about 10 per cent during 1886–1978 (see Figure I.2).[19]

Aluminium arrived to its status of everyday metal through an intense activity of R&D, which was not only carried out by firms individually, but which also implied diffusions and sharing through cartel channels.[20] Aluminium producers diverged from the other commodity suppliers, not only for their pricing system, but also because they did not limit their activity to sell standard products on the market. They provided a far-reaching governance to the development of the outputs, of the markets and of the applications of this metal. As Florence Hachez-Leroy had already and rightly epitomised for the French case,[21] aluminium had only limited ready markets at the beginnings of its history and the producers continuously cooperated in finding new applications. We add that price stability was the key competitive edge that the producers adopted on a global scale to convince customers to use aluminium in substitution of other materials. Moreover, price stability emerged as essential to provide funds necessary to firms to engage in new investments for the ongoing expansion of this industry.[22] Unlike the other non-ferrous metals, which since the nineteenth century had been traded into LME and whose prices were extremely volatile and unstable, aluminium emerged and competed with them thanks to its unique price stability. About the significance of price stability in the non-ferrous metals panorama, it is illuminating to quote Lord Carr of Hadley who, in his twofold figure of aluminium user (as manager of the fabricator John Dole Metal Co.), and of politician with a certain experience in the field of commodities governance, still claimed in 1977, a few months before aluminium entered LME:

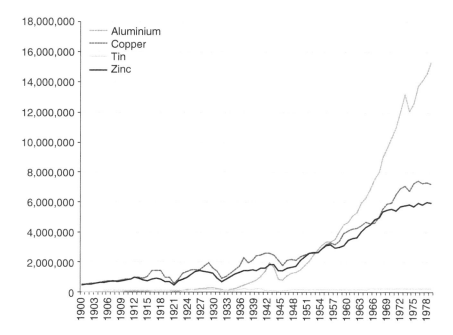

*Figure I.2* Global aluminium output, 1900–1978, compared with the other principal non-ferrous metals (copper, tin, and zinc), in metric tons (source: US Geological Survey, aluminum, copper, tin, and zinc statistics).

For most of my own industrial life the principal raw material with which I had to deal was aluminium. I always felt how lucky I was that it was aluminium and not copper. I had no doubt that manufacturers and fabricators in aluminium had, on the whole, a long-term advantage over fabricators in copper, simply because of the greater stability of aluminium prices compared with copper. When I say 'advantage', I am not just looking at short-term commercial advantage; I am looking too at the greater certainty with which one could plan ahead one's investment and marketing programmes when one was dealing in a raw material price movements of which were much more stable than those of some competing commodities.[23]

Cartelisation in other non-ferrous metals meant a certain degree of market 'manipulations' that aimed to reverse their intrinsic instability: while, due to their output structure and technical features, non-ferrous metals were volatile-priced commodities, cartels made attempts to stabilise their courses with alternate fortunes. The mining-logic of other non-ferrous metals and the distance from the place of extraction and the terminal market made these metals more sensitive to price fluctuation and made hedging operation necessary in the management of their markets. Recently, John Hilmann provided a far-reaching history of the international tin cartel and has shown several attempts that producers and suppliers made to cope with the constant boom and bust cycles of this metal, trying to provide some stability to an unstable industry.[24] Moreover, other examples, such as other non-ferrous metals and commodities, provided similar argumentation to the working of cartels that were artificially used to raise prices and to take advantage of the swinging market situation.[25] Aluminium essentially diverged from this experience: in spite of the few specific situations in which recessions reshaped it, the international aluminium industry has been a fast growing industry during its whole cartelisation. During this impressive growth, aluminium benefited from relative stability in prices. Being the outcome of one of the most energy and capital intensive industries, aluminium had not the same need of hedging operations that characterised the instable market of other commodities. Its high-technological features made aluminium diverse from other metals.

Stability is not to be intended as an 'average' stability: in aluminium trade, prices simply did not vary or vary only few times over months, while other metals were priced on daily basis. In this aspect the international aluminium industry is more similar to the steel industry, which knew a similar history of cartelisation and price stability.[26] As a young metal, its producers seized price stability as a competitive edge to overcome the older metals instead of speculating on the rise of demand to obtain higher prices. Even though, on the one hand, cartels reduced the competition within this industry, we can wonder if, on the other hand, they enacted this metal to compete with the older established non-ferrous metals. As we will see, aluminium producers learned their credo in price stability at the eve of the twentieth century, when their model was questioned by other means of governance. The long-lasting stability, which made it unnecessary for aluminium to adopt the tools of market governance that characterised other non-ferrous metals, should draw the attention of the historian. Cartels and cooperation were the leading thread of the aluminium industry for a century, not an exception from a model based on the competition. Firms in the aluminium industry have growth up in a cooperative environment, also obtaining spectacular achievements in terms of performance and economic effectiveness. This continuous cooperation continuously reshaped not only the strategies of firms, but also their structures thanks to common agencies on R&D, statistics, marketing, etc. One of the most challenging research questions for the aluminium industry is to wonder which were the causes that led this cooperative industrial model to end.

Cartels are a controversial subject for business and economic historians, not only because they are often believed to belong to a grey zone of non-codified and extemporary business practices. There is also little agreement about their nature or even on their definition. Deeper than simple business agreements, yet less cohesive than mergers, cartels were in many cases wrongly thought of as a pejorative synonym for oligopolies. In some other cases, cartels have been presented as forerunners of multinational enterprises.[27] Many scholars agree with Liefmann's definition that sees cartels as 'agreements between independent firms aiming to reduce competition'.[28] Some other studies also added to this definition 'and to raise profits'.[29] Some important studies, however, contested the power of cartels to erase competition.[30] Also many empirical studies showed both that competition rests within a cartel framework, aiming at least to measure the respective force of potential cartel members, and that it is extremely difficult to prove the relations between earnings and cartels.[31] As anticipated, a too rigid application of these suggestions to our study would lead to misunderstand the general positioning of aluminium as a young and competitive commodity in a market already dominated by other non-ferrous metals. Even if the problem of competition is strongly related to cartels, our case could disclose other suggestions that are related to both the problem of industrial cooperation and of international governance.

This is particularly evident if we consider that scholarly studies have often analysed cartels from the perspective of firms' behaviours, adopting game theory to explain how and why firms aimed either at entering cartel agreements, in spite of the risk of being charged under antitrust laws, or not entering, in spite of the desirability to join cartel schemes to raise prices.[32] Furthermore, it is often argued, following George Stigler's seminal approach, that, even if cartels were formed owing to the greed for extra earnings, they were not effective and short-lived because firms were constantly tempted to cheat (for instance underquoting cartel prices to increase sales) at the expense of other participants in the agreement.[33] Debora Spar, analysing some cartels with different fortunes (in the cases of diamonds, uranium, gold, and silver), concluded that, aside from market structures and governmental implications, commitment and credibility are the essential centrepieces to explain cartelisation.[34] More recently, the works of Dominique Barjot and of Harm Schröter had revitalised research questions about cartels. The key insights of their argumentation are that cartels should not be considered simply as collusive actions of firms, but as an historical form of business organisation. Like other institutions, cartels had proper rules that governed their working and the conduct of their members, which sometimes did not exclude some competition.

Barjot's and Schröter's studies tried to question the classical business history model as based on the single-competing firm: according to them, cartels were neither an exception in the historical evolution of firms, nor a sub-optimal form of business organisation.[35]

The long-lasting existence of cartels in the aluminium industry and the sharing of a pricing credo confirm these views. They also partially confute per se the beliefs about cartels as weak and short-lived institutions and confirm the high importance of commitment amongst cartel members. However, we argue that the degree of commitment of firms into a cartel agreement should consider Michael Porter's approaches about strategic groups. They can provide new insight about the historical studies of cartels because, according to Porter, the firms did not chose to compete or to cooperate only following their will; options are strongly related to their position within an industry and within the group of firms. While firms that are similar for their structure and for their strategy would tend to cooperate, economic actors with different strategies or goals would be led to compete. Using Porter's words, the faculty to compete depends on the existence of different 'strategic groups' within an industry.[36] Nappi has already pointed out that the emergence of a strategic group different from the one of the historical producers helped the success of LME. Here, one of the leading threads of our narration will be the description of the history of a consistent strategic group that, after being formed at the eve of the aluminium industry by common technology and shared marketing approaches, has lasted for many decades.

The problem of how and when cartels are settled still persists, even though we pointed out that their formation is easier when a robust strategic group exists. Several studies have tried to examine which factors stimulated the formation of cartels and which reshaped their forms. In a seminal and very influential study, Dominique Barjot rightly pointed out that the formation of cartels is strongly related both to exogenous factors (such as laws, economic cycles, and culture) and to endogenous ones (such as technology and industrial structure). Not all industrial sectors are suitable for cartels: both the technological features of the production and industrial structure of a branch, such as the existence of few firms, the standardisation of products, and the capital intensity of the production process, are some of the prerequisites that Barjot claimed to be useful in order to have a successful cartelisation. Also the general context worked as a factor that reshaped the formation of cartels: their general toleration during the interwar period helped the blossoming of the cartel movement, while a more hostile situation, even if it could not hamper the formation of agreements, influenced the way in which they were formed. It is also often believed that the general enthusiasm of economists and policymakers for cartels before the Second World War helped their formation, while after 1945 they were progressively criminalised in a more hostile institutional context.[37] From the standpoint of the exogenous factors, it is often believed that cartels are *Kinder der not.* Harm Schröter already pointed out that this idea should be revisited because in some cases crisis worked as a factor pushing firms more closely together; in others, it provoked the collapse of existing cartels.[38]

The problem of the nexus between the individual behaviours of firms and the collective action of a strategic group represents an important issue for our study.

Some divergences can still persist even within the same strategic groups and even in such a 'pro-cartel' industry as aluminium. This fact can deeply affect the effectiveness of cartels in pursuing their goals. In many cases, these divergences are not only related to the industrial structure, but they can also be the consequence of a changing political and institutional situation. As a consequence, Margaret Levenstein and Valery Suslow argued that in certain cases the degree of success of a cartel is measured by its ability to adapt to changing economic conditions, which may affect the strategies of firms. Instead of confining cartels to the neutral choice of firms or defining a sterile taxonomy of options to be adopted, Levenstein and Suslow claimed that cartels are indeed dynamic institutions whose forms are continuously reshaped by the economic context and by the bargaining process of firms. This adaptability made cartel agreements stronger than was believed by theoretical works and allowed them to survive historical changes, in spite of the never-ending problem of cheating and in spite of adverse legal situations. According to their studies, cartels revealed a certain capability to adapt their actual shapes to economic and institutional contexts, making them a kind of constant in the development of the international economy.[39] Previously, William Baumol had also claimed that the intrinsic weakness of cartel agreements was overestimated and that technology sharing could improve cohesion and make cartels more effective leading firms to reinforce their cooperation.[40]

However, we also believe that the continuity of the cartel phenomenon should be nuanced. In the case of the aluminium industry, the institutional change of the post-1945 cartelisation is central to our research: the transition from a phase of formal (and institutionally supported) cartelisation to new forms of industrial cooperation cannot be explained as the mere adaptation to the rise of antitrust law. Military, political, financial, and corporate considerations affected this change. Specific features of the cartel behaviours were intrinsically part of the 'business philosophy'[41] that characterised the interwar period, which was shared by policymakers and business administrators, according to which international cooperation of private business actors could serve in supporting public policies and international political actions. Afterwards, a certain divorce between cartels and policymakers occurred and it should be considered as an important factor in shaping the nature of international industrial cooperation. For that, we feel that, in spite of the continuity of the cartel experience that is often claimed, the actual nature of cartels and their desirability belonged for many aspects also to political and institutional levels. For many years, despite the rise of antitrust policies, institutionalised cartels have governed the actual evolution of several industries, in which not only firms, but also governments and intergovernmental bodies carried out an important role in the international cartelisation. The free evolution of market forces in itself was often subordinated to other considerations, which focused on practical solutions in a complex interplay of actors. Also the desirability of competition by governments is subjected to a historical process: in some cases it was reinforced; in others it was subordinated to other factors and cartel behaviour was tolerated.[42]

The historical evolution of commodity governance also draws a further research question, wondering why aluminium also diverged from the other commodities from the standpoint of intergovernmental implications in its cartelisation. Unlike other commodities, such as tin or rubber for instance, neither political bodies nor intergovernmental authorities were formed to administrate its cartel. As we will see, the aluminium cartel always belonged to a private sphere in which governments often played some roles, but have never taken over its administration. The nexus between producers and political powers followed a tortuous evolution, which swung from alignments to struggles. In order to explain this nexus, our study should take into account the cartel not only as a strategic option of firms, but also as a structure that belonged to an intra- and extra-firm need for cooperation, which tried to deal with the political need to regulate the production and trade of such an important commodity. We point out that, while firms and governments were the relevant actors of the business history of the aluminium industry, cartels were the informal institution that worked as the general scaffolding during the historical evolution of the international aluminium industry. In this institution, both firms and political powers interplayed, adapting their goals to the changing economic and political conditions. As a consequence, another key question of this study is not only how and why the cartel worked, but above all which were the causes that, in spite of its long-lasting existence and success, this cartel was doomed to its termination at the end of the 1970s.

Recently, scholarly studies have focused their attention on the links between cartels and the organisational and structural development of firms and on the industrial regulatory issues that lay beyond the formation of cartels. In particular, Jeffrey Fear pointed out that cartels should be considered as a form of economic regulation, going beyond the classical approached that focused either on the concept of markets and hierarchies or on the mere competition. Thanks to his insights, we understand the real nature of cartels better, considering them as structures governed with their own rules that can differ from the ones usually adopted in the business history.[43] Other scholars also suggested considering cartels as 'economic institutions' that belong, with proper rules and structures, to a given historical phase of industrial development.[44] In particular, Harm Schröter suggested considering cartels as historical economic institutions that characterised the European economy,[45] while Dominique Barjot pointed out that cartels were elaborated forms of industrial agreements that implied structures and rules.[46] The historical problem of cartels seems not too far from Douglass North's insights about the links between economic organisations and institutions. If we considered cartels as institutions, with proper codes of conduct, internal logics, and operating structures, we could imagine that each institutional change called for a transformation of their nature, or their work and also of their desirability.[47]

Our conviction is that this institutional approach can successfully deal with the study of cartels. However, if cartels can be thought of as more or less informal economic institutions shaped by both endogenous and exogenous factors, we should provide a deeper explanation about which kind of actors were involved in the international cartelisation and which were their interplays. Apart from firms, in this dynamic interplay of actors bargaining within cartels, governments played significant roles in many cases. In spite of the complexity of the relationships between business and politics,[48] cartels can disclose some important insights about the regulation of markets and the governance of industries. Historically, many public authorities were not only regulators of the cartel problem from an antitrust point of view. As already pointed out, in some cases cartels were not only endorsed, but also administered by political powers. The seminal studies of Alice Teichova demonstrated this, showing that governments played roles in the process either as supporters or as mere regulators, interfacing international industrial governance and national economic policies.[49] Clemens Wurm also carried out innovative research on the interwar steel and cotton industries and argued that governments used cartels in order to pursue international economic policies; specific interference of public policies was able to affect the specific shape and scope of cartels.[50] The role of public authorities in the construction and in the working of cartels deserves close attention: their involvement in negotiation affected the never-ending process of bargaining associated with cartels. Political support, sometimes following non-economic considerations, could be used by firms to strengthen their position during cartel settlements.[51]

We can add to this sketch that also the rise and falls of a globalised economy and of international trade played a key role in the process of formation of cartels and in the settlement of the specific features they had. While the role of political powers in the governance of economy is changing during history, too large an interference of political power can destabilise the cohesion of agreements. As a consequence, mismatches have been sometimes shown between international cartel schemes and national power.[52] We can wonder if, instead of the economic crisis, the phases of market opening influenced the formation of cartels as a private way to provide some governance to the liberalisation process and to tackle the risks derived from this process. While they were less desirable, from the standpoint of firms, when political protection already defended national markets, cartels could have played a key role during the phases in which globalisation was expanding. Moreover, the rising role of several governments in national industrial regulation during specific periods reshaped the ways undertaken by the international cartelisation.[53] The complexity of the links between globalisation and national economic policies affected the fate of many cartels beyond the mere issues linked to the settlement of competition policies. For instance, the endorsement of cartel schemes by political powers assured, in some cases, the prolongation of their activity after the Second World War – in spite of the general anti-cartel campaign and of the Americanisation of global business.[54] According to this link between cartelisation and globalisation, Levenstein and Suslow also formulated the hypothesis that the 1990s were a period of intense cartelisation.[55]

The aluminium cartel was indeed a kind of informal institution that has attempted, with more or less success, to regulate the production and trade of this metal during almost a century, coping continuously with institutional (both economic and political) change, with the changing nature of public authorities' intervention in this industry, and with the changing interplay within the 'strategic groups' of firms. During that time, it reduced, or rather, it regimented competition among a defined range of options; yet cartelisation also provided specific tools to firms to manage and regulate their industry, coordinating their actions and cooperating with the global evolution of their industry. Specific attention is provided to the interplay between economics and politics within the international aluminium cartel, in order to seize the role both of firms and of governments in this long-lasting history of cartelisation. It is still open to judgement whether this industry benefited from this long-lasting cartelisation or not; however, it cannot be denied that the cartel's framework has worked continuously as a structuring factor for both the whole industry and individual actors. Consequently, strategies and structures of single firms have never been the simple result of individual choices: they were reshaped by the dynamic relationships of the group of actors. From a theoretical point of view, this means that cartels can serve to bridge the macroeconomic evolution of the whole aluminium industry (from ores to finished products) with the microeconomic strategy of each firm, representing a kind of mesoeconomic dimension of business actors' choices.

Aluminium represented a kind of *idealtypus* for international cartelisation already before 1945: the general economic and political debate, which involved both supporters[56] and opponents[57] of cartelisation, used the aluminium industry as an example to show the pros and cons of the whole cartel movement. Also afterwards, the aluminium industry continued to play the role of key example in the regulation of commodity trade. This industry belongs perfectly to that kind of industry in which cartels are easier to form because aluminium is a standardised metal without producers' special qualities; its production is highly capital intensive and requires huge electrical resources; the lightness of this metal has made its market highly internationalised from a very early stage; finally, only a few actors were involved in its production, representing a strong international oligopoly. Until 1945, for instance, most firms represented national monopolies and a strong oligopolistic structure was kept afterwards. Furthermore, aluminium has an extremely rigid smelting technology: output stability is a key factor in maintaining optimal scale economies. Cuts of production are major technical and strategic issues for producers: stopping the smelting process involves significant increases in production costs and requires huge investments afterwards to restart it. The lack of flexibility of aluminium production pushed producers to collaborate in order to forecast market trends and to set common market analyses from the end of the nineteenth century. In case of a crisis, they collectively stockpiled to manage supply and/or coordinated a reduction of production. All of these factors, both endogenous and exogenous, not only facilitated the formation of cartels in the aluminium industry; they also shaped the specific forms of such organisations.

The book is organised as follows: each of the four main parts corresponds to a specific phase of cartelisation. The first part describes the 'rise' of an international cartel in the early history of the aluminium industry (1886–1914) and it is divided in three chapters in which we describe the birth of this industry and the first agreements on patents (Chapter 1), the settlement of the first real cartel (Chapter 2) and its evolution until the Great War (Chapter 3). The second part explores the 'boom' during the 1920s: after studying the Great War of aluminium and the impact of the conflict on the global governance of this industry until the eve of the 1920s (Chapter 4), the settlement of the European cartel in 1926 and its life until the late 1920s will be treated in Chapter 5, while the more complex situation that came with the great crisis will be the main argument of Chapter 6. The adaptation during the 1930s until its collapse in 1945 will be analysed in the third part: in Chapter 7, the full description of the creation of one of the most influential cartels, the Alliance Aluminium Compagnie, will be provided, and its evolution during the 1930s will be explored in Chapter 8, while its collapse during the war will be described in Chapter 9. In the fourth part, the narration will involve the cartel-like organisations that were revitalised after the Second World War: in Chapter 10, we will show how the aluminium producers handled both the liquidation of the Alliance and the rise of new forms of informal cooperation; Chapter 11's topic will be international aluminium governance during the 1960s, while its sunset during the 1970s will be shown in Chapter 12.

## Notes

1 University of Glasgow Documents (UGD), British Aluminium Company (BACO) Archives, 347/10/7/13, American Metal Market Forum, notes by J.S. Bridgeman, 30 October 1978.
2 (Not exhaustive) Christopher L. Gilbert, 'Modelling Market Fundamentals: A Model of the Aluminium Market', *Journal of Applied Econometrics*, vol. 10, no. 4, 1995, 385–410. Martin Gross, 'A Semi Strong Test of the Efficiency of the Aluminium and Copper Markets at the LME', *Journal of Futures Markets*, vol. 8 no. 1, 1988, 67–77. F. I. Figuerola, C. L. Gilbert, 'Price Volatility and Marketing Methods in the Non-ferrous Metal Industry', *Journal of Financial Economy*, vol. 27, no. 3, 2001, 169–177, and 'Price Discovery in the Aluminium Market', *Journal of Futures Markets*, vol. 25, no. 10, 2005, 967–988. Prosper Mouak, *Le Marché de l'Aluminium: Structuration et Analyse du Comportement des Prix au Comptant et à Terme au London Metal Exchange*. Unpublished PhD Thesis, Université d'Orléans, 2010.
3 Carmine Nappi, *L'Aluminium*. Paris: Economica, 1994. Réné Lesclous, *Histoire des Sites Producteurs d'Aluminium: Les Choix Stratégiques de Pechiney 1892–1992*. Paris: Presses des mines, 2004. Thierry Brault, 'L'introduction de l'Aluminium au London Metal Exchange (1978): Cause ou Effet de la Transformation du Marché Mondial?' *Cahiers d'Histoire de l'Aluminium*, no. 40, 2008. Isaiah Litvak, Christopher Maule, 'Assessing Industry Concentration: The Case of Aluminium', *Journal of International Business Studies*, vol. 15, no. 1, 1984, 97–104. Merton J. Peck (ed.), *The World Aluminum Industry in a Changing Energy Era*. Washington DC: John Hopkins University Press, 1988. George D. Smith, *From Monopoly to Competition: The Transformations of Alcoa, 1888–1986*. New York: Cambridge University Press, 1988.
4 Nappi, *L'Aluminium*.
5 Wilfried Kossmann, *Über die Wirtschaftliche Entwicklung der Aluminiumindustrie*. Strasbourg: Straßburger Druckerei, 1911. Carl Dux, *Die Aluminium-Industrie-Aktiengesellschaft Neuhausen und ihre Konkurrenz-Gesellschaften*. Luzern: Albins, 1911.
6 Donald Horace Wallace, *Market Control in Aluminium Industry*. Cambridge MA: Harvard University Press, 1937.
7 Charlotte Muller, *Light Metals Monopoly*. New York: Columbia University Press, 1946. Myron W. Watkins, 'The Aluminum Alliance', in *Cartels in Action: Cases Studies in International Business Diplomacy*, edited by George W. Stocking and Myron W. Watkins. New York: Twentieth Century Fund, 1946, 216–273. Joseph Borkin, 'The Aluminum Battle', in *Germany's Master Plan: The Story of Industrial Offensive*, edited by Joseph Borkin and Charles A. Welsh. New York: Sloan Long, 1943, 203–222.
8 Louis Marlio, *The Aluminum Cartel*. Washington DC: Brookings Institution, 1947. Ernst Rauch, *Geschichte der Hüttenaluminiumindustrie in der Westlichen Welt*. Düsseldorf: Aluminium Verlag, 1962.
9 Karl Erich Born, *Internationale Kartellierung einer Neuen Industrie: Die Aluminium-Association 1901–1915*. Munich: Berg, 1994.

10  Florence Hachez-Leroy, 'Le Cartel International de l'Aluminium du Point de Vue des Sociétés Françaises, 1901–1940', in *International Cartels Revisited: Vues Nouvelles sur les Cartels Internationaux (1880s–1980s)*, edited by Dominique Barjot. Caen: Editions du Lys, 1994, 153–162. Espen Storli, 'Cartel Theory and Cartel Practice: The Case of International Aluminium Cartels, 1901–1940', *Business History Review*, vol. 88, no. 3, 2014, 445–467, which is largely based on Espen Storli, *Out of Norway Falls Aluminium: The Norwegian Aluminium Industry in the International Economy, 1908–1940*. Unpublished PhD Thesis, Norwegian University of Science and Technology, Trondheim, 2010.

11  Marco Bertilorenzi, 'Business, Finance, and Politics: The Rise and Fall of International Aluminium Cartels, 1914–45', *Business History*, vol. 56, no. 2, 2014, 236–269.

12  John A. Stuckey, *Vertical Integration and Joint Ventures in the Aluminum Industry*. London: Harvard University Press, 1983.

13  Steven K. Holloway, *The Aluminium Multinationals and the Bauxite Cartel*. London: Macmillan, 1988.

14  Jeffrey Fear, 'Cartels and Competition: Neither Markets nor Hierarchies', *Harvard Business School Discussion Paper*, no. 07-011, 2006, 17–18.

15  John Hillman, *The International Tin Cartel*. London: Routledge, 2010.

16  Daniel Yergin, *The Prize: The Epic Quest for Oil, Money, and Power*. New York: Free Press, 2009.

17  Mimi Sheller, *Aluminum Dreams: The Making of Light Modernity*. Cambridge: MIT Press, 2014. Eric Schatzberg, 'Symbolic Culture and Technological Change: The Cultural History of Aluminum as an Industrial Material', *Enterprise and Society*, vol. 4, no. 2, June 2003, 226–271. Margaret Graham, 'Aluminum and the Third Industrial Revolution', in *The Third Industrial Revolution in Global Business*, edited by Giovanni Dosi and Louis Galambos. Cambridge: Cambridge University Press, 2013, 220–228. Luitgard Marshall, *Aluminium: Metal der Moderne*. Munich: Oekom, 2008. Dominique Barjot, Marco Bertilorenzi (eds), *Aluminium: Du Métal de Luxe au Métal de Masse: From Luxury Metal to Mass Commodity (XIXe–XXe siècles)*. Paris: Presses de l'Université Paris-Sorbonne, 2014.

18  See for instance, Hans Otto Frøland, Mats Ingulstad (eds), *From Warfare to Welfare: Business–Government Relations in the Aluminium Industry*. Trondheim: Akademika, 2012.

19  About the general story of aluminium, see Ivan Grinberg, *Aluminum: Light at Heart*, Paris, Gallimard, 2009; Paul Morel (ed.), *Histoire Technique de la Production d'Aluminium: Les Apports Français au Développement International d'une Industrie*, Grenoble, Presses Universitaires de Grenoble, 1991; Ivan Grinberg, Florence Hachez-Leroy, *Industrialisation et Sociétés en Europe Occidentale de la Fin du XIXe Siècle à nos Jours: L'Âge de l'Aluminium*, Paris, Armand Colin, 1997.

20  See Margaret B. W. Graham, Bettye H. Pruitt. *R&D for Industry: A Century of Technical Innovation at Alcoa*. Cambridge MA: University Press, 1990. Muriel Le Roux, *L'Entreprise et la Recherche: Un Siècle de Recherche Industrielle à Pechiney*. Paris: Editions Rive Droite, 1998.

21  Florence Hachez-Leroy, *L'Aluminium français: La Création d'un Marché, 1911–1983*. Paris: CNRS Editions, 1999.

22  See for instance, Louis Ferrand, 'Le Problème des Prix dans la Métallurgie de l'Aluminiun', *Revue d'économie politique*, vol. 51, March–April 1937, 299–3325.

23  Commons and Lords Hansard (CLH), House of Lords, Select Committee on Commodity Price, report 1977, 26 July 1977, vol 386, cc. 878–896.

24  Hillman, *The International Tin Cartel*.

25  See for instance (not exhaustive) Orris C. Herfindahl, *Copper Costs and Prices: 1870–1957*. Baltimore MD: Johns Hopkins University Press, 1957. Austin Coates, *The Commerce in Rubber: The First 250 years*. Oxford: Oxford University Press, 1984. Carmine Nappi, *Commodity Market Controls: An Historical Review*. Toronto: Lexington Books, 1979. Miguel Morel-Lopez, José M. O'Kean, 'Rothschilds' Strategies in International Non-ferrous Metals Markets, 1830–1940', *Economic History Review*, vol. 67, no. 3, 2014, 720–749. Mark Casson (ed.), *Multinationals and World Trade: Vertical Integration and the Division of Labour in World Industries*. New York: Routledge, 2011.

26 Philippe Mioche, 'La Vitalité des Ententes Sidérurgiques en France et en Europe de l'Entre-deux-guerres à nos Jours', in *International Cartels Revisited: Vues Nouvelles sur les Cartels Internationaux (1880s–1980s)*, edited by Dominique Barjot. Caen: Editions du Lys, 1994, 119–128.

27 Mark Casson, 'Multinational Monopolies and International Cartels', in *The Economic Theory of the Multinational Enterprise*, edited by Mark Casson and Peter J. Buckley. London: Macmillan, 1985, 60–97. Helga Nussbaum, 'International Cartels and Multinational Enterprises' in *Multinational Enterprise in Historical Perspective*, edited by Maurice Levy-Léboyer, Helga Nussbaum, and Alice Teichova. London: Cambridge University Press, 1980, 131–145.

28 Robert Liefmann, *Cartels, Concerns and Trusts*. London: Europa, 1932.

29 Karl Pribram, *Cartel Problems: An Analysis of Collective Monopolies in Europe with American Application*. New York: Brookings Institution, 1935. Temporary National Economic Committee (TNEC), *Competition and Monopoly in American Industry*. Investigation of Concentration of Economic Power Monograph no. 21, Washington, 1945.

30 Edward Chamberlin, *The Theory of Monopolistic Competition: A Re-orientation of the Theory of Value*. London: Harvard University Press, 1933. George Stigler, 'A Theory of Oligopoly', *Journal of Political Economy*, vol. 72, no. 1, 1964, 44–61.

31 Daniel Barbezat, 'Cooperation and Rivalry in the International Steel Cartel, 1926–1933', *Journal of Economic History*, vol. 49, no. 2, 1989, 435–447. Margaret Levenstein, 'Price Wars and the Stability of Collusion: A Study of the Pre-World War I Bromine Industry', *Journal of Industrial Economics*, vol. 45, no. 2, 1997, 117–137. Bishnupriya Gupta, 'Why did Collusion Fail? The Indian Jute Industry in the Inter-War Years', *Business History*, vol. 47, no. 4, 2005, 532–552; Valerio Cerretano, 'European Cartels and Technology Transfer: The Experience of the Rayon Industry, 1920 to 1940', *Zeitschrift für Unternehmensgeschichte*, vol. 56, no. 2, 2011, 206–244. Valerio Cerretano, 'European Cartels, European Multinationals and Economic De-globalisation: Insights from the Rayon Industry, c. 1900–1939', *Business History*, vol. 54, no. 4, 2012, 594–622. Alain Cortat, *Un Cartel Parfait: Réseaux, R&D et Profits dans l'Industrie Suisse des Cables*. Neuchatel: Éditions Alphil – Presses Universitaires Suisses, 2009.

32 Mancur Olson, *The Logic of Collective Action: Public Goods and the Theory of Group*. Cambridge MA: Harvard University Press, 1965. Christopher Leslie, 'Trust, Distrust and Antitrust', *Texas Law Review*, vol. 82, No. 3, 2004, 515–680.

33 Stigler, 'A Theory of Oligopoly'.

34 Debora Spar, *The Cooperative Edge: The International Politics of International Cartels*. London: Cornell University Press, 1994, 218–220.

35 See for instance, Harm Schröter, 'Das Kartellverbot und Andere Ungereimtheiten: Neue Ansätze in der Internationales Kartellforschung', in *Regulierte Märkte: Zünfte und Kartelle: Marchés régulés: Corporations et cartels*, edited by Margrit Muller, Heinrich R. Schmidt, and Laurent Tissot. Zurich: Chronos, 2011, 199–212. Dominique Barjot, Harm Schröter, 'General Introduction: Why a Special Edition on Cartels?' *Revue Économique*, vol. 64, no. 6, 2013, 957–971, and Harm Schröter 'Cartels Revisited: An Overview on Fresh Questions, New Methods, and Surprising Results', *Revue Économique*, vol. 64, no. 6, 2013, 989–1010, Special issue *Economic Cooperation Reconsidered*, edited by Dominique Barjot and Harm Schröter. Dominique Barjot, 'Cartels et Cartelisation: Des Instruments Contre les Crises?' *Entreprises et Histoire*, no. 76, 2014, 5–19.

36 Michael Porter, *Competitive Strategy: Techniques for Analyzing Industries and Competitors*, New York: Free Press, 1980, 129–141.

37 Dominique Barjot, 'Introduction', in *International Cartels Revisited: Vues Nouvelles sur les Cartels Internationaux (1880s–1980s)*, edited by Dominique Barjot. Caen: Editions du Lys, 1994, 9–70. Dominique Barjot, 'Un Nouveau Champ Pionnier pour la Recherche Historique: Les Cartels Internationaux (1880–1970)', *Revue d'Allemagne et des Pays de Langue Allemande*, no. 1, 1998, 31–54.

38  Harm Schröter, 'Cartelisation and Decartelisation in Europe, 1870–1995: Rise and Decline of an Economic Institution', *Journal of European Economic History*, vol. 25, no. 1, 1996, 129–153.

39  Margaret Levenstein, Valery Suslow, 'What Determines Cartel Success?' *Journal of Economic Literature*, vol. 46, 2006, 43–95. Margaret Levenstein, Valery Suslow, 'Breaking Up is Hard to Do: Determinants of Cartel Duration', *Journal of Law and Economics*, vol. 54, no. 2, 2011, 455–492.

40  William J. Baumol, 'Horizontal Collusion and Innovation', *Economic Journal*, vol. 102, no. 410, 1992, 129–137.

41  About business philosophy, see Leslie Hannah, *The Rise of Corporate Economy: The British Experience*. London: Johns Hopkins University Press, 1976.

42  Peter Hall, David Soskice (eds), *Varieties of Capitalism: The Institutional Foundations of Comparative Advantage*. Oxford: Oxford University Press, 2001.

43  Fear, 'Cartels and Competition'. Jeffrey Fear, 'Cartels', in *The Oxford Handbook of Business History*, edited by Geoffrey Jones and Jonathan Zeitlin. London: Oxford University Press, 2008, 268–292.

44  Akira Kudo, Terushi Hara, 'Introduction', *International Cartels in Business History*, edited by Akira Kudo and Terushi Hara. Tokyo: Tokyo University Press, 1993, 1–24. Schröter, 'Cartelisation and decartelisation'.

45  Schröter, 'Cartelisation and Decartelisation in Europe'.

46  Barjot, 'Introduction'.

47  Douglass C. North, *Institutions, Institutional Change and Economic Performance*. Cambridge: Cambridge University Press, 1990.

48  Mathias Kipping, 'The Changing Nature of the Business–Government Relationship in Western Europe after 1945', *European Yearbook of Business History*, no. 2, 1999, 35–51.

49  Alice Teichova, *An Economic Background to Munich: International Business and Czechoslovakia, 1918–1938*. London: Cambridge University Press, 1974.

50  Clemens Wurm, *Business, Politics and International Relations: Steel, Cotton and International Cartels in British Politics 1924–1939*. London: Cambridge University Press, 1993.

51  Wurm, *Business, Politics and International Relations*. Ervin Hexner, *International Steel Cartel*. Chapel Hill NC: North Carolina University Press, 1943.

52  Harm Schröter, 'The International Potash Syndicate', in *International Cartels Revisited: Vues Nouvelles sur les Cartels Internationaux (1880s–1980s)*, edited by Dominique Barjot. Caen: Editions du Lys, 1994, 75–92.

53  Harold James, *The End of Globalisation: Lessons from the Great Depression*. London: Harvard University Press, 2001. Harold James, Jakob Tanner (eds), *Enterprise in the Period of Fascism in Europe*. Farnham: Ashgate & Turner, 2002. Terry Gourvish, *Business and Politics in Europe, 1900–1970: Essays in Honour of Alice Teichova*. Cambridge: Cambridge University Press, 2003. Christian Kobrak, Paul Hansen (eds), *European Business, Dictatorship, and Political Risk, 1920–1945*. New York: Berghahn 2004.

54  Tony A. Freyer, *Antitrust and Global Capitalism*. London: Cambridge University Press, 2005. Wyatt Wells, *Antitrust and the Formation of the Postwar World*. New York: Columbia University Press, 2002. Luciano Segreto, Ben Wubs, 'Resistance of the Defeated: German and Italian Big Business and the American Antitrust Policy, 1945–1957', *Enterprise and Society*, vol. 15, no. 2, 2014, 307–336. Wendy Asbeck Brusse, Richard T. Griffiths, 'L'European Recovery Program e i Cartelli: Una Indagine Preliminare', *Studi Storici*, vol. 37, no. 1, 1999, 41–67. About Americanisation, see also Matthias Kipping, Ove Bjarnar (eds), *The Americanisation of European Business: The Marshall Plan and the Transfer of US Management Models*. New York: Routledge, 1998. Jonathan Zeitlin, Gary Herriger (eds), *Americanization and its Limits: Reworking US Technology and Management in Post-war Europe and Japan*. New York: Oxford University Press, 2000. Dominique Barjot (ed.), *Catching up with America: Productivity Missions and the Diffusion of American Economic and Technological Influence after the Second World War*. Paris: Presses de l'Université Paris-Sorbonne, 2002. Harm Schröter, *Americanization of the European Economy: A Compact Survey of American Economic Influence in Europe since the 1800s*. Berlin: Springer, 2005.

55 Simon J. Evenett, Margaret C. Levenstein, Valerie Suslow, 'International Cartel Enforcement: Lessons from the 1990s', *World Economy*, vol. 24, no. 9, 2001, 1221–1245.
56 Société des Nations, Section économique et financière, *Etude sur les Aspects Économiques de Différentes Ententes Industrielles Internationales*, Doc. Officiel n. E.614, Geneva: League of Nations, 1930. Clemens Lammers (ed.) *Ententes Internationales, Proceedings of the Congress of Berlin of the International Chamber of Commerce.* Paris: International Chamber of Commerce, 1937. Laurence Ballande, 'Prix de Cartels et prix de Concurrence: Etude Statistique Relative aux Métaux non Ferroux', in *Les Ententes Internationales de Matières Premières*, edited by William Oualid. Paris: Société des Nations, 1938, 13–32.
57 Muller, *Light Metals Monopoly*. Watkins, 'Aluminum Alliance'. Borkin, 'The Aluminum Battle'.

# Part I

# From patents sharing to cartels

The rise of the Aluminium-Association (1886–1914)

# 1 Scale, scope, and agreements

## The birth of the modern aluminium industry, 1886–1900

Unlike other metals, whose origins are lost in the mist of history, aluminium is a modern material and eventually had an exact date of birth: 1886. Before this date, aluminium was a rare and expensive metal, representing a paradox for the scientific community of the nineteenth century. Although 8 per cent of the Earth's crust is made of aluminium, this metal cannot be found pure in nature and it is always associated with oxygen, forming aluminium oxide ($Al_2O_3$), also known as alumina. The first tests to obtain pure aluminium started in 1807, when Sir Humphrey Davy tried without success to isolate aluminium for the first time. Even though it is theoretically possible to obtain aluminium from all clays, in 1823 Alexandre Berthier identified the key ore for the future aluminium industry, bauxite, in southern France. In 1827, Frederic Wöhler partially achieved the goal to isolate pure aluminium, obtaining some aluminium powder, but only in 1854 Henri Saint-Claire Deville tuned a chemical process to obtain pure metallic aluminium. This discovery was adopted in a small scale by the first world aluminium producer, Produits Chimiques d'Alais et de la Camargue (PCAC – also known as Pechiney), and by other littler business until the late 1880s. Through successive improvements, Saint-Claire Deville's process reduced the unitary production cost from 100 F/kg in 1854 (34 \$/lb) to 61 F/kg in 1886 (12 \$/lb). Due to these high prices, aluminium was considered a luxury metal, which was produced in very small quantities. For instance, in 1886, the global output was only about 2 tons and aluminium was often labelled 'silver from clay'.[1]

The status of aluminium was irreversibly changed after 1886, when the Frenchman Paul Toussaint Héroult and the American Charles Martin Hall concomitantly but independently discovered the process that is still today used to obtain aluminium, the electrolysis of a bath of alumina and cryolite.[2] Aluminium technology was one of the most curious coincidences in the history of technology because, not only did the two inventors make the same discovery at the same time in 1886, but they were also both born in 1863 and died in 1914. As a consequence, they often were reported as 'the aluminium twins'. Their inventions laid the foundation for a new industry and of its first movers.[3] These two inventors were directly implicated in the creation of the first movers of this industry and in the initial dissemination of the new smelting technology. Paul Toussaint Héroult initially worked for the Schweizerische Metallurgische Gesellschaft (SMG), in Neuhausen, Switzerland, which was turned into Aluminium Industrie Aktiengesellschaft (AIAG) one year later.[4]

AIAG disseminated Héroult's technology in the Old Continent: it provided licences to the Société Electrométallurgique Française (SEMF) in 1889 and to the British Aluminium Company (BACO) in 1894,[5] and it created subsidiaries in Germany (1895) and one in Austria (1897). Hall was implicated in the creation of the Pittsburgh Reduction Company (PRC), in the US in 1888 and it was renamed the Aluminum Company of America (ALCOA) in 1907.[6] Moreover, thanks to Hall's patent, PRC installed a production facility in Canada, creating the Northern Aluminium Company (NACO) in 1901. PRC also tried to license a new producer in Great Britain in 1890 and it sold its patent to a French company in 1895. After some financial turmoil, this French company was taken over by PCAC in 1897, which entered again the aluminium business after having been obliged to give up the old chemical process.[7] The group of first movers of this industry, who dominated it until the Great War, was the direct outcome of the initial diffusion of Hall's and Héroult's technologies.

The fact that aluminium was a 'patented' metal in the phase of its original development deserves great attention. The first movers modelled their original strategy after this factor from a twofold standpoint. On the one hand, the existence of these patents provided legal protection, which could be considered an early form of market control. On the other hand, the original strategy of Héroult and Hall in terms of patent registration provided a first international division between two spheres of influence: one dominated by Héroult's technology – where Héroult anticipated Hall in filing his patent (Europe), and one by Hall's (North America).[8] The standard narration about international cartelisation in the aluminium industry often reports that cartels followed the end of patent protection, which hitherto created national monopolies for the first movers of this industry. Actually, it is often claimed that cartelisation in the aluminium industry became necessary only when the legal protection of patents ended. As a consequence, these patents were often considered a key element in the strategy of control over the market in the late nineteenth century, because they helped to prevent the creation of newcomers. Many authors both in old publications[9] and in more recent ones[10] have repeated this explanation to show the reasons for the formation in 1901 of the first international cartel: the Aluminium-Association.

However, this standard explanation is questionable because links between patents and cartels were more complex. According to the different national legislations of that time, patents had different durations that made the expiry of aluminium patents not coincide with 1901.[11] Moreover, Hall and Héroult's patents were not registered in all the countries at the same time, this fact also delayed the actual duration of the patents. The patents' protection lasted over 1901 in the most countries, until 1905 in the UK, to 1909 in the US, and to 1904 in Germany. Only in France did Héroult's patent expire in 1901 but, as anticipated, the two patents were concomitantly adopted in this country after PRC's sale of Hall's technology. At that time, French patent legislation did not provide examination for inventions, which made it possible that both Héroult and Hall registered their process in this country and that two companies were present even during the legal period of patent protection.[12] Furthermore, the geographical dissemination of Héroult and Hall's technology was more complicated than the simple situation described by the patent registration. While AIAG tried to enter the US at the end of the 1880s, PRC aimed to 'invade' Europe investing in the UK at about the same time, before moving to France. In order to bring some order back to this dissemination of technology, already before the settlement of a first international cartel, AIAG and PRC reached an agreement about the geographical division of their 'sphere of influence', and managed other agreements, which aimed to underpin the legal situation of the international patents registration.[13]

Our main explanation of the inception of cartels in the aluminium industry is that neither patents nor these agreements were effective to protect the first movers from the risk of the early aluminium market. They could not prevent the metal from coming across borders under the action of the international metal traders. The history of the early aluminium industry should not be exclusively considered from the standpoint of either market control strategies or of institutional patent protection. Aluminium firms needed some tools to coordinate their actions and to provide some international governance to their industry that, as a matter of fact, was born as a global business. The aluminium market was insignificant for a long time and, instead of being controlled, firms had to develop it to compete with the older and more established non-ferrous metals markets. Moreover, the legal situation of patents was not sufficient to impose the producers' vision about the international development of this industry. While national markets were insufficient to absorb the scale output of the first movers, the international market was difficult to tackle. During the first decade of its life, the aluminium industry swung between two possible models of governance. On the one hand, the national monopoly was appealing for firms, which would have liked to create a reserved market for their production. On the other hand, when the firms recognised the need to run strategies that, borrowing from Alfred D. Chandler's model, we could define in 'scale and scope',[14] this choice made the geographical division of the markets short lived, because national markets were not wide enough to absorb the output. For that, the need to find some agreement was not a substitute for optimal management, but a consequence of it.

It was the impossibility of managing the conflicts among the different firms by relying on the instruments of patents laws that led the producers to negotiate some informal agreements at the end of the nineteenth century. The incompatibility of national legislations on patents and the international strategies of the firms led to the creation of a framework of agreements to rectify the situation. This system of agreements turned out to be ineffective because the firms could not avoid the implication of the non-ferrous metal traders in the administration of the aluminium market, which aimed to sell aluminium through prices fluctuations like other commodities. Once all the producers converged on the same business model of scale and scope strategies, they agreed on the necessity of finding a third way, between national control and international commodity trade, to assist in the development of their industry. During this convergence, firms understood the necessity of selling their metal at stable prices, in order to find a competitive edge against the other non-ferrous metals, whose price was intrinsically unstable. As we will see in the next chapter, in 1901, the first international aluminium cartel was created in order restore some order to the market and to impose this 'credo' on the international traders, reassembling the various agreements on patents and trade that had been previously signed.

## From patents to industry: Héroult's technology and the transformation of SMG into AIAG

The transition of electrolysis technology to an industrial scale and its international licence afterwards did not have a linear development. The history of the technological dissemination of Héroult's and Hall's discoveries was the outcome of a changing strategic vision of the two first movers in the aluminium industry. The investors' choices as regards the patent application for their discoveries laid the foundation on which AIAG and PRC built their investment and international licence strategies, thus defining the geographic zone and the modes of their expansion. The case of Héroult and Hall shows that patents are not only documents of a legal nature, but that they denoted, by the manner in which they were written and registered, a strategic vision of innovation.[15] At the beginning, AIAG was a much more internationalized company, making the holding of Héroult's patents the key to its expansion, as opposed to PRC, which tried to establish and protect its national monopoly, giving less importance to internationalisation strategies. The two first firms adopted similar strategies only when they recognised the need to invest in scale economies, during the mid-1890s when the former strategies were revealed to be a main cause of commercial disorder in international trade.

Héroult applied for his first patent for the production of aluminium from the electrolysis of alumina and cryolite in France in April 1886. Héroult also filed his patents abroad, in Great Britain and the USA. This strategy came from the familiarity of the inventor with the Anglophone world, because he had spent several years in England during his childhood in the 1870s, but also because of his particular entrepreneurial vision with regard to his inventions. Initially Héroult tried to sell the technology to PCAC, which was the major 'chemical aluminium' producer in the world, and then he addressed the Rothschild bank in Paris. Both refused to consider it, particularly Alfred R. Pechiney, the director of PCAC, who told Héroult that:

> Aluminium is a metal with limited markets; it is used to make opera glasses, no matter if you sold it at 100 or 10 F, you would not sell a kg more. If you made aluminium bronze, that would be different, because great quantities of aluminium bronze are employed, if you sold it at a good price, the bargaining would be interesting.[16]

This statement shows the special status of aluminium at that time. While pure aluminium was still considered a luxury metal, typical of jewellery, alloys such as aluminium bronze (5–20 per cent aluminium and the rest copper) were already appealing in selected metallurgic uses with high added value and whose global demand was increasing. When Héroult started his career as an inventor, it was already known that it was possible to produce aluminium bronze directly from raw materials, without passing through the pure aluminium stage, which at that time still represented a major technical puzzle. Before Héroult, the direct production of aluminium bronze had been started in 1885 by the American company Cowles Electric Smelting and Aluminum Company, which was created by the brothers Alfred and Eugene Cowles, and produced this alloy directly by means of a thermo-electric process and the use of a powerful arc furnace. This company was carrying out wide-ranging research in order to find metallurgic uses for the electro-technical equipment (dynamo) of the Brush Electric Company, of which Eugene Cowles himself was the director.[17]

Pechiney's refusal had the effect of redirecting Héroult's research towards aluminium bronze. Particularly, Héroult focused his research on the design of an arc furnace that could melt alumina with copper. This research was patented during 1887 in France, as an addition to his original patent and it was merged into the original patent that had already been patented in Great Britain and was applied for as a new patent in the USA (see Table 1.1). Thanks to the intermediation of an agent of Goldschmidt Bank in Paris, Emile Dreyfus, this new patent captured the attention of some leading electro-mechanical and metallurgical Swiss companies, which created SMG to take advantage of Héroult's research.[18] These companies were Nehers und Sohne, which was trying to diversify its production from its core production of iron and steel, the producer of dynamos Oerlikon, and the maker of turbines Escher Wyss.[19] In that period, Oerlikon and Escher Wyss had collaborated in the creation of the Brown system, a powerful electric generator invented by Eugene Charles Lancelot Brown, who had worked as an engineer for Oerlikon, before founding Brown-Boveri.[20] Like Cowles' firm, these companies were carrying out some wide-ranging research on the use of electricity in the metallurgic field, in order to widen their reference market for electrical equipment.

When Héroult met Gustav Naville, the director of Escher Wyss and George Neher's son-in-law, and Emil Huber-Werdmüller, the director of Oerlikon, aluminium bronze was an ideally suitable technology to test the efficiency of the Brown system, which was already installed at Neuhausen falls. The meeting between the French inventor and the Swiss electric companies led to the creation of SMG with a modest capital of 200,000 Swiss francs. Héroult was appointed technical director while Nehers became sales manager. Huber and Naville were respectively president and CEO.[21] According to the initial agreements, Héroult also became shareholder of SMG, as well as Dreyfus, while the company gained control over the foreign patents for which Héroult had applied so far, while Héroult and Dreyfus would create another company in France. SMG was also committed to continuing the international application on behalf of the company on payment of 1,000 francs for each country where they applied. Actually, SMG proceeded with the application of Héroult's patents in Germany, Austria-Hungary, and Belgium, for a process that was similar to the one described in the English patent, which presented both the production of pure aluminium from alumina and cryolite, and aluminium bronze using alumina and copper (see Table 1.1). Moreover, Héroult and the Swiss company committed to share every

Table 1.1 Héroult's patents, 1886–1889

| Application filed | Country | No. | Date patented | Specification | Registered by | Owned by, according to Héroult–SMG agreement | Licensed to |
|---|---|---|---|---|---|---|---|
| 23 April 1886 | France | 175,711 | 1 September 1886 | Pure aluminium (alumina + cryolite) | Héroult | Héroult | SEMF |
| 22 May 1886 | United States | – | Rejected | Pure aluminium (alumina + cryolite) | Héroult | SMG/AIAG | Lowrey/USAMC |
| 15 April 1887 | France | Addition to 175,711 | 14 September 1887 | Aluminium bronze (copper + alumina) | Héroult | Héroult | SEMF |
| 16 April 1887 | Belgium | 77,100 | ? | Pure aluminium + bronze | Héroult | SMG/AIAG | None |
| 21 May 1887 | Great Britain | 7,426 | 27 April 1888 | Pure aluminium + bronze | Héroult | SMG/AIAG | BACO |
| 7 December 1887 | Belgium | 79,834 | 14 June 1888* | Apparatus for aluminium bronze (alumina + copper) | SMG/AIAG | SMG/AIAG | None |
| 7 December 1887 | Italy | 22,658 | 14 June 1888* | Apparatus for aluminium bronze (alumina + copper) | SMG/AIAG | SMG/AIAG | None |
| 7 December 1887 | Spain | 8,112 | 14 June 1888* | Apparatus for aluminium bronze (alumina + copper) | SMG/AIAG | SMG/AIAG | None |
| 7 December 1887 | Great Britain | 16,853 | 7 December 1888 | Apparatus for aluminium bronze (alumina + copper) | SMG/AIAG | SMG/AIAG | BACO |
| 8 December 1887 | Germany | 47,165 | 3 June 1889 | Apparatus for aluminium bronze (alumina + copper) | SMG/AIAG | SMG/AIAG | AIAG |
| 7 December 1887 | France | 187,447 | 25 February 1888 | Apparatus for aluminium bronze (alumina + copper) | Dreyfus | Dreyfus/Héroult | SEMF |
| 27 December 1887 | United States | 387,876 | 14 August 1888 | Aluminium bronze (= addition) | Héroult | SMG/AIAG | Lowrey/USAMC |
| 27 December 1887 | United States | 473,118 | 19 April 1892 | Apparatus for aluminium bronze (Alumina + copper) | Héroult | SMG/AIAG | Lowrey/USAMC |
| 27 December 1887 | Canada | 29,033 | 28 April 1888 | Apparatus metals from their oxide | Héroult | SMG/AIAG | None |

Note
* Actual date unknown: this date refers to when Héroult was informed by AIAG's agent about patenting.

subsequent innovation to the production process for 20 years, because an improvement of the machinery was planned, for which the new patents were to be filed.[22]

In Neuhausen, Héroult conceived new machinery for the direct production of bronze, which was patented again in France, the USA, Germany, Austria, Great Britain, and other European countries during 1888 (see Table 1.1). Héroult's key concept was the creation of specific machinery that, through the use of a large amount of electricity, managed to melt alumina and copper to create aluminium bronze directly. Héroult himself thought that he could have created a universal arc furnace with his research, which was able to melt the majority of metals starting from their oxide, as for aluminium.[23] One of the main guidelines of this strategy was adopted in France, where Héroult's new patent was filed by Dreyfus, who committed to create a new company, SEMF, with a smelter in Froges. This plant was created in 1889 like SMG's in Neuhausen and it was equipped with Oerlikon–Escher Wyss machinery.[24] This international strategy was useful for Oerlikon and Escher Wyss to broaden their market for electric machinery through the selling of Héroult's technology. Already in the course of 1888, SMG tried to entrust Héroult's patents to possible foreign buyers (in Belgium, Scotland, and the USA) along with Oerlikon–Escher Wyss equipment. SMG wanted to be able to provide contracts for the creation of small smelters equipped with the Brown system to produce aluminium alloys, whose outlets were expanding at the end of the century. This strategy corresponds to a specific period in the history of the industrial application of electricity, where the producers of electrical machinery tried to widen their market through some key applications. Scholarly studies have often underlined the use of electricity for urban lighting as the main purpose of this strategy. However, aluminium alloys represented a commercial opportunity to widen the industrial use of electricity for the performing machinery that these firms produced.[25]

The strategy of SMG was also oriented to the US market. During 1888, a group of entrepreneurs, who were close to Thomas Alva Edison, became interested in Héroult's patents. In fact, Grosvenor P. Lowrey, who was an expert in patents and had contributed to the creation of the Edison Company,[26] became the *assignor* of Héroult's patent on aluminium bronzes in the US. Lowrey also tried to start a company, called the United States Aluminium Metal Company (USAMC) to adopt Héroult's technology: Walter Barnard and Franklin Pope, two engineers close to Edison and Lowrey, visited the Neuhausen establishments at the end of 1888 in order to advance this project.[27] In the course of 1889, Héroult himself came to the US to install his production process on bronzes along with Oerlikon and Escher Wyss machinery.[28] However, this venture was blocked by some legal issues that emerged concerning the aluminium patents. USAMC was accused by Cowles of violating his patent on aluminium bronzes.[29] Moreover, Charles Hall obtained his patent in April 1889, when the American Patent Office gave priority to Hall over Héroult's process on pure aluminium, rejecting the first application that Héroult had made in 1886. As is known, even if Hall filed his patent in July 1886, thus after the original patent that Héroult registered in France in April 1886, the US Patent authority gave priority to Hall because his sister testified that Hall obtained aluminium for the first time in February of 1886. Héroult, who came in the US to install his machinery, had no evidence to testify any prior dates and, since the US customs authorities did not admit Swiss electrical machinery, he was not able to prove the value of his inventions. This fact did not modify the situation of patents outside the US, but Héroult was precluded from this country when, as we will see, SMG's strategy turned to the pure aluminium business.[30]

At the beginning, SMG's strategy was not far from Cowles', which essentially focused on the marketing of electrical equipment and on the enlargement of metallurgical applications for electricity. At the end of the 1880s, the Swiss company changed its core business thanks to new synergies coming from the German business. Actually, SMG redesigned its initial strategy thanks to the implication of new actors in 1888, when it was informed that the Allgemeine Elektrizität Gesellschaft (AEG) was also working on the electrolysis of aluminium at its pilot unit in Berlin. German rules on patents required a field test, and this created issues for the application of Héroult's patent in Germany, where implementation is required to validate the application of a patent. Vice versa, AEG found its strategy for technological innovation stalled by Héroult's and SMG's patents abroad, which were already filed in many countries. This led to the idea of creating an *Interessengemeischaft* around aluminium, in order to gather the patents of Héroult, SMG, and AEG in one company. The closeness of AEG to Edison (AEG was born as a company licensed by the patents of Edison for Germany) helped to merge Swiss interests with the German electrical company. Lowrey himself acted as an intermediary during the first phase of the negotiation between AEG and SMG that led to the foundation of AIAG.[31]

In October 1888, Emil Rathenau, president of AEG, and Emil Huber-Werdmüller signed an agreement between the two companies to create AIAG.[32] Unlike SMG, this company was set up to invest in scale production and had capital of 10 million Swiss francs, with the participation of the *Gotha* of German banks that were already AEG's allies, i.e. Deutsche Bank and Berliner Handels-Gesellschaft. Héroult was replaced by an engineer from AEG, Martin Kiliani, who had performed experiments on copper electrolysis and was tackling the separation of pure aluminium at AEG's laboratory. AIAG's strategy quickly turned from the sale of Héroult's technology to the development of pure aluminium production and of its markets. Martin Schindler, a dealer from the paper industry, was appointed as sales manager, while Héroult was sent to work at the creation of USAMC.[33] Kiliani has worked on pure aluminium during 1889, uniting the research he had previously performed at AEG and applying it to the machinery for bronze designed by the French inventor. It is often believed that Kiliani's main contribution was the introduction of a rotatory movement to the anode, which served to break the crust of metal that, due to the lower temperature on its top, capped the electrolytic bath. However, his main contribution was the creation of an electrolyte, in which, in addition to alumina and cryolite, other *chemicalia* (i.e. different fluorides to reduce the melting point of alumina) allowed the production of pure aluminium.[34] In contemporary studies, this process is often called Héroult–Kiliani, to distinguish it from Héroult's process on bronze.[35]

AIAG's strategy shifted towards the production of pure aluminium, modifying SMG's original strategy. The plant in Neuhausen became the production centre of the company, thanks to support from the German financial world. New investments were made in order to increase the productive capacity and to vertically integrate the production. AIAG signed some stable contracts for the supply of alumina with Chemischen Fabrik Bergius in Breslau, which was subsequently acquired in 1894, and for the supply of artificial cryolite with Kundheim in Berlin, which was a company close to AEG and joined AIAG's capital. AIAG also created an atelier for the production of semi-finished and finished products, which also included cookware, thermos, and keys.[36] The increase of economies of scale and the previous integration allowed lowering of the production cost of the produced metal from 30 Swiss francs per kilo in 1889 to 19 in 1891, until reaching 6.5 in 1892. In the same time interval, the production of Neuhausen multiplied ten times, going from three to almost 200 tons per year, the majority of which was exported to Germany. This country represented the main world market of aluminium at the end of the nineteenth century and AEG was able to provide a widespread commercial network, which was managed by Schindler. Moreover, AIAG created an international commercial network, which included the principal European countries (such as Italy, Spain, Austria, Poland, Belgium, Netherlands, Germany), Russia, Egypt, and Japan.[37]

Considering the reduction of the production costs obtained in Neuhausen, AIAG's board decided in 1892 to start building a new plant in Rheinfelden, in Germany, near the Swiss border, along with the construction of a new hydroelectric power station. On the one hand, this investment would have allowed production on a much greater scale than the one existing in Neuhausen, and, as a consequence, lowering the unitary production costs in order to encourage the expansion of the market of this metal. On the other hand, the creation of this plant in Germany aimed at supporting the increasing demand for aluminium from the German metal industry, after obtaining some important contacts for the supply with Carl Berg AG, one of the first big buyers of aluminium for metallic construction.[38] This link between AIAG and Berg pushed AIAG to reorganise its sales strategy towards long-term contracts with stable prices, which is documented in the publication of its 'price list', which has been published since 1892.[39] Not only did this German investment mark the starting point of aluminium mass production, but it also aimed to shield AIAG from the imports that were beginning to be consistent from other countries.[40] Because of the huge size of this investment, its construction lasted until 1898. In the meanwhile, AIAG took the decision to build a third plant in Lend, Austria, which came on stream in 1899. Meanwhile, between 1892 and 1897, the plant in Neuhausen was involved in several investments, which took its productive capacity from around 200 tons per year to 700.[41]

## Hall, PRC, and the initial strategies of the American company

Unlike Héroult, Hall did not have the same international strategy as regards his patents: he started to spread them internationally only after the creation of PRC.

Actually, Hall registered his process abroad only in June 1889, when some patents were registered in Canada and the UK. Moreover, while Héroult focused his interest on machinery, the composition of the electrolytic bath captured Hall's attention, which led him to apply for different patents with different bath specifications. Particularly, Hall hypothesised that the production of pure aluminium could be performed through the electrolysis of alumina in different electrolytes, made of aluminium fluoride, chloride of calcium, and chloride of potassium. Other two fluorides and alkali metal were thought to be usable in this process. Following these considerations, he applied for three patents in the USA in July 1886, and two others in 1888. This choice was dictated by the more chemical view of his invention, that Héroult lacked and that was implemented in Neuhausen after the hiring of Kiliani. However, Hall wrote his patents with the intention of considering a series of hypothetical theories while waiting for validation through production, which would have made industrial experimentation available.[42] Hall addressed the company that would have in theory been the most interested in aluminium to test his process in the industrial environment: Cowles. However, after a trial of only few months in a pilot plant in Lockport, Hall was fired, and Cowles decided to keep his production process on bronze.[43]

Thanks to the history of the company ALCOA written by George Smith and, more specifically, the history of its R&D written by Graham and Pruitt, both the dynamics that led to the foundation of the American aluminium industry and its relationships with Hall are well known.[44] Once removed from his duties at the Cowles pilot plant, Hall came into contact with a group of engineers from the steel industry in Pittsburgh. These engineers decided to bet on Hall's research, creating PRC with an initial capital of $20,000. Production was started in an experimental smelter, called the Pittsburgh Testing Laboratory (PTL), owned by Alfred E. Hunt, who was one of the first admirers of Hall's process and the first president of PRC. Hall went there to produce with his method, starting the first production on a semi-industrial scale, from which he filed three other patents.[45] In a manner similar to the one in Neuhausen, this first plant worked as a kind of 'incubator' where Hall, along with Hunt and Arthur Vining Davis, an engineer who came to PRC in 1889, reached the production standard.[46]

Thanks to several innovations, the price of aluminium in the US was reduced from $6 in 1888 to $4 in 1889, reaching $2 in 1890. Encouraged by these initial results, PRC started the construction a new plant in order to achieve greater economies of scale and further lower the unitary production costs. In order to obtain the funds necessary to expand production, PRC used a strategy of international diffusion of Hall's process. After the international filing of his patent in Canada, Great Britain, and France during 1889, Hunt looked for potential buyers for the process abroad with the aim of finding financing channels useful for carrying out new investments in the US. In these countries, Hall filed the patents in which he described an electrolyte composed of a mixture of aluminium fluorides, sodium fluorides, calcium chloride, and alumina, which was different from the process described by Héroult (electrolysis of alumina with cryolite).[47] When PRC enacted this strategy, it was using this electrolyte to produce aluminium, using different salts and fluorides to lower the melting point of alumina instead of cryolite.[48] In 1890, PRC managed to sell a licence in Britain, where Reduction Metals Syndicate Ltd of Manchester was formed. This company was created as a joint venture between PRC and a producer of precious metals, Johnson Matthey & Co., which was the main English pure aluminium dealer at the time. Wilfried S. Sample, who had previously worked as chief chemist at PRC, was appointed director of this company.[49] Not much information about this company is available: it seems that it never went beyond a phase of experimentation on a small scale, replicating the experiments on electrolytes made in Pittsburgh, and that its production did not exceed 50 tons per year.[50] After making scale investments in the US, PRC adopted a strategy of exportation to Great Britain, limiting the production on site. As we will see, the creation of BACO led to the final closure of the plant in Manchester.

As it is known, PRC found its most important financial source in the alliance with one of the main American merchant banks. At the end of 1889, Hunt obtained financial aid from the Mellon Bank in Pittsburgh, one of the largest merchant banks in the country, which still remains one of the most important partners of ALCOA.[51] With a new capital of $1 million, PRC began to build a new plant in New Kensington, whose initial productive capacity was about 200 tons per year, compared to 5 tons that were initially produced in Pittsburgh. The price of aluminium produced in this period fell from $4/lb to about 60 cents. Thanks to the support of Mellon, in 1893 the company in Pittsburgh took over the Niagara Falls Power Company and began the construction of a new plant on site, where from 1895 it concentrated its production, integrating with the production of electricity. The plant in New Kensington was used for the production of the chemical materials of electrolytes first, and then the semi-finished products. Scale economies progressively went from 100 tons per year in 1892 to about 400 tons per year, and they reached 1,000 in 1896. In parallel with the growth of scale economies, PRC also adopted a strategy of productive integration towards semi-finished products and finished products and, subsequently, towards raw materials.[52]

The early history of PRC was shaped by the protection of its monopoly in the United States provided by Hall's patent. Once Hall's patent took precedence over Héroult's, a threat to the PRC's monopoly came from Cowles. At the time when PRC was incorporated, Cowles had already established itself as a pioneer company in the production of aluminium alloys, whose strategy also included a phase of internationalisation with a subsidiary in Great Britain, i.e. Cowles Syndicate Limited in Milton-on-Tyne. At the same time, Cowles also represented a threat to Héroult's process in Europe, where he had filed his patent in several countries. However, Cowles' technology could no longer compete in the electrolysis of aluminium used by PRC and AIAG since 1891, when the production costs were reduced by the improvements brought in the first production centres.[53] Cowles then decided to produce pure aluminium to recover the market shares that PRC was taking away. To legitimate this production from a legal point of view, Cowles made an agreement with another inventor, Charles Bradley, who has experimented with electrolysis on various metals since 1883. Cowles filed his patent in 1891, producing proof of the anteriority of Bradley's experiments over

Hall's.[54] For a short period, AIAG has tried to take part into the disputes about the anteriority between Cowles and PRC in order to take advantage to enter in the US market again. Several studies on the initial phase of aluminium production quote the attempts made by Lowrey to gain control over Bradley's patents, which had even led to legal action taken by Cowles.[55] In fact, Lowrey's initiative did not stand alone, but was a joint action carried out with AIAG, which at that time still hoped to reverse the decision about the anteriority of Hall over Héroult in the United States to enter the American market.[56]

For a brief period between 1891 and 1893 in the US there was a duopoly, interrupted by the lawsuit filed by the PRC against Cowles. PRC denounced Cowles for plagiarism of Hall's method, after proving that Cowles was using Hall's inventions in Lockport without the consent of the inventor. In 1893 the American patent office prohibited Cowles from producing, forcing him to leave the aluminium business and give PRC back its domestic monopoly that would last, as we will see, until 1941. Cowles decided to appeal and prove the anteriority of Bradley's patent over Hall's patent: the process lasted until 1903, when a new verdict overturned the situation of 1893, establishing the priority of Bradley. However, this verdict neither solved the issue of patents, nor could change the situation. The only company to possess the technique to produce aluminium was PRC, while Cowles could not use Bradley's technique, because it did not work. The verdict forced the two companies to seek a gentleman's agreement on their patents, so PRC decided to buy Bradley's patent and compensate Cowles, obtaining the absolute monopoly in the American market. Thus, PRC extended domestic protection provided by the patent for other five years (to 1909), because Bradley's patent, as we have seen, was filed in 1891.[57]

## The aluminium industry in France and Great Britain

France represented one of the main elements of the Swiss company's international strategy. AIAG inherited the agreements that had been reached between Héroult and SMG and between SMG and SEMF, updating them to the new strategy on pure aluminium. In 1890, when AIAG changed the production to pure aluminium through Kiliani's innovations, SEMF received this technology from AIAG as well, on payment of a royalty on the produced metal. AIAG also provided all the electrical machinery to build the hydroelectric power station in Froges and agreed to supply alumina to the French factory under an agreement with Bergius.[58] Even if SEMF was born as a sort of *franchise* of SMG and AIAG, it actually became more independent from the Swiss company in the course of the 1890s. In 1890, SEMF hired Héroult himself as a *consultant*, since once he came back from the USA in 1890, he could not keep working for AIAG, which had turned to Kiliani's method to produce pure aluminium. However, in Froges, Héroult designed a new technology, which proved to be better than Kiliani's. Héroult improved the electrolytic furnaces, lowering the production costs of SEMF to below those of AIAG, producing aluminium through only alumina and cryolite and reducing the consumption of electric power. From 1891, SEMF started studying the possibility of making new investments in order to build a new smelter in La Praz with greater scale economies (about 2,000 tons/year) and to integrate production upward (towards alumina) and downward (towards semi-finished products). Another important aspect of SEMF's R&D was the creation of new carbon electrodes, which made production even more efficient and the produced metal even purer.[59]

Like PRC and AIAG, SEMF was trying to abandon the small-scale test phase that had characterised the early 1890s, to start large-scale production. Notwithstanding the participation of Paris Goldschmidt Bank in the capital of Paris, SEMF could not count on the same financial power that supported AIAG or PRC. In fact, SEMF had been founded in 1888 with a fairly limited capital, i.e. only 650,000 francs, consisting almost only of the participation of small local interests, like those represented by the entrepreneurs Gustav de Munerel and Jules Viard – who came from the construction industry and were the main shareholders – along with Dreyfus and Héroult. The new development plans involved an increase in capital up to five million francs, which the French company could not obtain on the financial market. SEMF was convinced that only with a production on a particularly large scale, about 2,000 tons per year, they could have lowered the unitary cost of aluminium in order to make it a 'mass metal' and overcome the resistance of the market and, in particular, to prove the capability of aluminium to compete with copper in key applications.[60]

In the course of 1892, SEMF was in such a difficult situation that it could not implement its investments. The poor commercial situation of aluminium, which the management attributed to the relative narrowness of the market and the relatively high cost of the metal, affected the financial situation of the company. This situation inspired no confidence in the investors outside the aluminium field, because they did not share the optimism of the company that believed it could rapidly change the status of this metal through the proposed investments. Héroult entered into new negotiations with AIAG in order to merge the Swiss and the French companies and create a new common unit in La Praz. According to Héroult, only the joint companies could have achieved the scale economies necessary to modify the market of this metal. His new furnaces and the technology on electric carbons were used as a bargaining weapon with AIAG.[61] However, AIAG was already redirecting its strategy to the construction of the unit in Rheinfelden, since Germany was the main market for this metal. This decision led AIAG to refuse the merger with SEMF, but the Swiss company realised that Héroult's technology was superior to Kiliani's technology used in Neuhausen. The new technology designed by Héroult could halve the production cost, bringing it from 5 F/kg to 2.70 F/kg, and it made Kiliani's chemical solutions unnecessary. AIAG understood that this type of cost reduction made it truly possible to launch mass production of aluminium and it would be essential to pursue the outlined investment plans.[62] AIAG offered a new type of agreement to SEMF: in exchange for Héroult's new technology, it proposed a new cross-participation between the two companies and the end of the royalties that SEMF had to pay AIAG. AIAG also decided to buy SEMF's unsold stocks of metal in bulk, aiming to export to Germany. From a commercial point of view, SEMF would have the selling monopoly in France because AIAG refrained from selling in exchange for the export ban by SEMF.[63]

After these negotiations, SEMF could begin to build its new unit in La Praz, but on a more modest scale than the one that had been hypothesised in the beginning. The participation of the bank Cottet in Lyon also played a crucial role. The company was also reorganised from a managerial point of view: a new manager, Emile Vielhomme, was appointed director of the company to restore the accounts. The company's capacity was only 500 tons/year at the beginning and it was doubled before the end of the century.[64] These new agreements had led to a separation between the two companies. SEMF was born as a 'franchise' of AIAG on the French market; with Héroult's new technologies and the construction of a new modern smelter it became more and more autonomous from the Swiss company. This technological autonomy was further sanctioned in the course of 1894, when SEMF acquired new technology for the production of alumina and left the supplies from Bergius. The Austrian inventor Karl Joseph Bayer had patented an innovative process for the separation of alumina from bauxite, through a purification system based on caustic soda. This process allowed a reduction in the cost of alumina, which until then had always been obtained using the method designed by Saint-Claire Deville (dissolution based on sodium carbonate). Bayer had been in contact with some French entrepreneurs who had founded the Société Industrielle de l'Alumine Pure (SIAP), with a unit in Gardanne, in the south of France. However, this unit failed to achieve a continuous production and SIAP went out of business in 1893. On Héroult's recommendation, SIAP was taken over by SEMF; Héroult himself worked with Bayer to change the equipment in Gardanne and start production on an industrial scale.[65]

Once it had opted for the mass production of aluminium, AIAG decided to pursue his strategy of international licences in Great Britain anyhow. In Great Britain, AIAG had the advantage that Héroult had filed the electrolysis patent before Hall. However, while the British market was not much developed to sell great quantities of aluminium, it threatened the European markets because both Hall's production of Patricroft and the production of Cowles' aluminium bronze were re-exported to Germany, damaging AIAG in its main outlet. The possibility of licensing a producer close to the Swiss company turned out to be a crucial action to stop both the export from Great Britain to the continent, and to grant an organised development of the aluminium industry in this country. The opportunity arose at the end of 1893, when Emmanuele Ristori, an Italian-born engineer who worked as a director in a company producing weapons, Nordfolk Guns, managed to buy Héroult's patents for Great Britain.[66] Almost a year later, BACO was born.[67]

BACO was different from the other three companies that have so far been presented for three main reasons. First, BACO had never experienced the small-scale production phase and it was conceived as an integrated company and on a large scale. In fact, in 1894, also the other companies had already chosen this path and AIAG provided BACO with Héroult's more advanced technology. BACO's investment plan also involved full vertical integration, which included the purchase of raw materials mines (Irish bauxite), the erection of a scale production of alumina (at Larne, Ireland), the construction of hydroelectric capacities in

Scotland (at Foyes), and the production of semi-finished products.[68] Second, BACO was born as a large limited company, which would find the necessary financing in the City stock market: the inclusion of Lord Kelvin as scientific adviser, one of the main British scientists of the time, turned out to be crucial to give credibility to the project.[69] Third, Ristori did not only buy Héroult's patent: he acquired other patents on electro-metallurgical furnaces preceding Héroult and he also took over the patents and units of the Cowles brothers, who in the meantime were pushed out of the aluminium market by PRC, with the idea of obtaining the legal monopoly to produce and sell aluminium in the UK.[70]

A further important aspect of the creation of BACO was its control over Bayer's British patent on the production of alumina. This technological advantage put BACO on a different level from the other companies that had obtained the licences. On the one hand, AIAG provided BACO with the most advanced technology for the production of aluminium (Oerlikon and Escher Wyss electro-technical machinery and Héroult's new furnaces that he himself supervised in the course of 1897),[71] and on the other hand, BACO could provide Bayer's technology on the production of alumina in exchange. As we previously said, in these years AIAG was getting its supply of alumina from Bergius, which used the old Saint-Claire Deville method, and the problem of what type of technology was to be adopted for the production of this raw material was arising when AIAG implemented the plan for new investments in scale economies. The alliance with BACO, also established thanks to participation in its capital, allowed it to get its supply of alumina from the British company, while waiting to make their own investments. Moreover, the agreements granted BACO the British market exclusively, in exchange for the export ban.[72]

The creation of BACO led to the end of the British joint venture with PRC, which was forced to interrupt production due to several litigations started by BACO's board. PRC had never made investments to increase its scale economies in Great Britain, since – as we have previously seen – it preferred to put all its strengths into domestic production. The precarious situation of the Syndicate ventured by PRC worsened after the creation of BACO. In the course of 1894 and 1985, BACO sued other British traders of metals such as Armstrong Mitchell, who sold in the British market the metal produced by the PRC's venture in the UK. Thanks to the ownership of several patents on electrolysis of aluminium and on the production of alumina, Ristori's company claimed that aluminium was declared as its trademark. In fact, the British High Court of Justice established that BACO owned the legal monopoly on the production and sale of this metal.[73] However, PRC had continued to have a commercial strategy oriented towards Great Britain, exporting part of its growing production that could not be absorbed by the domestic market. To support this strategy a new company had been created, Aluminium Supply Company Ltd (ASCO), that soon also clashed with the legal actions of BACO.[74]

The British court's verdict, which overturned the situation in the US, did not represent a solution for a geographical division of the issue of the patents. After leaving Great Britain, in fact, PRC decided to sell its patent in France. Since 1887, another producer, i.e. Société Industrielle de l'Aluminium et des Alliages

Métalliques (SIAAM) had been trying to set up electrolytic production of pure aluminium. This company used the patent designed by Adolphe Minet in 1886, which involved the electrolytic smelting of a bath of alumina and aluminium and potassium fluorides that, according to some contemporary observers, was not very different from some experiments which were contained in Hall's patents.[75] After the test on a small scale in Creil, north of the Parisian region, thanks to the support of the bankers, Myrtil and Ernest Bernand, production on an industrial scale was tried at 'Calypso' plant, not far from Froges. However, SIAAM never achieved satisfying production and, after being paid off, it was reorganised in 1895, following the purchase of Hall's patents and under the direction of Wilfred Sample himself who was leaving the PRC's venture in Britain.[76]

Unlike the other countries, France did not require an evaluation of the patents, so it was impossible for SEMF to resort to legal action to invalidate Hall's patents, as BACO did in Britain. Moreover, Hall's patents for France described an electrolyte that was different from the electrolyte used by Héroult, and this made any legal action to demonstrate possible plagiarism difficult. However, SIAAM failed to obtain satisfying results from the point of view of the purity of the metal and it went through a severe financial crisis in the course of 1897. Héroult would have wanted SEMF to take over this company, but SEMF objected because of the financial commitments previously made. The acquisition of this company by SEMF would have led to a divide between the processes of Héroult and Hall from the geographical point of view on a continental level, because it would have actually banned Hall from France as well. Instead of SEMF, the unit in Saint-Michel was then taken over by PCAC, thanks to the intuition of the new director: Adrien Badin. Badin was placed by the side of the old president of the company who refused to provide assistance to Héroult, Alfred R. Pechiney, and gave new impetus to its strategy regarding aluminium. Thus, PCAC could go back into the business of aluminium, from which it had been excluded in 1889.[77]

## The difficult relationships between AIAG and PRC, between agreements and global clashes

The technological and productive proximity of AIAG and PRC made the two companies lean towards an agreement on the related spheres of influence, in order to avoid a dispute over the patents or the reference markets. However, the settlement of an international cooperation agreement was not reached easily, because of the early struggles necessary to find room in the relatively narrow aluminium market. AIAG had already suggested a meeting with PRC in the summer of 1889, when Hunt undertook a journey to Europe to look for buyers for Hall's patents that had led to the creation of the Metal Reduction Syndicate.[78] Even if this proposal failed to hamper the creation of a Hall unit in Great Britain, AIAG continued to negotiate an agreement with the American company to share their respective markets. In the first months of 1890, Rathenau also suggested PRC merge all the European and American interests in aluminium, including Cowles, aiming to follow a strategy that was similar to the one that had led to the creation of AIAG. Lowrey himself had been charged by Rathenau with testing the waters to see if a merger with the American companies was possible.[79] This offer was refused by Hunt, who wrote to Rathenau:

> My views regarding some unions, or at least, understanding, between your interests and ours, are not at all changed from what I have already written, said, and send to you, namely, that some understanding would be to the mutual advantages of both parties, without any doubts.[80]

In the course of 1890, the heads of PRC and AIAG mutually inspected the others' facilities to evaluate the state of the art of the production of aluminium and they shared information about the composition of the electrolytes and the construction of the furnaces. Huber's son performed an internship at PRC, during which he wrote a complete report on the equipment and technologies of the American company, while Hunt visited Neuhausen in the summer of 1890, inspecting both the smelter and the fabricating facilities.[81] In spite of these friendly relationships, AIAG kept working to consolidate its legal position, acquiring the patents that preceded Héroult's patents in several countries, like France and Germany, so to be covered from any possible hostile moves of PRC. For example, AIAG was interested in Lontin's patent on the electrolysis of cryolite of 1883 that, even if it did not work on an industrial level, could have become crucial if a legal dispute on the priority of the patents in the countries where PRC and AIAG were expanding was started. We have seen that in the case of Great Britain, AIAG preferred to license a third producer instead of investing in first person. When AIAG opted for a scale production in Germany, its commercial strategy became the defence of its monopoly in this country, which was the main mark of aluminium at the time.[82]

The year 1894 marked the change from small facilities to those with larger scale economies (see Table 1.2 and also Figure 2.1 in the next chapter). Before this date, aluminium production had still been relatively insignificant and AIAG and PRC did not seem to have great issues with each other. The existing small-scale production could satisfy the small market of this metal, even though it could not satisfy any increase in demand. As the productive capacity of the different companies increased, it became clearer that the market was not sufficient for all the scale productions. Since the beginning, both PRC and AIAG reached agreements on prices and then agreements on the geographical division of their markets in order to manage this situation. As a consequence, between 1894 and 1897, the market of aluminium could be described as a haze of agreements that prevented BACO and SEMF from exporting to foreign markets, while AIAG and PRC had saved for themselves Germany and the USA, respectively. In fact, PRC was 'authorised' to sell Hall's patent in France by AIAG, which agreed to supply it with German alumina coming from Bergius in exchange for an agreement on prices and the reference markets.[83]

In 1896, PRC also converged to the 'price-list' strategy, already started by AIAG. While, previously, PRC left international traders free to set prices, the

Table 1.2 Production (tons) and selling prices of aluminium producers, 1886–1901

| | PRC | | | AIAG | | SEMF | | PCAC* | | BACO | | Total | Exp. Price |
|---|---|---|---|---|---|---|---|---|---|---|---|---|---|
| | Prod. | $/kg | ChF/kg | Prod. | ChF/kg | Prod. | F/kg | Prod. | F/kg | Prod. | £/t | Prod. | DM/kg |
| 1886 | – | – | – | – | – | – | – | 2 | 67.00 | – | – | 2 | – |
| 1887 | – | – | – | – | – | – | – | 2 | 68.00 | – | – | 2 | – |
| 1888 | – | – | – | – | – | – | – | 2 | 66.00 | – | – | 2 | – |
| 1889 | 5 | 4.08 | 46.51 | 3 | 30.00 | – | – | 3 | 61.00 | – | – | 11 | 27.60 |
| 1890 | 20 | 2.00 | 22.80 | 41 | 19.00 | 31 | 29.60 | – | – | – | – | 92 | 15.20 |
| 1891 | 22 | 1.21 | 13.79 | 173 | 19.00 | 32 | 18.10 | – | – | – | – | 227 | 8.00 |
| 1892 | 40 | 0.86 | 9.80 | 242 | 6.25 | 47 | 6.80 | – | – | – | – | 329 | 5.00 |
| 1893 | 98 | 0.78 | 8.89 | 447 | 5.00 | 86 | 5.00 | – | – | – | – | 631 | 5.00 |
| 1894 | 224 | 0.61 | 6.95 | 615 | 3.75 | 180 | 5.50 | – | – | – | – | 1,019 | 4.00 |
| 1895 | 227 | 0.54 | 6.68 | 505 | 3.75 | 269 | 4.10 | – | – | – | – | 1,001 | 3.00 |
| 1896 | 454 | 0.48 | 5.78 | 602 | 3.00 | 307 | 4.20 | 56 | – | – | – | 1,419 | 2.60 |
| 1897 | 1,076 | 0.36 | 4.44 | 717 | 2.90 | 289 | 4.50 | 114 | – | 247 | 160.0 | 2,443 | 2.50 |
| 1898 | 1,357 | – | 3.48 | 843 | 2.80 | 465 | 2.90 | 147 | 2.89 | 381 | 140.0 | 3,193 | 2.20 |
| 1899 | 1,479 | – | 3.73 | 1,347 | 2.50 | 567 | 2.70 | 200 | 2.46 | 384 | n.a. | 3,977 | 2.20 |
| 1900 | 2,296 | – | 3.73 | 1,890 | 2.50 | 784 | 2.80 | 126 | 2.85 | 390 | n.a. | 5,486 | 2.00 |
| 1901 | 2,603 | – | 3.72 | 1,624 | 2.50 | 1,036 | 2.85 | 363 | 1.85 | 397 | 130.0 | 6,023 | 2.00 |

Source: various files from TMA, RPA, and UGD.

Note
* production costs.

frequentation of AIAG and the first agreements with this company pushed PRC to publish list prices in order to avoid oscillations in market prices. The 'credo' about price stability, which started with AIAG in 1891, was adopted also by PRC: in this period, it became evident for aluminium firms that price stability could serve as competitive edge against other non-ferrous metals. Moreover, stable prices appeared as the best choice to help the management of aluminium technology, whose rigidity and capital intensity made it diverge from other non-ferrous metals production. The concomitant idea of PRC to create ASCO to assist sales in the UK market was also driven by this will to take control over the selling process.[84] From 1897, also Metallgesellschaft, one of the world's main sellers of non-ferrous metals, based in Frankfurt am Main, started to publish AIAG's price list in its annual statistical yearbook along with some figures about the outputs of the principal countries.[85] However, neither of these agreements was sufficient to regulate the international market, nor was price stability achievable with ease. The main problem for the market in this period was that the different scale economies were too big for the existing markets. Who dealt with the history of the applications of aluminium showed that the assertion of this metal on the market required a longer time and that, in addition to the gradual reduction of production costs, intense activities of R&D were required for the creation of new outlets.[86]

This situation reveals a kind of dilemma for the companies that opted for a scale production in the early aluminium business: without investments in large productive capacities, the unitary production cost would not have fallen to such a low level to be able to set market prices as low as possible to compete with other metals. AIAG many times also decided to sell aluminium below its production costs (see Table 1.1), in order to extend the market for aluminium, but only new investments would bring cost to a satisfying level. However, these capacities tended to create a latent overproduction, which anticipated the expansion of the market itself. In the course of the second half of the 1890s, we witnessed a re-composition of the strategies of the productive companies to try to solve this dilemma. European companies, which adopted Héroult's technology, tried to reduce production to make it more suitable for the existing market. Thanks to the technologies developed by Héroult himself, part of the electric power that was freed from the production of aluminium was used for the production of other electro-metallurgical products, i.e. calcium carbide, sodium, and special alloys like iron-silicon. In fact, the new aluminium smelters had great productive rigidities, so a reduction of production was technically difficult and economically expensive. To balance the cost of these interruptions, which were necessary to adapt production to the conditions of the market, the companies tried a series of lucrative productions, like calcium carbide. This choice equated AIAG, SEMF, and BACO, and the latter also performed a more vigorous entering into the carbide business, taking control over Acetylene Illuminating Company Ltd.[87]

Almost all the companies resorted to help from the international non-ferrous metals traders to find additional outlets for their products. For example, SEMF got into business with a French trader, Maurice Bigillion, and then with

Metallgesellschaft. PRC signed an agreement with Aron Hirsch, another important German trader, and created ASCO, as we had anticipated.[88] These exports were made even if they were prohibited by the various agreements on the patents that had involved SEMF, BACO, and AIAG and by the agreements between AIAG and PRC. AIAG itself started to export to the USA, in reprisal for PRC exports in Europe. AIAG tried to forbid SEMF's exports through legal action. However, the civil court of Grenoble established that SEMF was not responsible for these exports and, examining the whole dossier of the patent agreement, added that AIAG did not have the right to sell Héroult's technology to BACO.[89] Even if this decision did not influence AIAG's business at all because it acted outside British legislation, it further fragmented the system of agreements on patents, showing their transience, and made more precarious the alliances between the Swiss and French firms. For instance, SEMF did not purchase Oerlikon dynamos for the new unit in La Praz, but it adopted the ones of Compagnie de l'Industrie Electrique et Mécanique of Geneva, which used René Thury's system, which was a competitor of Brown's system.[90]

In this picture, which was already marked by over-investment, AIAG decided to accelerate the launch of its unity of Rheinfelden, in order to better defend the German market with local production. A second initiative, started in this period, was to create another plant in Lend, in the Austro-Hungarian Empire, following the same considerations. Also PRC started to design its project in 1896 to build a smelter in Canada, to defend itself from the possible reprisals of the other European companies, particularly BACO and AIAG, against their exports. A partial solution to the issues of the international market was found in 1897, when BACO, which was waiting to implement its aluminium unit, and after the beginning of the production of calcium carbide, decided to buy the metal directly from PRC, withdrawing the charges against ASCO. The reduction of the American group's imports into France also led to the withdrawal of its legal action.[91] However, BACO was selling part of its metal to Merton Company, an international merchant that was close to Metallgesellschaft, and which exported the metal that was not sold in Great Britain to Germany.[92]

These dynamics had a twofold negative result on the aluminium business. On the one hand, the reduction of production increased the unitary costs of the companies. At the same time, the metal that was sold in this way made ineffective the haze of agreements worked out by AIAG and PRC. In several instances, AIAG tried to enter into negotiations in order to reach a general agreement on prices, but every effort was useless, because the formation of the prices on the main market for aluminium, i.e. Germany, was in the hands of the traders. Even though the market price was a sort of barometer for the aluminium business, it was not the only problem for the producers at that time. Since the merchants had played a major role in the trade of this metal, the producers had lost touch with consumers and were losing direct knowledge of the market. This made the creation of investment and production strategies difficult. It was for this reason that the 'haze of agreements' at the end of the century did not become a general agreement on the price, but a real international cartel, i.e. the Aluminium-Association of 1901.

# Notes

1 Robert Friedel, 'A New Metal! Aluminum in its 19th-Century Context', in *Aluminum by Design*, edited Sarah Nichols, Elisabeth Agro, and Elizabeth Teller. Pittsburgh: Carnegie Museum of Art, 2000, 66. Jacques Bocquentin, 'La Fabrication de l'Aluminium par l'Électrolyse', in *Histoire de la Technique de la production d'aluminium*, edited by Paul Morel. Grenoble: Presses Universitaires de Grenoble, 1991, 21–130. Claude Joseph Gignoux, *Histoire d'une Entreprise Française*. Paris: Hachette, 1955, 71–72.

2 Grinberg, *Aluminium*. Maurice Laparra, 'The Aluminium False Twins: Charles Martin Hall and Paul Héroult's First Experiments and Technological Options', *Cahiers d'Histoire de l'Aluminium*, no. 48, 2012, 85–105.

3 Warren S. Peterson, Ronald E. Miller (eds), *Hall–Héroult Centennial: First Century of Aluminum Process Technology 1886–1986*. Warrendale: Metallurgical Society, 1986.

4 About AIAG, see AIAG, *Geschichte der Aluminium-Industrie-Aktien-Gesellschaft Neuhausen 1888–1938*. Zurich: Fretz, 1942. Cornelia Rauh, *Schweizer Aluminium für Hitlers Krieg? Zur Geschichte der Alusuisse 1918–1950*. Munich: Beck, 2009. Adrian Knoepfli, *From Dawn to Dusk: Alusuisse, Swiss Aluminium Pioneer from 1930 to 2010*. Zurich: Jetz, 2010.

5 About BACO, Andrew Perchard, *Aluminiumville: Government, Global Business and the Scottish Highlands*. Lancaster: Crucible Books, 2012.

6 About ALCOA, see Smith, *From Monopoly to Competition*. Graham, Pruitt, *R&D for Industry*. Charles C. Carr, *Alcoa: An American Enterprise*. New York: Rinehart, 1952.

7 About SEMF and PCAC, see Gignoux, *Histoire d'une Entreprise*. Ludovic Cailluet, *Stratégies, Structures d'Organisation et Pratiques de Gestion de Pechiney des années 1880 à 1971*. Unpublished PhD Thesis, Lyon III University, 1995. Le Roux, *L'Entreprise et la Recherche*.

8 Graham, Pruitt, *R&D for Industry*. Le Roux, *L'Entreprise et la Recherche*. About Héroult's early carrier, see also Marco Bertilorenzi, 'From Patents to Industry: Paul Héroult and International Patents Strategies, 1886–1889', *Cahiers d'Histoire de l'Aluminium*, no. 49, 2012, 46–69.

9 Dux, *Die Aluminium-Industrie-Aktiengesellschaft*. Kossman, *Über die Wirtschaftliche Entwicklung der Aluminiumindustrie*. Wallace, *Market Control*. Watkins, 'The Aluminum Alliance'.

10 Smith, *From Monopoly to Competition*. Born, *Internationale Kartellierung*. Hachez-Leroy, 'Le Cartel International de l'Aluminium'.

11 See for instance, Henri Allart, *Traité des Brevets d'Invention*. Paris: Albert Rousseau, 2 vols, 1885. About the role of patents on international economic development, see Edith Penrose, *The Economics of the International Patent System*. Baltimore MD: Johns Hopkins University Press, 1951. Jacob Schmookler, *Invention and Economic growth*. Cambridge MA: Harvard University Press, 1966. François Caron (ed.), *Les Brevets: Leur Utilisation en Histoire des Techniques et de l'Économie*. Paris: IHMC-CNRS, 1985. François Caron, *La Dynamique de l'Invention: Changement Technique et Changement Social (xvie–xxe siècle)*. Paris: Gallimard, 2010.

12 About France, see Gabriel Galvez-Behar, *La République des Inventeurs: Propriété et Organisation de l'Innovation en France (1791–1922)*. Rennes: Presses Universitaires de Rennes, 2008; Alain Beltran, Sophie Chauveau, Gabriel Galvez-Behar, *Des Brevets et des Marques: Une Histoire de la Propriété Industrielle*. Paris: Fayard, 2001.

13 Marco Bertilorenzi, 'Big Business, Inter-Firm Cooperation and National Governments: The International Aluminium Cartel, 1886–1939', in *Organizing Global Technology Flows: Institutions, Actors, and Processes*, edited by Pierre-Yves Donzé and Shigehiro Nishimura. London: Routledge, 2014, 108–125.

14 Alfred Dupont Chandler, *Scale and Scope: The Dynamics of Industrial Capitalism*. Cambridge: Belknap Press, 1994, 8.

15 Christopher Beauchamp, 'Who Invented the Telephone? Lawyers, Patents and the Judgement of the History', *Technology and Culture*, vol. 51, no. 4, 2010, 854–878.

Carsten Burhop, Thorsten Lubbers, 'The Design of Licensing Contracts: Chemicals, Pharmaceuticals, and Electrical Engineering in Imperial Germany', *Business History*, vol. 54, no. 4, 2012, 574–593. Noemi R. Lamoreux, Kenneth L. Solokoff, Dhanoos Sutthiphisal, 'Patent Alchemy: The Market for Technology in the US History', *Business History Review*, vol. 87, no. 1, 3–38.

16

  L'aluminium est un métal à débouchés restreints; il s'emploie à faire des tubes de lorgnettes et, que vous les vendiez à 10 ou 100 F, vous n'en vendrez pas un kilo de plus. Si vous faisiez du bronze d'aluminium, ce serait une autre affaire, car il s'emploit des quantités considerable de bronze et, si vous en faisiez à bon marché, nul doute que l'affaire soit intéressante.

  Gignoux, *Histoire d'une Entreprise*, 68–69. Adolph Minet, *L'Aluminium: Fabrication, Emploi, Alliages*. Paris: Tignol, 1890, 124. Paul Héroult, *L'Aluminium à Bon Marché*. Saint-Etienne: Théollier & Thomas, 1900, 20.

17 Alfred Cowles, *The True Story of Aluminum*. Chicago IL: Henry Regnery Co., 1958. Smith, *From Monopoly to Competition*, 34–35.

18 Technoseum Mannheim, Archives (hereafter, TMA), AIAG Documents, box 91, Protokoll. Hotel National Zurich, 31 October 1887; box 63, Accord avec Héroult, 6 August 1887.

19 Bertilorenzi, 'From Patents to Industry'.

20 AIAG, *Die Anlage der Aluminium-Industrie-Actien-Gesellschaft*. Schaffhausen: Brodtmann'sche Buchdruckerei, 1890. Christian Müller, *Arbeiterbewegung und Unternehmerpolitik in der Aufstrebenden Industriestadt: Baden nach der Gründung der Firma Brown Boveri 1891–1914*. Zurich: Buchdruckerei Wanner, 1974. Serge Paquier, *Histoire de l'Électricité en Suisse: La Dynamique d'un Petit Pays Européen, 1876–1939*. Geneva: Passé et Présent, 1998, 487–489.

21 TMA, AIAG, box 1, Agreement beetwen Héroult, Huber, and Naville, 26 August 1887.

22 TMA, AIAG, box 1, Contract between Dreyfus and SMG, 31 December 1887; Contract between Héroult, Dreyfus, and SMG, 25 March 1888.

23 TMA, AIAG, box 63, Bericht der Velwantungrathes, 13 September 1888.

24 Institut Pour l'Histoire de l'Aluminium, Clichy (IHA), Documents de Henry Morsel, Convention avec M. Dreyfus et Sté Métall. Suisse, 26 October 1888.

25 William Hausman, Peter Hertner, Mira Wilkins, *Global Electrification: Multinational Enterprise and International Finance in the History of Light and Power, 1878–2007*. Cambridge MA: Cambridge University Press, 2008, 41–44. Luciano Segreto, 'Elettricità ed Economia in Europa', in *Storia dell'Industria Elettrica in Italia: Vol. 1, Le Origini, 1882–1914*, edited by Giorgio Mori. Rome-Bari: Laterza, 1990, 704–736. Albert Broder, 'L'expansion Internationale de l'Industrie Allemande dans le Dernier Tiers du XIXe Siècle: Le Cas de l'Industrie Électrique', *Relations Internationales*, no. 29, 1982, 65–87.

26 About Lowrey and his links with Edison, see Thomas Parke Hughes, *Networks of Powers: Electrification in Western Society, 1880–1930*. Baltimore MD: John Hopkins University Press, 1993, 25–26; Jocelyn Pierson Tyson, *Grosvenor Porter Lowrey: Thomas Alva Edison's Lawyer*. New York, Topp-Litho, 1978. Hausman, Hertner, Wilkins, *Global Electrification*, 77.

27 Franklin L. Pope, Walter T. Barnard, *Aluminium and its Alloys: A Report*. New York, 1888 – booklet found in Kassel library, Germany.

28 Rio Tinto-Alcan Archives, Zurich (RZA), SMG Documents, Paul Héroult's Correspondence, 1887–1889, Héroult to Lowrey, 21 March 1888.

29 Cowles, *The True Story*, 95–96. 'Cowles against Héroult', *Electrical Engineer*, 2 May 1890, 332.

30 Graham, Pruitt, *R&D for Industry*. Junius Edwards, *The Immortal Woodshed: The Story of the Inventor who brought Aluminum to America*. New York: Dodd Mead, 1955. Claude Pascaud, 'Le Développement du Procédé Hall-Héroult et son Accompagnement par la

Propriété Industrielle (1886–1994)', *Cahiers d'Histoire de l'Aluminium*, no. 20, 1997, 61–86. Wallace, *Market Control*. Louis Ferrand, *Histoire de la Science et des Techniques de l'Aluminium et ses Développements Industriels: Tome I – Le Passé*. Paris: Unpublished Manuscript, 1960, 220–227.

31 RZA, SMG, Héroult's correspondance, Héroult to Lowrey, 21 March 1888. TMA, AIAG, box 12, Rathenau to Lowrey, 15 October 1888.

32 TMA, AIAG, box 61, Frankfurt Preliminary Contract, 5 October 1888.

33 TMA, AIAG, box 63, Bericht des Verwaltungsrathes an die Generalversammlung in sachen der Gewinn vertheilung mit Herrn Héroult, 13 October 1888. Box 91, Protokoll, 24 April 1889.

34 TMA, AIAG, Box 29, P.E. Huber, Rhein Aluminium Fabrikation: Verfahren von Dr. Kiliani, 31 October 1888.

35 Adolphe Lejeal, *L'Aluminium le Manganèse, le Baryum, le Strontium, le Calcium et le Magnésium*. Paris: Baillière, 1894, 98. Joseph William Richards, *Aluminium: Its History, Occurrence, Properties, Metallurgy and Applications, including its Alloys*. London: Martson & Co., 1896, 25. Minet, *L'Aluminium*, 13. About Héroult's early carrier, see Bertilorenzi, 'From Patents to Industry'.

36 TMA, AIAG, box 91, Protokoll der AIAG, 24 April 1889. Protokoll der AIAG, 21 January 1889. Schweizerisches Wirtschaftsarchiv, Basel (SWA), Alusuisse Schweizerische Aluminium AG Chippis – H + I Bg 7, Jahresberichte 1894–1923, Sechter Geschaftbericht der AIAG in Neuhausen, das Geschaftjahr 1894, Schaffausen, 1895, 2. About the place of Germany in the early international aluminium market, see Born, *Internationale Kartellierung*, 15–16.

37 RZA, Vertretungen und Preis-Liste der AIAG, 1891.

38 About Carl Berg and aluminium, see Roman Köster, 'Aluminium for the Airship: Zeppelin and the Adaptation of a "New" Construction Material', in Barjot, Bertilorenzi (eds), *Aluminium*, 77–97.

39 TMA, AIAG, Preis-Liste der Aluminium Industrie Actien-Gesellschaft, Neuhausen (Schweiz), 1892. RZA, AIAG, Preis-Liste der Aluminium-Industrie Actien-Gesellschaft, Neuhanusen am Rehinfall (Schweiz), 1 January 1894.

40 TMA, AIAG, box 91, Protokoll der AIAG, 10 November 1892.

41 RZA, AIAG, Rothaluminium – Produktion in kg, 1889–1961. TMA, AIAG, box 91, Protokoll, 18 October 1895. Protokoll, 17 November 1897.

42 Laparra, 'The Aluminium False Twins', 90–95.

43 Oberlin College Archives (OCA), Charles Martin Hall collection, series III, box 2, List of Hall's foreign patents.

44 Smith, *From Monopoly to Competition*. Graham, Pruitt, *R&D for Industry*. See also Carr, *Alcoa*, and Edwards, *The Immortal Woodshed*.

45 Smith, *From Monopoly to Competition*, 25–28.

46 Graham, Pruitts, *R&D for Industry*, 29–30.

47 OCA, Charles Martin Hall collection, series III, box 2, Hall's foreign patents, Foreign Patent, Great Britain, Improvements in the production of aluminum, no. 5669, 1 June 1889.

48 Heinz History Center (HHC), ALCOA Documents (ALCOA), MSS#282, box 37, folder 4, Arthur Vining Davis, Statement of the process used by the Pittsburg Reduction Co., 1895.

49 University of Glasgow Archives (UGD), 351/21/26/10, Wilfried S. Sample, The Manufacture of Aluminium at Patricroft, 1894.

50 Alan S. Darling, 'The Light Metals, Aluminium and Magnesium', in *An Encyclopedia of the History of Technology*, edited by Ian McNeil. London: Routledge, 2002, 105, 112. Lejeal, *L'Aluminium*, 143.

51 David E. Koskoff, *The Mellons: Chronicle of America's Richest Family*. New York: Crowell, 1978, 110–115. Philiph H. Love, *Andrew W. Mellon, His Life and His Work*. Baltimore MD: Heath Cogging, 1929. David Cannadine, *Mellon: An American Life*. London: Allen Lane, 2006.

52  Smith, *From Monopoly to Competition*, 31–34, 78–83.
53  Joseph Rousseau, *Applications de l'Electricité à la Métallurgie: Fabrication de l'Aluminium*. Paris: Berger-Levrault, 1893, 16. Junius D. Edwards, Francis C. Frary, Zay Jeffries, *The Aluminum Industry: 2 vols, I, Aluminum and its Production*. New York, McGraw-Hill, 1930, 35–37. Cowles, *The True Story*, 91–93.
54  Carr, *An American Enterprise*, 49–50. Cowles, *The true story*, 98–9. Wallace, *Market Control*, 530.
55  Smith, *From monopoly*, 37. Wallace, *Market control*, 532. Cowles, *The True Story*, 60–63.
56  TMA, AIAG, box 91, Protokoll der AIAG, 3 October 1891.
57  Smith, *From Monopoly to Competition*, 35. Carr, *An American Enterprise*, 51. Muller, *Light Metals*, 51–53.
58  Rio Tinto Archives, Pechiney Documents (RPA), 072-13-29960, Conseil d'administration SEMF, 26 October 1888. IHA, Documents de Henri Morsel, SEMF. Rapports avec Ste de Neuhausen, 20 October 1890.
59  RPA, 072-1-9588, Héroult technical documents 1887–1903, Les cuves Paul Héroult. Laparra, 'The False Aluminium Twins'. Bocquentin, 'La Fabrication de l'Aluminium'.
60  RPA, 00-12-20029, Gustav de Munerel, Aluminium – Notice, 1891.
61  TMA, AIAG, box 91, Protokoll, Héroult to Huber, 31 May 1892.
62  RPA, 00-12-20020, SEMF, Conference de Berne avec AIAG, 26 June 1893. TMA, AIAG, box 91, Protokoll, 30 June 1893.
63  TMA, AIAG, box 61, Convention entre SEMF et AIAG, 5 August 1893.
64  IHA, Documents de Henri Morsel, Lettre de M. Dreyfus au Conseil sur l'advenir de l'Aluminium, 24 March 1893. RPA, Conseils d'administration SEMF, Conseil, 28 March 1893.
65  Philippe Mioche, *L'Alumine à Gardanne de 1893 à nos Jours: Une Traversée Industrielle en Provence*. Grenoble: Presses Universitaires de Grenoble, 1994. Philippe Mioche, 'Contribution à l'Histoire du Procédé Bayer: Le Procédé à Gardanne, 1893–2012', in Barjot, Bertilorenzi (eds), *Aluminium*, 27–62. IHA, Paul Soudain, *Historique Technique et Économique de la Fabrication de l'Alumine*, Compagnie Pechiney, May 1970, 13–15.
66  TMA, AIAG, box 91, Protokoll, 14 May 1893.
67  Perchard, *Aluminiumville*, 25.
68  UGD, 347/21/46/7, British Aluminium Co. E. Ristori, Summary report of the position of Affairs, 12 October 1894. Report of Lord Kelvin to the directors of the British Aluminium Company, 6 November 1894.
69  Perchard, *Aluminiumville*, 166–167.
70  UGD, 347/21/31/1, British Aluminium Company Ltd, Specification of Patents. Agreement between Cowles and Ristori, 9 May 1894. UGD, 347/21/46/7, E. Ristori, Notes on the Formation of the British Aluminium Company Ltd, 1 May 1894.
71  RPA, 072-1-9588, Héroult technical documents 1887–1903, Héroult to Vielhomme, 25 May 1897.
72  TMA, AIAG, box 61, Vertrag der Aluminium-Industrie AG Neuhausen und British Aluminium Company Ltd, London, 26 July 1894.
73  HHC, ALCOA, MSS#282, box 37, folder 4, Statements of claims between British Aluminium Co. Ltd and Sir W. G. Armstrong Mitchel and Co. in the High Court of Justice, B.N. 3822, 1895.
74  HHC, ALCOA, MSS#282, United States v. Alcoa, Equity, 73–85, Exhibits, ex. 478, PRC Annual Report, 1895, 17 September 1896. UGD, 347/21/46/7, The British Aluminium Company – Memorandum, 13 January 1896.
75  Richards, *Aluminium*, 396–397. Lejeal, *L'Aluminium*, 143–144.
76  RPA, 00-1-20029, Rapport du Conseil d'administration de la Société Indutrielle de l'aluminium et d'alliages métalliques – exercise 1896.
77  Gignoux, *Histoire d'une Entreprise*, 92.
78  RZA, AIAG director correspondance, 1888–1892, Schindler to Hunt, 15 July 1889.
79  TMA, AIAG, box 91, Fusion mit der amerikanischer Concurrenz, 13 March 1890.

80 TMA, AIAG, box 91, Protokoll, 31 December 1890, Hunt to Huber, 12 December 1890.

81 RZA, AIAG director correspondence, 1888–1899, Schildler to Hunt, 15 July 1889. TMA, AIAG, box 91, Rapport des Hrn E Huber uber die Aluminiumfabr. in Amerika, 12 November 1890. Prot., 10 July 1890.

82 TMA, AIAG, box 91, Frankfurt Prot. SMG-AIAG, 30 June 1893.

83 Some gentlemen's agreements were concluded between 1894 and 1897. HHC, ALCOA, MSS#282, United States v. Alcoa, Equity, 73–85, Exhibits, ex. 478, Prc Annual Report, 1895, 17 September 1896. TMA, AIAG, box 91, Preis Convention mit PRC, 21 February 1894. Prot. 2 May 1895. Prot. 21 May 1896. Frankfurt Convention mit PRC, 16 July 1896.

84 For instance, in 1894 PRC did not published its prices, while in 1896 it started to publish its prices for ingots and semi-finished works. RZA, AIAG, Pittsburg Reduction Company, manufacturers of aluminum, February 1894. Pittsburg Reduction Company. Price list, July 1896.

85 Metallurgischen Gesellschaft AG, *Statistische Zusammenstellungen uber Blei, Kupfer, Zink, Zinn, Silber, Nickel und Aluminium von der Metallgesellschaft*. Frankurt am Main: Metallgesellschaft, 1897.

86 Graham, Pruitt, *R&D for Industry*. Smith, *From Monopoly to Competition*. Le Roux, *La Recherche*. Hachez-Leroy, *L'Aluminium français*.

87 IHA, Documents Henri Morsel, SEMF, Lettre de M. Dreyfus au Conseil sur l'avenir de l'Aluminium, 24 April 1893. TMA, AIAG, box 91, Prot. 26 May 1896. UGD, 347/21/46/7, BACO, Chairman's report, 8 March 1897.

88 About German traders, see Susan Becker, 'The German Metal Traders', in *The Multinational Traders*, edited by Goeffrey Jones. New York: Routledge, 1998. Benjamin W. De Vries, *Of Mettle and Metal: From Court Jews to World-wide Industrialists*. Amsterdam: Neha, 2000.

89 IHA, Documents de Henri Morsel, SEMF-AIAG. Conclusion par le tribunal de Grenoble, 19 February 1897.

90 About this company and René Thury, see Paquier, *Histoire de l'Électricité en Suisse*.

91 HHC, MSS#282, ALCOA, Box 37, fold 2, Letter of Aron Hirsch & Sohn to PRC, 17 December 1897.

92 UGD, 347/21/45/1, BACO, Agreement between Pittsburgh Reduction Company, Alumnium Supply Company Ltd and British Aluminium Company Ltd, 5 July 1897.

# 2   The Aluminium-Association

## The dawn of international cartelisation, 1901–1908

At the beginning of the twentieth century, the international aluminium market appeared disorganised. The 'fog' of agreements that AIAG had created in the previous decade appeared inefficient. In spite of the international division of electrolysis patents that AIAG arranged to provide a reserved national market for each producer, international trade was out of control. Actually, the production that could not be absorbed into the national markets was too often exported to Germany, injuring the sales of AIAG and depressing the global prices. When AIAG started its German (1897) and Austrian (1898) smelters, this trend was intensified, leading to the saturation of these markets and putting in jeopardy the general architecture of the agreements. The concomitant starting of PCAC's and BACO's production created an even more serious situation that, despite the significant reduction of prices, led to an overproduction. In 1900, the starting of PRC's Canadian unit also led the American firm to find additional foreign market outlets. The search for opportunities in export markets through international merchants had a negative impact, leading not only to unsatisfactory prices in an increasing number of transactions, but also marking a progressive distance between producers and customers. In fact, the multiplication of actors involved in the trading of this metal was causing the loss of direct contact with the consumers.[1]

In the specific phase of the evolution of the aluminium industry at the end of the nineteenth century, the producers progressively realised that the reduction of unitary production costs was not sufficient to break through the resistance of the market and to win the competition with the older metals. The use of commercial logic, that involved fluctuating prices to meet the trends of other non-ferrous metals, was not able to consolidate the position of aluminium. AIAG had understood these dynamics, and, as a consequence, it tried to settle some important partnerships with big metal consumers, like Carl Berg AG, with which it preferred to sign long-term contracts with relatively stable prices. While orders of large volumes and long duration could encourage the extension of production capacity, a fluctuating trend in prices had the effect of destabilising the demand and of reducing the knowledge that the firms had of the market. AIAG wanted to change the general conditions of the market, reducing the weight of the traders in the aluminium business. As a consequence, a partial agreement on the prices was not proposed, even if Aron Hirsch & Söhne had volunteered as intermediaries between AIAG and PRC for the stipulation of a new agreement between the two leading companies.[2]

The case of the aluminium industry seems to confirm George Stigler's oligopoly theory. According to Stigler, cartel agreements on prices are intrinsically weak and doomed to fail, because every company is constantly given the opportunity to cheat on the agreement to sell more and at lower prices than those defined with the other companies, thus taking advantage of the possibility to achieve greater scale economies.[3] Also the economic sociologist Mancur Olson, taking up these issues, showed the existence in a group of economic actors of the dilemma between following the common interests, which were due to high prices, and to pursue individual goals derived from the increase in the volume of sales and achieve greater scale economies.[4] The situation was more complex in the aluminium industry between the nineteenth and twentieth century because the legal context of patents was still an element of market protection for most producers. The hope that patents could work as a commercial barrier, reserving domestic markets, represented the key point of the commercial strategy that had been the *leitmotif* of the agreements at the end of the nineteenth century. Not only did exports create a situation that made honouring the agreements impossible, but it also progressively broke the trust among the producers in the various agreements that they settled. Moreover, the new role of the international traders deprived the companies of the possibility of a direct and precise knowledge of the market. In this phase, AIAG played a crucial role in transforming a simple oligopoly of companies into a cohesive group of producers. In other words, AIAG managed to restore the confidence among producers and their commitment. In doing so, it paved the way for the formation of a group that had the same strategic vision on the evolution of this metal. This action led to the creation of the first international cartel, the Aluminium-Association (AA).

## The formation of the Aluminium-Association

Instead of carrying on the negotiations for an agreement on prices only with PRC, AIAG proposed the formation of an international cartel to all other producers. It suggested removing the aluminium market from the control of international merchants, proposing itself as an intermediary for all the companies. Moreover, it decided to share the German market with the other companies, thus ending the fog of bilateral agreements that had characterised the previous decade to preserve this market for the Swiss firm. According to AIAG, only a general and overall cartel should organise the market with more reliable rules. This initiative was undertaken at a time when, due to the slowdown in demand recorded between late 1900 and early 1901,[5] a worsening of the tendency to overproduction was feared. Without a cartel that fixed precise sale quotas for each company, it was impossible to turn over the preponderance of international merchants in export markets. Thus, in 1901 AIAG called a convention of all producers with the aim of concluding a comprehensive agreement that would reorganise all world markets.[6]

AIAG called a first general convention in Paris from 11 to 12 July 1901. Firms agreed on three major points that, in the following months, formed the framework of their first international cartel. First, they decided that it was necessary to stop the race to lower prices in order to avoid speculative behaviour on the part of buyers. Second, it was necessary to establish quotas so as to divide the international market among producers, avoiding a repetition of the hunt for additional outlets that was harmful to stable prices and led to over-investment. Finally, to ensure the effectiveness of these agreements, AIAG claimed its intention to establish a common *selling board* for all the aluminium producers, which would operate as a joint-commercial company. This company would also record the trend of the market and gather reliable statistics about the international markets. According to AIAG's opinion, this selling board would have managed the orders also to international merchants, reducing their bargaining power in the process of the formation of prices, and would have monitored the global business performance of the aluminium markets, providing feedbacks to firms about the evolution of their business. Without this type of organisation, the producers could not obtain reliable information about the market and, as a result, they were not able to plan production, investments, and amortisation schedules.[7]

The formation of this selling board appears to be the decisive difference between the agreements of the 1890s and a real cartel. According to Dominique Barjot, a cartel differs from a simple agreement because it implements the goal of the agreement with a specific organisation.[8] Even if agreements existed before 1901 in the aluminium industry, as it was showed, these were not equal to a real cartel. In order to achieve the goal of developing the aluminium business, AIAG shifted from the idea of adopting bilateral agreements with the other producers, to create a new multilateral organisation, able to coordinate the strategies of each actor. The idea of a board of this type was proposed by Carl Fürstenberg, the director of the bank Berliner Handels-Geschäft – one of the major financial partners of AIAG – who suggested it to Huber, inspired by the Swiss Portland cement cartel. In other word, it was not the non-ferrous metal trade that was inspiring the business organisation of aluminium, but the insights of a capital intensive industry, like cement, were used to switch to a new business model. Without such an organisation, the companies would not have been able to control the flow of metals that remained under the discretion of the traders.[9] The role played by Fürstenberg in the creation of the first international cartel confirms the hypothesis of Harm Schröter, according to which the movement of cartels in Europe began in financial circles and then became an instrument of industrial policy on the part of producers who 'learned how to construct reliable and long-lasting cartels', after a phase characterised by partial agreements on the price.[10]

Aluminium was part of a general movement of international cartelisation, which was being established from the late nineteenth century in major industries. Unlike simple business agreements, cartels represented in the 'business philosophy'[11] of the time a modern form of industrial organisation, that responded to specific management needs of production and trade.[12] A careful observer described this movement in 1902 in these terms:

> We can say that the cartels exist nowadays all around the world. There is not one country that escaped this contagion … Consequently, this universal movement leads us to conclude that unions are the answer to a modern idea

of the modern commercial needs and they are not the result of the mere fantasy of some financier or some big tycoons.[13]

Aluminium was part of this international movement, but the technological (heavy capitalisation and high energy intensity) and commercial (the struggle with merchants about which kind of business model to adopt for the aluminium trade) situations of this industry cast the specific shapes that its cartelisation assumed. AIAG played the role of the architect of the cartel, proposing the main guidelines. It proposed to divide the world aluminium market into two broad categories: the 'closed markets' and the 'open markets'. The 'closed markets' were the United States, France, and the sales made by companies to the following governments: the German, Austro-Hungarian, the British, and the Swiss. These markets were reserved for the national producers. The 'open markets' were instead all of the remaining markets where the five companies would share the sales quotas, entrusting them to the management of the unique selling board.[14] Germany, expecting the sales to the German government, was part of the 'open markets'. Actually, this division served to regulate the exports in Germany, which had been the main source of disunity for the producers in the late nineteenth century and the principal target of international metal traders. AIAG volunteered to become the intermediary of all the cartel companies in this market, instead to claim it as a reserved market – unlike what it did in the past. The new agreement gave to PRC the monopoly in the United States and, at the same time, an outlet on other European markets for its Canadian unit. The French companies were guaranteed their domestic market and an export quota, preventing this second activity from becoming, as in the past, a destabilising factor in the international market.[15]

The previous agreements between AIAG and SEMF, between AIAG and BACO, and between PRC and BACO were deleted by the new cartel agreement. Unlike the French companies and PRC, AIAG and BACO had only small reserved markets in accordance with the wording of the agreement: their 'closed' markets were represented only by the sales of their respective national governments. These sales corresponded to a small amount per year. For example, AIAG in 1900 and in 1901 sold to its reference governments (German, Swiss, and Austrian-Hungarian) about 10 per cent of its global sales. The decision to restrict these orders was aimed at building stable relationships with the reference governments, in order to help the adoption of aluminium for military applications, such as the manufacture of weapons or infantry equipment, in which aluminium had actual capacity for expansion due to its low specific weight. In exchange for such a small reserved market, the two producers were given quotas on the export markets sufficient to sell out their production.[16]

The most delicate point of the negotiations was the establishment of the quotas in the open market, which was the kernel of the cartel agreement. The quotas were the result of negotiation among the companies that adapted an initial proposal made by AIAG. AIAG made a first proposal following complex considerations, which took into account the real possibilities of absorption of the market, the outputs of each company, and their investments in progress. Thanks to its international sale agency that it had already established during the 1890s, AIAG was in position to forecast global sales better than the other companies. The Swiss company had calculated that the overall importance of 'open markets' for the year 1901 would be 3,100 tons. During the negotiations, each company tried to obtain a quota that was consistent with the sales that it had actually made the previous year, or with the production capacity that it had installed. PRC and AIAG tried to include in these units part of the capacity of the production of the productive units that were being completed. Moreover, AIAG and BACO received guaranteed minimum quotas (then called 'preferences' in the contract) on the open market. During the negotiations, the fixed quotas were as shown in Table 2.1.

The relatively small quotas of PRC and the French producers were the result of the importance of their reserved markets. PRC had a closed market of about 2,000 tons per year and exported about 25 per cent of its production in the open markets; the French companies had in turn a reserved market of approximately 900 tons and exported 40 per cent of their production. Unlike the other companies, BACO had a lower production and negotiated a small quota. So, the formation of the cartel did not change BACO's strategy that continued to produce little, and it seems that this company had not the same medium-term strategic vision as the other companies as regards aluminium. This choice was in part the result of its production strategy, which, as we have seen, was strongly oriented towards diversification into other electro-metallurgical products, such as carbides, because of the narrowness of the consumption of aluminium in Great Britain and the relatively high producing costs that BACO had in aluminium.[17] However, to avoid the specific position of BACO becoming a factor of disturbance, the companies gave to BACO a preference of 40 per cent in the British market in case it increased above 400 tons per year.[18]

Moreover, the agreement had a duration of five years and expired on 31 December 1906. The five-year duration was common in agreements of this type, because it corresponded to a short-term business cycle.[19] However, some specific clauses were added to make the agreement more adaptable to the changing trade situation. Regardless of the duration of the contract, the quotas were considered valid as long as the open market did not exceed 5,000 tons per year. Then, new quotas would be negotiated. If the importance of the open market had dropped

*Table 2.1* Aluminium-Association, 1901: cartel quotas and actual production of the members (tons and %)

| Firms | Preferences (tons) | Quotas (tons) | Total open market (tons) | % | Actual outputs 1901 (tons) |
|---|---|---|---|---|---|
| AIAG | 1,200 | 300 | 1,500 | 48.4 | 1,600 |
| PRC | – | 650 | 650 | 21.0 | 2,603 |
| BACO | 300 | 100 | 400 | 12.9 | 389 |
| SEMF and PCAC | – | 550 | 500 | 17.7 | 1,340 |
| Total | 1,500 | 1,600 | 3,100 | 1.0 | 5,932 |

Source: TMA and RPA.

below 50 per cent of 3,100 tons, the agreement would have been automatically cancelled. These agreements on the limitation of the validity of the agreement show that the companies were not very confident about the use of a cartel: on the one hand, they recognised the need to form an association to coordinate the development of their industry, on the other hand, they tried to create loopholes in the agreement to be used if the conditions in which the compromises were made had changed, making the agreement outdated.[20]

## The launch of the international cartel: AIAG's 'system'

After finding a compromise on the overall scheme of the cartel agreement, the companies had to determine which legal form to give it. Each company asked a legal expert about the official form to give to the cartel, and several hypotheses were formulated. The companies soon realised that the different national legislations were not coherent about this issue. Except the United States, which formally forbade them since the enactment of the Sherman Act in 1890, in other countries there was no specific legislation about cartels. It was also impossible to establish which was the competent jurisdiction in the event of an international cartel.[21] Consequently, the companies were venturing into a test ground in which the legal form would be subject to the strategic goals of the group. PCAC, which had previously taken part in similar international schemes,[22] suggested a free association, in which each producer would retain its autonomy in relation to the other associates, keeping its business service and the direct relationship with customers. The board of the cartel would have had only the task of fixing the price from time to time and to ensure that the quotas of each company were met, by collecting the sales statistics of all participants in all markets. The board, in addition to collecting statistical data, would take care of rebalancing periodically in case of discrepancy between the fixed quotas and actual sales.[23]

On the contrary, AIAG wanted a more centralised structure, similar to a kind of integration among the companies. The board, in addition to monitoring the fulfilment of the quotas and fixing the prices, would have to centralise sales to ensure that the business finally came out of the discretionary control of the traders and it was the same board that passed their orders on the open markets on behalf of all the members of the cartel. AIAG thought that the best way to build this board was to form a corporation: actually, archive documents attest the draft to create a limited company with a capital of one million Swiss francs, in which each of the five members held a participation in the capital.[24] The purpose of this new company (that could have been called *Comptoir uniques des producteurs d'aluminium*, or *Central Selling Board*, or also *Allgemeine Aluminium Verkaufe*) was to unify all the commercial services of the members of the cartel to act as a unique merchant on the behalf of firms. Forming a limited company, AIAG thought to give a more solid form to the cartel, that would enforce the cartel contract also from a legal point of view providing an institutional framework within which it could have worked.[25]

Between July and October 1901, an intermediate form between PCAC's and AIAG's proposals prevailed. According to the advice of their lawyers, and especially

Professor Friederich Meili, of the University of Zurich, who was considered one of the leading experts in Swiss private law with a strong expertise and knowledge of different national legislations,[26] the producers of aluminium decided not to set up a real corporation. Instead, a simple private association registered under the Swiss Code of Obligations was a safe and inexpensive way to make a solid agreement. Meili suggested that the name of this private association should be Aluminium-Association since, doing so, it would not have been necessary to translate it into various languages of the members. The association would not pay taxes, as a corporation would have done, and it would have benefited from legal arbitration before a Swiss public court, if there were any problems about the contract of association. Moreover, this type of association would have the necessary coercive power to enforce its contract, because it could have adopted, instead of a capital, guarantee deposits from which to draw in case of violation of the agreements. In other words, Swiss legislation, according to Meili, could provide firms with the right institutional backbone to set a workable agreement.[27]

Since AA was not a corporation, this type of partnership could not manage sales as an enterprise, puzzling the original idea of AIAG to merge sales to wrestle against the international traders. However, the companies aimed to follow the idea to have a unique vendor and they decided to entrust AIAG with the management of all the sales of the members of the Aluminium-Association, that were made in the open market. AIAG would set up an office of AA at its headquarters in Neuhausen, where it would collect all the data from the other companies. AIAG was the only enterprise in the group to own a true international network of agents. The European companies had recognised the supremacy of AIAG in international markets, due to the early formation of a commercial service since 1891, which had sales agents in all European markets and in the main Asian markets. The other firms could benefit from this unique and powerful sales network to expand their sales abroad, thanks to the intermediary of AIAG. AIAG asked for a commission of 10 per cent, but the other firms succeeded in reducing that to 5 per cent. Moreover, AIAG would negotiate orders from buyers on the open market on behalf of AA and would allocate the contracts according to the established quotas of the cartel.[28]

A delicate point was management of the relationships with the metal traders. AIAG was also appointed to work out an agreement with Metallgesellschaft according to which the cartel would provide the company with an annual fixed tonnage, paying some rather high commission on the sales, in exchange for the prohibition to negotiate contracts directly with individual companies. This measure designated the cartel as a universal manager of relationships with the merchants of metal. Davis from PRC had been instructed to make similar agreements with Aron Hirsch. In both cases, the cartel took the decision to pay a stable commission of 3 per cent to these traders, instead of leaving the traders free, as in the past, to speculate to obtain their own remuneration on the sales. In the final agreement between AIAG and Metallgesellschaft, the German trader obtained 10 per cent of the sales made by the cartel in exchange for accepting the pricing policy established by AIAG and to keep the firms constantly informed about the evolution of its sales.[29] This strategy aimed at bringing price stability in the aluminium business and it gained the agreement of the principal metal traders, such as Aron Hirsch and Metallgesellschaft, because they grasped the opportunity to benefit, in this way, in a less risky environment.[30]

Even though the new role of AIAG was the outcome both of its supremacy in international trade and of the specific need to patch up some pragmatic issues linked to the quick settlement of the cartel, the consensus towards AIAG was not general. In particular, PRC was reluctant to delegate such an important part of the business management to AIAG. As we have seen, PRC had created an export company in the UK, ASCO, which was used for its business operations abroad. With the launch of its Canadian plant, PRC was interested in getting bigger quotas in the international markets and was evaluating the institutional and political advantage of being able to count on a corporation on British territory. So, in exchange for the acceptance of AIAG as manager of the cartel and as a trade intermediary on the open markets, it proposed to enter into a secret agreement with the other companies in the cartel, according to which AIAG would give an additional 50 tons to PRC, actually dividing the quotas in 1,450 tons for AIAG and 700 for PRC, instead of 1,500 and 650, as shown in Table 2.1.[31]

The other companies accepted AIAG as manager of the cartel in a meeting, that was organised in Paris in October 1901, in which only the European companies took part.[32] AA's contract was ratified 2 November 1901, and AA began to operate immediately. AIAG assumed the role of manager, accumulating market information from all members. For five years, AIAG's offices became the international centre for the development of aluminium, where collective strategies were designed and market data gathered and shared.[33] After the formation of AA, PRC expressed the desire not to participate directly, but to use a Canadian subsidiary, the Northern Aluminium Company (NACO), which was created in the meantime to manage the production of the unit in Shawinigan Falls. This decision was derived from the fear that PRC could be prosecuted according to US antitrust law. For this reason, companies also decided not to reference the American market in the contract. It would be kept reserved for PRC in an informal way. These adaptations to the specific situation of American law were decisive for the participation of PRC in the cartel. These solutions were proposed again in the following decade to define the relationship between Europeans and Americans.

With the formation of AA, the companies had a stable and centralised service for statistics and sales. This service received orders and allocated them every month among the members, also negotiating with the metal traders. This monopoly of sales served to ensure price stability. Acting as an observatory through which to analyse the trends of the market, this organisation also made it easier to plan the use and extension of production capacities. An ongoing dialogue between each company and the cartel's central office was established and it influenced the strategic choices of individual companies, in harmony with the general policy decided by the *comité* of the cartel. In fact, not only did AA control the open markets, but it also had information on sales made by the members in their respective markets, which ensured an overall picture of the general evolution of the aluminium industry.[34] AA was not only a unique *comptoir* (selling board) for sales, but it represented a monopoly of information about trade.

The *comité* was formed by eight members: two each for PRC (Mellon and Davis), AIAG (Huber and Schindler), and BACO (Ristori and Wallace), and one each for SEMF (Vielhomme) and PCAC (Pechiney). The *comité* was the decision-making authority of AA: it used to meet at least twice a year and could be convened in an extraordinary way by one of its members if the need arose. It was up to the *comité* to design a common strategy for the overall development of the industry, setting the prices, and exchanging business information. The companies that participated in the cartel had in mind, even at this early stage of international cartels, the problem of possible cheating. It was common practice that the cartels were equipped with measures that could either prevent or keep an eye on these possible frauds.[35] Consequently, two members of the *comité* were alternately appointed to inspect the accounts of the other companies and to verify the accuracy of the data provided by the companies, in the headquarters of the AA. They were allowed to check the books of their partners also as regards the sales on the closed market. The accessibility of the accounts among the members shows a willingness to spread a feeling of trust among the members.[36]

One of the specific actions of AA was addressed to the pricing policy. The selling prices were set at 2.90 F/kg (2.3 Marks), with progressive discounts depending on the quantity purchased, and they came down to 2.75 francs (2 Marks). This price corresponded to what AIAG had already practised during 1900, but could not impose due to the variations determined by the actions of traders. However, in the closed markets, the price would have been 10 cents higher to prevent that part of the metal destined for the closed market being directed to the open market, thus altering the quota mechanism. It was also decided to establish from time to time some specific sale policies for promoting new uses of the metal through special discounts. An eloquent example of this strategy was represented by discounts for the use of aluminium in cables and electrical equipment. This measure seemed to be particularly useful for AEG, which was the reference shareholder and a customer of AIAG, so that it could count on favourable prices established with the consent of all the members of the cartel, but it had the effect of spreading the aluminium in a use that, up to that point, had failed to replace copper. AA also began to discount aluminium for use in the packaging of chocolate bars and, more generally, in the food industry.[37]

AA's working principle was mainly based on a sales forecast made by AIAG at the beginning of the year, followed by subsequent readjustments. During its first meeting in November 1901, AA decided to divide sales on the open market for 1902 among the members, that were estimated at a total of 3,100 tons, and also to balance the sales between July and December 1901 following the set quotas for a total of 1,400 tons (corresponding to five months). As it divided the quotas, the contracts with buyers were communicated to the companies for the monthly tranches, as to gradually fulfil the sales forecast for the current year for each member. This division into *tranches* was useful to ensure that, in the case that the sales were either inferior or superior than the anticipated quotas, the companies would share proportionally both reductions and surplus. At the end of each financial year, AIAG compiled a report, which summarised the sales made by each member and the 'delays' or the 'leftovers' that it had accumulated over the quota attributed by the contract.[38] Table 2.2 shows the data collected by AIAG for the first cycle of 17 months.

Table 2.2 Quotas and sales of AA members on the open market, 12 July 1901 to 31 December 1902 (tons)

| Firms | Quotas (tons) | Shares, July to December 1901 | Sales, July to December 1901 | Shares, January to June 1902 | Sales, January to June 1902 | Quotas, 17 months | Shares, 17 months | Sales, 17 months |
|---|---|---|---|---|---|---|---|---|
| AIAG | 1,500 | 677.60 | 617.97 | 750.00 | 605.10 | 2,178.00 | 2,104.67 | 2,119.50 |
| NACO | 650 | 294.00 | 209.57 | 325.00 | 332.90 | 945.00 | 913.19 | 852.00 |
| BACO | 400 | 180.60 | 140.52 | 200.00 | 244.40 | 580.50 | 589.46 | 630.50 |
| SEMF and PCAC | 550 | 247.80 | 66.91 | 275.00 | 270.70 | 795.50 | 769.68 | 775.00 |
| Total | 3,100 | 1,400.00 | 1,034.70 | 1,550.00 | 1,453.10 | 4,500.00 | 4,377.00 | 4,377.00 |

Source: TMA.

In the last five months of 1901, a slowdown in sales was recorded: the open market only absorbed 1,034 tons of the 1,400 tons provided for AIAG, which corresponded to five months of normal sales. However, in the first six months of 1902, sales were closer to the predictions made for the six months. At the end of 1902, less than the 4,500 tons expected in November 1901 to be sold during 17 months, was actually sold. Thanks to AIAG's 'system', this decrease in sales was split among all the companies in the cartel, thus sharing the sacrifices caused by the circumstance. This fact becomes more evident further analysing the data of each company. NACO sold less than its quota because of shipping delays from Canada during 1902: this *défaillance* was redistributed on the quotas of the other companies, which thus took some redundancies. BACO recorded a surplus with respect to its quota because, as we have seen, the agreement destined to BACO an important part of the British market, if it recorded sales exceeding 400 tons. The initial performance of its 'system' shows that AIAG was able to predict the course of business, managing the international market, and arranging readjustments that were needed from the forecast and the actual evolution of the market.[39]

## Readjustments to the agreement and sales strategy

Notwithstanding the measures taken to prevent a possible problem with relations among the members, from 1902 BACO began to remonstrate at the offices of AA to get a bigger quota than that fixed in the contract. The expansion of the British market at the beginning of the century revealed growth, which forced BACO to rethink its strategy. The change in BACO's strategy was also derived from the international crisis that hit the market of carbides, which penalised the choices made earlier to use its electricity to manufacture carbides instead of increasing its aluminium production.[40] Faced with this strategic mistake, the chairman (Ristori) and the vice-chairman (Wallace) of BACO were forced to resign and were replaced by Wolfenden and Bonner, who also entered AA's *comité*. The new representatives expressed their disappointment with the previous choices, because, while all the other companies had a contingent that took into account ongoing capacity or expansion, BACO owned a quota equal only to its current production in 1901. Without a modification of the quotas, this company could not follow its domestic market and feared not being able to properly plan the use of its electric power.[41]

Faced with this demand, AA requested again a consultation with Professor Meili about the modifiability of the quotas before the expiry of the contract. Meili categorically excluded this possibility from the legal point of view, because 'The intention of the parties could only be to fix a definitive and unchangeable prorate.'[42] Nevertheless, AIAG tried to propose a compromise to BACO, aiming to find a peaceful resolution to the conflict inside the group of producers. After the French companies and PRC objected to any increase in BACO's quotas at the expense of their quotas, AIAG proposed to BACO to unofficially reformulate the quotas from 1903, attributing to BACO an additional 100 tons per year to be sold into the British market only. As a consequence, the new quotas did not require sacrifices from the other companies, and satisfied BACO's requests. The new quotas are shown in Table 2.3.

*Table 2.3* Changes in AA quotas after BACO complaints, 1901–1903 (tons and %)

| Firms | Shares in 3100 tons | Quotas, 1901 (%) | Shares in 3200 tons | Quotas, 1903 (%) |
|---|---|---|---|---|
| AIAG | 1,500.00 | 48.40 | 1,500.00 | 47.50 |
| NACO | 650.00 | 21.00 | 650.00 | 20.10 |
| SEMF and PCAC | 550.00 | 17.70 | 550.00 | 16.80 |
| BACO | 400.00 | 12.90 | 500.00 | 15.60 |
| Total | 3,100.00 | 100.00 | 3,200.00 | 100.00 |

Source: TMA.

In addition to a review of the quotas, AA underwent further transformation compared to the original contract. BACO obtained, with the support of PRC, that AIAG no longer sold on behalf of the cartel in Britain. This market was entrusted to BACO and NACO that, together, began to act as intermediaries on behalf of the cartel, handling imports into Britain. In order to do this, BACO and NACO replicated in their offices the measures taken by AIAG, establishing a register that could be inspected at any time by AIAG and communicating monthly sales reports to the central office in Neuhausen. This compromise was not opposed by the French companies, that were interested in the continuation of AA, because it provided them with a large enough reserved market, where they could adopt selling prices significantly higher than in export markets. In fact, the prices on the French market amounted to 3 francs in 1904, compared to 2.75 francs in the open market. This gap was also caused by the customs duties that weighed 30 per cent on the price of the metal.[43]

This first episode shows that a successful cartel is one that is able change in order to follow the evolution of the economic environment in which it operates.[44] It also shows that at this stage, AIAG knew how to manage the group of producers as a leader: its primacy among the other members, as sanctioned by the fact that it was the manager of the cartel, led to conflict resolution, trying to protect the general interests of the group. Unlike AIAG, other companies tried to exploit this initial disagreement to their advantage: this is proved by the revival of the alliance between PRC and BACO, derived from the agreements at the end of the century with ASCO. Although AIAG was able to fix the situation, its position was weakened by the new autonomy of the British market. The real problem with this new configuration was the fact that decentralising and making control on sales more cooperative, there was a risk that centrifugal forces could be born in the cartel. AIAG decided to extend transparency in the group, distributing monthly reports on sales and other marketing information, because this would be an effective deterrent against any possible loosening of internal cohesion.[45]

The actual strategy of the cartel varied over time, according to the information on the market. AIAG functioned as statistical centre, as central manager of contracts, and as marketing office of aluminium in the first cartel. AIAG also designed a common commercial strategy, that aimed to promote progressive extension of the aluminium market through sale price stability. This policy had already emerged during the clash with the merchants at the end of the century and was sought by the main German customers of AIAG, but now it was clearly formalised and extended to the whole aluminium international trade. This stability consolidated a market that was not speculative, differently from other non-ferrous metals, and allowed scheduling of a gradual extension of production capacity of the companies, writing off the investments at a good rate. This strategy was summed up in the 'Rapport de Gestion' of 1903 with these words:

> Whereas before, some consumers were in the position to force the producers and the suppliers to sell Aluminium [*sic*] at different prices, these consumers realised that this strategy does no longer work since the management of the business has been merged in the hands of a single power. They also have to admit that the stability of the prices reigns over all the market, and it helps the development of the business. [...] Then, our efforts must aim to suppress these intermediaries that disturb the market uselessly.[46]

To facilitate this task, the AA instituted a common warehouse in Rotterdam where it accumulated stocks of metal from various sources (primarily British and Canadian), and it sold them on behalf of the cartel on the open market. From the establishment of this common warehouse, AIAG asked all the members of AA to mark the ingots with the producer's name – a practice that continues today – because it would have made it easier to store the metal and get feedback from buyers, who could know the origin of the metal and judge its quality. This feedback was included in the annual *rapports de gestion*. Between 1902 and 1905, AIAG was able to effectively control the market and prices and to design sales programmes without difficulty. Table 2.4 shows the overall evolution of AA's open markets.

The first AA was an effective tool in the management of sales and price control. The cartel encouraged a gradual increase in the market and, despite the unequal development of individual national markets, the companies were able to meet their quotas without producing serious imbalances. Prices remained stable

*Table 2.4* AA's sales in the open market, 1902–1905 (tons, %, and F/kg)

|  | AIAG | | NACO | | BACO | | SEMF and PCAC | | Total | |
|---|---|---|---|---|---|---|---|---|---|---|
|  | tons | % | tons | % | tons | % | tons | % | tons | prices |
| Quotas | 1500 | 47.50 | 650 | 20.10 | 500 | 15.60 | 550 | 16.80 | 3,200 | 2.75–2.90 |
| 1902 | 1442 | 48.42 | 555 | 18.63 | 453 | 15.21 | 527 | 17.69 | 2,978 | 2.85 |
| 1903 | 1,852 | 48.60 | 725 | 19.02 | 610 | 16.00 | 624 | 16.40 | 3,811 | 2.85 |
| 1904 | 2,576 | 45.47 | 1,168 | 20.60 | 1,002 | 17.68 | 920 | 16.23 | 5,666 | 2.85 |
| 1905 | 3,023 | 43.10 | 1,449 | 20.67 | 1,387 | 19.78 | 1,151 | 16.41 | 7,010 | 2.95 |
| Total | 9,571 | 45.89 | 4,191 | 20.09 | 3,632 | 17.41 | 3,470 | 16.63 | 20,855 | – |

Source: TMA and RPA.

despite the strong increase in demand that occurred during the early years of the cartel's activity. In fact, between 1901 and 1905, the market that was managed directly by the AA went from around 3,000 tons to more than 7,000 tons, while the world production of this metal increased by 100 per cent. However, 1905 was a critical year. Several extraordinary and unpredictable markets suddenly increased the demand of aluminium well above the installed production capacity and, while several outsiders began to undermine the AA, its internal cohesion was drastically reduced.

## Investments and technological control

Following the global growth of demand, the companies planned new investments. These investments were also instrumental in the negotiations for the renewal of AA because, as we have seen, the production capacity was an important element in the definition of the quotas of the cartel. Investments are not immediate in the aluminium industry. Actually, the construction of an integrated aluminium and electricity unit required a fairly long time, which could last from three to five years. BACO, that failed in the negotiations of 1901, did not want to be unprepared at the end of the cartel in 1906, and began planning the opening of a second plant in Scotland, in Kinlochleven, from 1902, whose construction started in 1904. BACO also started a strategy of foreign investment, showing an interest in the construction of a plant in Norway, in Stangfjorden – near Oslo – where there was already a hydroelectric power station.[47] These investments were also oriented to fill its growing national markets, because BACO was obliged to use the metal of other companies before the construction

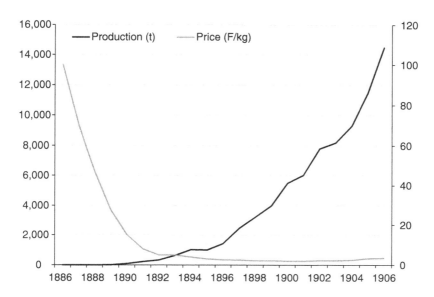

*Figure 2.1* Aluminium global production and prices, 1886–1907.

of these new units.[48] The other companies soon began to think about investments to follow the trend of the market and, at the same time, to prepare negotiations for the new cartel. In 1904, PCAC, in turn, began the construction of a second plant in Saint-Jean de Maurienne, that was completed only in 1909, and SEMF began the construction of a hydroelectric power station in La Saussat.[49] In 1904, AIAG had obtained authorisation to install a hydroelectric power station in Chippis, in Wallis in Switzerland, and in 1905 it began its construction.[50] PRC had launched its new plant in Massena in 1903, and during 1905 it was planning to increase its investments in hydroelectric installations at Niagara Falls and to increase the production capacity of its Canadian unit.[51]

Despite the investments made by AA, which aimed at following the upward trend of global demand, the news of the appearance of outsiders showed up several times from 1903 onwards. The main reason of these actions was not the lack of metal in the market, but the fact that aluminium became the focus of a diversification strategy carried out by actors outside the cartel group. These programmes came especially from electricity producers, who were looking for industrial applications for their electricity, from producers of alumina looking for outlets for their production, and from engineers who had dealt with aluminium, but had been removed from their office. The aluminium market was growing rapidly, as well as the production of hydroelectric energy: this metal was beginning to look like a good diversification of production in many countries, where the protection provided by Heroult's patents had ended, such as in France, or was about to end, such as in Britain.[52]

Faced with these threats, AA decided to lower its price from 2.90 F/kg to 2.75, despite the expansion phase that the market had been experiencing from 1903 onwards. The low prices would have kept away from aluminium a range of manufacturers who were suffering from the international competition in carbides, and, as a consequence, were looking for new and more profitable uses for the electric power that they produced.[53] In addition, AA also decided to hire or pay the engineers who had been removed from their offices. In particular, AA paid Adolphe Minet who, even if he did not manage to develop his process, could replicate Hall's and Heroult's process.[54] AA also decided to hire Emanuele Ristori who, after being removed from his office at BACO, had tried several times to get back into the aluminium business and had been contacted by a group in the UK. At the beginning, AA asked Ristori to survey some bauxite reserves in India, and later he was employed as a cartel consultant, who was charged with inspecting the various establishments of the members.[55]

Part of this control over technology was represented by the strategy on alumina. As seen in the previous chapter, only SEMF and BACO were able to obtain the best existing technology for the production of alumina, the one developed by Karl Bayer. At first, not all producers realised the importance of Bayer's process in reducing production costs and continued for a long time either to stock up from third parties or to look for other production processes.[56] With the expansion strategies at the beginning of the century, the control over Bayer's process became a way to encourage vertical integration, lowering production costs, and cutting off the market's potential producers. In the course of 1903, AA tried to involve Bayer in the cartel with an exclusive contract, offering him 25,000 francs. Even though he sold his technology to the cartel, the inventor refused to grant the exclusive, because he wanted to be free to negotiate the sale of the process with other companies. In particular, a major German producer of alumina, Gebrüder Giulini, began the construction of a large plant in Ludwigshafen with this technology. AA then negotiated an agreement with Giulini, in order to have stable supplies in exchange for a commitment not to sell alumina outside AA and not to produce aluminium independently. According to an agreement signed in 1904, Giulini was committed with AA for five years, in exchange for a stable market of 3,000 tons per year.[57]

With these manoeuvres aimed at hiring Minet and Ristori, AA was able to put on hold an initiative in the UK and one in France. The agreement with Giulini also prevented any possible newcomers from entering the market, because it created a monopoly in the supply of the main raw material for aluminium production. Moreover, Bayer's death in 1904 made it difficult to further spread his technology, because only the companies in the cartel or its allies, as Giulini was at this time, had the technical knowledge to start this type of production. The fact that the English and French ventures described above had been avoided placed the companies in the cartel in a seemingly comfortable situation. For instance, Vielhomme congratulated Huber on the success of this operation, stating that: 'We could avoid by linking the collaborations that would have started the production of aluminium and alumina, or by preventing them from buying the alumina, that they needed.'[58]

However, these agreements represented a major limitation for the individual strategies of the cartel members, which were planning extensions in alumina production to ensure stable supplies at a low cost in view of the increases in the production of aluminium. Vertical integration, as we have seen, was one of the main parts of the strategies of all aluminium companies, and, even after the conclusion of the cartel arrangements, this strategy did not disappear. In fact, the companies were encouraged to reduce production costs through integration to increase their profit margins in a situation of stable sales prices. As a consequence, several companies began to see the agreement with Giulini as a strong limitation to their earnings. For example, PRC, which was stably supplied by Giulini and until then had not been integrated towards alumina, proposed AIAG to negotiate a reduction of supplies. Even BACO, which produced alumina individually, with which it also supplied PRC and AIAG, doubted the opportunity to conclude these agreements with Giulini: in fact, a large part of the cartel lost its cohesion on the alumina affair, because almost all the members' individual goals were contrary to the collective interests of the group.[59]

## The cohesion of AA to the international business cycle test

Another proof that the cohesion of the cartel was crumbling under the centrifugal forces of the individual interests of the single companies came in the course of 1905. The investments made to support the increased demand needed time to be completed, and from 1905 the metal had become scarce in different markets. This situation was not caused by a mistake in the planning by AA's *comité*, but by the presence of impromptu demands linked to the rapid growth of the price of copper on the London market, which had increased from £59.60 per ton in 1904 to 87.12 over the course of 1905, and to 105 in 1906.[60] This sudden increase made aluminium even more appealing on the market as a replacement material in key applications and it suddenly changed the competitiveness of aluminium as a substitute for copper in key applications. In addition, important orders requested by the Russian government for military equipment for the Russo-Japanese War had led to a further increase in the demand.[61]

Since the beginning of 1905, the metal produced by the AA firms had seemed insufficient to satisfy the increasing demand. The situation became particularly severe at the end of 1905, when the metal became scarce and some merchants accumulated stock for speculation, creating an upward spiral in the international situation. This action created problems with the architecture created by AIAG because international traders were playing an important role in trade again, depriving AIAG of the monopoly of sales that it had built with AA. AIAG suggested to the other members of the cartel to sell metal with specific clauses that would prohibit the export or resale, but these solutions proved to be ineffective. Except for AIAG, all the other companies in the cartel proposed to increase the price to slow down the demand while waiting for the implementation of the new production capacity. An increase of the price would also have avoided speculative behaviour in the markets, because it would have reduced the profit margins of the merchants, curbing speculative corner operation.[62]

To ensure that the agreement was not broken by the strong tension that had arisen, the general director of AIAG and of AA, Huber, decided to accept the increases in prices proposed by the other members of the cartel. He decided to propose to the members to still consider the price as indicated in AA as a base rate, leaving the individual companies the opportunity to seek a higher price on behalf of AA. The main point was not to create market failures and AA's *comité* judged that the price increase was the most sensible way to reduce both the demand and the accumulation of stock by traders, while waiting for the launch of the new capacities. Actually, by 1908, the global production capacity of the AA would increase by 50 per cent compared to 1905. To prevent these increases from generating individualistic tendencies on the part of the cartel members, it was decided that the earnings derived from the increases would be pooled together and shared amongst the cartel members.[63] Thus, at first, the price on the markets increased from 2.5 to 3.45 F/kg in 1906, and it continued to increase up to 4 francs in the first half of 1907.[64]

However, the projects undertaken by outsiders wanting to come into the business were updated again by these increases. These actions were supported by Giulini, who was threatened to be deprived of important outlets by the integration strategies of the companies in the cartel. Giulini decided to break the agreement with AA and started an offensive against the cartel. In fact, the supply contract was not renewed in 1904, because the companies were not willing to commit to purchase alumina after 1907, as far as they were investing to integrate their productions. Instead of lasting five years, it was finally broken at the end of June 1906 after less than two years since its beginning.[65] This encouraged Giulini to take decisive measures towards the outsiders to encourage them to produce aluminium. Giulini produced about 10,000 tons of alumina, which were useful to produce about 5,000 tons of aluminium. Without the sales to AA, it was deprived of a market for more than half of its outlets.[66] Giulini was convinced that alumina was the key of success to produce aluminium and it provokingly declared in the newspapers specialising in the trade of metals: 'Donnez-moi de l'alumine et je ferai de l'aluminium sans le secours d'Héroult et de Hall.'[67]

Giulini started a deal with two French companies, the Société des Forces de l'Avre Motrices (SARV) of the Bergès group, and the Société d'Electrochimie (EC) to provide them the alumina needed to start production of aluminium. The Bergès group was a major producer of paper and had large hydroelectric capacities. It was allied with the leading enterprise in the field of hydroelectric production, Bouchayer & Viallet. Even EC owned hydro capacity in excess, that was derived from the crisis of carbides.[68] The group that was led by Bergès in France soon declared its intention to extend the production to other sites and founded a second company, the Société des Produits Electrochimiques et Electrométallurgiques des Pyrénées (PYR). Also two other firms were created in France, which were supplied by Giulini: l'Aluminium du Sud-Ouest (ASO) and the Société Electrométallurgique du Sud-Est (EMSE).[69] The strong connection with Giulini meant that these companies also benefited from the commercial channels of a commercial enterprise that was linked to the German producer of alumina, Beer, Sondheimer & Co., that became the reference trader of the group of outsiders.[70]

Because of the high prices and AIAG's strategies to cut out international merchants, aluminium became an appealing business also for other actors. Cecil Budd, chairman of the London Metal Exchange, created Aluminium Corporation Ltd (ALCOR) with a unit in Wales. This company, in turn, founded also a subsidiary in Norway, the Anglo-Norwegian Aluminium Corporation Ltd (ANCO). These companies were getting their supply of alumina from an independent Belgian producer, Gaetan Somze, who started test production in Salzaete and Mennesis, using an alternative process to the Bayer, the Peniakoff process.[71] In the course of 1905, Metallgesellschaft itself collaborated to launch aluminium production with a major German chemical company, Chemische Fabrik Griesheim Elektron (CFGE), which was developing an experimental process for the use of clay instead of bauxite in the production of alumina. AA was informed of the foundation of a new outsider in Italy, the Società Italiana per la Fabbricazione e la Lavorazione dell'Alluminio (SIFA), led by Lorenzo Allievi – a prominent Italian electrotechnical engineer, which had been created with the help of Beer, Sondheimer & Co. for integrated production from bauxite (extracted in Abruzzi) to semi-finished products.[72]

## The difficult renewal of the cartel and its crisis

These events happened just as the first cartel agreement was about to end. Even if the outsiders had further developed, AIAG had already sensed the danger of the situation by the end of 1905. AIAG decided to call a meeting in March 1906 in anticipation of the renewal of the cartel and it suggested a new system to manage the agreement, which was able to avoid the worst effects of boom–bust cycles

and the risk of advance from the outsiders. AIAG feared that part of the investments planned by the cartel members was merely linked to the renewal of the
cartel to negotiate higher quotas. As in 1901, AIAG tried to impose its vision in
the formulation of the cartel, aiming to increase centralisation of decisions, with
the aim of ensuring a more orderly development of the industry. AIAG proposed
to assign to the companies some guidelines for investments, allocating progressive
quotas, which varied with the expansion of demand. The new quotas took into
account the results of the sales between 1901 and 1905 (see Table 2.4), the
expansion in progress, and the predictions about the future.

The French companies refused these quotas, because they considered them too
low and they suggested reconstructing a different architecture for the agreement. In
particular, PCAC proposed the *comité* included the French market among the open
markets. According to this proposal, the French companies would have handled this
market on behalf of AA, in a manner similar to what happened in the German and
British markets, allowing imports. PCAC's proposal derived from the fear that the
new producers on the French market would be able to start production soon,
eroding the outlets of PCAC and SEMF. Second, PCAC's idea of the cartel was
completely different from AIAG's vision. According to PCAC's director, Adrien
Badin, the cartel would have to be reconstituted in a more cooperative way, including an equal role among the partners, which implied the end of AIAG's primacy in
the management of the cartel. This company was trying to make room for itself
among the producers with considerable investments, for which it would have
needed a much larger quota than the one which it had managed to get in old AA.[73]

The members of AA decided to satisfy the demands of the French companies
as regards the inclusion of the French market in the 'open markets', but AIAG
was able to keep its primacy in AA. SEMF and PCAC were given the quotas
corresponding to their French market in addition to the old export quota.
Although SEMF and PCAC demanded a quota of 31.67 per cent, the other
members were able to reduce this requirement to 30 per cent and to lead the
French companies to accept the new system developed by AIAG on progressive
quotas.[74] The new agreement was finally signed in April 1906 and started from 1
January 1907. It was expected to last five years, until 31 December 1911. AIAG
lost a consistent part of its quotas, in order to make the other firm accept the new
agreement. The quotas of new AA are described in Table 2.5.

The renewal of AA marked a deep modification of the structure of the cartel.
Although AIAG continued to manage the AA and sought to control the industry's development with guidelines for investments, now all the other companies
had become intermediaries for the sales of the AA: SEMF and PCAC in France,
BACO and NACO in Great Britain, and NACO in North, Central and South
America. AIAG's pre-eminent position was gradually eroded by the development
of other companies, which were becoming more and more similar in size and
quotas to the Swiss company.[75] The advance of outsiders in all major markets
forced the cartel to decentralise its management, in order to be able to follow the
progress of the individual national markets in a better way. However, this new
allocation of quotas displeased BACO who, as was the case with the first contract, tried to change its quota after the signing of the contract. However, this

Table 2.5 AIAG proposal and actual quotas for the new Aluminium-Association, 1906 (%)

| Firms | Up to 5000 tons | | From 5001 to 10,000 tons | | From 10,001 to 15,000 tons | | From 15,001 to 20,000 tons | | From 21,001 to 25,000 tons | |
|---|---|---|---|---|---|---|---|---|---|---|
| | Proposal | Actual | Proposal | Actual | Proposal | Actual | Proposal | Actual | Proposal | Actual |
| AIAG | 45.125 | 37.44 | 42.750 | 35.52 | 40.250 | 33.92 | 37.625 | 31.66 | 35.125 | 29.56 |
| NACO | 20.125 | 16.70 | 20.750 | 17.24 | 21.750 | 18.33 | 23.125 | 19.46 | 24.625 | 20.72 |
| BACO | 19.125 | 15.86 | 20.750 | 17.24 | 22.250 | 18.75 | 23.625 | 19.88 | 24.625 | 20.72 |
| SEMF&PCAC | 15.625 | 30.00 | 15.750 | 30.00 | 15.750 | 29.00 | 15.625 | 29.00 | 15.625 | 29.00 |
| Total | 100.00 | 100.00 | 100.00 | 100.00 | 100.00 | 100.00 | 100.00 | 100.00 | 100.00 | 100.00 |

Source: TMA and RPA.

time, BACO tried to force its hand by investing in Switzerland in order to directly threaten AIAG.[76] Although AIAG managed to prevent BACO from producing aluminium in Switzerland, in exchange, BACO was appointed as the sole seller of AA in the UK, by inserting a clause in the new agreement on territoriality. This displeased NACO, which would sell only on the American continent.[77]

However, AA turned out to be unsuitable to manage the situation. Although the members of the cartel had a national monopoly on sales, the rapid growth of outsiders between 1907 and 1908 made any attempt to control the market useless. The cartel then tried to change its strategy, driven by the demands of PCAC. PCAC proposed again its criticism towards the system of AA: since there were four separate vendors for AA, the association had become too slow to adapt to the market conditions and the 'monopoly of information' of AA no longer existed. Thus Adrien Badin from PCAC suggested that any company should be free to follow a personal business strategy, reducing the cartel to a control office, as in other associations 'de la nature même de l'AA', or that the *comité* would be summoned more frequently, such as once a month, to better coordinate its action.[78] The situation, which had already been delicate in the course of 1906, worsened at the end of 1907, when a severe international economic crisis replaced the euphoria that had marked the economic cycle at the beginning of the century, reducing the purchases of the major buyers.[79] Faced with falling demand, the cartel members seemed really unprepared: the lack of communication of commercial information among the members had meant that even in late August 1907 demand was largely overestimated, and that is why the members did not take into consideration either lowering of prices, or the risk that overproduction was near. For example, still in September 1907, Arthur Vining Davis was convinced that the annual total demand amounted to 15–20,000 tons, which encouraged PRC to operate its Canadian plant at full capacity. In fact, the total demand in 1907 was slightly less than 10,000 tons.[80]

Faced with the fear of a sudden decline in sales, the companies tried to run for cover: they suddenly decided to lower the selling price thinking 'employer les finances du Pool pour subventionner les entreprises destinées à consommer de grandes quantités d'aluminium'. After several negotiations, the companies of AA lowered the price to 2.50 F/kg, expecting to drop to 2 francs, and PCAC proposed to bring it to 1.5 francs by the end of 1907, but it did not get the consent of the other members.[81] The price was not lowered further for two reasons. First, AA had come to know that Beer, Sondheimer & Co. was the international trader of the companies linked to Giulini and that it systematically underquoted its price to compete against AA, in a range between 2.20 and 1.70 Marks/kg (2.75–1.90 F/kg). Second, excepting PCAC, the other members thought it best to accumulate more resources to lower the prices abruptly when outsiders would have ended their investments, i.e. when they had been running out of capital. As far as sales dropped down at the end of 1907, Davis cabled to AIAG 'further reduction will not stop competition only demoralize trade'.[82] Between 1906 and 1908, AA had the results shown in Table 2.6.

The AA of 1906 allowed too much freedom in the decision-making process to companies, damaging the structure of the monopoly of sales and of information that had characterised the first cartel from 1901 to 1905. The collection of data, that was

*Table 2.6* AA sales and prices in the open market, 1906–1908 (tons, %, and F/kg)

| | AIAG | | NACO | | BACO | | SEMF and PCAC | | Total | AA price |
|---|---|---|---|---|---|---|---|---|---|---|
| | tons | % | tons | % | tons | % | tons | % | tons | F/kg |
| 1905 | 3,185 | 36,8 | 1,395 | 16.1 | 1,303 | 15.1 | 2,766 | 32.0 | 8,649 | 2.95 |
| 1906 | 3,327 | 34,0 | 1,408 | 14.4 | 1,429 | 14.6 | 3,609 | 37.0 | 9,773 | 3.45 |
| 1907 | 3,097 | 36,7 | 1,430 | 16.9 | 1,386 | 16.4 | 2,535 | 30.0 | 8,450 | 3.65 |
| 1908* | 1,557 | 37,4 | 695 | 16.7 | 660 | 15.9 | 1,248 | 30.0 | 4,150 | 2.50 |
| Total | 11,166 | 35,9 | 4,901 | 15.7 | 4,778 | 15.4 | 10,158 | 32.7 | 31,022 | – |

Source: TMA and RPA.

Note
* Until September 1908.

divided among four companies, no longer allowed the AA system to get adequate knowledge of the market. This fact had a significant influence on the error of prediction made in 1907, which perpetuated the strategy of high prices, when the trend had reversed and the new producers were flourishing in almost all European countries. With the exception of AIAG, the members of the cartel were also afraid that the other companies were providing wrong data to show that their respective national markets were larger than they really were, to exploit in their favour the mechanism of progressive quotas. AA was neither as centralised as AIAG would have liked nor the free association that PCAC hoped to create. The companies were still too dependent on each other for sales and division of contracts, and this resulted in slowness in the decision-making process as regards production and commercial strategies.[83]

The international crisis had a severe impact on the market. By November 1907, all companies had to acknowledge that the market was now 'almost dead'.[84] The cartel companies had accumulated 4,100 tons of unsold stock (respectively AIAG 600 tons, SEMF 1,500, PCAC 1,000, NACO 500, BACO 500), equal to about six months of sales in normal conditions.[85] The production capacity of the outsiders was estimated at about 3,800 tons per year which, together with new investments by the cartel members, was further aggravating the overproduction crisis. In April 1908 PCAC decided to propose the dissolution of AA in order to fight the competition independently on each national market. This decision was supported by the fact that AA's manner of operating could not be fast and flexible enough to apply competitive prices successfully: the process of fixing prices involved the *comité* and took a longer time than the time it would take Beer, Sondheimer & Co. who, as a seller of many outsiders linked to Giulini, had greater and more effective decision-making power.[86]

At the same time, PCAC was trying to stand out among the producers. Since its return to the aluminium business, at the end of the nineteenth century, this producer had always been second to SEMF in the domestic market, both from the quantitative and qualitative point of view. From the new investments that it planned in the renewal period of the cartel, PCAC decided to increase its production capacity to turn over its balance of power in the national market with

SEMF. The imbalance between supply and demand that was emerging due to the arrival of outsiders on the French market, was aggravated by PCAC's behaviour, which was trying to make room for itself in the cartel, in this delicate moment. Overproduction in the French market, in fact, pushed the price down to 1.50 F/ kg in the summer of 1908.[87] Despite the fact that other producers preferred a continuation of the agreement, while also taking into account the possibility of establishing a quota for the outsiders in order to bring order to the market, it was PCAC that refused to continue because the inclusion of the outsiders at this time would have meant only a reduction of its quota.[88]

In a contemporary study published by Wilfried Kossman, it is explained that the failure of AA in 1908 was the fault of AIAG. According to this author, AIAG managed the cartel in a too individualistic way, taking too much profit for it, and it also decided to increase the prices in 1905. Also another author, Carl Dux shares part of these explanations.[89] However, we have showed that, in reality, AIAG was against the rise of prices and it managed the cartel in a fair way, even making individual sacrifices to save the whole structure of the cartel. Yet, the cartel as it was managed was not a perfect solution for an industry in full development, with some firms elbowing to emerge. In particular, it was PCAC's strategy that forced the change, while the vertical integration strategies of other firms made vain the attempts, made by AIAG, to gain control over Giulini. From an institutional standpoint, it was PCAC that asked for the termination of the cartel agreement at the court of Zurich, because it aimed to be free to compete with the outsiders in its national market without the limitation that AA represented to its quickness to respond to the Giulini group's underquotations. The French producers were actually the ones that were suffering most in the cartel due to harsh competition and the drop in sales.[90] The cartel was finally declared dissolved on 1 October 1908, more than three years in anticipation of its contractual end.

## Notes

1  TMA, AIAG, box 152, Huber to Fürstenberg, 7 March 1901.
2  TMA, AIAG, box 152, Aron Hirsch to AIAG, 12 November 1900. Bemarkungen zum Vorschlage Hirsch bez. Convention mit PRC, 11 November 1900.
3  Stigler, 'A Theory of Oligopoly'.
4  Olson, *The Logic of Collective Action*.
5  Metallgesellschaft, *Statistische Zusammenstellungen über Blei, Kupfer, Zink, Zinn, Silber, Nickel und Aluminium von der Metallgesellschaft*. Frankfurt am Main: Metallgesellschaft, 1901.
6  RPA, 00-2-15492, AIAG to SEMF, 1 July 1901. TMA, AIAG, box 223, PCAC to AIAG, 27 May 1901. A.V. Davis to Huber, 30 July 1901.
7  TMA, AIAG, box 223, Convention, Proposal Agreement, 6 July 1901.
8  Barjot, 'Introduction'. Barjot, 'Un Nouveau Champ Pionner'.
9  TMA, AIAG box 223, Fürstenberg to AIAG, 1 May 1901.
10  Schröter, 'Cartelisation and Decartelisation in Europe', 133.
11  Hannah, *The Rise of Corporate Economy*.
12  Francis Laur, *De l'Accaparement: Essai Doctrinal*. Paris: Publications scientifiques et industrielles, 1900. Paul de Rousiers, *Syndicats Industriels des Producteurs en France et à l'Étranger: Trust – Cartells – Comptoirs*. Paris: Armand Colin, 1901. Arthur Raffalovich, *Trusts, Cartels and Syndicats*. Paris: Librairie Guillaumin, 1903. Robert Liefmann, *Schutzzoll und Kartelle*. Jena: Fischer, 1903.

13

On peut dire que les cartels existent aujourd'hui dans le monde entier. Il n'est plus un seul pays qui ait échappé à la contagion … On est donc porté à conclure de ce mouvement universel que les syndicats répondent à une conception moderne des besoins commerciaux et ne sont pas déterminés par la seule fantaisie de quelques financiers ou gros brasseurs d'affaires.

Archives Nationales, Paris, F/12/8850, Ententes et Cartels, Jullemier (attaché commercial in Berlin) to Théophile Delcasse (French Minister of Foreign Affairs), 13 October 1902.

14 TMA, AIAG, box 223, Convention, Proposal Agreement, 6 July 1901.
15 TMA, AIAG, box 100B, Resultate der Konferenz berichte Huber am 18.7 und 22.7.1901.
16 TMA, AIAG, box 225, Aluminium-Verkäufe, 1902.
17 UGD, 347/21/46/2, BACO Chairman Reports of 1901. Report on continental visit. October 1901.
18 TMA, AIAG, box 223, Convention. Proposal Agreement, 6 July 1901. RPA, 00-2-15940, Convention. Aluminium-Association, 1901.
19 Valerie Suslow, 'Cartel Contract Duration: Empirical Evidence from Inter-war Period', *Industrial and Corporate Change*, vol. 14, no. 5, 2005, 705–744.
20 TMA, AIAG, box 223, Convention. Proposal Agreement, 6 July 1901.
21 UGD, 347/21/52/7, BACO, Legal opinion on aluminium syndicate or alliance, opinion by JF Iselin, 13 August 1901. J. F. Iselin was a barrister and expert in the Swiss and German laws and in industrial properties and patents. Justin Hughes, 'A Short History of "Intellectual Property" in Relation to Copyright', *Cardozo Law Review*, vol. 33, no. 4, 2012, 1293–1340, 1307–1308.
22 Henri Morsel, 'Contribution à l'Histoire des Ententes Industrielles, à Partir d'un Example, l'Industrie des Clorates', *Revue d'Histoire Économique et Sociale*, vol. 54, no. 1, 118–129.
23 TMA, AIAG, box 223, Proposition faite par M. E. Collin de la Société de Saint-Michel (PCAC), 18 July 1901.
24 RPA, 00-2-15940, Convention Préapratoire. Aluminium-Association, 1901.
25 TMA, AIAG, box 152, Aluminium-Association, 9 March 1901. Observations et proposition juridiques concernant la Convention d'Aluminium, 24 July 1901. Proposal of the Convention Agreement, 16 August 1901.
26 'In Memoriam: Friederich Meili', *American Journal of International Law*, vol. 8, no. 2, 1914, 347–349.
27 TMA, AIAG, box 157, Meili to Huber, 24 July 1901. Convention pour la Vente de l'Aluminium. Rédaction après les conseils de Mr. Le Professeur Dr. Meili à Zurich, 1901.
28 RPA, 00-2-15942, AIAG to SEMF, 5 August 1901. AA Circular letter, 9 December 1901.
29 TMA, AIAG, box 223, Metallsgesllchaft to Huber (AIAG), Schindler (AIAG), and Dreyfuss (SEMF), 15 October 1901. Vertrag zwischen der Aluminium-Industrie-Aktien-Gesellschaft und der Metallgesellschaft zu Frankfurt a/M.
30 TMA, AIAG, box 157, AA, Séance du Comité à Paris, 17 December 1901, Compte-Rendu, 23 December 1901. Box 223, A.V. Davis to AIAG, 19 August 1901. A.V. Davis to BACO, 2 October 1901.
31 TMA, AIAG, box 157, Proposition PRC, 9 August 1901.
32 TMA, AIAG, box 223, Aluminium-Association, Bemerkungen und Ergänzungen zu der Gedruckten Vorlage über die Pariser Konferenz von 10.11 und 12 Oktober 1901.
33 RPA, 00-2-15940, Aluminium-Association, Marché Commercial, 2 November 1901.
34 TMA, AIAG, box 153, Aluminium-Association, Convention, 2 November 1901.
35 Valerie Suslow and Margaret Levenstein. 'What Determines Cartel Success?' *Journal of Economic Literature*, vol. 44, no. 1, 2006. Levenstein, Suslow, 'Breaking Up is Hard to Do'.
36 TMA, AIAG, box 153, Aluminium-Association, Convention, 2 November 1901.

37 TMA, AIAG, box 223, AIAG to AA members, 12 November 1901.
38 TMA, AIAG, box 152, Die Entwicklung des Aluminium-Absatzes im offenen Markt der AA seit Juli 1901.
39 TMA, AIAG, box 152, Betrucht über die Entwicklung der Aluminium-Association, 31 December 1902.
40 Anne-Catherine Robert-Hauglustaine, 'Le Carbure de Calcium et l'Acétylène, de Nouveaux Produits pour de Nouvelles Industries, 1885–1914', in *Des Barrages, des Usines et des Hommes: L'industrialisation des Alpes du Nord entre Ressources Locales et Apports Extérieurs*, edited by Hervé Joly, Alexandre Giandou, Muriel Le Roux, and Ludovic Cailluet. Grenoble: Presses Universitaires de Grenoble, 2002, 101–116.
41 TMA, AIAG, box 152, PV de la Réunion à Paris le 12 Janvier 1903. Box 224, SEMF to AIAG, 2 December 1902.
42 Quote in original language – 'l'intention des parties ne pouvait etre que celle-ci: fixer un prorate définitif et invariable'.
43 RPA, 00-2-15492, AIAG to SEMF, 11 August 1902. TMA, AIAG, box 157, AA, Rapport de Gestion sur l'exercise 1903, 21 July 1904.
44 Suslow, Levenstein, 'What Determines Cartel Success?'
45 TMA, AIAG, box 157, AA Angelegenheit: Sitzung von 12 Januar 1903. PV de la Réunion tenue à Paris le 12 Janvier 1903.
46

Tandis qu'auparavant certains consommateurs important étaient en position de forcer les fabricants – fournisseurs à vendre l'Aluminium à un meilleur marché que l'autre, ces consommateurs ont vu que cette tactique ne prend plus depuis que la gestion des affaires se trouve concentrée dans une seule main. Ils doivent même reconnaître que la stabilité des prix règne dans tout le marché, et favorise le développement des affaires. [...] Nos efforts doivent donc tendre à supprimer ces intermédiaires qui inquiètent inutilement le marché.

RPA, 00-2-15940, Rapport de Gestion AA, Excise 1902.
47 UGD, 347/21/46/2, On Loch Leven Scheme Agreement, 1904. On Loch Leven Water Power Scheme, 12 September 1905. On visit to Norway, 14 July 1905. Perchard, *Aluminiumville.*
48 TMA, AIAG, box 157, PV séance AA. Paris, 18 Décembre 1904.
49 Anne Pezet, *La Décision d'Investissement Industriel: Le Cas de l'Aluminium.* Economica, Paris, 2000, 29–30.
50 AIAG, *Geschichte*, vol. 1, 125–129, 134.
51 Smith, *From Monopoly to Competition*, 94–96.
52 Wallace, *Market Control*, 38–39
53 TMA, AIAG, 157, PV, Séance du Comité, 7 September 1904. Box 227, Schindler to BACO, 15 July 1904. SEMF to AIAG, 18 November 1904.
54 RPA, 00-1-20029, Accord entre A. Minet et SEMF, 10 November 1903. TMA, AIAG, box 226, SEMF to AIAG, 6 December 1903.
55 TMA, AIAG, box 167, Note Private and Confidential, 1905. Box 157, PV Séance AA Zurich, 18 November 1905.
56 Wolfran Bayer, 'So Geht es ... L'alumine pure de Karl Bayer et son Intégration dans l'Industrie de l'Aluminium', *Cahiers d'Histoire de l'Aluminium*, no. 49, 2013, 21–46.
57 TMA, AIAG, box 157, Items and Proposal for the Committee-Convention of the AA to be held on December 18th 1904. Giulini Business.
58 'Nous avons pu empecher en liant les collaborations qui les auraient initiés à la fabrication de l'aluminium et à celle de l'alumine, ou en leur enlevant toute possibilité d'acheter de l'alumine qui leur était indispensable'. TMA, AIAG, box 227, SEMF to AIAG, 19 January 1904.
59 RPA, 00-2-15942, A.V. Davis to Huber, 25 May 1904.
60 Metallgesellschaft, *Recueil Statistiques sur les Métaux Plomb, Cuivre, Zinc, Etain, Nickel, Aluminium, Mercure et Argent*, vol. 1898–1907. Frankfurt am Main: Metallgesellschaft, 1908, 95–96.

61 RPA, 00-2-15942, AA circular letter, 23 February 1905.
62 TMA, AIAG, box 227, BACO to AIAG, 17 June 1905. Box 157, PV séance AA, 22 September 1905.
63 TMA, AIAG, box 157, Résumé et appéciation sur quelques points des conventions intervenues entre les parties conctractantes de l'AA, 21 September 1905.
64 TMA, AIAG, box 166, AA. Reklamation des Franzosischen, 1908.
65 TMA, AIAG, box 157, PV Séance AA 16 Juin 1906 – Affaire Giulini.
66 TMA, AIAG, box 166, A.V. Davis to Schindler, 1 August 1907.
67 TMA, AIAG, box 163, AIAG to PCAC 5 July 1906.
68 Louis André, *Aristide Bergès, une Vie d'Innovateur: De la Papeterie à la Houille Blanche.* Grenoble, Presses Universitaires de Grenoble, 2013. Ludovic Cailluet, *Chedde: Un Siècle d'Industrie au Pays du Mont-Blanc.* Grenoble: Presses Universitaires de Grenoble, 1997, 27–28
69 Louis André, 'Les Stratégies des Papeteries des Alpes face à l'Aluminium, 1888–1914', in Barjot, Bertilorenzi (eds), *Aluminium*, 63–76.
70 TMA, AIAG, box 166, PCAC to AIAG, 26 August 1907. 00-1-17773, Historique. La Sté des produits alumineux de Salzaete, 1912.
71 TMA, AIAG, box 169, AIAG to NACO – Confidentiel, 30 March 1908.
72 RPA, 00-2-15942, AA circular letter, 7 July 1905. Archivio Storico Banca Intesa San-Paolo, Documents Banca Commerciale Italiana (ASBCI), Cart.1, Fasc.2, Società Italiana per la Fabbricazione dell'alluminio, 1906–1921.
73 TMA, AIAG box 62, PV, Séance 12, 13 and 14 March 1906. Box 166, Reklamation des Französischen, 1908.
74 TMA, AIAG, box 166, Reklamation des Franzosischen, 1908.
75 RPA, 00-2-15940, Aluminium-Association, Convention 1906.
76 UGA/UGD, 347/21/45/2, BACO, Note on the Swiss Power Scheme, 14 June 1906.
77 TMA, AIAG, box 161, Konferenz mit Herrn Bonner in Zürich am 20 Oktober 1906. Betrieb Walliser Affaire.
78 TMA, AIAG, box 116, PCAC to AIAG, 21 August 1907. Memorandum de PCAC, 22 July 1907.
79 TMA, AIAG, box 163, PV de la Séance de l'AA, tenue à Paris, 28 November 1907.
80 TMA, AIAG, box 166, A.V. Davis to AIAG, 4 September 1907.
81 TMA, AIAG, 166, Rapport sur la Réunion ufficieuse de l'AA, tenue à Paris le 24 October 1907.
82 RPA, 00-2-15942, Cable de M. Davis, 29 November 1907.
83 TMA, AIAG, box 163, Various letters from July to October 1907.
84 TMA, AIAG, box 163, PV de la Séance de l'AA, tenue à Paris, 28 November 1907
85 TMA, AIAG, box 166, BACO to AIAG, 4 November 1907.
86 TMA, AIAG, box 167, Davis to Huber, 12 August 1909.
87 TMA, AIAG, box 167, Note. L'avis de Froges, 1908. Vielhomme to Huber, 28 August 1909.
88 TMA, AIAG, box 167, PV séance AA, Paris 22 and 23 September 1908.
89 Kossmann, *Über die Wirtschaftliche Entwicklung der Aluminiumindustrie*, 16–17. Dux, *Die Aluminium-Industrie-Actiengesellschaft.* These two studies were for long time the only information available about the pre-1914 cartel; for instance they were the main sources that Wallace used for his study in the 1930s (*Market Control*).
90 TMA, AIAG, box 168, Mémoire de l'Arbitrage, 1908. Notes prises à la première séance du tribunal arbitral tenue a Zurich le 29 juin 1908. Conclusions par la Compagnie des Produits Chimiques de'Alais et de la Camargue, 29 June 1908.

# 3 Changes at the top

## The new Aluminium-Association, 1909–1914

The dissolution of the Association in 1908 opened a brand new phase from two points of view. First, the aluminium industry had never been so 'disorganised'. The sharing of the same technological system, electrolysis, had linked the aluminium producers since the end of the nineteenth century, facilitating the creation of the first cartel. In fact, ever since the companies had chosen scales and scopes strategies during the 1890s, the agreements had always functioned as a scaffold for this industry during its early development. In the situation opened by the crisis of the cartel, firms appeared for the first time as completely disconnected. Moreover, as a consequence of the creation of newcomers, such as the outsiders that came to the fore between 1906 and 1909, the group of producers was much less homogeneous than in the past. As a consequence, they both shared a less common basis on which to build a new agreement and were less dependent on the former leader of the Association, AIAG, to which they did not recognise any authority in the organisation of the international markets.[1]

The first Association was not a simple trade agreement. It worked as an institution to which companies outsourced part of their activities, such as the collection of business and statistic information of marketing activities, an important part of international sales, and research activities on new applications. During the entire first phase of the cartelisation, AIAG had worked as manager of the cartel, by making available its facilities for its partners. Now, the authority of AIAG was heavily contested and the Swiss firm had lost its powers to lead the reconstruction of the cartel. Already in the renewal of the AA in 1906, AIAG had lost an important part of its pre-eminence in the group of producers, which had tried to get increasing autonomy from the protection of the Swiss company. AIAG's position had been weakened by the progressive growth of the other companies, which had increased their influence in the cartel. With the end of AA, AIAG had lost its role as leader of the group, but none of the other companies could still take the role. Before creating a new cartel, a new leader would have reconstitute the cohesion of the group and suggest new model of international cartels that was more suitable to the new situation.[2]

## ALCOA's repositioning manoeuvres: agreements and international strategies

Unlike European countries, where there was a proliferation of outsiders, in the United States PRC kept its monopoly. This was the aftermath of a specific legal confrontation that opposed Hall to Cowles and that ended with the purchase by PRC of Bradley's patent. This fact extended the legal monopoly of PRC until 1909, allowing the company to face the wave of new producers unscathed. Also high customs duties allowed PRC to maintain relatively higher prices in the domestic market, protecting the US company from the turmoil of the business cycle. Furthermore, PRC had consolidated its monopoly with an important strategy of investments in new scale economies and upstream integration that aimed both to saturate the national market and to hamper access to the best production factors by other possible producers. This upstream integration had been partly the reason for the rupture between the cartel and Giulini, from which the wave of outsiders started. In 1908, PRC took the name of Aluminum [*sic*] Company of America (ALCOA), underlining its position as the only aluminium producer in the US market.[3]

When AA was to be finally liquidated, ALCOA expressed the idea of forming a new agreement among the old members as soon as possible. ALCOA was aware that the safeguard of its monopoly would be weakened without any control over imports into the US market. As regards the outsiders, ALCOA thought that they would soon be driven out of the market, because the current prices could not compensate for the huge investments that had been made to enter this industry. For this reason, Davis wrote to AIAG in the summer of 1908:

> My opinion is it will be better if present members make new arrangements if we cannot get competitors in. Trade depression cannot last much longer, meantime it will be of mutual advantage to maintain prices. Competitors do not get much business. Separately, the Association members will get reduced prices, whereas together will get increased prices.[4]

However, BACO and the French companies were not ready to negotiate an immediate agreement and the crisis period was proving to be excruciating for relations among the former members of AA. On the one hand, BACO went through one of the most serious crises in its history and its former directors were removed. On the other hand, PCAC's strategy to increase its influence in the cartel was doomed to be highly destabilising for any compromise. In the course of 1908, AIAG and ALCOA made alone an agreement to reserve their respective markets. NACO concluded this agreement with AIAG on behalf of ALCOA, according to which NACO committed not to sell directly in continental Europe, where AIAG would work as an intermediary for the American company, while AIAG would not sell directly in North America, where NACO would act as sales agent for both companies. Moreover, in Europe, AIAG and NACO agreed to create sales quotas at 75 per cent for the Swiss company and 25 per cent for NACO, while in America this proportion was reversed. In the rest of the markets, AIAG and NACO shared sales of 50 per cent, NACO would function as an intermediary for AIAG in English-speaking countries, while AIAG for everyone else. This agreement was valid until 1 January 1910, when it would be renewed from year to year.[5]

The purpose of this agreement was to reorganise the commercial strategies of the two firms. The result of seven years of the AA system was that none of the old members could dispose of an international sales network, excepting AIAG, which was the only company that had continued to play an important role in the international marketing of this metal. For that, ALCOA found an important commercial partner in AIAG. On the other hand, AIAG understood the importance to find a high priced outlet in the US, where ALCOA could help the Swiss firm to find room. Thanks to this agreement, AIAG and ALCOA tried to partially reconstruct this network of sales exploiting each other's advantages: AIAG obtained an outlet in the US market, that, despite the international crisis, was becoming one of the main outlets for aluminium overcoming Germany; ALCOA benefited from the widespread diffusion of AIAG's international network. This agreement was also used by the two companies to exchange technical information on the new uses of aluminium, which were judged as sensitive to redress the bad market situation.[6]

Moreover, this agreement was functional to ALCOA's strategy in international markets and in the defence of its national monopoly. In fact, ALCOA took advantage of the international crisis and the difficulties of BACO to try to re-enter the UK market, from which it had been excluded during renegotiation of the cartel in 1906. ALCOA recreated a sale structure similar to that at the end of the century, without relying on international intermediaries, such as Aron Hirsch & Sohne. As a consequence, ALCOA opened a commercial subsidiary of NACO in London in 1909, under the direction of resident manager, Ernst C. Darling.[7] With a stable and permanent sales office, Great Britain came back into the sphere of influence of the American company, at a time when BACO was in big difficulties. By taking control over the imports of AIAG into its domestic market, ALCOA neutralised the action of one of the most dangerous international actors, saving its market from too harsh reductions of prices.[8] As he wrote to AIAG, Davis did not exclude the possibility of extending this agreement to other companies in order to raise the price to 2 F/kg, after the collapse to 1.30–1.50.[9]

However, this agreement could not replace the Aluminium-Association. At the beginning of 1909, the first signs of recovery in the market encouraged the return to some speculative behaviour on the international metal trade. Although ALCOA and AIAG managed to prevent speculative behaviours from Metallgesellschaft and Aron Hirsch, with which they were on good terms, they could not control Beer & Sondheimer which, during the crisis, was one of the main proponents of international trade of the outsiders. Once the crisis was over, this trader was trying to obtain large stocks of metal at bargain prices, to resell later at higher prices.[10] Faced with an intensification of these speculative activities, the sale director of AIAG, Martin Schindler, compared the merchants of metals to 'vampires' and he claimed the necessity to hamper their power in order to establish a common strategy to stabilise the market.[11] Since the beginning of 1909, AIAG and ALCOA began to try to reconstruct an international association among the former members of AA, in which they also sought to involve outsiders who had managed to escape the crisis.

## The oligopoly looking for a deal: the failure of AIAG's proposal

AIAG again proposed itself as the negotiator for a new cartel. The Swiss company considered that the installed production capacities would have been a good basis on which start the negotiations. The companies had over-invested in the last years and, only knowing the actual outputs, the new cartel could establish quotas that represented the strength of the companies, thus avoiding unfair attitudes on the part of the participants. In fact, until the market had reached a capacity to absorb new installed capacities, the producers were forced to reduce their outputs. According to AIAG's directors, a cartel based on 'impartial' and 'objective' capacities would have made objective the sacrifices that each member would have to do.[12] However, it was not possible to measure the global output with ease, because the situation of the outsiders was not clear. Some had not survived the crisis, while others gave no sign of surrendering, and the issue was whether to include them in the cartel and, if so, what criteria to follow.[13]

Faced with this impasse, AIAG did not give up on proposing a new international cartel in the spring of 1909, based on production capacity. BACO and SEMF demonstrated willingness to start negotiations on this basis. The Swiss company obtained the commitment of the other ex-partners not to start the sales for 1910 yet, so as to have greater freedom in the event that a cartel would be re-established by the end of 1909. However, the time was not yet right because some investments were still being completed and, therefore, it was impossible to determine the quotas on the basis of productive capacities. Moreover, negotiations on capacities alone were not sufficient to achieve a cartel; it was necessary that a solution was found for the British and French market, where the presence of outsiders made it more difficult to define a quota for the old members. In spite of the fact that the French companies also tried to involve some outsiders, this initiative was halted abruptly in August 1909, when SEMF communicated to AIAG that it was impossible to reach a compromise on the French market.[14] As a consequence, each producer began sales for 1910 without waiting longer.[15]

At the same time, news came of the failure and the recapitalisation of BACO. BACO was oppressed by large investments, that were made just before the crisis: in addition to the new plant in Loch Leven in Scotland, BACO was active in Orsières near Martigny in Switzerland, and in Norway, in Stangfjords. These investments in aluminium had also led it to expand the production capacity of alumina in Larne and to take direct control of the bauxite mines in the south of France.[16] As argued by Andrew Perchard, probably the choice of investing in Switzerland in 1906 turned out to be a major handicap for the financial situation of BACO, since it damaged the other investments that it had made, and kept its focus away from its domestic market.[17] When the crisis hit the aluminium market, BACO had not yet completed its investments. All of a sudden, its profits began to decline along with the fall in prices in the UK market. BACO's shares on the London stock market went from a nominal value of £4 in 1908 to £0.50 in August 1909, while the value of the bonds that the company subscribed to on the financial market to finance its expansions went from £100 to 76.5.[18] In 1909, the chairmanship of BACO was assumed by Andrew Tait, an entrepreneur who represented the new financiers of the City, and by Arthur Pollen, who was close to the government department of defence.[19] Led by the new leaders, BACO did not agree with the basis of the previous negotiations.[20]

The crisis in the UK market not only damaged BACO; even ALCOR and ANCO suffered major losses. In the course of 1908, before going bankrupt, BACO had tried to take over these two companies, aiming to rebuild its national monopoly. BACO was especially interested in taking control of ANCO, because this achievement was aligned with the chronic lack of cheap power that, from early in the twentieth century, pushed BACO to invest abroad. This strategy targeted Norway, a country in which the competitive advantages of cheap hydro-electric capacity was decisive for BACO, which already operated deep integration of the aluminium market with Great Britain. The takeover of ANCO would have meant BACO bringing back full control over Norwegian production. However, one of the main financial and strategic troubles for BACO came from its starting-up Swiss investment. In the context of the poor relations that followed the end of the cartel, this operation was followed with an ambivalent attitude by the other former members of AA. On the one hand, its success would eliminate two outsiders; but, on the other hand, it would give BACO too much power. However, because of its financial difficulties, BACO failed in its attempt and ANCO and ALCOR found new investors and remained independent producers on the international aluminium market.[21]

Since 1909, PCAC started working towards the creation of a national cartel in France with the goal to help, in this way, the inclusion of the outsiders in a new international agreement. Moreover, this union could bring out the group of French producers in the oligopoly.[22] Adrien Badin come to the fore as the main architect of this general strategy, for which he decided to implicate also the other ex-AA members from an initial stage. In the aftermath of the failure of AIAG's proposal, Badin communicated to the other ex-members of AA that the sole solution to bring order to the international aluminium market was to build a national cartel in France, specifically designed to manage sales in the domestic market and to prepare participation in an international cartel. PCAC already started negotiations with Bergès' group (PYR and SARV) and tried to involve also the Italian company, which exported the bulk of its production to France for lack of outlets in its domestic market.[23] However, these outsiders were not disposed to follow Badin's scheme because they were part of a strategic group different from that of SEMF and PCAC. These producers were not willing to negotiate quotas, because they were associated with Giulini for the supplying of alumina and with Beer & Sondheimer for the selling of aluminium. Both were hostile to the old Association: the cartel has been a threat to their strategy of development. Moreover, the achievement of this agreement was hampered also by an ongoing restructure of the French aluminium industry. The Bergès group was in a deal to absorb ASO, which was in severe financial difficulties, while PCAC was negotiating the takeover of EMSE. Bergès' group was also willing to sell PYR, which was revealed not to be a rentable unit, to PCAC. EC was still in business and it invested in producing alumina independently in La Barasse, carrying out a strategy of vertical integration. Giulini had a major share of its stocks and also served as an intermediary to export to the German market.[24] Giulini also started production of aluminium in Martigny, Switzerland, in 1909, making the situation even more complicated.[25]

## Metallgesellschaft's almost successful attempt

Faced with these dynamics, AIAG gave up the negotiations and left the initiative to other actors.[26] Despite the crisis of demand being over in 1910, the price of the metal on the market was still low. The main cause of the persistence of low prices was the presence of several traders, which debased the level of prices. Since the attempts by the producers failed, in 1910 Metallgesellschaft (MG) took the initiative to call a meeting in order to reconstruct an international cartel. In these years, MG was emerging as a powerful international business, which had direct participation in various mining affairs and merged with financial activities. At the same time, MG became the organiser of some international cartels in other metals, reformulating its original strategy of international metal trader.[27]

MG's intent was to encourage a price increase to 2 F/kg, i.e. a level that was considered a minimum to ensure a profitable investment by the producers.[28] MG was one of the most important international traders and its statistical yearbook was the main instrument of knowledge in the trade of all non-ferrous metals. The publication of trade statistics and prices was able to influence the market trend and to serve as a reference for customers during the period in which the cartel lost its control over international prices. For the ex-members of the cartel, the alliance with MG meant the ability to spread positive information on the industry, which could help reduce the power of the more speculative traders. MG acted in this case following a complex strategic vision: on the one hand, MG was not opposed to the formation of a new cartel, because it already understood that the aluminium market could not benefit from speculative actions because, in this period, demand was less sensitive to price variation than other non-ferrous metals. On the other hand, MG adopted a long-term strategy, hoping to improve its position in relation to aluminium producers, overturning the subordination that was derived from the first cartel of 1901. MG thought it could obtain the management of the cartel and its sales, substituting AIAG.[29]

The president of MG, Zachary Hochschild, called a meeting in Brussels in October 1910 to which the old members of AA were invited. His idea was to reach a compromise, first among the former colleagues of the cartel, and then including outsiders. Hochschild suggested establishing quotas based on sales for the current year. This commercial approach was opposed by AIAG, which wanted to measure the actual production capacity in order to better match production with demand. MG's proposal ended up with a compromise between these two visions. Badin acted as a mediator, expressing the idea that a practical solution would have to ask to each company to indicate the minimum production for 1911 and, thus, to propose a quota to all outsiders, based on sales figures.[30] The data collected during the meeting in Brussels are summarised in Table 3.1.

In 1911, the global production capacity would be twice the expected demand at the end of 1910. Even the sum of all the minimum required production was greater than the demand, not to mention a quota to be allocated to the outsiders. To deal with the outsiders, the former members of AA thought to offer them only 3,000 tons, excluding the companies that were not yet able to produce at full capacity (like EMSE and Giulini's unit in Martigny). In addition to the quotas, the former AA members also spoke about the form to be given to their cartel. After the failure of AIAG's system, it appeared that any centralisation of sales in the hands of a producer was to be a workable solution. However, this did not mean that individual companies wanted to maintain their commercial independence outside the national markets because it would be expensive to create an autonomous network of sale agencies. Hochschild proposed MG as sole manager of sales in export markets, providing access to an existing integrated network of sales to the firms. The cartel would have set up a control office to align the commercial actions of the producers with MG.[31]

After the meeting in Brussels, the companies planned to continue negotiations calling another meeting in Paris in November 1911, for which they committed to review their proposals and to negotiate more realistic quotas. However, at this stage NACO showed an intransigent attitude, increasing its demands regarding the future quota of the cartel. ALCOA was trying to make more room for NACO on the international markets, thanks to a greater quota in the cartel, because it was planning to expand its domestic production capacity, eroding imports from its Canadian plant.[32] After the end of the legal protection of patents in 1909, ALCOA could not afford to leave free space for imports into the US market and planned investments to saturate the domestic market.[33] Davis did not accept a quota of 10 per cent because it was much lower than that held in the previous cartel, even though, as seen in Table 3.1, it corresponded to the sales that were actually made by NACO outside the United States in the previous years. The companies tried to reformulate the quotas, offering Davis a quota of 12.5 per cent, but NACO also rejected it.[34]

In addition to these difficulties with NACO, the outsiders refused the miserable quota that the former AA members were willing to grant. Since the Brussels conference, the old AA members would have liked to get the outsiders to accept fixed quantities as quota. Instead, some outsiders asked for a percentage of the total market, like the former members of AA, so they could increase their production in the case of expansion of demand and to enter the aluminium business more fully.[35] A last point that put on hold MG's proposal was the refusal by some former AA members to employ MG as sole international trader. NACO did not want to give up its sales agency in the UK market and also AIAG showed a fierce opposition to this idea. AIAG was not disposed to give this new role to MG, which meant giving up its sales network in its main market, Germany.[36] In an attempt to mediate, BACO then proposed to create a *comptoir*

Table 3.1 Brussels conference: sales by former members of AA and of the new outsiders during 1909 and 1910, production capacities, minimum production requested, and proposed quotas (tons and %)

| AA | Sales, 1909 | % AA | Sales to August 1910 | % AA | Production capacity, 1911 | % AA | Minimum production | % AA | Proposal (%) |
|---|---|---|---|---|---|---|---|---|---|
| PCAC | 2,800 | 14.81 | 2,100 | 13.46 | 4,200 | 11.14 | 3,000 | 12.76 | 15.4 |
| SEMF | 4,400 | 23.28 | 3,000 | 19.23 | 8,500 | 22.54 | 5,000 | 21.28 | 21.0 |
| BACO | 4,700 | 24.86 | 3,500 | 22.43 | 7,500 | 19.89 | 5,000 | 21.28 | 21.0 |
| NACO | 1,700 | 8.99 | 1,700 | 10.89 | 7,500 | 19.89 | 3,000 | 12.76 | 10.0 |
| AIAG | 5,300 | 28.04 | 5,300 | 33.97 | 10,000 | 26.52 | 7,500 | 31.91 | 32.6 |
| Total | 18,900 | 99.98 | 15,600 | 99.98 | 37,700 | 99.98 | 23,500 | 99.99 | 100.0 |

| Outsiders | Sales, 1909 | % OUT | Sales to August 1910 | % outsiders | Production capacity, 1910 | % outsiders | Maximum allowed | % OUT | Proposal (tons) |
|---|---|---|---|---|---|---|---|---|---|
| SARV | 1,000 | 50.00 | 1,500 | 62.50 | 800 | 12.30 | – | 36.67 | 1100 |
| PYR | | | | | 1,200 | 18.46 | – | | |
| EMSE | | | | | 600 | 9.24 | – | – | – |
| EC | | | | | 600 | 9.24 | – | 16.66 | 500 |
| SIFA | 500 | 25.00 | 450 | 18.75 | 1,000 | 15.38 | – | 16.66 | 500 |
| ANCO | 500 | 25.00 | 450 | 18.75 | 1,000 | 15.38 | – | 20.00 | 600 |
| ALCOR | – | – | – | | 500 | 7.69 | – | 10.00 | 300 |
| Giulini | – | – | – | | 800 | 12.30 | – | – | – |
| Total | 2,000 | 100.00 | 2,400 | 100.00 | 6,500 | 99.99 | 4,000 | 99.99 | 3000 |
| TOTAL | 20,900 | – | 18,000 | – | 44,200 | – | 27,500 | – | – |

Source: RPA, 00-2-15940, Conférence de Bruxelles du 22/X/1910.

of sales among the companies in the cartel for the German market, outside the direct control of MG, but also this proposal was rejected by AIAG and these negotiations were interrupted.[37]

## The rise of Aluminium français: the new French national cartel

The situation that had arisen made it extremely difficult to re-compose the different strategic visions of the companies. This prevented the producers from acting as a consistent strategic group, so continuing their individualist visions. After this failure, the group of companies divided into two distinct strategic groups. Some companies were favourable to the new role of MG, because it guaranteed the end of AIAG's dominance. This opinion was the starting point of setting up a new alliance in France. PCAC, SEMF, and the Bergès group formed a first national cartel a few days after the last international conference, the Syndicat des Fabricants Français d'Aluminium (SFFA). SFFA allotted quotas on the French and international markets, which were established giving 48 per cent to SEMF, 36 per cent to PCAC, and 18 per cent to Bergès. While in the domestic market each producer kept its commercial freedom, MG had been appointed as the sole intermediary of SFFA in export markets.[38] This new alliance immediately proved to be effective, because, thanks to MG as the sole negotiator, SFFA was able to get an order from some important German customers, that were historically linked to the Swiss company, i.e. Carl Berg and Krupp. This fact alarmed AIAG who formed an opposing alliance with NACO and BACO to weaken the force of the other coalition.[39]

At this point, the French producers tried to rebuild international relations through a targeted strategy aimed at reducing the position of these three companies and so to accept the vision of the French companies, and especially of PCAC, as regards the future of international cartels. Adrien Badin was the main author of what may be called *ingénierie de l'accord*, a term coined by Anne Pezet to describe how strategic decisions within a company are always the result of a compromise among its various components such as financiers, managers, and technicians.[40] Badin implemented a strategy to alter the balance of power in the international aluminium industry, in order to make it possible to reconstruct a more cohesive cartel than the cartel that ended in 1908. Badin's strategy can be summarised in the various projects related to the formation of Aluminium français (AF), the national cartel of French producers that replaced SFFA in December 1911. As shown by Florence Hachez-Leroy, Badin was able to link negotiations for the construction of AF to those for the formation of an international cartel, managing to persuade all companies, including the outsiders, to make the necessary sacrifices and to believe in a common project. Badin's action turned antagonistic firms into commitment players. The sharing of new technology for the production of alumina helped this transformation.[41]

Actually, Badin's strategy was based on a technological promise: a new production process for the production of alumina, developed by the Austrian inventor Ottokar Serpek. Serpek's process was designed to be able to simultaneously produce alumina from aluminium nitride and ammonia sulphate. This process encouraged hope for very low production costs: the Bayer alumina had a production cost of about 180 F/ton, while with Serpek's process the estimated cost was only 60 francs. In addition to this economy of 120 F/ton, the earnings from the sale of ammonia allowed the complete eliminatation of its cost of production. Since the cost of alumina influenced the final cost of aluminium by about 25 per cent in these years, the use of Serpek's process promised a decisive reduction of the production costs compared to those who used the Bayer process.[42] In 1910 PCAC obtained participation in the capital of the growing Société Générale des Nitrures (SGN), a company that was created to control Serpek's patents in France and abroad, and Badin became the CEO.[43] Badin promised to share this process with the French outsiders, AIAG, and ALCOA, in exchange for the role of leader in negotiations for the international cartel.[44]

Once in possession of this patent, PCAC tried to exploit it as a strength factor to encourage all the French producers to join AF.[45] Encouraged by the possibility to use this patent, SEMF accepted a lower quota than the one it had before 1906 during the negotiations with PCAC. In addition, Badin obtained the adhesion of EC, which broke its relationship with Giulini. This change was decisive in eroding the power of Giulini because EC provided the electricity for Giulini's plant in Martigny. Without energy, the starting of Martigny suffered a major slowdown. Later, the French companies consolidated their association forming a specific society, Aluminium français, which, in addition to sharing sales, launched the construction of a large common alumina unit to use the Serpek process, with large-scale economies (approximately 40,000 tons per year to be used to produce 20,000 tons of aluminium), which were needed to supply all the French units.[46] As Florence Hachez-Leroy showed, AF was not only a cartel, it was a major project of integration, of creation of scale economies and marketing.[47] In addition to investing in France, AF began to plan the construction of a smelter and a Serpek unit in the United States, in which also MG was involved.[48]

Other action was taken in the field of alumina, in order to hamper supplies to other outsiders. AF decided to take over two alumina plants of Gaëtan de Somze, that were in a critical situation after the failure in trying a new alumina process, the Peniakoff process. AF converted them to Bayer's process and began supplying French companies, definitively depriving Giulini of them, while waiting for Serpek's process to be completely developed. Controlling the Somze group also had another strategic value, i.e. these companies supplied alumina to ANCO and ALCOR: controlling them would also force these outsiders to accept a compromise cartel.[49]

## AF and the creation of the new international cartel

Encouraged by these successes, in early 1911 AF contacted AIAG, BACO, NACO, and SIFA, showing them the benefits of Serpek's process. Meanwhile, the alliance among BACO, NACO, and AIAG had been wrecked, because the three companies had failed to find a satisfactory agreement on the British market: while BACO asked for too large quotas, NACO rejected any agreement on prices because it wanted commercial autonomy in order to expand its sales in

Europe.[50] By virtue of the old ties that bound SEMF and AIAG, SEMF was appointed by the other French companies to propose a truce on prices, which would allow the opening of negotiations for the new cartel. AIAG and BACO agreed to enter into these new negotiations. Despite Davis considered sharing Serpek's process 'a good basis for the new Association',[51] NACO refused any agreement on the price. In doing so, Davis used the same arguments that had led him to refuse the continuation of the alliance with AIAG and BACO: commercial autonomy was judged key to expanding its European sales after the investments that both NACO and ALCOA had made.[52]

This attitude strengthened the connections among other European companies against Americans. In this situation, the idea of investing in the United States to force NACO to accept the agreement came up.[53] As a result of negotiations between the French firms and the other European producers, the strategy about Serperk technology was reshaped to meet this international goal. SGN gave an international Serpek patent licence to Aluminium français (as SFFA changed its name in July 1911) in order to produce up to 70,000 tons of alumina per year in Europe and up to 12,000 in the United States. In the agreement between SGN and AF, it was recognised also the right for the French cartel to create a subsidiary in the United States and to assign a part of its European licence to BACO, AIAG, and the Italian firm SIFA, with which some talks about it entering in the agreement were carried out. In the AF–SGN contract, AF did not have exclusive rights for the United States: AF probably still aimed to leave the door open to ALCOA in this affair. As a consequence, the interplay behind the Serpek technology was not a pure anti-ALCOA action, but it seemed to be a 'co-opetitive' action that aimed to force the American firm into a global agreement.[54]

After the definition of the AF–SGN agreement, PCAC started semi-industrial and industrial experimentation of the Serpek process. This was consistent both to carry out an investment strategy that was necessary for the French firms, which forecasted them to be in to be facing a shortfall in alumina, and to implement the actual technology. In spite of the reputation that this process enjoyed in scientific milieux, it was still a mere industrial promise. Its actual production costs, and thus its viability as a substitute for the Bayer process, were still to be fully determined. After some encouraging small-scale tests, AF formed a subsidiary that would have produced hydroelectric energy exclusively dedicated to the full development of Serpek alumina, the Société de l'Eau d'Olle. At the same time, SEMF started negotiations with AIAG, giving it three-eighths in this company capital in exchange for a quota that would be three-fifths of AF's quota in the new international cartel. This arrangement would have allowed the Swiss company to benefit from the new patent like the French companies, and gain a decisive advantage in the international oligopoly.[55]

AIAG considered this proposal very profitable. From an industrial standpoint, participation in this technological venture was decisive for AIAG. The Swiss company would fulfil its requirements of alumina, receiving 26,000 tons per year at very low costs. In a similar condition, AIAG accepted this in exchange a lower quota in the cartel, because it would earn greater unit profits on sales. In addition, AF told AIAG that it had not treated BACO in the same way because the British company was not admitted to participate directly in the development of the new process. This led AIAG to accept AF's strategy, also its antagonism with BACO stimulated this outcome, accepting SEMF's proposal and also agreeing to merge their efforts despite Davis' reluctance.[56] At this stage, even if PCAC was the creator of the entire scheme, it was SEMF that worked out the negotiations with AIAG, by virtue of the old ties that the two companies had had since the early 1880s. Dreyfus himself, who until then had played a very marginal role in the cartel, was appointed to conclude these agreements in May 1911. This strengthened the interests between AF and AIAG, and Dreyfus and Huber were convinced that their alliance constituted a kind of critical mass in the power balance, that would guarantee the stipulation of the international cartel.[57]

The Serpek affair had radically overturned the relationships among the companies: with these bases AF and AIAG negotiated some quotas in view of the formation of an international cartel, in which AIAG accepted a predominant quota for AF in exchange for the new technology on alumina, as showed Table 3.2.

The main problem with the negotiations was to make NACO accept a relatively low quota of just 8–9 per cent. To do this, Badin was convinced that a direct investment in the United States would lead Davis to accept this quota. As anticipated, AF involved Metallgesellschaft in the project: its American subsidiary American Metal Company, agreed to subscribe a participation of 10 per cent into the investment and played a decisive role in its design. This Franco-German deal in the US was a very isolated case in the history of foreign investment there and it was mainly motivated by the long-run nexus that linked Metallgesellschaft to the French companies and by the occasion that Serpek represented in the short run.[58] During the negotiations for the settlement of the US venture, SEMF also obtained participation in this affair from AIAG. The Swiss company agreed that, once the new American plant started, its subscription into it would have been equal to three-fifths of AF's share. This joint operation in the United States, made by the two most important European producers (AIAG and AF) with the leading international non-ferrous metals traders represented a critical threat to Davis, urging him to join the cartel.[59]

This American investment was not only instrumental in the foundation of the cartel. After the crisis of 1908, the demand for aluminium in the United States began to increase as in no other country between 1909 and 1912 (see Table 3.3), due to the demand in the automotive industry. This fact turned this country into the largest import market, overtaking Germany itself. With the end of protection of the patents in 1909, more possibilities were open to invest. Despite its strategy to protect its monopoly, characterised by the control of all the national reserves of bauxite and the best hydroelectric installations at Niagara Falls, ALCOA had failed to follow this increase in demand.[60] Imports from Europe began to be increasingly important, driven also by the low prices on the international market and higher prices in the American market. Until then, the entering of a new producer into the American aluminium industry was hampered by the total control that ALCOA had on national mineral resources. The Serpek process made an investment possible, lowering production costs even when bauxite imported from Europe was used. For this reason, Badin's action was aimed to strongly downsize Davis' requests, directly threatening him in its national market.[61]

Table 3.2 Towards the new AA: various proposals for quotas for the new cartel negotiations, 1910–1912 (tons and %)

| | Brussels, October 1910 | | May 1911 | | September 1911 | | December 1911 | | Quotas AA, June 1912 | |
|---|---|---|---|---|---|---|---|---|---|---|
| | | | *with* | *without* | | | | | | |
| | *tons* | *%* | *NACO %* | *%* | *tons* | *%* | *tons* | *%* | *tons* | *%* |
| AIAG | 10,000 | 22.62 | 26.00 | 28.26 | 9,000 | 21.95 | 10,000 | 23.14 | 10,000 | 21.4 |
| BACO | 7500 | 16.96 | 19.00 | 20.65 | 6,500 | 15.85 | 7,500 | 17.36 | 7,500 | 16.0 |
| ANCO | 1,000 | 2.26 | Ton. fix 900 | | 1,500 | 3.65 | – | – | 1,800 | 3.9 |
| ALCOR | 500 | 1.15 | Ton. fix 500 | | 500 | 1.20 | – | – | 900 | 1.9 |
| SIFA | 1,000 | 2.26 | Ton. fix 600 | | 1,000 | 2.45 | – | – | 900 | 1.9 |
| Giulini | 800 | 1.80 | Ton. fix 300 | | 800 | 1.95 | – | – | – | – |
| NACO | 7,500 | 16.96 | 8.00 | – | 3,500 | 8.55 | 7,500 | 17.36 | 7,500 | 16.0 |
| AF* | 15,900 | 35.97 | 47.00 | 51.09 | 18,200 | 44.40 | 18,200 | 42.12 | 18,200 | 38.9 |
| Total | 44,200 | 99.99 | 100.00 | 100.00 | 41,000 | 100.00 | 43,200 | 99.98 | 45,000 | 100.00 |

Source: author's elaboration from various files in TMA and RPA.

Note
AF includes SEMF, PCAC, SARV, PYR, EMSE, and EC.

Table 3.3 The US market and ALCOA's position, 1906–1914: production, consumption, imports, prices, and tariffs

| | ALCOA production (tons) | | | Consumption USA (tons) | Price (¢/lb) | Price (F/kg) | Tariffs (¢/lb) | Imports | | | |
|---|---|---|---|---|---|---|---|---|---|---|---|
| | USA | Canada | total | | | | | Canada (tons) | Europe (tons) | total (tons) | % |
| 1906 | 6,407 | 1,663 | 8,070 | 6,410 | 35.75 | 4.11 | 8.00 | – | 270 | 270 | 4.21 |
| 1907 | 7,405 | 2,685 | 10,090 | 7,410 | 45.00 | 5.17 | 8.00 | 68 | 518 | 586 | 7.90 |
| 1908 | 4,844 | 441 | 5,285 | 4,840 | 28.70 | 3.30 | 8.00 | – | 51 | 51 | 1.05 |
| 1909 | 13,191 | 2,759 | 15,950 | 15,500 | 22.00 | 2.53 | 7.00 | 501 | 424 | 923 | 5.95 |
| 1910 | 16,058 | 4,376 | 20,434 | 21,650 | 22.25 | 2.55 | 7.00 | 2,166 | 3,453 | 5,619 | 25.95 |
| 1911 | 17,416 | 4,390 | 21,806 | 20,900 | 20.07 | 2.30 | 7.00 | 887 | 1,944 | 2,831 | 13.54 |
| 1912 | 18,963 | 5,456 | 24,419 | 29,800 | 22.01 | 2.53 | 7.00 | 4,357 | 2,357 | 6,714 | 22.53 |
| 1913 | 21,445 | 6,379 | 27,824 | 32,000 | 23.64 | 2.71 | 2.00 | 3,049 | 9,179 | 12,228 | 38.21 |
| 1914 | 26,296 | 6,600 | 32,896 | 33,700 | 18.63 | 2.14 | 2.00 | 2,184 | 7,241 | 7,241 | 21.48 |

Source: HHC, RPA, and US Geological Survey.

In Badin's vision, an investment of 2–3,000 tons should be quickly developed to force Davis to negotiate. However, this plan was hampered by the impossibility of finding a supplier of electricity cheap enough to compete with ALCOA.[62] After several attempts, the Bank Leu, that was taking care of business in the United States on behalf of an ally of Metallgesellschaft, the Motor AG, looked at the prospect of taking over a hydroelectric company in bankruptcy, the North Carolina Power Company (NCPC), located in North Carolina.[63] The Banque Franco-Americaine had financed NCPC: Badin contacted the bank with an offer to gain control of both the hydroelectric plant and the Banque Franco-Americaine itself.[64] At this point, the size of the plan of the US changed drastically: Badin planned production of alumina with Serpek's process to produce 12,000 tons per year, used to produce 6,000 tons of aluminium. The total cost of the operation would have been $4 million and a production cost of 0.85 F/kg was estimated, which was 0.50 lower than that of ALCOA.[65] The financial aspect of the project was much more important, and at this point it led Badin to look for possible partners, including AIAG.

The creation of the Southern Aluminum Company (SACO) in Badinville, a town that took its name from Adrien Badin himself, was a real wakeup call for Davis, who changed his attitude towards European companies. In exchange for the possibility of using the Serpek process, Davis was willing to give SACO a share of 8,000 tons of the American market and to supply alumina until Serpek's process was completely developed. It also agreed to a quota of only 7,500 tons for NACO in a future cartel, ending his resistance to enter into the agreement. In December 1911, Badin obtained the agreement of all the old companies of AA for the quotas of a new cartel in which, thanks to previous negotiations, NACO and AIAG accepted a quota of respectively 7,500 tons and a participation equal to three-fifths of AF's participation. AIAG's quota was negotiated in a separate agreement that was kept secret to the other members of the cartel.[66] While in spring 1912 work on the construction of SACO began, the outsiders were involved in negotiations for the cartel with the promise of being able to take advantage of Serpek's alumina.[67] Only Giulini refused to join the cartel, but now the importance of this company was strongly downsized by both the *diaspora* of its French allies to Badin's camp and by the new alumina technology.[68]

There was also another factor behind the change in ALCOA's strategy. In addition to the technological relevance of Serpek's process, which was intertwined with the investment strategy in alumina by the American company,[69] Davis was forced to accept the formation of SACO by some legal issues, which were also reshaping the general attitude of ALCOA towards international cartelisation. In 1912, in the US a period characterised by the widespread actions of the antitrust authorities began and it affected a number of major companies, such as Standard Oil and American Tobacco, which were accused of monopolistic action according to the Sherman Act.[70] ALCOA was inspected by the antitrust authorities, since it was a monopoly, and the agreement that was concluded in 1908 by NACO with AIAG was discovered by the authorities as a result of a number of inspections that were carried out during 1911. The initial reluctance of ALCOA to enter the cartel agreement was also the aftermath of this complex legal situation. This agreement resulted in a legal charge to ALCOA in January 1912.[71] On the international level, the legal process slowed down Davis' action, with him procrastinating about which strategy to undertake with ALCOA's Canadian venture. As Paul Héroult referred to SEMF's board, while he was in the US to assist the creation of the American affair, Davis claimed to him during a meeting at Niagara Falls in November 1911 that

> We are completely willing to collaborate complying with the law, reducing the dimension of our plant or, in case of need, even selling you this plant, that is the only one that exports to Europe. It is very probable that the political orientation will change and that, in a few months, the pursuit against our trusts will be abandoned. Anyway, there is no need to force me.[72]

This legal situation influenced ALCOA's action. Since exports were vital to NACO, its fate appeared very precarious, according to Davis' dialogue with Héroult. This contests the literature on the aluminium cartel that shows the Canadian subsidiaries of ALCOA as a means for the American firm to enter into cartel agreements.[73] The positioning of NACO in the international aluminium market was more complex, due to its double role of big exporter and of leading player in the US market. In fact, the archive documents of the cartel rather suggest that ALCOA was in an uncomfortable position managing its Canadian investments during a period in which the international market was already exposed to over-investments. It had decided to set up this unit during the battle of the patents at the end of the century, and its production prevented ALCOA from investing more in the United States, because it had to leave a space for Canadian imports. Every investment cycle of ALCOA forced Davis to seek a growing quota from the cartel to find new international outlets for the Canadian unit to replace a portion of the imports to the United States. For this reason, the links between NACO and the cartel have been unstable since 1908, when Davis' extremist tactics often created discontent with other members of the cartel.[74]

Even if it broke ALCOA's national monopoly, the creation of SACO solved the legal risk of the American pioneer. Thanks to the creation of SACO, ALCOA was absolved from the antitrust process that it had had to face during 1912 and allowed Davis to negotiate NACO's participation in the international cartel with the American judicial authorities.[75] It was because of this external factor that finally ALCOA decided to reorganise its global strategy: it gave up a share of its domestic market in exchange for Serpek's technology and of a small export quota for NACO.[76] In June 1912, the new Association was finally created and its duration was set at ten years. AA was the result of intense negotiation that had lasted for four years. During this period, we have witnessed the end of AIAG's dominance and the rapid rise of the French companies, led by Adrien Badin, who was able to fundamentally alter the balance of power within the international oligopoly. The final quotas of AA were claimed to be allotted following the installed capacity but the actual respective quotas of AIAG, NACO, and AF were adjustments derived from these agreements.

## The new association: strategies and structures of the international cartel 1912–1914

The new Aluminium-Association marked a large-scale organisational change compared to the previous cartels. While the cartels of 1901 and 1906 were a direct 'emanation' of AIAG, the new cartel of 1912 was created following PCAC's ideas. Rather than acting as manager of the cartel, PCAC wanted to leave a great autonomy to cartel members. According to Badin's opinion, the cartel should work as an office of statistical control, in charge of balancing sales with quotas at the end of each financial year. Each company should be left free to employ its own commercial and investment strategies, without the interference that AIAG performed in the two former cartels. However, not all the companies were equal: the old founders of this industry were recognised as first class members while the latecomers (SIFA, ANCO, and ALCOR) were included only as second-tier partners.[77]

From an institutional standpoint, AA was formed by a *comité* consisting of five members, one for AF, one for BACO, one for NACO, one for AIAG, and one for the three outsiders that had agreed to join the cartel (SIFA, ALCOR, and ANCO), who alternated their representation at the meetings of the cartel. The *comité* was the decision-making body and was supported by an assembly, where every company had a right to vote in proportion to its own quota. It was decided that the offices of AA would not be located at one of the members' headquarters, but that the cartel would have an independent office. Although BACO preferred the creation of the cartel's office in a neutral country, and it suggested Brussels for its hometown, the headquarters of AA were established in Paris in the district of the Grands Boulevards, not far from the Opéra. AA also hired autonomous staff, who were paid directly by the cartel, without any connection with the companies. This staff only carried out administrative tasks, such as statistical data collection and their control. The director of the central office was Guy D'Ussel, a 34-year-old accountancy expert with many language skills (he knew French, English, and German), who came from the wool and fabric trade.[78]

The assembly met twice a year. During its meetings, it fixed prices, it validated the balances of the association, and it debated all the issues relating to the operations of the association. The *comité*, instead, managed the current business of the cartel and met at least once a quarter. Compared to the old AA, the *comité* was a decision-making organ, while the old *comité* resembled more the assembly of the new AA (also because AIAG was the real manager of the former cartels). This measure was aimed at preventing the recurrence of communication problems, like had happened in 1908, when the *comité* was not able to cope with the arrival of outsiders. The bureau, instead, represented the true sign of managerial innovation: it daily recorded all contracts made by the companies and drew up a report of monthly sales and stock. The task of the bureau was to send a monthly quotas report, functioning as a general rebalancing of sales. As for control, it was expected that each member would make its account available for an annual inspection by the personnel appointed by the *comité* itself.[79]

As regards the commercial operation of the cartel, each year the *comité* made available some tranches of metal, divided into quotas for each member, that each company had to try to sell. This quota could be either exceeded or not reached, in which case annual compensation would balance the quotas. As a consequence, each member maintained direct relationships with customers and was responsible for the quality of the metal and the conditions of sale. In addition, the quotas set by the cartel did not only include aluminium ingots, but also almost all semi-finished products, whose minimum prices were fixed by the assembly. Each member was free to sell where it wanted, without territorial restrictions or reserved markets, but it had to respect the fixed prices.[80] Finally, in AA's contract of 1912, the United States completely disappeared, with the contract not including anything for this market, where sales were made outside the quotas, and out of the control of the cartel. This was necessary because of US antitrust legislation that, as we have seen, had investigated ALCOA a few months before the definitive signing of the cartel.[81]

In spite of this construction, AA had had different relationship problems to fix from the beginning. As in the other cases, BACO proved not to be satisfied with the quotas. In July 1912, a few days after signing the contract, BACO made known to the other members that it had concluded negotiations to take over ANCO. Probably BACO's behaviour was aimed to improve its status in the cartel because its quota was relatively low (see Table 3.3) and it did not benefit from Serpek technology. Obtaining control over ANCO after the conclusion of AA's contract, BACO thought to automatically merge its quota with ANCO's, thus increasing its overall quota.[82] AF opposed this type of reasoning, because the British company wanted to cancel the contracts for the supply of alumina that ANCO had with Somze's group, which was controlled by AF, and aimed to supply its new Norwegian subsidiary with its own alumina. In spite of AF opposition, BACO was allowed to incorporate ANCO's quota without resorting to arbitration in order not to delay activation of the cartel's work.[83] However, this initial disagreement represented a first serious disturbance in the equilibrium reached in the negotiations and revealed a deep fragility of the whole architecture of the agreement.

AA began to operate on 1 January 1913. The *comité* allotted some progressive quotas that the companies bargained on the market through their commercial services, respecting the price decided by the *comité*. The tranches were allocated to the companies well in advance. A first lot of 25,000 tons was assigned in August 1912 to be accounted for sales on 1913. Once the first lot was completed, another lot of 15,000 was put on sale at the end of 1912. These orders, made by the cartel well in advance, were designed to accommodate both the evolution of the market and to manage the production in a better way. While the tranches were allotted according to the proportions set by the cartel contract, individual companies could conclude contracts for larger quotas at the end of the year. In case of differences between quotas and actual sales, a counterbalance through shipments of metal was performed, paying a prime to a company that had signed the contract. The operation of AA can be described as shown in Table 3.4.

Table 3.4 Quotas, sales, and difference between quotas and sales in AA, 1913–1914 (tons and %)

| | % AA | 1913 | | | | 1914 (7 months) | | | |
|---|---|---|---|---|---|---|---|---|---|
| | | quotas | sales | difference | % sales | quotas | sales | difference | % sales |
| AF | 38.9 | 16,532 | 16,155 | 377 | 39.58 | 11,670 | 10,476 | 1,194 | 40.07 |
| AIAG | 21.4 | 9,095 | 8,670 | 425 | 21.25 | 6,420 | 5,954 | 456 | 22.84 |
| BACO | 19.9 | 8,457 | 8,160 | 297 | 20.00 | 5,970 | 5,434 | 536 | 20.78 |
| NACO | 16.0 | 6,800 | 6,313 | 487 | 15.46 | 4,800 | 3,493 | 1,307 | 13.36 |
| SIFA | 1.9 | 807 | 870 | -63 | 2.13 | 570 | 474 | 96 | 1.81 |
| ALCOR | 1.9 | 807 | 642 | 165 | 1.57 | 570 | 297 | 273 | 1.13 |
| Total | 100.0 | 42,500 | 40,810 | 1,688 | 99.99 | 30,000 | 26,138 | 3,862 | 99.9 |

Source: author's elaboration from various files in TMA and RPA.

As we can see, AA distributed a total of 42,500 tons for 1913 assigning new tranches as the old ones were negotiated by the companies. The companies in the cartel had actually negotiated 41,000 of this tonnage. This system meant that companies that had a good commercial service, such as AF and AIAG, could have orders for higher percentages than those of their own quota. On the contrary, other companies, such as NACO and ALCOR, remained chronically below their quota: NACO because it preferred to export in the United States to saturate this market that was not included into the cartel quotas, and ALCOR because it could not get contracts due to its reduced commercial network compared to those of the older companies, especially of BACO in the British market. AA's mechanism forced the companies to try to sell as much as possible because the system penalised the companies that failed in reaching their quota. The companies that accumulated delay had to provide their metal to the firm in advance below the market price, paying a fee as commission to the company that had negotiated the sale. This established a system of commercial competition within the cartel that stimulated sales without pushing the companies to lower the market price below what had been agreed.[84] At the same time, this system avoided a repetition of the situation created in 1905–1906, when, faced with a sudden and unexpected increase in demand, the companies tried to slow down demand by raising prices.[85]

AA's strategy regarding the selling prices confirmed the fact that aluminium producers believed stable prices gave a competitive edge to boost the consumption their metal. The decision in 1905 to raise prices and the subsequent fall of 1907 had crystallised even more the idea that only a stable price, not influenced by the fluctuations of demand and offer, could ensure the orderly growth of this industry. Rather than changing the price, the cartel preferred to adjust supply, through the tranches system. Thanks to this strategy, the cartel members were now able to sell on the market in compliance with the agreed price, both through international merchants and using their own sales network. This can be clearly seen from AA's operation in 1913: the increase in demand from 25,000 tons, which had been stated as the normal level of the marked during the negotiations of 1912, to 41,000 tons of actual sales, did not prompt a rise in selling prices, which remained stable throughout the year. On the contrary, the *comité* spread the information about the uprising state of the market, encouraging companies to produce more and to reach their full scale economies. This strategy was possible thanks to the over-investments that had characterised the aluminium industry since the crisis of 1907: the increase in demand encouraged the producers to run their maximum theoretical output at the lowest unitary costs.

The increase in demand at the beginning of the 1910s was caused by a series of crucial innovations in the use of the metal. Between 1909 and 1912, aluminium started to be used for new applications that were destined to revolutionise the status of this metal. On the one hand, the processes for the reduction of aluminium to powder paved the way for the use of aluminium in paint and explosives. In particular, the use of Amonal, an explosive consisting of aluminium powder, spread so rapidly in the mining industries that it was called 'the explosive of the future'.[86] Two years later, this explosive was even more widespread due to the First World War. On the other hand, a new revolutionary alloy – the duralumin – was invented in 1909 by Alfred Wilm, who became the 'father' of the so-called strong alloys. This alloy, consisting of about 90 per cent aluminium and 10 per cent copper, paved the way for aluminium for all high performance applications for this metal, which asked for a higher resistance to creaking forces. Since its first applications from aviation to cars, duralumin favoured an expansion of demand in the transport sector which turned aluminium into a key metal for mobility.[87]

## A house of cards: the crisis of the Aluminium-Association

The analysis of the formation of the new AA shows that the nature of this type of organisation was based on relationships. Moreover, aluminium companies learned from the mistakes and weaknesses of the first cartel. These two aspects confirm the assumptions made by Levenstein and Suslow on the ability of the cartels to adapt to the economic environment in which they operate, despite the constant tendency to disintegration emphasised by Stigler.[88] In addition, Barjot's ideas about the exogenous and endogenous causes of cartelisation are confirmed: in particular, the impact of institutional change caused by intervention of the American antitrust authorities or of new technologies represented key factors in shaping the actual form of the cartel.[89] However, the case of the new Association shows another aspect related to technological innovation. The formations of both the French national cartel, AF, and the international cartel, AA, were mainly based on sharing of Serpek's patents and his technology. This new technology managed to connect the interests of the producers, creating a cohesive strategic group. Since the keystone of the new Association's architecture was the Serpek process, it is not hard to guess what happened when this process turned out to be a fiasco.

The quotas that had been divided by AF, NACO, and AIAG in the cartel were derived from the agreements on Serpek's patent and were conceived considering that by the beginning of 1914 production with this technology would begin to supply the French, Swiss, and American companies. When it was clear that the Serpek process would not work, AF's quota appeared overestimated. While AF was entitled to obtain orders for 18,000 tons, it was not able to produce more than 15,000 because of the bottleneck caused by the delay on the Serpek process. Even in the American market, there was a delay: once the construction of SACO has started, ALCOA gave up expanding its production because, as agreed in 1912, it left a space of 8000 tons to the subsidiary of AF in the US market.[90] When it became evident that SACO could not come on stream, because of the troubles of the Serpek process, the American companies were not able to fulfil the US market. The discrepancy between orders and production capacity of the companies created a kind of 'domino effect' which, until Serpek's patent was working and SACO started, the whole system of agreements that led to the founding of AA appeared very precarious (see Table 3.5).

While AA attributed quotas for 45,000 tons, which the companies' commercial services managed to turn into orders in the market during 1913, the actual production of AA did not exceed 35,000 tons. AF had a real quota of only 35.3

Table 3.5 AA actual production, sales, and quotas, 1913 (tons and %)

| | AA 1912 | | Commercial | | | Productive | | | | |
|---|---|---|---|---|---|---|---|---|---|---|
| | tons | % | quotas | sales | delay | AA | for US | stocks | total | % |
| AF | 18,200 | 38.9 | 16,532 | 13,199 | 3,333 | 13,199 | 1,500 | 1,000 | 15,699 | 35.3 |
| AIAG | 10,000 | 21.4 | 9,095 | 8,534 | 561 | 8,534 | 2,000 | 606 | 11,140 | 25.0 |
| BACO | 9,300 | 19.9 | 8,457 | 6,742 | 1,715 | 6,742 | 1,500 | 128 | 8,370 | 18.8 |
| NACO | 7,500 | 16.0 | 6,800 | 5,319 | 1,481 | 5,319 | 2,000 | 538 | 7,857 | 17.7 |
| SIFA | 900 | 1.9 | 807 | 800 | 7 | 800 | 50 | 18 | 832 | 1.9 |
| ALCOR | 900 | 1.9 | 807 | 449 | 358 | 449 | 150 | 24 | 575 | 1.3 |
| Total | 45,000 | 100.0 | 42,500 | 35,043 | 7,457 | 35,043 | 7,200 | 2,230 | 44,473 | 100.0 |

Source: author's elaboration from various files in TMA and RPA.

per cent, while AIAG could cover 25 per cent of the entire production of the cartel. In the course of 1913, PCAC was not able to start using Serpek's technology on an industrial scale.[91] Faced with the situation of strong limitation due to quotas, AIAG continuously asked to inspect the Serpek pilot plant, which was denied repeatedly. As a consequence, after a few months of hesitation, AIAG began to ask both for a revision of the quotas and to be able to produce in excess of its quota. However, given the secretive nature of the agreement with AF, AIAG could not simply file a formal request, as BACO had done when it merged with the quota of ANCO, so it tried to protest privately with AF. These underground negotiations came to a real break when AIAG withdrew from both French and American Serpek ventures.[92] When some information about the delays and ineffectiveness of the Serpek technology leaked, SGN's stocks quickly lost value at the stock exchange of Lyon, forcing the Banque Franco-Americaine to carry out expensive operations, creating a funding crisis to support its value at the stock exchange. SGN then decided to sell some of its patents, only those concerning the production of ammonia, to a Norwegian company, which had large hydroelectric capacity. In doing so, it thought that it could also test Serpek's technology on a large scale, solving most of the technical problems of PCAC's pilot plant. In 1914 the Det Norsk Nitrid (DNN or Société des norvégienne nitrures (SNN)) was founded by joint participation among PCAC, SGN, and the Norwegian company Elektrokemisk.[93]

Faced with serious delays in complying with the orders of his quota, in 1914 Badin decided to start the production of aluminium at DNN. This aspect definitely spoiled relations with AIAG and broke the balance of power within AA.[94] After this episode, AIAG began to build a new plant for alumina in Bayer, Martinswerk, near Cologne, and began to plan a legal complaint against AF to modify the contract of the Aluminium-Association.[95] It is impossible to tell what would have happened if the Great War had not broken out a few months later. The neutral form that the cartel had assumed would probably have enabled the companies to continue to use this institution as a regulatory element of their strategies, but it was clear that the quotas would have to be to completely revisited. However, since the nature of these associations is based on relationships, it is difficult to think that the relationship between AIAG and PCAC could have been resolved in a peaceful manner. This is proved by what happened during the First World War and in the aftermath, as we will show in the next chapter. Almost prophetically, Badin, who entered into the mechanisms that regulate international cartels and the relationships among the companies with great clarity, predicted that the balance of a cartel was weak and that no compromise would last forever. In fact, in 1909, Badin observed that:

It is a constant rule that it is impossible to avoid that the cartels in those industries in which the cake to share is always the same, the portion of the small ones grows ceaselessly at the expense of the big ones until the day when the fight puts everyone in their place. In the agreements such as those we aim to sign for Aluminium [*sic*], it will be even worse and we have already experienced it. Everybody, seeing the consumption increase, will expand in order to get a bigger place when the agreement is renewed than the one they had already occupied and as a consequence: at every renovation of the agreement there will be, like nowadays, an intense overproduction and a fight that will make all the profits of the period of peace disappear.[96]

## Notes

1 Olson, *The Logic of Collective Action*.
2 Leslie, 'Trust, Distrust and Antitrust'. Suslow, Levenstein. 'What Determines Cartel Success?'
3 Smith, *From Monopoly to Competition*.
4 TMA, AIAG, box 167, A.V. Davis to Huber, 12 August 1908.
5 TMA, AIAG, box 167, Agreement between AIAG and NACO, 25 September 1908.
6 TMA, AIAG, box 229, Besprechung mit Herrn Edward K. Davis im Hotel Baur-au-Lac, Zurich, 3 November 1911.
7 UGD, 347/28/3/2, A History of Northern Aluminium Company Limited, 1909–1952.
8 Smith, *From Monopoly to Competition*.
9 TMA, AIAG, box 167, A.V. Davis to AIAG, 2 March 1909.
10 TMA, AIAG, box 167, AIAG to A.V. Davis, 25 November 1908. A.V. Davis to Schindler, 1 December 1908.
11 TMA, AIAG, box 171, Schindler to Fürstenberg, 12 January 1909.
12 TMA, AIAG, box 167, Huber to A.V. Davis, 19 February 1909.
13 TMA, AIAG, box 167, Vielhomme to Huber, 27 August 1908.
14 TMA, AIAG, box 171, Cablegram, SEMF to AIAG, 12 August 1909.
15 RPA, 00-12-20019, SEMF to PCAC, 13 August 1909.
16 Perchard, *Aluminiumville*.
17 Perchard, *Aluminiumville*. About Norway, Espen Storli, 'The Norwegian Aluminium Industry, 1908–1940: Swing Producers in the Hands of the International Oligopoly?' *Cahiers d'Histoire de l'Aluminium*, Special Issue 2, 2007, 11–26.
18 UGD/21/41/23, Proceedings of the annual meeting of BACO, 1910.
19 Perchard, *Aluminiumville*.
20 TMA, AIAG, box 171, Tait (BACO's receiver) to Davis, 20 August 1909. Huber to Badin, 25 August 1909.
21 TMA, AIAG, box 169, AIAG to NACO, 30 April 1908.
22 Hachez-Leroy, *L'Aluminium français*.
23 TMA, AIAG, box 171, Badin to AIAG, 12 October 1909. Badin to Sawyes (BACO), 18 August 1909.
24 Hachez-Leroy, *L'Aluminium français*, 33–36. RPA, 00-500-1-17767, Convention passée entre la EC et Giulini, 16 April 1908.
25 Dominic Ruch, *Une Route Ardue pour un si Léger Métal: 100 Ans d'Aluminium Martigny AS*. Zurich: Orell Fussli, 2009, 35–37.
26 TMA, AIAG, box 171, Gegenwärtiger Stand der Verhandlungen betr. Neues Syndicat, 26 October 1909.
27 Stefanie Knetsch, *Das Konzerneigene Bankinstitut der Metallgesellschaft im Zeitraum von 1906 bis 1928: Programmatischer Anspruch und Realisierung*. Munich: Franz Steiger Verlag, 1998, 53–60. Susan Becker, *Multinationalität hat Verschiedene Gesichter: Fromen Internationaler Unternehmenstätigkeit der Société Anonyme des Mines et fonderies de Zinc de la Vielle Montagne und der Metallgesellschaft AG*. Stuttgart: Franz Steiner, 1999, 247–249.
28 TMA, AIAG, box 171, Hochschild (MG) to Schindler, 1 July 1910. Schindler to Davis, 10 October 1910.
29 Hessische Wirtschaftsarchiv (HWA), Metallgesellschaft (MG) Documents, Juristisches Büro, A2, Aluminium-Agenturvertrag der franzosischen Kutten mit M.G, 25 November 1910. Vertrag mit Froges, Hochschild to SEMF, 25 November 1910.

30  RPA, 00-2-15940, Conférence de Bruxelles du 22/X/1910.
31  RPA, 00-2-15940, Conférence de Bruxelles du 22/X/1910.
32  TMA, AIAG, box 228, A.V. Davis to Schindler, 31 October 1910.
33  Smith, *From Monopoly to Competition*.
34  TMA, AIAG, box 229, PV. Réunion des fabricants d'aluminium, Paris, 16, 17 and 19 November 1910.
35  RPA, 00-2-15941, Cecil Budd (ANCO) to Badin, 3 November 1910.
36  RPA, 00-2-15941, Tait to Badin, 28 October 1910.
37  TMA, AIAG, box 228, Huber a Badin, 12 October 1910.
38  RPA, 500-1-17767, Convention régissant l'Association en participation des producteurs français d'aluminium, 25 November 1910. Convention avec la Metallgesellschaft pour les Ventes d'aluminium hors de France, 25 November 1910. HWA, MG Documents, A2, Aluminium-Betrieb, 25 November 1910. Lamy (SEMF) to Metallgesellschaft, 16 February 1911.
39  TMA, AIAG, box 228, A.V. Davis to AIAG, 28 November 1910. AIAG to A.V. Davis, confidential, 3 December 1910. AIAG to NACO, 14 December 1910.
40  Pezet, *La Décision d'Investissement Industriel*, 27.
41  Hachez-Leroy, *L'Aluminium français*, 33–34.
42  RPA, 001-16-20607, Note sur la fabrication du nitrure par le ferro-aluminium, 1911. Note sur le nitrure d'aluminium et la fabrication simultanée d'alumine et de sulfate d'ammoniaque par les procédés de la Société Générale de Nitrures (Procédés Serpek), 1910.
43  Archives du Crédit Agricole, Crédit Lyonnais Documents (ACL), DEFF, 30181, Note 3940, Société Générale des Nitrures, 30 July 1912.
44  RPA, 001-16-20607, Note sur l'Aluminium-Français, par M. A. Badin, 25 September 1910.
45  Hachez-Leroy, *L'Aluminium français*, 49–50.
46  RPA, 500-1-17767, Repartition des quantités aux termes du contrat entre SGN et SFFA, 1911. Convention entre SGN e SFFA, 27 April 1911.
47  Hachez-Leroy, *L'Aluminium français*, 51.
48  To complete its projects, AF negotiated a bond issue of 20 million francs with two major French banks, Crédit Lyonnais and Société Générale. RPA, 500-1-17767, Note Financière Concernant l'Aluminium français, 15 December 1911. Archives historiques de la Société Générale (AHSG), 3268, Dossier 1764, Note Confidentielle. L'Aluminium-Français, 1912.
49  RPA, 00-2-19540, La Sté des produits Alumineux, 1912. RPA, 500-1-17773, Note sur les livraisons d'alumine calcinée faites aux participants et sur les livraisons des participants entre eux, 5 March 1913.
50  TMA, AIAG, box 228, AIAG to NACO, 14 December 1910.
51  TMA, AIAG, box 228, NACO to AIAG, 3 February 1911.
52  TMA; AIAG, box 228, A.V. Davis to Schindler, 3 February 1911.
53  TMA, AIAG, box 228, SEMF to AIAG, 4 February 1911. BACO to AIAG, 3 March 1911.
54  RPA, 500-1-17767, Convention entre SGN et SFFA, 27 April 1911.
55  TMA, AIAG, box 229, AIAG to SEMF, 11 June 1911.
56  RPA, 001-16-20607, Calcul de pourcentage en vue de l'Entente internationale, 1911.
57  TMA, AIAG, box 229, Besprechung mit Herrn Dreyfus am 23 Mai 1911 in Paris.
58  Mira Wilkins, *The History of Foreign Investment in United States, 1914–1945*. Cambridge MA: Harvard University Press, 2004, 33–34. Mira Wilkins, *The History of Foreign Investment in United States to 1914*. Cambridge MA: Harvard University Press, 1989, 283–284. Rondo Cameron, B. I. Bovykin, *International Banking 1870–1914*. Oxford: Oxford University Press, 1991, 240. Becker, *Multinationalität hat Verschiedene Gesichte*, 235–237.
59  TMA, AIAG, box 229, Besprechung mit Herrn Dreyfus am 23 Mai 1911 in Paris.
60  Smith, *From Monopoly to Competition*.

61 RPA, 500-1-17770, Note sur l'Aluminium Co. Of America et la Northern Aluminium Cy. Entreprises de M. Davis, 30 September 1911.

62 RPA, 500-1-17770, Badin to Vielhomme, 24 September 1911.

63 RPA, 500-1-17770, Motor AG to Leu AG, 26 October 1910.

64 About this bank, Cameron, Bovykin, *International Banking*, 240. Wilkins, *The History of Foreign Investment in United States to 1914*, 528–530.

65 RPA, 500-1-17770, Note sur l'Aluminium Co of America et la Northern Aluminium Cy. Entreprises de M. Davis, 30 September 1911.

66 RPA, 001-16-20607, Calcul de Pourcentage en vue de l'Entente internationale, 11 December 1912. RPA, 00-2-15942, Projet de Contrat 'Nitrures' pour la Société de Neuhausen, 31 January 1912.

67 RPA, 00-2-15940, Réunion des Fabricants d'Aluminium, Paris les 1 et 2 avril 1912.

68 TMA, AIAG, box 177, Conditions auxquelles la Maison Gebruder Giulini Gmbh entre dans l'Association internationale des Fabbricants d'Aluminium, 29 April 1912.

69 Graham, Pruitt, *R&D for Industry*.

70 Arthur Jerome Eddy, *New Competition: An Examination of the Conditions Underlying the Radical Change that is Taking Place in the Commercial and Industrial World – The Change from a Competitive to a Cooperative Basis*, New York: Appleton & Co., 1912. Wells, *Antitrust*, 25–30.

71 Spencer Weber Waller, 'The Story of Alcoa: The Enduring Questions of Market Power, Conduct, and Remedy in Monopolization Cases', in *Antitrust Stories*, edited by Eleanor M. Fox and Daniel A. Crane. New York: Foundation Press, 2007, 125.

72

> Nous sommes tout disposés à coopérer dans la mesure des possibilités que nous laissent la loi, au besoin en réduisant la proportion de notre usine ou même en vous vendant cette usine qui est la seule qui exporte en Europe. Il est aussi très probable que l'orientation politique va changer et que, d'ici quelques mois, les poursuites contre les trusts soient abandonnées. Dans tous les cas, il ne faut pas me presser.

RPA, 500-1-17770, Héroult to Dreyfus, 20 November 1911.

73 Wallace, *Market Control*. Watkins, 'Aluminum Alliance'. Muller, *Light Metals*.

74 TMA, AIAG, box 229, Besprechung mit Herrn Edward K. Davis im Hotel Baur-au-Lac, Zurich, Freitag den 3 November 1911.

75 HHC, ALCOA, MSS#282, US v. ALCOA, Exhibit. 1011, A.V. Davis to J. A. Fowler, Assistant to Attorney General, Department of Justice, Washington DC, 17 January 1912.

76 TMA, AIAG, box 230, AA Vertrag Protokole 1912, Réunion des fabricants tenue à Paris, 1–2 April 1912.

77 RPA, 00-2-15940, Contrat de l'Aluminium Association, 6 June 1912.

78 TMA, AIAG, box 177, AA Deuxième Assemblée Générale, 11 June 1912. Box 233, Guy D'Ussel's Curriculum.

79 TMA, AIAG, box 177, Reglèment du comité et de l'assemblée de AA, 1912.

80 RPA, 00-2-15940, Contrat de l'Aluminium Association, 6 June 1912.

81 TMA, AIAG, box 177, PV de la Réunion de l'AA, 14 August 1912. UGD/21/41/23, Proceedings of General Meeting of BACO, 1913.

82 RPA, 00-2-15940, Contrat de l'Aluminium Association, 6 June 1912.

83 TMA, AIAG, box 192, Dossier Affaire Baco – Anglo Norvegiènne, 1913. RPA, 00-2-15940, Aluminium-Association, Assemblée Générale, 5 February 1913 and 7 October 1913.

84 RPA, 00-2-15940, Contrat de l'Aluminium Association, 6 June 1912.

85 TMA, AIAG, box 182, PV réunion comité AA, 7 October 1913. Guy D'Ussel to Huber, 13 September 1913.

86 UGD, 321/19/4, BACO, Aluminium, 1909.

87 Olivier Hardouin Duparc, 'Alfred Wilm et les Débuts du Duralumin', *Cahiers d'Histoire de l'Aluminium*, no. 34, 2005, 63–76. About the cultural transformations of aluminium,

see Schatzberg, 'Symbolic Culture'. Eric Schatzberg, *Wings of Wood, Wings of Metal: Culture and Technical Choice in American Airplane Materials 1914–1945*. Princeton NJ: Princeton University Press, 1999.

88  Suslow, Levenstein, 'What Determines Cartels Success?' Stigler, 'A Theory of Olygopoly'.

89  Barjot, 'Introduction'.

90  Smith, *From Monopoly to Competition*, 88–90.

91  RPA, 001-16-20607, Note au sujet des nitrures, 19 March 1913.

92  TMA, AIAG, box 180, Projet confidentiel, étude juridique de M. Borel, 13 March 1913. Box 183, AIAG to AF, confidential, 14 May 1914.

93  René Bonfils, 'Pechiney au Pays des Vikings, 1912–1958', *Cahiers d'Histoire de l'Aluminium*, no. 27, 2000/2001, 18–42. Espen Storli, David Brégaint, 'The Ups and Downs of a Family Life: Det Norske Nitridaktienselskap, 1912–1976', *Enterprise and Society*, vol. 10, no. 4, 2009, 763–790.

94  RPA, 001-14-20486, Louis Marlio, Note historique SNN, 1918.

95  RPA, 00-2-15940, Aluminium-Association. Assemblée Générale tenue à Paris le 17 Février 1914.

96

c'est une règle constante à laquelle on ne peut se soustraire que dans les Syndicats [sic] où le gâteau à se partager reste toujours à peu près le même, la part des petits augmente sans cesse au détriment de celle des plus grands jusqu'au jour où la lutte remet chacun à sa place. Dans des ententes comme celles que nous voulons faire pour l'Aluminium ce sera bien pire et nous en avons déjà l'expérience. Chacun voyant la consommation grandir s'augmentera en vue de prendre aux renouvellements de l'entente une place plus grande que celle qu'il occupe et résultat: à chaque renouvellement on se trouvera comme aujourd'hui en présence d'une surproduction intense et d'une lutte qui fera disparaître pendant sa durée tous les profits de la période de paix.

TMA, AIAG, box 171, Badin to BACO, 18 August 1909.

# Part II

# Competition and cooperation from the First World War to the Great Depression (1915–1930)

# 4 The Great Aluminium War, 1914–1921

In 1914 both Héroult and Hall died, one a few months before the other. The 'aluminium twins' left the stage when their metal was about to become a mass commodity. The events that happened after 1914 accelerated this process because the Great War played the crucial role of spin-off for this metal.[1] During the war, aluminium became a strategic material and it was employed both to substitute other non-ferrous metals in old applications and to improve the performance of war equipment in new ones. Technical research carried out during the previous decades, which had already increased global demand for this metal, enabled it to be used to improve the performance of weapons and war craft. In particular, Allied camp's firms became key partners of governments in R&D activity for warfare. Moreover, commercial blockades of international trade in non-ferrous metals made aluminium emerge as a key substitute for copper and tin in many new applications, particularly in the Central Empires where the urgency of the war accelerated this process. The Great War represented a decisive step in the transformation of aluminium into a mass commodity.[2] This had a direct outcome on world production, which passed from about 80,000 tons in 1914 to about 180,000 tons in 1918 (see Table 4.1).

Here, it is not possible to give an account of all the new uses of aluminium found during the war, but it is important to point out the growing importance into some key applications. Aluminium became one of most important strategic materials that was extensively used in the production of weapons, of equipment for soldiers, of explosives, and of aircrafts. In particular, aluminium became the metal of aviation: until the 1910s, aeroplane technologies had been based on wood and textiles. Then, planes started to be produced with growing quantities of aluminium that was employed for the construction of engines and also frameworks. The adoption of aluminium improved the resistance and the performance of the planes and, by 1917, the first all-metallic planes were being built in both belligerent fronts. The research on the strong alloys carried out in the former decade, such as duralumin, made further research during the war period possible.[3] Aluminium also became a key material for the construction of the all-metallic dirigibles in both fronts, but especially in the Central Empires where Zeppelin AG stood out.[4]

The Great War also provoked deep institutional and corporate changes. During the war, the governments had played a new role in the administration

Table 4.1 Global aluminium production, 1914–1923 (thousands of tons)

| | 1914 | 1915 | 1916 | 1917 | 1918 | 1919 | 1920 | 1921 | 1922 | 1923 |
|---|---|---|---|---|---|---|---|---|---|---|
| France | 10.55 | 6.25 | 10.05 | 11.40 | 12.55 | 8.95 | 12.45 | 8.90 | 6.70 | 14.05 |
| UK | 7.50 | 7.10 | 7.70 | 7.10 | 8.30 | 8.10 | 8.00 | 5.00 | 5.00 | 8.00 |
| Switzerland | 8.00 | 11.00 | 14.00 | 13.00 | 15.00 | 8.00 | 12.00 | 12.00 | 13.00 | 15.00 |
| Germany | 1.25 | 1.40 | 6.40 | 11.75 | 14.65 | 14.50 | 10.55 | 10.00 | 15.00 | 15.90 |
| Austria | 1.85 | 1.65 | 2.80 | 2.75 | 2.85 | 1.50 | 2.00 | 2.00 | 2.00 | 1.50 |
| USA | 40.80 | 44.90 | 63.10 | 90.70 | 102.00 | 81.60 | 62.60 | 24.50 | 33.60 | 58.50 |
| Canada | 6.60 | 8.35 | 9.60 | 10.05 | 10.70 | 9.80 | 10.15 | 2.90 | 5.85 | 11.00 |
| Norway | 2.50 | 2.30 | 4.30 | 7.60 | 6.90 | 3.10 | 5.60 | 4.00 | 4.90 | 13.30 |
| Italy | 0.90 | 0.90 | 1.10 | 1.70 | 1.70 | 1.70 | 1.70 | 0.70 | 0.80 | 1.50 |
| Total | 79.95 | 83.85 | 119.05 | 156.05 | 174.65 | 137.25 | 125.05 | 70.00 | 86.85 | 138.75 |

Source: Metallgesellschaft statistical yearbook, 1920.

of the aluminium industry and of its trade, which modified the international governance of this industry. Before the war, governments had played a marginal, if not inexistent, role in the creation and in the administration of this industry. Governmental intervention implied a huge corporate change, which shaped the new international aluminium industry in the post-war era. New actors, such as a powerful German producer, emerged from the war, while the relative power of the old producers was dramatically changed by four years of hostilities. This transformation continued during the early 1920s, when public policies still operated a great influence over this industry. The international geography of the aluminium industry was transformed by the war, because new centres of production appeared along with the old ones. This statement is valid not only for the metal, but also for bauxite extraction, which was extensively started in Eastern Europe in substitution for the Central Empires, which historically came from southern France.[5]

For these reasons, the conflict caused a shock in the cartel, not only in the short run, but also in the longer period: its activities were interrupted and the equilibrium that the producers had reached before the war in the cartel was definitively broken by the four-year-long conflict. All these changes played an important role in the future cartelisation of the 1920s and 1930s. Not only was the Great War a general displacing factor for European industry, it continued to affect the European economy during the interwar period, as Ingvar Svennilson rightly point out in his seminal study.[6] In the case of the aluminium industry, the war sharpened old rivalries amongst the firms and new clashes delayed the reconstruction of the cartel after the conflict. The war investments reshaped this industry on a global level, playing the role of a huge boom–bust cycle. While the war could create new markets, the conversion from military uses to civil ones was not taken for granted once peace arrived. As happened to other strategic industries that showed a great growth spurt during hostilities, the Great War represented a big legacy for the global output of the aluminium industry. Even if aluminium was a young industry, and its demand has been constantly increasing during this period, it would take about seven years for global output to reach again the peak of 1918.

As a consequence, the period between 1914 and 1921 can be considered as a Great Aluminium War, during while 'parallel wars'[7] were fought among the former members of AA, who tried to benefit from the military demand in their respective national context. This created a rupture with the price policy that inspired the aluminium market before 1914 because its stability was questioned. Actually, inflation and the possibility of negotiating higher prices with political powers, due to the lack of production in the first phase of the war to meet military demand, caused a great rise in prices everywhere. Moreover, the firms invested not only to meet military demand, but also to improve their position on the national and international levels. The strategies developed during the war served to prepare the post-war period whether a new cartel was formed or not. At the same time, the appearance of new producers disturbed the pre-war equilibrium, making a deeper modification of the cartel background necessary.

## The destiny of AA at the outbreak of the war: the first campaign against AIAG

At the outbreak of the war during the summer of 1914, the fate of AA was still undefined. According to the rules written in its contract, the cartel was valid for ten years and the procedure for its liquidation could have started only once per year not before the end of 1914. Since this date, the termination of the cartel could have been requested by at least three members of the committee and the procedure would have been effective in September of the following year with a delay of nine months. In spite of the difficulties linked to the failure of the Serpek process, none of the members was willing to ask for the termination of AA. AIAG was willing to modify the quotas of the agreement, in order to rectify its quota in the cartel taking into account the termination of their secret agreement on the Serpek process. The respective quotas of AF and AIAG, according to the Swiss claim, should have changed from 38.9 and 21.4 per cent to 31.7 and 30.1 per cent respectively. Actually, AIAG claimed that the Swiss and the French groups had almost the same production capacities that, once the agreement on the Serpek was terminated, should have corresponded to these quotas into the cartel.[8]

However, AIAG could not modify the situation because AF had disregarded these claims. AF officially replied that the quotas were not modifiable, as it was in the former cartels. However, the modification approved after the takeover of ANCO by BACO during 1913 opened the door to a more pressing position for AIAG, which requested another revision. The struggle between AF and AIAG progressively ruined their relationship in the cartel. Thus, AIAG tried to damage AF with some sales under the cartel price in the French market, while in February 1914, AF started to discuss with Metallgesellschaft the possibility to hit AIAG in its main market, creating a new joint venture to produce aluminium in Germany.[9] This plan was never implemented because PCAC chose Norway to invest in new aluminium production, as we have seen. Yet, the new Norwegian unit asked for a further modification in AA. Since the quotas were linked to production capacity, it became necessary for AF to ask for the inclusion of this production into AA's mechanism.[10]

The inclusion of the new French venture in Norway in the cartel was a complex operation. On the one hand, this investment was linked to the attempts to use the Serpek process in alumina production, as it has been showed. On the other hand, AF opted to turn this unit into a smelter during 1914 because the French company needed additional output to reach its quota in the cartel, which had been overestimated. AIAG accused AF of cheating on the other members during AA negotiations, declaring production capacity was too large. As a consequence, the Norwegian venture of PCAC risked creating a general conflict within the cartel. Again, AIAG proposed to change its quota, trying to link the negotiations for the Norwegian unit with its claim. In May 1914, the Swiss firm asked for a quota of 26 per cent in exchange for helping to find a compromise on the new Norwegian unit.[11] However, the meeting in which this issue would have been debated was never summoned because the war interrupted cartel activity, putting on hold the cartel's whole agenda.

In the emergency of the war, the links among firms were interrupted and the meetings of the cartel suspended. During the first months of the war, each company used its energies to reorganise production for coping with the new war markets that, as we will see, requested relevant modifications of the business of this metal. Moreover, the firms had to find a way to manage their cartel during the conflict: even though it was logical to put it on hold and to resume it after the conflict, there was also the possibility to either terminate it immediately or to maintain it in activity. Actually, at the beginning of the war the nationality of all members of AA belonged either to the Allied camp (French, British – including Canadian) or in neutral countries (Swiss and Italian – Italy was neutral until spring 1915), excepting for the two little units that AIAG had in Germany and Austria. No formal aspect would have prevented the continuation of the cartel during the war. Initially, AIAG proposed to the other members of AA to move the bureau of the cartel to Switzerland where, thanks to its neutrality, its continuation would have been guaranteed, along with its activity of general coordination. Naville served as intermediary to negotiate this change with the other producers.[12]

Behind this operation, we may see a last attempt made by AIAG to regain its leadership in the cartel. Proposing the move of the central bureau of the cartel from Paris to Neuhausen, AIAG certainly aimed to bring the cartel back to the time when the Swiss firm was the manager of the Association. Furthermore, AIAG could have inspected the data of the cartel, in order to gather proof about the overestimated output of the French group. The Great War, along with the AF's difficulties with the Serpek process, offered this opportunity. Naville tried to gain the favour of the British and Italian producers and started some personal investigations with NACO, SIFA, and ALCOR during autumn 1914. However, this attempt turned out to be unrealistic because, even though these firms were still open to possible continuation of the cartel, they were strongly opposed to AA's move to Switzerland. As an alternative, they proposed to move the bureau to Genoa, in Italy, which was still a neutral country in December 1914. The Swiss group considered this proposal an insult and, since then, AIAG gave up the idea to continue the cartel during the war.[13] At the end of April 1915, AIAG sent a circular letter to the other members, asking for the termination of the cartel, which would be effective from the beginning of 1916 after having been accepted by the other members.[14]

In the meanwhile, the position of AIAG became very precarious. AF, and PCAC in particular, denounced AIAG as controlled by German interests to the French authorities in order to assist to a sequestration of AIAG's properties in France. It has to be remembered that, even though AIAG was a Swiss company, the situation of its ownership and its strategic focus is more complex. Not only was AIAG born as a German-Swiss corporation, it also had important interests in the Central Empires, such as one smelter in Austria (Lend), and two alumina plants (Martinswerk and Goldschmieden) and another smelter in Germany (Rheinfelden). Even though the weight of the German interest was reduced since the late nineteenth century and the majority of AIAG's capital in 1914 was not owned by Germans, AIAG's production became part of the Central Empire's war efforts, which compulsorily included AIAG's units in its military production.

Emil Rathenau's death in 1915 helped further the transition to a more 'neutral' ownership of the firm, but his son, Walter Rathenau, who worked at Neuhausen in 1892, became the head of the German war materials board, Kriegsrohstof-fabteilung (KRA). AIAG was quickly considered to be a mere expression of German interests, which were supposed to use a Swiss firm to continue to either exploit or to sabotage the Allied economic and industrial resources during the war. For instance, in October 1914, Badin wrote to Tait referring to AIAG 'We will get, I hope, joining our efforts, to make the Barbarians disappear, our common enemies, in the field of aluminium, as our brave soldiers will make them disappear from the battle field.'[15]

Actually, PCAC started a campaign to assimilate AIAG to 'the German Octopus',[16] if we may employ for France a term that the historian Simon Ball adopted to describe the campaign against the German penetration into the metal industry of Great Britain. Also Giulini, in spite of its Italian origins, was claimed to be a mere representation of German interests. PCAC worked to modify the relationships of the other firms with AIAG, establishing a coalition against the Swiss firm. AF quickly found cooperation with BACO, which acted jointly with the French firms in order to coordinate their efforts with their respective governments. Their goal was to enact the necessary measures to control the international aluminium trade, hampering the exports of this metal and its raw materials to Germany, both directly and indirectly. The goal of AF and BACO was to cut AIAG and Giulini from their supplies from the Allied camps and Badin actively implicated BACO in a campaign to include aluminium as soon as possible into the strategic materials whose trade was under military control. BACO shared the same vision because

> At present, we are not only 'Allies' in name, but by the blood that we have shed together fighting the Huns of the XXth century! … It would be necessary that the [French] government prevents the plant in Marseille from working and it also should prevent aluminium and bauxite to be sent to Switzerland. We know that Giulini has received some bauxite and that Neuhausen sends the metal to the German government. This should not happen and the French government can prevent it. It is also its duty to do so, because, in this case, they cannot obtain it [alumina] from alternative sources.[17]

Since the outbreak of the war, PCAC manoeuvred French public powers in order to confiscate AIAG's French subsidiary, Société Française pour l'Industrie de l'Aluminium (SFIA), which controlled some French bauxite deposits and an alumina unit that the Swiss firm erected at Saint-Louis les Aygalades, near Marseille, in 1906. AF also obtained permission to use AIAG's properties during the war. The use of this unit was necessary for AF because at the outbreak of the war it had lost its alumina plants in Belgium, which were formerly owned by Somze's group, due to German invasion.[18] AIAG was not ready for such an action. At about the same period in which AIAG was still convinced it could continue to move AA to Switzerland, its properties were confiscated. Any possibility at continuing the AIAG production chain was hampered by the French government, which enforced trade control on aluminium and its raw materials, in order to block exports in the neutral countries as well. In spite of attempts made by Naville to manoeuvre at the highest Swiss diplomatic channels to cease confiscation of the Swiss interests in France,[19] AIAG was cut out from its normal supplies for the whole duration of the war. This fact radically changed AIAG's position in the international geography of aluminium and compromised its relationships with the other firms after the war for a long time.

## The national monopoly of ALCOA and its international war supplies

On the other side of the Atlantic Ocean, the Great War offered the opportunity to ALCOA to keep its national monopoly closing down the AF venture. The construction of SACO was interrupted and after a passing crisis, this company was taken over by ALCOA. At the end of 1914, AF had not yet finished the construction of SACO, also because fruitless attempts to make the Serpek process delayed the project. The controls over the international transfer of capital, which were enacted during the conflict, blocked the flow of funds that AF needed to invest in this venture to complete the construction of the unit. The whole project, which was carried out with a German partner (Metallgesellschaft), was also in an uncomfortable political position, which led the French government not to help AF in the continuation of the project.[20] After failing to find other US firms or a bank willing to invest in this venture, and after unsuccessfully asking BACO, AF was obliged to accept ALCOA's offer to take over SACO.[21]

A series of studies of the late 1940s, which were essentially based on documents produced by the antitrust investigations, stated that SACO's takeover was part of the general strategy of ALCOA to keep its national monopoly. According to these studies, the influence of the Mellon Bank and of its chairman, Andrew Mellon, stopped AF in its search for a financial partner in the US to continue the project, which needed important investments before starting the production. It is usually narrated that the force of the Mellon bank and the ramification of ALCOA into the American big business were sufficient to hamper any alliance of other American interests with AF.[22] By obtaining its monopoly back, ALCOA was obliged to negotiate this takeover with the Federal Trade Commission (FTC), because it recreated the antitrust problem that the US aluminium industry faced during 1912. Nonetheless, the attitude of the US antitrust authority had changed since 1912, because it authorised SACO's takeover, claiming that it was not possible for justice to act *ex ante* about ALCOA's legal behaviour.[23]

Yet this outcome was not only the outcome of Mellon's manoeuvring. It was also the consequence both of the war situation and of the former technical issues of the project. Since the Serpek technology turned out to be a fiasco, SACO would have been converted to a more reliable technology for alumina production, such as the Bayer process. However, without any control over American bauxite deposits, AF would have been obliged to import bauxite and, in this case, the production costs would have been higher than ALCOA's costs. Thus, this solution did not represent an effective basis for an investment in the long run.

Moreover, bauxite was included in the list of goods that could not be exported from France, as we have already seen. Even though AF had much benefited from these French measures in its struggle with AIAG, it had not been possible to negotiate such a trade because it would represent a threat to the domestic production of alumina.[24] Once ALCOA obtained its monopoly back, it accelerated investments both in the US and in Canada in order to hamper any other possible investment in its home market. As a consequence, ALCOA emerged from the Great War as the biggest aluminium corporation in the world, owning about half of the world output.[25]

Unlike the United States, France and Great Britain reduced their aluminium output during the first phase of the war. In particular, the hydroelectric capacity of the members of AF was largely used for the production of other goods, such as explosives and other electrochemical products.[26] At the same time, during the war and until his death in 1917, Badin continued his plans to extend the importance of his firm within AF. The termination of the American venture freed capital and enabled him to carry out a policy of mergers and acquisitions in the national field. In particular, PCAC took control of Bergès' units (SARV and PYR). As a consequence, PCAC became the first aluminium producer in France, forestalling SEMF.[27] Furthermore, PCAC continued the construction of the unit in Norway, converting the Serpek attempt to a smelting unit and starting the erection of a second unit. These expansions were supplied with alumina thanks to the confiscation of AIAG's interests in France, which emerged as a key strategic tactic of the French firm. Finally, it invested in Italy, where it built a new smelter and obtained control over SIFA, because the assets owned by the German interests that controlled this company were confiscated when Italy entered the war in 1915.[28] Badin was able to manoeuvre the French political powers, obtaining advantages during negotiations with the Italian authorities and receiving substantial governmental subsidies for ongoing investments in French hydroelectrical equipment.[29]

In Britain, BACO was not in a position to extend its production. The hydroelectric capacity of BACO's plants was close to full utilisation. As a consequence, an increase of its output would have needed the creation of a new hydroelectric power station, which was not possible in a short time. As we will see, BACO started the construction of a new integrated unit only after the war.[30] This lack of aluminium production in the Allied camp at the beginning of the war was caused by a rather evident lack of understanding of aluminium as a material for modern warfare. The actual demand for this metal slowed down when the war started and, only during hostilities, did aluminium come to fore as a performance material in key applications, such as in aviation, military equipment, and others. Even if AF was able to enter into the Italian market and BACO extended its Norwegian production, their production was not sufficient to meet military demand. Due to its Canadian nationality, NACO joined the British war effort, offering ALCOA the possibility to participate in the highly remunerative war markets.[31]

This situation of lack of metal, however, was uncomfortable for the French and British governments. Deliveries from North America were the object of German submarine attacks, which made this trade very precarious. When the US entered the war in 1916, the role of NACO as supplier for the British Ministry of Munitions was questioned, because the Canadian smelter was no longer supplied with US alumina. Actually, even though it was an internal trade to ALCOA, this export of alumina from the US to Canada was hampered by the US government, which included aluminium and its raw materials in the list of strategic goods under the control of the War Industry Board. As a consequence, the Allied governments started to ask for supplies directly to ALCOA. This strong position on the war market provoked a rapid increase in aluminium prices in all the Allied countries (see Table 4.2). Even though ALCOA became the largest supplier of the Allied camp, this solution was too expensive, also because the governments of France, Great Britain, and Russia found themselves in competition for this supply.[32]

This rapid increase of prices, which were also harmful to the US government,[33] led the Allied powers to take control of the aluminium trade. Since the Allied economic conference held in Paris during September 1916, the Inter-Allied Munitions Board (IAMB) became central controller over almost all inter-allied trade of strategic materials, and was charged with allocating production and sales. Aluminium was included in IAMB's monitoring role, but with a main difference as regards the other materials. While the other materials were organised forming some national *comptoirs* that were linked to IAMB through their respective ministries, in the specific case of the aluminium industry, AF, BACO, and ALCOA became the direct reference for IAMB, also resuming their old links to assure the coordination of the war effort. IAMB was charged with the international repartition of production and supplies, in order to bring some order back to the international trade of this metal, and to take control over the formation of prices.[34]

## The 'war cartel' and the second campaign against AIAG

Due to its capacity to regulate the international trade of aluminium, an attentive observer of the international aluminium industry and intimate friend of Badin, Robert Pitaval, compared the network of aluminium producers in IAMB with a 'war cartel'.[35] In spite of its similarities with a cartel, industrial organisation during the war showed a substantial difference with the pre-war governance of this industry. From a general standpoint, the Great War reshaped the relationships that existed between private firms and public powers. The suppliers were implicated in many public offices during the war, while a progressive interconnection between public and private interests reshaped the administration of many industries.[36] In the specific case of the aluminium industry, this represented a new factor in the balance of relationships that had shaped international cartelisation until then. Badin managed to become very intimate with the French authorities, in particular with Albert Thomas and with Louis Loucheur, who were consecutive Ministers of Munitions in France during the War. When he died in 1917, Adrien Badin was substituted by Louis Marlio, who was a civil servant at the Ministry of Public Works. Marlio, as we will see, became one of the main actors of the international cartel movements after the war.[37]

*Table 4.2* Average prices in the Allied countries and variation (1913 base 100), 1913–1918

| | 1913 | | 1914 | | 1915 | | 1916 | | 1917 | | 1918 | |
|---|---|---|---|---|---|---|---|---|---|---|---|---|
| | *base* | *price* | *var.* | *price* | *var.* | *price* | *var.* | *price* | *var.* | *price* | *var.* | *price* |
| FR-F/kg | 100 | 2.25 | 93 | 2.10 | 155 | 3.50 | 177 | 4.00 | 302 | 6.80 | 333 | 7.50 |
| UK-£/t | 100 | 81.00 | 111 | 90.00 | 197 | 160.00 | 247 | 200.00 | 278 | 225.00 | 284 | 230.00 |
| US-¢/lb | 100 | 23.64 | 79 | 18.59 | 144 | 34.13 | 257 | 60.73 | 217 | 51.25 | 142 | 33.60 |
| RU-F/kg | 100 | 2.50 | – | n.a. | – | n.a. | 174 | 4.35 | 292 | 7.30 | – | n.a. |
| IT-L/kg | 100 | 2.55 | 106 | 2.70 | 176 | 4.50 | 431 | 11.00 | 530 | 13.50 | 200 | 5.11 |

Source: author's elaboration from various files in TNA, RPA, AN, and NARA.

BACO's situation appeared more complicated. BACO became a key firm for the British war effort. The director of BACO, Andrew Tait, served as a civil servant in the British War Munitions Board (WMB). He was appointed to survey German interests in Great Britain during the confiscation of Alien proprieties operations and worked also studying other dossiers that belonged to the financial world, such as an inspection of some Italian interests in Great Britain.[38] Also other managers of BACO played a crucial role in the British war effort, becoming officials at WMB. In spite of this political legitimation, BACO's business was put in jeopardy. The lack of production by BACO was exploited by NACO which, thanks to its Canadian nationality, was in a comfortable position to supply the British war market, exploiting the high prices that were derived from the general lack of metal. Only when the United States entered into the war and NACO's production was sacrificed to ALCOA, did the need of additional British production became pressing. As seen, ALCOA's price increases were causing anxiety in all the Allied countries. New visions about the position of BACO in war supplies emerged as a key strategic necessity for British political powers, who tried to help BACO to recover its position in the global context.[39]

In this context, from 1916 BACO and the British government planned to take over AIAG. This proposal was not only the outcome of the stronger bonds settled with their respective governments, which were exploited by Allied firms to support their respective positions within the international oligopoly. This second attack to AIAG aimed to injure the Central Empires' supply chain of aluminium, distracting an important supply from Germany and including it in the Allied war effort. The death of many of AIAG's key shareholders from 1914 to 1916 led the British to try a takeover of the majority of the Swiss firm's shares on the market: not only the death of Emil Rathenau in 1915, which has been already mentioned, but also the death of Emil Huber-Werdmüller, AIAG's president, at the end of 1916, left a provisional vacancy in the Swiss group' ownership. BACO was actively willing to exploit this opportunity because of both its poor relationships with AIAG and its necessity to recover its position into the oligopoly. The poor relationships between the British and the Swiss group were an aftermath of BACO's failed attempt to install production in Switzerland in 1906. Since then, the relationship between the two companies never recovered.[40]

Andrew Tait was the main crafter of this attempt and he was supported by the complicity of his government. Tait's programme wanted the British government to take over AIAG and leave BACO with direct control over its units during the war. It was calculated that AIAG's output in Switzerland was about 15,000 tons per year: this amount would have quickly incremented the Allies' production of aluminium in a critical period. Other outputs were insufficient and this fact also led to other investments, such as PCAC's in Norway and Italy. The use of AIAG's Swiss output would have redressed this critical situation, leading to a possible change in the global war. According to Tait's vision, after the war, BACO would have purchased the whole properties of AIAG from the British government. This operation would have dramatically changed the position of BACO amongst the other producers, giving to the British enterprise European leadership in the aluminium industry. Yet, since Swiss production was using alumina from

the Central Empires that would be interrupted after this takeover, this programme needed to find an alternative supply. As a consequence, the British
authorities investigated, through IAMB, French powers as regards the possibility
to give SFIA back to AIAG, in order to be used by BACO in the eventuality that
the takeover would be successfully achieved.[41]

This situation created a 'parallel war' in the Allied camp. Without SFIA's
output, the French producers would have been deprived of a substantial part of
their alumina requirements. Actually, SFIA's production was used not only to
supply the French units, after the loss of the Somze units located in Belgium
(which was occupied by German troops), but also to supply the new Italian and
Norwegian units. This fact puzzled the original programme established by Tait
because, even though the takeover of AIAG would have deprived the Central
Empires of an important output, it would have also deprived the French war
effort of its most substantial material basis.[42] Consequently, Badin manoeuvred
the French Ministry's Albert Thomas in order to block this operation, so attract-
ing the attention of French public powers on the hazardousness of this operation
from the national standpoint. A second aspect was pointed out by Badin as
regards to Norway's position in the war. Without French alumina, the Norwegian production of PCAC would have closed down and other Norwegian actors
next to the Central Empires, such as the newcomer Norsk Aluminium A/S,
would have exploited the situation. In 1916, Norsk had already tried to erect an
alumina plant in France, with which to supply the Central Empires.[43]

Badin was able to bridge national security to the international strategy of his
firm. He persuaded the French authorities that a collateral effect of endorsing
BACO's programme could be the loss of control over an important part of the
national war resources. His confidential notes alerted Albert Thomas of the
damage that this operation would have caused to the national aluminium industry
because it would allow foreign control over part of national resources. Actually, a
further argument was that, while the French and Norwegian units were safely far
from the front, AIAG's unit was too near to the German boundaries. This fact
was presented as extremely hazardous, even though a German invasion of Switzerland could not be taken seriously into account in retrospect. A final point,
which Badin exploited in his argumentation, was that Norway's production
would have covered an important part of the Russian supplies, as a consequence
of the arrangements already made within IAMB. The failure to supply Russia
would have helped ALCOA to build up a unit in this country, a fact that created
anxieties both in Great Britain and in France for diplomatic reasons.[44]

As a consequence of Badin's manoeuvring, Thomas did not help BACO to
take control over AIAG and claimed it impossible to bring SFIA back to Swiss
group. Meanwhile, the possibility of purchasing Swiss group's shares on the
market faded, delaying Tait's proposal to take over AIAG. In this context, BACO
and the British government reoriented their national strategy over aluminium
towards an important increase of the domestic smelting capacity and, for the first
time, the construction of a new smelter in Scotland was prospected.[45] As Andrew
Perchard showed, the Lochaber project, whose prospected output would have
been about 20,000 tons, became the most ambitious British aluminium

programme of the interwar period even though, as we will see, its construction was procrastinated until 1924.[46] However, the victory of the French position over AIAG affair neither meant that the Swiss group was safe nor that it would keep its international position during the war and afterward.

## The aluminium industry in the Central Empires

Aluminium played a new strategic role in the Central Empires since the outbreak of the war. Since Germany and the Austro-Hungarian Empire were great importers of non-ferrous metals before the war, which came from geographic areas under the British influence, the military preparedness of the Central Empires was seriously compromised by the commercial blockades and trade controls. Then aluminium came to the fore as a key substitute material and the adoption of this metal was strongly encouraged by political powers to substitute tin, copper, and other non-ferrous metals. Aluminium was included in the reorganisation of the war material production that followed the creation of KRA by Walter Ratheanu in autumn 1914. KRA's action was focused on coordinating the action of the German public powers and of private actors, which aimed at the creation of a national aluminium industry. Before the end of 1914, KRA started a general inspection of Germany's and the Austro-Hungarian Empire's mineral resources and extensive bauxite deposits were found in Hungary, Romania, and Istria. From then, the plan to use aluminium in substitute for other non-ferrous metals became feasible. A new state company, the Kriegsmetall AG (KMAG), was formed in 1915 to allocate bauxite from Eastern Europe among the different users.[47]

Before the war, the German output of aluminium was about 1400 tons concentrated in AIAG's Rheinfelden unit, and Austria's was about 2300 tons. This output was completely dependent on bauxite imports from France. The main part of Germany's aluminium needs, as showed, was satisfied by imports, which predominantly came from AIAG's Swiss smelters. In 1918, this situation was completely changed. The total output of the Central Empires reached about 18,000 tons and this production was self-sufficient for the German economy. Initially, Germany relied on war contracts signed with AIAG, which was also led to increase its Swiss outputs in order to meet the German war requirement. However, this production was not sufficient for the German plan to adopt aluminium in substitution of other non-ferrous metals. The Allied operations on AIAG (both the sequestration of SFIA and the takeover attempt) reshaped the German strategy for aluminium, making the German authorities opt for stronger national production. AIAG was in an ambivalent position: on the one hand, it aimed to show its neutrality in order to get back its peacetime industrial chain; on the other hand, it was dependent on German supplies of bauxite and on war contracts with the Central Empires to keep its position within the aluminium business during the war.[48]

In autumn 1914, AIAG was not able to prevent the action by the German authorities, which would have determined the loss of its strong position in the German metal market. AIAG also tried to avoid this outcome by establishing a temporary smelter at Martinswerk, which was supplied with expensive thermo-electric power. Even though AIAG believed that any German production, like that at Martinswerk, would not have the competitive advantage needed to continue to produce aluminium after the war, it acknowledged the risk of the implication of its old adversaries in the German war effort.[49] Actually, KRA involved many of AIAG's old enemies into the war programme for aluminium. The first was Giulini, which already produced alumina at Ludwigshafen. KRA also allowed Giulini to use PCAC's Belgian units and endorsed a big plan to build new smelting facilities in Germany. Beer & Sondheimer, which was planning to enter into alumina production before the war, also received government help to start a unit in Duisburg. Finally, and most importantly, Metallgesellschaft was actively involved in the German war plans. Metallgesellschaft resumed its experiments jointly made with CFGE to produce alumina from alternative ores. During the war, the blockade of international commerce and the rise of aluminium prices made this technology more reliable.[50]

The creation of new capacities was not limited to bauxite extraction and alumina production. MG–CFGE's venture formed three temporary aluminium smelters at Rummelsburg (near Berlin), at Horrem, and at Bitterfeld, whose total output was about 6,000 tons.[51] Giulini joined forces with other big German groups to make a decisive step towards the production of aluminium as well. Giulini collaborated with Rheinish-Westfalisches Elektrizitatwerk (RWE), which was part of the powerful Hugo Stinnes' economic empire, to build a new 6,000 tons capacity smelter near Erftwerk, where RWE owned a thermo-electrical plant. During the war, Giulini went through a situation as precarious as AIAG's: its Swiss-Italian nationality was not sufficient to save it from confiscation in France. The Martigny unit, which was located in Switzerland but whose electricity came from France, was shut down. As a consequence, this firm turned its attention to the German war trade and it also moved all the Martigny engineers to Erftwerk. For example, Ernst Rauch, who later became a leading actor of the interwar aluminium cartelisation, worked for the creation of Erftwerk after moving from Martigny. Giulini's contribution to the German war effort led him to be accused of high betrayal and sentenced to perpetual reclusion by the Allied public powers, as was the director of Martigny, Giulini's son-in-law, Mermod.[52]

Unlike what AIAG believed, all these plants supplied with thermo-electric power were not a simple temporary war investment. They were the start of a more consistent plan, which also lasted after the war. In the pre-war aluminium panorama, the adoption of thermo-electric power was not considered a reliable basis for the development of this industry. However, during autumn 1916, German public powers started to elaborate a plan to reorganise the industry, in order to help it to compete with the older aluminium firms. This plan involved saving the most performing investments and protecting them with tariffs. The German aluminium business was reorganised according to the elaboration of Hildenburg's plan.[53] German production would increase to 24,000 tons and a new company, Vereinigte Aluminium Werke (VAW), was created in 1917 as a joint venture of KRA, MG, and CFGE. Moritz 'Max' Von der Porten became the chairman of this venture, and, with Rauch, also played an important role in the interwar aluminium cartel. Von der Porten was previously the director of the

Octavi Mining AG, an enterprise that was appointed by KMAG for the exploitation of East European bauxite deposits. VAW was appointed to build an integrated alumina–aluminium unit at Lautawerk, whose scale economy was considered large enough (12,000 tons per year) to be competitive with the hydroelectric technology that has dominated aluminium until then.[54]

Before the end of the war, Giulini started one last big project, which would represent a heavy legacy for the post-war aluminium industry. With complicity of AEG and Siemens Schuckert Werke (SSW), construction of the largest German hydroelectric aluminium smelter was started at Toging am Inn, near the Austrian border, in Bavaria. A new enterprise was formed under the name of Bayerische Aluminium Werke (BAW) and the output of this unit, which is often called Innwerk, would have been 11,000 tons per year. Even though neither Lautawerk nor Innwerk started working during the war, they represented the solid basis for post-war German expansion, whose unitary production costs would have been able to compete with foreign production. During the war, production in Germany passed from 1,400 tons per year to about 40,000 (see Table 4.3). Even though many provisional plants were shut down because of their too expensive production costs, three units (Lautawerk, Innwerk, and Bitterfeld) continued to live in the post-war era.[55]

## The continuation of the conflict by other means during the 1920s

Allied firms tried to maintain their coalition after the war. From November 1918, the chairmen of ALCOA, AF, and BACO met in Paris with the aim to continue their 'war cartel' against AIAG and the German producers. They aimed to explore again the possibility of taking over AIAG jointly, and to share technology to achieve a competitive edge against the German producers. Actually, AIAG was an exporter, and its acquisition by ALCOA, BACO, and AF aimed both 'to tame' a dangerous global supplier and to get rid of its force from the oligopoly. Allied producers were convinced that AIAG came out of the war with a weaker position. AIAG lost its principal outlet (Germany) and its principal adversaries of the pre-war period gained prominence in this country due to the war. Without access to its French properties, which lasted until 1922 under French control, AIAG's situation appeared very precarious. From the financial standpoint, the big German post-war inflation reduced its margins of profits. An intelligence report informed that these facts made an important portion of AIAG's share available on the market, which induced the Allied producers to consider again taking over the Swiss group.[56]

These two programmes were functional, in the minds of the Allied producers, to a quick re-establishment of their former cartel, which would have excluded AIAG and the German producers.[57] In this phase, the American authorities were making plans to allow American firms to join international export cartels thanks to the enactment of the Webb–Pomerene Act.[58] Also in the British and French contexts, the adoption of private cartels was considered a possible way to help transition to a peace economy and to reduce the influence of German business in the post-war economy.[59] This would have helped a possible resumption of the

Table 4.3 German aluminium units with type of electricity adopted, 1915–1919

| Unit | Type energy | Ownership | Year | Production capacity | 1915 | 1916 | 1917 | 1918 | 1919 |
|---|---|---|---|---|---|---|---|---|---|
| Rheinfelden | H | AIAG | 1897 | 1,500 | 1,400 | 1,365 | 905 | 1,548 | 1,100 |
| Rummelsburg | T | CFGE/MMG | 1914 | 3,650 | 29 | 1,710 | 3,737 | 3,214 | 3,200 |
| Horrem | T | CFGE/MMG | 1915 | 2,400 | – | 1,824 | 2,940 | 2,484 | 1,600 |
| Bitterfeld | T | CFGE/MMG | 1915 | 3,000 | – | 1,501 | 3,588 | 3,754 | 3,100 |
| Erktwerk | T | Giulini/RWE | 1916 | 6,000 | – | – | – | 3,450 | 2,100 |
| Lauta – VAW | T | CFGE/MMG | 1917 | 12,000 | – | – | – | 200 | 3,400 |
| Innwerk | H | Giulini/AEG/SSW | 1918 | 11,000 | – | – | – | – | – |
| Total | | | | 41,050 | 1,429 | 6,400 | 11,170 | 14,650 | 14,500 |

Source: HWA.

Note
H = hydro-electric, T = thermal-coal.

old Aluminium-Association, in the case in which AIAG would have been taken over by the Allied firms. Furthermore, Allied firms were convinced that German production would be shut down after the war and that Germany would become an important outlet for them after the takeover of AIAG.[60]

Once it became clear that German production could survive, this takeover appeared useless, and was dismissed along with the 'war cartel' project.[61] The German government aimed to encourage national production with tariffs and aids to exports, in order to save a strategic industry in the post-war period. As Louis Marlio reported in 1919, the news about the corporate restructuring of the German aluminium industry

> Makes the interest in taking over Neuhausen less important for us since that will not get rid of the German plants, and at the same time, this must make the ambitions of Neuhausen less high, since it will lose its main costumer [Germany].[62]

However, AIAG's situation was less precarious than the Allied producers thought. During the war the Swiss firm was able to substitute its supply chain and, as soon as the war ended, launched a campaign of mergers and acquisitions in order to take control over the bauxite deposits in Hungary and Istria. While German inflation was not harmful as was believed for the Swiss group, which exploited it as a competitive advantage for its production (both alumina and aluminium were less expensive), AIAG implemented a strategy of international expansion. AIAG reconfigured its commercial strategy in order to find an alternative to the loss of its positions in Germany. It started to sell in the North American market, in Far Asia, and at the beginning of the 1920s this firm appeared as one of the most performing actors on the international scene. Moreover, AIAG had not the same downturns of the other producers, which had to manage a difficult inventories situation in the post-war era, and this enabled the firm to run its Swiss smelters at their scale outputs with low production costs.[63]

The continuation of the 'war cartel' turned out to be unrealistic, but the situation was not yet ready to include AIAG and new German actors in a new cartel agreement. Aside from old and new rivalries, the post-war economic disorder forced firms to postpone arrangements. The producers that had expanded their production during the conflict, could not find outlets in national markets, in which termination of war contracts reduced the global demand for aluminium. The Great War stimulated new applications for this metal, but when the conflict ended civil consumption was not yet ready to absorb the new outputs. The global production of aluminium dropped from about 180,000 tons in 1918 to 140,000 tons in 1919 to reach the lowest level during 1921, when only 70,000 tons were produced (see Table 4.1). As a consequence, in the post-war period, the global situation was characterised by a dangerous overproduction, which led firms to compete for outlets. Moreover, firms aimed to improve their own positions before starting negotiations for a new cartel. The post-war crisis of 1921 sharpened these conflicts, prolonging the existence of two coalitions in the aluminium industry (former Allies and former Central Empires) and even provoking struggles inside each of these coalitions.[64]

During the post-war recovery, stronger bonds were established between producers and national policymakers in the Allied camp, and each producer was fully shielded from international competition. This fact delayed the resumption of private agreements among producers. One of the most important aspects of the links between firms and governments was the management of war stock. Governments owned important quantities of aluminium, stocked during the war for military production, that were considered surplus as soon as the conflict ended. If this metal was sold on the market, it would seriously damage the producers. As a consequence, aluminium producers managed to negotiate some disposal programmes, which accompanied reduction of output with an activity of stock buffering. Aluminium français was appointed as official administrator of surplus stock in France and Italy and the governments of both countries protected AF from imports during the disposal. At the same time, the French government continued to survey exports of bauxite, adopting a system of licences to avoid any foreign control over these national resources and to hamper exports of bauxite.[65]

In Great Britain, the Non-Ferrous Metal Industry Act of 1918 provided BACO with similar protection, establishing a system of trade licences for aluminium. As in the French case, this measure granted BACO control over the stock situation, which was useful to plan the reduction of production while war stock was depleted. The British government also aimed to increase the imperial sources of strategic materials and it supported the construction of a new BACO smelter in Scotland, which was completed during the 1920s.[66] In the United States ALCOA was in a comfortable position to dispose of the absolute monopoly. Moreover, the American government adopted new measures to protect ALCOA during this phase of intense competition for international outlets. Post-war exports at very low prices, which did not only involve aluminium but almost all raw materials, led the US authorities to raise the tariff and to enact a new anti-dumping legislation in 1921. Furthermore, in the domestic market, ALCOA benefited from political control over aluminium prices, which helped to keep prices stable while demand was slowing down.[67]

The German government adopted similar policies to support its national production, promoting an export cartel formed by Metallgesellschaft, AIAG, and VAW to dump the metal on international markets.[68] At the same time, the disposal of war stock was assigned to a unique actor, Metallgesellschaft.[69] The government also restructured national production, shutting down uneconomic units and investing in more efficient ones to improve competitiveness.[70] In fact, all five smelters built during the war were supplied with expensive electricity produced in coal or lignite electric facilities. Only three of them had production costs low enough to survive after the war, even if tariff protection was necessary. Also the new project in Innwerk, which was started by Giulini, SSW, and AEG, was taken over by VAW and its construction was continued during the 1920s. Private interests were liquidated because, during post-war inflation, AEG and SSW preferred to divest from aluminium production. Even Giulini, in spite of its great role into the German war effort, was obliged to sell its shares and to divest from aluminium (but not alumina) production.[71]

The restructuration of the German aluminium industry was completed in 1923 when VAW was included in the Vereinigte Industrieunternehmungen Aktiengesellschaft (VIAG), the state-owned holding company. VAW became the owner of Lautawerk and Erftwerk and it continued the construction of Innwerk during the 1920s. Metallgesellschaft and CFGE kept ownership of Bitterfeld Aluminium-Werke but it was managed by VAW until 1925.[72] The last actor that entered the aluminium industry during the war, Beer & Sondheimer, settled a strategic alliance with the Norwegian group Norsk Aluminium, which started its production in the second half of 1918. Beer & Sondheimer supplied this firm with alumina, because the Norwegian group, as we have seen, failed to keep control over bauxite and alumina production in France. Norsk was included in the Metallgesellschaft export cartel after the war as well.[73] The action of the German export cartel focused its strategy to the United States, where the German producers aimed to find outlets for their production. On the one hand, this fact pushed the US government to enact stronger tariffs and to pass new laws about antidumping measures. On the other, it pushed ALCOA to start an international policy to tame the most dangerous exporters. In this phase, ALCOA developed again an international strategy of investments that focused on taking over Norsk Aluminium. At the same time, ALCOA obtained control over a certain quantity of the bauxite deposits in Istria, probably considering reducing German production through this takeover. As a consequence, ALCOA emerged from the war not only as a new American monopoly, but also as a powerful multinational corporation. As we will see in the next chapter, this strategy also continued in the 1920s.[74]

The international crisis of 1921 provoked another important corporate transformation in the panorama of aluminium. The two principal firms of AF, SEMF and PCAC were pushed to merge into the Compagnie des produits chimiques et électrométallurgiques d'Alais, Froges et Camargue (AFC). This new company was created to rationalise the production of the two leading French actors, in order to be more competitive in the post-war period that promised to be difficult for the aluminium business. In AF, the French national cartel, AFC became the leading firm while EC was relegated to the background. During the following decades, AF became almost synonymous with AFC in the nexus of relationships with the other firms of the oligopoly. Furthermore, AFC launched new investments to recover its alumina production before giving back AIAG's units.[75] As we will see, AFC did not only play the role of a leading actor in the international oligopoly, but its chairman, Louis Marlio, became the most important personality of the inter-war cartelisation. As we will see, Marlio was able to transform the situation of hostility, which reigned among the producers, into a more cohesive group of loyal partners.

## Notes

1 Clive Trebilcock, '"Spin-Offs" in British Economic History: Armaments and Industry, 1760–1914', *Economic History Review*, vol. 22, no. 3, 1969, 474–490.
2 Smith, *From Monopoly to Competition*, 128–131. Wallace, *Market Control*, 43–47.
3 Gaëtan Py, *Progrès de la Métallurgie et Leur Influence sur l'Aéronautique*. Paris: Mémoires de la Société des ingénieurs civils de France, 1928, 19–21. Charles Grard, *Aluminium and its Alloys: Their Properties, Thermal, Treatment and Industrial Application*, London,

Constable, 1921, 80–85. Jean Escard, *L'Aluminium dans les Industries: Métal pur et Alliages*. Paris: Dunod et Pinat, 1918, 25–30.

4   Schatzberg, *Wings of Wood, Wings of Metal*. Margaret B. W. Graham, 'R&D and Competition in England and the United States: The Case of the Aluminum Dirigible', *Business History Review*, vol. 62, no. 2. 1988, 261–285. Emmanuel Chadeau, *De Bériolt à Dassault: Histoire de l'Industrie Aéronautique en France, 1900–1950*. Paris, Fayard, 1987. Guilleaume De Syon, *Zeppelin! Germany and the Airship, 1900–1939*, Baltimore MD: John Hopkins University Press, 2002. Roman Köster, 'Zeppelin, Carl Berg and the Development of Aluminium Alloys for German Aviation (1890–1930)', *Cahiers d'Histoire de l'Aluminium*, no. 50, 2014, 72–87.

5   Wallace, *Market Control*. James E. Collier, 'Aluminium Industry of Europe', *Economic Geography*, vol. 22, no. 2, April 1946, 75–108.

6   Ingvar Svennilson, *Growth and Stagnation in the European Economy*. Geneva: United Nations Economic Commission for Europe, 1954.

7   Giogio Mori, 'Le Guerre Parallele: L'Industria Elettrica in Italia nel Periodo della Grande Guerra (1914–1919)', *Studi Storici*, vol. 14, 1973, 292–372.

8   TMA, AIAG, box 183, Huber to Vielhomme, 13 June 1913.

9   RPA, 00-12-20014, MG to Bergès, 12 February 1914, referring to a meeting between AF and MG held 11 February 1914. MG to Bergès, 18 February 1914.

10   RPA, 00-2-15940, PV du comité AA, 13 March 1914.

11   TMA, AIAG, box 183, AIAG to AF, 15 May 1914.

12   TMA, AIAG, box 116, Besprechung mit Herrn Oberst Naville über die Notizen in Angelegenheit AIAG von heute, 19 August 1914.

13   TMA, AIAG, box 118, Huber to Schindler, 12 December 1914.

14   TMA, AIAG, box 183, AIAG circular letter, 30 April 1915. Betriff Aluminium-Association, 10 December 1915.

15   'Nous arriverons, je l'espère, en unissant nos efforts à faire disparaitre les Barbares, nos ennemis communs, du champ de l'aluminium, alors bien que nos valoreux soldats les feront disparaitre dans le champ de bataille', RPA, 00-12-20014, Badin (AF) to Tait (BACO), 8 October 1914.

16   Simon Ball, 'The German Octopus: The British Metal Corporation and the Next War, 1914–1939', *Enterprise and Society*, vol. 5, no. 3, 2004, 451–489.

17
    Au present, nous ne sommes pas seulement 'Alliés' en nom, mais par le sang que nous avons perdu ensemble en combattant les Huns du XXe siècle! [...] Il faudrait que le gouvernement [français] ne devrait pas permettre l'usine de Neuhausen à Marseille de fonctionner et aussi devrait empecher qu'aucun aluminium et bauxite soit envoyé en Suisse. Nous savons que Giulini a reçu de la bauxite et que Neuhausen envoie le métal au gouvernment allemand. Cela ne devrait pas etre et le gouvernment français peut l'empecher. C'est meme son devoir de le faire, car alors ils ne peuvent l'obtenir de nulle part.

    RPA, 00-12-20014, Sawyer (BACO) to Barut (AF), 29 September 1914.

18   RPA, 00-12-20014, Note sur la Société de Neuhausen et ses intérêts en France, 15 November 1914. Note pour M. le Préfet des Bouches du Rhone sur l'industrie de l'aluminium et son exercice en France par des sociétés allemandes, September 1914. Badin to Robert Pinot (Comité des forges de France), 10 December 1914. AN 94 AP 114, Documents Albert Thomas, Note sur l'aluminium, 6 December 1915.

19   TMA, AIAG, box 118, Navile to Lady (Swiss Foreign Affairs Minister), 12 February 1915.

20   Hachez-Leroy, *L'Aluminium français*, 83–85. Becker, *Multinationalität hat Verschiedene Gesichter*, 235–238.

21   UGD 347/21/45/5, Badin to BACO, Southern Aluminium Co. Whitney NC, 26 February 1915.

22   Muller, *Light Metals*, 106–109. Watkins, 'Aluminum Alliance'.

23 HHC, ALCOA, MSS#282, box 2, folder 17, Paul Fuller (SACO) to Attorney General, 17 August 1915. Carroll Todd (Assistant to Attorney General) to Fuller, 5 September 1915. Smith, *From Monopoly to Competition*, 109–113; United States Federal Trade Commission, *Report on Cooperation in American Export Trade*, Washington DC: Government Printing Office, 1916, 122–123.
24 RPA, 500-1-17770, Etat des affaires de la Southern Aluminium Company à Whitney en fin 1914, 1 November 1914. Pezet, *La Decision de l'Investissement*, 33–34.
25 Smith, *From Monopoly to Competition*.
26 RPA, 500-1-17772, Note sur la production et les disponibilités d'Aluminium en 1916, 5 November 1915. Emploi pour les besoins militaires, 1917.
27 Hachez-Leroy, *L'Aluminium français*, 95–97. RPA, 001-0-11332, Nouveau Programme de l'AF, 3 March 1916.
28 About Norway, see Storli, Brégaint, 'The Ups and Downs'. About Italy, see Marco Bertilorenzi, 'The Italian Aluminium Industry: Cartels, Multinationals and the Autarkic Phase, 1917–1943', *Cahiers d'Histoire de l'Aluminium*, no. 41, 2008, 43–72.
29 Ludovic Cailluet, 'L'Impact de la Première Guerre Mondiale et le Rôle de l'Etat dans l'organisation de la branche et des entreprises', in Grinberg, Hachez-Leroy (eds), *Industrialisation et Sociétés*, 95–105. Hachez-Leroy, *L'Aluminium français*, 98–106.
30 Perchard, *Aluminiumville*.
31 The National Archives, Kew Garden, London (hereafter TNA), MUN/4/5402, Contract between Ministry of Munitions and NACO, 25 January 1916. Imperial Munition Board to Ministry of Munitions, 15 June 1917.
32 TNA, MUN/4/5402, Edward K. Davis (NACO), Memorandum A, 3 February 1917. National Archives and Records Administration, College Park (hereafter NARA), RG 61, Box 1, Jacob Schmuckler (US War Industries Board), Memorandum to Colonel Arnold. Sub. Explanation of Allies Requirements, 20 June 1918. Note. Aluminum, 10 June 1918. AN 94 AP 114, Papiers Thomas, Note pour Monsieur le Sous-Secrétaire d'Etat de l'Artillerie et des Munitions sur le prix de revient et le prix de vente actuel de l'aluminium, s.d. but second half of 1916.
33 Henry R. Aldrich, Jacob Schmuckler, *Prices of Ferroalloys, Nonferrous Metals and Rare Metals*, Washington DC: United States War Industries Board, 1919, 54–55.
34 TNA, BT/55/46, Committee of Non-Ferrous Metals. Report, 10 October 1916. MUN/4/724, Aluminium. Extract from Minutes of meeting of the IAMB, 3 March 1917. MUN/5/207/1830, Report on Aluminium, June 1918. Hachez-Leroy, *L'Aluminium français*, 90. Perchard, *Aluminiumville*. Cauillet, 'L'Impact de la Première Guerre Mondiale'. Robert D. Cuff, *The War Industries Board: Business–Government Relations during World War I*. Baltimore MD: Johns Hopkins University Press, 1973, 228–229.
35 Robert Pitaval, 'Les Ententes dans l'Industrie Mondiale de l'Aluminum', *Journal du Four Électrique*, vol. 46, no. 3, 1937, 83–85.
36 Cuff, *The War Industries Board*. John F. Godfrey, *Capitalism at War: Industrial Policy and Bureaucracy in France, 1914–1918*. Leamington: Berg, 1987. David Edgerton, *Warfare State: Britain 1920–1970*. Cambridge: Cambridge University Press, 2006.
37 About Marlio, see Alfred Pose, *Notice sur la Vie et les Travaux de Louis Marlio (1878–1952)*. Paris: Firmin-Didot, 1955. Henri Morsel, 'Louis Marlio, Position Idéologique et Comportement Politique d'un Dirigeant d'une Grande Entreprise dans la Première Moitié du XXes', in Grinberg, Hachez-Leroy (eds), *Industrialisation et Sociétés*, 106–112.
38 Perchard, *Aluminiumville*. Giuseppe Telesca, *Il Mercante di Varsavia: Giuseppe Toeplitz: Un Cosmopolita alla guida della Banca Commerciale Italiana*, Unpublished PhD thesis, Università degli studi di Firenze, 2010, 64–65. See also Ball, 'The German Octopus'.
39 TNA, MUN/5/207/1830/3, Memorandum. Aluminium, 3 February 1917. MUN/4/5402, Contract between Ministry of Munitions and NACO, 25 January 1916. Edward K. Davis (NACO), Memorandum A, 5 February 1917. Ministry of Munitions to Imperial Munitions Board, 19 May 1917.

40 TNA MUN/5/207/1830/1, Memorandum re-Neuhausen Works, 21 June 1917.
41 TNA MUN/5/207/1830/1, Memorandum re-Neuhausen Works, 21 June 1917. AN 94 AP 114, Papiers Thomas, BIAM-IAMB to Albert Thomas 21 May 1917.
42 AN 94 AP 114, Papier Thomas, Alumine pour Neuhausen, 17 May 1917. Albert Thomas to Sawyer (BACO-WMB), 5 June 1917.
43 AN 94 AP 114, Alumine pour Neuhausen. Complèment Sécret, s.d. but 17 May 1917. Note sur une nuovelle usine d'aluminium en Norvège, 28 March 1916.
44 AN, 94 AP 114, Note pour le Ministre des Armements et des Fabrications de Guerre, 28 June 1917. Copie d'une note confidentielle adressée par M. Badin (peu de temps avant sa mort) à M. Pitaval, sur l'industrie de l'aluminium en France, June 1917. TNA, MUN 4/3022, Aluminium Production in Russia: question of monopoly by an American Firm, 21 March 1917.
45 TNA, MUN/5/207/1830/1-5, Non Ferrous Metals Conference, Report on Aluminium, June 1918.
46 Perchard, *Aluminiumville.*
47 Roger Chickering, *Imperial Germany and the Great War, 1914–1918.* London, Cambridge University Press, 2004, 43–46, 143–147. Rauch, *Geschichte der Huttenaluminiumindustrie*, 105–106. Knetsch, *Das Konzeneigene Bankinstitut der Metallgesellschaft*, 141–142.
48 Anne Von Steiger, 'A "German" Firm in France, AIAG during World War One', unpublished working paper, EBHA, Geneva, 2007.
49 TMA, AIAG, box 116, Huber to Schilder, 24 October 1914.
50 MGA, Juristisches Buro V-3/1 Ansfuhrungen betreffend neue Tonerde und neue Aluminiumfabriken. 9 November 1916, Besprechung betr. Vereinigte Aluminium-Werke im kleinen Sitzungssaal des Reichssochatzamt, 9 December 1916. Abt.119/813, Geschichte der Bitterfled, 220.
51 MGA, Abt. 119/814, Geschichte der VAW, 1939, 75–77. V-3/1, Alfred Merton, Denkschrift Betreffend Vereinigte Aluminium-Werke AG, Berlin, 30 October 1918.
52 Rauch, *Geschichte der Huttenaluminiumindustrie*, 117. Ruch, *Une Route Ardue pour un si Léger Métal*, 55–56.
53 Hunt T. Tooley, 'The Hindenburg Program of 1916: A Central Experiment in Wartime Planning', *Quarterly Journal of Austrian Economics*, vol. 2, no. 2, 1999, 51–62.
54 HWA, MG Documents, Juristisches Buro V-3/38, Aschrift, Kreigministerium, 3 March 1917. Walther Däbritz, *Fünfzig Jahre Metallgesellschaft, 1881–1931*, Frankfurt am Main: Metallgesellschaft, 1931, 216–217.
55 HWA, MG Documents Juristisches Buro V-3/2, Betr. Aluminium-Preis nach dem Kriege unter Zugrundelegung der Selbstkosten, 20 August 1917. V-3/1, Alfred Merton, Denkschrift Betreffend Vereinigte Aluminium-Werke AG, Berlin, 30 October 1918.
56 TNA, MUN/4/724, Swiss Neuhausen Aluminium Company, 19 January 1919.
57 RPA, 001-0-11335, Conférence avec M. Davis, 2 December 1918.
58 Cuff, *The War Industries Board*, 224–225. William Notz, 'Export Trade Problems and an American Foreign Trade Policy', *Journal of Political Economy*, vol. 26, no. 2, 1918, 105–124.
59 TNA, CAB 24/90/85, War Cabinet, Alfred Mond, Combines Bill. Memorandum from the first commissioner of works, 22 October 1919. AN, F12, 8053, Rapport général au Comité Consultatif des Arts et Manufactures, Chapitre 7, La Métallurgie de l'Aluminium, Rapport de M. Sejournet, 1919.
60 RPA, 00-2-15942, Déjeunér avec M. Davis, 15 November 1918. Note n.1 Aluminium, 9 September 1918. Note n.2 Ce que dit M. Davis (ce que dit aussi M. Baruch), 9 September 1918.
61 RPA, 001-0-11333, Marlio (PCAC) to Tait (BACO), 20 October 1920.
62

Rend pour nous moins capital l'intérêt de mettre la main sur Neuhausen puisque cela ne nous débarrassera pas des usines allemandes, et en même temps ceci doit rendre les prétentions de Neuhausen moins élevées, puisque son principal client [l'Allemagne] va lui échapper.

RPA, 001-0-11335, Note de M. Marlio, 16 January 1920.

63 RZA, Berichte über die allgemeine Geschäftslage, 1920–1939, box. 1920–1924, Berichte, 15 March 1920.

64 RPA, 001-0-11332, Louis Marlio, Note sur la crise actuelle de l'Aluminium, 2 August 1921.

65 Archives historiques du Ministrère des affaires etrangères (AHMAE), B/49/3, Note sur la bauxite et l'aluminium, March 1920. RPA, 056-00-15949, A la réunion du comité interministeriel pour la liquidation de l'industrie de guerre, 22 January 1919.

66 UGD/347/21/19/1, British Aluminium Company Annual Report, 1919. TNA, MUN/5/207/1830/1-5, Non Ferrous Metals Conference, Report on Aluminium, June 1918. CAB/24/34/91, Final Report After the War, 1917. On the specific post-war context which led to the Non-Ferrous Metal Industry Act and to the new smelter, see Perchard, *Aluminiumville*, 87–91; Ball, 'The German Octopus', 455–458.

67 Smith, *From Monopoly to Competition*, 125. Cuff, *The War Industries Board*, 229.

68 RZA, AIAG Berichte Protokolls, box. 1920–24, Bericht über die allgemeine Geschäftslage, 15 March 1920. See also Rauch, *Geschichte der Huttenaluminiumindustrie*, 106.

69 Rauch, *Geschichte der Huttenaluminiumindustrie*, 120.

70 HWA, MG Documents, V-3/1, Alfred Merton, Denkschrift Betreffend Vereinigte Aluminium-Werke AG, Berlin, 30 October 1918.

71 HWA, MG Documents, Abt. 174, Betr. Geschäftsführungsvertrag Horren-Vaw, 20 January 1920.

72 HWA, MG Documents, Abt.119/813, Geschichte der Vereinigte Aluminium Werke AG', 220–224. Rauch, *Geschichte der Huttenaluminiumindustrie*, 105–106. Manfred Pohl, *VIAG Aktiengesellschaft 1923–1998: Vom Staatsunternehmen zum Internationalen Konzern*. Munich: Piper, 1998, 28–29.

73 RAZ, AIAG Direktionen Protollen, box 1920–1923, Direktion Protokoll der 19 August 1921. Abmachungen mit Herrn Von der Porten detr. Berkauf in Deutschland.

74 Smith, *From Monopoly to Competition*, 139–142.

75 Hachez-Leroy, *L'Aluminium français*, 80–82. Cailluet, *Stratégies, Structures d'Organisation et Pratique de Gestion de Pechiney*.

# 5 The return of cartelisation

## The European Aluminium-Association, 1922–1928

Although the Allied producers maintained constant relations since the end of the war, this was not sufficient to recast an international cartel. In fact, every effort made to set a price agreement on international sales, though favoured by the bonds that AF, ALCOA, and BACO had formed during the war, could not function without the agreement of the Swiss and German producers. Even when the 'war cartel' against AIAG was set aside, it was not easy to include again the Swiss company in their framework. The relationships with AIAG had been severely compromised by the manoeuvres that AF and BACO tried against the Swiss firm. AIAG's specific situation in the global trade made things even more complicated because, having lost its main pre-war market (Germany), the Swiss firm was on the hunt for new outlets, eroding the positions of the other manufacturers. In November 1920, a first attempt at reconciliation failed because AIAG refused to enter into a price agreement that AF, BACO, and NACO were trying to implement.[1]

The reasons for delaying reconstruction of an international cartel were not only due to the poor relationships between the Allies and AIAG. The emergence of new producers in Germany required a rebuild from scratch of a new possible agreement. The same German producers were in a very problematic situation: strong monetary instability, and in particular the hyperinflation that plagued the German Mark, gave enormous advantages to German companies in the export markets without, however, guaranteeing a satisfying level of earnings and the pay-back of investments. Moreover, the presence of antagonists to the cartel in Germany, such as Giulini and Beer & Sondheimer, made any agreement with Germans more complicated. In this context, AFC and BACO worked for a rapprochement with AIAG and started some first exploratory contacts with the German producers to understand their real strength before including them in their networks.[2] Once German production was reorganised under the ownership of VIAG, the relationship among the various producers began gradually to normalise. The nationalisation of the aluminium industry in Germany had excluded Giulini from aluminium production in this country, confining it only to the small Swiss unit in Martigny. As a consequence, the international aluminium industry got rid of an uncomfortable antagonist, who would not come to terms with the other producers both for historical reasons and for its present expansion strategies. Even the liquidation of all other private interests, which had began to deal with the aluminium industry during the war, created the conditions for more manageable relations among the former belligerents. The old Allies were aware of these problems and, once they had accepted the fact that Germany would be a major producer in the post-war period, considered its nationalisation as a positive fact. As Tait pointed out to Marlio, this modified 'the situation at present in the aluminium works in Germany, which are now the property of the State, and which we understand are being worked to a reasonable capacity'.[3]

However, the international crisis of 1921 slowed any possible rapprochement. Only the end of the economic crisis created favourable conditions for a new approach of the Swiss and German groups. At the same time, the gradual normalisation of international economic relationships, with the end of export controls and the re-opening of the market, led the season of political control over strategic industries to an end. Also the re-establishment of the international monetary order worked to appease the relationships. However, the 'relational' factor behind the rapprochement of the Swiss group needed to be worked out and a new inclusive attitude had to be settled. Since 1921, Louis Marlio had become the leading exponent of the thesis according to which international cartels were no longer to be intended as an anti-German allied weapon, as they were in the immediately preceding years, but rather as a vehicle to bring together the international economy to overcome the nationalism fuelled by the war. This thesis, which would be formalised in the early 1920s by Louis Loucheur and then openly debated during the Economic Conference of the League of Nations (LoN) in 1927,[4] was the ideological substratum that motivated Louis Marlio's actions. A practical application of Loucheur's proposal was the Entente Franco-Allemande de la Potasse of 1924.[5] Marlio aimed to prove that aluminium as well would became a material for peace.

Since 1921, Marlio promoted three major operations, which were intended to re-establish strategic group solidarity and unity among the various aluminium producers. First, Marlio recognised the possibility of accelerating the international post-war recovery by sharing the technology on new uses that emerged from the war. In particular, Marlio promoted the establishment of the Association de Propagande de l'Aluminium, in order to formalise the exchange of technological information on the new uses of aluminium and to facilitate the spread of such information to users.[6] This project was intended to expand internationally what AF was doing in the country. As Florence Hachez-Leroy has shown, AF was able to transform itself into one of the most active organisations for research and new applications of aluminium and its spread among users.[7] Although the creation of such an international system was delayed by the crisis and postponed until 1927, it was one of the major creations of the aluminium cartelisation in the 1920s, which tried to institutionalise the flow of technologies among the firms.[8]

Second, Marlio used his political influence to assist an international rapprochement. In 1921, Marlio was appointed President of the Chambre Syndicale de l'industrie et électrochimique électrométallurgiques and, in this role, he served as political adviser to suggest the gradual abolition of export duties for bauxite. This operation aimed to help BACO, which imported the bulk of its mineral resources from the south of France, where it owned several mines. This was followed by strong integration with BACO that Marlio obtained in the early 1920s. The French producers were still in short supply of alumina and this deficiency would be even more severe when the French establishments of AIAG returned under the supervision of the Swiss firm. On the contrary, BACO had inherited from the war alumina production that was oversized compared to its aluminium production. AF and BACO formed an alliance so that BACO supplied AF with alumina, while the latter sent aluminium to the British firm to complete its orders.[9]

Third, Marlio promoted progressive normalisation of the relationships with the German and Swiss groups. After trying to gather information about the real strength of German production by means of intense economic intelligence, Marlio managed to create direct relationships with some German firms between the end of 1921 and the first half of 1922. Marlio succeed in meeting the heads of Metallgesellschaft and of Beer & Sondheimer, tightening relevant ties with both firms. Even if it was one of the major German firms to contribute to the war effort, Metallgesellschaft tried to overcome the conflict and rebuild the ties it used to have with the French firms. In particular, MG suggested finding new alliances with French aluminium producers proposing to negotiate some agreements on patents on very innovative alloys, such as Alpax and Silium. These alloys were made of aluminium and silicon and, for their very promising mechanical properties, were judged a key advantage for the growing outlets of aluminium into automotive industries.[10]

These alloys opened the doors to the manufacturing of die casting products in aluminium. The name of Alpax derived from Aladar Pacz, its inventor, but it seems that it was also chosen to evoke the large applications for the civil demand that this alloy could open at the end of the war (Al: aluminium; pax: peace).[11] The economic implications of aluminium and silicon alloys were very important, comparable to those of the duralumin in the early 1910s, because their spread was emerging at a time of intense expansion of the automobile industry and, more generally, the mechanical industry. The aluminium–silicon alloys allowed production of aluminium extrusions that were resistant and performing, and that could be used for the production of engine parts and chassis of vehicles. Since the early 1920s, both ALCOA and the German firms carried out intense research to develop this production. The various international registrations of patents on these alloys, that both ALCOA and MG were doing, could create friction about anteriority. AF was able to relate ALCOA and MG in the creation of an international pool of several existing patents.[12]

## The revival of international cooperation: the first general meetings

The technology agreements on aluminium–silicon alloys between MG and the old Allies enacted a first rapprochement with the Germans. Moreover, Beer & Sondheimer proved to be an important ally to manage the relationships with AIAG, helping Marlio to bring back cordial behaviour of the Swiss firm. In addition to keeping Marlio and the other firms informed about the state of the

German aluminium industry, Beer & Sondheimer also signed some agreements with AF. AF agreed to provided bauxite to the German firm to receive alumina in exchange, according to a strategy that was similar to that decided by BACO. Beer & Sondheimer was bound to a Norwegian producer (Norsk), which ALCOA was trying to take over. This operation would reduce the outlets for alumina produced by Beer & Sondheimer. Moreover, the reorganisation of the German production of aluminium left no space for this independent producer of alumina. In this situation, the proximity to the French producers turned out to be crucial to continue the business of this German producer.[13]

Thanks to the interests shared with Beer & Sondheimer, which profoundly changed its status of 'trader of the outsiders' that had characterised it before the war, AF could count on a valuable ally in managing relationships with AIAG. The German firm offered several times to help AF to renew contacts with AIAG. Although AF refused the direct mediation of Nathan Sondheimer, the information that the German firm provided about the national and international situation was crucial for the initiation of a phase of international cooperation. Nathan Sondheimer informed Marlio that during 1922 an agreement on export markets between the German producers, AIAG, and Norsk was reached. Sondheimer informed Marlio that Arnold Bloch, the new general manager of AIAG, had criticised 'les propositions d'accord émanant des négociant ou des grands marchands' and that he claimed that 'il attendait que une conversation aurait lieu entre Industriels', in order to get to manage exports to the North American market. This information was also confirmed by Richard Merton, chairman of Metallgesellschaft, who informed Marlio that AIAG would be willing to renew its relationship with AF and BACO.[14]

From this time, Marlio realised that it was the right time for a reconciliation: he arranged for AIAG to get its French properties back on favourable terms (also because now the alumina situation of the French producers was more comfortable thanks to BACO and Beer & Sondheimer supplies), while he began to work at a new international cartel proposal.[15] Thanks to this operation, AF obtained AIAG's agreement to meet up with the former members of AA in London in May 1923. As had been hoped for by both coalitions at the end of the conflict, AF, AIAG, ALCOA, and BACO negotiated an agreement, which could coordinate a common international price policy. Meanwhile, governments' control systems on the aluminium market gradually began to be cleared, along with war stock. The various measures that had accompanied the post-war conversion, such as political control on prices and exports, were also being deleted in almost all countries. The aluminium producers were persuaded that the market would soon return to its normal situation, while demand reached again the levels of the record obtained during the war.[16]

The conference in London in May 1923 marked the restart of a multilateral approach to the regulation of the aluminium market, putting an end to the continuation of the two alliances, i.e. the group of old Allies and the German–Swiss group. The directors who met in London were able to create a joint policy on international prices, which aimed to merge the agreements that had been concluded separately by AF, BACO, and NACO, on the one hand, and by AIAG,

VAW, and Norsk, on the other. Moreover, facing the new expansion of demand, the producers decided to adopt a policy of stable and moderate prices, which aimed to lower the market price for aluminium over time to promote growth of demand. In fact, it was decided to lower the 'Allied' international price of £150 per ton and raise the 'German' price of £100, suggesting a single world price of £115 per ton. Although fluctuations of the major currencies compared to British sterling would cause problems for the effective adoption of a common universal price, the firms thought that this was the first step for the revival of a cartel.[17]

In fact, at the London conference the producers also spoke openly about the re-establishment of an international cartel. The firms discussed rebuilding the old Aluminium-Association, but it was not possible to find a compromise on quotas in a possible agreement, not even on a temporary basis while waiting for the involvement of the German group in negotiations. Production capacity could not serve as a basis, because all of the firms were either in the process of increasing their capacity or were completing some important investments. Not even the sales in recent years were useful in determining quotas, because they were too altered by currency fluctuations, by the crisis, and by buffering of the war stock. Faced with these difficulties, the firms decided to postpone the formation of a cartel to 1924, and simply start a monitoring phase, during which they would schedule meetings bimonthly. Two months later, at another meeting held in Paris the producers decided to involve the German producers into these meetings and AIAG was appointed to act as an intermediary between the assembly of producers and the German group.[18] At the end of October 1923, Max Von der Porten, director of VAW, was welcomed at the third meeting of the post-war period and this fact was considered by Marlio as 'la reprise des réunions des producteurs mondiaux d'aluminium depuis la guerre'.[19]

This meeting was very important because it finally sanctioned the acceptance of VAW by the old members of AA. When in 1923 VAW was reorganised under the ownership of the German state-holding company, this firm appeared to be a reliable partner for other aluminium firms. At that time VAW also managed the production of Aluminiumwerke Bitterfeld, i.e. the unit of Metallgesellschaft–CFGE: as a consequence, participation of AIAG and VAW in the agreements represented the inclusion of 100 per cent of the German production. VAW was also ready to follow the strategy of price stability that well suited the social and economic goals that the firm wanted to reach as part of the Weimar Republic economic policy. The reason for the new management's reliability was given by the will of the German state to use the participation of its firms in the cartels taking foreign policy into consideration, which was aimed at the normalisation of Germany's position in the international post-war economy. On the one hand, the negotiations for the Dawes plan for the war reparations contributed to this goal. On the other hand, the progressive definition of Loucheur's proposal to use international cartels for economic re-integration, which was shared by the economy minister of the Weimar Republic, Rathenau, was a solid guarantee.[20]

In the original plans that had been outlined in 1923, the price agreement and its extension to German producers would revive negotiations for the formation of a real cartel. Official resumption of negotiations was expected by all European producers in 1924, also due to the good results obtained by their agreements on prices, which were gradually extended to semi-finished products. However, in the course of 1924 there was not the opportunity to recreate the Aluminium-Association and a period of waiting and impasse took over. The beginning of an investigation by the American antitrust authorities against ALCOA influenced determinedly this decision.[21] Although this investigation did not lead to legal proceedings during the 1920s, after this incident, NACO interrupted its participation in the meetings. This established a situation characterised by a strong ambiguity between the European group, which continued to meet up to coordinate its market strategies, and the American group, which abandoned the meetings and the negotiations.[22] From this moment, the Europeans alone continued reconstruction of the international cartel, which was created in 1926. ALCOA did not join it, but it did not even become an outspoken opponent.

## Cooperation and rivalry between ALCOA and the Europeans during the 1920s

The end of ALCOA's involvement in the negotiations for the cartel represented a new situation in the relationships that the American firm had with the other producers. During the war, the American firm was not only back to being a monopoly, but it had become the biggest firm in the aluminium business world, with a production capacity that was equal to the sum of the production of all other producers. The American market, which had already experienced a relevant expansion before the war, had become the largest market in the world, where new applications in the field of transport encouraged an impressive growth of domestic demand. The war had encouraged intense R&D activity on new aluminium alloys. In all countries, these new applications helped the global growth of this industry, but in the US this trend was particularly strong, because in the 1920s the automobile industry alone consumed about 40 per cent of national production.[23] The growth of this market was one of the main reasons why, at the end of the conflict, the United States became one of the main targets for exports from the oversized European enterprises.

The European firms were aware of the new strength of ALCOA and, as a consequence, they tried to start negotiations early, to which Arthur V. Davis had responded favourably since the first meetings in late 1918. In particular, Europeans were afraid of ALCOA's enormous production capacity and of the strategy of overseas expansion that ALCOA demonstrated on several occasions. Over the 1920s, Davis began to have an original vision as regards the development strategies of the aluminium industry. Unlike European firms, which mainly continued to produce metal ingots, ALCOA became the company with the strongest vertical integration towards semi-finished products. The opportunity offered by die-casting technology was considered by Davis as a method to increase not only outlets in the US, but also to extend its sales abroad. Thus, ALCOA aimed to implement integration investments to 'educate the market', as Davis declared many times to his European colleagues. This strategy also involved the creation of Foreign Selling Subsidiaries at ALCOA, with resident managers in the major markets. In London, NACO already existed before the war. During the 1920s, ALCOA also opened sales offices in Japan, Germany, and France. In France, André Henri-Couannier was appointed resident director. To summarise this strategy, Davis wrote to Kloumann, the director of Norsk:

> Even if the War is one of the main causes for the reduction of consumption, the main reason seems to be the absence of 'culture' of the European territories. These territories can be divided into two parts: a war zone and a zone that has never been cultivated and is still uncultivated at present.... We believe, however, that the wisdom shows that the aluminium industry must be revitalised in the war zone and cultivated in the uncultivated zone. While it is dangerous for everybody not to undertake this task and that starting it is profitable for the aluminium industry in general, it is still true in similar cases that the real reward will be obtained by those who fulfilled the task.[24]

Even if, according to former literature about aluminium cartelisation,[25] ALCOA was often considered a silent partner in the European cartel during the 1920s, cartel archives and ALCOA's documents suggest that the Europeans failed to include the American firm in their association. Europeans believed that ALCOA's reluctance was due only to the antitrust investigations pending against it throughout the 1920s that, even though they did not come to trial, worked as a deterrent to joining the cartel.[26] However, archive sources suggest that ALCOA had a more complex attitude towards its participation in the international cartels during the 1920s. Apart from the fear of sanctions, the study of archive documents shows that other reasons pushed ALCOA not to join the cartel and to perform a strategy of penetration in international markets that was incompatible with a cartel agreement with Europeans. As it was for the period that preceded the foundation of the Association in 1912, ALCOA had an ambivalent vision towards cartelisation because it aimed at creating room for its Canadian production. Unlike the pre-war period, ALCOA had a tougher international strategy, which in certain cases was considered hostile by the European companies.

ALCOA initially showed a collaborative attitude with the Europeans. In 1923, AFC shared the ownership of DNN, the Norwegian unit that PCAC created in 1914, with ALCOA and BACO. This company, after working to support the Allied war effort, was in a precarious situation at the beginning of the 1920s and the French owners shut it down during the international crisis, also because they ran out of alumina to supply their Norwegian unit. One year later, the three owners took over the Beer & Sondheimer alumina plant at Duisburg, in order to supply DNN, and restarted its production.[27] In 1924, AFC offered participation in its Italian investments both to ALCOA and AIAG, that was accepted only by ALCOA.[28] One year later, the French company invested in Spain, trying again to settle a joint venture with BACO, AIAG, and ALCOA, which was called Aluminio Espagnol (AE). While BACO refused, AIAG and ALCOA joined the scheme.[29] Although they were often considered synonymous with cartelisation,[30] joint ventures have not the same strength as an official cartel with quotas and established rules concerning

*Table 5.1* International joint ventures, 1923–1925.

| Firms | Country | Production capacity (tons) | Year | Shares in % | | | | | |
|---|---|---|---|---|---|---|---|---|---|
| | | | | AFC | ALCOA | BACO | AIAG | VAW | Total |
| SNN | Norway | 16,000 | 1923 | 33.33 | 33.33 | 33.33 | – | – | 99.99 |
| AI | Italy | 2,000 | 1924 | 50.00 | 50.00 | – | – | – | 100.00 |
| AE | Spain | 1,200 | 1925 | 33.33 | 33.33 | – | 33.33 | – | 99.99 |

Source: author's elaboration from various files in RPA.

outputs and markets. Actually, the draftsman of these ventures, Louis Marlio, claimed that the final goal of these ventures was to create stronger bonds to help the creation of a cartel, not to substitute its formation.[31]

However, these collaborations were contradicted by other aggressive strategies of the American giant, which showed a certain ambiguity in ALCOA's actions. In the early 1920s, ALCOA gained control over some bauxite deposits in Italy, Yugoslavia, and France. As we have seen, ALCOA took control of Norsk in 1923. In 1925, ALCOA also took over some hydroelectric facilities in France. Three years later it invested in alternative alumina technologies in Italy, forestalling the French firms and some Italian interests. In 1926, ALCOA started expansion abroad for semi-finished products production. It took over Birmingham Aluminium Castings, an important British producer of alloys. In 1927, ALCOA tried unsuccessfully to buy one-third of Vereinigte Leichtmetall Werke (VLW), the semi-finished division of VAW and Aluminium Werke. Afterward, it incorporated Aluminium Die Casting in Nuremberg, entering Germany into the semi-finished aluminium business. In the same year, it also purchased half of the stock of Fonderies de Précision from AF, an important French producer of alloys. Finally, in 1928, a joint venture with Sumitomo in the fabricating branch was formed in Japan.[32]

In his pre-eminent history of ALCOA, George Smith suggested three reasons that underpinned this intense foreign expansion. First, Smith explains that many of these European assets were sold at discount prices, because of financial liabilities derived from post-war economic disorders and because of the relative strength of the American dollar. Second, ALCOA wanted to penetrate the European market to elude growing national protectionism. Third, thanks to these acquisitions, ALCOA wanted to take control over imports to the United States.[33] However, these explanations appear questionable, at least for the period that followed 1924. In 1927, ALCOA tried to buy VLW's shares at a 400 per cent premium, and other assets were paid at their nominal costs.[34] Italian alternative technologies were expensive, although they were often claimed in scientific milieux as technical 'absurdities'.[35] The American market was already well protected by the anti-dumping legislation enacted in 1922 and by high tariffs that in 1921 replaced the more liberal pre-war duties.[36] Finally, ALCOA had scale economies large enough to undercut European suppliers, which benefited less from political protection after 1925, as it was showed.[37]

Here it is suggested that ALCOA's hostile international activities were linked to a gargantuan project in Canada that demanded a repositioning of the American firm in the global markets and, consequently, in the international oligopoly. During this repositioning, ALCOA was not willing to enter cartel agreements with Europeans and tried to extend its outlets at their expense. This is the main cause that forced ALCOA not to join the cartel. In 1924, Arthur V. Davis was informed about the construction of a huge power scheme in Canada to produce aluminium. The outstanding electric firm Duke & Price incorporated a new company with the involvement of some important North American consumers of this metal, such as Bausch Machines Tool and Ford Motor Company. They formed a new company, the International Aluminum Company Ltd, of which George D. Haskell of Bausch Machine Tool was the chairman, and William B. Mayo, a Ford engineer expert in hydroelectric matters, its technical director.[38] Davis succeeded in stopping this competitor in 1925 when Duke agreed to merge with ALCOA.[39]

However, the output of the smelter inherited from the merger, Arvida, whose name stands for the initials of AR(thur) VI(nig) DA(vis), was too large for the given outlets. Its capacity of 40,000 tons per year made this smelter the world's biggest aluminium unit at that time. Its arrival overturned the global demand–supply balance of the North American market and demanded the repositioning of ALCOA in the global context. The problem with ALCOA's investment strategy was that it had been implemented in a period of general over-investments undertaken during the euphoric 1920s. Even in Europe, producers were trying to increase their exports to the US, a market in which ALCOA was also expanding its outputs. ALCOA's executives knew that they had been on the verge of a crisis of overproduction since 1926, when Moritz, the director of NACO, wrote to Davis

> I'm quite convinced that we are now at the beginning of an era of overproduction of aluminum not only in so far as our Company is concerned, but also an account of the fact that European companies are increasing their production ... I fear the matter of disposing of all of our product in the future is going to be a very serious problem, and I am strongly of the opinion that small fabricating plants will assist us very materially in controlling the general situation.[40]

As a consequence, it is debatable whether ALCOA did not reach a cartel agreement with the Europeans only for antitrust considerations. The antitrust menace played an important role in the American firm's behaviour, but ALCOA needed to have the freedom also to perform the above-mentioned hostile investments in order either to assist imports from Canada or to manoeuvre political powers to set favourable tariffs. This strategy was already outlined before 1924, when ALCOA started its foreign investments and planned to extend its capacity in fabricating units, but the merger with Duke accelerated it, because of the huge new capacity inherited by the takeover of the new Canadian unit at Arvida. Before Arvida started, the United States needed to import to fulfil demands. Afterward, this changed dramatically, as shown in Table 5.2.

Table 5.2 The American market during the 1920s: inner production, European imports, and prices

| | North America | | National prices | | | | | Aluminium Association | | |
|---|---|---|---|---|---|---|---|---|---|---|
| | Total production, US + Canada | US demand | US price | | US tariff | | | Production | Imports in US | AA price |
| | | | ¢/lb | £/t | ¢/lb | £/t | | | | £/t |
| 1925 | 77,100 | 80,000 | 27.18 | 126.50 | 5.00 | 23.27 | | 106,736 | 14,000 | 110 |
| 1926 | 84,500 | 106,000 | 26.99 | 124.40 | 5.00 | 23.27 | | 94,600 | 16,000 | 105 |
| 1927 | 112,700 | 100,000 | 25.40 | 117.00 | 5.00 | 23.27 | | 93,660 | 13,500 | 105 |
| 1928 | 136,000 | 124,000 | 23.90 | 110.00 | 5.00 | 23.27 | | 99,414 | 7,200 | 95 |
| 1929 | 144,800 | 137,000 | 23.90 | 110.00 | 5.00 | 23.27 | | 106,331 | 8,500 | 95–85 |
| 1930 | 144,000 | 95,000 | 18.77 | 86.38 | 4.00 | 18.61 | | 100,536 | 5,500 | 85 |

Source: author's elaboration from various files in RPA and HHC.

## The foundation of the new European Aluminium-Association

In 1926, the European firms alone formed a cartel, called the Aluminium-Association (hereafter AA). AIAG convinced AF and the other member to implement a formal cartel without the Americans following two considerations. AIAG emerged from the Great War as one of the most internationalised companies within the oligopoly and it had a clear vision about the tendencies that were reshaping the international aluminium market during the mid-1920s.[41] First, the new smelters that were planned at the end of Great War, such as those of VAW and BACO, were almost completed. Meanwhile, some companies also began to engage in strategies to improve their international position in view of the upcoming negotiations. AIAG in 1925 increased its production capacity in Switzerland and decided to invest in Italy, entering into a relationship with political and economic interests linked to the development of the industrial zone of Porto Marghera, near Venice.[42] VAW also took an interest in Italy, and proposed to form a joint venture with Montecatini, the leading chemical company in the country, to take advantage of a new process for the production of alumina, the Haglund, which was used to replace coal and caustic soda used in the Bayer process with an electrolytic reduction of bauxite.[43] In this context of investments and of starting new outputs, firms aimed to fix quotas to avoid the disruption of European demand–supply balance.

Second, the re-opening of international trade after the re-establishment of the international payment system put an end to the former protections. Producers aimed to manage this transition with the support of a cartel to implement the former price agreements. In 1925 import under licence established in the UK by the Non-Ferrous Metal Bill ended, control on the aluminium trade in France was also over, and in Germany VAW ceased to control the entire national production, because the Bitterfeld unit came back to Metallgesellschaft–CFGE.[44] In 1925, CFGE became part of the big German chemical *Konzern* IG Farben: also this transformation was seen with anxieties by the cartel members, who feared that IG Farben, as a new powerful organisation, would modify the balance of powers in the German aluminium industry, expanding its activities in this metal's production.[45] In turn, German production was also threatened by the return of imports, because there were strong pressures from big business consumers of aluminium (steel industry and electrical industry) to eliminate quotas on the import of non-ferrous metals.[46] In the summer of 1926, AIAG observed that these concomitant transformations of the global aluminium economy were making the former agreements on prices unworkable. As a consequence, the Swiss firm proposed to the other European companies to settle a real cartel as soon as possible, in order to handle the situation.[47]

Since the cartel provided a reliable statistical survey that allowed forecasting of market trends, it was considered useful to set optimal output rates in this context of growth. Furthermore, the market quotas allotted by the cartel imposed equilibration of sale, determining some improvements to the agreements on prices. This meant that, if a member exceeded its quota, it was compelled to buy metal from the others.[48] In any case, after two years of frequent meetings a cartel was in the air and, as was observed by an attentive international observer, 'the creation of the new aluminium cartel represent[ed] another step in the on-going process that, long the last month, is linking again the principal European countries with a grid of international economic agreements'.[49] However, AA was also a crucial entrepreneurial action for Europeans, which, since 1923, had oriented many of their investments looking at this goal. Producers had been preparing the resettlement of a cartel since their first reunion in London in 1923, when they decided that installed capacities were a 'barometer' for measuring the effective strength of firms. As a consequence, Europeans firms invested in new capacities to be ready when the cartel would be re-cast. In some cases, they also invested abroad, like AIAG and VAW, which both became leading integrated producers in Italy, and AFC, AIAG, and ALCOA, which did in Spain. When the Aluminium-Association was formed in September 1926, the producers did not forget their former discussions, and used the sales of 1925 to bargain quotas because, due to the extraordinary commercial record of this year, they corresponded to the closest figure to scale outputs.[50] The evolution of capacities and quotas are shown in Table 5.3.

The European cartel was formed with a contractual duration of only two years, which was shorter than the five year average of the interwar period.[51] This choice aimed at allowing the Americans to join the cartel when its antitrust concerns were fixed. Actually, in October 1926, Marlio was appointed by the other European firms to investigate Mortiz (ALCOA's delegate in Great Britain, and director of NACO), who refused to join the cartel due to antitrust reasons. However, Mortiz claimed that Davis wanted to follow European prices and hoped that Europeans did the same in the US market. The strong links that ALCOA had with European companies, thanks to the direct frequency of contact or joint ventures, were judged sufficient for the Europeans to believe that ALCOA would have been informally following cartel policies, in spite of the refusal to participate in their cartel. Europeans also obtained oral engagement that ALCOA would have reduced its production to make room for European exports into the US. This belief shaped the life of AA, until the moment in which, as we will see, the situation deteriorated as a consequence of ALCOA's foreign expansion, that was outlined above.[52]

Louis Marlio tried to manage the ambiguous relations between the European and American producers. As foremost a business diplomat, he believed that a minimal and short-lived cartel suited this waiting situation about American participation in the cartel.[53] Although it lasted two years, the European producers decided to model the new cartel after the Aluminium-Association of 1912, with a *comité* of eight members (two for each firm) and an assembly that approved of the *comité*'s decisions by a majority.[54] Unlike 1912, ad hoc offices were not created, but the management of statistics and documentation was entrusted to AIAG, which proved to be the most international firm of the group. This did not mean a return to the time when the cartel was the mere expression of AIAG's strategies. Each of the four companies would play an important operative role in the cartel, which was managed as a collegial and reciprocal organisation. Marlio,

*Table 5.3* The aluminium industry during the 1920s: the evolution of capacities of European and American producers, Aluminium–Association quotas (tons and %), 1919–1929, and production in 1929

| AA | Capacity 1919 | | Capacity 1926 | | AA | Capacity 1928 | | AA | Production 1929 | |
|---|---|---|---|---|---|---|---|---|---|---|
| | tons | % | tons | % | 1926 % | tons | % | 1928 % | tons | % |
| AF | 30,000 | 34.5 | 33,000 | 31.1 | 33.1 | 39,500 | 28.8 | 31.0 | 32,778 | 29.5 |
| AIAG | 20,000 | 23.0 | 25,000 | 23.6 | 23.8 | 33,000 | 24.1 | 22.4 | 25,701 | 23.2 |
| BACO | 12,000 | 13.8 | 17,000 | 16.0 | 16.0 | 29,000 | 21.2 | 18.0 | 19,932 | 18.0 |
| VAW | 25,000 | 28.7 | 31,000 | 29.2 | 27.1 | 34,000 | 24.9 | 22.6 | 32,520 | 29.3 |
| Total | 87,000 | 100.0 | 106,000 | 99.9 | 100.0 | 136,500 | 100.0 | 100.0 | 110,931 | 100.0 |

| ALCOA | Tons | % | Tons | % | | Tons* | % | | Tons** | % |
|---|---|---|---|---|---|---|---|---|---|---|
| USA | 90,000 | 90.0 | 80,000 | 61.5 | – | 105,000 | 61.8 | – | 102,100 | 65.0 |
| Canada | 10,000 | 10.0 | 40,000 | 30.8 | – | 50,000 | 29.4 | – | 42,700 | 27.2 |
| Europe | 0 | 0 | 10,000 | 7.7 | – | 15,000 | 8.8 | – | 12,300 | 7.8 |
| Total | 100,000 | 100.0 | 130,000 | 100.0 | – | 170,000 | 100.0 | – | 157,100 | 100.0 |
| World | 187,000 | – | 236,000 | – | – | 306,500 | – | – | 268,031 | 100.0 |

Source: author's elaboration from various files in RPA and HHC.

Note
ALCOA's data are indicative; * before ALTED incorporation; ** Canada and Europe are controlled by ALTED in 1929.

from AFC, was named president, Pollen, from BACO, vice president, AIAG, as already mentioned, was charged with the task of managing statistics in its office in Neuhausen, and Von der Porten, from VAW, with the task of auditing.[55]

The contract provided that there would be neither sales agencies in common, nor the territorial division of sales. AA would only ensure that each firm would sell its annual share respecting the selling price fixed by the cartel and, in the case where a company breached the sales, every three months there would be a rebalancing in order to meet the assigned quotas. This rebalancing operation would be carried out through methods that would be decided from time to time but which allegedly foresaw the purchase or the sale of metal amongst the firms of the cartel. The firms that made more sales than was allocated by their quotas would purchase from the firms which are in deficit. The price of these operations would be lower than that of AA (a price defined 'rebalancing price'). In this way, the 'rebalancing price' represented the lower limit for market quotations, which worked as a guarantee to avoid unfair attitudes of the cartel members. However, the new AA was shaped by a certain instability: it was recognised that also the quotas were modifiable after two years, because the plants of BACO, of AIAG, of VAW, and of the French, which were planned since 1923, would be completed. This need for instability was created to leave the door open to ALCOA, which could decide to join the agreement afterwards. The Europeans considered this to be cohesive enough to make the agreement work even with this fragile ground.[56]

These choices were instrumental to the situation of emergency that accompanied the formation of the cartel: firms feared that a decline in sales and the consequent accumulation of unsold stock would further alienate the possibility of forming a cartel. As a consequence, they tried to create a cartel as soon as possible with the idea, on the one hand, of making decisions on production and management of stock in the immediate future and, on the other, to improve the agreement on the way.[57] Right after the formation of the cartel, the European firms tried to manage the risk of overproduction. Consequently, they decided to lower the selling prices of ingots from £115, i.e. the standard price adopted in 1923 during the meetings, to £105, also lowering the prices of semi-finished products and also setting prices for alloys. In addition to setting a price in sterling, which was valid for all markets, AA decided to fix prices in national currencies as well, so that the price was not affected by the fluctuation of currencies.[58] One of the innovations in the management of the new cartel was integration of the analysis of stock as data in order to better understand and manage the market. In fact, the members of AA also exchanged information on the global stock that was accumulated during 1926, offering a coordination of sales to gradually clear them reducing the production. In October 1926 it was calculated that the various members of the cartel owned the metal reserves shown in Table 5.4, and programmes for their clearance were established in 1927.

By means of central management of stock, AA was trying to prevent market instability, which would create a speculative trend in sales.[59] It is not possible to determine why and what were the reasons that led the different firms to choose to clear their stock to varying degrees, but it is clear that the firms were affected

*Table 5.4* Stocks held by AA's members in 1926 and to be buffered in 1927 (tons and %)

| Firm | Sales 1925 (A)* | | Stocks 1926 (B) (tons) | B/A (%) | Stocks to be buffered in 1927 (C) (tons) | C/B (%) |
|---|---|---|---|---|---|---|
| | Tons | % | | | | |
| AIAG | 25,426 | 23.8 | 8,800 | 34.61 | 4,450 | 50.56 |
| VAW | 28,736 | 27.1 | 5,493 | 19.11 | 5,160 | 93.93 |
| AF | 35,366 | 33.1 | 2,900 | 8.19 | 2,260 | 77.93 |
| BACO | 17,007 | 16.0 | 3,627 | 21.32 | 1,417 | 39.06 |
| Total | 106,736 | 100.0 | 20,820 | 19.50 | 13,797 | 66.26 |

Source: author's elaboration from various files in RPA, 00-2-19540.

differently by the drop in demand. While AF was able to maintain an acceptable level of stock in 1926, VAW and BACO had too much stock and AIAG was in a very delicate situation. In fact, the accumulation of stock by AIAG was particularly fearsome for all the other aluminium firms: since AIAG did not have a defined national market, this firm could have represented a threat to all international markets.[60]

The cartel of 1926 was endowed with another important innovation compared to previous experiences. In 1927, a common organisation of R&D was founded: the Bureau International de Propaganda et Reinsignements (BIEP) in the form of an independent agency based in Paris.[61] BIEP was a direct continuation of the projects Marlio and Tait created at the end of the war. The difficult business situation that was arising because of too many investments, again created problems similar to those at the end of the war, i.e. finding new outlets thanks to intensive research. From a purely operational plan, the cartel also became the driving force for scientific and technological research and the spread of new technologies among the members, planning studies on the applications of the metal, and carrying out sectorial analyses. These operations were considered useful to spread, in a better way, technical knowledge about aluminium applications, which would lead more consumers to choose aluminium in substitution of other metals. The creation of BIEP confirms Baumol's thesis that cartelisation can stimulate innovation, which in turn can function as an instrument of cohesion for the members of a cartel.[62]

BIEP worked as follows: the office was divided into sections corresponding to the industry that used aluminium (i.e. automobile, electrical industry, food industry, etc.), and within each section the directors of the R&D departments of each firm met to create a kind of agenda on the topics to be discussed, the various problems of how to expand uses, and technical solutions to find new applications for the metal. Research was divided among the members of BIEP, that later compiled summary reports. BIEP also undertook a thorough standardisation of all alloys which, until then, had lacked a certain nomenclature, and their composition was based on the almost artisanal savoir-faire of the foundries. Moreover, in addition to these sections the 'propaganda' section was also formed and was in charge of promoting competition, taking part in exhibitions, and dividing the cost of publication of brochures and manuals designed to increase demand among the members.[63]

## The European Aluminium-Association and the outsiders

To provide more effective control on overproduction, AA adopted a consistent policy of control over the outsiders that still existed in the aluminium business. Compared to the period before the war, in the 1920s Giulini had a much weaker position and was almost cast out from the production of aluminium after the nationalisation of VAW.[64] After the war, Giulini could no longer count on obtaining big markets outside Germany. All of the firms had already integrated production so they no longer depended on his supplies. However, Giulini was also freer from the foreign aluminium producers because, when VAW was reorganised, he was able to negotiate important annual supplies, which absorbed the bulk of its production.[65] While Giulini's alumina production was to some extent integrated in the post-war configuration of the German aluminium industry, the smelter that Giulini still controlled in Martigny was considered a possible threat for the cartel. This smelter started production again in 1925 with a theoretical production capacity of 1,800 tons per year. During the creation of AA, the cartel members asked AIAG to enter into negotiations to convince Mermod, the director of this unit, to sell his entire production to AIAG, which would use it as part of its cartel quota, but this attempt failed.[66] In the same way, VAW was asked to negotiate a similar agreement with Stern & Hafferl Steeg, a small Austrian producer that was also called 'Lissauer'. This small actor had a theoretical maximum capacity of 600 tons per year and, even though it was created during the First World War, it started to produce only during the 1920s thanks to alumina supplied by Giulini.[67] VAW managed to sign a contract to buy up to 600 tons per year all the aluminium that it could not to sell at a cartel price on the market. In return Steeg would not expand its production capacity and would not provide metal to firms outside the cartel. One last case of the control strategy of the outsiders was represented by a similar agreement between BACO and ALCOR.[68]

In the three above-mentioned cases, the new AA behaved very differently from the old AA of 1912. Before the war, all the outsiders were forced to join the cartel after a long period of crisis and decline in sales prices, with second-class participation with fewer rights and without decision-making capacity. In the new association, the four major European firms considered it more useful to forge a strong bond of cooperation among them and monitor the firms through external agreements, which in broad terms provided the purchase of metal at prices lower than those of AA for average durations. While the cartel members considered these actions useful to make the price policy effective, because they avoided marginal sales that would have affected the global price, the outsiders also considered them partially advantageous. That ensured them a production scale without spending to much on marketing. Taking over their sales, AA controlled the international market, monitoring the effectiveness of its stable prices policy. Europeans acted this way also because they believed they could export part of this metal to the US, where ALCOA promised to make room for their sales. Also other markets were considered 'safety valves' for these sales, such as Japan or the UK, where BACO could not meet growing domestic demand with its own capacities.[69]

The cartel also carried out a specific policy for Metallgesellschaft. This firm agreed to include the production of Aluminiumwerke Bitterfeld into VAW's quota during the negotiations for the 1926 cartel. As we have seen, MG already had good relationships with the various aluminium producers from the period that preceded the revitalisation of international meetings, thanks to its policy on special aluminium alloys and silicon. Metallgesellschaft also collaborated with VAW in the field of special alloys of aluminium, for which they had formed a joint venture in Horrem. In addition, Metallgesellschaft was part of VLW, along with VAW, Thyssen, Krupp, and Berg & Selve.[70] Thus, the management of Bittereld's participation in the cartel was relatively simple: this production unit would be part of a unique German group with VAW, which would then distribute the respective quotas independently. These quotas were fixed following the reached production capacities, i.e. 85 per cent for VAW and 15 per cent for Bitterfeld.[71]

With the constant monitoring of stock and control on the production of European outsiders, AA was considered to be in a position of controller for the global market. The Europeans tried to bring the European production surplus to a level that did not exceed the absorption capacity of the American market and other export markets. In fact, selling on export markets was the only way to stabilise growing overproduction, which would be even greater in the near future when all investments were completed. For this reason, European firms tried to collaborate with ALCOA even after the creation of the cartel, in order to clear increasing amounts of metal in the US market.

## ALCOA and the Association: a slow rift

Although European firms aimed at cooperation with the American enterprise, the relationship between Europeans and ALCOA progressively degenerated after the creation of AA. ALCOA's strategy could not be easily reconciled with the persistence of imports in the American market by European firms. The balance between production and demand in the North American continent, as shown in Table 5.2, was deeply changing when the Arvida smelter started its operations. Underestimating the extent of this change, the European firms tried to negotiate a fixed quota of exports to the United States several times; in fact, according to their calculations it would have to consist of 20,000 tons per year – this figure was equivalent to the exports to this country in 1926 to be sold at the same price as ALCOA's. At the end of 1926, the European firms charged Marlio with negotiating with ALCOA a quota for the American market that was close to that figure.[72]

After the failure of this proposal, at first the Europeans restricted their sales prospects to 16,000 tons per year in total, but they decided to underquote ALCOA's price of 0.50 cents per pound, so as to try to force cartel sales in the US. Along with this tactic, AA also decided to reduce its production to 85 per cent of capacity, because the European firms feared that the result of the reduction in imports in the United States, which was concomitant with the agreements with the outsiders, would start a trend of excess of supply over demand.[73] As a reply, ALCOA then began to sell some amounts of semi-finished products at very low prices, below the price that the cartel had set for the metal ingot, which was about £100 per ton on German and English markets. At the end of 1927, AA tried to renegotiate exports to the American market with ALCOA limiting them to 4,000 tons for the first semester, but this did not eliminate the competition of the American semi-finished products in Europe, which, starting in February 1928, appeared more and more as a provocation by the American group to AA. Marlio tried several times to communicate with Davis, but he did not get any kind of warranty and Davis proved to be very skilled at buying time with AA's proposals.[74]

In the course of 1928, during the meetings of the cartel, a debate started on what to do about American competition in the semi-finished products market and how to expand sales in Europe. The members of AA took several measures to make special discounts to promote the extension of demand. First of all, AA decided to allow AF to enjoy special discounts for sales to be made to car companies in France (£1 per ton). Moreover, AA allowed VAW and AIAG to make additional discounts (£2 per ton) on large supplies of aluminium required by AEG and Siemens, both equal to 1,500 tons, for the manufacture of electric cables. In addition, in February, they decided to implement a policy of discount for exports to the semi-finished products industry: manufacturers, in fact, agreed to repay £10 per ton to rolling mills and foundries for the sales which were made on export markets, so as to help them fight against the offensive of ALCOA.[75]

However, these measures were not sufficient to handle the new situation that was arising. In May 1928, AA decided to lower the standard price for the sale of metal from £105 per ton to £95 per ton, also gradually reducing prices for all the semi-finished products. The relationship problems that AA was having with ALCOA in the field of semi-finished products forced the European firms to fix prices for these products as well. This was possible thanks to the fact that almost all firms had made decisive steps towards a robust strategy of vertical integration during the interwar period. A single negotiator was not desirable due to the fact that they controlled the chain of downstream production, which allowed the aluminium firm to form agreements similar to those in the steel industry, where, along with a cartel on general ingots, prices and quotas for the main semi-finished products were set as well.[76] These measures had the effect of increasing the sales of metal ingots in Europe and reducing the quota allotted to exports in the United States, as described in Table 5.5.

Europeans tried also in vain to force ALCOA to join their cartel, when it was due to be renewed in 1928, by means of competitive prices in the American market. For instance, the Association initially underquoted ALCOA's price in 1927, then agreed to follow the American price considering this choice an act of goodwill to force ALCOA into their agreement.[77] The original idea to fix the duration of AA to only two years turned out to be senseless, because ALCOA systematically refused all of the proposals of AA. However, this short duration of the cartel had two weak points, which had a negative influence over the international situation of the aluminium industry. First, Europeans made investments that were oriented to negotiate bigger quotas during the cartel renewal of 1928,

Table 5.5 European production, consumption, and exports in the US, 1926–1928 (tons and %)

| | Production AA | Production Europe | AA price | European consumption | AA's exports to US | | | | |
| | | | | | Total | AF | BACO | VAW | AIAG |
|------|---------|---------|---------|---------|--------|-------|-------|-------|-------|
| 1926 | 94,600  | 110,800 | 110–105 | 78,100  | 20,000 | n.a.  | n.a.  | n.a.  | n.a.  |
| 1927 | 93,660  | 108,037 | 105     | 93,600  | 13,500 | 2,300 | 4,300 | 3,000 | 3,900 |
| 1928 | 99,414  | 119,363 | 105–95  | 103,600 | 7,200  | 1,200 | 2,500 | 500   | 3,000 |
| 1929 | 106,331 | 131,506 | 95      | 122,300 | 8,500  | 1,700 | 3,500 | 800   | 2,500 |

Source: author's elaboration from various files in RPA, 00-2-19540.

even above market possibilities (see Table 5.3). Second, the wait for ALCOA shows a low-profile policy, which made the Association un-enterprising at the mercy of American actions.[78] From the archive documents of the cartel and the minutes of the meetings of the European producers, it is clear that European firms were in a difficult situation due to the attitude of the American company. In March 1928, Davis had told Marlio that he considered the formation of the cartel and its strategy of low prices as a 'war machine' against ALCOA and that is why the American company could not agree to enter into negotiations with the Europeans. Two months later, Marlio had learned that ALCOA was equipping a dam for hydroelectric power generation in France, in Valle d'Aspe, for the production of 3000 tons per year of aluminium.[79]

In spite of the Association's actions to force ALCOA's participation in their cartel, or at least to consent to an agreement over European exports in the United States, ALCOA always refused AA's proposals. In June 1928, Aluminium Limited (ALTED) was formed as a Canadian holding company to take over all of ALCOA's foreign activities.[80] Its creation is often presented a mere escamotage to bypass American antitrust law and to enter into agreements with the Europeans. On the contrary, an internal history of ALCOA argued that the formation of ALTED was also linked to a long-run strategy of the American firm to penetrate the British market. Recently, Andrew Perchard argued that this strategy also aimed to assist imperial defence programmes of the British government with a more comfortable Canadian nationality.[81] From the standpoint of our narration, it is important to state that ALTED did not immediately join a cartel with the Europeans and its actions exacerbated ALCOA's hostile policies, which disrupted the formerly cordial relationships between ALCOA and the Europeans. Actually, in June 1928, when ALTED was formed, Marlio broke the news to Murray-Morrison, general manager of BACO, declaring that probably this event would make 'les rapports plus faciles entre les filiales américaines et les producteurs européens'. However, he did not come forward with an upcoming participation of ALTED in the cartel.[82]

## Notes

1 RPA, 001-0-11333, Tait (BACO) to Marlio (AF), 17 November 1920.
2 RPA, 001-0-11333, Marlio (AF) to Murray-Morrison (BACO), 7 March 1921.
3 RAP, 001-0-11332, Tait (BACO) to Marlio (AF), 26 October 1920.
4 About Loucheur's proposal and LoN conference, see Terushi Hara, 'La Conférence Économique Internationale de 1927 et ses Effets sur la Formation des Cartels Internationaux', in Barjot (ed.), *International Cartels*, 265–272. Dominique Barjot, 'Les Cartels, une Voie vers l'Intégration Européenne? Le Role de Louis Loucheur (1872–1931)', *Revue Economique*, Vol. 64, No. 6, 2013, 1043–1066. About LoN conference see also Eric Bussière, 'La SDN, les Cartels et l'Organisation Économique de l'Europe Entre les Deux Guerres', in Barjot (ed.), *International Cartels*, 273–283.
5 About the potash agreement, see Schröter, 'The International Potash Syndicate'.
6 RPA, 001-0-11332, Marlio, Propagande de l'Aluminium, 1921.
7 Hachez-Leroy, *L'Aluminium français*.
8 Bertilorenzi, 'Big Business, Inter-Firm Cooperation and National Governments'.
9 RPA, 001-0-11332, Marlio (AF) to Tait (BACO), 15 September 1920. Tait (BACO) to Guignard (AF), 26 November 1920.

10  RPA, 001-1-11332, Metallbank und Metallurgischegesellschaft Metallgesellschaft in Frankfurt, 17 December 1921.

11  Léon Guillet, 'Un Nouvel Alliage d'Aluminium: L'Alpax', *Le Génie Civil*, 1923, 23; 'Les Progrès et les Avantages de la Construction Métallique en Aviation', *Revue de l'Aluminium*, no. 1, 1924, 8–9. Graham, Pruitts, *R&D for Industry*, 131–132, 139.

12  HHC, ALCOA, MSS#282, US v. ALCOA, Equity, 73–85, Exhibits, ex. 1086, Arthur V. Davis to Eduard K. Davis (ALCOA), 2 November 1923. RPA, 001-5-19036, Arthur V. Davis (ALCOA) to Marlio (AF), 19 September 1923.

13  RPA, 001-1-11332. Conversation de M. Marlio avec M. Sondheimer, 20 July 1922. Resumé de la conversation de M. Louis Marlio avec M. Nathan Sondheimer, 12 October 1922.

14  RPA, 001-1-11332, Renseignements recueillis par M. Marlio au cours de la tournée à Frankfort le 19 et 20 juin 1922. Compte-Rendu de la visite de M. Sondheimer à M. Marlio, 24 July 1922.

15  RPA, 001-0-11332, Marlio (AF) to Schindler (AIAG), 12 October 1922. Note historiques et renseignements pour M. Bouchayer sur nos rélations avec Neuhausen, 20 September 1922. RPA, 001-0-11333, Mortiz (NACO) to Marlio (AF), 4 May 1923. Revisions des contingents AA, 17 July 1922.

16  RPA, 001-0-11335, A.V. Davis (ALCOA) to Marlio (AF), 14 March 1923. Mortiz (NACO) to Marlio (AF), 4 May 1923. UGA, UGD/347/21/19/1, Annual Reports of the British Aluminium Company Ltd, 1923, TNA, CAB/24/160/15, Board of Trade advisory council, 26 April 1923.

17  RPA, 00-2-15940, Minutes of Meeting held at the offices of the British Aluminum Company Limited on Friday, 11 May 1923. RPA, 00-2-15942, Murray-Morrison (BACO) to Marlio (AF), 25 May 1923.

18  RPA, 00-2-15940, Reunion à Londres du 11 mai 1923, Deuxième Séance, 15 h 1/2. Procès-Verbal de la réunion tenue à l'Aluminium-Français, 6 July 1923.

19  RPA, 00-2-15940, Conférence des producteurs de Zurich, 23 October 1923.

20  RPA, 00-2-15942, Dalmais (AF) to Murray Morrison (Baco), 18 July 1923.

21  Aluminum Co. of America v. Federal Trade Commission, Circuit Court of Appeals, Third Circuit, June 24, 1924, no. 2721. About ALCOA legal problems during 1920s, see Waller, 'The Story of Alcoa', 125.

22  The last meeting at which a NACO representantive (Esperson) was present was one in April 1924. RPA, 00-2-15940, Agreement decided upon at a meeting held in London on Friday, 4 April 1924.

23  Wallace, *Market Control*, 60–61.

24  
   Quoiqu'il soit vrai que la Guerre est une des grandes causes de la réduction de la consommation, la raison principale semble être l'absence de 'culture' (cultivation) des territoires européens. Ces territoires peuvent être divisé en deux parties: une zone de guerre et une zone n'ayant jamais cultivée et à l'heure actuelle encore inculte…. Nous croyons cependant que la sagesse indique que l'industrie de l'aluminium doit être revivifié dans la zone de guerre et cultivé dans la zone inculte. Alors qu'il est dangereux pour tous de ne pas entreprendre cette tâche et que l'entreprendre est profitable à l'industrie de l'aluminium en général, il est encore vrai en pareil cas que la récompense réelle revient à ceux qui ont accompli le travail.

   RPA, 001-0-11333, Extrait d'une lettre de Mr. Arthur V. Davis to Mr. S. Kloumann en date du 23 mars 1923.

25  Muller, *Light Metals Monopoly*, 115–118, Watkins, 'Aluminum Alliance', 251–252.

26  Waller, 'The Story of Alcoa', 121–143.

27  RPA, 001-0-11333, Marlio, Note sur la SNN, March 1922. UGD, 347/21/35/6/2, BACO, Murray-Morrison (BACO), Report on visit to Norway and Inspection of Det Norske Nitrid Company's factories, June 1922. See also Bonfils, 'Pechiney au pays des Vikings', 18–42, Storli, Brégaint, 'The Ups and Downs', 763–790.

28  RPA, 056-00-12347, Note sur l'industrie de l'Aluminium in Italie, 21 June 1924. Marlio, Memorandum pour Davis, 16 July 1924. PV de la réunion du lundi 25 aout 1924, Alluminio Italiano. See also Bertilorenzi, 'The Italian Aluminium', 43–72.
29  RZA, AIAG Berichte Protokolls, 1925–1928, Bericht über die allgemeine Geschäftslage, 29 December 1925. RPA, 072-1-9589, Pollen (BACO) to Davis (ALCOA) and Marlio (AF), 9 December 1925. About Spain, see René Bonfils, 'Pechiney en Espagne, 1925–1985', *Cahiers d'Histoire de l'Aluminium*, no. 38–39, 2007, 77–101. About post-1945 developments, see also Ludovic Cailluet, Matthias Kipping, 'Ménage à Trois: Alcan in Spain, 1950s to 1980s', *Cahiers d'Histoire de l'Aluminium*, no. 44–45, 2010, 79–106.
30  Joseph F. Brodley, 'Joint Ventures and Antitrust Policy', *Harvard Law Review*, vol. 95, no. 7, 1982, 1521–1590. On the aluminium industry this interpretation is endorsed, for the 1960s and 1970s, by Stuckey, *Vertical Integration and Joint Ventures*, and transposed to the interwar period by Storli, Brégaint, 'The Ups and Downs'.
31  RPA, 056-00-12347, Marlio, AI historique et reinsignements generaux sur la société, 1924.
32  All these initiatives are resumed in Muller, *Light Metals*, 111–117; Smith, *From Monopoly to Competition*, 138–147.
33  Smith, *From Monopoly to Competition*, 140.
34  HWA, MG Documents, Juridische Büro, 84a/2, Von der Porten (VAW) to Merton (MG), 25 November 1927. Alfred Merton, Notiz Unterhalung mit Herrn Edward K Davis von der Aluminium Company of America, 14 October 1927. RPA, 056-00-12348, Actions 1928 – Alluminio Italiano.
35  Archivio Storico Banca d'Italia (ASBI), carte de Stefani, 22.7 sfasc 42, Pro-Memoria sulla fabbricazione in Italia dell'alluminio metallico in dipendenza degli accordi: Società Italiana Potassa (brevetti Blanc) con Società prodotti chimici Napoli (ALCOA), 1929. Archivio Storico Istituto per la Ricostruzione Industriale (ASIRI), Serie Rossa, 020152, Studi su concimi potassici e leucite, 1930.
36  RPA, 001-0-11335 Rose & Paskus (American attorneys of AF) to Marlio, 20 May 1929.
37  United Nations Archives (UNA), R2741/8000/6955, League of Nations files, 10c 1928–1932, Réponses au questionnaire du Comité. Abaissement des Tarifs, Aluminium, 26 November 1928.
38  HHC, ALCOA MSS # 282, US v. ALCOA, Equity 85–73, Exhibit 42, International Aluminium Company Co., s.d. (but 1925). About Mayo, see Ford R. Bryan, *Henry's Lieutenants*. Detroit: Great Lakes Books, 1993, 219–224.
39  David Massell, *Amasing Power: J.B. Duke at Saguenay River, 1897–1927*. Quebec City: McGill-Queen's University Press, 2000, 176–177; Smith, *From Monopoly to Competition*, 154–159.
40  HHC, ALCOA MSS #282, US v. ALCOA, Equity 85–73, Exhibits, Ex.n.1092, Mortiz (NACO) to A.V. Davis (ALCOA), Re: European Manufacturing Subsidiaries, 12 July 1926.
41  RPA, 00-2-15942, Bloch (AIAG) to Marlio (AF), 19 May 1926. Bloch (AIAG) to Marlio (AF), Von der Porten (VAW) and Murray-Morrison (BACO), 30 June 1926.
42  RZA, Aiag Direktion Protokollen, DP nr. 171–340, 1923–1927, Direktion Protokoll, 14. November 1925. Direktion Protokoll, 26 June 1926.
43  ASBCI, Società finanziaria industriale italiana (Sofindit), SOF 327/5, L'alluminio Italiano. Nota sulle società, 1937. About Montecatini, see Franco Amatori, Bruno Bezza (eds), *Montecatini, 1888–1966: Capitoli di Storia di una Grande Impresa*. Bologna: Il Mulino, 1990.
44  RPA, 00-2-15940, Réunion de Berlin le 3 Avril 1925. Rauch, *Geschichte der Huttenaluminiumindutrie*, 122–123.
45  About IG Farben, see Peter Hayes, *Industry and Ideology: IG Farben in the Nazi Era*, Cambridge: Cambridge University Press, 1987. Gottfried Plumpe, *Die I.G. Farbenindustrie AG: Wirtschaft, Technik und Politik, 1904–1945*. Berlin: Duncker & Humblot,

1990; Raymond Stokes, 'From the IG Farben Fusion to the Establishment of BASF AG (1925–1952)', in *German Industry and Global Enterprise: BASF: The History of a Company*, edited by Werner Abelshauser, Wolfgang von Hippel, Jeffrey Allan Johnson, and Raymond G. Stokes. New York: Cambridge University Press, 2004, 206–301. Stephan H. Lindner, *Inside IG Farben: Hoechst during the Third Reich*. New York: Cambridge University Press, 2008.

46  RPA, 00-2-15940, Procès-Verbal de la Réunion du 15 Janvier 1926 à Bale.

47  RPA, 00-2-15942, Bloch (AIAG) to Murray-Morrison (BACO), Von der Porten (VAW) and Marlio (AF), 30 June 1926. Recently, Espen Storli pointed out that AIAG issued an ultimatum to other firms about the settlement of the cartel. Storli, 'Cartel Theory and Cartel Practice', 451. It seems from cartel archives that AIAG, thanks to its international economic intelligence (and not by a mere 'ultimatum'), was able to gather global data about the context and to convince the other firms about the desiderability not to procrastinate the settlement of a cartel.

48  RPA, 00-2-15940, Procès Verbal de la Quatrième Réunion du Comité de l'Aluminium-Association, 10 February 1927. HWA, MG Documents, 6b-2/7, Notiz. Aluminium-Association, 29 April 1927.

49  ASBI, Studi e Pratiche, cart. 20, fasc. 1, Delegazione di Berlino, Corvino Milkowski Stanislao, Sindacato europeo alluminio fra i maggiori paesi europei, 29 November 1926.

50  RPA, 00-2-15940, Procès Verbal de la Première Réunion du Comité de l'Aluminium-Association, 11 September 1926. 3ème cartel. Contrat de l'Aluminium-Association, 11 September 1926.

51  Suslow, 'Cartel Contract Duration'.

52  RPA, 00-2-15942, Marlio (AF) to Bloch (AIAG), 4 November 1926. AIAG, Exposé confidentielle, 2 May 1928.

53  RPA, 00-2-15940, Procès-Verbal de la Réunion du 25 Avril 1926 à Stresa.

54  HWA, MG Documents, Juristisches Buro, 6b-2/1, Statute. Abschrift. Projet de Status pour une Association Coopérative entre les Producteurs d'Aluminium, 26 August 1926.

55  RPA, 001-0-11333, Bloch (AIAG) to Marlio (AF), 27 August 1926. Marlio to Bloch, 6 October 1926.

56  RZA, Berichte über die Allgemeine Geschaftslage, 1920–1929, Verwaltungeretsitzung von 25 Dezember 1926. RPA, 00–2–15940, Contrat 11.9.1926, 3eme cartel.

57  RPA, 00-2-15941, Von der Porten (VAW) to Marlio (AF), 17 September 1926.

58  As follows: £105 = 1,680 Fr, 210 M, 260 CHF, 3.55 Austrian schillings. For the Japanese market the price would be determined by firm representatives and residents of Japan notified by AA. RPA, 00-2-15940, Procès-Verbal de la première Réunion du Comité de AA, tenue à Paris le 11 septembre 1926.

59  RPA, 00-2-15940, Procès-Verbal de la Deuxième Réunion du Comité de AA tenue à Paris le 15 octobre 1926.

60  RPA, 00-2-15942, Bloch (AIAG) to Murray Morrison (BACO), 30 June 1926.

61  RPA, 00-2-19540, Procès Verbal de la Cinquième Réunion du Comité de AA, 4 May 1927.

62  Baumol, 'Horizontal Collusion and Innovation'.

63  RPA, 00-2-19540, Statut du Bureau de Propagande & Reinsignements, 1927.

64  Ruch, *Une route ardue*, 53–4.

65  RPA, 001-0-11333, Marlio, Note. Visite de M. Schwartz de Metallgesellschaft, 1 December 1925.

66  RPA, 00-2-15940, Procès Verbal de la Deuxième Réunion du Comité AA, 15 October 1926.

67  RPA, 001-0-11333, Marlio (AF) to Steck (AIAG), 20 August 1924. Bloch (AIAG) to Marlio, 26 January 1926.

68  RPA, 00-2-15940, Procès Verbal de la Cinquième Réunion du Comité de AA tenue à Paris, le 4 Mai 1927.

69 RPA, 00-2-15940, Procès Verbal de la Troisième Réunion du Comité de AA, tenue à Paris le 10 Décembre 1926.

70 HWA, MG Documents, Abt.119-84a/1, Vereinigte Leichtmetall Werke, Gmbh, Notiz 1927.

71 HWA, MG Documents, 6b-2/2, Niederschrift uber das Ergebnis der Besprechung mit der Metallbank und Metallurgischen Gesellschaft AG, vom 12 Oktober 1927.

72 RPA, 00-1-15940, Procès Verbal de la Troisième Réunion du Comité de AA, tenue à Paris le 10 Décembre 1926.

73 RPA, 00-2-15942, Procès-Verbal de la Quatrième Réunion du Comité de AA, tenue à Bale le 10 Février 1927.

74 RPA, 00-2-19540, Procès Verbal de la Cinquième Réunion du Comité de AA, 4 May 1928. Procès Verbal de la Dixième Réunion de AA, tenue a Bale le 17 Février 1928.

75 RPA, 00-2-15942, Conversation de Marlio avec André Henry-Couannier, le 13 Mars 1928, 14,30 à 17 h.

76 Hexner, *The International Steel Cartel*. John Gillingham, *Coal, Steel, and the Rebirth of Europe, 1945–1955: The Germans and French from Ruhr Conflict to Economic Community.* Cambridge: Cambridge University Press, 1991, 26–28. Daniel Barbezat, 'Cooperation and Rivalry'.

77 RPA, 00-2-15940, Procès Verbal de la Quatrième Réunion du Comité de AA, 10 February 1927. Procès Verbal de la Neuvième Réunion de AA, 29 December 1927.

78 RPA; 00-2-15942, Note sur le fonctionnement de l'Aluminium-Association, 1928. Von der Porten (VAW) to Marlio (AF), 2 May 1928.

79 RPA, 00-2-15942, Conversation de Marlio avec André Henri-Couannier, le 13 Mars 1928, 14,30 à 17 h.

80 Duncan C. Campbell, *Global Mission, The History of Alcan*. 3 vols. Don Mills: Ontario Publishing, 1985–1992, vol. I, 2–5; Matthias Kipping, Ludovic Cailluet, 'Mintzberg's Emergent and Deliberate Strategies: Tracking Alcan's Activities in Europe, 1928–2007', *Business History Review*, no. 84, 2010, 79–104.

81 HHC, ALCOA MSS #282, Box 48, Fold. 1, John Saint-Peter, The Alcoa Bible, 1942, vol. 1, 74–75. About imperial defence strategies, see Perchard, *Aluminiumville*, 41–47.

82 RPA, 00-2-15941, Marlio to Murray Morrison, 5 June 1928.

# 6 European Cartel versus American Trust

## Cooperation and rivalry in a difficult economic environment, 1928–1930

The birth of ALTED was one of the main changes in the corporate landscape of the aluminium industry in the period between the two world wars. Unlike NACO, ALTED was not a mere subsidiary of ALCOA, but it was born to be an autonomous firm.[1] The separation between the two firms was achieved through exchange of ALTED's shares for the property of ALCOA. After the creation of ALTED, this firm gave all its shares to ALCOA in exchange for the foreign investments of the American firm. As a consequence, ALTED became the owner of the two smelters in Canada (Shawinigan and the new plant of Arvida), those in Norway (one-third of DNN and 50 per cent of Norsk), the one in Spain (one-third of the investment in the joint venture with AFC and AIAG), and one in Italy (50 per cent of the joint venture with AFC). In addition, ALTED obtained control over bauxite properties outside the US (apart from the deposits in Guyana, that remained under the direct control of ALCOA to support its expansion) along with all the processing companies (in France, Britain, Germany, Japan, and Canada). ALTED's direction was taken by Edward K. Davis, the younger brother of Arthur.[2]

As anticipated, after the news of the creation of ALTED, Europeans immediately tried to renew negotiations aimed at the conclusion of an agreement for a quota for European imports in the American market. Edward K. Davis replied at first that he could not conduct any kind of negotiation until the two firms were effectively separated and postponed any discussion until the autumn of 1929. BACO and AF were convinced that a collaboration was possible, and even near, thanks to this corporate transformation. According to them, ALTED represented a step closer to a new agreement. However, this idea clashed with the views of AIAG and VAW, which saw the formation of ALTED as an additional barrier to cooperation because it aimed to increase the competitive force of the North American producer in the global scene. On the contrary, these two firms thought that the Europeans would have to find a better form of organisation to wage tougher competition against ALCOA.[3]

In the months that followed ALTED's refusal, it became increasingly clear that the new Canadian firm had not been created to enter into a cartel agreement with the Europeans, but to allow ALCOA to find a new position in the international market as a result of the huge investment by Arvida. According to its official history, Duncan Campbell argued that the creation of ALTED corresponded to a new corporate organisation created to manage a strategy of large-scale exports, that ALCOA's sales subsidiaries, created in the 1920s, were not able to manage. Arthur V. Davis achieved the separation of the American business, to which ALCOA could devote itself entirely, from foreign affairs with the aim of directing them through an ad hoc structure.[4] When questioned by the inspectors of the antitrust authorities, Davis in 1937 said that the choice to form ALTED was guided by this observation:

> The disadvantage of handling the business the way we were handling it was that we were not a foreign organisation; our people naturally preferred to sell in large quantities in the United States rather than to bother, as they perhaps may have considered it, with smaller quantities abroad.... I considered that it was necessary for the advancement of business in Italy to do it by Italians in an Italian manner, and to do it in Germany by Germans in a German manner, and so on. I don't mean by that the German, Italian and other branches of the company were to be entirely divorced from jurisdiction on this side, but the various active selling officers, particularly, and also to a somewhat less extent the manufacturing operations, I conceived should be nationalized to a very much greater extent than we had so far done.[5]

The start of Arvida marked a decisive step in the history of the international aluminium industry and made quite a stir, even outside the world of the industry of non-ferrous metals.[6] The new amount of metal on the market only resulted in creating global overproduction, because it saturated the North American market and forced ALCOA to take extraordinary measures to export and accelerate market strategies on semi-finished products initiated since 1923, as described in the previous chapter. ALCOA tried to force sales into each market in which it was already present. ALCOA tried to extend its sales to Great Britain and in India, where acting through its Canadian company it could count on imperial preference for exports. ALCOA also carried out aggressive commercial activity in Spain and Italy. Also Japan was an important target of the American expansion, given its geographical proximity. The need for export was becoming more urgent as the situation worsened in the American market due to the beginning of the recession.

From 1929 onwards, ALTED acquired an aggressive commercial structure. It created several commercial agencies in the major markets, which depended on the headquarters in Montreal. For the British market, the old NACO was reorganised and extended taking over the management of all sales and of the manufacturing firms. This new organisation was called Aluminium Limited (II), based in London and it was directed by Walter Esperson. The European markets as a whole were placed under the management of Aluminium Limited (III) based in Geneva, and assisted by André Henri-Couannier in Paris and Sigmur Kloumann, CEO of Norsk, in Norway, who was charged with managing the Scandinavian markets and exports to the continent. In addition to these sales agencies, ALTED also created Aluminium Limited (IV) based in Sao Paulo, in Brazil, which was in charge of sales in Latin America, and Aluminium Limited (V) with headquarters

Table 6.1 AA in 1927: quotas, production, authorised sales, actual sales, and exports in the US (tons and %)

| Firms | Quota AA, % | Production, 1927 | | Actual sales, 1927* | | Sales authorised, 1927** (B) | Sales to US, 1927*** (C) | A−B, tons | A+C, tons | A+C, % |
|---|---|---|---|---|---|---|---|---|---|---|
| | | tons | % | tons (A) | % | | | | | |
| AF | 33.1 | 28,003 | 29.90 | 16,926 | 22.06 | 25,394 | 2,126 | −8,466 | 19,052 | 21.27 |
| BACO | 16.0 | 16,253 | 17.35 | 11,640 | 15.18 | 12,274 | 4,153 | −634 | 15,793 | 17.63 |
| AIAG | 23.8 | 23,600 | 25.20 | 19,945 | 26.00 | 18,259 | 3,619 | +1,685 | 23,564 | 26.30 |
| VAW | 27.1 | 25,804 | 27.55 | 28,204 | 36.76 | 20,790 | 2,962 | +7,414 | 31,166 | 34.80 |
| Total | 100.0 | 93,660 | 100.00 | 76,717 | 100.00 | 76,717 | 12,860 | – | 89,575 | 100.00 |

Source: author's elaboration from various files in RPA, 00-2-19540.

Notes

* From October 1926 to September 1927; ** according to AA's contract quotas; *** out of the AA's agreement.

in Osaka and a subsidiary in Shanghai, which managed sales in the Asian markets and administered a joint venture for the production of cables and semi-finished products with Sumitomo. This structure was modified only in 1933, when a more vertical form was established under the central control of a Swiss holding company, Aluminium Union.[7]

As a result, this new commercial strategy cancelled the tacit agreement that had been established since 1924, according to which ALCOA and the cartel would respect their selling prices. As we have seen, the relationship between the Americans and Europeans had actually progressively deteriorated after the formation of AA, when, on the one hand, the firms of the Old Continent repeatedly tried to force ALCOA to sign an agreement through moderate competition in the US market and, on the other hand, ALCOA had made hostile investments in different European countries. The bad relations between the two groups did not degenerate into an open conflict, only because the European firms were convinced that ALCOA's reluctance to enter into a cartel was the mere result of the actions of American antitrust authorities. When ALTED also refused to join the cartel in 1928 using as an excuse the same fear of antitrust laws again,[8] the Association's wait turned out to be meaningless. Relations between the two sides degenerated into an open conflict while a period of negative economic conjuncture was taking the place of the 1920s' euphoria. The firms experienced growing competition for outlets, which provoked price wars in some 'far' markets, such as Japan and India, and in many countries in which ALTED had good positions as regards production or manufacturing, such as Italy, Great Britain, and Spain.[9]

## The imperfect cartel: between intrinsic weaknesses and strategic downturns

The cartel as it was designed was not ready to compete with ALTED in the global market. In 1927, the year prior to the renewal of the agreement, the internal cohesion of the members seemed very precarious and the expected renewal in 1928 was not only made difficult by relations with the American group, but also by the internal dynamics of the cartel. Acting on a level that we call 'meso-economic', the cartel aimed to distribute the costs and benefits of the international economy among its members through mediation between the strategies of the firms and the various national markets. The short duration of AA led the different firms in the cartel to invest in new production capacities hoping to change quotas in their favour.[10] This broke the strategic unity of firms, which was the guarantee for internal cohesion of the cartel. Three distinct strategic groups emerged, causing an internal struggle in the cartel: AF was in overproduction, AIAG and VAW were undersized compared to their needs, and BACO was mostly in balance (see Table 6.2).

AF's quota did not seem to be justified and threatened to put the French firm in a delicate situation compared to its partners. In 1928, AIAG and VAW were compelled to purchase respectively 4,437 and 805 tons of aluminium from AF, which could not sell its quota. In fact, AIAG and VAW had insufficient production compared to their markets because, at the time of AA's negotiations, their

Table 6.2 The modifications of the Aluminium Association's quotas in 1928

| | Quotas AA 1926, % | Production capacity at 31 December 1926, tons | Production capacity, % | Quotas AA 1928, % | Production capacity at 31 December 1928, tons | Production capacity, % |
|---|---|---|---|---|---|---|
| AF | 33.1 | 33,000 | 31.13 | 31.0 | 39,500 | 28.93 |
| BACO | 16.0 | 17,000 | 16.03 | 18.0 | 29,000 | 21.24 |
| VAW | 27.1 | 31,000 | 29.24 | 22.6 | 34,000 | 24.90 |
| AIAG | 23.8 | 25,000 | 23.58 | 22.4 | 33,000 | 24.17 |
| Total | 100.0 | 106,000 | 99.98 | 100.0 | 136,500 | 99.94 |

Source: author's elaboration from various files in RPA, 00-2-19540.

quota had been calculated on the basis of their capacity. Taking into account production destined for the US, AF produced about 10,000 tons more than it actually managed to sell. The difficult commercial position of the French firms was caused by the revaluation of the franc, which caused a recession in the automotive industry, one of the main outlets for aluminium at this time. On the contrary, Germany and Great Britain greatly increased their national market thanks to the policies of electrification of the territory, from which aluminium firms benefited as suppliers of wires and other electrical equipment.[11]

In order to prevent its position from being reduced in the new cartel due to the economic problems of the French market, AF decided to expand abroad in the late 1920s, looking for new markets to sell its production. While AF was reluctant to extend its sales in the United States, where it would cause problems with ALCOA that threatened to invest in France, AF looked for outlets in less developed markets.[12] Thanks to the intermediation of its own government, in 1927, AF was able to enter into negotiations with Russia for a contract sale of about 10,000 tons per year. AF decided to share this trade with the members of AA, in order to manage its position in the cartel in a *do ut des* tactic, and also proposed a quota to ALCOA in order to confirm the spirit of cooperation towards this firm.[13] However, to achieve this important deal with the Russians, AF agreed to help the Soviet Union by providing the necessary technology to create a national aluminium industry as was decided within the Second Five-Year Plan. Although AF informed the other firms in the cartel of these negotiations, minimising the danger of possible Russian exports, this represented a first important antecedent of technology transfer to a country outside the cartel.[14] A second outlet that AF found was Japan, where it established stable business relationships with some of the top Japanese groups such as Mitsubishi and Mitsui.[15]

At the same time, Louis Marlio tried to act on a political level with the French government in order to receive political help to support AF's quota into the cartel. In fact, he obtained that his government implemented measures to help AF to maintain its quota in the cartel through an artificial increase of sales. So Marlio required the establishment of a military stock of about 8000 tons, asking also for the deletion of semi-finished aluminium goods from the list of goods that Germany could have given to France as reparations within the settlement of the Dawes Plan.[16] This is a case that contradicts the existing historiography as regards the relationship between political powers and international cartels. It showed several instances in which the various governments tried to use international cartels in order to achieve economic objectives and foreign economic policy goals. In this case, the relationship between the cartel and the political power appeared more complex, showing that the policy could be conceived as one of the various weapons available to the firms to compete in a situation of cartelisation.[17]

European firms that had an insufficient quota tried to change this situation by investing. In the German case, the new plant of VAW in Innwerk, which was almost complete, would improve the firm's ability to meet the demand of its national market. Without any reserved national market, AIAG thought that production that was allowed by the cartel was insufficient because, as an actor with a highly developed international sales network, it needed a greater amount of stock (and therefore additional production). For this reason, AIAG made new investments in Switzerland, which went hand in hand with an intensification of its activities in export markets in Far Asia and North America. In addition to these 'home investments', AIAG and VAW also developed a strategy for foreign direct investments. As anticipated, both firms decided to invest in Italy: in this country, the production from AFC and ALCOA's joint venture was insufficient to meet the demand of the domestic market, which was in a phase of rapid increase. The two firms, in fact, regarded Italy as a country in which to concentrate their exports, rather than investing.[18] AIAG and VAW decided to invest in order to remedy the insufficient output in the cartel and accelerated the investments during 1927 and 1928, in view of the negotiations. AIAG founded a firm in association with an Italian group interested in the development of Porto Marghera, for the construction of a corporate structure, that would ensure the 'full cycle' of aluminium (from bauxite to semi-finished products), the Società Anonima Veneta Alluminio (SAVA), with 6,000 tons per year as capacity, thanks to the supplies given by the Società Idroelettrica del Cismon (SIC) of Marco Bernabo.[19] VAW got in contact with Montecatini, as it wanted to find a partner to join aluminium production to diversify its production and find an industrial use for its hydro-power capacity in excess.[20] VAW and Montecatini created a joint venture for the construction of an alumina plant in Porto Marghera, i.e. the Società Italiana Allumina (SIA), and a manufacturing plant in Mori in Trentino, the Società dell'Alluminio Italiano (SIDA), which had a production capacity of 4,000 tons per year. Both investments began to produce by the end of 1928.[21]

BACO's situation looked different from that of the other firms. Although its new plant in Lochaber had a production capacity of 8,000 tons and it improved its position in the domestic market, BACO could not find a monopoly strategy for its domestic market. In fact, the UK market was much greater than what BACO produced on the whole (production in the UK and Norway amounted to approximately 17,000 tons per year) being estimated in 1927 at about 30,000 tons. Consequently, during the 1920s Great Britain represented an export market for NACO (then for ALTED) and AIAG. Despite this, BACO had become a strongly internationalised actor during the interwar period.[22] It did not concentrate its sales in Great Britain, but over the 1920s it had built an effective sales agency in New York, thanks to which it was one of the major importers of aluminium in the United States.[23] Compared to its domestic industry, BACO had a very different view from the other firms in the cartel, that instead thought of their domestic demand as the backbone of the sales strategy and considered export markets simply as momentary 'safety valves' for their production.

The extension of BACO's production in the UK was not intended to saturate its market to replace imports: it was started for military-strategic issues with the support of the British government. The British executive adopted two special measures to support high levels of production and strong integration of production, which affected BACO's strategy. The first measure consisted of increasing duties for imports of tableware made of aluminium, the other was aimed at knowing the bauxite resources that Great Britain had and creating preferential channels among the companies belonging to the empire for the exploitation of these resources.[24] What the British government needed was not self-sufficiency, but certainty that aluminium production in peacetime was sufficient to support any military need in the event of war. This British government strategic vision clearly appears in a Committee of Imperial Defence document of 1928, which states: 'In time of war British demands for aluminium for the manufactures of aeroplanes, airships, etc. would largely increase but could be met by diverting the metal from use in hollow-ware industry, etc.'[25]

The existence of these divergences in the cartel and the uncertainty related to the refusal of the Americans to join made the renewal of AA in 1928 very difficult. Revision of quotas was made following arbitrary rules: they were neither related to capacity, nor to the sales that were made, but were the result of bargaining ton per ton. As in the case of AA in 1926, also in 1928 it was decided that the cartel should last only two years, again because of strong uncertainty of relations with the US group. However, the short duration and negotiations weakened the association, because they placed the new cartel in a sort of 'limbo' in which the firms might try to compete with each other by investing and forcing sales in order to get a larger quota in the next revision. While establishing the new quotas, it was decided not to include into the cartel the investments in Italy and Spain, which had not yet begun production.[26]

## Growing rivalries between Americans and Europeans

Despite the renewal of the cartel in 1928, AA was not able to cope with the ongoing international economic crisis. The relationships between the European and American groups deteriorated further, leading to clashes in some key markets. The transition from a difficult but cordial situation to a situation characterised by direct confrontation took place during 1928, when the strategies planned by AFC to find forms of cooperation with the Americans were completely reorganised. ALTED's assets in Spain were exchanged with AFC's assets in Italy. The separation of interests in these markets, which were becoming theatres of competition between the Europeans and Americans, showed that the former strategy of cooperation with ALCOA was ending. Among the three joint ventures formed during the 1920s, only DNN continued to exist. In the specific case of Italy, AF already aimed to divest its holdings there because of overproduction created there by the starting of AIAG's and VAW's smelters.[27]

In 1928, ALCOA definitely put aside the construction of a smelter in France, which created many anxieties for the French group. On the one hand, this decision was judged by Marlio as a sign of goodwill towards AA; but on the other hand, this judgement ended up with increasing ambiguity in the relations between the Americans and Europeans. This choice corresponded to the change of direction in the strategy of the American trust that occurred after the creation of ALTED. The American enterprise was now concentrating its forces on exporting the Canadian metal in Europe directly, putting on hold all the other projects that were distracting funds from this goal. This was revealed by the flow of cheap imports of semi-finished products that affected Spain and Italy, when ALTED

*Table 6.3* Production and consumption in North America, 1927–1930 (tons)

| | 1927 | | 1928 | | 1929 | | 1930 | |
|---|---|---|---|---|---|---|---|---|
| | *Production* | *Consumption* | *Production* | *Consumption* | *Production* | *Consumption* | *Production* | *Consumption* |
| United States | 72,600 | 100,000 | 95,500 | 124,000 | 102,100 | 137,000 | 103,900 | 95,000 |
| Canada | 38,500 | – | 40,000 | – | 42,000 | – | 34,900 | – |
| Total | 111,100 | 100,000 | 135,300 | 124,000 | 144,000 | 137,000 | 138,800 | 95,000 |

Source: author's elaboration from various files in RPA and HHC.

Note
In the statistical sources, consumptions of United States and Canada are always merged. However, at this time, the Canadian market is negligible.

tried to reduce outputs of the joint venture that it had with the European firms to make room for Arvida's metal. The board of the cartel was also informed that ALTED was proposing to pay the cost of customs duties for European customers, in order to find additional outlets at the expense of the cartel members.[28] ALTED launched a real campaign of commercial conquest abroad that in many cases threatened to weaken the position of the European firms. The Japanese market deserves a particular attention. All AA's members, but especially AIAG, were strongly threatened in this market, where ALTED (V) had even lower prices and better payment conditions for consumers. At the same time, AIAG and VAW were threatened in the Italian market, where ALTED (II) set very low prices, thereby increasing its imports. On the contrary, BACO was threatened in India and in the UK, where ALTED (III) was stealing many customers including English carmakers. In all these markets, European companies tried to oppose the American firm acting individually. Sometimes, they allowed for exemptions on the sale price of the cartel, but this only resulted in debasing prices.[29]

If during the euphoria of the 1920s, the tacit agreement with the Americans was sufficient to save the price strategy of the European cartel, in the international economic crisis an explicit agreement with ALTED became of outmost importance. The European cartel realised that friendly relations that it had tried to keep with ALCOA and with ALTED would not lead to any agreement with the American group, which aimed to expand sales at any cost. In Marlio's mind, the cartel behaviour should be implemented with some moderate competition, which was necessary to convince ALTED of the opportunity to join the cartel. AIAG and VAW strongly supported an open conflict against ALTED, while BACO claimed the necessity to impose a détente with the Canadian firm. In spite of these disagreements, Europeans recasted their strategy to contrast against the American expansion. AA progressively lowered its official price, from £105 per ton to £95 in late 1928 and to £85 at the end of 1929. In the British market, Europeans agreed to pool their sales to share the losses of low quotations. They also allowed special discounts for car producers in France, the UK, and Germany. The cartel also decided to update the agreements with the outsiders, asking for output curtailments, in order to shield their official price in European markets from ALTED's low quotations.[30]

However, in some markets an open confrontation arose, as in the case of Japan. This market had progressively attracted vigorous export strategies by all Western firms, because it had proved to be a very lucrative market. Historically, this market was dominated by AIAG, which had installed a sales agency in 1891, but also all the other firms consolidated privileged relations with the principal Zaibatsu: AF had stable trades with Mitsubishi, BACO with Furukawa, AIAG with Nichisui, and VAW with Illies.[31] Compared to European firms, the American group had initiated a more serious strategy of market penetration latterly, when it had founded a joint venture with Sumitomo in 1928 for the production of electrical cables and semi-finished products.[32] The presence of an American vigorous export policy in Japan gradually led to open conflict, the outcome of which was to progressively lower prices, in some cases even below the cost of production. From the official cartel price of £107 per ton of 1926, the price in this market gradually fell to £90 after the formation of ALTED, to £85 at the end of 1928, and to £70 between 1929 and 1930. Some sales were made even at £55.[33] The competition between AA and ALTED was made even harder by the fact that they were not negotiating with small and disorganised business groups, but with powerful buyers that, in some cases, also formed coalitions to get the same treatment from the sellers. If a European firm offered a special discount, this particular treatment was expected also in future negotiations to the whole group of aluminium producers. When ALTED, through its sales agency in Tokyo, began to propose special credits on payments, prices fell to the levels described above. In many cases, prices were also negotiated by ALTED after the delivery of metal. Moreover, the problem was not only the lowering of sales, but also the deep change that was affecting sales in the Japanese market. Price instability and hard negotiations for each sale were substituting the policy of stable price list that characterised aluminium, risking also infecting other markets outside Japan.[34]

Faced with this major risk, in September 1929 AA took extraordinary measures to defend the position of producers in the markets that were most affected by competition. It was decided to put the sales of AA under single management, to build special quotas out of the general cartel quotas and to indemnify suppliers sharing the financial burden of price competition, reimbursing the individual producers of the difference between the obtained market price and the official price of AA.[35] This type of sales organisation and this strategy were initially tried in Japan, then they were also tried in India, where the quotas shown in Table 6.4 were shared amongst AA members.

These quotas were fixed according to the average of sales made by each individual member of AA between October 1926 and the end of June 1929. Since in both markets there were firms that had more deeply rooted and strong commercial structures, it was pretty easy to decide how to organise the joint sales. The firms of AA, in fact, decided to entrust respectively AIAG and BACO with sales on the territory and moved a decisive step towards the formulation of a much more cohesive and compact cartel, in which the members decided to give full confidence to the ability of one of the commercial associates and its impartiality in allocating sales following the quotas. The complex relationships with ALTED obliged AA to change its features, implementing some measures that transformed the commercial structure of the cartel. As for the Japanese market, this decision was made even stronger by the decision to forge the ingots with the mark 'Europe' printed on, instead of the typical name of the producer.[36]

*Table 6.4* AA quotas on the Japanese and Indian markets after the special agreement of 26/27 September 1929 (%)

|  | *AF* | *BACO* | *AIAG* | *VAW* | *Total* |
|---|---|---|---|---|---|
| Japan | 25.00 | 5.00 | 50.00 | 20.00 | 100.00 |
| India | 20.00 | 50.00 | 15.00 | 15.00 | 100.00 |

Source: author's elaboration from various files in RPA.

The clash between the Americans and Europeans was also tough in the Italian market. After the departure of AFC from this market, AIAG (SAVA) and VAW–Montecatini (SIDA) were not able to keep cooperative attitudes with ALTED's subsidiary. Both SAVA and SIDA's production started in 1929, with the result of bringing Italian production above the national demand. AA encouraged the formation of a national cartel, called ASA (Alluminio Società Anonima), for fixing prices in accordance with AA's policies and to balance production with consumption. However, the specific situation of VAW in this market was ambiguous: even if VAW had the duty to administrate the Italian joint-venture, Montecatini was an uncomfortable partner that did not accept a reduction in the production of aluminium. Moreover, AA's firms feared that simply reducing SIDA and SAVA's production would not be sufficient to face the competition from ALTED. As a consequence, Italy became one of the main battlefields of the struggle between the Americans and Europeans, and AA decided to support Italian companies against Canadian imports.[37]

In this situation, Guido Donegani, the chairman of Montecatini, was able to manoeuvre to gain special benefits for his firm. In spite of the lack of Italian demand and the general slowdown due to the international crisis, Donegani managed to avoid a reduction in Italian production. Donegani claimed to have several sales contracts with the Italian government that required him to keep production running. In particular, he foresaw a market for 9,000 tons during 1930, parts of which would be utilised for the manufacture of energy transmission cables. This was a promising market that, according to Donegani, was directly encouraged by the government in order to substitute the use of copper in the electrification of Italy.[38] It is not clear if Donegani really had the support of the government or if his statements were only a bluff, but the members of the cartel considered him to be a very dangerous competitor if left free from any engagement with the cartel. In particular they feared that if they had not taken some measure, Mussolini's regime could finance Italian exports at dumping prices, perturbing the general situation of the international aluminium markets.[39]

AA explored the possibility of negotiating with Donegani to take control over SIDA, but he refused to sell the shares of this firm to AA members. Consequently AA allowed VAW to negotiate with Donegani to put an end to further expansions of SIDA, following the basis of the other outsiders that entered in agreement with the cartel.[40] In return, the cartel would purchase the unsold metal at a price of £5 below AA's official price. Once SIDA obtained this agreement, AIAG demanded the same treatment for SAVA, and finally AA signed a special agreement for the duration of five years with ASA at the end of 1929 to take over all Italian overproduction.[41] Recent historiography has questioned whether Donegani was really fully aligned with the Fascist regime, in particular Franco Amatori suggested that a deliberate strategy of *do ut des* shaped the relationships between Montecatini and the regime.[42] No documentary evidence of government aids to SIDA was found during this research. Yet the most important aspect in our analysis is that the belief shared in the board of AA that political intervention was sufficient to push the cartel to negotiate special agreements with Italian companies.

While the cartel was alerted by the competition made by ALTED, AA also took some measures to update control over the sales of outsiders, aiming to prevent them from disturbing the cartel price policy. In particular, ALCOR was in severe financial difficulties and threatened to further disturb the international market by opening another front in addition to the clash between AA and ALTED. This firm was in an excessive financial exposure that derived from the decision to invest in a new plant producing 10,000 tons per year in Norway, while the onset of the international crisis slowed down its sales.[43] ALCOR could represent an even greater risk for AA's firms, because it had settled an agreement with Giulini to supply a new alumina unit. After the integration strategies of the German firms, which deprived Giulini of some very important outlets for its production, this firm entered in deals with ALCOR. AA decided to make an arrangement with ALCOR to break the alliance with Giulini. According to this agreement, the cartel would buy 3,000 tons per year at AA's price less £7, with the possibility to extend this purchase to further 1,000 tons at AA's price less £15.[44]

These facts proved to AA's members that, where they had established a collective sales organisation, they were able to compete with ease against ALTED. On the contrary, the cartel was concerned about the agreements with the outsiders, because they forced the cartel to purchase approximately 10,000 tons per year that, in the context of a great drop in sales, would not find an outlet with ease. Thus, AA members debated transforming the whole cartel to compete with ALTED. At a meeting of AA in June 1930 it was put on record that

> It is unanimously recognised that the issue, that has become urgent, of the extension of the association agreement beyond 1931, is subordinate to that of a fundamental reorganisation of AA. This reorganisation should create some financial interests and technical solidarities among the associate producers and allow a rapid and effective action towards the completion.[45]

## The Aluminium-Européen project

At the end of this meeting, AA entrusted Marlio and Bloch with processing certain propositions entirely devoted to the creation of a stronger and more cohesive structure for the cartel, with the aim of submitting them to the *comité* one month later. Marlio considered three different possibilities of action. First, the merger of all the European producers under a single enterprise; second, the exchange of shares among the different firms to create a strong interconnection and financial solidarity among them; finally, the creation of a cartel that would have some implementation to achieve the same result as a merger or stock sharing.[46]

The fusion of all the firms was not a workable solution: the firms were too heterogeneous in the formation of their capital (VAW was an state-owned firm) and in productive structure (AFC had a big part of its active budget devoted to chemical production while BACO was strongly oriented in the production of semi-finished products) to merge their assets to create a big aluminium business. The exchange of shares could only be effective if it involved a large share of the capital stock of any firm: as a consequence, the different firms would have to increase their capital and they were afraid of not being able to quickly find capital for operations of this type or the consent of their shareholders. As regards these hypotheses, the preferred form to reach a deeper cohesion of the four firms would be to create a new form of cartel. This project took the name of Aluminium Européen (ALEUR).[47]

The ALEUR project aimed to merge the commercial division of each firm, forming a common selling agency to oppose ALTED. Moreover, ALEUR was also designed to take control over new smelters: in particular, the creation of a new smelter directly owned by ALEUR in the United States was planned.[48] Harm Schröter pointed out that cartels could represent the substitute of fusions.[49] Moreover, some pioneering studies about international cartels claimed these organisations as forerunners of modern multinational (or transnational) corporations.[50] ALEUR epitomises these ideas, showing that the urgency of economic crisis enabled and accelerated this process. Actually, according to Von der Porten, who was one of the main supporters of this project within the board of governors of AA, 'The expression "Aluminium Européen" is a strong term that is equal to ALCOA. It is a term that conveys a unity that is rather complete.'[51] This opinion was shared by Bloch, according to whom

> For the Americans, there is only one man who holds the flanges and leads everybody. On our part, there are from four to six companies, that believe they can follow their own path. It is the weakness of the European Alumium industry ... We would need some financial interests, either a 'pool' of financial results, or the sharing of all or a part of the product of our sales. Otherwise our agreement will never be strong enough to dominate the particular interests in a decisive way.[52]

In fact, the ALEUR project considered the creation of a pool: it would buy from the market all the metal sold at a price that was lower than that fixed by the cartel in order to control prices. The cost of this operation would be divided among the members according to the quotas of each firm in the cartel. To strengthen even more the community of interest that would be created around ALEUR, each member that produced in a market protected by custom tariffs would share with the other members of the cartel the difference between the official price of the cartel and the market price, in the case in which it was set at a higher level. The sales of metal in all its forms would be made in each country by a single member that would sell the metal on behalf of all members: BACO would sell in the countries of the British Empire, AF in France and in the French colonies, VAW in Germany, and AIAG in all export markets.[53] As a general sale policy, ALEUR would give priority to selling as much as possible, going so far as to question the price stability that had dominated up to now the strategy of the cartel. In the proposed reorganisation of the cartel in fact it was stated that

> The integral flow of the production of the Associates seems to us more important than the strict keeping of the official selling price for all the

deliveries, and this from the point of view of the financial result of each Associate and from the point of view of the vulgarisation of the use of aluminium'.[54]

For this purpose a central committee was to be established and it would keep the overall management of sales, dividing a quantity for each market to sell, a common selling price, and a maximum cost of production to achieve. The duration of such an association was originally set at ten years, renewable for another ten. As regards the management of quotas, in the original proposal for ALEUR they were fixed once and for all. None of the associates would have built more plants alone, but that all new investments would be made in common and managed by a dedicated limited company in which each of the four firms of the cartel would have held 25 per cent of the capital. In a similar way, ALEUR would be in charge of buying and jointly managing the outsiders if it was the case and of building firms for manufacturing and processing the metal.[55]

The ALEUR proposal was the resumé of the overall experience of aluminium cartelisation. In this proposal, European firms tried to set up the 'perfect cartel' to manage their industry in the future. However, this proposal involved never-ending debates because while AIAG, VAW, and AF supported its settlement, BACO was strongly opposed.[56] In July 1930, the *comité* of AA met to discuss the proposed reorganisation of the cartel, according to the proposals of Marlio and Bloch. In spite of the cohesion shown in front of the successes of the new sales organisations in Asia, not all members could accept a formula like ALEUR's. While AF, AIAG, and VAW were partisans that supported the formation of the new cartel, BACO tried to delay the formation of this cartel, arguing that it was preferable to seek an agreement with ALTED rather than such a long-lasting cartel. In addition, BACO made it known that it could not accept any pool mechanism in sales and could not give up its commercial service in foreign markets. Finally, BACO, taking account of certain developments in its relationship with ALTED, thought that a general agreement with the Canadian firm was closer than ever.[57] Faced with this resistance, AF, AIAG, and VAW also thought of creating Aluminium Européen by themselves and leaving BACO out.[58]

## The Japanese truce: the Zurich agreement of 1930

However, these reflections on what form to give the cartel were interrupted abruptly, before the tensions between the three companies in favour of the ALEUR project (VAW, AF, and AIAG) and BACO degenerated. In late July 1930, in fact a few days after the meeting in which the four firms discussed the formation of Aluminium Européen for the first time, ALTED let the firms in the cartel know that it would be willing to come to an agreement over the Japanese market. ALTED's leaders had already proposed a price agreement for that market, but with neither a written contract nor sales quotas. After the discussions on ALEUR, instead ALTED was willing to sign a written contract with quotas about Japan. ALTED also wanted to negotiate a very advanced agreement: the agreement should be in the form of a simple commercial contract and a joint sales agency in Japan, managed by ALTED (V), that was to be set up to share sales among the members of the agreement. The goal of this specific design was to show the Japanese market that the organisation was not governed by a cartel agreement but simply by a joint commercial office. ALTED aimed at forming a 'ghost cartel' without the appearance of an ordinary cartel showing once again its antitrust concerns.[59]

ALTED decided to move to this agreement, albeit its legal situation, also because the Japanese market was very dangerous for ALCOA. Given its geographical proximity, the metal sold at low prices in Japan could be re-exported to the United States, circumventing the anti-dumping law and creating a difficult situation for ALCOA from a commercial point of view.[60] This risk was even more dangerous due to the fact that the new US tariffs, established by the Smoot-Hawley Tariff Act, actually lowered import duty on aluminium from $0.05 to 0.04/lb, although they were generally regarded as hyper-protectionist.[61] The European firms cautiously negotiated this agreement with ALTED, because they were afraid of losing their commercial autonomy in this key market. However, the situation on the market was so compromised that they agreed. They succeeded in obtaining that AIAG retained formal control of the office of the joint Japanese sales agency with the aim of constant control over the activities of ALTED (V). With regard to quotas, the European firms decided to negotiate on the basis the last two years' sales to maintain the status quo achieved thanks to their central European sales office and ended up with a division between the two groups, i.e. 48 per cent for AA and 52 per cent for ALTED.[62] This agreement, signed 18 July 1930, took the name of 'Zurich agreement', because it was signed at AIAG's trading headquarters in Zurich. The quotas of this agreement are summarised in Table 6.5.

After negotiation of this agreement and with the risk of the formation of an organisation such as ALEUR, ALTED eventually changed its strategy and, after years in which it had postponed any kind of general agreement, it communicated to Marlio that Edward K. Davis was willing to reach a compromise with the European cartel. It is not possible to know if ALTED already had a strategy to enter into an agreement with AA when it signed the Zurich agreement. However, we can argue that the project of ALEUR contributed to the general appeasement between the two sides of the aluminium business. The news of the formation of ALEUR frightened André Henry-Couannier and in September 1930 he wrote to Edward K. Davis to advise him to prepare to adopt a new counter-offensive, because in Europe there would soon be a new firm that would merge all the old firms of AA and would place ALTED in a very difficult position to manage. Couannier suggested breaking the cohesion of ALEUR proposing a separate agreement with AFC, or to indirectly compete with ALEUR taking control of a small number of outsiders, such as SIDA and ALCOR.[63]

After this communication, Arthur V. Davis went to Europe in October 1930 and told the cartel that his brother, Edward K. Davis, would be willing to meet with the members of AA and to host a delegation from the Aluminium-Association in Montreal, at ALTED's headquarters, during the following spring. Faced with this news, the *comité* of AA interrupted negotiations for the formation

Table 6.5 Zurich agreement: ALTED and AA's quotas and sales in the Japanese market, 1929–1930

| Firms | Sales 1929 | | Sales 1930 | | Agreement AA | Zurich | AA in | AA in |
|---|---|---|---|---|---|---|---|---|
| | tons | % | tons | % | 13 November 1929 | 18 July 1930 | 48% | 100% |
| AIAG | 4,561 | 39.31 | 5,215 | 47.84 | 50.00 | 48.00 | 41.00 | 19.70 |
| BACO | | | | | 5.00 | | 21.00 | 10.10 |
| AF | | | | | 25.00 | | 21.00 | 10.10 |
| VAW | | | | | 20.00 | | 17.00 | 8.10 |
| ALTED | 7,039 | 60.69 | 5,685 | 52.16 | – | 52.00 | – | 52.00 |
| Total | 11,600 | 100.00 | 10,900 | 100.00 | 100.00 | 100.00 | 100.00 | 100.00 |

Source: author's elaboration from various files in RPA.

of ALEUR and focused on how to engage the most fruitful negotiations with ALTED.[64] These negotiations would lead a few months after to a new international cartel, the Alliance Aluminium Companies that, as we will see in the next chapter, represented the most sophisticated form of cartel adopted in the international aluminium industry in the period between the two world wars.

## Notes

1 Kipping, Cailluet, 'Mintzberg's Emergent and Deliberate Strategies'.
2 Campbell, *Global Mission*, vol. 1, 18–19.
3 RPA, 00-2-15940, Procès Verbal de la Treizième Réunion de la Aluminium-Association, tenue a Paris le 5 et 6 septembre 1928.
4 Campbell, *Global Mission*, vol. 1, 15–19. Smith, *From Monopoly to Competition*, 145–147.
5 Campbell, *Global Mission*, vol. 1, 11.
6 Michal Kalecki, 'The World Production of Aluminium', originally published in 1928, now in *Collected Works of Michal Kalecki: Volume VI, Studies in Applied Economics 1927–1941*, edited by Jerzy Osiatynski. Oxford, Clarendon Press, 1996, 8–10.
7 HHC, MSM #282, ALCOA, US v. ALCOA, Equity 85–73, Exhibits, Ex.n.448, Shipping instruction of United States Aluminum Company, 15 May 1929. Campbell, *Global Mission*, 29–30.
8 RPA, 00-2-15942, Conversation de Marlio avec André Henri-Couannier, le 13 Mars 1928, 14h30 à 17h.
9 RPA, 00-2-15940, Procès Verbal de la Quinzième Réunion de la Aluminium-Association, 14 December 1928. Situation actuelle du marché japonais. Note de Mitsubishi à l'Aluminium français, 1929.
10 HWA, MG Documents, 6b-2/7, Aluminium-Association, Notiz, 29 April 1927. RPA, 00-2-15942, Note sur le fonctionement de l'Aluminium-Association, 1928.
11 UGD, 347/21/19/1, Proceedings of the ordinary annual meeting of the British Aluminium Company Ltd., 1928. Vereinigte Aluminium Werke AG, *Hauszeitschrift der Vaw und Erftwerk AG*, 1930.
12 RPA, 00-2-15941, Note sur les Relations avec l'Aluminium Company of America, 1925. Note pour M. Marlio. Points essentiels à porter à la conaissance du cartel, 4 May 1927.
13 RPA, 001-5-19036, Marlio to Level, 1 August 1927. Marlio to Level, 10 August 1928. Projet du Comptoir Franco-Russe, 1928.
14 RPA, 00-2-15940, Procès-Verbal de la Réunion du Comité de l'Aluminium-Association, tenue à Bale le 10 février 1927. Réné Bonfils, 'Pechiney au Pays des Soviets: Le Contrat Russe de 1930', *Cahiers d'Histoire de l'Aluminium*, no. 23, 1998, 29–41. Bertilorenzi, 'Big Business'.
15 RPA, 00-2-15940, Situation Actuelle du Marché Japonais. Note de Mitsubishi à l'Aluminium français, 1929.
16 RPA, 00-2-15942, Note pour M. le Ministre sur le fonctionement de l'Aluminium-Association, 1928.
17 Wurm, *Business, Politics and International Relations*, 36–42.
18 Bertilorenzi, 'The Italian Aluminium Industry'.
19 RZA, S.17, Verhehlungen betr. Gründung der SAVA u.d. Marco Bernabò (SIC) to Bloch (AIAG), 27 November 1927. Promemoria consegnato a S.E. il Generale Dallolio il 27 Novembre 1927. About the Italian aluminium industry during the 1920s, see also Rolf Petri, 'Acqua Contro Carbone: Elettrochimica e Indipendenza Energetica Italiana degli anni Trenta', *Italia Contemporanea*, no. 168, 1987, 63–96. Rolf Petri, 'L'Industrie Italienne de l'Aluminium à la Veille de la Seconde Guerre Mondiale', in Grinberg, Hachez-Leroy (eds), *L'Âge de l'Aluminium*, 143–152. Amatori, Bezza, *Montecatini*, 40–42.

20  HHC, MSS #282, ALCOA, US v. ALCOA, Equity 83–75, Exhibits, Ex. no. 1082, Mortiz (NACO) to A.V. Davis (ALCOA), Re: Donegani, 25 September 1925. Mortiz to A. V. Davis, Re: Montecatini, 24 August 1926.
21  Archivio Edison, fondo Montecatini, Corsico – Milano (AEC), Box 3 fold. 5, SIDA, Verbale della seduta del consiglio del 1 settembre 1928. ASBCI, SOF 327, fold. 5, L'alluminio Italiano. See also, Mario Perugini, *Il Farsi di una Grande Impresa: La Montecatini tra le due Guerre Mondiali*. Milan: Franco Angeli, 2014.
22  Perchard, *Aluminiumville*.
23  UGD, 347/21/12/14, British Aluminium Company Ltd. Statements and Accounts of New York Trading A/C, 1925 and 1927.
24  Walter G. Rumbold, *Bauxite and Aluminium: Monographs on Mineral Resources with Special Reference to the British Empire*. London, Imperial Institute, 1925. Board of Trade, *Safeguarding of Industries: Report of the Committee on Aluminium Hollow-Ware*. London: HMSO, 1925. About the relationships between industries and political powers in the post-First World War era, see Edgerton, *Warfare State*. About the specific case of aluminium, see Perchard, *Aluminiumville*.
25  TNA, SUPP 3/70, Committee of Imperial Defence. Principal Supply Officers Committee. Board of Trade Supply Organisation, Memorandum on Aluminium, 14 December 1928.
26  RPA, 00-2-15940, Procès-verbal de la Douzième Réunion du Comité de l'Aluminium-Association tenue à Cologne le 13 Juillet 1928. MGA, 6b-2 Internationale Aluminium – Konvention, Grundung & Organisation, Doc.3, Generalverstulungs Protokolle, Aluminium-Association, Paris, 5 September 1928.
27  RPA, 00-2-15941, Marlio (AF) to Von der Porten (VAW), 29 October 1928.
28  RPA, 00-2-15940, Procès Verbal de la Dix-septième Réunion de la Aluminium-Association, tenue a Londres le 16 et 17 avril 1929.
29  RPA, 00-2-15940, Procès-Verbal de la Dix-huitième Réunion du Comité de l'Aluminium Association tenue à Paris le 27 et 28 juin 1928. Procès-Verbal de la Dix-neuvième Réunion du Comité de la Aluminium-Association tenue à Paris le 26 et 27 septembre 1929.
30  RPA, 00-2-15940, Procès Verbal de la Dix-Neuvième Reunion du Comité de l'Aluminium Association, 26 and 27 September 1929.
31  RPA, 00-2-15940, AA Circular Letter no. 120, Japanese market, 15 November 1929.
32  Campbell, *Global Mission*, vol. 1, 209–210.
33  RPA, 00-2-15940, AA. Accord Japan 1929, Note: Situation Actuelle du marché japonais, 4 October 1929.
34  RPA, 00-2-15940, AA. Note: Situation actuelle du marché japonais, 4 October 1929.
35  RPA 00-2-15940, Procès-Verbal de la Dix-Neuvième Réunion du Comité de l'Aluminium-Association tenue à Paris le 26 et 27 septembre 1929.
36  HWA, MG Documents, 6b/1, Aluminium Japan, Von der Porten to Jllies & Co, Betr. Gemeinsame Verkaufsorganisation in Japan, 4 November 1929. RPA, 00-2-15940, Convention concernant la vente de l'aluminium brut, des alliages et des produits mifabriqués au Japon, 13 November 1929.
37  RPA, 00-2-15933, Note. Italie, 1929.
38  AEC, Sc.3, fasc. 5, SIDA, Consiglio del 16 dicembre 1929, Consiglio del 23 marzo 1930.
39  RPA, 00-2-15933, AIAG correspondance, Note. Italie, 1929.
40  RPA, 00-2-15940, Procès verbal de la 19e reunion du comité de l'Aluminium-Association, 26–27 septembre 1929. RPA, 00-2-14942, Bloch to Marlio, 10 December 1931.
41  RPA, 00-2-15940, Procès verbal de la 20e Reunion du Comité de l'Aluminium-Association, 19 et 20 décembre 1929. AEC, Sc.3 fasc. 5 SIDA, Consiglio del 13 Marzo 1931. Box 7. fasc.3, ASA, Consiglio del 22 marzo 1930.
42  Franco Amatori, 'Italy: The Tormented Rise of Organizational Capabilities between Government and Families', in *Big Business and the Wealth of Nations*, edited by Alfred

D. Chandler, Franco Amatori, and Takashi Hikino. Cambridge: Cambridge University Press, 1997, 246–276. Franco Amatori, 'The Fascist Regime and Big Business: The Fiat and Montecatini Cases', in *Enterprise in the Period of Fascism in Europe*, edited by Harold James and Jakob Tanner. Aldershot: Ashgate, 2002, 62–77.

43 RPA, 00-2-15941, AA, Conversation avec MM. Morrison & Steel à Londres le 19 Juillet 1929 de 10 H.1/2 à 13 H.3/4, Copie pour M. Dalmais (AF) 4 November 1931.
44 RPA, 00-2-15940, Procès verbal de la 19e Réunion du Comité de l'Aluminium-Association, 18 and December 1929.
45

Il est reconnu que à l'unanimité que la question, devenue urgente, de la prolongation du contrat d'association au-delà de l'année 1931, est subordonnée à celle d'une réorganisation fondamentale de l'AA. Cette réorganisation devrait créer des intérêts financiers et techniques solidaires entre les producteurs associés et permettre une action rapide et efficace en face de la concurrence.

RPA, 00-2-15942, Procès verbal de la 22e Réunion du Comité de l'Aluminium Association tenue à Bruxelles le 2 Juin 1930.
46 RPA, 00-2-15940, Projet de Reorganisation de l'Aluminium-Association, 4 June 1930. Note du 4 Juillet 1930.
47 RPA, 00-2-15940, Note sur la Réunion de l'AA du 11 Juillet 1930 au Chateau D'Ardenne, 11 July 1930.
48 HWA, MG Documents, Juristisches Buro, Internationale Aluminium – Konvention, Aluminium Association, Grundung & Organisation, 6b-2/1 Statuten, Abschrift. – Aluminium-Européen, 1930. RTA, 00-2-15935, Contrat d'Association de l'Aluminium Européen, 20 August 1930.
49 Harm Schröter, 'Cartels as a Form of Concentration in Industry: The Example of the International Dyestuffs Cartel from 1927 to 1939', in *German Yearbook on Business History*, edited by Hans Pohl and Rudolf Bernd. Berlin: Springer, 1988, 113–144.
50 Casson, 'Multinational Monopolies'. Nussbaum, 'International Cartels and Multinational Enterprises'.
51 Original quote – 'L'expression "Aluminium Européen" est un terme très fort qui équivaut celui d'ALCOA. C'est un terme qui exprime une unité assez complète', RPA, 00-2-15940, Aluminium-Association, Notes Dactilographés de l'AA, Réunion du 7 août 1930.
52

Chez les Américains, c'est un seul homme qui tient les brides et dirige tous. De notre coté. Il y a de quatre à six compagnies, dont chacune pense pouvoir suivre son propre chemin. C'est là la faiblesse de l'industrie européenne de l'Aluminium … Il nous faudra des intérêts financiers, soit par un 'pool' des résultats financiers, soit par la mise en commun de tout ou partie du produit de nos ventes. Sinon notre liaison ne sera jamais assez forte pour prédominer d'une façon décisive sur les intérêts particuliers.

RPA, 00-2-15940, Aluminium Association, Notes Dactilographés de l'AA, Réunion du 2 juin 1930.
53 RPA, 00-2-15935, Aluminium Européen, 11 September 1930.
54

L'écoulement intégral de la production des Associés nous paraît être plus important que le maintien rigide du prix de vente officiel pour toutes livraisons, et cela au point de vue du résultat financier de chaque Associé et au point de vue de la vulgarisation de l'emploi de l'aluminium.

RPA, 00-2-15940, Projet de Reorganisation de l'Aluminium Association, 4 June 1930.
55 RPA, 00-2-15940, Projet de Reorganisation de l'Aluminium Association, 4 June 1930.

56 In the intention of AF, AIAG, and VAW, the creation of ALEUR was possible even without BACO, with which they did not exclude reaching a separate agreement in a second time. RPA, 00-2-15942, Level (AF), Note pour M. Marlio, 5 August 1930.

57 RPA, 00-2-15942, Résumé des principales observations présentées par les Membres du Conseil de la British à M. Marlio le 20 Septembre 1930. Also Metallgesellschaft showed to be not disposed to endorse this proposal. HWA, MG Documents, 6b-2/2, Aluminium-Association, Vertaulich Betr. Aluminium-Association, 26 August 1930.

58 RPA, 00-2-15940, Réunion AA du 7 août 1930.

59 RPA, 00-2-15940, Réunion AA du 11 juillet 1930. Note au sujet du Rapport de M. Kaufmann, 1930.

60 HHC, MSS #282, ALCOA, US v. ALCOA, Equity 85–73, Exhibits, Ex.814, E.K. Davis to A. Henry-Couannier, 5 May 1930.

61 Smith, *From Monopoly to Competition*, 139.

62 RPA, 00-2-15940, Marché Japonais, Accord du 18 juillet 1930 (Accord de Zurich)

63 HHC, MSS #282, ALCOA, US v. ALCOA, Equity 85–73, Exhibits, Ex.n. 743, A. Henry-Couannier to E.K. Davis, 19 September 1930.

64 RPA, 00-2-15940, Procès-Verbal de la Vingt-Cinquième Réunion du Comité de l'Aluminium Association, Tenue a Londres le 15 octobre 1930.

# Part III

# Business, finance and politics

The rise and fall of the Alliance
(1931–1945)

# 7 The new global cartel

The inception of the Alliance
Aluminium Compagnie, 1931–1933

The trip in Europe organised in October 1930 by Arthur V. Davis to meet Louis Marlio represented the starting point of a general detente between the Americans and Europeans. Even if he excluded ALCOA's participation in an agreement, Davis wanted to help a first rapprochement between ALTED and the Europeans finalised with the creation of a new global cartel. He confided to Marlio that both ALCOA and ALTED were in an extremely difficult position, which represented a global threat for the aluminium market. Due to the crisis and the investment strategies of the previous years, the two firms had accumulated about 150,000 tons of unsold stock, equal what they produced in one year. Mario suggested to Davis that ALTED could become a member of AA to manage this difficult situation with the methods of the cartel, before the European firms concluded the creation of ALEUR. However, Davis criticised AA's modus operandi and its policy on stable prices that, according to him, did not suit the condition of the market, contributing to depressing the sales.[1]

Despite these criticisms, Davis volunteered as an intermediary to arrange a meeting with the Canadian firm and with his CEO, Edward K. Davis, to try to create a framework for cooperation with the European cartel. Some of the companies of AA thought that the American company was trying again to buy time to continue its aggressive commercial strategy. Until ALTED made its cooperation more explicit, the European firms continued to adopt competitive strategies against the Americans. Immediately after the meeting between Marlio and Davis, in fact, the cartel lowered the selling price from £95 to £85 per ton. In addition, the ALEUR project was not immediately stopped, because AIAG and VAW considered that this new organisation could be used to strengthen the European position, if not to defeat ALTED, at least to achieve a strong point during negotiations, as had happened with the agreement for the Japanese market.[2]

The clash between the Europeans and Americans that had characterised the late 1920s had coincided with the start of a series of investments, some of which were quite oversized for the actual market. ALTED's strategy of trying to break through the resistance of the market with aggressive commercial policies had not given the expected results. When the international economic crisis started, the already difficult situation turned into the most serious crisis of overproduction that the aluminium industry had ever known. In addition to ALTED's stock, even European firms had accumulated some stock during 1930 because, without an agreement with the American firms, they had delayed the reduction of production. Actually, the characteristic technical rigidity of aluminium technology, for which output reductions are extremely expensive, made both fronts reticent to curtail production before finding a compromise, even if global consumption was slowing down during 1929 and 1930. This struggle for global outlets resulted in a huge accumulation of inventories, evaluated by Louis Marlio at 13 months of world production.[3]

Without a global agreement between the two parties, the firms that had reduced production would have simply found themselves 'overwhelmed' by the competition's metal. However, the weight of the inventories in the balance sheets eroded the profit of the firms and created incessant needs for liquidity to producers, that worsened their financial positions. Davis was very concerned by the possibility that the Europeans could organise a real war machine against the American company, such as ALEUR was designed for, because his company could not withstand further confrontation without seriously compromising its financial situation. In turn, Marlio wanted to involve ALTED as early as possible in a cartel, because he knew that the world situation in the aluminium market was close to collapse, and without an agreement with the Americans they would soon be 'invaded' by very low quotations from Canadian unsold stock.[4] For this reason, he informed ALTED's French delegate, André Henry-Couannier, about the progress of ALEUR's project, who did not hesitate to report to Davis in December 1930 that 'The reorganisation of the European association and its transformation into a war-machine against ALTED would probably happen if they [the Europeans] have still longer the impression that you intend to postpone the convention.'[5]

ALEUR was definitively interrupted in December 1930, when André Henry-Couannier confirmed to Marlio that Edward K. Davis wanted to meet a delegation of the cartel and communicated that Davis had prepared a new draft for an agreement between the two groups, that he wanted to show personally to the members of AA.[6] The cartel decided to send AF and BACO representatives to negotiate with the Americans, because these two were the firms that had proved less intransigent towards the Americans, while AIAG and VAW were in poorer relations with Davis. Although on several occasions BACO had proved too pro-American and, contrary to a too close association with other European firms, its participation in the negotiations was solicited both for linguistic reasons and because, in doing so, it would have prevented a new change of mind. Moreover, Bloch and Von der Porten had great confidence that Marlio's ability of mediation could avert the risk of a separate agreement between Murray-Morrison and Davis. The other member of the French delegation was Hyppolite Bouchayer who, more than being member of the board of AF since its creation in 1911, was one of the most authoritative hydroelectric engineers in France and would have been able to appreciate the actual power of the US installations.[7]

The meetings between ALTED and AA were held in Canada and the United States in April 1931. ALTED showed the European delegation the huge mass of accumulated stock in the yards of some plants. The delegation saw 30,000 tonnes of unsold metal in Massena and other 30,000 in Arvida. While travelling in Canada, the Europeans also received a visit from Arthur V. Davis, who led them in person to visit Arvida. During this meeting, the attempt to involve ALCOA in the negotiations was interrupted several times by a lawyer, who advised Davis to end the meeting. On the way back, the cartel delegation described with apprehension the amount of unsold stock and the close legal situation to which ALCOA was subjected. In addition, this was the first visit to Arvida, which turned out to be a huge investment, far larger than expected by the cartel members. But the aspect that most impressed the European firms was the agreement that Edward K. Davis outlined to the Europeans.[8]

## ALTED's proposal: the Aluminium International Company

The main goal of the journey in North America was to start discussions for the formation of an agreement between AA and the Canadian company. ALTED led the creation of this cartel and provided the general guidelines about its actual shape. Edward K. Davis highlighted that, instead of joining the European cartel or transforming AA to include ALTED into the old agreement, a new 'finance company' should be created to replace the former cartelisation. He distributed a draft document to Europeans about this finance company, which was provisionally called the Aluminium International Company (AIC). According to this draft, its

> Shareholders will be free to produce, fabricate and sell aluminium in all its forms ... without any price agreement, territorial divisions or other regulations except those imposed by AIC, as before described, but nothing prevents a continuance of any existing, or the making of any future, arrangement among any of the shareholders for a convention of prices, or partitioning of any given market (such as the arrangement now in effect in Japan), nor the organisation of such present and future cartels as the shareholders, or any of them, may desire to form amongst themselves. This company will only buy and sell aluminium or warrants representing aluminium.[9]

ALTED wanted to create a financial device to take control over the whole surplus, freezing the overproduction until market conditions would buffer it. In other words, AIC would have managed unsold stock, buffering them on the market. This company would buy metal from firms to avoid too low quotations and sell metal when prices would be too high. According to Davis, AIC could have been created in the Netherlands, which was a country with no producers installed and with low taxation. Davis predicted that it would take three years to recover the stock situation. This managerial creativity confirms Dominique Barjot's hypothesis about endogenous and exogenous factors which reshaped the constitution of cartels.[10] Not only did the general situation of economic depression and overproduction lead ALTED to cooperate with the Europeans, but cartelisation was also reshaped by the specific poor financial situation of the Canadian company. Actually, ALTED was financially exhausted by an extraordinary inventory accumulation that severely eroded earnings and created liabilities in its balance sheets.[11]

The AIC proposal meant a deep rupture with past cartelisation. Instead of a cartel with market quotas and fixed prices, as AA was, ALTED aimed to create a new type of corporation whose main task was to 'freeze' the inventories of the firms. As we have seen, AA also in 1926 considered the stock situation as vital to analyse the market situation. Yet, ALTED now placed a mechanism on inventories at the centre of market governance. ALTED considered three specific advantages while proposing this scheme. First, the 'finance company' shielded Americans on the legal side: the scheme represented the substitute for a cartel because it did not have any manifest quota and price fixing. Formally it was a trading company. Second, the foreseen mechanism of buying and selling would work more effectively than purely fixing prices in this period of economic disorder: the buying price was conceived to work as a 'ceiling' for low quotations, and the selling one as a 'roof'. Finally, the Canadian firm considered it possible to continue a scale production, in spite of the economic crisis, because the finance company would purchase the excesses, improving the cash flow situation.[12]

This last point deserves particular attention. From the theoretical standpoint, the accumulation of stock requires additional liquidity and, in some cases, ad hoc loans to level balance sheets. When liabilities become too high, weaker firms without easy access to financial facilities are forced to sell stock, even at low prices, to obtain liquidity. Price stability through inventories devices represents a far-reaching innovation in commodities markets during the 1930s. For instance, John Maynard Keynes proposed inventories devices as possible solutions to economic instability and inflation.[13] Actually, buffer stock schemes had been effectively adopted to stabilise prices in tin, copper, rubber, and wheat markets since the mid-1930s. In these cases, the difficulty of outlining general plans for private actors led public authorities to intervene directly: in the case of tin and rubber, the old cartel agreements of the 1920s were reshaped during the 1930s under the control of political authorities, which reduced output and stockpiled the excess of production caused by the crisis. Instead of simply reducing production, the involved governments administrated output keeping part of the unsold stock out of the markets with the twofold goal of manoeuvring prices and keeping a minimal scale output.[14]

More than being innovative because it anticipated both the theoretical debate and its practical application, the aluminium proposal diverged from the other commodity schemes on stock because it was conceived without the political involvement and commitment that characterised these schemes. Aluminium producers aimed to ensure stability of both production and prices for technological issues and ALTED's fear of the antitrust authorities during the discussions for its creation.[15] European producers had understood that control over stock was a key device to control market prices. As shown, AA already seized the importance of controlling the unsold stock when it decided to buy the metal from ALCOR and Italian firms during 1929: their relative financial weakness could have caused the buffering of the unsold stock at low prices, which would have disrupted the attempts made by the cartel to keep stable prices. But, AIC aimed to control the global market with a collective stock cushion, which was judged able to curb individual behaviours of firms. According to the draft, the firms could subscribe to up to 90 per cent of their participation in AIC in warrants on the metal. This measure aimed to de-charge immediately their assets and to consent to the firm to form AIC without reducing their liquidity. The firms understood the opportunity disclosed by this mechanism to improve their cash flow.[16]

The finance company proposed by Davis would set production quotas, hidden in the phrasing of the contract. In fact, Davis did not exclude the need to link the clearance of stock on the market with a reduction in production to alleviate the international situation in the most acute phase of the crisis. That was conceived as a fallback solution if the levels of stock were out of control. To do this, he proposed to link the shares that each company owned into the capital of AIC with a production right. In this way, AIC shares would represent the global production capacity of the European companies and of ALTED. AIC would have a capital of £3,100,000, each action would have a nominal value of £1,000 for a total of 3,100 shares. At first only 1680 of these actions would be issued and 1,000 would be assigned to AA, 500 to ALTED, 120 to SNN, and 60 to Norsk. When the 'rights' of production were restored to the maximum and all stock in excess cleared, the remaining 1,420 shares would be issued, respectively, 900 for ALTED, 300 to AA, 60 to Italian firms, and 160 to all the other outsiders. The original idea of the project was that the shares were not transferable and that only a decision of the Board of Governors could authorise buying and selling of shares.[17]

The Europeans feared that, without modifications, this project would introduce elements of instability into the pricing policy of aluminium. Davis envisaged eliminating the practice of explicitly setting a list price that characterised the former cartel experience, using instead purchases and sales that the finance company would have made to the members as a way to influence market prices. The system of warrants on the metal would in fact eliminate too low quotations, removing from the market the metal that could be sold at a price lower than the value expressed by the warrant. This mechanism would work as a kind of 'paramount' for prices that, differently from the past, would be left free to fluctuate. Control over stock was the new coordinate of cartelisation proposed by ALCOA–ALTED, that aimed to replace sales quotas and fixed prices for the sale of AA.[18] We can wonder if the Americans wanted to move from a 'régulation par volumes', which characterised the former cartel experience, to a 'régulation par les prix', to use the terminology employed by Carmine Nappi.[19] As we will show, the second type of governance came only after 1978, when aluminium was introduced at the London Metal Exchange. Yet, the introduction of financial instruments, such as warrants on the metal that were already adopted in other more volatile commodities, reveals a process of convergence towards a different trading model that could be called 'commodisation' of aluminium.[20]

## The compromise: the creation of the Alliance Aluminium Compagnie

The AIC project was considered very clever by the members of AA, who were impressed by this mechanism. Von der Porten thought it was a very powerful mechanism to carry out effective market control in such a delicate situation. A new role of finance in commence was emerging, introducing a new system that both helped comprehension of the economic cycle and gave a definite advantage for the companies' financial statements. In fact, control over sales only, as had been adopted by AA until then, neither helped avoiding overinvestments, nor coordinating production rates. The difference from the former cartel experience was huge. As noted by Bloch at the meeting held at the return of the European delegation from North America 'The main idea of Mr. Davis' project is control over production and a complete buffering through the l'Aluminium International Co. as a clearing house, while at present we have no restrictions on production but on sales.'[21]

In spite of overall positive feedback on the outlined structure of AIC, some aspects of the draft perplexed the Europeans. In particular, the European firms aimed to modify some specific features that were not aligned with their vision of cartelisation. Europeans particularly aimed to stop ALTED's scale production, which was the main cause of unsold inventories. Moreover, this scheme was conceived to be a 'global' system, but it did not entail any agreement with ALCOA, which owned around 40 per cent of world output in 1931 and more than 100,000 tons of unsold stock. Europeans also wanted ALCOA to enter the agreement because they feared that ALTED could have taken over and resold the unsold inventories of ALCOA to the finance company. This menace was critical because ALCOA was the owner of large amounts of stock, which it could have transferred to its Canadian sister, compromising the working of the prospected financial company. Finally, according to the European firms, the feasibility of the scheme depended on available finance facilities to start the device on stock.[22]

During negotiations, the quotas of the cartel, 'hidden' behind the shares that each firm would own, were an issue particularly difficult to modify. In fact, if every share was tied to a production right, it emerged from AIC's proposal that ALTED and AA would have a proportion of 33.33 per cent compared to 66.66 per cent of the world production (1,000 shares for AA and 500 for ALTED). When the market expanded again after the overall clearance of stock, this distribution would be about 52 per cent compared to 48 per cent (1,300 shares to AA in total, compared to 1,400 for ALTED). These shares were unacceptable for the European companies as they were not willing to offer such a great advantage to ALTED. The quotas that Davis had indicated would allow new expansion to Arvida's production, which would eventually overwhelm the European companies. The European companies, in turn, thought that their production capacity was bigger than the proportion indicated by ALTED and that, in the future, they would preserve, thanks to the investments that had already been programmed, the majority of the total production capacity without ever getting to a situation of almost equality.[23] AA's strategy towards ALTED was to get the majority of the shares both at present and in the future, avoiding Davis' attempt to obtain a too large quota of production, which would ultimately undermine the cartel's members from their positions. As a consequence, AA's firms thought that the respective shares of the two groups would have followed the installed production capacity and sales made during the last years, without altering the balance of powers that had been established during the 1920s. In other words, AA wanted to avoid ALTED exploiting the creation of the finance company to create room for the expansion of Canadian production at their expenses. As a consequence, the counter-project of AA agreed that ALTED could improve its position in the future, but without getting to hold the majority of shares in the new company.[24]

The companies also agreed on how to deal with the outsiders: while in ALTED's project virtually all companies formally external to the two groups were regarded as outsiders, AA thought that the firms that were under its control had to be included in the quotas. For this reason, in AA's amendments to ALTED's project Steeg, Lissauer, and ALCOR were considered part of the group of outsiders, while the other companies such as SNN, Norsk, and AE were included either in the quotas of AA or of ALTED. The Italian companies were also considered in the counter-project as outside the direct control of the share-holders of the future finance company, because of the special agreements that AA had negotiated with SAVA and SIDA in December 1929. In reality, the inclusion or exclusion of outsiders in the project was used to determine the balance of power between AA and ALTED and to negotiate the output that would be allowed to each group. The decision whether to include firms like AE, SNN, or SAVA in the quotas of their respective groups was instrumental in obtaining a greater quota and this risked arousing again some hostility between the groups.[25] In order to overcome this impasse, AA and ALTED first decided to fix the shares between them, in order to avoid the re-emergence of hostility between the two groups, and then start separate negotiations about the role of the outsiders in the scheme. In June 1931, a new division of shares was proposed to Davis as the basis of the agreement and a compromise was reached. Table 7.1 describes the compromise and shows the quotas for the European cartel (I), for ALTED (II), and for the outsiders (III).

The main criticism that the Europeans had for AIC's project was the absence of a cartel price, which seemed too risky. AA's firms were faithful to the idea that the international aluminium industry could only expand through stable and reliable market prices, which, in turn, sanctioned a kind of pact between producers and consumers in order to avoid any speculation. The main idea, expressed on several occasions during the meetings of AA's *comité*, was that only stable prices could allow consuming firms to be able to plan the replacement of other metals with aluminium. Second, stability prevented consumers from obtaining stock with speculative goals, ensuring stability in the production of aluminium and avoiding the consumers employing a great part of their liquidity into hedging operations. According to European firms, this stability could only be achieved through a cartel system, in which there were fixed sale quotas, rebalancing, and a common market price, also announced in trade publications, as it had actually been up to that time.[26]

*Table 7.1* AIC's proposal to AAC: quota negotiations of AA (I), ALTED (II), and outsiders (III) (shares and %)

| | AIC – ALTED's proposal (April 1931) | | | | Counter-proposal AA (May 1931) | | | | Compromise AAC (June 1931) | | | |
|---|---|---|---|---|---|---|---|---|---|---|---|---|
| | initial shares | % | final shares | % total | initial shares | % | final shares | % total | initial shares | % | final shares | % total |
| I | 1,000 | 59.52 | 1,300 | 43.33 | 1,074 | 63.0 | 1,389 | 61.73 | 1,000 | 71.42 | 1,500 | 57.69 |
| II | 500 | 29.76 | 1,400 | 46.66 | 402 | 23.5 | 584 | 25.95 | 400 | 28.58 | 900 | 34.61 |
| III | 180 | 10.71 | 300 | 10.00 | 231 | 13.5 | 277 | 12.31 | – | – | 200 | 7.69 |
| Total | 1,680 | 99.99 | 3,000 | 99.99 | 1,707 | 100.0 | 2,250 | 99.99 | 1,400 | 100.0 | 2,600 | 99.99 |

Source: author's elaboration from various files in **RPA**, 00-2-19532 and 00-2-19533, and in **HHC**.

In spite of this criticism, Davis' plan contained an idea that interested European firms and that was not rejected. The creation of a holding company that could manage the market through immediate reduction of stock from the firms' balance sheets was very interesting also for the Europeans. Actually, the proposal would allow off-balance financing facilities for the unsold inventories that, because of the crisis, weighed on the firms' balance sheets. This represented for the Europeans an idea that could have been used without problems because, by controlling the level of stock, the firms would be discouraged from establishing low prices and competing with each other. Control over stock looked very different from how the European producers had imagined improving their old cartel. Compared to ALEUR's project, which involved a kind of merger in sales and in future investments, AIC allowed a great deal of freedom to producers. According to Marlio, in fact, this was the goal of the proposal 'que M. E.K. Davis avait remis à Montréal: limitation de la production, liberté absolue des ventes'.[27]

The members of the European cartel believed that AIC's mechanism could be adapted to the policy of stable prices. To do this, they wanted to implement a proposal providing fixation of a list price and of other two prices that worked as referral for the market. The first was the value of the initial warrants, which was fixed at £55 per ton. This price was close to the cost of production of most of the producers and was considered fair to pay only the production costs for this initial amount of unsold stock. Then, they settled a 'purchase price' for future buys that would made from the members, which was set at £70 per ton. Finally, the third was for the 'selling price' at which the finance company would sell to the members. This price was set at £77 per ton. This mechanism would also create a profit margin with which AIC could self-finance part of its operations.[28] AIC, after the acquirement of stocks of metal when it was created, would continue to buy from the members that could not sell all their production at a price of £70 per ton, which would be the minimum market price. Leaving this price unchanged, instead of changing it as Davis wanted, the companies would be able to continue the policy of stability. European firms also insisted on securing a 'semi-official' list price of £80 per ton that would work as a standard price guide as in the case of the old Association.[29]

The core of the European amendments to ALTED's proposal had the goal of providing guarantees about the fair attitude of the Canadian company vis-à-vis the Europeans. In particular, the Europeans requested immediately setting a policy to reduce production, aiming to avoid overflows of Canadian metal. The original mechanism, proposed by Davis, to link shares with production rights was improved. The shares of the finance company were linked to a 'right of production' expressed as a percentage of total possible output: for instance, 100 meant the full utilisation of outputs, 50 half, and so forth. Each firm became owner of shares proportional to its respective production capacity (one share for 100 tons of capacity production). As a consequence, these shares meant effective production quotas for its members. By assigning production rights, firms were able to set global output. The Board of Governors, in which only producers were represented, had the task of defining rates, brackets of prices, and stock depletion.[30]

In order to reduce the influence of ALTED over the assets of the new company, it was also established that only a part of unsold inventories was to be taken over by the cartel: firms kept the rest according to specific 'holding rights'. It was too expensive to purchase the whole stock surplus. So the finance company was appointed to take over only extraordinary inventories above a certain surplus, also fixed by the Board of Governors. These corrections saved the general sense of the 'off balance' financing system, but restricted the unlimited freedom expected by ALTED, as Europeans requested.[31] The last modification was to obtain an agreement about the American market. ALCOA did not join the cartel and the Europeans did not obtain any written engagement about its behaviour in the future. The Europeans were asked to believe that ALCOA would limit its activities to its national market, as a consequence of the choice already made in 1928, and that only ALTED continued to act abroad. However, Europeans asked and obtained from ALTED extra rights of production of 14,000 tons to be exported to the United States, and that were not included in the Alliance plan. This measure aimed to secure ALCOA's fair attitude because, even if it was not a formal agreement, it showed that ALCOA was willing to accept sacrifices, like all the other firms. Only Europeans signed this agreement, called *contrat avenant* (pre-requisite), but ALTED endorsed it during a preparatory meeting in June 1931.[32]

In the summer of 1931, ALTED approved many of these points and agreed to create the Alliance Aluminium Compagnie (hereafter Alliance or AAC). Incorporated in Basel as a holding company with a capital of 35 million Swiss francs, its shares were subscribed by the four Association members and by ALTED. Its duration was set at 99 years, but each of the five shareholders had the right to denounce the agreement after five years with six months' advance notice.[33] The nationality of the firm was chosen after fiscal, monetary, and financial consideration. Switzerland was a cheap country in terms of taxation. Furthermore, even in aluminium international trade, prices were set in British sterling, in 1931 the Swiss franc was a relatively stable currency that could help good achievement of operations on stock allowing their expression in British gold–sterling. Finally, the support of Société de Banque Suisse and of Crédit Suisse was obtained to finance inventories operations.[34]

The participation of Swiss banks in the scheme was decisive for the settlement of the cartel. They accepted financing the scheme because AIAG, which was one of the main Swiss businesses during this period, had strong ties with these banks. In particular, Arnold Bloch was a member of the board of both banks. Moreover, the banks also considered the financial appeal of the operation. Actually, this investment held little risk for them, because the repayment of Alliance's securities was guaranteed by the existence of the cartel, which reduced risks of insolvency. Rudolf G. Bindschedler (vice-president of Crédit Suisse) and Max Staehelin (chairman of Société de Banque Suisse) were appointed to the administration board of Alliance in order to cement their support. Marlio was nominated chairman, after Edward K. Davis' refusal. Cooper of BACO became vice-president of Alliance. Bankers Trust of London was also involved in these operations. This bank was perhaps an ally of ALTED's (and ALCOA's) main financier, Andrew Mellon, who also endorsed the Swiss banks' participation.[35] Mellon was not only

ALCOA's principal backer since the early 1890s and a substantial stock-owner of both ALCOA and ALTED, but he also was part of the American financial elite and the US secretary of treasury between 1921 and 1932.[36]

Since Swiss law required that at least half of the directors of the board were of Swiss nationality, Marlio thought of limiting the problem by forming a 'conseil panaché'. Apart from Bindschedler and Staehelin, who were designated in the board of Alliance respectively as representatives of VAW and BACO, other Swiss personalities were selected. Professor Maurice Lugeon of the University of Lausanne, an expert in the geology of mountains, agreed to represent AF in the board of AAC, after being invited to join Alliance's board by Hippolyte Boucha-yer.[37] This council would have a purely representative ratification role with respect to the decisions made by the producers that formed alone a real executive board (the so-called 'board of governors'). Essentially, the designated role of the board was to approve the budget and hold a general meeting every year. Marlio also thought that this was the best way to create a partnership with the financial world. In fact he said to the other members that

> The advantage of a 'mixed' committee whose members would be the repre-
> sentatives of the great Swiss banks, would be to get us all the money that we
> may want immediately .... It is necessary to choose very influential people
> and we wonder whether these Businessmen would be willing to play the
> role they are given.[38]

The AAC was formed with a proper office and with paid staff to manage the daily business of Alliance, keeping statistics, gathering the correspondence among the firms, and carrying out studies on production, stock, and the market. This office was entrusted to Ludwig Braasch, who previously was the delegate for the German market of ALTED (II). ALTED took into account the fact that, in addi-tion to these offices, Alliance would continue the experience of scientific and technological research started by BIEP, which would keep its headquarters in Paris at the same location as AF, but changing its name and becoming the Bureau International de l'Aluminium (BIA). The last aspect of this global compromise was to involve Price, Waterhouse & Co., a standing audit company with a global network of agencies, in the scheme. This firm was employed to verify and to assess the level of output and of stock in each unit of Alliance's members. The adoption of an independent auditing consultant was motivated by previous poor relations between the two sides. To avoid cheating, Price, Waterhouse & Co. was also charged with determining the exact level of initial inventories, which were evaluated at 90,000 tons.[39]

## The start of Alliance: from finance company to clearing house

Alliance shows how cartels can be sophisticated structures. It also was a *chef d'œuvre* of bargaining features specific to cartel frameworks. ALTED was the main architect of the plan, and it also named it. Actually, the name was proposed by

Henry-Couannier in June 1931, when he was invited with Edward K. Davis to a meeting of AA to discuss the settlement of the new global cartel.[40] Yet Europeans carefully negotiated each term and its modus operandi and were able to transform the original proposal to a safer agreement against the power of the American firms. The main issue to figure out during the launch of Alliance was to establish rates to manage the global balance of supply and demand. Firms deliberated to subscribe Alliance's capital for 25 per cent in cash and for 75 per cent in warrants at nominal price of producing costs (£-gold 55 per ton) supported by the bankers' loans. In this way, the mere incorporation of Alliance alleviated inventories levels of about 20,000 tons. The firms' inventories were authorised up to 40 tons per share. As a consequence, Alliance was committed to purchase a further 15,000 tons to 'reset' market conditions and Alliance's production rate was fixed at 80 per cent (see Table 7.2). Three years would have been sufficient to buffer all the unsold stock (90,000 tons) because the firms estimated that the annual demand would be at least 140,000 tons and they considered it sufficient to reduce output by 20 per cent in order to both buffer inventories and keep scale economies.[41]

However, the firms were not able to forecast that, as soon as Alliance started to work, the new financial partners would demand to play an important role in the decision-making process. Finance overcame the initial industrial considerations, affecting the work of the cartel and displeasing some national politics. Actually, these figures appeared too optimistic. Consumption during the second half of 1931 only reached about 50,000 tons, and inventories reached a new peak. The choice to take 80 tons per share for the final phase of 1931 was part of the compromise between AA and the Canadian firm. ALTED proposed during a preparatory meeting of AAC in June 1931 to maintain a high level of production and even proposed to start with 100 tons per share and then decrease from 1932. BACO would have wanted to lower directly to 80 tons, while the producers from Germany, France, and AIAG were convinced that it was necessary to go down at least below 70 tons. ALTED thought that Alliance was supposed to help the firms maintain high production in order to achieve the scale economies through the forfeiture of unsold surplus even during a period of crisis. On the contrary, the European firms were more inclined to think that a large reduction of the surplus was necessary because the accumulation of stock was considered too risky, since it would allow continuation of ALTED's excessive production that was, according to them, the main cause of the market slump.[42]

This different vision derived from the different production structure of the two groups. The Europeans could 'spread' the reduction of production more successfully on their units because they had smaller size plants than the North American units. In this case, to reduce production, it was possible to completely close an inefficient units and maintain the production of scale economies in those with lower unit production costs. In retrospect, we know that AFC in 1932 took the decision to close down the old unit of Calypso and La Praz and to stop the small output of the more recent smelter of Beyrède and Saint-Aubain, which were not able to give satisfying cost figures. At the same time, AFC kept the output from the more performing units.[43] Also AIAG operated a similar choice, closing down the old Neuhausen unit and focusing production in the most performing smelters.[44] VAW focused the

Table 7.2 Alliance Aluminium Compagnie: shares, initial subscription, and metal inventories to be kept and to be depleted

| | Shares | Capacity in AAC (tons)* | AAC initial subscriptions | | | Inventories (tons) | | | |
| --- | --- | --- | --- | --- | --- | --- | --- | --- | --- |
| | | | Cash £ (25%) | Metal £ (75%) | Actual tons | Total | Less subscription | Authorised | Further purchase |
| AF | 299 | 29,900 | 74,750 | 224,250 | 4,100 | 13,000 | 8,900 | 11,960 | −3,060 |
| AIAG | 216 | 21,600 | 54,000 | 162,000 | 2,900 | 12,000 | 9,100 | 8,640 | 460 |
| BACO | 210 | 21,000 | 52,500 | 157,500 | 2,850 | 12,000 | 9,150 | 8,400 | 750 |
| VAW | 275 | 27,500 | 68,750 | 206,250 | 3,750 | 18,000 | 14,250 | 11,000 | 3,250 |
| ALTED | 400 | 40,000 | 100,000 | 300,000 | 5,450 | 35,000 | 29,550 | 16,000 | 13,550 |
| Total | 1,400 | 140,000 | 350,000 | 1,050,000 | 19,050 | 90,000 | 70,950 | 56,000 | 14,950 |

Source: author's elaboration from various files in RPA, 00–2–19532 and 00–2–195433.

Notes
* Capacities were the outcome of negotiations: they are different from the real ones of Table 7.1.

reduction in Lautawerk and Erftwerk, concentrating production in the most performing unit at Innwerk.[45] Instead, ALTED, with two plants producing respectively 20,000 and 40,000 tons per year, had greater scale economies at full speed, but also great rigidity in handling fixed costs in the case of a too important reduction of production. These profoundly different situations led the two parties to a mediation that set a first right of production of 80 tons per share for the second half of 1931, which corresponded to the minimum ALTED could accept to run its unit in Arvida but also to the maximum the Europeans could allow.[46]

The different views on production rate also derived from the terms of the AAC contract and from the former links that the Europeans had established with the outsiders. European companies could count on production quotas destined to the United States, which remained outside the control of the scheme. In addition to production for the American market, the old firms of AA continued contracts with outsiders to buy from them amounts of metal at low prices, in exchange for a reduction in production. Keeping these old contracts for the purchase of metal from the outsiders, the European companies also had other metal to either be handled or, eventually, to be sold to AAC. Both these facts led the Europeans to ask for a right of production lower than that desired by ALTED.[47] However, these two factors did not allow AAC to have an objective idea about the international situation while deciding the production right to be applied. This fact negatively influenced AAC's ability to operate as an international clearing house causing a failure to clear stock, and persistent overproduction.[48] Actually, during the second half of 1931, rather than make room in the market to sell the unsold stock, all the firms of AAC had an excess of production of about 5,000 tons. In addition to over-estimating demand, firms produced outside the quota and also bought metal from outsiders. According to the plans, as we have seen, AAC would have had to clear instead a total of 14,000 tons of stock (half of the annual 28,000). Instead in the first six months of operations, an increase in unsold stock was recorded, rather than their progressive clearance as showed in Table 7.3.

AAC funds did not allow other purchases to present a regular balance. Unlike what Marlio thought about the financial partners of the cartel, these proved to be extremely averse to allow loans to finance a further accumulation of stock. The strategy of the cartel was strongly influenced by the vision that the banks had of the aluminium industry. Instead of serving as mere *conseil panaché*, the administration board of the company imposed its vision on the industrial executives. Actually, the Swiss banks were alarmed by this increase of unsold stock, and during 1932 requested a substantial curtailment of production to the Board of Governors. Swiss bankers forced Alliance to favour the buffering of stock instead of keeping scale production because, if these guidelines were not accepted, warrants risked not being repayable at the banks' outlay.[49] Aluminium producers also tried to involve other banks in the scheme, such as the Société Générale and Crédit Lyonnais (at that time the main financial backer of French producers), without success.[50] The producers were compelled to renounce further inventory purchases due to this veto, and endorsed a plan for their faster liquidation at the expense of scale production. Financial supporters endeavoured successfully to curb unlimited stock accumulation rectifying the whole scheme.[51]

Table 7.3 The start of Alliance: output, stocks, and transfer of metal to AAC and purchases from AAC and outsiders (tons and %), second half of 1931

| | Stocks 1931 at 31 December | Production | | Purchases from | | | A + B | Sales |
|---|---|---|---|---|---|---|---|---|
| | | allowed | actual (A) | outsiders | AAC | total (B) | | |
| AF | 12,369 | 11,960 | 12,912 | 1,592 | -4,800 | -3,208 | 9,704 | 8,514 |
| AIAG | 9,745 | 8,640 | 9,713 | 4,294 | -4,200 | 94 | 9,807 | 8,478 |
| ALTED | 16,918 | 16,000 | 16,133 | 300 | -4,400 | -4,100 | 12,033 | 12,420 |
| BACO | 8,323 | 8,400 | 8,959 | 841 | 1,100 | 1,941 | 10,900 | 9,510 |
| VAW | 11,677 | 11,000 | 11,934 | 3,600 | -4,600 | -1,000 | 10,934 | 9,948 |
| Total | 59,032 | 56,000 | 59,651 | 10,627 | -16,900 | -6,273 | 53,378 | 48,870 |

Source: author's elaboration from various files in RPA, 00-2-19532 and 00-2-195433.

Swiss banks refused to finance further purchases of stocks during 1932. AFC and AIAG were compelled to lend ten million Swiss francs to Alliance in order to complete the purchase of some inventories that were still in the hands of the producers. However, this was not sufficient to allow Alliance to take control over all extra-inventories. Thus, AFC and AIAG obtained that the cartel board raised 'holding rights' up to 53 tons per share and modified Alliance's policies.[52] Production rights were lowered from 80 per cent in the summer of 1931 to 70 per cent in the autumn of the same year, to 57.5 per cent in the spring of 1932, and, finally, to 50 per cent in the summer of 1932, when smelters worked at half capacity for the rest of the year and during 1933. This curtailment stabilised prices at £-gold 70 per ton, and kept this price stable until late 1934. At the same time, Alliance started to liquidate stock using some markets as a 'relief valve', such as Japan, India, and the Soviet Union.[53] The activity of Alliance progressively changed, as showed in Figure 7.1.

This uniform reduction was very effective to redress the international balance, but it was hardly adaptable to specific national conditions. BACO feared that its government would not accept a reduction that big. In addition to the strategic policies of the British government towards the aluminium industry, the British economic policy was oriented towards the construction of a system of imperial preferences aimed at import substitution, the creation of new tariffs, and the construction of an intra-imperial trade sanctioned by the Ottawa Conference of 1932. The British demand for aluminium, as we have seen in the previous chapters, had long been satisfied in large part by imports

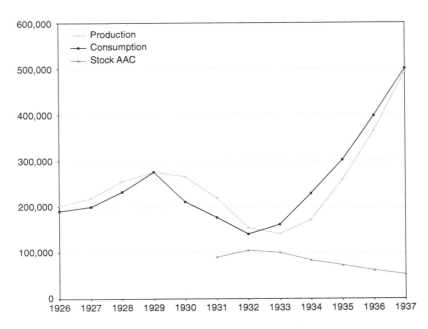

*Figure 7.1* Alliance control over the global aluminium market.

coming from Switzerland, Germany, and Norway – as well as from Canada – and the British government expected that BACO would gradually reduce and replace these with domestic or imperial production. Rather than import increasing amounts of Canadian metal, military circles preferred to maintain a high level of employment in establishments in Scotland to be ready to quickly meet military demand in case of need.[54]

In addition, the action of Alliance was also modified by British monetary policy. As we have seen, the whole framework of the cartel had been built using British sterling as the reference currency. This was the result of two considerations. First, this currency had standing in the interwar period as a reference in the prices of all other non-ferrous metals (after 1945, quotations would be mainly in US$). As a result, the international price of aluminium had also begun to be listed in this currency, as this would allow greater efficiency in competition with other metals such as tin and copper that came from the sterling area. Second, the system of international payments, the Golden Metal Exchange, was rebuilt in 1926 on the basis of the convertibility of its currency with gold. The decision to stop the convertibility of British sterling at the end of 1931 and the devaluation that followed created an advantage for BACO, which could lower its sales prices. In fact, the standard price of AAC of £-gold 70 per ton corresponded to £-paper 110, and this price was too high for its own domestic market.[55]

These curtailments particularly provoked opposition from the German government. VAW endorsed output reductions during 1932 and agreed to import metal, but during 1933 Von der Porten was concerned by the growing hostility of his government, which aimed to increase national production and to cut imports in order to cope with unemployment and harsh deficits of national commercial balance. German monetary authorities obstructed the flow of foreign currencies to Alliance's cashier and started to support low price exports of semi-finished goods in aluminium, especially towards the sterling area, endangering the stabilisation of the ingots market.[56] German semi-fabricated imports endangered the position of the British market, which was already affected by the devaluation of British sterling. Alliance's stabilised price of £-gold 70 per ton corresponded to about £-paper 110, which BACO and ALTED claimed was too high to win the competition of other metals.[57] High prices of aluminium, which were the consequence of the specific monetary situation of British sterling devaluation, favoured copper producers operating in the sterling area, thus threatening a key outlet for aluminium. High prices were a threat also for ALTED. The Canadian company was able to refocus its strategy into this market, taking advantage of the new economic policies of the British government. As a consequence of the Ottawa conference and of imperial preferences, ALTED imports passed from 3,382 (40 per cent of the total) tons in 1932 to 10,036 in 1933 (90 per cent of the total). BACO and ALTED obtained that Alliance chose to employ a special price strategy for the British market, where special prices were set to meet copper lowest quotations and allowed reductions for electrical conductors up to £-gold 45, pooling losses.[58]

## The weaknesses of Alliance: outsiders, monetary situation, and cost of operations

Despite these measures, Alliance had some weaknesses that caused a problematic situation on several markets. As anticipated, AAC tried to use some markets as a relief valve for stock, such as the Russian and Japanese markets. The Japanese market, as we have seen in the previous chapter, followed special arrangements and ALTED managed all exports on behalf of the Western companies. Acting as intermediary for the cartel, ALTED's strategy was to lower selling prices on this market to help raise sales. This measure was intended to adapt price to the devaluation implemented by the Japanese central bank[59] and to prevent the government from supporting the emergence of local production as it had seemed to happen several times.[60] In 1932, ALTED proposed to the firms of the group to form a strategic stock of 10,000 tons, which was intended to clear the Western part of the surplus and to ensure to the Japanese government the presence of an adequate supply of metal for military purposes. In this case ALTED provided the bulk of this stock and managed the supply of the other companies with metal swaps.[61]

The Russian market appeared to be more problematic. Towards the late 1920s, when the global crisis began to reduce consumption in European markets, several companies consolidated trade with the USSR to find additional outlets. As mentioned above, AF was among the companies that tried to take advantage of this outlet the most by establishing business contacts through its government and forming an appropriate sales office, the Comptoir Franco-Russe. However, this trade was very risky because the firms received late payments compared to the shipping and in some cases payment was not completed due to the chronic lack of foreign currency in the Soviet Union. At the beginning of the 1930s a flow of international trade to the Soviet Union based on a system of state guarantees and private insurance was imposed.[62] The problem with this system was that the governments were not always willing to provide their guarantees to the whole trade, but only on part of the value, leaving much of the risk to private companies. The governments in fact provided guarantees only if this trade was functional to their commercial policy and this did not take into account the needs of the aluminium producers (or of AAC). From 1932 onwards German and Italian firms, which hoped to export part of their surplus to the Soviet Union, no longer had government guarantees. At the same time, in France several companies that emerged to promote foreign trade with the Soviet Union lost the support of the financial world for their operations. In this situation, Norway was one of the few countries that adopted a policy of assurance and encouragement of exports of aluminium in Russia. Faced with the nationalism and protectionism of other countries, the Soviet Union became one of the few outlets for an exporting country such as Norway, from which also ALTED, BACO, and AF took advantage to export thanks to their subsidiaries.[63]

In addition to these strategies, AAC tried to reduce the purchase of metal to outsiders. In particular, the situation of ALCOR appeared very dangerous for the whole scheme. This company had a large enough capacity, approximately 9,000 tons per year (1,000 in the UK and 8,000 in Norway), which was unlikely to be reduced because the energy used for the production of aluminium was purchased from the Norwegian government and because this supply contract foresaw an increase to expand production to 12,000 tons in Norway at the end of 1932. At the beginning, ALTED suggested that Norsk should buy out this firm taking advantage of the financial problems of ALCOR that had arisen with the crisis. The companies of AAC thought to make Norsk buy it out, because its CEO, Sigmur Kloumann, was very influential with its government and could easily renegotiate a reduction in energy contracts and a drastic reduction in production up to 4,000 tons per year.[64] For a second time, however, the European companies opted for another procedure to avoid ALTED expanding its influence in Norway. At the end of 1931, AAC prospected to take over directly ALCOR, in order to reduce its production and to stop the purchase of its unsold stock. Thanks to the intermediation of BACO, AAC entered into negotiations to take over ALCOR. BACO contacted the bank that financed this firm, the T.T. Lee Bank in London, and held a large block of shares as a pledge of the overdraft accumulated. BACO obtained a purchase option for the company on behalf of AAC and, at the same time, Kloumann negotiated a reduction in the supply of electricity with his government to slow down production accordingly, presenting himself as the final purchaser of Norsk. These operations were completed successfully at the end of 1933, when the Alliance Aluminium Holding (AAH), a British company that would manage ALCOR on behalf of the cartel, was founded.[65]

Differently from ALCOR, Alliance had big problems slowing down Italian production. This was a real paradox, because the companies in the cartel were convinced that the Italian companies would surrender to the will of Alliance without difficulty. We also have seen that Davis forecast that they would be part of the cartel by 1934. Instead, the existence of the contract signed among VAW, AIAG, SAVA, and SIDA in December 1929, when they were competing with ALTED, represented a bothersome legacy in the new context. VAW and AIAG, in fact, were bound by contract to purchase all of the two firms' surplus regarding Italian demand until 31 December 1934 in exchange for the prohibition to export and to increase the production capacity for SAVA and SIDA. The continuation of this agreement was considered effective in taming a possible export policy of the fascist regime. As we have seen, this agreement was the outcome of the specific corporate situation of SIDA, which was not fully controlled by VAW, and of the request of AIAG to see SAVA treated in the same manner as SIDA. When AA was liquidated, VAW and AIAG did not end up with an obligation to buy the metal from the two companies which, thanks to their contract, did not reduce production in the harsher core of the international market slump.[66] The metal VAW and AIAG had to buy was included in the system of warrants of AAC and, consequently, it deeply affected the financial situation of the cartel, spoiling the relationship among the members of Alliance.[67]

The Italian case represented a main source of anxiety for Alliance in this period: while the cartel was struggling to redress the global market situation, Italian production, in spite of the almost total control that the companies of the cartel had over it, was out from the general output curtailments. All the companies of AAC in this period had reduced their production by 50 per cent of their capacity, while the Italian companies were producing at full capacity thanks to their former agreements. AF and BACO found this intolerable and thought VAW and AIAG were taking advantage of the situation too much. AAC tried to outline various plans to rectify this situation, but they all failed because the contract of 1929 was too convenient for SIDA and SAVA to lead them to accept any other solution. In addition, thanks to this contract AIAG could count on additional production which was considered as compensation for the quota that it accepted in the cartel.[68] This situation should have continued until the end of the contract in 1934, but surprisingly it found relief some months before, when public authorities decided to close down SIDA's smelter for environmental reasons. The alumina produced with VAW's new technology, the Haglund process, was indicated as one of the main causes of this turmoil and generated an escalation of difficulties between Montecatini, which aimed to continue production, and VAW, which was not in position to continue the flow of capital necessary to tune the process.[69] In 1934, at the same time that SIDA was closed down, the Italian government included aluminium in its trade restrictions scheme, which was launched in the same year to solve its balance of trade and payments problems.[70] Considering the importance that was ascribed to aluminium in the construction of full metal planes and the growing role of air power in modern warfare, the Italian government encouraged the increase of national production and consumption over the limits imposed by Alliance, banning also the exports of this metal. This radically altered the situation: exports were no longer a problem for Alliance and the Italian aluminium industry was effectively removed from the international panorama. VAW, as it was no longer possible to finance further experiments with the Haglund process, liquidated its interests in Italian production at the beginning of 1935, ending its uncomfortable venture with Donegani.[71]

The new strategy of AAC was a mixture of heavy reduction in production for the members, strong control over the stock of the outsiders, and a ductile export strategy into the 'relief valve' markets. Aside from the Russian and Japanese markets, the US market deserves specific attention in our narrative. Due to the antitrust law, it was not possible to set an agreement with ALTED about this market, even though the former AA firms set up a *contrat avenant* about the export to US to keep outside from Alliance's regulation. From 1932, AF changed its sales structure in the US in order to help find customers in this outlet, improving its former sales agency. AF had been present in the US market since the end of the Great War, but in 1932, AF reorganised its American business forming a new company, which was used to sell also French chemical products, named International Selling Corporation (ISCO). ISCO director was Ernst Darling, who before the Great War was ALCOA's agent in the British market. The reorganisation of ISCO was not a weapon against ALCOA; on the contrary, the peace made with ALCOA and the room made in the US market by the tacit agreement with ALTED led AF to enter this market with much efficacy. During the 1930s, two main customers emerged: Fairmont and Reynolds Metals Company.[72]

This composite strategy guaranteed a more or less successful control over the situation, allowing an overall control of surpluses from 1932 onwards. It allowed companies to bring the level of the owned stocks back to an acceptable limit with much benefit for stabilisation of the market price. However, AAC failed to implement the plan developed in June 1931, according to which every year 24,000 tons of stock would be sold on the market. The companies belonging to AAC reduced their production below demand between 1932 and 1933 to leave space progressively for the sale of stock and of the metal that they had to buy from outsider firms. When demand increased again in 1934, the firms continued to keep production far below demand to allow a sale of almost 17,000 tons that had previously been accumulated. The overall operations of Alliance on the world market are summarised in Table 7.4.

Alliance succeeded through its compromises to keep low production even when demand increased again above the levels of 1931, but it was not able to clear the stock by the end of 1934, as was originally proposed. AAC only partially worked as a clearing house: it gave up buying all the stock due to lack of funds, and decided to gradually increase the surplus in the hands of producers and to reduce their level of production, thus passing over the original idea contained in Davis' draft of 1931. AAC's operation was much influenced by sales policies of the outsiders and the presence of a large producer like ALTED, that was virtually landlocked and could not dispose of its annual production, forcing AAC to repeat purchases. In order for Alliance's system to work and to reduce overproduction some companies endured great financial sacrifices (AF, BACO, and, to a lesser extent, VAW), while others (AIAG and especially ALTED) were forced to sell the metal to AAC at low cost as determined by the foundation contract.

As regards prices, AAC was not able to keep the price of AA of £-gold 85 per ton (2,125 Swiss francs), and stabilised it around the level of £-gold 70 (1,750 Swiss francs) preventing falls below this limit and avoiding downward speculations. The risks that the market price fell to £60–55, as had happened in 1930 in the Japanese market, was thus averted. In the event that AAC was not able to check the prices, they would generate a total loss over 100,000 tons of about 25 million Swiss francs. On total sales of approximately 335,000 tons between 1932 and 1934 this loss would have been about 84 million Swiss francs. AAC's system avoided a global loss that would have been more than double its capital. We must also add that the capital of AAC of 35 million was not lost, as in the case of a simple reduction of price, but it was 'invested' in AAC. Sales of stock would have regenerated profit when the demand grew again. While the financial mechanism seems very effective to prevent losses that would have been caused by a rapid decline in prices, AAC could not guarantee a quick clearance of stock, which continued to influence the international aluminium market negatively after 1934. To ensure that the surpluses were paid, a significant increase in demand was needed, which, as we will see, came only with sudden military demand in the second half of the 1930s. We will see in the next chapter that the military demand and strategies of the various governments, primarily the German one, for the aluminium industry did not just provide a new stimulus to demand, but profoundly altered the operation of AAC, which underwent a deep transformation. Due to military and strategic policies, AAC was no longer able to operate correctly during the second half of the 1930s and was reorganised in order to take account of the individual national conditions of each producer.

Table 7.4 Production, sales, exports, purchases from outsiders, stock, and rights established by the Alliance, 1932–1943 (tons)

| | Rights | | Production | | Stocks at 31 December | | | Purchases | | Sales | | A + B − C |
|---|---|---|---|---|---|---|---|---|---|---|---|---|
| | production | stock | actual (A) | allowed | individual | AAC | outsiders | total (B) | exports* | total (C) | | |
| 1932 | 53.7 | 48.0 | 79,218 | 74,692 | 69,595 | 35,300 | 11,173 | 20,473 | 20,437 | 98,859 | 6,833 |
| 1933 | 50.0 | 50.5 | 75,859 | 68,254 | 62,954 | 36,900 | 12,361 | 11,161 | 11,981 | 99,649 | −12,629 |
| 1934 | 55.0 | 53.0 | 97,061 | 91,343 | 52,935 | 28,100 | 14,899 | 22,699 | 16,339 | 136,670 | −16,910 |
| Total | – | – | 252,138 | 234,289 | – | – | 38,433 | 54,333 | 48,757 | 335,178 | −22,706 |

Source: author's elaboration from various files in RPA, 00-2-19532 and 00-2-195433.

Note
* To USSR, Japan, and United States.

Table 7.5 Money transfers between AAC and its members, 1931–1934 (in Swiss francs)

| | AF | AIAG | ALTED | BACO | VAW | Total. AAC |
|---|---|---|---|---|---|---|
| 25% initial capital | -1,868,750 | -1,350,000 | -2,500,000 | -1,312,500 | -1,718,750 | 8,750,000 |
| Transfers to AAC | -5,960,000 | 12,500,000 | 21,900,000 | -8,260,000 | -520,000 | -19,660,000 |
| Further contributions | -1,100,000 | -800,000 | -1,460,000 | -760,000 | -1,000,000 | 5,120,000 |
| Total | -8,928,750 | 10,350,000 | 17,940,000 | -10,300,000 | -3,238,750 | -5,790,000 |

Source: author's elaboration from various files in RPA, 00-2-19532 and 00-2-195433.

Note
Numbers are negative when the firm paid to AAC, they are positive when AAC paid to firms.

# Notes

1  RPA, 00-2-15940, Note Dactylographiée de la réunion du Comité de l'AA de 15 Octobre 1930.
2  RZA, Berichte über die allgemeine Geschaftslage, fold. 1929–1930, Berichte 18 October 1930.
3  Marlio, *The Aluminum Cartel*, 37, 42.
4  RPA, 00-2-15940, Procès-Verbal de la Vingt-Cinquième Réunion du Comité de l'Aluminium-Association tenue à Londres le 15 Octobre 1930.
5  HHC, MSS #282, ALCOA, US v. ALCOA, Equity 85–73, Exhibits, Ex.800, Henry-Couannier to E.K. Davis, 10 December 1930.
6  RPA, 00-2-15940, Procès-Verbal de la Vingt-Sexième Réunion du Comité de l'Aluminium-Association tenue à Zurich le 16 janvier 1931. 00-2-15931, Bloch to Marlio, 19 May 1931.
7  RPA, 00-2-15940, Note dactylographiée de la Réunion du comité de l'AA de 15 Janvier 1931. About Bouchayer, see Robert J. Smith, *The Bouchayers of Grenoble and French Industrial Entrerprise, 1850–1970*. Baltimore MD: John Hopkins University Press, 2001.
8  RPA, 00-2-15933, Marlio, Résultats des conversations avec M. E.K. Davis, 26 June 1931.
9  HHC, MSS #282, ALCOA, US v. ALCOA, Equity 85–73, Exhibit 784, Draft Project for the Aluminium International Company, April 1931.
10 Barjot, 'Introduction'.
11 ALTED registered a net deficit of around $1 million in its 1931 balance sheet. SWA, ALCAN Jahresberichte Bg 1132–1968, Aluminium Limited, Fourth annual report 1931, Montreal 1932, 5.
12 RPA, 00-2-15928, Murray-Morrison, Memorandum Re Document for the proposed formation of a Finance Company by Aluminium Producers, Private and Confidential, 19 May 1931. HHC, MSS #282, ALCOA, US v. ALCOA, Equity 85–73, Exhibit 784, Draft Project for the Aluminium International Company, April 1931.
13 John Maynard Keynes, 'The Policy of Government Storage of Food-Stuffs and Raw Materials', *Economic Journal*, vol. 48, no. 191, 1938, 449–460. The original idea was presented by Benjamin Graham, *Storage and Stability: A Modern ever Normal Granary*. New York: McGraw-Hill, 1937.
14 Hillman, *The International Tin Cartel*. Coates, *The Commerce in Rubber*. Colin Barlow, Sisira Jayasuriya, Choo Suan Tan, *The World Rubber Industry*. London: Routledge, 1994, 260–270.
15 RPA, 00-2-15928, Murray-Morrison, Memorandum Re for the proposed formation of a Finance Company, 19 May 1931.
16 RPA, 00-2-15940, Note Dactylographiée de la réunion du Comité AA, 27 May 1931. Note Dactylographiée de la réunion du Comité AA, 8 May 1931. Bloch (AIAG) to Marlio (AF), 19 May 1931.
17 HHC, MSS #282, ALCOA, US v. ALCOA, Equity 85–73, Exhibit 784, Draft Project for the Aluminium International Co., April 1931.
18 HHC, MSS #282, ALCOA, US v. ALCOA, Equity 85–73, Exhibit 784, Draft Project for the Aluminium International Company, April 1931.
19 Nappi, *L'Aluminium*.
20 About financial tools for trading in commodities, see Carlo Fumian, 'Commodity Trading', in *The Palgrave Dictionary of Transnational History*, edited by Akira Iriye and Pierre-Yves Saunier. Basingstoke, New York: Palgrave Macmillan, 2009, *ad vocem*.
21 'L'idée fondamentale du projet de M. Davis est contingentement de la production et une équilibration complète avec l'Aluminium International Co. comme clearing house, tandis qu'aujourd'hui nous n'avons pas de restriction de la production mais des ventes.' RPA, 00-2-15928, Memorandum Re the proposed formation of a Finance Company, 19 May 1931.

22 RPA, 00-2-15931, Von Der Porten to Marlio, 2 June 1931. RPA, 00-2-15933, Marlio, Résultats des conversations avec M. E.K. Davis', 26 June 1931.
23 RPA, 00-2-15940, Note Dactylographiée de la réunion du Comité de l'AA de 8 Mai 1931.
24 RPA, 00-2-15928, Alliance Aluminium Compagnie, Contre-Projet, 29 May 1931. Note Explicative, 12 May 1931. RPA, 00-2-15931, Von der Porten, Remarques sommaires concernant la proposition des Canadiens pour la création d'une société internationale pour la valorisation de l'aluminium, 23 May 1931.
25 RPA, 00-2-15940, Note Dactylographiée de la réunion du Comité de l'AA de 27 Mai 1931.
26 RPA, 00-2-15940, Note Dactylographiée de la réunion du Comité de l'AA de 8 Mai 1931. Note Dactylographiée de la réunion du Comité de l'AA de 27 Mai 1931.
27 RPA, 00-2-15933, Résultats des conversations avec M. E.K. Davis, 26 June 1931.
28 RPA, 00-2-15932, Bloch to Marlio, 19 May 1931.
29 RPA, 00-2-15940, Note Dactylographiée de la réunion du Comité de l'AA de 27 et 28 Mai 1931. RPA, 00-2-15928, Memorandum Re the proposed formation of a Finance Company, 19 May 1931.
30 RPA, 00-2-15928, Marlio, Note Explicative, 12 May 1931.
31 RPA, 00-2-15928, Contrat des Associés de l'Alliance Aluminium, Fonctionnement de l'AAC, 3 July 1931. Bloch (AIAG), Contre-Projet, 29 May 1931. Von der Porten (VAW), Remarques sommaires concernant la proposition des Canadiens pour la création d'une société internationale pour la valorisation de l'aluminium, 23 May 1931.
32 RPA, 00-2-15928, Decisions 18 et 19 Juin 1931 concernant l'application du contrat sur la fondation de l'AAC. RPA, 00-2-15933, Contrat avenant au contrat de fondation de l'Alliance, 3 July 1931.
33 RPA, 00-2-15928, Contrat Alliance Aluminium Compagnie, 3 July 1931. Decisions 18 et 19 Juin concernant l'application du contrat sur la foundation de l'AAC.
34 RPA, 00-2-15940, Note Dactylographiée de la réunion du Comité de l'AA, 2 and 3 July 1931. RPA, 00-2-15928, Conditions envisages pour la Constitution de l'Alliance Aluminium Compagnie, 3 July 1931. On these points see also Marco Bertilorenzi, 'L'Alliance Aluminium Compagnie, 1931–1939: Organisation et Gestion de la Branche International de l'Aluminium entre Grande Crise et Guerre Mondiale', in *Contribution à une Histoire des Cartels en Suisse*, edited by Alain Cortat. Neuchatel: Editions d'Alphil, Presses Universitaires Suisses, 2010, 219–253.
35 HHC, MSS #282, ALCOA, US v. ALCOA, Exhibits, ex.781, E.K. Davis to A. Henry-Couannier, 1 August 1931.
36 Cannadine, *Mellon: An American Life*; Koskoff, *The Mellons*; Love, *Andrew W. Mellon*.
37 Alliance's board was formed by Louis Marlio (AF), Robert W. Cooper (BACO), Rudolf G. Bindschedler (Crédit Suisse), Arnold Bloch (AIAG), André Henry-Couannier (ALTED), Maurice Lugeon (Université de Lausanne), Max Von der Porten (VAW), Max Staehelin (Société de Banque Suisse), Gérard Steck (AIAG). SWA, b.851, Alliance Aluminium Compagnie, Exercise de l'Alliance Aluminium Compagnie de Bale, 1931.
38

L'avantage d'un conseil panaché qui aurait comme membres des représentants de grandes banques suisses, serait de nous procurer immédiatement autant d'argent que nous pourrions en désirer ... Il faudrait choisir des gens très influents et la question se pose de savoir si ces Messieurs seraient disposés à jouer le role que nous leur attribuerions.

RPA, 00-2-15940, Note Dactylographiée de la réunion du Comité de l'AA du 2–3 Juillet 1931.
39 RPA, 00-2-15928, Procès Verbal. 1ère Réunion du Board of Governors, 21 October 1931.
40 RPA, 00-2-15940, Note Dactylographiée de la reunion du Comité de l'AA, 18 and 19 June 1931.

41 RPA, 00-2-19528, Répercussions de l'accord américain au point de vue souscription en numéraire et stocks initiaux. Capital initial correspondant aux deux groupes fondateurs. 26 June 1931.
42 RPA, 00-2-15928, Proces-Verbal de la Réunion de l'Alliance, tenue à Bale le 3 Juillet 1931.
43 RPA, 00-1-20028, Production Aluminium des usines AFC, 1913–1938.
44 RZA, S2 T2, Rohaluminium – Produktion in Kg, 1889–1983.
45 HWA, MG Documents, Abt.119, Nr.896–900 Erzeugung an Hutter-aluminium (in t), 1931–1940.
46 RPA, 00-2-15940, Note Dactylographiée de la réunion du Comité de l'AA du 18–19 Juin 1931.
47 RPA, 00-2-15940, Note Dactylographiée de la réunion du Comité de l'AA du 20 et 21 Octobre 1931. RPA, 00-2-15928, Minutes of the 2nd Board of Governors AAC, 21 October 1931.
48 RPA, 00-2-15933, Note sur l'Alliance, 17 August 1932.
49 RPA, 00-2-15933, Braasch (Alliance) to Marlio (AF), 30 January 1932. Marlio to Staehelin (Société de Banque Suisse), 9 March 1932.
50 AHSG, 6350/2845, Note. Visite de M. Dupin, Directeur de Péchiney et de M. Braasch, Directeur de l'Alliance Compagnie à M. de Méeus, 2 June 1932.
51 RPA, 00-2-15929, AAC 8ème Réunion du Board of Governors, Ostende, 18, 19, and 20 July 1932.
52 RPA, 00-2-15933, Résultats des mouvements de fonds depuis l'origine entre l'Alliance Aluminium Cie et ses actionnaires, 3 December 1934.
53 RPA, A00-2-15938, Actif de l'AAC, 5 January 1935.
54 TNA, CAB/24/234, Cabinet, Imperial Economic Conference at Ottawa, 1932. Summary and Proceedings and Copies of Trade Agreements. See also Perchard, *Aluminiumville.*
55 RPA, 00-2-15929, AAC 10ème Réunion du Board of Governors, 15 December 1932.
56 RPA, 00-2-15929, AAC 12ème Réunion du Board of Governors, 15 June 1933. See also Rauh, *Schweizer Aluminium für Hitlers Krieg?* 69–71.
57 TNA, CAB/24/234, Cabinet, Imperial Economic Conference at Ottawa, 1932. Summary and Proceedings and Copies of Trade Agreements.
58 RPA, 00-2-15933, Note sur le nouvel accord pour les ventes de metal destiné aux conducteurs électriques, 17 August 1932.
59 W. Miles Fletcher III, 'Japanese Banks and National Economic Policy, 1920–1936', in *The Role of Banks in the Interwar Economy*, edited by Harold James, Hakan Lindgren, and Alice Teichova. New York: Cambridge University Press, 1991, 25–71, Karl E. Born, *International Banking in the 19th and 20th Century*. New York: Leamington, 1983. Ishii Kanji, 'Japan', in Cameron, Bovykin (eds), *International Banking, 1870–1914*, 214–232.
60 RPA, 00-1-20047, Marché Japonais – Aspects du Marché, 1933. RPA, 00-2-15932, Organisation de vente au Japon, 18 April 1932.
61 RPA, 00-2-15928, AAC, Procès-Verbal de la 6ème Réunion de l'AAC, 1 June 1932. Procès-Verbal de la 7ème Réunion de l'AAC', 19–20 July 1932.
62 Andrew J. Williams, *Trading with the Bolsheviks: The Politics of East–West Trade, 1920–39.* Manchester: Manchester University Press, 1992.
63 RPA, 001-14-20501, Note sur la monnaie de paiement des contrats russes, 17 February 1932. See also Bonfils, 'Pechiney au Pays des Soviets'. Espen Storli, 'Trade and Politics: The Western Aluminium Industry and the Soviet Union in the Intewar Period', in Frøland, Ingulstad (eds), *From Warfare to Welfare*, 69–99.
64 RPA, 00-2-15940, Note Dactylographiée de la réunion du Comité de l'AA du 18–19 Juin 1931.
65 UGD, 347/21/6/35, Alliance Aluminium Holding Ltd, Reports and Accounts, Report of 1934. RPA, 00-2-15933, Allaince Aluminium Holdings Limited, 1933.

66 RPA, 00-2-15933, Alliance Aluminium Cie., July 1935. 4 Années d'existence de l'AAC, 5 July 1935.

67 RPA, 00-2-15933, Marlio to E.K. Davis, 22 December 1932.

68 RPA, 00-2-15933, Alliance Aluminium Cie., July 1935. AEC, Box Montecatini, Fold. 3/5, SIDA, Verbale del consiglio d'amministrazione, 11 July 1933.

69 About this aspect of history, see Guido De Luigi, Edgar Meyer, Andrea Saba, 'Industrie, Pollution et Politique: La "Zone Noire" de la Società Italiana dell'Alluminio dans la Province de Trente (1928–1938)', in Grinberg, Hachez-Leroy (eds), *Industrialisation et Sociétés*, 314–323.

70 Luigi Spaventa and Franco Cotula (ed.), *La Politica Monetaria tra le due Guerre, 1919–1935*. Rome-Bari: Laterza, 1993. Felice Guarneri, *Battaglie Economiche fra le due Guerre*. Milano: Garzanti, 1953. See also the recent Alessio Gagliardi, *L'impossibile Autarchia: La Politica Economica del Fascismo e il Ministero Scambi e Valute*. Milano: Rubattino, 2006.

71 ASBCI, 6. Archivi Aggregati, Società finanziaria industriale italiana (Sofindit), Archivio Sofindit, Presidenza e Direzione, SOF 327, fasc.5 (società diverse), L'alluminio Italiano, 1937.

72 RPA, 001-14-20477, Historique de nos agences américaines aux Etats-Unis, ISCO, Note sur l'International Selling Co., Janvier 1933. Réorganisation de l'International Selling Corp., 1932.

# 8 The 'great transformation' of Alliance

## An international cartel in an autarkic world, 1934–1938

After Hitler's takeover, VAW's position in the cartel strongly changed, questioning the working of the whole cartel. Hjalmar Schacht, the German Minister of Economics and Reichbank's president, reinforced monetary and trade controls hampering both imports in Germany and VAW's payments to Alliance for its operations. At the same time, both Von der Porten and Ernst Rauch – the German delegates who had been part of the network of producers since 1923 – were removed from VAW's and Alliance's boards.[1] Von der Porten was replaced with Karl Schirner, while Rauch was replaced with Rudolf Westrick.[2] When Schirner and Westrick joined Alliance's board, they both worked to change Alliance's rules.[3] For instance, during a meeting in February 1934, Schirner argued

> It was a mistake to think of regulating the aluminium market through Alliance. The steel international cartel had made the same mistake ... It is the reason why I am convinced to organize the exports from my county immediately, in order to be able to ask you to organize the export market together.[4]

Before their appointment, Schirner and Westrick played a key role in the international steel industry. They were kind of 'industrial diplomats', who – being members of the German deputation into the steel cartel – were able to recast the International Steel Cartel (ISC) in the first half of 1933 following the directives of the German authorities. They succeeded in establishing a system based on national monopolies and quotas for the export markets.[5] The previous cartel, the Entente Internationale de l'Acier (EIA) had worked between 1926 and 1931 by means of production quotas and a system of fines for those that exceeded the allowed production. With this system, an expansion of demand in Germany between 1927 and 1929, that was higher than its quota in the cartel, had forced Vereinigte Stahlwerke to pay various penalties. The penalties were forfeited by the Belgian and French groups, because their production was smaller than their quotas, and had been used to dump their exports in the British market and in Germany in 1930 and 1931. These manoeuvres led to the end of the EIA in 1931 and opened new negotiations for the resettlement of the cartel. After about a couple of years of negotiations, ISC was created with a system of reservations for 'home markets' of its members. Each group was completely free to produce for the domestic market without quotas, while ISC only fixed export quotas.[6]

The steel cartel of 1926, which was replaced in 1933 by the ISC's home markets system, was rather similar to Alliance. Like Alliance, it settled universal rights of production that did not take into account the individual national economies. Even if it was not explicitly stated at first, Schirner was appointed in the board of Alliance to gradually erode the internationalism of the finance company and to progressively adopt strategies that best suited the nationalistic policies of the German government. European companies were inclined to change Alliance in this sense because they were not completely satisfied with its work, since it was not successful either in clearing the unsold stocks or maintaining sales prices at a level higher than £70 per ton during a period of severe decline in sales. Moreover, Alliance had showed it was not to be able to adapt its international tools with ease with the national policies of each member.[7]

Since his arrival in the board of Alliance in 1933, Schirner tried to present the way in which the steel cartel was reshaped as a model for the reform of Alliance. The new German policies placed VAW in the position not to be able to fulfil Alliance's rules. Schirner's goal was to serve the deep change that was reshaping the German aluminium industry and his government's policies for this metal. The reduction of production that VAW made to follow the guidelines of AAC became incompatible with the plans of Hitler's regime to boost domestic demand, and reduce imports and unemployment. In fact, according to the measures taken by AAC, increases in demand would have to be satisfied with the liquidation of stocks. When the demand in Germany increased, VAW would have to import metal from abroad (mainly from Canada, where the bulk of stock was concentrated) instead to increase its production. This was contrary not only to Schacht's measures for reducing imports, but also to the German law on cartels, because it discriminated against the domestic industry in favour of foreign production.[8]

The policies of the German government were a big institutional change. They represented a clear path towards Polanyi's 'Great transformation', that led to the end of the liberal economy and to the emergence of states as industrial planners.[9] After the extraordinary measures that were taken during the Great War, aluminium became again the object of consistent measures in Germany, which aimed to make this metal a cornerstone of economic policies relying on import substitution. These policies boosted domestic demand for aluminium making it a compulsory substitute for other non-ferrous metals, which mainly came from the British sterling area. New demands began to increase gradually in the second half of 1933, and doubled in the next year. Contemporary observers called the German aluminium industry a real 'economy of aluminium', to explain the role of this metal in the plan for import substitution.[10] Schirner pointed out to the cartel that the German group would not be able to follow the policies of Alliance for political and monetary reasons, that he called force majeure, asking for exceptions to the rule of the cartel to allow VAW to produce for the home market.[11]

The change in direction of the steel cartel, which Schirner used as an example for reform of Alliance, shows how the international economic situation had changed between the late 1920s and early 1930s. The public debate on international cartels followed this change. With the start of nationalistic and protectionist economic policies, which were eliminating multilateralism in international trade,[12] cartels would no longer play the political role that they had played over the 1920s. They lost their role of tools for the progressive integration of markets, as the Economic Conference of LoN claimed in 1927. On the contrary, they became part of the international economic policies of the states in the 1930s, when cartels became instruments of economic policy to combat the effects of the crisis and of international monetary disorders. The steel cartel constituted in the mind of politicians and economists a kind of avant-garde of what was the kind of agreement best suited to the new context.[13]

## The ambivalent situation of the German group

The German government implemented special programmes to reduce imports of other non-ferrous metals, complying with Schacht's new monetary policies, and started to replace them with aluminium. New policies in Germany led to spectacular expansion in the aluminium industry, which was not recorded in any other country. This programme was launched in 1933, then implemented within the Goering four-year plan in 1936. At its launch, the demand for aluminium doubled in 1934, and was multiplied by five in 1936. Substantial increases in the consumption of this metal occurred in the transportation industry, with gradual adoption of aluminium by the major car manufacturers. In the field of electrical equipment, German consumption of aluminium also experienced the most spectacular increases, rising from 1,000 tons in 1933 to 7,000 in 1934 and 15,000 in 1935.[14]

In addition to these measures, the German government supported a decisive increase in production and started huge investments, that since 1934 involved not only VAW but also private producers such as Aluminiumwerke (owned by Metallgesellschaft and IG Farben) and AIAG, with its plant in Rheinfelden.[15] These were the dynamics that lay behind the derogations that the German group asked for, and obtained, to the rules about the output restrictions of Alliance. The German government aimed to have free hands from the cartel control over aluminium, which became a key commodity for its commercial, monetary, and strategic policies. Without the obligation of Alliance's rules, German production grew, fostered by political powers that programmed and financed spectacular expansion. In 1936, Goering's four-year plan launched new investments linked to rearmament programmes, which settled the goal of 210,000 tons of output capacity for 1940.[16] From 1936, in fact, serial production of the new Junkers aircraft entirely made of aluminium alloy was launched, while airpower was turning out to became a key strategic factor in modern warfare, as the massacre of Guernica, one of the first bombing of civil targets, recalls.[17] From our standpoint, the key fact of this governance transition towards direct state control meant that, by 1939, German production became the largest in the world.[18]

Moreover, a national research institute for aluminium was formed in 1935, the Aluminium Zentrale (AZ) of Düsseldorf, aiming to help the substitution of other metals with aluminium in selected applications. AZ was responsible for centralising all the scientific and technological research that was previously carried out separately by the three firms producing primary metal and all other firms present on

German territory. When it was created, AZ was also linked to the BIA, the R&D office of Alliance, replacing the membership that previously was given to VLW and VAW.[19] From the institutional standpoint, a mandatory selling agency set prices and quotas for German producers (VAW, AW, and AIAG), the Aluminium-Verkaufs Gesellschaft (AVG). Its duties were to fix prices, centralise sales and planning, follow the instructions of the government, and make investments to increase output.[20] The new system deeply changed the management of the German aluminium industry. Planning production, investment, and consumption were outlined at the political level, escaping from the mechanism of Alliance.[21]

As a consequence of the start of the German programme for aluminium, VAW's rights of production became insufficient to cover national consumption. The German group also accumulated debts to AAC for about 15 million Swiss francs because of the lack of foreign currencies to participate in the costs of carrying out the activities of the cartel. At first, Schirner was not willing to ask for a liquidation of AAC, but asked that the German group was authorised to produce above its quota for special applications in the automotive and electrical industries. This proposal was intended to save the general Alliance system, but getting exceptions to the rights system.[22] The main risk for the other producers was that the German government, as an alternative, would have required the withdrawal of the German group from the cartel and included aluminium in the policies of export assistance that were also interesting other commodities.[23]

German exports represented a threat on the international markets that could have destroyed the efforts of AAC to preserve the international price. The threat came not only from the ingot market, but also from that of semi-finished products. Unlike AA, AAC had not any control over the markets of finished and semi-finished products. German export policies would have therefore directly influenced the international market of semi-finished products, eventually affecting the price of ingots. The Reich could have financed exports at low prices, through the Bond-Geschäfte (special loans to export). Even if the actual debate in the cartel was whether to recast Alliance with national preferences, AAC agreed, not without difficulty and reluctance, to grant special rights of production to the Germans to temporarily patch the situation. Schirner and Westrick obtained to produce 13,000 additional tons in 1934. Also AIAG's unit was included into the special measures of other German producers.[24] In 1935, since these measures were not sufficient to meet national demand, the German group asked and was authorised to be free to produce until the fulfilment of domestic demand.[25] In return, VAW reduced its exports dramatically (see Table 8.1). To reach this compromise, VAW agreed to buy 4,000 tons of stock in order to contribute to clearance of the surplus and to make the cartel benefit from the expansion of the German aluminium market.[26]

The cartel board adopted these ad hoc measures following a twofold consideration. On the one hand, all members aimed to maintain their cartel agreement whatever the cost because they were still going through the international crisis and inventories were not liquidated yet. The disruption of the cartel could have meant the release on the international market of a huge quantity of unsold stock. In particular, firms aimed to keep the Germans in the agreement because

Table 8.1 Capacity and production of each German producer, domestic consumption, and exports of primary metal, 1932–1939

| | VAW | | Aluminiumwerke* | | AIAG-Rheinfelden | | Total | | Domestic demand | Exports |
|---|---|---|---|---|---|---|---|---|---|---|
| | Capacity | Production | Capacity | Production | Capacity | Production | Capacity | Production | | |
| 1932 | 30,400 | 12,987 | 8,400 | 2,306 | 4,000 | 4,415 | 42,800 | 19,708 | 19,100 | 2,542 |
| 1933 | 30,400 | 10,993 | 8,400 | 2,930 | 4,400 | 4,432 | 43,200 | 18,932 | 25,955 | 3,182 |
| 1934 | 39,000 | 25,435 | 8,400 | 5,862 | 4,800 | 4,715 | 52,200 | 37,158 | 48,776 | 702 |
| 1935 | 68,500 | 52,352 | 16,500 | 10,456 | 6,700 | 6,570 | 91,700 | 70,779 | 83,550 | 249 |
| 1936 | 68,500 | 68,514 | 16,500 | 16,583 | 14,000 | 10,346 | 99,000 | 97,460 | 102,316 | 246 |
| 1937 | 104,000 | 91,689 | 26,000 | 19,502 | 14,000 | 13,774 | 144,000 | 127,543 | 128,567 | 1,334 |
| 1938 | 130,200 | 112,219 | 31,500 | 26,636 | 21,000 | 18,463 | 182,700 | 157,318 | 176,451 | n.a. |
| 1939 | 142,700 | 136,878 | 36,500 | 32,642 | 21,000 | 21,314 | 200,200 | 190,834 | 203,145 | n.a. |

Source: HWA.

Note
* A joint venture of Metallgesellschaft and IG Farben.

of the fear of exports at very low quotations. On the other hand, the solution adopted for Germany was aligned with reform of the cartel that many other members would have undertaken. But, Alliance's delegated aim was to involve the German authorities in the formulation of a new policy, in order to have guarantees before endorsing the requests that Schirner and Westrick made. In this context, finding a compromise with German political issues were meant to save the whole cartel: the specific policy that the cartel aimed to adopt for Germany was to 'rip off' this market from the rest of the world, where Alliance would continue to rule. Hjalmar Schacht himself received a cartel delegation formed by Marlio (AFC), Cooper (BACO), Bloch (AIAG), and Merton (Metallgesellschaft) during 1935 and both guaranteed an export ban for aluminium ingots and endorsed a plan to pay back German debts to AAC.[27]

This compromise seemed like a victory for the members of the cartel. Obtaining that the German group did not export at low prices was regarded as a reassuring event.[28] By cutting out Germany from the world market, the members of Alliance thought they could also remedy other delicate situations that were created with Giulini, the non-integrated producer of alumina that supplied many outsiders of the cartel (such as ALCOR). Since ALCOR was placed under the control of AAH in 1933, Giulini was back to being an insidious threat for the cartel. The takeover of ALCOR deprived Giulini of a market of over 10,000 tons of alumina per year. According to the plans of development formulated by ALCOR in the previous chapter, Giulini was also expecting to double production in the near future to supply the extensions of the new Norwegian installations. When AAC stopped this expansion and greatly reduced the production of ALCOR, Giulini sought alternative outlets, unsuccessfully negotiating contracts with other members of the Alliance. The German group accepted a deal with Giulini, but, by the end of 1934, IG Farben would launch its own production of alumina to supply the Bitterfeld smelter, jointly owned with Metallgesellschaft, cutting out Giulini as supplier.[29]

Since it feared being left without suitable outlets, Giulini started some ambitious investment policies, trying to involve several governments in his projects. In fact, in 1932 Giulini asked the German government for permission to build a new smelter in Bavaria, counting on taking advantage of the government help to curb unemployment that was already discussed in the Weimar Republic before Hitler's takeover. In addition, he negotiated with the Dutch and Swedish governments the construction of two aluminium plants that would use his alumina importing it from Germany.[30] While AAC was able to discard the risk associated with building a new plant in Germany thanks to the intervention of Von der Porten, who was then still head of VAW at that time, it was seriously worried by the other two investment attempts.[31] After trying to stop Giulini through French and British diplomatic channels, which stopped the venture in the Netherlands, Norsk managed to anticipate Giulini in Sweden, negotiating the formation of a new company, Svenska Aluminium A/S. This downsized Giulini's expansion strategy and his claims to the cartel.[32]

After this operation, Giulini decided to make terms with AAC, demanding a guaranteed outlet for his alumina. To arrive to this end, he proposed to the cartel to join AAC with a market quota of aluminium production of 10,000 tons per year. The companies were opposed to this option, as they considered it too risky to let Giulini integrate to aluminium production.[33] In 1934, AAC was able to reach a compromise with Giulini, signing an agreement according to which Giulini was given an outlet for alumina equal to the minimum amount required to produce 12 per cent of the production allowed by the production rights of AAC. Also a guaranteed minimum of 21,000 tons of alumina was settled. The contract had a duration of five years starting from 1 January 1934. This agreement set the price at which AAC bought alumina, fixing it at 15 per cent of AAC's purchase price. Although it was not optimal for AAC's companies, because it forced them to purchase alumina at quite a high price by reducing their production of alumina, the contract in exchange prevented Giulini both from investing directly in the field of aluminium and from providing technical assistance to outsiders that, as we will see, were growing in different countries.[34]

The negotiations with Giulini were made simultaneously with those of VAW for the additional quotas. Schirner was able to tie his demands to the Giulini affaire: in exchange for the right to be free to produce, VAW committed to purchase all the alumina that AAC would have to buy from Giulini according to the contract signed in January 1934, freeing the cartel from this duty. By allowing the German group to freely produce for its domestic market, Giulini would definitely be denied the possibility of launching his own smelter in Germany and its alumina production was integrated into the system of the so-called 'economy of aluminium' that the German government was implementing. In addition, validating Giulini as a supplier of alumina for German production actually paused the investment of IG Farben, which was seen with concern in the board of the international cartel. Overall, the detachment of VAW from the rules of the cartel would solve in a pragmatic way the various problems that underlay the relationship between AAC and all German producers (including Giulini and IG Farben). Since 1935, the German group was allowed to produce out of the quota without limit, ignoring the rules set by AAC also with regard to payments and purchases of stocks.[35]

Even if the delegates of Alliance welcomed the German compromise as a success of the cartel's industrial diplomacy and of its head, Louis Marlio, its collateral effect was to damage the cohesion of the cartel. On the one hand, the initiative of ALTED–Norsk created a big clash in AAC. The European members harshly criticised ALTED, because the creation of Svenska continued, even if Giulini was cut from it. In fact, Davis was unable to divert the Swedish government from this investment, or at least he declaimed this as a reason to continue this investment. Tensions were resolved only when Davis agreed to include half of Svenka's production in ALTED's quota into Alliance.[36] On the other hand – and in a more relevant way – instead of being perceived as an amputation of the German market from the global Alliance system, the new German situation meant the creation of a two-speed system in the cartel board, which represented an antecedent for other amendments of global governance previously defined by the producers. When other countries launched special policies for aluminium during the mid-1930s and demand skyrocketed following the upward trend of military purchases, Alliance's utility was toughly questioned.[37]

## National policies during the 1930s and Alliance's control strategy

During the mid-1930s, Germany was not the only country in which aluminium became a 'political metal', as was often declaimed during the second half of the 1930s.[38] In many countries, ad hoc policies were outlined to expand or create new aluminium facilities for both strategic and economic issues. These projects represented a threat for the international cohesion of Alliance because, on the one hand, these projects questioned the role of the cartel as general administrator for this industry; on the other hand, in many cases the cartel members were also directly implicated in the erection of these programmes and often exploited the opportunities that governmental policies offered them.[39] These projects became possible in a context in which, on the one hand the international economy was led towards a progressive end of globalisation, which altered and modified the former comparative advantages of countries. On the other hand, political powers emerged as administrators and planners in the economy, reshaping the nexus between business and politics.[40] An actual alternative to the governance of the international cartel appeared, being represented by the policies of government in fixing prices, in allocating production quotas, and in settling political driven demands. The disruption of the international monetary system also fragmented the global market that Alliance aimed to manage.

As we have seen, the Russian market had been used as a relief valve for excess production when AAC was created. In 1934, the start of production in the USSR posed a big problem on the continuation of AAC's clearing strategy, significantly reducing the exports of the cartel members. In 1935, the companies that were mostly implicated in the exports to Russia – AF, ALTED and Norsk – signed an agreement to divide some quotas in this market. These three companies were favoured politically in trade with the Soviets: in May 1935 the French government had signed an agreement for technical assistance, while the Norwegian government was already a major trading partner of the regime in Moscow in the late 1920s, thanks to the guarantees which it provided to its domestic firms that exported in this country. ALTED, as an ally of Norsk, the leading and most influential Norwegian aluminium company, was able to use this channel for export to the Soviet Union. However, this turned out to be a progressively saturated market, and only in the course of 1938 was witnessed a resumption of imports, due mainly to an unexpected delay in the achievement of the installations.[41]

In 1934, the Japanese government supported the birth of national production to emancipate the country from cartel control, by financing technical research on alternative alumina processes, and setting new very high tariffs. The lack of bauxite in the Japanese territories led the government to focus its strategy on the research of alternative ores for which specific processes were tuned to substitute the Bayer process. Alliance tried to adopt a more offensive strategy that would hamper domestic production and would make imports last as long as possible. The conception of a national industry of aluminium in Japan was born for the first time in the mid-1920s, when Western companies, as we have seen, charged high prices and investments for the national electrical grid boosted the demand

Table 8.2 Soviet trade: domestic production, imports, and national demand, 1934–1939 (tons and %)

| | Soviet Union | | | Imports | | | | | Import/ production, % | Import/ consumption, % |
|---|---|---|---|---|---|---|---|---|---|---|
| | Production | Demand | Capacity | AF | ALTED | Norsk | Total | | | |
| 1934 | 14,400 | 19,500 | 15,000 | 4,900 | – | – | 4,900 | | 34.02 | 25.12 |
| 1935 | 24,500 | 25,000 | 27,000 | 508 | 405 | 1,120 | 2,000 | | 8.16 | 8.00 |
| 1936 | 37,900 | 38,000 | 52,000 | 135 | 107 | 297 | 500 | | 1.31 | 1.31 |
| 1937 | 47,600 | 47,000 | 52,000 | 310 | 250 | 690 | 1,250 | | 2.62 | 2.65 |
| 1938 | 48,000 | 55,000 | 100,000 | 2,910 | 1,940 | 4,850 | 9,700 | | 20.20 | 17.63 |

Source: RPA, HHC, and Marlio, *The Aluminium Cartel.*

for aluminium. Yet, the lack of competitive advantages always made aluminium production unrealistic. From time to time, Japanese economic and political milieux resumed this idea but the lack of raw materials and progressive lowering of market prices caused by competition between AA and ALTED minimised this risk during the second half of the 1920s.[42]

In the early 1930s, monetary policies to redress the balance of payments of the country mixed with the military demand stimulated by the invasion of Manchuria in 1931 urged the Japanese government to propose again the creation of a domestic aluminium industry. This time, the context of progressive end of globalisation made the lack of specific competitive advantages less determinant and the government showed its will to protect a future national aluminium industry. Faced with this risk, AAC decided to negotiate with the Japanese government for the formation of a strategic stock of 10,000 tons. In order to propitiate the benevolence of the Japanese government, Alliance also tried to involve the country's large processing firm, such as Furukawa, Sumitomo, Mitsui and Mitsubishi, in the sales activities of the cartel companies in the Japanese market. Moreover, ALTED began to lower prices to discourage private enterprises from taking an interest in this production.[43] However, AAC's strategy in Japan was hit hard during 1934, when the first national manufacturing industry was created by an independent producer well linked with the political powers, the Showa Denko.[44]

After the invasion of Manchuria, some Japanese groups were able to take control of the extensive alunite mines, a mineral with high aluminium content that was found in the occupied territories, and extensive investment was carried out into the construction of hydroelectric facilities. Among these companies was the Showa Denko of Nobutero Mori, an entrepreneur very close to the conservative and the Japanese military milieu. After intense research, funded by the government and military apparatus, Showa was able to start production of alumina with two processes alternative to Bayer, called Tanaka and Suzuki after the name of their inventors. These initiatives also affected Mitsui and Mitsubishi, two of the largest Zaibatsu in the country, which left their strategic alliance with the Western cartel members.[45] This production did not provide good quality aluminium, which was necessary in the production of special alloys useful for aviation or electric cables. Actually, both of these applications required a quality of aluminium higher than 99 per cent, compared to 96.5–97 per cent obtained with the Tanaka alumina. Yet it represented a first bulk of production, which served to learn the know-how of aluminium smelting technology. Several Japanese groups tried to import Bayer alumina to improve the quality of their aluminium, waiting their national process to be tuned.[46]

Faced with the demands of the Japanese government, AAC refused to negotiate the supply of alumina several times. Thanks to the agreement with Giulini, it also managed to prevent the Japanese industry from finding other suppliers. After the first results obtained with the start of production in 1934 and in response to the strategies of the international cartel, the Japanese government took decisive steps towards the extension of aluminium production and obtained the support of the largest industrial groups in the country, such as Mitusi and Mitsubishi, that formed Nippon Soda Aluminium in 1936. The Japanese government, in fact, promoted national production thanks to higher customs duties and tried to adopt a policy of import substitution modelled after the German one. At the same time, the government began to survey all neighbouring regions to obtain bauxite. Actually, Japanese interests linked to Mitsui obtained the control over important bauxite deposits, which were discovered in the Dutch East Indies during the 1930s. National powers also promoted policies of technological research on the substitution of other non-ferrous metals with aluminium, following the German model.[47]

However, Japanese investments began to produce only after 1936, which enabled Alliance's firms to continue a strategy of export. In particular, ALTED found important outlets for its production, which, as the sole manager of exports in this country, consolidated some privileged commercial channels, leading also to the export of 18,000 tons of aluminium in 1938 (see Table 8.3). This was a turning point for ALTED who, after years of declining production, was able to have the appropriate outlets for expanding production again and to achieve scale economies. Probably ALTED also provided the technical assistance necessary to start production of aluminium and alumina to Sumitomo, the company with which it had been linked due to the creation of a joint venture in the field of semi-finished products since the 1920s, although studies on the history of ALTED failed to provide information about it.[48] In fact, in 1936 AAC's board ruled on technology transfer, banning technical assistance to those who possessed subsidiaries, but excluding Japan from this clause. Since ALTED was the only Western company to have a subsidiary in Japan, this rule should have been introduced at its request.[49]

Market conditions were also changing in Italy. The market was progressively reoriented to autarkic policies after 1935, when exports were banned. This changed the former position of the Italian companies, which benefited from their particular agreements with the cartel. Italian authorities took control over the fixation of prices, and new plans for output expansion were outlined within the *corporativismo*.[50] After VAW was divested from Italy, AIAG and Montecatini continued to follow their strategy in the aluminium industry, considering the new direction of the fascist regime as a great opportunity to expand sales after years of recession. Montecatini liquidated the old company and set up a new one, called Società Nazionale Alluminio (SNAL), to manage the Mori unit and a new Bayer alumina plant.[51] At the same time, AIAG grasped the opportunity provided by the new involvement of the Italian government and promptly started investments to expand its Italian aluminium output. AIAG also significantly increased its alumina production, starting a new plant in Porto Marghera in order to supply Montecatini as well, before its own plan was completed.[52] The two companies engaged in a joint venture, integrating their downstream operations: Lavorazione Leghe Leggere (LLL), a producer of alloys and metal sheets, which benefited from Swiss technological capabilities in this field filling the gaps of Montecatini.[53]

The joint market-ward integration of Montecatini and AIAG's Italian unit (SAVA) in LLL was linked to the emergence of new markets created by the fascist regime. Previously the main customers of both companies had been car and electro-technical producers, which principally bought metal ingots. At

Table 8.3 The Japanese situation: domestic production, AAC exports to Japan, consumption, tariffs (per ton), and sale prices (per ton), 1932–1939

| | Domestic production | | | | AAC exports | | | Total supply | Consumption^ | Tariff | Prices |
|---|---|---|---|---|---|---|---|---|---|---|---|
| | Showa Denko | Sumitomo | Nippon Soda Mitsui | Total | ALTED | Ex-AA | Total | | | £-paper | £-paper |
| 1932 | – | – | – | – | 2,570 | 2,538 | 5,288 | 5,288 | 5,300 | 3.2 | 82.0 |
| 1933 | – | – | – | – | 1,795 | 1,657 | 3,452 | 3,452 | 4,000 | 3.2 | 93.0 |
| 1934 | 1,002 | – | – | 1,002 | 2,120 | 1,937 | 4,077 | 5,079 | 5,800 | 3.2 | 85.0 |
| 1935 | 4,211 | – | – | 3,211 | 3,133 | 2,892 | 6,025 | 9,236 | 12,500 | 3.2 | 80.0 |
| 1936 | 5,720 | 872 | – | 5,592 | 4,948 | 3,077 | 8,025 | 13,617 | 17,000 | 13.0 | 90.0 |
| 1937 | 9,539 | 1,066 | 953 | 11,658 | 12,563 | 3,511 | 16,074 | 28,637 | 22,000 | 13.0 | 95.0 |
| 1938 | 12,513 | 2,494 | 2,753 | 17,759 | 15,235 | 9,231 | 24,446 | 42,205 | 40,000 | 13.0 | 100.0 |
| 1939 | 12,753 | 3,113 | 4,413 | 21,658 | 18,000 | n.a. | n.a. | n.a. | 50,000 | 13.0 | 120.0 |

Source: author's elaboration from various files in RPA.

present the main market for aluminium became light alloy sheets for aeroplane production. At first glance the purpose of the government seemed to be to boost aluminium consumption as a substitute for imported metals, even though it did not provide any defined plan. But, since expansionism increasingly dominated Italian foreign policy, the demand for aluminium became driven by war needs.[54] The Ethiopian war of 1936 was a good opportunity to increase consumption in the field of aircraft production and thus provided a quick and easy alternative to the export agreement signed with the cartel in 1929. The sanctions introduced by the League of Nations during the war against Ethiopia made this policy all the more effective, since it cut the Italians from international trade.[55]

In this new context, AIAG and Montecatini found common ground and planned to enlarge their production following a joint national strategy. The two companies planned to increase their capacity with the help of the government. In February 1935, AIAG approached the government to build an alumina plant in Porto Marghera for production of 30,000 tons per year with the possibility of increasing capacity to 60,000 tons in a second stage. This new political context affected AIAG's whole strategy, which aimed to use the Porto Marghera alumina plant to support its production in Switzerland and also to export part of it in Germany, where the Swiss firm was expanding its Rheinfelden smelting capacity to follow the German programmes.[56] At the same time AIAG and Donegani consolidated their joint efforts: in 1935 AIAG provided Montecatini with Bayer technology.[57] Montecatini started to build a second aluminium smelter in Bolzano, Industria Nazionale Alluminio (INA), with initial production capacity of 8,000 tons per year.[58] The market for electrical goods and cables provided a good outlet for this expansion, along with the demand for military aircraft stimulated by the Ethiopian war of 1935–1936.[59]

Italian government policies towards aluminium were not simply limited to encouraging sales: Italian production turned out to be insufficient to meet Italian war requirements during 1936, and this also obliged Italian firms to import a certain amount of metal from Switzerland and France. This fact pushed some political strategists to claim the need for self-sufficiency in aluminium.[60] The government therefore increased its support for the aluminium industry by making it a pillar of the so-called Autarchia, for which it opened special lines of credit to help firms to expand their output. At the same time, the government fixed the schedules of expansion in output, following the German model. In 1937, after a certain period of incubation, a general plan for expansion of aluminium production was launched at the direct order of Mussolini. The political powers became the centre of trade, production, and, most importantly, investment regulations for the Italian aluminium industry. In a similar way to a cartel, the Autarkic Committee fixed prices, quotas, and planned expansions.[61]

## The struggle for new markets and the political factor in Eastern Europe

In other countries, Alliance members cooperated with governments supplying technology in exchange for long-term contracts to furnish aluminium, such as in

Yugoslavia, Poland, Hungary, Bulgaria, and Czechoslovakia. Even if Alliance recommended a policy similar to the one adopted in Japan, to negotiate the constitution of a strategic stock of aluminium instead of providing technology, several members entered other deals with the political powers of Eastern Europe. As anticipated, Alliance defined a common rule only in 1936, when technology transfer was banned. Yet, its members disregarded this rule in many cases. In the specific context of the Great Depression, technology transfer could play an important role in helping the opening of new commercial channels. As a consequence, the formation of these new producing countries entailed competition amongst cartel members that took commercial advantage from these technology transfers. As was stated several times in the board of Alliance, only specific agreements about spheres of influence would have prevented the progressive disruption of the cartel's cohesion.[62]

A specific position in this trend was played by Hungary and Yugoslavia because these countries were becoming the largest producers of bauxite in the world during the early 1930s, also overcoming France. This competitive advantage was an important factor in the strategies adopted by cartel members. Hungary was a country rich in bauxite and many mines were opened during the First World War to supply aluminium production in Germany. At the end of the Great War, most of these mines were reorganised under a firm, the Bauxit Trust (BT), a Swiss holding company founded with German and Hungarian capital. VAW directly owned about 15 per cent of this holding company's capital and other shares belonged also to the German government, but without holding control over this venture, which was publically claimed as Swiss from the end of the Great War also for diplomatic reasons. This firm ensured the continuation of control from German interests on the mining of bauxite in this country and it gradually promoted investments and expansion from 1934 onwards, along with the policies for aluminium.[63]

In 1934, BT started an alumina factory and said it wanted to enter aluminium production as well. This initiative was undertaken with the help of one of the largest Hungarian companies involved in BT, Manfred Weiss of Budapest, a large mining and metallurgic trust close to Hitler's regime. At first, this firm aimed to produce only a small amount of aluminium for Weiss' alloy needs, which were linked to its core business, i.e. steel production.[64] After 1936 it began to expand its production capacity with the intention of supplying German demand and to integrate in the expansion of the aluminium industry started with the Goring four year plan. Schirner neither took the initiative of these investments, nor recognised any indirect role of VAW in the action made by BT–Weiss, but he strived to manage an agreement between the German and Hungarian governments in order not to damage the working of Alliance. Also in this event, it was chosen to cut off this production from the area in which Alliance operated.[65] Since 1936 Weiss was fully integrated into Goring's plan and also became a producer of aircraft under licence for the Luftwaffe, expanding its production capacity to 6,000 tons per year.[66]

Thanks to the support of the government in Yugoslavia, Fabrika Aluminiuma A.D. (FAAD) was built in 1935 with a capacity of 1,500 tons per year. It was supplied by a small alumina plant in Ljubljana, belonging to the Giulini group since the aftermath of the Great War. This firm represented a threat for the cartel because the Yugoslavian market was very small, amounting to about 100 tons per year. The company would have been obliged to find outlets on the export market for nearly its whole output. The enactment of the Petite Entente (a military alliance that included Yugoslavia, Romania, and Czechoslovakia) was considered to work as a privileged channel to export FAAD's production to Romania and Czechoslovakia, eroding the outlets that AF, Norsk, and AIAG had in these markets.[67] In this new context, also the military milieux in Romania, Poland, and Czechoslovakia had tried several times without success to obtain technical help from the companies of the cartel for the construction of national production. After opening the plant in Yugoslavia, there was a risk that these countries would begin to stock up from FAAD that, as a consequence, would increase its annual production capacity to over 5,000 tons to supply the allied countries.[68]

The cartel systematically proposed the formation of strategic stocks to governments as an alternative to starting production. Yet this strategy gradually crumbled in the second half of the 1930s. The main cause of this change was represented by the difficulties of the international market that led the cartel members to use their technological know-how as a bargaining chip in negotiations for contracts for the metal's supply. In this new context, in which globalisation faded and national military demand grew, aluminium firms saw the policies of the various countries as opportunities to increase sales, to extend the geographical spans of their outlets, and to find financial aid for new investments. AFC forestalled AIAG and ALTED in Czechoslovakia and Poland in 1937,[69] as well as ALTED and VAW in Romania in 1938. AFC benefited substantially from the diplomatic and military relationships that French authorities had established with these countries. Furthermore, AFC was able to find good national partners, including Skoda in Czechoslovakia and Concordia in Romania.[70] These initiatives of newcomers developed too late to be achieved before the war. When in March 1938 the Sudetenland in Czechoslovakia was annexed to Germany, the investments had not yet been started and were postponed for an indefinite time. Then also the project in Poland was abandoned because of growing international political and military tension.[71]

Alliance had not been able to oppose a common line against these initiatives because it was gradually changing its internal structure, abdicating its role as a regulator of international production. Its members were increasingly focusing their strategy on the respective domestic markets where military demands were bringing the rate of production back to full speed. Yet, as shown in Table 8.4, the outcome of this transformation was to deprive Alliance of the management of global output.

This new role of the political powers in the aluminium industry was linked to technological change involving this metal. A new series production of fully metallic planes was replacing the small scale prototypes of the 1920s, and airpower started playing a central role in warfare.[72] Existing facilities could not fulfil the substantial new demands for aluminium created by these changes. However,

Table 8.4 State driven investments during the 1930s, the evolution of capacity outputs (in metric tons) outside Alliance regulation (1933–1939), and comparison with Alliance's production and use of its capacity

| | Germany | | Italy | Soviet Union** | Japan | Others*** | Total state driven | ALCOA | AAC | |
| | Capacity | AAC right | | | | | | | Production* | Use (%) |
|---|---|---|---|---|---|---|---|---|---|---|
| 1933 | 44,200 | 18,932 | 12,000 | – | – | – | – | 38,612 | 76,390 | 50.0 |
| 1934 | 44,200 | 37,158 | 15,000 | 15,000 | 1,000 | – | 16,000 | 33,650 | 97,693 | 55.0 |
| 1935 | 53,700 | – | 17,000 | 27,000 | 5,000 | 1,000 | 103,700 | 54,111 | 86,068 | 53.0 |
| 1936 | 93,700 | – | 20,000 | 52,000 | 7,000 | 3,000 | 175,500 | 102,026 | 105,177 | 70.0 |
| 1937 | 101,700 | – | 27,500 | 52,000 | 12,000 | 4,500 | 197,700 | 132,757 | 154,747 | 100.0 |
| 1938 | 153,400 | – | 36,000 | 100,000 | 20,000 | 7,000 | 316,400 | 130,127 | – | – |
| 1939 | 200,200 | – | 40,000 | 140,000 | 25,000 | 9,000 | 414,200 | 148,365 | – | – |

Source: author's elaboration from various files in RPA, HWA, and Metallgesellschaft's statistical yearbooks.

Notes

* Since 1935, Alliance production included only AF, BACO, AIAG, and ALTED output. It did not contain German figures because Germany was free to set national production; 1937 is the last year of production control; ** USSR's capacity is not certain, official figures are not available; *** others are Yugoslavia and Hungary.

the firms invested only when they received the clear support of political powers because, otherwise, these investments would have created overproduction after this trend of military demand. Without this help, firms were reticent to invest and preferred to use Alliance's stock. The tension between civil markets, which were still virtually supplied by former stock accumulation, and new military need pointed out a major issue in the governance of aluminium firms. In many cases governments disputed control of outputs to Alliance and fixed prices above the ones guaranteed by the cartel. In Germany, for instance, prices went from 1.6 Mark Reich/kg in 1933 to 1.4 in 1936 to be fixed at 1.33 between 1937 and 1939.[73] These prices were relatively high compared to the international situation. In 1938, the price of 1.33 RM/kg corresponded to £108 per ton, while in France the market price was £75, in the United States £88, in Switzerland £92, and, finally, in Italy £113.[74]

## The unachieved reform of Alliance

Despite the fact that Alliance had avoided a fall in prices and a serious loss of profitability in aluminium trading during the hardest years of the Great Depression, its effectiveness was actually nonexistent if compared to what a government could do for the aluminium industry in the specific context of the second half of the 1930s.[75] Autarkic policies, economic planning, and rearmament were proving to be more effective than the cartel to assist the general development of this industry. Unlike the early 1920s, when government intervened in the economy almost exclusively through tariffs, the different experiences of the 1930s had shown that direct intervention in support of the demand for aluminium could support the extension of aluminium's applications more than any effort made by an international cartel or the service of propaganda of each firm. Faced with this transformation, the head of AF proved to be an attentive observer of this change, claiming that

> Consequently, we can face the world situation in the present conditions, with the natural reserved domains, having to deal only with our compatriots and to take into account only our own national interests and the desires of our own government in the same zones, but being ready to share the free zones.[76]

This change reshaped the behaviour of Alliance's members, threatening the structure of the cartel. The 'home markets' proposal, outlined by Schirner in 1934, was achieving a certain consensus in Alliance's board. While political planning progressively influenced production and investment, Alliance lost its original sense and obliged the cartel board to explore a change to its rules.[77] A new strategic group emerged in the cartel, in which firms understood the key importance of national policies in the specific market situation of the second half of the 1930s. This was particularly the case for AIAG. While AIAG grew as the more international firm of the oligopoly during the 1920s, it experienced a strong implication in national policies, benefiting from both the German and Italian policies for aluminium.[78] AIAG was not alone in this transformation because, a few months after the German compromise, BACO's delegates claimed in the cartel board that, in the near future, they would ask for the same treatment in order to meet the British government's demands.[79] Actually, also BACO and ALTED forecasted they would be in a position to benefit as a result of government rearmament programmes, particularly of aircraft production when the first industrial series of Spitfires was started.[80] The British market was deeply changing during the 1930s: BACO found itself in a serious position because both its lack of output and its quota in AAC determined a growing position for ALTED, which, by 1936, forestalled BACO as supplier of this market. Also other importers benefited from the British market's expansion during the 1930s (see Table 8.5).

Although the British government's policy never reached the same depth as the German or Italian solutions, it strongly influenced the strategies of three companies in the cartel: ALTED, BACO, and also AIAG, which found a way to enter this market. In particular, ALTED perceived interest in focusing on this market, which became a key outlet for its output. Further expansion was forecast in the second half of the 1930s, which made this market even more attractive. In July 1936 the British government decided to create a stock of 36,000 tons and asked for an increase in national output of semi-finished goods in aluminium alloys from 6,000 to 40,000 tons per year by the beginning of 1939. Also an additional output of 23,000 tons was prospected by the end of 1939.[81] The demand for aluminium was met mostly through imports, as BACO could not produce in its homeland more than 25,000 tons per year due to the lack of hydroelectric facilities. Since the production of primary metal was insufficient to meet the government programmes, room was available for new ventures. In 1938, AIAG prospected to start a smelter in Wales, where the construction of a thermal power plant would have supplied the new unit, and it found the alliance of Philip Hill, an important producer of non-ferrous alloys. This plant with a capacity of 12,500 tons, in spite of the prospected high producing costs of £70 per ton, was encouraged by both the Secretary of the Treasury and the military milieux because, by removing the monopoly of BACO, they thought they could maximise domestic production and reduce prices sales.[82] This fact alarmed ALTED and BACO, which after long negotiations within the board of the cartel, were included in the capital of the new venture, the South Wales Aluminium Company (SWACO), with a participation of 25 per cent each.[83]

While the strategies of firms and governments' programmes were close, Alliance attempted reform to save the cartel from dissolution. In this new context, each member had specific interests to reshape the agreement following Schirner's ideas.[84] The multi-nation implications of each firm made a real 'home market' division unworkable. As a consequence, Marlio proposed to amend the 'home markets proposal' with the creation of five markets, where companies could manage both production and sales. AF would have obtained France and its colonies, VAW would have got Germany with the exclusion of part reserved for AIAG, with which it would have collaborated with the management of this market. The Swiss firm would also have obtained Italy and a part of Great Britain. In turn ALTED would have obtained Canada and a part of the British Empire to

Table 8.5 The British market and BACO: BACO's domestic consumption, exports, imports, production, and sales (with exports to United States), and sales prices, 1932–1937 (tons and £/t)

| | Production BACO | | Sales BACO | | Consumption | Exports | Imports | | | Prices in GB£ | | |
|---|---|---|---|---|---|---|---|---|---|---|---|---|
| | Actual | Allow AAC | Total | US | | | ALTED | Others | Total | AAC | Gold | Paper |
| 1932 | 12,529 | 11,173 | 18,570 | 971 | 17,500 | 3,637 | 3,382 | 4,819 | 8,202 | 72.0 | 70.65 | 89.0 |
| 1933 | 13,484 | 10,115 | 18,096 | 3,141 | 19,000 | 4,050 | 10,036 | 1,744 | 11,780 | 73.0 | 68.50 | 96.0 |
| 1934 | 15,081 | 11,401 | 20,016 | 3,558 | 23,000 | 1,535 | 11,736 | 2,714 | 14,450 | 69.0 | 61.72 | 100.0 |
| 1935 | 17,601 | 13,451 | 18,313 | 1,451 | 28,400 | 2,569 | 15,423 | 2,848 | 18,271 | 67.0 | 59.87 | 100.0 |
| 1936 | 19,499 | 14,700 | 19,596 | n.a* | 35,000 | 2,048 | 16,926 | 5,141 | 22,067 | 62.1 | 60.60 | 100.0 |
| 1937 | 25,649 | 21,187 | 29,462 | n.a.* | 49,000 | 4,023 | 20,567 | 11,512 | 32,079 | 64.0** | 60.60 | 100.0 |

Source: author's elaboration from various files in RPA and TNA.

Note
* Since 1936, AAC stopped organising sales to the US; ** in 1937, Swiss franc left its exchange to gold, which put AAC prices in gold-£ to an end. Gold-£64 refers to the last change before the end of the exchange.

negotiate with BACO, which, finally, would have got the rest of the British Empire and would have cooperated with AIAG and ALTED in the UK. In all other markets some *comptoirs* would have been created to allocate quotas for the sales of each firm, using the model of the agreement that was made for Japan.[85] These quotas, about which European companies had been thinking since mid-1934 would probably have been 40 per cent for ALTED, 32 per cent for AIAG, 7 per cent to VAW, 11 per cent to AF, and 10 per cent to BACO.[86]

However, during 1935 ALTED was not comfortable with Alliance and it wanted to reshape the cartel in a different way. The position of ALTED was a watershed for the whole reform of the cartel, which was procrastinating, putting on hold the 'home markets' proposal. The position of ALTED was linked to the worsening of the legal situation of ALCOA, its sister company. In 1931, Bausch Machine Tool sued ALCOA, accusing it of antitrust law violation. During the interrogations that followed, Arthur V. Davis was questioned directly about ALCOA's involvement in the international cartel, about the American extra-right of production permitted to Europeans since 1931, and even about each journey to Europe that Davis made during the previous 30 years. Also the role of ALTED in the international aluminium industry was surveyed, along with its relationships with ALCOA. In early 1935, FTC initially fined ALCOA about $3 million, but the firm avoided this payment in September 1935 after overturning the initial verdict.[87] The German compromise was reached while the situation was troubled by these legal concerns. As a consequence, ALTED endeavoured to fix them along with reform of the cartel agreement.

Hence ALTED proposed to the other members to eliminate the system of rights, and to replace it with royalties to be paid in the case of production exceeding a certain level. According to Edward K. Davis, this fee was sufficient to generate a virtuous circle in each market for which the members could choose between producing more (gaining scale economies but paying fees), and buying stock (keeping a lower rate of production but saving in new investments). ALTED's reforms aimed to turn Alliance into a 'merchant firm', whose task was merely to liquidate the metal still in its possession to its members, achieving buffering of the unsold stock gathered during the harsher phase of the Great Depression. Davis did not exclude that other agreements on export markets could have been formed, modelling them on the Japanese agreement that was still in force, but his main goal was to reshape Alliance in order to persuade American authorities that it was not a cartel. This implied putting an end to production rights, to price fixing and its stabilisation, and, especially, to export quotas to United States.[88]

The 'home markets' proposal was more attractive for European firms, which all claimed the right to exploit particular national advantages without paying any royalty. In 1934, AIAG was charged with implementing this proposal with an agreement only on export markets of semi-finished goods. Its goal was to reach a broader cartel focused on geographical sharing of markets, which would have also involved the non-integrated producers of aluminium and aluminium alloys.[89] The overall idea for Alliance reform was to set up a new agreement in the shape of the steel cartel, with the implementation of specific clauses modelled on the Japanese

Table 8.6 Alliance Aluminium Compagnie: production rights, actual production, purchases from outsiders, and sales, 1934–1939

| | Stocks at 1 December of each year | | | | Production | | | Purchases | Sales | Stock/actual production % |
|---|---|---|---|---|---|---|---|---|---|---|
| | Rights, t/share | AAC | Firms | Total | Rights, t/share | AAC** | Actual | | | |
| 1934 | 53 | 28,500 | 54,996 | 83,496 | 55 | 91,343 | 97,061 | 14,889 | 133,593 | 86.02 |
| 1935 | 63 | 22,800 | 50,014 | 72,814 | 53 | 76,082 | 148,056 | 12,605 | 194,170 | 49.18 |
| 1936 | 45 | 18,300 | 43,308 | 61,608 | 70 | 76,372 | 189,674 | 16,228 | 246,432 | 32.48 |
| 1937 | 45 | 5,200 | 47,680 | 52,880 | 100 | 111,101 | 266,168 | 18,931 | 317,280 | 19.86 |
| 1938 | – | 7,419 | 57,461 | 64,880 | – | – | 348,400 | – | 349,280 | 18.62 |
| 1939 | – | 5,792* | 50,526 | 56,318* | – | – | 404,600 | – | 400,544 | 13.91 |

Source: author's elaboration from various files in RPA, 00-2-19532 and 00-2-195433, and in HWA.

Note
* At 1 June 1939; ** since 1935, German producers were free to produce for the domestic market.

agreement of 1929. The Europeans planned to settle a certain number of regional markets to include fabricated goods in which, to please ALTED, a middleman would work to hide effective quotas.[90] In July 1935, Marlio convinced other Europeans to accept a compromise agreeing to go ahead with a two-step reform of Alliance. ALTED's proposal was accepted under the condition of starting negotiations for export agreements and national preferences as soon as possible.[91] A few months later, the plan on royalties was outlined aiming to continue the agreement on export markets. Initially, production rights, below which production was free of fines, were settled at 70 tons per share and then they were progressively brought to 100 tons during 1937. Production rights were recognised to be senseless at the beginning of 1938 because demand boomed, driven by rearmament programmes, and fees were no longer applied to producers. Meanwhile, almost all political authorities started to fix prices while rearmament programmes were definitively launched.[92]

In the new context, AAC came to an almost complete clearance of stocks and the regulation on royalties led to the formation a surplus in the balance sheet of Alliance. In addition to repaying the debts previously contracted with banks, AAC accumulated a total profit of about 19 million Swiss francs until 1938, when the system of royalties was also abolished. The members of ACC did not really know how to use these funds: in some cases it was indicated by some companies (AIAG and AF) that they would rather share them in the form of dividends, while BACO and ALTED thought that this treasure was to be kept aside to be reused in the event of a crisis to fund a new system of stock purchase.[93] These funds would have been insufficient for financing a mechanism for stock in a situation such as that of 1938–1939: the increase in production and demand meant that these funds would be enough to purchase stock on a limited scale. When AAC would be reformed according to the mechanism of home markets, the firms considered that these funds could have been used to finance stock for export markets, reproducing the Alliance system on a smaller geographical scale. Until that time, these funds were kept waiting to be used and also to facilitate the preservation of value, AAC decided to invest them 50 per cent in gold and to keep them at 25 per cent in sterling and at 25 per cent in Swiss francs. After a further devaluation of sterling in 1939, AAC converted part of its possessions in US dollars.[94]

However, the structural change of AAC has neither implied a reformulation of the agreement as regards the home markets, nor the formation of separate agreements for the regional markets. The rearmament programmes and the final collapse of the international monetary system by the end of the gold block at the end of 1936 made international governance of production and sales unnecessary. This opinion was clearly expressed by Level, President of AF, at the beginning of 1938:

> The arbitrary decisions of the German and Italian governments have led the German group and the Swiss group to a disproportionate increase in their outputs. Today British rearmament policy puts the UK market in such an abnormal situation. These conditions make it impossible to implement the 1931 agreements. We can no longer rely on the production right to balance the aluminum market.[95]

Further cartel reforms were prevented by another factor. ALCOA avoided fines in 1935, but it could not prevent further investigations. In early 1937, when Alliance should have started settlement of the home markets proposal, the American government started one of the largest antitrust actions of its history against ALCOA. Since it feared to aggravate the position of its sister company, ALTED refused to deal with the Europeans and stopped attending cartel meetings. Once rights were suspended in 1938, the Board of Governors became a mere observatory.[96] The definitive break of Alliance was represented by some concomitant decisions of investments by firms: as anticipated, AIAG went into business to erect a new smelter in the UK, provoking an harsh reaction from both BACO and ALTED, while AF signed some technology transfer agreements with East European countries, injuring the other firms' expansion in those countries.[97] Louis Marlio's resignation from the presidency of Alliance at the end of 1938, to protest against the German annexation of Sudetenland that followed the Munich agreement, definitively marked the end of the meeting of Alliance before the start of the Second World War.[98]

## Notes

1 HWA, MG Documents, Abt 119/886, Liste der Teilnehmer an den Sitzungen des Board of Governors des Alliance Aluminium Cie. Cornelia Rauh claimed that the substitution of Von der Porten was pushed also because of his Jewish origins. Rauh, *Schweizer Aluminium für Hitlers Krieg?* 72.
2 RPA, 00-2-15933, Alliance, Correspondance, 'Conversation de M. Braasch (AAC) avec M. Dupin (AF), le 5 Septembre 1933'. AEC, Montecatini, 3/5, SIDA, Verbale del consiglio d'amministrazione, 14 March 1934. They kept their position in Alliance until 1938, then Schirner moved to the oil industry and Westrick to VIAG. Westrick in the post-war era became the State Secretary of the West German Economic Ministry. See Raymond G. Stokes, *Opting for Oil: The Political Economy of Technological Change in the West German Chemical Industry 1945–1961.* Cambridge: Cambridge University Press, 1994, 77–78.
3 RPA, 00-2-15933, AAC, Notes, 'Observations de VAW au sujet des indications données par M. Marlio', 1934.
4

   C'était une erreur de penser de régler le marché de l'aluminium par l'entremise de l'Alliance. Le cartel international de l'acier a commis la même faute … C'est pourquoi je suis decidé d'organiser tout d'abord l'exportation dans mon pays, afin de pouvoir vous demander ensuite de nous arranger sur les marches d'exportation.

   RPA, 00-2-1529, AAC, Comité de Direction, 'PV 15ème Réunion du Board of governors', 10 February 1934.
5 Françoise Berger, *La France, l'Allemagne et l'Acier (1932–1952): De la Stratégie des Cartels à l'Élaboration de la CECA.* Unpublished PhD Thesis, Paris-I Panthéon-Sorbonne University, 2000, 107–108.
6 Hexner, *The International Steel Cartel*, 82–83. Barbezat, 'Cooperation and Rivalry'. See also Daniel Barbezat 'A Price for Every Product, Every Place: The International Steel Export Cartel, 1933–39', *Business History*, vol. 33, no. 4, 1991, 70–86.
7 RPA, 00-2-15933, AAC, Notes diverses, Marlio, Note pour les membres de l'Alliance, 3 July 1933. Quelques Observations sur l'AAC, 28 December 1933.
8 Rudolf K. Michels, *Cartels, Combines and Trusts in Post-war Germany.* New York: Columbia University Press, 1928, 59–60. Sigfried Tschierschky, *Etude sur le Nouveau Régime Juridique des Ententes Économiques (Cartels etc.) en Allemagne et en Hongrie: Préparé*

*pour le Comité Économique de la Société des Nations.* Geneva: League of Nations, Doc. E. 529, 1932. Heinrich Kronstein, *The Law of International Cartels.* London: Cornell University Press, 1973, 228–229.

9  Karl Polanyi, *The Great Transformation.* New York: Ferrar & Rinehart, 1944.

10  Robert J. Anderson, 'Germany's Aluminum Economy', *Iron Age*, 20 June 1940, 40–44. Frederich L. Neher, *Kupfer, Zinn, Aluminium.* Leipzig: Wilhem Goldmann Verlag, 1940, 324–325. See also Plumpe, *Die I.G. Farbenindustrie AG*, 409. Rauh, *Schweizer Aluminium für Hitlers Krieg?* 69–71.

11  RPA, 00-2-15929, AAC, Comités de directions, PV 13ème Réunion du Board of Governors, Paris, 22 September 1933.

12  Heinrich Liepmann, *Tariff Levels and the Economic Unity of Europe: An Examination of Tariff Policy, Export Movements and the Economic Integration of Europe, 1913–1931.* London: Allen & Unwin, 1938, 352–355.

13  Heinz Wolfgang Arndt, *The Economic Lessons of Nineteen-Thirties.* London: Oxford University Press, 1944, 182–183. Svennilson, *Growth and Stagnation*, 39. Political and Economic Planning, *Report on International Trade: A Survey of Problems Affecting the Expansion of International Trade, with Proposal for the Development of British Commercial Policy and Export Mechanism.* London: PEP, 1937. Hexner, *The International Steel Cartel*, 32.

14  RPA, 00-2-15933, Marlio to French Foreign Affairs Minister, 20 October 1934 and 1 April 1935.

15  HWA, MG Documents, Abt.119/5, Verkaufsgemeinschafts-Vertrag zwischen der Vereinigte Aluminium-Werke Aktien Gesellschaft und der Metallgesellschaft AG, 24–25 May 1935.

16  Hayes, *Industry and Ideology*, 179–180.

17  Edward L. Homze, *Arming the Luftwaffe: The Reich Air Ministry and the German Aircraft Industry 1919–39.* Lincoln NE and London: University of Nebraska Press, 1976.

18  HWA, MG Documents, Abt.119, nr. 890, AVG, Stastitische Zusammenstellungen der AVG, 1940.

19  RPA, 00-1-20035, Bureau International d'Etude et de Propagande pour le Développement des Emplois de l'Aluminium, BIA communication mensuelle, various issues.

20  HWA, MG Documents, Abt.119 nr890/6, AVG. Quotenvertag, 24–25 June 1935.

21  RZA, Berichte über die allgemeine Geschaftslage, fasc. 1938–1939, Berichte 26 August 1938.

22  RPA, 00-2-15933, Alliance Aluminium Compagnie, Observations de Vaw au sujet des indications données par M. Marlio et qui sont parvenues aux Membres de l'AAC le 27 Juillet 1933.

23  RPA, 00-2-15929, Notes sur la 15ème Conférence de l'Alliance Aluminium Cie, tenue à Paris le 10 Février 1934. On Schacht's whole policy for the redressing of German commercial balance during 1934 and 1935, see Frédéric Clavert, *Hjalmar Schacht, Financier et Diplomate (1930–1950).* Brussels: Peter Lang, 2009, 46, 214–215. Richard Overy, *War and Economy in the Third Reich.* Oxford: Clarendon Press, 1994, 96, 103, 177–184.

24  RPA, 00-2-15928, Procès-Verbal de la 17ème Réunion de l'AAC, 26 September 1934.

25  RPA, 00-2-15929, Alliance Aluminium Cie, 17ème Réunion du Board of Governors, 26 September 1934. Note sur la conférence straordinaire de l'Alliance. Réunion à Berlin avec M. Schacht, 5 April 1935. Situation Allemande, 19 June 1935.

26  RPA, 00-2-15929, Notes sur la 15ème Conférence de l'Alliance Aluminium Cie, tenue à Paris le 10 Février 1934.

27  RPA, 00-2-15929, Alliance Aluminum Cie., 19e bis, Procès verbal de la réunion extraordinaire, Négociations avec M. le dr. Schacht, 20 March 1935.

28  RPA, 00-2-15929, Alliance Aluminium Compagnie,Situation Allemande, 19 June 1935.

29  RPA, 00-2-15933, Note sur l'AAC, 19 May 1934. Merton (MG) to Marlio, 7 July 1933.

30  RPA, 00-2-15933, Circular letter of AAC n.190, 25 August 1933.
31  RPA, 00-2-15933, Conversation de M. Braasch (AAC) avec M. Dupin (AF), 7 September 1933. Marlio to Level, 29 August 1933.
32  RPA, 00-2-15933, Questions dans lesquelles l'attitude de l'Aluminium Limited apparait un peu trop personelle, 3 January 1934.
33  RPA, 00-2-15933, Circular letter of AAC n.160 – Giulini, 25 August 1933.
34  HWA, MG Documents, 6b/14, Alliance – Giulini Agreement February 1934.
35  RPA, 00-2-15928, Procès-Verbal de la 16ème Réunion de l'AAC, 25 May 1934.
36  Actually, ALTED owned 50 per cent shares in Swenka, while the other 50 per cent was in the hands of Norsk. RPA, 00-2-15933, Questions dans lesquelles l'Attitude de l'Aluminium Limited apparait un peu trop personelle, 3 January 1934.
37  RPA, 00-2-15933, Note sur l'Alliance, 5 December 1934.
38  W. Schmidt, 'Sviluppo e Stato Attuale dell'Industria Internazionale dell'Alluminio', *Alluminio: Rivista Tecnica del Gruppo Metalli Leggeri della Associazione Nazionale Fascista fra gli Industriali Metallurgici Italiani*, no. 5, 1938, 219.
39  On the role of governments as substitute for cartels in aluminium industry, see Bertilorenzi, 'Business, Finance, and Politics'.
40  James, *The End of Globalisation*. Gourvish, *Business and Politics in Europe*. Kobrak, Hansen (eds), *European Business*. Dominique Barjot, Olivier Dard, Jean Garrigues, Didier Musiedlak, Eric Anceau (eds), *Industrie et Politique en Europe Occidentale et aux Etats-Unis (XIXe–XXe Siècles)*. Paris: Presses de l'Université Paris-Sorbonne, 2006.
41  RPA, 001-14-20501, AFC, Note sur l'accord commercial avec les Sovietiques, 11 January 1934. About monetary issues, see also Carley Michael Jabara, 'Five Kopecks for Five Kopecks: Franco-Soviet Trade Negotiations, 1928–1939', *Cahiers du Monde Russe et Soviétique*, vol. 33, no. 1, 1992, 23–57.
42  RPA, 00-2-15932, Bruce (ALTED-Japan), Memorandum on the present status of various schemes for producing aluminium in Japan, September 1933. Kaufmann (AIAG), Marché Japonais. L'Industrie Nationale de l'Aluminium, 23 May 1935. See also Jerome B. Cohen, *Japan's Economy in War and Reconstruction*. Minneapolis MN: University of Minnesota Press, 1949, 230–231. John A. Krug, James Boyd, *The Japanese Aluminum Industry: Prepared for the Department of Interior*. Washington DC: Department of Interior, 1949.
43  RPA, 00-2-15932, E.K. Davis (ALTED) to Steck (Aiag), 29 March 1932. RPA, 00-2-15933, Note sur l'AAC, 1933.
44  RPA, 00-2-15933, Painvin (French military attaché in Tokyo) to Marlio, 4 September 1933. RPA, 00-2-15932, Bruce (Alted (V), Memorandum on the present status of various schemes for producing aluminium in Japan, September 1933.
45  'Japan to Develop own Aluminum Industry', *Far Eastern Survey*, vol. 4, no. 6, 1935, 45–46. About Japanese patents, see Ferrand, *Histoire de la Science*, 556; Rauch, *Geschichte der Huttenaluminiumindustrie*, 202. About Mitusi and the aluminium industry, see John G. Roberts, *Mitsui: Three Centuries of Japanese Business*. New York: Cambridge University Press, 1973, 261, 327. About Mitsubishi, see Claude Hamon, *Le Groupe Mitsubishi (1870–1990): Du Zaibatsu au Keiretsu*. Paris: L'Harmattan, 1995, 199–200. About Showa Denko KK, see Cohen, *Japan's Economy in War and Reconstruction*, 230–231. Chalmers Johnson, *Miti and the Japanse Miracle: The Growth of Industrial Policy, 1925–1975*. Stanford CA: Stanford University Press, 1985, 132, 167.
46  RPA, 00-2-15932, Marché Japonais. L'Industrie Nationale de l'Aluminium, 23 May 1935.
47  Hiroshi Saito, 'Japan's Foreign Trade', *Annals of American Academy of Political and Social Science*, vol. 186, July 1936, 178–182. Catherine Porter, 'Mineral Deficiency versus Self-Sufficiency in Japan', *Far Eastern Survey*, vol. 5, no. 2, January 1936, 9–14.
48  Campbell, *Global Mission*, vol. 1, 215–218.
49  RPA, 00-2-15933, Aide Techniques aux Outsiders. Extraits de procès-verbaux des réunions de l'Alliance Aluminium Compagnie, 7 July 1936.
50  In Italy, the *Piano autarchico per l'alluminio* fixed the goal of 48,000 tons for the end of

1939. Archivio Thaon de Revel, Fondazione Luigi Einaudi (ATR), 5.58–59.14, Corporazione della Chimica, Piano Autarchico. Voll.II. Bozze di Stampa (Riservato), vol. 14. Potassa e Alluminio, 1937, 39–82.

51 AEC, Montecatini, Box 3/5, SIDA, Consiglio del 12 novembre 1934. RPA, 00-15-20452, Italie 1927–52, Entretien de M. Donegani avec M. Level, le 27 septembre 1935.

52 RZA, AIAG Direktion Protokollen, 1935–1937, Direktion Protokoll, 8 July 1936.

53 ASBI, Sconti, pratiche no. 580, f.1, Direzione Banca d'Italia, Sede di Venezia, Società Veneta Alluminio Anonima, 23 March 1937.

54 ABISP, BCI, 6, Archivio Sofindit, Presidenza e Direzione, SOF 327/5, L'alluminio italiano, 1937. 'I Consigli delle corporazioni e i problemi da discutere in sede corporativa', Alluminio, no. 6, 1934, 326.

55 'Creazione di un comitato tecnico inter-corporativo per l'alluminio e la potassa', *Alluminio*. no. 1, 1937, 33–34.

56 ASBI, sconti, box 580/1, Venezia 1935–1938, Andamenti delle attività economiche di Venezia, 24 gennaio 1936, riferito all'anno 1935. See also Bruna Bianchi, 'L'Economia di Guerra a Porto Marghera: Produzione, Occupazione, Lavoro, 1935–1945', in *La Resistenza nel Veneziano: La Società Veneziana tra Fascismo, Resistenza, Repubblica*, edited by Giannantonio Paladini and Maurizio Reberschak. Venezia: Istituto veneto per la storia della resistenza, 1985, 167–169.

57 RPA, 00-15-20452, Italie, 1935, Relations entre AFC et Neuhausen, Question Italienne, 1937.

58 AEC box 29/54, INA, Verbali consiglio d'amministrazione, Consiglio del 9 dicembre 1936. See also Amatori and Bezza, *Montecatini*, 43–44. ATR, 5.58–59.14, Corporazione della Chimica, Piano Autarchico, voll.II, Bozze di stampa (riservato), vol. 14. Potassa ed Alluminio, Roma, 1937, 39–82.

59 About the Italian aircraft industry, see Fortunato Minniti, 'La Realtà di un Mito: L'industria Aeronautica durante il Fascismo', in *L'Aeronautica Italiana: Una Storia del Novecento*, edited by Paolo Ferrari., Milano: Franco Angeli, 2004, 43–67.

60 ASBI, Consorzio Sovvenzioni, Sede Principale, Prat. n. 73, doc. n. 2, 18 November 1937.

61 ATR, 5.58–59.14, Piano Autarchico. Silvio Golzio, *L'industria dei metalli in Italia*, Torino: Einaudi, 1942, 109. For some technical aspects on the uses of aluminium and the spread of its applications see *Alluminio: Rivista Tecnica del Gruppo Metalli Leggeri della Associazione Nazionale Fascista fra gli Industriali Metallurgici Italiani*, various issues, 1932 to 1939.

62 RPA, 00-1-15930, Alliance Aluminium Cie, 16ème Réunion du Board of Governorns, 24 May 1934. RPA, 00-1-15933, Aide Technique aux Outsiders. Extraits de process-verbaux des reunions de l'AAC.

63 Harold James, *The Nazi Dictatorship and the Deutsche Bank*. Cambridge and New York: Cambridge University Press, 2004, 175–176. Rauch, *Geschichte der Huttenaluminiumindustrie*, 213–214.

64 RPA, 00-2-15929, Alliance Aluminium Cie, 16ème Réunion du Board of Governors, Basilea, 24 May 1934.

65 RPA, 00-1-20047, Création d'une industrie de l'aluminium en Hongrie, 28 January 1937.

66 I. Berend, Gy Ranki, 'Die Deutsche Wirtschafliche Expansion und das Ungarische Wirtschaftleben zur Zeit des Zweiten Weltekriegs', *Acta Historica Academiae Scientiarum Hungaricae*, vol. 5, 1958, 313–359. David Turnock, *The Economy of East Central Europe, 1815–1989: Stages of Transformation in a Peripheral Region*. New York: Routledge, 2006, 277.

67 RPA, 00-1-20047, AFC, Projet de Fabrication d'aluminum en Pologne et en Tchecoslosvachie, 4 November 1936.

68 RPA, 00-1-20047, AFC, Fabrication de l'Aluminium en Yougoslavie. Rapport établi par M. Lacreon à la suite de son voyage en Yougoslavie, 1 March 1938. Note sur l'Aluminium en Yougoslavie, 1 February 1939.

69 RZA, Allgemeiner Bericht an den Verwaltungsrat der AIAG Neuhausem, Sitzung vom 8 Juli 1936; RPA, 00-1-20047, Relations avec les pays Etrangers, Note. Projet de Fabrication d'aluminum en Pologne et en Tchecolosvachie, 4 November 1936.

70 RPA, 00-1-15933, Etat de la question Aluminium et Alumine vis-à-vis de l'Alliance Aluminium Compagnie, 6 July 1938. RPA, 00-1-20047, Note. Aluminium. Marchés de l'Europe Centrale. Tchécoslovacquie, Pologne, Roumanie, Hongries, 20 October 1938.

71 RPA, 00-1-20047, AFC, Aluminium. Marchés de l'Europe Centrale. Tchécoslovacquie, Pologne, Roumanie, Hongries, 20. October 1938.

72 See for instance, Homze, *Arming the Luftwaffe*. Richard Overy, *The Air War, 1939–1945*. Dulles VA: Potomac Press, 2005. Sebastian Ritchie, *Industry and Air Power: The Expansion of British Aircraft Production, 1935–1941*. London: Frank Cass, 1997.

73 Rauch, *Geschichte der Huttenaluminiumindustrie*, 193.

74 RZA, AIAG Berichte Protokolls, box. 1938–1939, 'Bericht über die allgemeine Geschäftslage', 26 August 1938.

75 RPA, 00-2-15933, Alliance. Notes. '4 années d'existance de l'AAC', 5 July 1935.

76 Nous pouvons donc envisager la situation mondiale dans les conditions où elle se trouve actuellement, avec ses domaines naturels réservés, chacun n'ayant à traiter qu'avec ses compatriotes et à ne tenir compte que de ses intérêts nationaux et des desiderata de son propre gouvernement dans ces mêmes zones, quitte à se repartir les zones libres.
   RPA, 00-2-15933, Alliance. Notes. 'AAC, Note du 3 décembre 1934'.

77 RPA, 00-2-15933, Alliance. Notes. Level (AF), 'Note sur l'Alliance', 13 June 1934.

78 Rauh, *Schweizer Aluminium für Hitlers Krieg?*; Knoepfli, *From Dawn to Dusk*.

79 HHC, MSS #282, ALCOA, US v. ALCOA, Equity 85–73, Exhibit 835, Cooper (BACO) to E.K. Davis (ALTED), 28 May 1935.

80 TNA, SUPP/3/82/271, Committee of Imperial Defence. Principal Supply Officers Committee. Board of Trade supply organisation, Memorandum on Aluminium, 3 July 1935. UGD/347/21/41/23, Murray-Morrison (BACO), Position of the Aluminium Industry in UK, 31 December 1936. See also Perchard, *Aluminiumville*, 93–96; Ball, 'The German Octopus', 468–470; Edgerton, *Warfare State*, 42–45.

81 TNA, BT 64/5039, War Industries Stories, Official History of Aluminium and Aluminium Alloys, 1945.

82 TNA, Tresaury, T 187/55, The Swiss Aluminium Co. Philip Hill & Partners Ltd, Sir Alan Barlow (Tresaury Minister) to Palmer (War Minister), 28 May 1938. Initiative was taken after the refusal by BACO to increase its national production of 20,000 tons.

83 RPA, 00-1-20046, Pays Etrangers. Angleterre. Cooper (BACO) to Buber (AIAG), 9 June 1938. E.K. Davis (ALTED) to Marlio (AF).

84 RPA, 00-2-15933, Alliance. Notes. 'Note sur l'Aluminium Association et sur l'Alliance Aluminium Cie', 14 January 1936.

85 RPA, 00-2-15933, Alliance. Notes. 'Reforme de l'Alliance Aluminium Cie', 4 December 1935.

86 RPA, 00-2-15933, Alliance. Notes. 'Note sur l'AAC', 19 May 1934.

87 RPA, 00-2-15933, Alliance. Réunions diverses, 'Conférence des producteurs européens d'aluminium', 11 July 1935. RPA, 00-2-15928, AAC, Conseils de direction, 'Exposé de M. Davis', 19 June 1935. About the process, Wallace, *Market Control*, 481–484. Smith, *From Monopoly to Competition*, 194–195.

88 Davis indeed claimed that ALTED was disposed to continue Alliance only if 'puisse produire ce qu'elle veut, soit libre de vendre où elle veut, puisse coter les prix qu'il lui plaira' [it can produce how much it want, can sell where it want, and it can free to fix prices]. RPA, 00-2-15933, AAC, Notes diverses, 'Reforme de l'AAC', 4 and 5 December 1935.

89 During September 1934, firms summoned also a special meeting in London to analyse AIAG's proposal. RPA, 00-2-15929, AAC notes sténographées du conseil de direction,

'17ème Réunion du Board of Governors', 29 September 1934. RZA, AIAG Berichte Protokolls, box. 1931–1935, 'Bericht über die allgemeine Geschäftslage', 10 July 1934.

90  RPA, 00-2-15933, AAC, Projects. 'Draft Minutes of the First Meeting of the Executive Committee of the Export Agreement', s.d. but June or July 1935. This idea was endorsed as basis by Davis. HHC, MSS #282, ALCOA, US v. ALCOA, Equity 85–73, Exhibit 834, E.K. Davis to Marlio, 26 June 1935.

91  RPA, 00-2-15928, AAC, Réunion diverses, 'Conférence des producteurs européens', 11 July 1935. RPA, 00-2-15933, AAC, Notes, Level (AF), 'Note sur l'Aluminium-Association et l'Alliance Aluminium Cie', 14 January 1936.

92  RPA, 00-1-20028, AFC, Aluminium, 'Note sur l'Aluminium. Programme production 1939', 23 November 1938, These measures interested also France, see Hachez-Leroy, *L'Aluminium français*, 228–229.

93  RPA 00-2-15928, AAC. Conseils de direction, 'PV du 33e conseil de direction de l'AAC, tenu à Zurich le 17 February 1939'.

94  RPA, 00-2-15933, AAC, Notes, 'La Tresorerie de l'Alliance Aluminium Cie', 10 February 1939.

95  Les décision arbitraires des Gouvernements allemand et italien ont entrainé, pour le groupe allemand et pour le groupe suisse, une augmentation disproportionnée de leurs moyens de production. La politique britannique de réarmement met aujourd'hui le marché anglais dans une situation aussi anormale. Ces conditions rendent impossible la marche des accords de 1931. On ne peut plus baser sur le droit de production l'équilibre du marché de l'aluminium.
RPA, 00-2-15933, AAC, Notes diverses, Philippe Level, 'Note sur l'Alliance', 12 January 1938.

96  RPA, 00-2-15928, AAC, Autres réunions, 'Conférence des producteurs Européens', 4 March 1938.

97  TNA, T/187/55, Swiss Aluminium Company, 'Note on the Swiss Aluminium Company Limited', 20 July 1938; RZA, AIAG Berichte Protokolls, box. 1937–1939, 'Bericht über die allgemeine Geschäftslage', 23 December 1937. RPA, 00-1-20047, AFC. Aluminium. Notes sur les pays etrangers, 'Marchés de l'Europe Centrale. Tchécoslocquie, Pologne, Roumanie, Hongries', 20 October 1938. AN F/23/343 Direction des fabrications d'armements, 'Note sur l'Industrie française des metaux legers', 15 November 1938.

98  UGD 347 21/45/9, Alliance Correspondance, Marlio to AAC, 14 December 1938.

# 9 A cartel in the turmoil of the war

## The causes of Alliance's termination, 1939–1945

After a decade of economic depression, the production of aluminium stagnated in those countries in which no political programmes were carried out to support the expansion of this metal. The global conflict sharpened this trend and reshaped the global aluminium industry, pushing many countries to become new producers and increasing the output of the old producing countries. Compared with the output of about 400,000 tons recorded in 1938, the global aluminium output skyrocketed to the peak of about 2,000,000 tons in 1943. This dramatic increase was not the same in all countries. Yet war investments showed that many countries arrived unprepared for the war (such as the US and France). The old mismatch between private strategies and public policies was sharpened during the first months of the war. In some other countries, the war programmes launched during the 1930s granted an optimal output, such as in Germany, which became the world leading country to produce aluminium in 1939, or in Japan whose production spurted during the conflict.

Not only did the aluminium industry emerge from the war totally changed from a quantitative standpoint, but also it was modified in its institutional background. If Alliance proved already during the last phase of the 1930s not to be able to conjugate private and public policies, neither its end was still decreed nor a substitute for the cartels was ready to take over the international governance of this industry. As we will see in this chapter, Alliance did not survive the war and some particular governmental policies, in particular those of the United States, hampered its resurgence after the conflict.[1] In this chapter, the process that led to the end of Alliance will be described. Its collapse was not the mere outcome of antitrust policies, which had already affected the evolution of the relationships between Americans and Europeans during the last decade. The emergence of new governance and strategic, read military, issues in the US had an international impact over the cartel, leading to its conclusion in 1945. Cartel regulation and strategic material governance flow together in the administration of the aluminium industry, which was definitively changed by the Second World War.

The issues of industrial governance behind a strategic material such as aluminium are evident looking at the French and American cases at the eve of the conflict. In 1939, both countries had a theoretical maximum output equal to that of ten years before. In the specific case of France, the Great Depression, before, and Alliance's policies after, had delayed key investments in the early 1930s, ending

Table 9.1 Production of aluminium in the principal countries during the Second World War, 1939–1946 (thousand of tons)

| | France | USA | Canada | Germany | UK | Norway | Italy | Switzerland | Japan | USSR | World |
|---|---|---|---|---|---|---|---|---|---|---|---|
| 1939 | 52.5 | 148.4 | 75.0 | 195.1 | 25.0 | 31.1 | 34.2 | 27.0 | 32.8 | 55.0 | 695.3 |
| 1940 | 61.7 | 187.1 | 98.8 | 204.6 | 28.0 | 27.8 | 38.8 | 28.0 | 45.9 | 62.0 | 807.2 |
| 1941 | 63.9 | 280.4 | 193.7 | 223.5 | 35.0 | 17.5 | 40.8 | 26.0 | 79.8 | 60.0 | 1,063.7 |
| 1942 | 45.2 | 472.4 | 308.6 | 254.2 | 50.0 | 20.5 | 45.4 | 24.0 | 110.5 | 57.0 | 1,445.6 |
| 1943 | 46.5 | 834.7 | 449.1 | 242.0 | 56.5 | 23.5 | 47.2 | 19.0 | 149.6 | 65.0 | 2,006.6 |
| 1944 | 26.1 | 753.2 | 418.6 | 236.1 | 36.1 | 15.0 | 18.8 | 10.0 | 118.4 | 71.0 | 1,769.0 |
| 1945 | 37.2 | 453.5 | 195.7 | 0.7 | 32.4 | 4.6 | 4.3 | 5.0 | 8.1 | 86.3 | 842.3 |
| 1946 | 47.8 | 371.8 | 176.0 | 0.6 | 32.0 | 16.6 | 10.9 | 13.1 | 3.2 | 90.0 | 773.4 |

Source: RPA, 00-1-20028, Pechiney Collection Historique, Aluminium Statistiques, Croissance de l'Aluminium dans le monde, s.d. but 1956.

up with severely slowing the growth of production in this country.[2] Only in 1938 did the problem of military needs of aluminium in case of war start to attract the interest of the French government. In particular, the formulation of a plan for the production of military planes showed a possible scarcity in raw materials needed to support it. In 1938 AF had had an installed production capacity of 45,000 tons per year of which only 28,000 tonnes had outlets in the domestic market. The French war ministry asked AF to maintain production at full capacity to be able to easily start military production in wartime. Even if the government could neither guarantee to stockpile the metal nor to provide other aids to find additional outlets, the French companies planned expansion of production capacity up to 60,000 tons per year to follow military demands.[3]

The French government was not willing to implement any measures similar to the policies that Germany, Italy, and, to a lesser extent, Great Britain had undertaken during the 1930s to help the expansion of the aluminium industry. For instance, it neither provided specific programmes to private producers, nor enacted compulsory substitutions of other non-ferrous metals, such as copper and tin. The complex interplay between private business and public policies, that in other countries was reshaped towards a more robust public implication in the administration of national aluminium industries, in France produced only timid modifications to the governance of this industry. In 1937 the French government formed the Groupement d'Importation et de Repartition de l'Aluminium (GIRA) that, in spite of its public guardianship, was under the complete control of AF. GIRA's main tasks would be to administrate imports from the United States in case of war to support the production of aeroplanes.[4]

The government adopted an ambiguous policy towards AF: the organisation of imports from the United States was a sort of replica of the situation that had arisen in 1915, when there was a shortage of aluminium for the war effort. It was, as the French authorities recognised, their lack of war preparedness and their faintness in encouraging investments in national aluminium production. However, unlike 1915, the French government introduced political control over prices. This measure was undertaken to avoid AF increasing its prices to pay back investments to increase production capacity.[5] Although this measure was aimed to prevent the uncontrolled increase in prices that had occurred in 1915, it caused problems to production planning and investment in a period of severe monetary instability. This aspect reveals the profound contradiction that existed in the late 1930s between future military demand and the current civil market. Military demand required a latent overproduction, whose burden weighed on the producers. While production was overestimated for civil markets, it would not be enough in wartime, and it would require new investments. AF partially tried to solve this contradiction looking for outlets abroad, as in Eastern Europe and in the North American market, not without causing tensions in the cartel.

This type of situation was hiding another pitfall. The upward trend of sales was led in the late 1930s by rearmament programmes that were not doomed to last in the future. Even if they pushed companies to produce at full capacity, these programmes did not allow investments over the long term. At the end of 1937, a decrease in the purchase of military goods was recorded in many countries, which in turn caused a slowdown on all areas related to the policies of rearmament, including aluminium.[6] Without any defined programme, private companies could not take the investment risk to meet military demand, because this would lead them to overcapacity. This was valid for the French companies, but to a lesser extent also for ALTED, BACO, and, in part, AIAG. In fact, also BACO and ALTED were involved in ambiguous plans in Great Britain. The British government had set guidelines for the producers of the Commonwealth, but without establishing policies comparable to those of Hitler's Germany or fascist Italy.[7] BACO's reluctance to invest in new capacities encouraged the British government to involve AIAG in the construction of a new plant.[8] The behaviour of AIAG emphasises this nexus between private strategy and public policies. The Swiss company increased its outputs in those countries where clear political programmes supported it, such as in Germany (Rheinfelden went from a capacity of 2,500 tons in 1929 to 20,000 tons in 1940) and Italy (SAVA went from 2,000 tons to 16,000 tons). On the contrary, AIAG kept the Swiss capacities unchanged: the plant in Chppis, in fact, experienced the greatest reduction being used at 25 per cent of its capacity.[9]

## ALCOA, its monopoly, and US war programmes

In the case of the United States this complex link among national policies, business strategies, and models of corporate governance seemed even more difficult to manage. Antitrust policies made the situation more critical for ALCOA because it mingled with the strategic considerations of the company and the military visions of the government. ALCOA was not a member of Alliance and followed strategies that were independent from the directives of the cartel, even if the cartel in 1931 was possible only because a complete separation of the American market from the rest of the world was operated by ALCOA. In fact, since the creation of ALTED, ALCOA had concentrated entirely on its domestic market and it neither invested abroad, nor exported.[10] The autonomy of ALCOA from the international cartel appears clearly by comparing its policies on prices, production, and stock buffering with AAC during the 1930s (see Table 9.2).

Unlike Alliance, whose minimal production was set at about 50 per cent of capacity, ALCOA's production was lowered by 70 per cent (using about 30 per cent of total capacity) during the harsher period of the crisis. The crisis had a much greater intensity in the American market compared to Europe and the recovery was not as stimulated as in many European countries by military demand. ALCOA also had to face a new severe crisis in 1938, the year in which unsold stock was again accumulated quickly. ALCOA implemented a policy of reduction in selling prices which, even if they offered a decisive advantage in their domestic market between 1933 and 1936, they failed to increase the demand that long stagnated. Moreover, this advantage was gradually lost after the abandonment of the convertibility by the Swiss franc in 1936, because the prices of AAC, as shown in Table 9.2, were again lower than those of ALCOA. Despite these restrictive policies, in the 1930s ALCOA continued to invest in order to maintain its national monopoly, preventing new groups from taking advantage of

Table 9.2 Alliance and ALCOA rate of production, sales, prices (in ¢/lb) and inventory levels, 1930s

| | Alliance Aluminium Compagnie | | | | | Aluminum Company of America | | | | |
|---|---|---|---|---|---|---|---|---|---|---|
| | production** | rate | sales | stocks | prices* | production | rate | sales | stocks | prices |
| 1932 | 79,218 | 53.5 | 98,859 | 104,895 | 15.52 | 47,576 | 39.0 | 44,369 | 140,470 | 21.76 |
| 1933 | 75,859 | 50.0 | 99,649 | 99,854 | 20.16 | 38,612 | 32.0 | 42,421 | 136,898 | 19.30 |
| 1934 | 97,061 | 55.0 | 136,670 | 83,496 | 25.28 | 33,650 | 28.0 | 65,667 | 113,240 | 18.95 |
| 1935 | 148,056 | 53.0 | 194,170 | 72,814 | 23.30 | 54,111 | 45.0 | 78,041 | 88,278 | 18.75 |
| 1936 | 189,674 | 70.0 | 246,432 | 61,608 | 21.74 | 102,026 | 84.0 | 115,589 | 76,231 | 18.82 |
| 1937 | 266,168 | 100.0 | 317,280 | 52,880 | 17.69 | 132,757 | 97.0 | 143,224 | 74,651 | 19.56 |
| 1938 | 348,400 | – | 349,280 | 64,880 | 16.56 | 130,127 | 84.0 | 78,886 | 125,889 | 19.44 |
| 1939 | 404,600 | – | 400,544 | 56,318 | – | 148,365 | 74.0 | 143,573 | 97,364 | 19.86 |

Source: RPA and HHC.

Notes

* Prices of AAC were stable at a level of about 70 gold British sterling; however the fluctuations of British sterling and US dollars affected price expressed in $; ** includes the production of all members (AF, AIAG, ALTED, BACO, VAW).

the business recovery to invest in this industry. In addition to extending the old plant, the company began to make investments to build a new smelter in Tennessee, in a city that was called Alcoa. Due to this investment, it could sign long-term supply contracts for electricity at low cost with the Tennessee Valley Authority.[11] While the production capacity of ALCOA stagnated in the peak of the international crisis between 1932 and 1935 (125,000 tons per year), the decision to make various investments increased its capacity tons per year which in 1937 reached 135,000 and 155,000 in 1938. In the early 1940s, ALCOA had a total production capacity of over 200,000 tons per year.[12]

The new crisis of demand in the American market in 1938 prevented ALCOA from continuing its investments beyond this limit. However, faced with a progressive deterioration of the international political situation, ALCOA wondered if its capacity was adequate to meet military needs in case of war. At that time, the American government made it known to the company that it was planning to produce 9,000 aircraft (which required approximately 90,000 tonnes of aluminium). Faced with this plan of production of aircraft and the realisation that the installed capacity was already oversized for the civilian market, ALCOA changed its mind about investing beyond what its finances would allow, which were already weighed down by the inventory holding.[13] The outbreak of war in Europe in 1939 prompted a rethinking for ALCOA, which thought to seize the opportunity to play again in the Second World War, the role of supplier of aluminium for the allied field as it did during the First World War. Thus, ALCOA started an expansion plan that included the construction of a new plant in Vancouver, a second plant for the refining of alumina, and an increase in production capacity of the old plants to reach a production capacity of 400,000 tons during the subsequent three years.[14]

During 1941, however, this programme proved to be inadequate to meet the United States' new plans for the production of aircraft, when this country entered the global conflict. The Truman Committee, established in May 1941 to investigate the preparation of the American economy for war, calculated that at least 50–60,000 planes per year were required, which demanded an aluminium production capacity of 600,000 tons per year. With such a programme, not even the new capacity of ALCOA of 400,000 tons per year would have been sufficient. Meanwhile, also, aviation production began to conceive larger planes for long-range campaigns, requiring on average more aluminium than the first planes built in the late 1930s.[15] The need for additional production for military needs was added to the problem, not yet resolved, of ALCOA's monopoly in the American market. Even if FTC had failed to prove any ALCOA anti-competitive action in terms of the current antitrust law, its position as sole supplier of such an important strategic metal proved to be a danger for military preparedness. As a consequence, during the war antitrust action and military policies were tied up together.

Before the war, FTC took note that the position of ALCOA was difficult to modify, because there was no actor that was actually willing to enter the aluminium market where the dominant position of ALCOA was overwhelming. Even the measures that FTC could take in the event of a prosecution would not have guaranteed the transition from a monopoly to a competitive environment.[16] In fact, FTC explored several hypotheses to break the monopoly of ALCOA. The first hypothesis was splitting ALCOA into four companies, one for each plant that ALCOA had at that time (the fifth plant of Vancouver had not yet been designed when FTC was surveying ALCOA's monopoly). Although this solution aimed to keep a scale production, however, it did not grant that new actors entered the US primary aluminium industry. In fact ALCOA also controlled the best hydroelectric productions, the higher aluminium-grade bauxite deposits, and, until the late 1930s, only one large alumina plant with huge scale economies that supplied all of its facilities. This explains why no investor would risk capital, even to take over one of ALCOA's plants, because this 'piece' of the American trusts would not be integrated and could not defend itself against the competition that ALCOA would have engaged against a newcomer. At the end of the 1930s, aluminium was no more a little business and the barriers to entry were even higher than they were a few decades earlier.[17]

Another hypothesis formulated by the FTC was the division of the trust into four separate companies, but without the implication of new interests. According to FTC, ALCOA could have been divided among the four groups of shareholders that already had the control of the company: Davis, Hunt, Mellon, and, finally, the Duke group, that had entered ALCOA's capital at the time of the construction of Arvida, in 1925. Moreover, FTC considered worthwhile that ALTED had to change its ownership.[18] Also in this case, however, this division would have reduced the integration of ALCOA, with detriment to its efficiency. Faced with this impasse, the solution proposed by FTC in the late 1930s was to establish a commission that should monitor the prices and profits of ALCOA, which also the representatives of the major consumers of aluminium in the country would participate.[19] This solution created doubts among the old antagonists of ALCOA. For instance, Haskell, the chairman of Bausch Machine Tool Co. (BMTC) who had promoted the Arvida project before it passed under the control of ALCOA, told FTC that the formation of a government commission on prices did not guarantee that any newcomers could compete with ALCOA. The problem was the inability to create another company from scratch that was as vertically integrated and high performing as ALCOA.[20]

The lack of overwhelming evidence that proved direct participation of ALCOA in the international cartel or, at least, that ALCOA had a national monopoly because of the agreement signed with European companies, frustrated every action of FTC. The American authorities were unable to find the smoking gun that accounted for a restrictive agreement between the American company and the cartel for the American market. The huge amount of archival documents that FTC seized from ALCOA, in fact, showed a much more complex situation, made up of cooperation and rivalry at the same time. ALCOA had some cooperation with the European firms during the interwar period, such as joint ventures or the agreements for the Japanese market, but this had no criminal relevance for ALCOA in the United States. According to antitrust legislation in force at the time, a company was guilty according to the provisions of the Sherman Act, not if it had a monopoly, but if this monopoly was derived from agreements with other companies or by unfair trade practices.[21]

In a last attempt to nail ALCOA, FTC also interrogated Philippe Level, chairman of ISCO, AF's sales subsidiary in the US, and son of Jacques Level – who was president of AFC and of AF. This interrogation risked creating a diplomatic incident between France and the United States because the French military authorities had expressed concern that Level could reveal sensitive information about the French aluminium industry.[22] During his interrogation, Level told FTC's investigators that ALCOA's monopoly was reinforced by American protective measures, i.e. antidumping and high customs duties, which had prevented European producers from exporting more in the US or to invest directly in the interwar era.[23] A last attempt was made at the end of 1940, when FTC also interrogated Louis Marlio – who came to the US at the beginning of the conflict, as we will show – about Alliance and other links between the European and American groups.[24] As much as the antitrust authorities wanted to break the monopoly of ALCOA, they failed to find any compelling evidence of any unlawful conduct by the company of Pittsburgh. This led to a first judgment of acquittal by Judge Caffey in October 1941, a few months after the report of the Truman committee. In this verdict, it was decided that ALCOA's monopoly was granted not by unfair restrictive practices, but by its extreme efficiency and integration.[25] Recently, Wyatt Wells has shown that when the US entered the conflict, the American antitrust authorities made a sort of truce with big business in order to help military preparations.[26] ALCOA as well benefited from this truce to concentrate on the war effort.

Although ALCOA was acquitted in 1941, its monopoly still represented a problem for military preparation, implying a key national security issue. As it emerged when the American government realised that domestic production of aluminium was insufficient for production in wartime, a monopoly was not the best choice to have a strong military preparedness. In this context, the action of the antitrust linked the problem of ALCOA's monopoly to the military security and military capacity of the United States. This point was clearly declaimed by the head of the American antitrust authorities between 1938 and 1943, Thurman Arnold, who became known in history as one of the main 'trust-busters'.[27] In the course of 1941 Arnold said in response to the data presented by the Truman Committee that showed the inadequacy of American production of aluminium with this phrasing:

> This is a war between industrial armies, not between military armies. It is a war in which the country which produces the fastest will win. It is a test to see whether an industrial democracy can make itself more efficient than a dictatorship. . . . But I do say that it [the big industrial business] indistinctively fears expansions. It fears that overproduction will hurt its dividends after the war is over. Expansion may mean that its dominating position will be lost. . . . For instance, even the collapse of France failed to wake up the aluminum industry to the dangerous shortage which their policy of limiting production had created.[28]

## Reynolds Metals Co., Louis Marlio, and the strategic policies of the United States

As anticipated, these ideas were not followed at the end of the first verdict of the ALCOA case, which acquitted the American company. ALCOA's reluctance to make private investments led the government to take charge of all the investments to be made to increase the production capacity of aluminium useful for the extension of the production of aeroplanes, following the new directions of the Truman Committee.[29] In June 1941, the United States government implemented a major programme of expansion of aluminium production, which was funded through the Reconstruction Finance Corporation (RFC). This programme aimed to extend overall capabilities up to 725,000 tons per year through the construction of nine aluminium plants and four alumina plants. The government decided to retain ownership of these plants and placed them under the control of a separate government agency, the Defense Plant Corporation (DPC), a subsidiary of RFC. Although DPC was still the owner of the new plants for aluminium and alumina, ALCOA was appointed to design and administer these units because, as the only company in the United States, it was the only one, according to military circles, that could manage a plan on that scale.[30]

In spite of this, ALCOA was close to losing its monopoly. The first independent producer of aluminium appeared about the same time: Reynolds Metals Company (RMC). RMC became a producer of aluminium on its own, breaking ALCOA's monopoly. The government supported Reynolds, after several financial circles refused to back its investment strategies in this field. Several studies have emphasised the importance of Reynolds joining the production of aluminium. In fact, the investment of this firm showed that, despite FTC's pessimistic studies to solve the problem of ALCOA's monopoly, it was possible for a new investor to overcome the barriers to join this industry. Moreover, Reynolds played an important role in convincing the United States government that the aluminium production was insufficient for the war. Reynolds began his investments at the end of 1940, when Richard Reynolds persuaded, thanks to the intermediation of Senator Lister Hill, RFC to provide the necessary capital to invest in this sector. Jesse Jones, head of RFC, decided to grant a loan at 4 per cent interest of $15,800,000 to RMC, in which it mortgaged all of its properties as a guarantee to pay back this loan. RMC used these funds to build an alumina plant and two aluminium smelters with a total capacity of 80,000 tons per year.[31] After this first 'breach' into ALCOA's monopoly, DPC also assigned the management of one small smelter to Olin Corporation, which divested from aluminium at the end of the war.[32]

Although compared to ALCOA's production it could appear as marginal, RMC's output was bigger that the output of France or Great Britain in those days. Until then, no other company, even more important than RMC, had succeeded in entering ALCOA's business. This was made possible by the particular context of the war and by RMC's long-term path. Reynolds entered the aluminium field through a policy of diversification of production started a few decades earlier. Before the Great War, Reynolds was a leading producer of cigarettes (Camel) based in Richmond, Virginia. It was led to produce metal sheets to wrap its cigarettes following above all some marketing considerations. Initially, the packets of cigarettes were produced with tin foil; after the Great War, the vulgarisation of aluminium led Reynolds to opt for sheets of this metal. In 1926, Reynolds invested further in the metallurgy of aluminium and formed RMC, which extended into the production of other finished and semi-finished products. The historical supplier of aluminium for RMC had always been ALCOA, but in 1938 Reynolds negotiated provision from AF because ALCOA was short of metal to supply. In that year, Richard Reynolds went on a journey to Europe and, following a trip to Germany, discovered that Germany was achieving a huge military programme. This vision led Reynolds first to try to convince ALCOA to invest, and then to invest directly in this production.[33] As we will see, Reynolds could count on a special consultant to enter this industry: Louis Marlio himself.

Despite the first round of investments started by the US government and the beginning of Reynolds' production, at the end of 1941 the American government realised that production was still insufficient. Further investments were needed to increase the production of aeroplanes that, from the very beginning of the conflict, were proving to be the main military tool in the war.[34] To plan a second round of investments, the American administration did not consult ALCOA, like the first time, but it asked for collaboration from Louis Marlio. In January 1942, he was commissioned to carry out a study about how aluminium would be necessary to win the war. The decision to ask Marlio to carry out a study of this kind may seem a little surprising: Marlio had been sent on a mission in the United States directly by Marshal Petain a few days before the armistice of France with Germany, and his mission was to restore the reputation of France after the defeat in the American political and economic environments.[35] In fact, the secret purpose of Marlio's mission was to push the Americans to enter the conflict. This was also supported by the British Foreign Office that met Marlio in Madrid before he left the Old Continent in June 1940.[36]

When he arrived in the United States, Marlio began a series of lectures in several universities where he showed the need for the United States to enter the war to turn the tide of the conflict by imposing the economic and political superiority of the American military machine over the dictatorships. During his lectures, he got to know the Brookings Institution, a powerful American counselling agency close to the Democratic Party that supported the intervention of the United States in the war. As requested by Harold Moulton, president of Brookings, Marlio was hired as an expert in economics and international affairs at Brookings, that financed the publication of several studies on the possibility that the United States entered the war, the military superiority of this country compared to dictatorships, and which strategy to adopt towards Japan and Germany. This role entrusted to Marlio aimed at mobilising a by-partisan consensus in the Democrat and Republican environments about the opportunity that the United States entered the conflict as soon as possible.[37] In particular, Moulton commissioned Marlio to produce a pamphlet on the entry of the USA into the war and the influence that the American industrial machine would have in turning the tide in the conflict.[38] Until summer 1941, Marlio reported to the French authorities about the American movement to enter the conflict.[39]

Marlio took an active part in the rapid rearmament of the American industry and his lobbying was aimed at the universities,[40] power seats, and even country clubs.[41] According to the reconstruction that Marlio made of his activities in the United States, RFC helped Marlio's nomination as Reynolds' economic adviser during 1941.[42] Also Reynolds' documents confirm RFC endorsed Marlio's participation in RMC and eventually consented to his employment at this company.[43] Without Marlio's help, in fact, Reynolds would not have been able to start production of primary aluminium in such a quick time and to carry out this business successfully.[44] At first Marlio thought that Reynolds would have left aluminium production after the war and that AFC would have continued to supply RMC with all the aluminium that it required. With this idea to serve both the US government and his company, he accepted working for Reynolds.[45] During the conflict, Reynolds decided to stay in the aluminium business and Marlio also became the author of Reynolds' strategy for the post-war period, helping the company to consolidate its position. Marlio, moreover, could also offer his help in American political circles, thanks to his interconnection with Brookings. In addition to the Reynolds' appointment, Marlio actually became the economic and strategic adviser for the Department of War, following Harold Moulton's advice. The US government commissioned two studies: one on the production of aluminium in the US[46] and the other on electrical energy for American military production.[47]

Due to the fact that he had been president of Alliance before the war, Marlio had played a main intelligence role during the war, which profoundly reshaped the structure of the global aluminium industry. Marlio knew the productive capacities of all countries and could recommend a plan to achieve the capacity necessary to win the war.[48] The presentation of what we may call the 'Marlio report' also occurred in a very difficult time for the fate of the war: German penetration into Soviet territory to Stalingrad had deprived the Soviet Union of more than half of its production capacity of aluminium, which was damaged by shelling during the advance. Great Britain could not produce more than 50,000 tons due to lack of electricity. On the contrary, the Axis powers, which in the meantime had conquered Norway, where they were starting to build a huge plant under the direct leadership of Herman Göring,[49] had placed Yugoslavia's and France's production under control, and were extending the production capacity of other occupied countries or allies such as Hungary, Romania, and Czechoslovakia.[50] In 1941, Marlio could calculate the total production capacity of Axis at approximately 400,000 tons, and he foresaw that it would increase up to 650,000 by 1943 to reach 780,000 in 1944.[51] In reality, Hans Otto Frøland showed that this programme had different scales,[52] but Marlio was the only person in the US during these days who could provide reliable figures about the German plans at that time.

Marlio criticised DPC's first programme for the extension of American production capacity, because it did not take into account a global vision of the aluminium industry and how much this metal was needed for aircraft production sufficient to defeat the Axis. Marlio advised the American government to take charge of all the extensions necessary to double the overall production capacity of the United Nations with regards to that of the Axis. In fact,

Marlio suggested bringing production capacity to 1,300,000 tons by 1943 and to achieve the goal of 1,560,000 tons by 1944. In addition to these guidelines for the production of aluminium, Marlio described in detail what stock policy management the government should have adopted. He suggested considering the amount of three or four months of production as rolling stock, and since it was intended to increase the turnover of the metal between production plants and transformation units, it always had to be available to the government.[53] The American government, following this advice, extended its American production capacity and also financed the extension of Canadian production, which, when added together, brought the total production capacity of these two countries to exceed 1.3 million tons in 1943 (about 800,000 in the United States and 500,000 in Canada, see Table 9.1).[54]

In his report, Marlio also suggested other measures to be taken immediately. First, he advised the US government to fund research on new technology for refining alternative raw materials, which was at Reynolds' disposal, to make use of the vast deposits on American soil that until then had not been exploited. This would eliminate a major bottleneck in the supply of raw materials and breach into ALCOA's business. Second, Marlio proposed to the government to launch a comprehensive programme for the production of aluminium from scrap that would further extend the production of metal. In addition Marlio also provided a full list of bombing targets in order to neutralise German production of aluminium. In particular, he advised destroying the alumina plants instead of the hydroelectric installations, because they were extremely vulnerable and difficult to reconstruct in a short time.[55] Later, Marlio in a book published by Brookings also supported the need to completely destroy the German productive capacity of aluminium, as it was the only way to ensure world peace after the war.[56] Marlio's role during the conflict was threefold. Relying on Brookings, he started a public campaign for the entry of the US into the war and for the end of American isolationism. In addition, he contributed decisively to the end of ALCOA's monopoly, helping a new actor to join the aluminium industry and to carry out a consistent strategy to keep this business after the war. Finally, he decisively contributed to military planning and to the elaboration of a strategy focused on aluminium and aircraft production.[57]

Although his work was secret, Marlio deeply influenced the production level of the main weapon during the conflict: aviation.[58] The aeroplane production programme in the United States, in fact, was a major factor in winning a decisive superiority over the Axis powers, as shown in Table 9.3.

The contribution of the United States was decisive for the productive superiority of the Allied camp. Between the two sides there was such a large spread because the forecast made by Marlio in 1942 actually proved to be overestimated for the Axis. The Axis global production of aluminium not only never reached the objectives of Goering's plan, but also failed to reach the 750,000 tons that Marlio had foreseen.[59] Its maximum capacity stood at 500,000 because it failed to implement its plans for the construction of a new unit with capacity of 100,000 tons per year in Norway.[60] The programme established with the help of Marlio, and his role played in Reynolds' entering the aluminium business, can be

*Table 9.3* Military aeroplane production by countries during the Second World War, 1939–1945

|  | 1939 | 1940 | 1941 | 1942 | 1943 | 1944 | 1945 |
|---|---|---|---|---|---|---|---|
| United States | 5,856 | 12,804 | 26,277 | 47,836 | 85,898 | 96,318 | 49,761 |
| Soviet Union | 10,382 | 10,565 | 15,735 | 25,436 | 34,900 | 40,300 | 20,900 |
| Great Britain | 8,190 | 16,149 | 22,694 | 28,247 | 30,963 | 31,036 | 14,145 |
| Total Allies | 24,178 | 39,518 | 64,706 | 101,519 | 151,761 | 167,654 | 84,806 |
| Allies without US | 18,572 | 26,714 | 38,429 | 53,683 | 65,863 | 71,336 | 35,045 |
| Germany | 8,295 | 10,247 | 11,776 | 15,409 | 24,807 | 39,807 | 7,540 |
| Japan | 4,467 | 4,768 | 5,088 | 8,861 | 16,693 | 28,180 | 11,066 |
| Italy | 1,750 | 3,257 | 3,503 | 2,821 | 2,024 | 0 | 0 |
| Total Axis | 14,562 | 16,815 | 19,264 | 26,670 | 43,100 | 67,987 | 18,606 |

Source: Overy, *The Air War*, 150.

considered, in retrospect, amongst the most important factors that reshaped the international aluminium industry after the war. One of these changes was, as we will see, the end of the formal cartelisation that had lasted before 1945. Ironically, one of the leading *cartel-matador*, as Harm Schröter defined the high influential personalities of the international cartelisation,[61] was also a leading but involuntary architect of its end.

## Alliance during the war: a 'dead cartel walking'?

Proceeding with order, at the eve of the war, the destiny of Alliance was not yet decided and its members were not sure about its desirability for the post-war period. Even before the outbreak of war, the members of the cartel were not sure about what to do with their association. A quick dismantling was not possible due to the presence of VAW's pending debt. However, some companies were aiming at least to reduce Alliance's capital in order to reallocate some of the funds that were frozen in its mechanisms. AF volunteered this proposal on many occasions because it saw no immediate utility in this company. According to the French company, in 1939 AAC would no longer be able to influence the market because, due to output expansion, a capital at least five times larger was necessary to play the role it played in 1931. In the new context, AAC could only take over a small quantity of stock or, in alternative, a few small outsiders; as a consequence, Alliance represented no ready utility for the aluminium producers.[62] However, some tactical reasons convinced the firms that participated in this cartel to keep Alliance's destiny on hold.

In spite of the divergences that emerged at the end of the 1930s, which caused the failure of cartel reform following the 'home markets' proposal, the firms agreed not to exclude using the devices of Alliance after hostilities again. The continuation of Alliance would have avoided the long procrastination that had delayed the formation of a new cartel after 1918. At the outbreak of war, Alliance was modified in order to help it survive. All its funds were exchanged into gold ingots and kept safe in banks in the United States and Switzerland. The members of the board resigned and they were substituted with Swiss citizens, chosen from among the most reputed scholars and politicians, in order to reduce the risk of confiscations. The chairmanship of Alliance, which had been vacant since Marlio's resignation in 1938, was now assigned to Heinrich Haeberlin, a very influential and reputed Swiss personality who had been the president of the Helvetic confederation during the 1920s.[63] Being the owner of a British company, AAH, which controlled one smelter in Norway and another in the UK, the cartel also needed a director of British origin to avoid the risk of sequestration. As a consequence, Ludwig Braasch, who had directed AAC since 1931, was replaced by Robert Hodson, a British citizen and ex-employee of ALTED.[64]

However, these measures were not sufficient to avoid confiscations in the Allied countries. The fact that the German group owned 20 per cent of shares in Alliance forced British authorities to put this firm on the black list of enemy properties. When they joined the war, the United States also included this company in their black list, sequestrating gold ingots and shares in the hands of US citizens. The various attempts made by Maurice Lugeon and Heinrich Haeberlin to re-enable it between 1942 and 1944 proved to be useless.[65] According to the British authorities, the majority of AAC's shares, although represented by people of neutral nationalities, was in the hands of interests belonging to the Axis. The French group was in fact assimilated to the Axis powers, because the Vichy government was supplying Germany, while AIAG was directly involved in Italian and German war production. The British authorities indicated that only 616 shares (i.e. 400 of ALTED and 216 of BACO) of Alliance out of the total of 1,400 clearly belonged to the Allies; even AAH and SWACO, in which AIAG held 50 per cent of the capital, were sequestrated during hostilities.[66]

Even if this legal situation complicated the position of the cartel, the companies continued to debate the future of Alliance during the conflict. During his stay in the US, in 1941, Marlio had the opportunity to discuss the post-war period with Edward K. Davis. In spite of the enormous size that ALTED was planning to reach, Davis was optimistic about the quickness of post-war conversion to civil uses for aluminium. Davis explained to Marlio the need to fix very low prices in the post-war period to extend the use of aluminium as much as possible. Davis thought that, by lowering prices below 15¢/lb (about £60 per ton charged on the UK market), aluminium could immediately find new uses, thanks to the immense technological spin-off that the war represented. Davis also expressed this idea before the British and American authorities, prospecting a new era characterised by mass consumption of aluminium that would absorb the huge war output. This idea was also spread by independent studies in the final phase of the war, which outlined a 'golden' future for aluminium.[67] Nevertheless, Marlio and Davis agreed on the need to keep Alliance in stand-by until the end of hostilities, when the network of directors could be restarted and then its destiny could be discussed.[68]

However, even if the companies agreed on the stand-by of Alliance during the hostilities and about the desirability to continue this cartel after the war, it was not clear how Alliance could have actually worked in the future. In 1941 the head of AF produced a study to analyse whether Alliance would ease the burden of economic conversion from war to peace economy at the end of the conflict, avoiding a recurrence of the serious imbalances between supply and demand that had occurred at the end of the Great War.[69] In a similar manner, even Metallgesellschaft reasoned how it would be possible to restart Alliance after the hostilities.[70] Both studies were strongly opposed to the simple reactivation of Alliance after the war. In fact, new investments had completely altered the balance of powers among its members and Alliance's resources were insufficient to pursue the control scheme on stock.[71] Nevertheless, the system of control of stock and production was still interesting. Its stock-buffering work, in theory, could provide effective control over surplus, eliminating the negative effects that would be caused by the quick sale of military stock on the market. This idea was expressed also by Lugeon, a temporary member of Alliance's board, who wrote to the British authorities in Basel in December 1941 that

> Alliance has been quoted several times as a type of international association. It is a sort of prototype of what it should have been done for other products that have become indispensable to men and of what we will have to do after the war if we want to achieve a real peace. We know perfectly, regarding the metal aluminium, what will inevitably happen when peace comes, for the time will come when the cannons are silent. We risk an economic war after another and perhaps just as deadly. So maybe it will be recalled that this international organisation [AAC] exists.[72]

During the war, Marlio was a supporter of these ideas in the United States. On several occasions, he suggested entrusting the transition from wartime to peacetime economy to a system of international cartels. He tried to show Alliance as a prototype of future cartels, praising its conduct during the Great Depression. During the 1930s, Alliance already represented a kind of *idealtypus* for 'private' international cartelisation and, in many publications that aimed to explore the general nature of the international cartel movement, aluminium often figured amongst the most effective and 'fair' cartels. From the political standpoint, for its 'private' nature, Alliance was often counterposed to the case of the tin and steel industry.[73] During the Second World War, however, Marlio aimed to actively support these ideas, with new fresh information and to provide the insider vision of the more difficult issues that the cartel faced, such as trade with the Soviets and, above all, the relationships with German rearmament. For this reason, Marlio also wrote a book, which was published by Brookings itself,[74] to balance the negative public opinion that was derived from the book by Borkin and Welsh, *Germany's Master Plan*. According to Borkin and Welsh, Alliance symbolised (along with a few other cartels) the evil of international cartelisation that was used by Hitler to reduce the military preparedness of the Allies. Actually, in their well-known book about cartels, Joseph Borkin and Charles Welsh summarised those claims writing in 1943 'through the cartel device Germany achieved a victory which a thousand bombers could not have won'.[75] However, only few copies of Marlio's memoirs were published and its publication was delayed for two years due to some issues linked to the translation from French. Marlio's book was anticipated by two other studies on the aluminium cartel, manoeuvred by the US antitrust authorities, which disclosed many documents gathered during ALCOA's process, reinforcing the thesis of Welsh and Borkin.[76]

In any case, when Marlio's book was published in 1947, the debate about the continuation of Alliance was no longer up to date. Its continuation in the future was hampered by the inclusion of aluminium in a more general debate about which policies the Allied governments would want to adopt for cartels during the post-war period. During 1943 and 1944, when the war changed course in favour of the countries of the United Nations, London and Washington began a debate on which policy to adopt for post-war problems of conversion. During these talks, specific attention was addressed to the formulation of coherent international governance to regulate the trade of major raw materials useful in the event of another war. These problems in the United States mingled with the problems related to antitrust legislation because, in addition to aluminium, a number of other useful materials for the war were severely scarce in the first part of the conflict: magnesium, steel, synthetic rubber, raw materials for explosives.[77] As pointed out by the historians Wells and Freyer in their respective studies, during the war the American antitrust authorities functioned as intelligence about strategic problems for the United States government, which was able to impose its own agenda in the peace negotiations.[78]

Following the interpretation method initiated by Arnold and taken up by an inquiry committee on war mobilisation created by Senator Kilgore, FTC supported the thesis that the American industry's lack of preparation in the first phase of the conflict was mainly due to its participation in international cartels. For this, the post-war period would have to be characterised by rapid general decartelisation that would allow, according to the staff of the antitrust authorities, both peace and international prosperity.[79] FTC's staff also produced a series of popular books on this topic aimed at raising public awareness.[80] As we have seen, in the first phase, the movement of international cartels was subjected to public 'criminalisation', to which in 1944 ad hoc journalistic campaigns were added during the campaign for the presidential elections. Even Cordell Hull, state secretary, and President Roosevelt on several occasions pointed to the need to end the experience of international cartels, identifying them as a mere instrument of Nazi foreign policy.[81] This public campaign against cartels was triggered by an investigation of the CIA, which discovered in 1944 a Nazi plan to use cartels as a tool to allow Germany to regain control of the world economy post-war period.[82] This fear became so widespread that, for instance, part of this discourse was also present in a blockbuster of that time such as *Gilda*, in which Gilda's husband, Ballin Mudson, secretly planned with some former German Nazis to establish a tungsten cartel in South America.[83] This general averse context to cartels was also reshaping the public 'narration' of the most important actors of Alliance. For instance, in January 1945, William Murray-Morrison, the president of BACO and one of the leading figures of Alliance, publically declaimed that

[Alliance] is a finance company but is sometimes erroneously referred as to a 'cartel'. It has a large capital and unlimited borrowing powers, and its main functions were to take over by purchase large accumulations of metal from its Shareholders and to resell this stock to the Shareholders as required. The Alliance did not fix selling prices to the public, nor lay down a partition of territories as is generally supposed.[84]

Despite this public debate, which affected the social perception of the cartel problem in the US and abroad, the military and strategic issues that lay behind the cartel problem drew more pragmatic attitudes.[85] Moreover, the international policies that should have been adopted for cartels were not designed by the US alone, but they were the outcome of the negotiations with Great Britain about the post-war order. Very pragmatic features reshaped the attitude to international cartels because, more than being a matter for the antitrust authorities, they were also considered a key issue in international industrial diplomacy.[86] In 1943, the United States government established an office on cartels and monopolies to study their working. At the same time, an office on raw materials and international trade was also created to develop a plan to prevent the recurrence of serious misconduct in the case of a new war. These two offices thought about proposing an intergovernmental control instead of simply eliminating the cartels. For example, Corwin Edwards in 1943 wrote to Myron Watkins

> We should not bury our heads in the sand by offering a liberal program and saying that it is not applicable to the great bulk of large industry. Instead we should face the difficulty and propose a line of adjustments between liberal principles of trade and safeguard for national security.[87]

At the same time, also in Great Britain the Board of Trade prepared an extensive study on all international cartels with British participation and on all national cartels aiming to prepare substantial documentation before taking any decision in this regard.[88] These studies were possible because the government of Great Britain implemented a policy of control on cartels at the outbreak of war, in order to prevent enemy companies from influencing war efforts with cartels. This information led the British government to put Alliance in the black list of enemy companies.[89] During the negotiations, Great Britain and the United States came to a compromise and instead of adopting an anti-trust law and banning international cartels, they planned to put their work under intergovernmental control, through the creation of an appropriate agency.[90] During the last phase of the war, this compromise was dictated by the fact that the problem of cartels was linked to the trade on raw materials. Due to strategic issues, both governments agreed that the self-control provided by private cartels was to be progressively replaced by governmental control. Governments would have avoided restrictions on strategic supplies in order to meet military needs.[91]

This idea was not a novelty. The debate about governmental control over cartel agreements also implicated the League of Nations and the International Chamber of Commerce during the 1930s.[92] The tin and rubber cartels, which had been under the control of the British Foreign Office since the 1930s, represented a model for other raw materials. Their working through stock buffering schemes had represented an innovation during the Great Depression, when – unlike Alliance, which remained a private cartel – the international schemes of these two raw materials came under intergovernmental control. Aside from tin and rubber, which epitomised the new fashioned 'intergovernmental commodity agreements' according to the definition that the International Chamber of Commerce conferred to these understandings at the end of the 1930s, aluminium was instead a key sample of the 'private cartels' movement, as Marlio pointed out at the congress about cartels, organised by the International Chamber of Commerce in 1937.[93] For instance, the steel industry – due to its strong links with public powers – was often presented as something that stood in the middle of the two models.[94] The aims of controlling the stock of raw materials was to combine the struggle against overproduction, caused by the extension of production capacities and the end of military demand. This scheme, outlined by the Board of Trade and also supported by John Maynard Keynes, was very similar to the finance company proposed by Davis in 1930, but stock was placed under the control of governments instead of private enterprises.[95]

The new aspect of this debate was its inclusion in the programmes for post-war international policy. Actually, during various meetings among the Cartel Committee, the American Raw Material Committee, and the British Board of Trade, which had occurred between 1943 and 1945, the possibility of enacting an international policy for cartels and raw material trade was debated. The main possibilities forecasted to tackle the cartel problem were to establish a register of cartels, to implement the strategies of international stock buffering to provide governmental control over key raw materials, and to suggest the inclusion of governments into the administration of cartels. The agreements in the future would not have been as systemic as in the past, but they would have intervened only in cases of serious imbalance between supply and demand. Their work would have ensured the stability of production and prices through mechanisms of forfeiture of overproduction.[96] In 1945 the United States also involved the Canadian government in the formation of an international registry of cartels. The Canadian government looked forward to active participation in the construction of this register and, in order to support its involvement in the post-war agenda on international trade, published an extensive study on the international cartels that involved Canadian industries.[97] These ideas were linked to negotiations for the formation of the International Trade Organisation (ITO), which would control the cartels and the coordination of agreements among governments for raw materials. The negotiations for the formation of ITO continued until the conference in Havana in the spring of 1948, but this the register was never created. As is known, the idea to form ITO was replaced by the construction of a multilateral tool to manage the international trade, the General Agreement on Trade and Tariffs (GATT).[98]

## The end of Alliance and preparation of the post-war aluminium trade

Therefore Alliance could not last after the war because it was a private cartel, without any kind of control from governments. In the case of the creation of

ITO and of an international register of cartels, Marlio was confident about the possibility of continuing Alliance, this solution 'n'est pas dangereuse, au contraire, pour les organisations comme le cartel de l'aluminium, qui ont ont toujours eu une politique des prix extremement modérée'.[99] However, the serious accusations that were addressed to Alliance during the war made its situation even more precarious. In this context, the American antitrust authorities decided to stop the cartel in an unilateral way because, in addition to considering it a threat to American security, it had a real power to curb it thanks to the legal issues of ALCOA. This was the outcome of the pending judgement that ALCOA was awaiting. Unlike other commodities, aluminium escaped control by an intergovernmental agreement, which did not replace Alliance after the war, because it was considered a special case due to the specific legal and political situation of ALCOA. Moreover, 55 per cent of American aluminium output was directly under the control of the government, which had a decisive power to set its policies.[100]

This fact reshaped the specific policy for aluminium in the post-war era. The crucial importance of aluminium in the production of planes, which proved crucial to assure correct military preparedness at the beginning of the Cold War, led American authorities to opt for a solution that would assure national control over this metal. In order to avoid any shortage in the future, the American authorities asked for the dismantling of the cartel and for the end of ALCOA's monopoly. Actually, during the Second World War, the destiny of the cartel and the process against ALCOA were tied up together by FTC. The end of the cartel and the prevention of its resurgence were led by the action of the American authorities, which used the process pending against ALCOA to achieve this goal. Even though American authorities failed to find the 'smoking gun' as regards the direct participation of ALCOA into Alliance, they took possession of Alliance's board minutes about German exceptions, which authorised the increase of output in this country after 1934. Immediately, ALCOA's monopoly ended being only an issue for the antitrust authorities and became a matter of national and international security.[101] In reality, as we have seen, the rise of German output was the outcome of political choices that endangered the cartel as well, while the United States had underestimated the importance of the aluminium industry and air power before 1941.[102]

Consequently, when American political powers organised a special board to assess the impact of cartels on the international economy and on American security, Alliance was thoroughly inspected. Supervising Alliance, in March 1945 the Board of Economic Warfare (BEW) finally concluded that

> The cartel [has to] be dissolved by vote of the allied representatives on order of allied governments. Either the British or the Canadian stockholders can dissolve the corporation by exercise of their notice rights.... The activities of this corporation have been outstandingly harmful to the war interest of the United States, in hampering wartime aluminum [*sic*] production.[103]

Afterward, this judgement affected the future history of the international aluminium cartel because BEW's opinion was used during the final phase of the process against ALCOA. The history of this case is well known both by business and law historians. After being cleared of the accusations in 1941, ALCOA was convicted for monopolisation of the American market in the second circuit in March 1945. Yet, none of the former studies outlined that this decision arrived a few days after BEW's memorandum. ALCOA avoided fines and dissolution because the situation was considered repaired for two reasons. First, the formation of the first independent aluminium producer in 1941, Reynolds, put the actual monopoly of ALCOA to an end. Second, ALTED promised that Alliance would not reappear in the future.[104] This last 'remedy' to ALCOA's situation had the effect of preventing the idea of the other members to continue with Alliance during the post-war period. To a certain extent, the American antitrust authority, supported by strategic reasons, had in this specific case an unprecedented global effect because it hampered the reconstruction of the international cartel afterward.

When the war in the European theatre ended, ALTED was compelled to follow BEW's memorandum to save its sister company from serious legal consequences. The Canadian firm sent a letter to Alliance's headquarters in Basel asking for its definitive, immediate, and irrevocable dissolution in May 1945, without procrastination, a few days after the end of the war in Europe.[105] ALTED acted in this way in order to save ALCOA in the final phase of the process, providing consistent reparation to the situation observed by FTC. Moreover, ALTED did not want to damage ALCOA during the post-war period. The main part of the war expansion in the American aluminium industry, which reached the capacity of over 1.5 million tons, was directly under the control of the War Industries Board. Even if ALCOA had managed these new smelters during hostilities, in 1945 the government owned about 33 per cent of the world output. Until the disposal of these plants, ALCOA was forced to accept the government's vision on the aluminium industry.[106]

## Notes

1 Bertilorenzi, 'Business, Finance, and Politics'.
2 Pezet, *La Decision d'Investissement*.
3 AN F/23/343, Services extraordinaires des temps de guerre, 1933–1940, Métaux Non Ferreux, Aluminium et Magnesium, fold. 12, Aluminium 1938–1939, Note dur l'industrie française des métaux legers, 15 November 1938. About French air programme, see Chadeau, *De Blériot à Dassault*, 359–360.
4 Hachez-Leroy, *L'Aluminium français*, 228–229.
5 AN F/23/343, Services extraordinaires des temps de guerre, 1933–1940, Métaux Non Ferreux, Aluminium et Magnesium, Fold. 12, Aluminium 1938–1939, Compte-Rendu, Métaux et Alliages Légers, 17 January 1939.
6 Charles Poor Kindleberger, *The World in Depression, 1929–1939*. London: Penguin, 1973, 106–107.
7 TNA, SUPP 3/82, no. 271, Committee of imperial defence, principal supply officers committee, Board of Trade supply organisation, Memorandum on Aluminium, 3 July 1935. BT 64/5039, War Industries Stories, Secret, Official History of Aluminium and Aluminium Alloys Industry, 1945.
8 TNA, T 187/55, The Swiss Aluminium Co. Sir Alan Barlow (Treasury Ministry) to Palmer (Ministry of the War), 28 May 1938.
9 RZA, S2 T2, Rohaluminium – Produktion in Kg, 1889–1983. About AIAG's participation in German rearmament, see Rauh, *Schweizer Aluminium für Hitlers Krieg?*

10  HHC, MSS #282, ALCOA, Box 48, f.2, Saint-John, The Alcoa Bible, 207. SWA, H+I, Bg 1200, Alcoa, Zeitungsausschnitte 1913–, The Aluminum Company of America, note by Clark, Doyle & Co, Confidential, 15 February 1939.
11  Smith, *From Monopoly to Competition*, 214–215.
12  Watkins, 'The Aluminum Alliance', 247.
13  HHC, MSS #282, ALCOA, Box 58, fold. 2, The Alcoa's Bible, 203–209. United States Tariff Commission, *Aluminum: Prepared in Response to Requests from the Committee on Finance of the United States Senate and the Committee on Ways and Means of the House of Representatives, War Changes in Industry Series, Report no. 14*. Washington DC: US Government Print Office, 1946, 70–72.
14  Smith, *From Monopoly to Competition*, 243–244.
15  United States Tariff Commission, *Aluminum*, 81–82.
16  NARA, RG, 122, Prewitt Documents, Federal Trade Commission Records, box 1, fold. Aluminum Industry, Memorandum for assistant general Jackson, US v. Alcoa, 5 March 1938.
17  NARA, RG 122, Prewitt Documents, box 1, Aluminum Co., Draft Memo, 2 November 1938.
18  NARA, RG 122, Prewitt Documents, box 1, Corwin Edwards, Memorandum for Mr. Arnold in re: Aluminum Co., 14 December 1938.
19  NARA, RG 122, Prewitt Documents, box 1, Corwin Edwards, Memorandum to George Comer, 30 November 1938.
20  NARA, RG 122, Prewitt Documents, box 1, Memorandum for Mr. Rice, Re: Edwards Plan, 9 December 1938. George D. Haskell to Thurman Arnolds, 6 September 1938.
21  Waller, 'The Story of Alcoa'. Wells, *Antitrust*, 59–64.
22  AN, F23-343, Métaux non ferreux, aluminium et magnesium, Fold. 12, Aluminium et Magnesium, 1938–1939, Philippe Level to French Munitions Minister, 22 May 1938. Direction des Fabrications d'armement, Note pour le Secrétariat Général (Section des Etudes Générales), Secret – Urgent, May 1938.
23  RPA, 072-9588, AFC, Resumé de l'Interrogatoire subi par M. Ph. Level aux Etats-Unis pour le procès Alcoa au début juillet 1938, 22 July 1938.
24  IHA, Documents de Henri Morsel, Marlio to Launay (ISCO), 17 November 1940.
25  Smith, *From Monopoly to Competition*, 254–255. Waller, 'The Story of Alcoa'. United States v. Aluminum Co. of America, 44 F. Supp. 97, S.D.N.Y. 1941.
26  Wells, *Antitrust*, 68–69.
27  Wells, *Antitrust*, 40–42.
28  HHC, MSS #282, ALCOA, box 58, fold. 1, An Address by Arnold W. Thurman before the American Business Congress, 13 June 1941.
29  Wells, *Antitrust*, 80–82.
30  NARA, RG 107, War Department. Office of the Under Secretary of War, box 23, War Production Board. List of project sponsored by Aluminum & Magnesium Division, Confidential, January 1943.
31  Peck, *Competition in the Aluminum Industry*, 43–46. United States Tariff Commission, *Aluminum*, 75.
32  Smith, *From Monopoly to Competition*, 217–218. Peck, *Competition in the Aluminium Industry*, 11–12.
33  Virginia Historical Society (VHS), MSS3, R3395a, Series 3, Papers of Richard Reynolds Sr., box 33, fold. Aluminum, The Record. Reynolds Metals Company, The First Independent Producer of Aluminum, 1942.
34  Overy, *The Air War*.
35  IHA, Documents Morsel, Alibert, Presidence du Conseil, Note pour M. le Ministre des affaires etrangères, 22 June 1940. Marlio to Petain, 23 June 1940. See also Morsel, 'Louis Marlio'.
36  TNA, FO 371/24354, Sir Samuel Hoare (British ambassador in Madrid), Reported mission of M. Marlio to United States of America, 30 June 1940.

37 Brookings Institution Archive, Washington DC (ABI), Personal documents of Mr. Louis Marlio, Harold G. Moulton to Louis Marlio, 25 August 1941.

38 Louis Marlio, *A Short War through American Industrial Superiority*, Washington DC: Brookings Institution, 1941 (Brookings Pamphlets no. 28). This book was published in 600,000 copies, see ABI, Personal Documents of Mr. Louis Marlio, Harold G. Moulton to Louis Marlio, 22 August 1944.

39 British authorities also intercepted a letter by Marlio in 1941, which confirms the scope of his mission. TNA, FO 371/28576, Marlio to Gen. Weygand, 30 June 1941.

40 For instance, 'Louis Marlio says we should make a Choice between a Long or a Short Conflict: French Economist asserts we can Produce on a Scale Germany cannot Match', *New York Times*, 1 August 1941.

41 ABI, Personal Documents of Mr. Louis Marlio, Harold Moulton to Director of Columbia Country Club, 22 October 1942.

42 RPA, 001-14-20047, Louis Marlio to Raoul De Vitry (AFC), 22 March 1944.

43 VHS, MSS3, R3395a, Series 3, Papers of Richard Reynolds Sr., box 35, fold. Louis Marlio, Richard Reynolds Sr. to Louis Marlio, 7 February 1942. Louis Marlio to Richard Reynolds Sr., 17 February 1942.

44 RPA, 001-14-20047, Pechiney-AFC, Etude sur nos relations avec les Etats-Unis. Historique sur nos agences, 1944.

45 IHA, Documents de Henry Morsel, Note. Contract 1936 entre Pechiney et Reynolds; Reynolds to Marlio, 12 December 1940.

46 NARA, RG 107, War Department. Office of the Under Secretary of War, box 4, Louis Marlio (Brookings Institution) to Mr. Robert P. Patterson (Under Secretary of War), 12 January 1942. ABI, Personal Documents of Mr. Louis Marlio, Marlio to Moulton, 5 February 1942.

47 Louis Marlio, *Will Electric Power be a Bottleneck?* Washington DC: Brookings Institution, 1942.

48 NARA, RG 107, War Department. Office of the Under Secretary of War, box 4, Arthur H. Bunker (Chief of Aluminum Division – War Production Board) to Robert P. Patterson, 3 February 1942.

49 Alan S. Milward, *The Fascist Economy in Norway*. Oxford: Clarendon Press, 1972, 171. Fritz Petrick, *Der 'Leichtmerallausbau Norwegen' 1940–1945: Eine Studie zur Deutschen Expansions – Un Okkupationspolitik in Nordeuropa*. Frankfurt am Main: Peter Lang, 1992, 213–220. Hans Otto Frøland, 'Nazi Planning and Aluminium Industry', in *Alan S. Milward and a Century of Eurpean Change*, edited by Fernando Guirao, Frances Lynch, and Sigfrido M. Ramirez Pérez. London: Routledge, 2012, 168–188.

50 Collier, 'Aluminium Industry of Europe'.

51 NARA RG 169, Foreign Economic Administration, Records Relating to Monopolies and Cartels, box 8, fold. Aluminum, Louis Marlio, The Present and future production of Aluminum in the United Nations and in the Axis, 24 January 1942.

52 Frøland, 'Nazi Planing and Aluminium Industry'.

53 NARA RG 169, Foreign Economic Administration, Records Relating to Monopolies and Cartels, box 8, fold. Aluminum, Louis Marlio, The Present and future production of Aluminum in the United Nations and in the Axis, 24 January 1942.

54 US Tariff Commission, *Aluminum*, 83. Donald M. Nelson, *Arsenal of Democracy: The Story of American War Production*. New York: Harcourt, Brace & Company, 1946, 354. Canadian Department of Trade and Commerce, Census of Industry, *The Non-Ferrous Smelting and Refining Industry in Canada*. Ottawa, 1947, 3, 9.

55 NARA RG 169, Foreign Economic Administration, Business organization staff, Records Relating to Monopolies and Cartels, box 8, fold. Aluminum, Louis Marlio, The Present and future production of Aluminum in the United Nations and in the Axis, 24 January 1942.

56 Harold G. Moulton, Louis Marlio, *The Control of Germany and Japan*. Washington DC: Brookings Institution, 1944.

57 IHA, Documents de Henry Morsel, Marlio to Dupin (AF), 20 August 1940.

58  Robert Pitaval, *Histoire de l'Aluminium: Metal de la Victoire*. Paris: Publications minières et métallurgiques, 1946.
59  HWA, Metallgesellschaft, Abt.119, Nr.890, Statistische Zusammenstellungen der
AVG 1936–1945.
60  Hans Otto Frøland, Jan Thomas Kobberrød, 'The Norwegian Contribution to
Göring's Megalomania: Norway's Aluminium Industry during World War II', *Cahiers
d'Histoire de l'Aluminium*, no. 42–3, 2009, 131–149. Frøland, 'Nazi Planning and Aluminium Industry'.
61  Schröter, 'Cartel Revisited'.
62  RPA, 00-2-15933, AAC, Notes. Tresorerie de l'Alliance Aluminium Cie, 10
February 1939.
63  RPA, 00-2-15928, AAC, Comité de Direction, Internal communication from the
Secretary to the board of directors, 11 January 1940.
64  RPA, 00-2-15933, AAC, Note sur l'Alliance Aluminium Compagnie, October 1941.
65  RPA, 00-2-15939, Maurice Lugeon to M. Galland (British consul in Basle), 9
December 1941. Haeberlin to Galland, 19 September 1941. Lugeon to British
Consul in Berne, 23 November 1944.
66  TNA, BT 64/387, Board of Trade, International Cartels, fold. Aluminium, Note 4.
Aluminium, s.d. but 1942.
67  Nathaniel H. Engle, Homer E. Gregory, Robert Mosse, *Aluminum: An Industrial
Marketing Survey*. Chicago IL: Irwin, 1945, 256–258.
68  IHA, Documents de Henry Morsel,Marlio to De Vitry, 1 February 1941.
69  RPA, 00-2-15933, Note sur l'Alliance Aluminium Compagnie, October 1941.
70  HWA, MG Documents, Abt. 6b/3, Notiz betreffend Reinstaluminium-Produktion in
Rahmen der AAC-Vertage des Quotenvertrages und des Verstandigungsabkmmens, 21
January 1942.
71  RPA, 00-2-15933, Note sur l'Alliance Aluminium Company, 15 January 1943. Situation Interntionale de l'Aluminium, 9 July 1944.
72

L'Alliance a été citée plusieurs fois comme type d'une association internationale.
Elle est en quelque sorte le prototype de ce que l'on aurait dû faire pour d'autres
produits devenus indispensables à l'homme et ce que l'on sera obligé de faire après
les hostilités si on veut assurer une vraie paix … Nous savons parfaitement, en ce
qui concerne le métal aluminium, ce qui va nécessairement se passer quand la paix
viendra, car il viendra bien le jour où le cannons seront silencieux. On risque une
guerre économique succédant à l'autre et peut-être autant meurtrière. Alors on se
souviendra peut-être qu'il existe cet organisme international [l'AAC].
RPA, 00-2-15939, Maurice Lugeon to M. Galland
(British consul in Basle), 9 December 1941.

73  Ballande, 'Prix de Cartels et prix de Concurrence'. Lammers, 'Ententes Internationales'. About the debate on cartels during the 1930s, see Marco Bertilorenzi, 'Legitimating the International Cartels Movement: League of Nations, International
Chamber of Commerce, and the Survey of International Cartels', in *Regulating Competition: Cartel Registers in the Twentieth Century World*, edited by Susanna Fellman and
Martin Shahannan. London: Routledge, forthcoming 2015.
74  Marlio, *The Aluminum Cartel*. Marlio also continued to write in favour of a system of
cartels after the war, see Louis Marlio, *Le Liberalisme Social*. Paris: Fortin, 1946.
75  Joseph Borkin, Charles A. Welsh. *Germany's Master Plan: The Story of Industrial Offensive*. New York: Sloan Long, 1943, 211.
76  Watkins, 'Aluminum Alliance'. Muller, *Light Metals Monopoly*.
77  NARA, RG 122 Prewitts Documents, box 6, Cartel Memo no. 1, draft, s.d. but end
of 1943.
78  Wells, *Antitrust*. Freyer, *Antitrust*.
79  Wells, *Antitrust*, 80–82.

80 See for instance, Corwin D. Edwards, *Economic and Political Aspects of International Cartels: A Study made for the Subcommittee on War Mobilization of the Committee on Military Affairs of United States Senate.* Washington DC: Government Printing Office, 1944, 49–61; Corwin D. Edwards, Theodore J. Kreps, Ben W. Lewis, Frits Machlup, Robert P. Terill, *A Cartel Policy for the United Nations.* New York: Columbia University Press, 1945; Borkin, Welsh, *Germany's Master Plan.* Thurman W. Arnold, *Cartels or Free Enterprise?* Washington DC: Public Affairs Press, 1945; Wendell Berge, *Cartels: Challenge to a Free World.* Washington DC: Public Affairs Press, 1946; George W. Stocking, Myron W. Watkins, *Cartels or Competition? The Economics of International Controls by Business and Government.* Washington DC: Twentieth Century Fund, 1948.

81 TNA, BT 64/317, Board of Trade, Discussions with the Americans on International Cartels, 1944, various clippings, September 1944. See also Freyer, *Antitrust and Global Capitalism,* 49–51; Wells, *Antitrust,* 108–110.

82 TNA, BT 64/397, Board of Trade, International Cartels. German participation in International cartels, 1946, A report on a meeting of German industrialists to make post-wars plans, Strasbourg, 10 August 1944. However, this document has been classified by TNA as a probable historical false. About this plan, see also Édouard Husson, 'Idéee Européenne, Europe Allemande, ordre Nouveau Nazi', in *Penser et Construire l'Europe (1919–1992),* edited by Dominique Barjot. Paris: Editions Sedes, 2007, 122–123.

83 Cf. *Gilda,* directed by Charles Vidor, United States, 1946. Ballin is the owner of an illegal high-class casino and he is characterised as a unscrupulous businessman. He explains his plans about tungsten with these words: 'A man who controls a strategic material can control the world.'

84 UGD, BACO, 347/21/51/8, Managers' meeting – Chalfont park, January 1945. Opening address to the first general conference by Sir Murray-Morrison, 22 January 1945.

85 Graham D. Taylor, 'Debate in the United States over the Control of International Cartels, 1942–1950', *International History Review,* vol. 3, no. 3, 1981, 385–398.

86 Theodore J. Kreps, 'Cartels, a Phase of Business Haute Politique', *American Economic Review,* vol. 35, no. 2, 1945, 297–311.

87 NARA, RG 122 Prewitts Documents, box 2, International Cartels, C. Edwards, Hasty comments on your draft re Cartel Policy, 17 August 1943.

88 Board of Trade, *Survey of International Cartels and Internal Cartels,* 2 vols. London: Board of Trade, 1944–1946.

89 TNA, BT 64/387, Board of trade, International Cartels, Note 4. Aluminium, s.d. but 1942.

90 TNA, BT 64/317, Board of Trade, Discussions with the Americans on International Cartels 1944, Prof. Allen, Note for Habakkuk, 12 April 1944.

91 NARA, RG 122, Prewitts documents, Box 3, fold Cartels Committee Minutes, July 1943 to December 1944, Cartel Committee Minute no. 4, 29 October 1943; Cartel Memo no. 16, A positive program for dealing with international cartels, 11 December 1943.

92 Bertilorenzi, 'Legitimating the International Cartels Movement'.

93 UGD, 347 21/40/16. International Aluminium Cartel. International cartels, Berlin Congress of the International Chamber of Commerce, 1937, Publ. No. 4, Published by International Handelskammer, Paris. Lammers, *Ententes Internationales.*

94 Lammers, *Ententes Internationales.* See also Bertilorenzi, 'Legitimating the International Cartels Movement'.

95 TNA, BT 11/2336, Post War Commodity Policy – Aluminium, Habakkuk, Post War reconstruction. The light metal industry, 24 August 1944. About Keynes, see Wells, *Antitrust,* 84. About the transformation of cartels into intergovernmental agreements, see Edward S. Mason, *Controlling World Trade: Cartels and Commodity Agreements.* New York: McGraw-Hill, 1946, 262–268. Wells, *Antitrust,* 114–116.

96   NARA, RG 169, Foreign Economic Administration, Business organization staff, box 10, Office of Economic Programs Foreign Economic Administration. Trends and Opinions concerning British Post-War Foreign Trade, British Trends and Opinions Through Mid-Febraury, 1945.

97   Combines Investigation Commission, *Canada and International Cartels: An Inquiry into the Nature and Effects of International Cartels and other Trade Combinations*. Ottawa: 1945.

98   Brusse, Griffiths, 'L'European Recovery Program e i Cartelli'. Wells, *Antitrust*, 114–116, 120–121.

99   IHA, Documents de Henri Morsel, Marlio to De Vitry (AFC), 25 May 1945.

100   Sara Nocentini, 'Building the Network: Raw Materials Shortages and the Western Bloc at the Beginning of the Cold War, 1948–1951', *Business History on-line*, vol. 2, 2004. Accessed: www.thebhc.org/sites/default/files/Nocentini_0.pdf.

101   These findings are described in NARA, RG 169, box 1, Study of the FEA drafting committee of the treatment of German participation in international cartels from the standpoint of international security, 1 August 1945.

102   About ALCOA, see Mats Ingulstad, 'We want Aluminium not Excuses! Antitrust and Business–Government Partnership in the American Aluminium Industry, 1917–1957', in Frøland, Ingulstat (eds.), *From Warfare to Welfare*, 33–68. This point is confirmed also in the internal story of ALCOA: HHC, box 58, folder 2, The Alcoa's Bible, 207–208.

103   NARA, RG 169, box 8, Foreign Economic Organisation, Records Relating to Monopolies and Cartels, fold. Aluminum, Memorandum on Alliance Aluminum (*sic*) Company to Irene Till, 10 March 1945.

104   Smith, *From Monopoly to Competition*, 207–208. Peck, *Competition in the Aluminum Industry*, 8–14. Waller, 'The Story of Alcoa', 129–138. The process against ALCOA ended 12 March 1945 and the end of Alliance, declaimed by ALTED, was considered as a remedy. See US v. Aluminum Co. of America, 148F.2d 416,424 (2nd circuit), 12 March 1945.

105   RPA, 00-2-15939, Dullea (ALTED-Montréal) to Alliance Aluminium Compagnie, 17 May 1945.

106   Smith, *From Monopoly to Competition*, 256–258; Peck, *Competition in the Aluminum Industry*, 18–19. Ingulstad, 'We want Aluminium', 54–55.

Part IV

# Resumption, collapse, and criminalisation of aluminium governance (1945–1978)

# 10 Post-war governance for the aluminium industry

## The sunset of Alliance and the rise of the 'Club', 1945–1953

The unilateral decision of ALTED to ask for the dissolution of Alliance, which was led by the strategic considerations of the US government and by the legal concerns of its American sister company, prevented the re-establishment of the cartel after the war. Although other members aimed to recast Alliance after the war to stabilise the balance between supply and demand,[1] ALTED's decision recreated the scenario of 1918, when cartelisation abruptly knew a pause. However, unlike 1918, the resurgence of the cartel was not only procrastinated, but it was deleted from the vision of firms for the post-war period. In a context of war preparedness, led by the settlement of the Cold War, states cemented their links to national producers.[2] In particular the United States and the United Kingdom endorsed the formation of national devices for inventories similar to Alliance's but, this time, in public powers' hands and conceived to respond to military and strategic necessities. These creations contributed to hampering the recasting of the old cartel in the post-war era, but they did not avoid the adaptation of international industrial cooperation to the new institutional situation.[3]

After the formal request for the liquidation of Alliance, which ALTED sent to the other members in May 1945, it took ten years to definitively dissolve the cartel. The internal documents of Alliance suggest that this long liquidation was the outcome of a deliberate strategy by the European firms, which aimed to use the cartel board to manage the transition from a war to a peace economy.[4] Actually, the old members of Alliance resumed their meetings a few days after the end of the war in the European theatre. The first meeting was motivated by the need to discuss ALTED's request for the immediate dissolution of the cartel. While the Germans and the Canadians did not participate in this first post-war meeting, representatives of the other members claimed that 'il serait souhaitable que les Anglais, les Suisses et les Français fissent une nouvelle alliance'.[5] According to what AF, AIAG, and BACO had discussed, it was confirmed that the mere continuation of Alliance was impossible. The impressive change in production capacities and, in particular, the spurt of American output deeply questioned the former system established by Alliance. Yet these firms aimed to resuscitate international cooperation as soon as possible, which could be more consistent with the new situation. In particular, the main threat that the Europeans aimed to debate was the new situation of the North American aluminium industry.[6]

Table 10.1 Production in selected countries, 1939 and 1945–1952 (tons×1,000)

| | France | US | Canada | Germany | UK | Norway | Italy | Switzerland | USSR | World |
|---|---|---|---|---|---|---|---|---|---|---|
| 1939 | 52.5 | 148.4 | 75.0 | 195.1 | 25.0 | 31.1 | 34.2 | 27.0 | 55.0 | 695.3 |
| 1945 | 37.2 | 453.5 | 195.7 | 0.7 | 32.4 | 4.6 | 4.3 | 5.0 | 86.3 | 842.3 |
| 1946 | 47.8 | 371.8 | 176.0 | 0.6 | 32.0 | 16.6 | 10.9 | 13.1 | 90.0 | 773.4 |
| 1947 | 53.4 | 518.6 | 270.0 | 0.5 | 29.4 | 21.7 | 24.3 | 18.4 | 100.0 | 1,060.4 |
| 1948 | 64.8 | 563.7 | 333.0 | 7.3 | 30.5 | 30.1 | 32.3 | 19.0 | 125.0 | 1,248.2 |
| 1949 | 54.1 | 546.7 | 335.0 | 28.9 | 30.8 | 35.0 | 25.6 | 21.0 | 155.0 | 1,297.0 |
| 1950 | 60.7 | 651.8 | 360.0 | 27.8 | 29.9 | 46.6 | 36.8 | 21.0 | 200.0 | 1,506.8 |
| 1951 | 91.1 | 758.2 | 405.0 | 68.6 | 28.2 | 50.0 | 49.3 | 27.0 | 250.0 | 1,831.7 |
| 1952 | 106.1 | 849.2 | 454.0 | 100.5 | 28.4 | 52.5 | 52.0 | 27.0 | 235.0 | 2,040.0 |

Source: Metallgesellchaft's statistical yearbooks (1939 and 1955).

The absence of the Canadian company at the first post-war meeting was due to the complicated legal situation of ALCOA that ALTED did not wish to aggravate. ALTED clearly pointed out this idea to the French firm during summer 1945.[7] However, it was not perceived as a real problem by the other firms because it gave the opportunity to the European companies to debate the new global situation and the new impressive force that the Americans obtained during the conflict. In particular, the new North American production situation provoked anxieties, because the end of the US monopoly disrupted the pre-war relationships with ALCOA. Even if the relationships with ALCOA had not always been easy during the interwar years, the European companies were aware that the general compromise of 1931 had been possible only because in the United States there was only one company, which promised to focus its activities uniquely on the national market. Now the presence of new actors, with strategic visions that could differ from the one that had led the evolution of the aluminium industry until then, was potentially dangerous for the continuation of the pre-war cartel strategy. The fact that Marlio worked for Reynolds during the war was not a guarantee for future cooperation between the two aluminium sides of the Atlantic. As a consequence the European companies aimed to cooperate to shield their positions against a possible invasion from the American metal.[8]

While the Canadians were not present at the first official meeting, they joined the old Alliance's members afterwards. However, the Germans did not participate in the meetings until the beginning of the 1950s. Alliance's board was not able to contact the directors of VAW to invite them and the extremely precarious situation of Germany put on hold the continuation of aluminium production there. Some Allies' plans aimed even to hamper the reconstruction of aluminium output in Germany. In 1945, this idea prevailed in international post-war negotiations and it was partially confirmed also by the Potsdam conference.[9] The German aluminium industry was in any case seriously injured. While almost all alumina units were bombed, the principal German smelter, Lautawerk, was unbundled and transported to the Soviet Union by Russian occupying forces. AIAG's Rheinfelden unit was under French control, while the British and US authorities took over all the stock available in the country. All the installations of Metallgesellschaft–IG Faben had undergone the same fate of Lautawerk – being in the Soviet occupation zone – while IG Farben was dismantled by US occupying forces.[10] As a consequence, it was predicted that Germany was out of the aluminium business if not forever, at least for a certain time after the war, and this fact did not urge the other producers to try to implicate the Germans in their first meetings.[11]

In spite of these absences from the Alliance's board meetings and of the lack of adherence of this cartel to the new international situation, the board of the old cartel was an optimal occasion to bridge the pre-war to post-war aluminium economy. Differently from what had happened after the Great War, when the continuation of hostilities 'by other means' had hampered the recomposition of the old network for almost five years, in 1945 the quick rapprochement of BACO, AIAG, and AF made it possible to set up a common strategy very quickly. In spite of its indirect participation to the German and Italian war efforts,[12] the situation of AIAG was deeply different from the end of the Great

War. AIAG avoided the ostracism that hit the Swiss company after 1914.[13] The Swiss firm also concluded an agreement with AF before the war to avoid the repetition of the situation of 1914–1918, when AIAG's alumina unit in southern France was confiscated by the French authorities and the Allied producers tried to take over the Swiss company after damaging it. According to this agreement, in case of war, AIAG would supply Germany neither with its French alumina, nor with its Swiss aluminium. Instead, AF agreed to include AIAG in supplies of alumina and aluminium to the French government in case of need.[14] This was part of the global strategy of AIAG to be implicated in several rearmament programmes at the end of the 1930s on both fronts. After the Second World War, some friction resulted from French control over AIAG's Rheinfelden smelter, but the Swiss firm obtained it back soon thanks to the intermediation of AFC.[15]

However, an official cartel was not set up again for the post-war period and cartelisation in the aluminium industry became a more intricate institution, as we will see. This was not the outcome of antitrust enforcement in Europe. The belief that often shows the interwar period as a 'cartel wisdom' in opposition to the post-war pretended era of competition policies and free trade has already been questioned by many researchers, who have showed a more blurred division of the two periods.[16] Many commodity agreements were continued in the post-war era and, even if they were not called 'cartels', they were in any case the direct heirs of the pre-war organisations. In many cases, these cartels were transformed into stock buffering schemes, which became accepted operations in the institutional context of the post-war period.[17] Also competitive policies in Europe did not play a real barrier in the settlement of cartels because, even though they were included in the Treaty of Rome, they were implemented in 1962 and became effective only during the 1970s.[18] According to Jeffrey Fear 'cartels boomed in the 1920s, peaked in the 1930s, reappeared strongly after 1945 before they gradually faded away, especially after the 1970s'.[19] The aluminium industry perfectly fits with this insight.

## The specific international post–war governance for the aluminium industry: the British proposal

The path that led the cartel network to reappear after the Second World War was accompanied by deep institutional change. A proper cartel, like the one represented by the interwar organisations, was not recreated, because a kind of protection framework that governmental policies played during the 1940s and the 1950s shielded firms from international competition. Differently from other commodities, in which governments had already taken a position in their international administration during the 1930s, Alliance's governance turned up to be a suboptimal tool to bridge the gap between governments' policies and private firms' strategies. Five years of war crystallised the links between private business and public policies, asking for a change in the international governance of the aluminium industry after the war. The start of the Cold War finally brought this change and during this time almost all countries included important strategic materials such as aluminium in their programmes. In almost all countries, policies that supported the 'national champions' represented the framework in which new international cooperation was established.[20]

During the war, the British authorities formulated a proposal to reshape the international governance of the aluminium industry into an international commodity agreement. This proposal aimed at modelling aluminium after the tin or rubber industries, which were considered the masterpieces of British international governance and diplomacy during the interwar period. Both tin and rubber were administrated 'buffer stock schemes' by the British authorities and, instead of being dismantled after the war, they became a model for the future regulation of commodity trade because they represented a successful way of administrating the relationships between producing and consuming countries.[21] Certainly, also, these organisations collapsed during the conflict and were revitalised afterward not without some changes and adaptations, but in the broad sense these industries had a certain institutional continuity. It should also be remembered that the buffer stock schemes were also a fundamental part of Keynes' ideas expressed, not only during the 1930s but also during the Bretton Woods conference, both to stabilise the international monetary system and to provide consistent governance to the trade of key commodities.[22] Some observers in the United States shared this point of view at the end of war and, as is known, during the following decades.[23]

Looking at a post-war policy for aluminium, Great Britain tried to make aluminium converge to this model, even though it did not succeed in achieving this goal. This choice was driven by a twofold consideration about the future of the aluminium industry in the UK. On the one hand, the UK could never become a huge producer of primary metal. The lack of cheap energy sources, such as hydroelectricity, hampered the settlement of a workable programme to turn the UK into a massive producer of primary metal. Production from coal electrical power, such as SWACO, proved to be inefficient to assure a long-term supply. On the other hand, the UK was emerging as one of the most important international outlets for aluminium.[24] Not only did the development of the aircraft industry lead to this outcome, but also a clear policy that Great Britain aimed to adopt for the conversion to civil uses was promising great developments in the post-war period. Just to provide a size of the expected development, many observers considered that in the post-war period the UK national market could have absorbed even 300,000 tons per year of aluminium, while during the mid-1930s, before the rearmament programmes, the national consumption was only about 30,000 tons. The key for the success of this quick conversion was, according to the British authorities, a price as low as possible that would have assisted the diffusion of the uses of aluminium.[25]

From 1943, the Board of Trade and the Ministry of Air Production (MAP) debated which policy to adopt for the post-war aluminium industry. The specific position of Great Britain led the British authorities to start some policies that were contrary to the continuation of Alliance. This position was far different from the one that the United States adopted: while the US aimed to set a general policy to increase domestic production of aluminium, which led the to Board of Economic Warfare asking for the dissolution of Alliance, the United Kingdom did not consider the raising of national production as crucial. Since the beginning of the rearmament programmes, the relationships between BACO and its national government had been changing. The support that the British government provided to BACO during the whole interwar period was revealed to be useless in assuring a consistent policy to increase the primary production of aluminium. Not only the lack of cheap electricity frustrated the expansion programmes of BACO, but also the specific position that BACO had in Alliance revealed a weakness in the relationships with its government.[26]

Alliance was considered by the British authorities as the main cause of higher prices on the UK market that, as a consequence, also negatively affected the position of semi- and finished aluminium goods in this country. In particular, the price on the continent was fixed by Alliance at £-gold 80 per ton and by ALCOA in the US at about £-paper 90 per ton (equal to 20¢/lb), while in the UK it was about £-paper 100 per ton. In reality, the devaluation of British sterling, as we have seen, was the main cause of this negative influence on the national prices of aluminium. To follow the price set by the cartel board during the 1930s, BACO was obliged to adopt a relatively high price which clashed against cheap imports from Germany and Canada. However, this fact proved that BACO was not able to choose between the international regulation offered by Alliance and the desiderata of its government. This fact damaged the image of BACO in many political mileux and, if it is also true that BACO continued to benefit from important public help, the British government was well aware that it was not possible to set a military programme relying only on this company's output.[27]

The alternative was represented by ALTED, which came to the fore as the main supplier for the British aluminium industry.[28] While the output of BACO was almost unchanged during the war, the other Commonwealth producer – ALTED – increased its output five times, jumping from about 100,000 tons per year to almost 450,000. ALTED, which was renamed ALCAN (Aluminium Company of Canada) in the 1950s, at the end of the war was the second largest world producer and was second only to ALCOA.[29] During the war, the official price of aluminium in the US and in Great Britain had fallen from 20¢/lb to 17¢/lb, because the US and British governments were able to negotiate this reduction in return for the heavy financial implications that these governments had in new war investments. In the huge governmental contracts linked to military supplies, the authorities of these two countries were able to avoid the tremendous inflation that had affected the aluminium trade during the Great War. Also the arrival of new producers in the North American market, such as Reynolds and, as we will see, Kaiser Aluminum, were the cause of this reduction decided by ALCOA. These reductions became possible also because the new scale economies brought the aluminium business to a new gigantic dimension. During the war, global aluminium production overcame global copper output for the first time, before consolidating its rank of first non-ferrous metal during the 1950s.[30]

The Canadian company took the opportunity that the war was disclosing to the aluminium industry: the technological spread, if linked to a decisive cost reduction, could allow aluminium to win the competition with other non-ferrous metals and start to be a threat to steel in many applications.[31] In particular, ALCAN reached a very low production cost, thanks to the full development of its scale economies. Arvida's 'dream', as we can define the idea that paved the way for the construction of this 'mammoth' smelter during the 1920s and according to which huge scale economies could lead to new mass consumption for aluminium, finally could find a material basis to be fulfilled. That led ALCAN to elaborate a policy of strong development after the war. Edward K. Davis had already discussed this programme in private meetings with Marlio during 1941, but this idea started to play a consistent role in the post-war policy debate when ALCAN's representatives claimed to MAP and the Board of Trade their willingness to reduce the price to 12¢/lb, and even to 10¢/lb, which were equal to, respectively, about £60 and £50 per ton. This proposal was applicable only if ALCAN could fully developed its scale economies and, thus, if the British authorities were willing to provide a guarantee for its outlet. Of course, this proposal represented a problem for BACO, which was not able to meet this price (its production costs were declared at about £60–70 per ton).[32]

However, the possibility of relying on the Canadian supplier represented a big weakness, according to the British authorities. The configuration of the British aluminium market as a big importing outlet from a unique source, which was controlled by the American giant ALCOA, reminded MAP and Board of Trade officials of the injurious situation of the Great War, when the American firm was left free to raise prices at the expense of European countries. The risk of relying on a unique source was neither safe enough to grant the continuation of low cost and mass production of aluminium, nor ideal to set a consistent strategic policy. The British authorities feared that if a new international political crisis was to begin, ALCAN could enter into cartel agreements again with other European firms, also providing a general compromise on prices as had been done in 1931. These reports about the future of the aluminium industry were perhaps aware of the fact that the actual working of Alliance was not too far from a stock buffering scheme, at least in its original idea. Yet in the mind of the British authorities the main fault of Alliance was to have failed in governing the UK market and in having sacrificed national interests to the international industry. Consequently, Alliance was not a good example of 'private' stock buffering schemes in non-ferrous metals, but it embodied the worst features of cartelisation: high prices and output restriction.[33]

A possible way to avoid the risk that in the future another cartel could hamper the military preparedness of Great Britain was, according to MAP, to create an international authority for the aluminium industry that, under the political control of both the producing and the consuming countries, could have administered a general stock buffering scheme to prevent an increase in pricing and shortages in production. This scheme would not forcedly exclude some measure to hamper competition, such as quotas of production and sales, but governmental control over these actions would prevent this authority from acting against public welfare, unlike a private cartel. It would also assure a great development to the international aluminium industry, thanks to the inclusion both of producing and consuming countries – as was often decided for other authorities that governed the commodities trade. It was recognised that, without this multilateral political authority

> Soon or later the main world producers will be driven to agreement on restriction of outputs and maintenance of prices either by private cartel agreements or governments planes.... These arrangements would not, and indeed must not, preclude the holding independently of a strategic reserve by the UK Government, nor need they preclude the UK Government from buying, if it thought fit, to augment this reserve.[34]

Even if this policy was recognised as the best option to provide a new international governance to the aluminium industry, a public authority for the administration of the aluminium trade in the post-war era was never created. No further action was undertaken to substitute the cartel with some other kind of agencies because no consensus was achieved during negotiations between Great Britain and the US. The difference with other raw materials and, in particular, with other non-ferrous metals, is striking. In many cases, such as tin, rubber, or copper, the United States endorsed the constitution of some intergovernmental commodity agreements, which continued the experiences made during the 1930s with the direct involvement of the governments. In these cases, the concentration of production in a few determined countries and their relative distance from the terminal markets pushed the United States and Great Britain to establish some multilateral approaches already before the end of the war.[35]

In the case of aluminium, the British authorities decided to postpone this proposal for two reasons. As claimed in the text quoted above, the British authorities decided to build up a public stockpile of aluminium, which would control the amount of metal necessary to produce war aircraft for five years. This reserve would be a decisive source in case of a new war because, as an importing country, the UK feared being cut off from its suppliers. As a consequence, a vast stockpile was established in Great Britain, in which ALCAN entered with stable long-term contracts with low and stable prices. The purchase of the Canadian metal lasted until 1953, with a rate of about 250,000 tons per year.[36] Moreover, the British government until this date remained the unique administrator for the British aluminium market, gathering all the metal and administrating market supplies through the management. In 1945, the British authorities took also the decision not to leave the LME (London Metal Exchange) to administrate the handling of aluminium stocks in the post-war period, because the government aimed to keep in its hand the full monopoly of such a vital strategic material and aimed to pursue the low and stable price policy outlined during the discussions with ALCAN.[37] In other words, the British Authorities decided to adopt a pragmatic strategic policy to hamper a new international cartel that, in the worst of the possible scenarios, would have increased prices and restricted outputs. This shift from an international programme to a concrete national policy shows which were the basis of the 'rescue of the nation-state' generally pointed out by Alan Milward.[38]

Even if the British authorities claimed the desirability of an international aluminium agency, MAP was convinced that the British authorities should not have to propose the creation of this authority for diplomatic and strategic reasons. First, Great Britain should have in any case subsided the construction of a stockpiling scheme for its national strategic goals. Second, Great Britain should enter such a scheme if its proposition had come from another producing country:

> It does not by any means follow that we should take the initiative in proposing the international regulation of aluminium. We shall probably be in a better position to impose our terms as an importing country if we leave that to other.[39]

The public agency for aluminium, which was prospected by the British authorities, has never been brought into existence. Aluminium greatly diverged to other commodities, which needed the operation of a stock buffering scheme to stabilise their prices. Also thanks to the British stockpile, which provided a price discipline to the main world exporter (ALCAN), aluminium never experienced a serious fluctuation of prices during the 1940s and 1950s to require the settlement by an agency. Other firms shared the same policy about stable prices. At the end of the war, the US adopted similar policies to the UK stockpile, which had important macro-economic outcomes in avoiding the risk of a generalised unbalanced development of this industry. This delayed the overcoming of both serious price instability and of flows of metal to the European markets. This fact also delayed the moment in which the main firms would try to resuscitate a cartel, as MAP feared. National policies again were the main substitute for international cartels.

## Post-war strategic policies for aluminium in the United States

Not only did North American output spurt during the conflict, but also a deep institutional change affected the aluminium industry in the country. The end of ALCOA's monopoly was encouraged by both strategic policies and legal measures, which brought new producers in the scene. The political powers were also assigned a new brand role in the regulation and governance of this industry. In particular, the trial to ALCOA was used in its last phase, not only to curb North American participation in the international cartel, but also to find a 'remedy' in the national context to the aluminium monopoly. The American government bet on the development of Reynolds after the war and supported the arrival of new producers on the scene, Kaiser Chemical and Aluminum Company. At the same time, Olin Corporation did not keep its position immediately after the war. The goal of the strategic policies of the United States was to introduce some competition in the American aluminium industry, which could have improved American war preparedness. The American antitrust authorities played a main regulatory role in this transition because they pushed ALCOA to accept the new situation.[40]

As Merton Peck outlined in his book about the post-war American aluminium industry, the US government played a decisive role in the creation of a competitive industry in this country. All the possible remedies that FTC tried to adopt to figure out the problem of ALCOA's monopoly turned out to be unworkable in the context of the late 1930s. All the plans of FTC were linked to the idea to unbundle ALCOA, sharing the pieces of its industrial power to new potential entrants. The war and the creation of a huge government-owned output changed this situation. According to Peck, US government policy used the disposal of the DPC plants erected during the war to give an advantage to Reynolds and Kaiser to catch up with ALCOA.[41] Following the ideas expressed in a report compiled by Irving Lipkowitz, a leading figure in the group of lawyers and economic experts of the FTC that inspected ALCOA during the 1930s, ALCOA was excluded from the bid to take over the plants that this company had built and managed during the war. Stuart W. Symington, a democrat senator from Missouri, was appointed chief administrator of the Surplus Property Board, which took over DFC's plants and adopted Lipkowitz's vision, hampering any reclamation for attributions to the Pittsburgh's trust.[42] Symington was the crafter of the post-war market structure of the American aluminium industry, which was changed as showed by Table 10.2.

Even if ALCOA avoided its divestiture as a radical remedy to its monopoly, the American aluminium industry remained under court jurisdiction until 1956. The US aluminium industry was kept under the direct control of FTC, which was charged to control the market price in order to save the earnings of the new entrants. This did not change the price policy of the aluminium industry, which remained stable and did not undergo any decisive reduction in the long run. The public authorities aimed to keep prices stable in order not to introduce speculation in this metal trade, which would lead to hamper the development of civil markets for this metal. George Smith and Merton Peck also discussed in their studies the US pricing policy as an outcome of both the oligopolistic situation of the American aluminium industry and the 'discipline' drawn to such a capital intense industry.[43] From our standpoint, it is interesting to state that, as in the British case, the strategy of price stability introduced by the cartels at the beginning of the century was also kept in the post-cartel situation as one of the main features. Moreover, we can add that stable prices also fit with the general economic stability that was sought by the Bretton Woods system. The US and UK governments used war stock to implement this policy. In the US case, it also served the structuring of a competitive industry in which ALCOA had a reduced market force. The Civilian Production Administration, which took control over the metal after the war, understood the importance of stock in the future policy of aluminium and aimed to provide assistance to new competitors through its action. As an official report about the aluminium industry in the US published in 1956 reported,

> If the inventories were not released in an orderly fashion, the price structure of the industry would be threatened, primary production would be cut back, and the disposal of DPC aluminum facilities would be almost impossible since there would be little incentive for new producers to enter the field.[44]

A further step was made in the early 1950s. Since 1947, the US government was planning an overall transformation of its stockpile policy, considering adopting a

Table 10.2 US aluminium industry, 1944–1950 (capacities in tons and %), and expansion programmes (I, II, and III)

| | 1944 Capacity | 1944 % | 1946 Capacity | 1946 % | 1950 Capacity | 1950 % | Exp. I 1950 | Exp. II 1951 | Exp. III 1952 | Actual capacity 1955 |
|---|---|---|---|---|---|---|---|---|---|---|
| ALCOA | 415,000 | 38 | 295,000 | 50 | 335,000 | 50 | 120,000 | 205,000 | – | 653,750 |
| ALCOA DPC | 576,000 | 53 | – | – | – | – | – | – | – | – |
| Reynolds | 81,000 | 7 | 172,000 | 30 | 216,000 | 32 | 100,000 | 180,000 | – | 414,500 |
| Olin DPC | 21,000 | 2 | – | – | – | – | – | – | – | – |
| Kaiser | – | – | 117,000 | 20 | 117,000 | 18 | 100,000 | 228,000 | – | 408,200 |
| Harvey-Anaconda | – | – | – | – | – | – | 72,000 | 50,000 | 54,000 | 60,000 |
| Apex | – | – | – | – | – | – | 54,000 | – | – | – |
| Olin–Mathieson | – | – | – | – | – | – | – | – | 110,000 | 60,000 |
| Wheland | – | – | – | – | – | – | – | – | 50,000 | – |
| Total | 1,093,000 | 100 | 584,000 | 100 | 668,000 | 100 | 446,000 | 663,000 | 214,000 | 1,596,450 |

Source: US Material Survey, Aluminum, NARA, and VHS.

larger scope and with more stable functioning. In 1950, the US government implemented its policy with a new expansion programme, which aimed to expand US output in order to supply the military effort necessary for the Korean War. Three further 'rounds' of expansion were programmed by DPC in 1950, 1951, and 1952 to increase national output, accordingly, of about 450,000 tons, 600,000 tons, and 200,000 tons. These measures aimed to reduce to zero the risk in investing in aluminium and solved one of the main issues that had emerged since the rearmament programmes of the 1930s. The arrival of new marginal producers, such as Harvey Aluminium and Olin Mathienson, was also encouraged and was helped through financial facilities, even though not all the new entrants succeeded. Above all, the assurance that all the metal produced would be purchased by the government and included in the stockpile helped much the expansion and the entrance of new firms. Even if the 'third round' of DPC was stopped in 1954 and none of these investments was achieved, this strategic policy was able to bring the US's capacity from about 700,000 tons in 1950 to about 1,600,000 tons in 1955 (see Table 10.2). This would have represented a solid basis for the military needs of the Cold War; moreover, this measure reduced ALCOA's strength, pushing Reynolds and Kaiser to emerge and other industrial groups to enter the aluminium field.[45]

A further concomitant decision, taken by FTC in 1950, reshaped the configuration of the North America aluminium industry as a whole. Judge Knox's final decision on the ALCOA process was to indicate, as a necessary remedy to the monopolistic situation of ALCOA, separating ALCAN from its mother company. In this new situation, the fears expressed by the British authorities about relying on Canadian supplies for its aluminium market were overcome, showing that the policies of these countries were very aligned. In this way, in the North American aluminium industry there would be four 'majors', which would compete: ALCOA, ALCAN, Reynolds, and Kaiser.[46] After 1950, also ALCAN was included in the stockpile policy of the US government. As a consequence, the stockpile consequently provided a major macro-economic regulation to the international aluminium industry. The need to break the monopoly of ALCOA led the US government not to propose an international board, but to directly administrate this industry for many years after the conflict: as a matter of fact, until 1956, the US government and the FTC continued to fix market prices and to survey this industry.[47]

This great expansion of North American production, which was encouraged by a thorough set of public policies for aluminium, was the outcome of a great institutional change that reshaped again the nexus between strategic policies and antitrust considerations. As Louis Marlio reshaped US policy on aluminium production during the war and outlined some features of the post-war governance, another one of Reynolds' advisers played a crucial role in establishing the future policy for the aluminium industry: Irving Lipkowitz. As already said, Lipkowitz was one of FTC's lawyers who had inspected ALCOA during the 1930s and during the war, when he was one of the leading actors of the post-monopoly strategies for the US aluminium industry. He proposed in the FTC to use the disposal of the DPC plants to curb ALCOA's monopoly, finding the consensus of Symington. In 1948, Lipkowitz left FTC and was appointed as chief economic and legal adviser of the Reynolds Metal Company. We anticipate that during the 1950s and 1960s, he also played a high influential role in the Aluminum Association (AAA), the US trade association for aluminium. When he was appointed at RMC, Lipkowitz prepared a study, which was distributed to the American military and political milieux called 'Mobilizing the Aluminium Industry for Peace and for Victory' in which he outlined the future orientation that the US government should have undertaken to promote a healthy aluminium industry. This report also circulated into the military milieux, thanks to a certain lobbying activity that Reynolds was able to set.[48]

In this study, Lipkowitz declared that the current production of aluminium was insufficient in case of war, albeit by far the largest in the world. He pointed out that at least an increase of 1,300,000 tons would be necessary to face a new global conflict. It was calculated that in the case of a 'hot' war, about 2,200,000 tons of aluminium per year would be necessary for the construction of aeroplanes and weapons. However, US national demand was only about 600,000 tons in 1948 and, even if new expansion was forecast by several analysts, this figure was too far from the level of military needs. A private industry, without public incentives, would never have decided to invest in such an overcapacity. As a consequence, according to Lipkowitz, it was necessary to conjugate the civil expansion of outputs with the military needs thanks to a specific policy of stockpiling. Thus, the US needed to develop as soon as possible new programmes to invest in new outputs that, on the one hand, would satisfy the growing civil demand for aluminium and, on the other hand, would build up a new enormous strategic reserve. Lipkowitz proposed the creation of an enormous reserve, in which all the aluminium that was not consumed by the civil market would be kept aside to be used in case of war.[49]

Following this idea, the chief of the General Service Administration, the agency that controlled the strategic stockpiles of the United States, Samuel Anderson, completely reformulated the working of the stockpile as regards to aluminium. Also the shortages during the Korean War imposed this change during the early 1950s, when a new shortage of metal threatened to hamper the US victory against the little communist country. Anderson actually proposed that the stockpile should have been the 'residual legatee' of the US aluminium industry. The government would define programmes for expansion and provide financial help to private companies to achieve this expansion; all the aluminium that was not consumed by the civil market, should be integrated into the stockpile in order to provide a material basis to face a future war. Following an approach similar to the insights provided by 'Mobilizing Aluminum', Anderson explained that a massive reserve of aluminium was also an optimal way to increase the invulnerability of American military power because it reduced the risk that shortages in raw materials or in electrical supplies during the war would affect war production. As a consequence, aluminium was declaimed an 'ingot of electricity and raw materials', which should have been stockpiled to free other resources in case of emergency.[50]

Other historians that analysed the US post-war aluminium industry also claimed that the stockpile was a decisive tool in controlling prices because, theoretically, it could work as a mechanism of bracket prices that ended up with favouring price stability. Also the US authorities pointed out that the stockpile served this goal. The Korean war in 1950 and the temporary scarcity of aluminium also pushed the creation of a huge stockpiling device, which supported the military–industrial complex of this strategic material. The main outcome of the US stockpile was to have managed with great efficiency the historical problem of the coordination between civil demand and military need of a strategic material.[51] From our standpoint, it is important that, as Lipkowitz and Anderson outlined, the stockpiling policy tried to find a definitive solution to the mismatch between public and private goals in the aluminium industry. As we will see in the next chapter, Lipkowitz was also a key figure in the global governance of this industry during the 1960s, which was incepted in this phase. Actually, the complex nexus between national and international industries and, moreover, between public and private actors, was reshaped by the need to foster the US national output in a environment of political controls. In retrospect, the US stockpile was a method to stimulate the production also in time of peace because it reduced the risk of investment, which also had a major macro-economic influence until the middle of the 1960s because it hid from the market a consistent bulk of stocks that, otherwise, would have affected market price.

In spite of these measures on the national level, the US government provided only a few direct policies for the international aluminium industry during this period. Even if the American authorities pushed ALCAN to ask for the liquidation of the cartel in 1945, there was no consensus about how the global aluminium industry would be regulated in the post-war era. Certainly, serious overproduction was predicted, because it was not taken for granted that the increase of output would find ready civil outlets with ease. The future of this industry as a whole was uncertain because, in spite of the big strategic value of

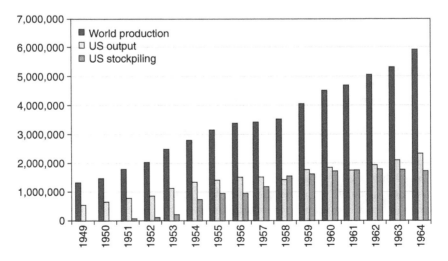

*Figure 10.1* The 'weight' of the US stockpile on US and global output, 1949–1964.

aluminium, it was not clear how the civil markets could have absorbed the new impressive outputs. Almost half of the US war output was closed down after the conflict because it had too high production costs (see Table 10.1). Yet, many observers bet on the future expansion of aluminium, not only because the war provided a wide range of new applications for this metal, but also because the new oligopolistic situation of the US industry could have encouraged a massive adoption of aluminium in the car industry, which for instance had started to disregard aluminium after the merger of ALCOA with Duke in 1925.[52] Louis Marlio also shared this vision and, as adviser of Reynolds, he suggested to the newcomer to continue to invest in aluminium production after the war in order to be ready to catch the uprising trend.[53]

In the settlement of this policy, the United States did not adopt a multilateral approach to the post-war need of international governance. It is also true that the strategic policy of the United States had some international fringes: in particular, it enabled through the Economic Cooperation Administration consistent loans to develop bauxite extraction in Jamaica and it also financed the construction of a new smelter in Norway, whose production was included in the supply of the stockpile, as Mats Ingulstad showed in his studies.[54] Also specific policies were settled in regards to the control over bauxite deposits in Central and Southern America. But the main international outcome of the strategic policies of the United States avoided a dangerous flow of metal, which could have disrupted the international balance between supply and demand. As a consequence, we may suggest that the US policies served indirectly to tame the international markets: both the stockpiling policy and the control over prices, even if they aimed to create a competitive national industry, ripped North American producers out from the international trade and provided continuity to the pricing structure of the international aluminium industry. Moreover, the controls over imports and exports that all European countries maintained after the war hampered the free development of an international market for commodities.[55]

## The long liquidation of the cartel and its legacy

If aluminium was fundamentally different from other non-ferrous metals from the institutional standpoint of its international governance, this metal diverged also from the steel industry. Actually, a sort of European Coal and Steel Community (ECSC or CECA) was never created for the aluminium industry. It is allowed to believe that ECSC was in a certain fashion the legacy of the inter-war cartelisation of the steel industry because the progressive implication of public powers into this industry reshaped the private cartelisation and provided the ground to build up a new kind of institutional regulation. This was the basis on which the ECSC was finally built in 1950: on the one hand, the French and the German governments wanted to avoid the return to mere 'private' cartels; on the other hand, cooperation was considered necessary to avoid the ruinous effects of too strong competition between these two countries. As a consequence, ECSC is often considered in part as linked to the former steel cartel.[56] The transformation of Alliance into 'an aluminium ECSC' was impossible because its essentially private feature made it impossible to transform Alliance into a kind of governmental sponsored industrial cooperation.

This did not mean that aluminium firms were not touched by national policies after 1945. For instance, the French aluminium industry was hit by the nationalisation of electrical production and by the settlement of the 'Plans' that characterised the French public economy, while in Germany the private actors disappeared.[57] However, Alliance could not support a general rapprochement at the end of the war. Thanks to its Swiss nationality, Alliance was a solid institution to assure post-war meetings to aluminium producers that, as anticipated, restarted a few days after the end of the war in the European theatre. The main goal of the first meeting was to debate the attitude to adopt towards ALCAN and American output. In particular, BACO was already aware of the post-war price strategy of ALCAN, which was potentially harmful for its primary aluminium production in the UK. At the same time, BACO wanted to show to its government a certain autonomy and extraneousness about a possible attempt to recast an international aluminium cartel. Consequently, BACO's delegates aimed to use Alliance as an observatory and, to achieve this goal, 'son intention serait de faire une douce obstruction aux opérations de liquidation et de les retarder pratiquement au maximum'.[58] The task of liquidation was given to an independent audit company, Price, Waterhouse & Co (PWC), which already knew Alliance's dossier because it had been the cartel's external auditor for the past ten years. PWC would work with a consultative committee, in which the directors of the firms would lead the effective liquidation. Arnold Bloch was named director of the consultative committee and AIAG was charged to find a way to represent the German interest while waiting for their return on to the scene. Also Piaton (AF), De Souza (ALCAN), and Cooper (BACO) were named as consultants to assist the liquidation.[59]

In the phase that immediately followed the end of the conflict, BACO was willing to set stronger bonds with the French company to obtain some advantages over ALCAN. BACO did not exclude the possibility of a three member agreement with AF and AIAG, but it tried to set a strong technical alliance with the French firm in order to share patents and technical innovations with the final goal of reducing the costs in both countries. BACO was still reticent to begin cordial relationships with AIAG again because of the attempt of the Swiss company to take a position in the UK with the SWACO venture. However, the emergence of the competition with ALCAN led the British firm to include AIAG in its strategic alliance. Also Raoul de Vitry, the president of AFC (which in 1950 changed its name to Pechiney) who replaced Marlio at the beginning of the war, claimed the necessity to create a technical study group to share technology and to reduce production costs of the European firms.[60] Yet at the end of summer of 1945, the technical cooperation planned by AF and BACO appeared an insufficient basis to resume any deeper form of industrial cooperation. The French firm proposed again a 'home markets' scheme, which was reinforced by the sharpened links between producers and national economies. According to this proposal, firms should reformulate their cartel defining each internal market, in which they would be free to act, and the exports markets, in which they would settle market quotas.[61]

This shows that firms naturally opted for solutions in certain continuity between the experience of the 1930s after the war. AF proposed that each of the three firms would direct the sales for the other members of the agreement in all the export markets, virtually continuing the negotiations that were interrupted in 1937. For instance, AF would have acted as middleman for the sale of the three companies in Belgium, Holland, Poland, Hungary, and Czechoslovakia, while BACO would have served as seller in Norway, Sweden, Denmark. AIAG was supposed to carry out this task in Russia, Finland, Estonia, Lithuania, Yugoslavia, Bulgaria, and Portugal. Also the Asian and American markets, excluding the United States, were detailed in the proposal. AF was in a position to be confident about the quick formation of a post-war cartel because, unlike BACO, it was fully supported by its government in this operation and it was in the comfortable position to be the sole supplier in its national market. Even if some projects to create a national anti-cartel policy were discussed in France, this neither affected seriously the working of AF, nor prevented the French firm from considering a quick resettlement of an international cartel. Also AIAG would be willing to enter in the negotiations for the creation of this scheme.[62]

Yet, this proposal was not accepted by BACO which aimed to follow the policy of the Board of Trade.[63] We have already showed the public position of BACO, which even denied the fact that Alliance was a cartel in order not to displease its national authorities. However, even though a cartel was not the most consistent solution with the new institutional situation, the problem about how to provide governance to the aluminium industry persisted. Nobody, either in public administration or in private business, would dare to deny the risk of over-production which the aluminium industry would have been experiencing. Before the settlement of the US and British policies concerning stockpiles and industrial restoration, an overall incertitude persisted in the aluminium industry because the political implication in this industry was a key factor in reshaping post-war policy. Without a clear indication whether the government should continue to administrate this industry or not, it was not possible to set a coherent policy for future international governance. The place of a possible future international cartel in the post-war era, for that, deemed extremely improbable, because, as BACO reported to Reuters

> The global aluminum surplus is currently more important than ever, but it seems unlikely that the problem will be resolved internationally and in any case by the cartel system ... The US government, which controls 3/7 of the capacity of the US, or 1/3 of the global capacity, wants to break the domestic monopoly and stands against an international cartel, without excluding 'intergovernmental' cartels.[64]

As a consequence, BACO tried to reorient its tactic, showing a waiting attitude. BACO's structure was also far different from the other European firms. Unlike them, which had a semi-finished goods division with a capacity largely smaller than their primary aluminium capacity, BACO had a fabricating branch with a capacity six times bigger than its primary capacity. After the war BACO was a big producer of semi-finished works and it could benefit from low cost imports. This strategy was endorsed by the Board of Trade that, as we have seen, aimed to increase this branch in order to promote both its national production and the military preparedness of Great Britain. This field, however, was highly competitive because BACO's challengers relied on cheap Canadian supplies. Furthermore, this choice was risky also because ALCAN planned to develop a semi-finished division in the UK as well as to extend its business abroad. Cooper and Boex, the delegates of the British firm, preferred to explore the possibility that AF could supply BACO with its metal and to help BACO finding an export market for its semi-finished products. Also a far reaching cooperation on bauxite supplies was in the deal. In other words, BACO would aim to conclude an agreement in the semi-finished market, in order to 'barrer l'afflux immédiat de métal américain … avec de sous-quotations permettant de barrer certains marchés'.[65]

Both the proposals formulated by AF about export markets quotas schemes and by BACO about an agreement on the semi-finished markets turned out to be out-dated in the new context. Thanks to the US and UK strategic policies, the flow of the American metal revealed to be almost inexistent in the European markets until the end of the 1950s. The control that the British authorities provided over this market also revealed that the position of BACO was less precarious than expected. In spite of the general overproduction that was feared by the European firms, each national market for aluminium started to grow in the immediate post-war period and many smelters that were closed down at the end of the war were reactivated to cope with the upward trend of the market. Instead of a policy of output restriction, almost all firms were compelled to carry out a strategy of investment to meet new uprising consumption. For instance, George Messud in his 'internal' history of Pechiney in the post-war era, gives account of the fact that, in spite of the optimistic vision that the French company had about the increase of the aluminium market in the post-war era, it was obliged to upgrade its investments plan in order to catch up with market development.[66]

It turned out that not only the ghost of overproduction had been overestimated during the second half of the 1940s, but also that the international trade situation proved to be very different from the one that had been imagined in the immediate post-war period. Instead of a general trend to trade liberalisation, the negotiations for the creation of a more open international system in trade proved to be a hard task. While the ITO was never ratified by the United States, which feared that a too open policy in international trade would interfere with the national strategic policies of this country, the implementation of a general policy for the opening of trade was settled only at the end of 1947 with the creation of the General Agreement on Tariffs and Trade (GATT). Unlike ITO, GATT was not an international body charged to survey the effective governance of raw materials. Its main policy was to establish a progressive reduction of tariffs through the successive settlement of 'rounds', during which multilateral negotiations tried to achieve this goal.[67] Before the Geneva and Kennedy round in the 1960s, aluminium was never influenced by this trend of trade liberalisation.[68] Thus, not only the conversion from military to civil markets was achieved in a relatively short period of time, but also during this conversion almost all the aluminium producers were shielded from international competition by direct and indirect barriers to the international trade of this metal.[69]

At the end of 1945, the first meeting for the liquidation of Alliance was nostalgically summoned at the Hotel des Trois Rois in Basle, where the first meeting of this company had been organised in 1931.[70] We will not dwell on the liquidation itself, even if it took a very long time. Reading the voluminous dossier about this operation that was left in the archives, the overall impression is that, in spite of the initial idea to procrastinate it, the process of liquidation escaped from the hands of the aluminium firms, becoming a never-ending bureaucratic issue. Alliance had to deal with a too complex interconnection of national legislations about capital transfers and enemy properties. It was a Swiss company, which was partially owned by German interests and which had its main assets in the UK, United States, Canada, and Norway. This process created a bureaucratic labyrinth of attestations, procedures, and authorisations. In particular, the blockage that the US, Great Britain, and Canada imposed on the transfer to ownership of German assets complicated the liquidation. Moreover, the control over the currency exchanges made even transferring the assets of AAH from UK to France an uneasy task. The situation began generally to improve only after general appeasement in regards to Germany that followed 1948 and after the creation of the European Payment Union in 1950.[71] Yet the revitalisation of the German actor in 1953 delayed again the liquidation of the cartel, because it opened new discussions about repayment of the old German debts. Alliance was finally liquidated in 1955.[72]

## Towards new forms of business self-regulation in Europe

In spite of this general procrastination, it could be pointed out that all these bureaucratic difficulties were also exploited as a pretext by the firms to continue their meetings. For example, in 1947 De Sousa (director of Stand Société Anonyme – the Swiss holding firm that ALCAN used to manage part of its assets in Europe and which took over the former Aluminium Union) told Piaton (director at Pechiney) that he strongly aimed to end the liquidation as soon as possible because 'on supsonne le Comité Consultatif de n'etre qu'une renaissance du Board of Directors, avec toutes ses attributions'.[73] Even if it is caricatural to compare the control that Alliance's board had over the global market with the activity of the Consultative Committee, it is true that the board for the liquidation of Alliance represented a good observatory from which to follow the evolution of the international aluminium industry – even though the content of these meeting often remained out of records. It was summoned about four times in each year from 1946 to 1949 and it also gave the opportunity to call more informal meetings several times. After the initial absence of ALCAN, also the Canadian firm attended these meetings. Since both AF and BACO's proposal to recast a cartel was revealed to be impracticable once the British and American strategic policies were settled, the role of Alliance in the international aluminium market was turned in a mere observatory in which firms had the possibility to share information about the specific national situation, about international prices, and about the development of each national industry.[74]

As a consequence, we provide the hypothesis that the liquidation of Alliance was a kind of passive channel for international cartelisation that, even though it was never reactivated, stood by during the whole transition from the war to peace economy providing major institutional continuity to the firms. The new role of Alliance was not anodyne for three reasons. First, the consultative board of Alliance was able to observe the general modification of international policy and, in particular, the lingering of a national approach to the international governance problem. Second, this board was able to bridge the old guard of aluminium managers with the new directors of the post-war period. The principal actors of the post-war aluminium industry became used to the overall international cooperation that characterised this industry since its birth. Third and more important point is that this consultative board could have reactivated more active cooperation if the situation had demanded it. Even if the minutes of the meeting surprisingly do not report very often any discussion about market conditions, sometimes personal notes taken by the directors who participated in these conventions showed that real exchange of opinions about market conditions were normal in such meetings.

For instance, in September 1948 Raoul de Vitry, the CEO of Pechiney, travelled to the United States where he also organised a meeting with the headquarters of ALCAN, which aimed to discuss Alliance's liquidation. During this visit he personally discussed with Ray Powell, the CEO of ALCAN, the situation of the international aluminium industry. Powell provided fresh information about the situation of the North American market and about the strategy that ALCAN would have liked to undertake. First, he pointed out that production was not sufficient to cover the growing market and that ALCAN was also supplying three US firms in order to avoid market failure. He advocated the need to avoid a lack of supplies, which could create a dangerous increase of the market price that, instead, should be kept as low and stable as possible. Second, ALCAN was investing in new capacities with the aim of following the uprising trend of global demand and, above all, to keep prices low and stable in the ingot market. If we consider that ALCAN was the main international actor in the aluminium panorama, whose price was often used by metal traders as a barometer for understanding the trend of the aluminium industry, and that it was still part of ALCOA (ALCAN became independent only in 1950), we can understand the far reaching importance of this kind of information and conversation. Once shared with the European companies through Alliance's board, this information became an important factor in reshaping the investment and pricing policies of the other firms.[75] This informal coordination was a leading thread of the international aluminium industry until the beginning of the 1950s.

However, this new informal coordination was an inefficient regulatory option. It had not any kind of power to play an active role in case of need. Actually, it was meaningless if compared with the refined statistical committee of the Aluminium-Association during the 1920s or with the impressive data that Alliance had collected during the 1930s. Without structured working and rules, it was not possible to create a reliable corpus of statistical data to be used by the firms to determine investments and commercial strategies. It could be observed that, in any case, firms benefited from the new national statistics and economic programmes, which in a certain way assisted post-war investments. Also, the new governmental stockpiles took over part of Alliance's work. However, no real international coordination was possible on this basis because such a structure lacked the coercive tools to impose, or at least to influence, each firm's strategy. As we have shown in the former chapters, cartelisation was a managerial action with its structures and codes. It is not possible to consider that an effective cartelisation could be achieved only with informal talks: the well-known literature about the 'cheating' of agreements clearly shows the impossibility of saving agreements from their implosion. A further aspect nuances this informal cooperation: the five members of Alliance were too little a group to have a real influence on the global governance of this metal. Not only were the US firms excluded from direct implication in these talks, but also other important European actors such as Italian and Norwegian companies did not take part in these meetings.[76] Although, until a real international market for aluminium was hampered by public controls, monetary authorities, and high tariffs, the consultative board was sufficient for aluminium firms.

An institutional modification of the meeting was started during the 1950s. The Korean War created a new shortage in the aluminium market because it absorbed almost the whole North American production of aluminium. This fact created some shortages of aluminium also in European markets. The Organisation for European Economic Co-operation (OEEC) decided to create an ad hoc study group on aluminium to help the growth of production in Europe, the Centre pour le developpement de l'industrie de l'aluminium (CIDA). This study group had the goal of reducing imports of aluminium from the dollar zone. In order to achieve this goal, it provided statistics to European firms to be able to decide the extension of their production capacity more easily and to share technological improvement to lower production costs. It is not surprising that OEEC took this initiative: as a legacy of the Marshall Plan, this organisation was an important actor for the rebuilding of multilateral approaches to the international economy. OEEC already served as a study group for the other non-ferrous metals and it was guarantee against the reformation of a private cartel system. It has to be remembered that, among the several propositions about the future CECA, the creation of this authority under the control of OEEC was also prospected.[77]

Unlike the liquidation board of Alliance, CIDA was open to all the producers that were not members of the cartel, such as German, Italian, Austrian, and Norwegian firms. Moreover, its membership was not firm based but nation based. Not firms but national R&D agencies were admitted to its works. The important diplomatic aspect of CIDA was the inclusion in its working of Aluminium Zentrale in 1950, which followed the decision taken by the inter-allied powers to admit the resurgence of German production. In this way, German production was politically reintegrated in the international aluminium panorama. Moreover, it also included the consuming countries that were emerging after the war as big outlets for the primary producers, such as Benelux and Holland. In broad words, CIDA was not too far from the pre-war BIA: it focused on technological aspects, sharing R&D amongst its members and providing a general labour division around big research projects. CIDA was divided into further sub-sections, dedicated to big classes of uses, such as transport, architecture, packaging etc. Also cross-visits of smelters and manufacturers were organised within CIDA.[78]

However, CIDA did not fit with the necessity of governance that, during the 1950s, had started to be required by several aluminium producers. Using the channels of CIDA, Pechiney succeeded in forming an alternative board, which escaped from the public control that OEEC provided to CIDA. This shifting to a private board was also the outcome of some perplexities that were expressed by the Economic Cooperation Administration about the tendency in the non-ferrous metals committees of OEEC also to debate prices and other 'collusive' topics.[79] In 1953, Pechiney succeed in settling the 'Club', as the informal board of directors is called in the archive records. Its creation aimed to gather all the European firms in order to debate some gentlemen's agreements to manage the international market of aluminium, which was starting to re-open during the early 1950s. Also some coordination about international prices was considered important.[80] In this regards, at the second meeting of the Club, Roehr (VAW's delegate) pointed out that 'il faut en tous cas éviter d'utiliser nos accords pour tenir des prix élevés et que les prix de vente soient en rapport des prix de revient'.[81] The price credo of pre-war cartels was also transmitted to the post-war period through the Club. The summoning of the Club happened few months after Marlio's death, which occurred in 1952. Even though after the war he did not return to the aluminium industry, his influence as one of the global actors of interwar cartelisation persisted. As we will see, the settlement of the Club, such as a new form of international cooperation, also marked the definitive enfranchisement from the pre-war model of international governance.

## Notes

1 TNA, BT/11/2336, Post-war Commodity policy, Aluminium, H.J. Habakkuk, Note Aluminium, 29 August 1944. HWA, MG Documents, Abt.6, Alliance, no. 3, Notiz betreffend Reinstaluminium-Produktion in Rahmen der AAC-Vertage des Quotevertrages und eder Verstandingungsabkmmens, 21 November 1942. RPA, 00-2-15933, AAC Notes, Situation internationale de l'Aluminium, 9 July 1944. See also Marlio, *The Aluminum Cartel*, 116–121.

2 For a general discussion of the new role of states in the economy after the Second World War, see Alan S. Milward, *The European Rescue of the Nation-State*. London: Routledge, 2000, 21–45.

3 TNA, BT/11/2336, Policy proposal with regard to virgin aluminium. Note by MAP, 28 September 1944. TNA, BT/67/5039, Official History of Aluminium Industry, 1939–1946, 7 September 1950. United States Tariff Commission, *Aluminum*, 87–90. United States Office of Defense Mobilization, *Materials Survey: Aluminum Compiled by United States Department of Commerce. Business and Defense Services Administration*. Washington DC: Government Printing office, 1956, II 8–19, VII 25–29.

4 RPA, 00-2-15939, Alliance, Dossiers liquidation. Réunion de Londres, 17–18 July 1945.

5 RPA, 00-2-15939, Alliance, Dossiers liquidation. Réunion du comité executif de l'Alliance, à Zurich, 5 June 1945.

6 RPA, 00-2-15939, Alliance, Dossiers liquidation. Visite de AIAG à Zurich, 3 July 1945.

7 RPA, 00-2-15939, Alliance, Dossiers liquidation, Entretien De Vitry avec Hodson et De Sousa, 2 and 6 July 1945.

8 RPA, 00-2-15939, Alliance, Dossiers liquidation, Réunion avec BACO à Londres, 17–18 July 1945.

9 Hans Pohl, 'Die Wiederaufnahme des Metallhandels durch die Metallgesellschaft nach dem Zwiten Weltkrieg', in *Witschaft, Unternehmen, Kreditwesen, Soziale Probleme. Ausgewahlte Aufsatze*, edited by Hans Pohl. Munich: Franz Steiner Verlag, 2005, 82–83. Manfred Knauer, 'A Difficult New Beginning : The Race of the German Aluminium Industry to Catch Up with the Competition in the 1950s and 1960s', *Cahiers d'Histoire de l'Aluminium*, no. 51, 2013, 65–77, 66–67.

10 TNA, FO 371/65368, German industry, file no. 68, German aluminium industry, 1947.

11 RPA, 00–2–15939, Alliance, Dossiers liquidation, Entretien de M. de Vitry avec le professeur Lugeon, le 2 et 6 Juillet 1945 à Genève. AF, Réunion avec BACO et AIAG, 3 August 1945.

12 Rauh, *Schweizer Aluminium*. Knoepfli, *From Dawn to Dusk*, 22–24, 30–32. Bertilorenzi, 'The Italian Aluminium Industry'.

13 Knoepfli, *From Dawn to Dusk*, 40–41.

14 RPA, 00-12-20015, AFC, Accord entre la Société Anonyme pour l'Industrie de l'Aluminium à Neuhausen (Suisse) et la Société de l'Aluminium français, 27 July 1938.

15 RPA, 00-2-15939, Alliance, Dossiers liquidation, Confidentiel. Relations avec Neuhausen, 20 June 1946.

16 See for instance Barjot, 'Introduction'. Segreto, Wubs, 'Resistance of the Defeated'. Schröter, 'Cartelisation and Decartelisation'.

17 Mason, *Controlling World Trade*. Joseph S. Davis, 'Experience Under Intergovernmental Commodity Agreements, 1902–45', *Journal of Political Economy*, vol. 54, no. 3, 1946, 193–220. Carmine Nappi, *Commodity Market Controls*.

18 Eric Bussière, 'La concurrence', in *La Commission Européenne. Mémoires d'une institution*, edited by Commission Européenne. Brussels: Commission Européenne, 2007, 315–329; Laurent Walrouzet, 'The Rise of European Competition Policy, 1950–1991: A Cross-disciplinary Survey of a Contested Policy Sphere', European University Institute Working Papers, RSCAS 2010/80.

19 Fear, 'Cartels and Competition'.

20 Florence Hachez-Leroy (ed.), 'L'Europe de l'aluminium (1945–1975)', Special Issue no. 1, *Cahiers d'Histoire de l'Aluminium*, 2003. About 'national champions', see Oliver Falck, Christian Gollier, Ludger Woessmann (eds), *Industrial Policy for National Champions*. London: MIT Press, 2011. Robert A. Pollard, *Economic Security and the Origins of the Cold War, 1945–1950*. New York: Columbia University Press, 1985.

21 Hillman, *The International Tin Cartel*. Coates, *The Commerce in Rubber*.

22 Claude Schwob, 'Keynes, Meade, Robbins et l'Organisation Internationale du Commerce', *L'Actualité Économique*, vol. 83, no. 2, 2007, 255–283.

23 Michael K. Bennet, *International Commodity Stockpiling as an Economic Stabilizer*. New York: Stanford University Press, 1949. Milton Friedman, 'Commodity-Reserve Currency', *Journal of Political Economy*, vol. 59, no. 3, 1951, 203–232. Albert G. Hart, Nicholas Kaldor, Jan Tinbergen, *The Case for an International Commodity Reserve Currency*. Geneva, UNCTAD, 1963. About the debate on these inventory schemes, see also Alfred Maizels, *Commodity in Crisis: The Commodity Crisis of the 1980s and the Political Economy of International Commodity Policies*. Oxford: Clarendon Press, 1992. David Atsé, *Commodity Futures Trading and International Market Stabilization*. Uppsala: Acta Universitatis Upsaliensis, 1986.

24 Perchard, *Aluminiumville*.

25 TNA, BT/11/2336, Problems of the transition from war to peace. Light metals industry. Aluminium, 4 January 1944.

26 TNA, BT/11/2336, Policy proposal with regards to virgin aluminium. Note by MAP. Appendix C. Note on international commodity policy, 1944. Forres (MAP) to Murray-

Morrison (BACO), 28 September 1944. British Air Commission. Note to MAP, 2 September 1944.

27  TNA, BT/11/2336, Aluminium. Note on cartels, 1944. Aluminium Prices (1928–1939), 1945.

28  Perchard, *Aluminiumville*, 21–22.

29  About ALCAN, see Campbell, *Global Mission*. Pierre Lanthier, 'ALCAN de 1945 à 1975: Les Voies Incertaines de la Maturation', in Hachez-Leroy (ed.), *L'Europe de l'Aluminium*, 63–84. Kipping, Cailluet, 'Mintzberg's Emergent and Deliberate Strategies'.

30  Peck, *Competition in the Aluminum Industry*. Smith, *From Monopoly to Competition*. TNA, BT/11/2336, Policy proposal with regards to virgin aluminium. Note by MAP. Appendix A, 1944.

31  Nations Unies, Conseil Economique et Social, La Concurrence entre l'Acier et l'Aluminium. Geneva: Document E/ECE/184, 1954.

32  TNA, BT/11/2336, Policy proposal with regards to virgin aluminium. Note by MAP. Appendix C. Note on international commodity policy, 1944.

33  TNA, BT/11/2336, Aluminium. Note on cartels, 1944. Aluminium Prices (1928–1939), 1945.

34  TNA, BT/11/2336, Aluminium. Policy proposal with regards to virgin aluminium. Note by MAP. Appendix C. Note on international commodity policy, 1944.

35  NARA, RG 169, box. 1, Special Committee on monopolies and cartels, general, Lines of Policy, 20 July 1944. Memos: Relationship between the cartel program and the commodities program, 24 July 1945. Draft. International commodity agreement, 16 July 1945. About post-war commodity and strategic policies, see also Nocentini. 'Building the Network'.

36  UGD, BACO, 347/10/6/1, Memorandum of agreements with the Ministry of Supply, 3 April 1946. TNA, BT/11/2336, Problems of the transition from war to peace. Light metals industry. Aluminium, 1 March 1944. Perchard, *Aluminiumville*, 58–59.

37  TNA, BT/11/2336, Note on aluminium, 31 October 1944.

38  Milward, *The European Rescue*.

39  TNA, BT/11/2336, Aluminium. Policy proposal with regards to virgin aluminium. Note by MAP. Appendix C. Note on international commodity policy, 1944.

40  Peck, *Competition in the Aluminum Industry*. Smith, *From Monopoly to Competition*.

41  Peck, *Competition in the Aluminum Industry*, 52–62.

42  Smith, *From Monopoly to Competition*, 276–277.

43  Smith, *From Monopoly to Competition*. Peck, *Competition in the Aluminum Industry*.

44  United States Office of Defense Mobilization, Materials survey. Aluminum, VII-20.

45  Peck, *Competition in the Aluminum Industry*, 153–155. US Office of Defense Mobilization. Materials Survey. Aluminum, VI-14–15.

46  About this separation, see Smith, *From Monopoly to Competition*. Campbell, *Global Mission*.

47  Peck, *Competition in the Aluminum Industry*.

48  VHS, MSS3, R3395a, Series 4, Papers of Richard Reynolds Jr., box 33, fold. 1297, Reynolds Metals Company (Irving Lipkowitz), Mobilizing the aluminum industry for peace and for victory, 9 January 1948. RMC, Aluminum for military aircraft. Memorandum sent to Vice Admiral AW Radford, 2 April 1948.

49  VHS, MSS3, R3395a, Series 4, Papers of Richard Reynolds Jr., box 33, fold. 1297, Mobilizing the aluminum industry for peace and for victory, 9 January 1948.

50  The French company obtained a copy of Anderson's programme from the US producer, during a journey to the US in 1952. See RPA, 001-14-20478, Samuel W. Anderson, La question de l'aluminium aux Etats-Unis, strictement confidentiel, 1952. About Anderson's policy, see also Ingulstad, 'We want Aluminium'.

51  Robert D. Cuff, 'Stockpiles and Defense Escalation, 1965–1968', *Public Historian*, vol. 9, no. 4, 1987, 44–64. Peck, *Competition in the Aluminum Industry*. Smith, *From Monopoly to Competition*. United States Office of Defense Mobilization, Materials survey. Aluminum.

52 See for instance Engle, Gregory, Mosse, *Aluminum*. Marlio and E.K. Davis are quoted as persons consulted for this study.
53 VHS, MSS3, R3395a, Series 4, Papers of Richard Reynolds Jr., box 6, fold. 181, Louis Marlio, Report on post-war production of aluminum, 1943. Marlio also sent a report to Pechiney, in which he outlined a great expansion for the post-war period. RPA, 00-1-20046, Louis Marlio, Etude sur ALCOA et sur l'industrie américaine de l'aluminium, 1947.
54 Mats Ingulstad, 'Cold War and Hot Metal: American Strategic Materials Policy, the Marshall Plan and the Loan to the Sunndal Smelter', *Cahiers d'Histoire de l'Aluminium*, Special Issue no. 2, 2007, 125–145. Mats Ingulstad, 'National Security Business? The United States and the Creation of the Jamaican Bauxite Industry', in Robin S. Gendron, Mats Ingulstad, Espen Storli (eds), *Aluminium Ore: The Political Economy of the Global Bauxite Industry*. Toronto: University of British Columbia Press, 2013, 107–137.
55 OEEC, *Interim Report on the European Recovery Programme: Report of the Non-Ferrous Metals Committee*. Paris: OEEC, 1949, 48–50.
56 Matthias Kipping, *La France et les Origines de l'Union Européenne: Intégration Économique et Compétitivité Internationale*. Paris: Cheff, 2002. Berger, *La France, l'Allemagne et l'acier (1932–1952)*. Gillingham, *Coal, Steel and the Rebirth of Europe, 1945–55*. Philippe Mioche, *Le Plan Monnet: Génèse et Élaboration, 1941–1947*. Paris: Presses de l'Université Paris-Sorbonne, 1987. Philippe Mioche, *Les Cinquantes Années de l'Europe du Charbon et de l'Acier*. Luxembourg: Commission Européenne, 2004.
57 Henry Morsel, 'Pechiney et le Plan Marshall', in *Le Plan Marshall et le Relèvement Économique de l'Europe*, edited by René Girault and Maurice Lévy-Leboyer. Paris: Comité pour l'Histoire économique et financière de la France, 1991. Knauer, 'A Difficult New Beginning'.
58 RPA, 00-2-15939, Alliance, Liquidation, Réunion avec BACO à Londres, 17–18 July 1945.
59 RZA, Alliance Liquidation, 1938–1945, Bloch (AIAG), Notiz. Alliance Aluminium Cie en Liq. Basel, September 1945. RPA, 00-2-15939, Alliance en liquidation, Dissolution éventuelle de l'Agence 'Aluminium Compagnie', 17 July 1945.
60 RPA, 00-2-15939, Alliance, Liquidation, Réunion franco-britannique à Paris, 27 August 1945.
61 RPA, 00-2-15939, Alliance, Liquidation, Réunions officieuses des 28 et 29 aout 1945.
62 RPA, 00-2-15939, Alliance, Liquidation, Projet d'accord avec la British et Neuhausen, 29 September 1945. About French post-war anti-cartel fears, see also Hachez-Leroy, *L'Aluminium français*.
63 RPA, 00-2-15939, Alliance, Liquidation, Conversation franco-anglaise, 1 October 1945.
64

> Le surplus mondial d'aluminium est actuellement plus imporntat que jamais, mais il semble peu probable que la question soit résolue internationalement et en tout cas par le système du cartel … Le gouvernement des USA, qui controle les 3/7 de la capacité des USA, soit le 1/3 de la capacité mondiale, veut briser le monopole intérieur et se dresse contre un cartel international, sans exclure des cartels 'intergouvernementaux.

RZA, 00-2-15939, Alliance, Liquidation, 1938–1955, Commentaires sur la dissolution de l'Alliance Aluminium Cy (du correspondant économique de Reuters à Londres), 4 December 1945.
65 RPA, 00-2-15939, Alliance, Liquidation, Conversation franco-anglaise, 1 October 1945. Réunion officieuse des membres de l'Alliance, 1er Octobre 1945.
66 IHA, Documents imprimés, G. Messud, De la suite dans les idées. Pechiney 1945–1970. Paris: Unpublished manuscript, 1971, 35–36.
67 Regine Perron, *Histoire du Multilateralisme: L'Utopie du Siècle Américain de 1918 à nos Jours*. Paris: Presses de l'Université Paris-Sorbonne, 2014. Till Geiger, Dennis Kennedy,

*Regional Trade Blocs, Multilateralism, and the GATT: Complementary Paths to Free Trade?* London: Pinter, 1996.

68 Matthieu Ly Van Luong, 'L'aluminium Européen dans les Négociations Commerciales du Kennedy Round', *Cahiers d'Histoire de l'Aluminium*, no. 28, 2001, 43–59.

69 Manfred Knauer, 'Les "trente glorieuses" de l'industrie européenne de l'aluminium dans le boom économique de l'après-guerre', in Hachez-Leroy (ed.), *L'Europe de l'Aluminium*.

70 RZA, Dossiers Liquidation Alliance, 1938–1945, Bloch (AIAG), Notiz. Alliance Aluminium Cie en Liq. Basel, September 1945. Alliance Aluminium en Liquidation, Assemblée générale à l'Hotel les Trois Rois à Base, 1 December 1945.

71 RZA, Dossiers Liquidation Alliance, 1938–1955, Auszug aus Memorandum Price Waterhouse & Co, Zurich, 25 March 1947. RPA, 00-2-15939, AAC, Résumé des décisions prises à la séance du 21 Novembre 1946. R. de Vitry (AFC) to Chantreuil (AFC) Re: Entretien avec Edw. K. Davis, 3 October 1946.

72 RPA, 00-2-15939, Alliance, Liquidation, Compte-Rendu du Comité Consulative de Liquidation de l'Alliance, 8 January 1954. RZA, Alliance Aluminium Liquidation, Compte Rendu de l'Alliance Aluminium Compagnie à l'Hotel des Trois Rois à Bale, 15 December1955.

73 RPA, 00-2-15939, Alliance, Liquidation, R. de Vitry (AFC), Entretien avec M. De Sousa (ALTED), 20 September 1947.

74 See various meetings reports from 1946 to 1949 contained in RPA, 00-2-15939.

75 RPA, 00-2-15939, Alliance, Liquidation. Entretien à New York le 22 septembre avec MM. Powell, McDowell, Hodson and Dullea (ALTED), 23 September 1948.

76 For instance, in 1948, Bloch (AIAG), De Sousa (ALCAN), Hodson (ALCAN), Peacock (BACO), Chaintreuil (AFC), Schnorf (AIAG) met up together at the headquarters of ALCAN's holding company Stand S.A in Geneva. RZA, Dossiers Liquidation Alliance 1938–1955, Réunion du Comité Consultatif de Liquidation de l'Alliance, 16 March 1948.

77 Archives OECD (après AOECD), Fonds OECE, fold. 50, file 99, Recommandation du Conseil relative à l'accroissement de la coopération technique entre les industries de l'aluminium des pays membres, 5 June 1950.

78 RPA, 001-16-70257, CIDA Première réunion du comité directeur, 9 October 1950.

79 TNA, FO/371/87/262, Complaint by the ECA London Mission about the activities of the international Non-Ferrous metals manufacturers, 27 September 1950.

80 RPA, 001-8-20514, Aluminium, Ententes, Réunion internationale, 17 July 1953.

81 RPA, 001-8-20514, Aluminium, Ententes, Réunion des produceurs d'aluminium, 10 December 1953.

# 11 Institutional innovations

Towards a new balanced equilibrium
in the aluminium industry, 1953–1969

The creation of the Club in 1953 can be considered, in retrospect, the first step towards the creation of the European trade association for aluminium that would happen about 15 year later. Actually, in the course of the 1950s and 1960s the informal network of producers was reshaped with new attributions that contributed to create the European Primary Aluminium Association (EPAA) in 1969. Before this date, the European producers had already experienced a progressive reformulation of their cooperative strategies to provide an optimal method for the international governance for aluminium from the institutional standpoint. EPAA was also an optimal organisation to deal with similar institutions that were already working for regional economic governance in the US, such as the American Aluminium Association (AAA), which was born in 1934 and, after the creation of an oligopoly in the US, became a regulatory body for this industry. Before the creation of EPAA, the Club had become a key agent for regulation of the international aluminium market on the global scale while the actual market was opening again, after post-war political controls.[1]

Another historical category, with which business historians are less familiar, enters here in our explorations about aluminium cartels: trade associations. In broad terms, it is questionable to compare trade associations with cartels. In a seminal work about US trade associations, Louis Galambos argued that the main goals of these organisations were to share statistical information and provide information about pricing and costs. Taking the sample of the US cotton industry from 1926 to 1935, the scholar argued that the construction of a 'regulated cooperation' helped to keep stable prices and markets shares of producers. Of course, this meant that trade associations could hamper the deployment of a 'too' free competition; yet, as the author recognised, they also provided a context in which a 'workable' competition should be possible. Moreover, according to Galambos, trade associations were created in a specific economic and political context, in which the new institutional role of the American government in economic regulation implied some coordination between public powers and private actors.[2] Coming back to this topic, Galambos pointed out that, even if they were informal tools to control the market, trade associations offered firms the opportunity to regulate their own industry through a process of institutionalisation that led to their political recognition. From this standpoint, it is interesting to see whether trade associations can be considered a substitute, at least for certain aspects, for cartels, playing a crucial role in the process of institutionalisation of international industrial cooperation.[3]

In the specific case of aluminium, it is questionable that the Club before and EPAA after belonged to the same field as cartels, since they did not have the same attributions and working methods of cartels. Not only did they diverge from the business model of the cartels that had characterised the pre-war era; the participation into these schemes also represented an entrepreneurial action less consistent and intrusive for the strategic policies of the companies. Having neither sales, nor production quotas, the creation of trade associations did not affect the investments and commercial policies of the firms. In return, their works responded to almost the same need for an inter-firm structure for governance that had led the settlement of cartels before 1945. As a consequence, international governance knew a big institutional change in the aluminium industry because it asked for the creation of new organisations that, while providing effective devices, should also be able to enter into dialogue with national and international authorities and with the new international institutional context. The pattern chosen by the European producers was the adaptation of their decennial experience on statistical analysis of the market, of their coordination, and of their credo in price stability to the new institutional context.

This transformation, however, followed a tortuous path during the 1950s and 1960s and was reshaped by the international development of this industry during this time. We anticipate that, during this period, antitrust laws represented only a marginal threat for the coordination of aluminium producers. The analysis of this phase should consider another factor, which influenced the decision to form a European trade association: the industrial structure of the international aluminium industry and the changing relationships with national political powers at a global level. In the US, the national industry passed from the public guardianship to a phase of global expansion, which was partially helped by US foreign policy. In European countries, the interactions between governments and firms, which may be defined as 'national champion' support, did not exclude the active participation of firms in the global market. That explains the long incubation of the organisation. The changing interactions between national and international levels, which lay behind the process of European construction, reshaped the dialogue amongst the producers.[4] As we will see, they partially asked for new forms of governance to encourage an ordered development of this industry.

## The Club in the 1950s: a first ring for the international aluminium industry

Other studies have already revealed the existence of many interconnections amongst the aluminium producers since the 1950s. In particular, John Stuckey argued that the core of post-war 'collusion' was the aftermath of the long-lasting associations that firms had in several joint ventures, which came from bauxite mining to fabricating facilities.[5] It was already argued in the previous chapters that joint ventures cannot be equated with cartelisation, even though they may help arrangements. This is also true for the post-war period because, in spite of the intricate interlocking directorships that joint ventures represented, the actual governance of the international aluminium industry was obtained through other means and in other places. In a seminal article about Norway's position in the post-war international aluminium trade, Haral Rinde described this governance as an 'industrial order', which was carefully kept through occasional meetings organised in Zurich at the headquarters of AIAG (which in the meanwhile was renamed Alusuisse) during the 1960s.[6] In spite of this insight, meetings were less occasional than has been pointed out and had started long before, at the eve of the 1950s.

The creation of the Club meant a shift away from the former informal talks that were carried out on a regular basis during the liquidation of Alliance or on an irregular basis outside this organisation. Within the Club, the European companies were supported by the creation of a statistical structure, which was also partially linked with OEEC's aluminium group (CIDA). The Club had also frequent meetings with North American producers, both individually and collectively from the mid-1950s within specific 'study groups' that, as we will see, were created to coordinate some collective projects that the producers aimed to carry out in the African continent. The goal of the Club was not to fix prices or to merely 'collude', but was overall to keep stable prices through a continuous observation of the global balance between supply and demand. To use Carmine Nappi's words, the Club served to continue the 'régulation par les volumes' that had characterised this industry in the post-war era until the late 1970s.[7] However, the activity of the Club diverged a lot from the 1950s to the 1960s: the re-opening of the international market at the end of the 1950s reshaped the strategies of firms and, as a consequence, also the original attributions of the Club.

The Club was created by the leading European companies in the summer of 1953. Initially, only Alusuisse, VAW, Montecatini, and Pechiney participated in this first meeting. After the retirement of Guido Donegani from the head of Montecatini at the end of the war, the Italian company became a more reliable partner for the old cartel members, which had aimed to include this company into their meetings since the beginning. From the second meeting also BACO, which initially procrastinated its membership into the Club to please the Board of Trade, became a stable member as well. The role of the Club was rather undefined in 1953: the producers expressed the need to be 'loyal' amongst them and to keep themselves informed about 'all the important decisions' that were made. The goal of the Club was not to 'résusciter les ententes d'avant guerre', as was claimed, but to coordinate the international strategies of the firms with action 'in the style of gentlemen's agreements'. It was also recognised that this Club should not have acted clandestinely, even if a more discrete profile than the pre-war cartel was judged necessary. The Club would be summoned every six months in the various headquarters of its members. There was neither a president nor a secretary, but the hosting firms would organise the meeting and its CEO would serve as president.[8]

In order to have an idea about the working of the Club, we can list a series of topics that were debated thanks to the minutes of these meetings. At the beginning of each convention, each producer used to present its own national situation:

productions, sales, prices, key uses, and general tendencies of the national economy. Also activities of 'concurrence' were often reported: in many cases, the producers referred to the actions of ALCAN in their markets and abroad. For instance, the European producers were alerted by the news about construction at Kitimatt, in Canada, of a new smelter by ALCAN that would have increased the capacity of the Canadian firm from about 650,000 tons per year to one million tons. The situation of ALCAN was already alarming because, after the end of British governmental control over the aluminium market in 1953, the Canadian firm was experiencing an intensification of its penetration in European markets. The Club asked BACO to gather information about this investment and, in a meeting in 1954, George Boex – director of BACO – reported the intention of ALCAN was to use this new smelter to supply the American market that was far expanding at the US authorities' request, reassuring the Club about the future situation of the European markets.[9]

During these meetings, several times the topic of prices was debated. The previous chapter already described that the Club adopted the credo of price stability from its inception, declaiming as a general rule putting prices in relation with production costs. As regards international price, the Club decided to adopt ALCAN's export price as the universal reference. This choice was not autonomously made by the Club, but it was already a common 'price list' published in the leading traders news, such as the *Metal Bulletin*, as a referral price. Actually, ALCAN was the leading exporter firm of aluminium ingots and its low production costs ensured that this price list could serve as a kind of lower limit for all quotations. Not only was ALCAN a decisive partner of the pre-war cartelisation, which focused on price stability as a competitive edge to develop aluminium, but also general stability in prices was aligned with the economic system that was settled at the Bretton Woods conference. For these reasons, the idea to follow ALCAN's export price served the twofold strategy of finding a way to manage an agreement on prices and bridging the pre-war price policy with post-war developments. Apart from this lower limit on the international markets, each member of the Club made the decision to follow the producer's price in each national market that belonged to the Club.[10]

However, it would be overestimated to consider these meetings like a price cartel because, until the late 1950s, the international market for aluminium was not much developed. While ALCAN mainly focused its expansion in the UK and in the US, where the Canadian firm had another list-price that converged with that of the US producers, the European producers focused on their respective national markets where prices were very often set by public authorities in consultation with their 'national champion', such as in France, Italy, and Germany. During the 1950s, only marginal sales of the Club came across the Atlantic. The commercial strategies of the American companies were negligible outside the US as well. Each European market was still shielded by tariffs and other direct and indirect forms of protection (see Table 11.2 about tariffs before the creation of EEC). The 'spirit' of the Club until the end of the 1950s had been to assist the stability of market prices in a period of great market expansion in order to coordinate the action of each production after the respective national authorities in terms of prices and policies. During the 1950s, aluminium over-came copper, definitively becoming the first non-ferrous metal for global output and demand. These achievements happened in almost absolute price stability: the increasing demand for this metal never provoked an uprising trend of prices. This policy was clearly debated in the Club and, even though a cartel was not formed again, the principles that governed the pre-war cartel experience were transmitted to the new post-war world.[11]

During the meetings of the Club, firms also reported on their current produc-tion capacities and investments, providing some details (such as producing costs, target markets). For instance, in 1954 Alusuisse informed the other members about its intention to invest in a new smelter in Norway,[12] while in 1955, BACO also informed the other firms about the investment plans that it was programming at Baie Comeau in Canada, claiming its too short position as a producer of primary aluminium.[13] Since 1956, the sharing of production and market figures became more stable because the firms recognised the necessity of providing ele-ments for the construction of a consistent strategy within the group in order to coordinate the global evolution of their industry.[14] Unlike the pre-war cartel, the Club was an informal association without any written rule or implementation and this cooperation was working on a voluntary basis. The backbone of the Club was the mutual trust and the voluntary commitment that firms decided to gave one other. Some folkloristic actions were organised to improve the bonds amongst firms. For instance, in 1955 the Club decided to create a European ski competition for the employees of the aluminium firms, which since 1956 became the Thropée Européen de l'Aluminium.[15]

It is questionable that this could be a consistent basis on which to build a workable agreement. However, the cohesion of the European firms proved to be reliable and it was expanded to new fields. During the 1950s, the cooperative attitude of the Club's five members was focused on the settlement of a coherent policy for the development of an aluminium industry in Africa. These pro-grammes also pushed the firms to make common forecasts that, in turn, showed the need for international governance and for settling ways to analyse the inter-national balance between supply and demand. From 1954, Pechiney offered to share with the other Club members the details of a series of African programmes, which the French firm was debating with its own national government both in the Afrique Equatoriale Française (AEF – such as Congo) and in Afrique Occi-dentale Française (AOF – such as Guinea). Pechiney was amongst the pioneers of an investment strategy in Africa, because it started the construction of a smelter in Cameroon in 1954, ALUCAM, that came on stream in 1957.[16] However, unlike this first case, Pechiney decided to implicate the other members of the Club in further investments, seeing in a collective African strategy the opportunity to merge part of their activity.[17]

We can anticipate that almost none of these projects came on stream. In par-ticular, while the original projects always included the construction of an integ-rated aluminium industry, the actual realisation was often confined to bauxite extraction and only few industrial achievements were created in the following decades. In some interesting publications about the relationships between aluminium multinationals and Africa linked to the New Economic Order debate, this outcome is often offered as an example for the control that the 'North' had exerted on the natural resources of the 'South'. According to these studies, the combination of interests in these ventures was declaimed as detrimental for African economic development.[18] From our standpoint, it is important to reveal that cooperation on the African projects gave a twofold opportunity to the Club to reshape the institutional context of their cooperation. First, African projects represented a way to collectively study the future of the aluminium industry, which pushed the firms to implement their meeting with specific devices for international governance. Second, these projects provided a direct link to American producers that, in the meanwhile, had become interested in African resources as well. This was the actual way in which the Club started to implement its work to achieve actual governance of the international aluminium industry.

## Programming the future: the 'Eurafrican' momentum of the aluminium industry

Since the beginning of the 1950s, many programmes started to envisage a strategy that today we may define as 'delocalisation' of production to the African continent. In many cases, these programmes had already been conceived during the interwar period, but the international economic crisis had postponed them.[19] Also the relatively small size of the aluminium business before 1945 made these projects not attractive. The uprising trend of aluminium demand and the progressive scarcity of electricity and raw materials in the post-war era provided new support for these projects and pushed the reactivation of investment programmes in the colonial milieux of France, Great Britain, and Belgium. Not only the presence of larger deposits of aluminium-grade bauxite, but also the immense hydroelectrical capacities of Gold Coast (today Ghana), Guinea, Congo (today Republic of Congo), and Belgian Congo (today Democratic Republic of Congo) drew the interest of the governments. For its very energy intensity, aluminium appeared an ideal industry to plan the industrialisation of these African countries. These projects were too huge to be carried out by a single company and the international aluminium industry formed some 'study groups' to cooperate in this field. The Club served as coordinator of these programmes from an early stage.[20]

The African projects were well linked to the last phase of colonisation and swung from being an actualisation of the idea of 'Eurafrica', which was the plan to integrate the European market with the African continent in the last phase of colonisation, to became a privileged target of US expansion abroad.[21] At the beginning, European firms explored the idea of merging their initiatives in Africa to provide a common development of African mining and hydroelectric resources. The European producers were aware that European hydroelectric capacities would not have been sufficient in future to provide the energy necessary for the growing aluminium output.[22] Africa represented one huge collective programme of future aluminium production, with the idea of a productive integration between the two continents and of a path towards self-sufficiency of the future European, or Eurafrican as it was called, market for aluminium. The Treaty of Rome served as an actual spin-off for this programme.[23] In 1955, Pechiney formed a study group called AFRAL (Société Européenne pour l'Etude de l'Industrie de l'Aluminium en Afrique) in which also Alusuisse, VAW, and Montecatini were implicated. BACO initially preferred not to join this group, because of its implication in the Volta River project in Gold Coast that was in some competition with it, but it expressed the desire to be informed about its evolution, not excluding future participation.[24] AFRAL was settled to study the possibility of developing aluminium production in Sub-Equatorial French Africa because, as the head of Pechiney recognised,

> The European aluminium producers can no longer perform their essential task that is to provide their own country with aluminium if they do not resort to external sources of supply. The French Black Africa presents unique opportunities that can be developed in the framework of a European cooperation. On the industrial side as in terms of policy, it is time to go ahead and give a concrete form to a European cooperation.[25]

However, this European strategy was questioned by the presence of ALCAN and some new entrants to the aluminium industry. ALCAN had already been implicated in some exploration in Guinea before the war, while it threatened the leadership of BACO in the Volta River project in Gold Coast. The Belgian Société Générale de Belgique (SGB) was the initiator of the programmes in the Belgian Congo, which risked stealing the prominence of the members of the Club.[26] These projects were in concurrence at a certain level because it was not possible to develop them concomitantly. Together, the hydroelectric potential of all the African projects represented about 27 billion kWh, with which it was possible to produce up to almost 1.2 millions tons of aluminium (see Table 11.1). In 1954, when the first debates about these programmes started in the Club's meetings, the global production of aluminium was about three millions tons: it was clear that the African potential should not have been developed at the same time and that its actual realisation would have needed coordination with the global evolution of this industry and of its market.

At the beginning, the creation of AFRAL was linked with some difficult relationships with ALCAN. The Canadian firm was penetrating in Africa at the

*Table 11.1* African hydroelectric and aluminium projects during the 1950s

| Colony | Colonial country | Place | kWh per year max. | Aluminium, tons per year |
|---|---|---|---|---|
| Cameroun (AEF) | France | Edéa | 900,000,000 | 45,000 |
| French Guinea (AOF) | France | Konkouré | 3,000,000,000 | 150,000 |
| Gold Coast | Great Britain | Volta River | 4,200,000,000 | 210,000 |
| Congo-Brazzaville (AEF) | France | Kouilou | 6,500,000,000 | 250,000 |
| Belgian Congo | Belgium | Inga | 12,500,000,000 | 500,000 |
| | Total | | 27,100,000,000 | 1,155,000 |

Source: author's elaboration from various files in AGR2 and RPA.

expense of Pechiney and BACO. While in Ghana, ALCAN was forestalling BACO in obtaining the favour of the British Colonial Office to carry out the Volta River Project, in Guinea ALCAN used a French subsidiary that managed the bauxite field in southern France in order to draw French colonial ministry favour.[27] If ALCAN had forestalled Pechiney in Guinea in creating some production facilities, the Canadian firm would have accessed the French market with ease, eroding the position of the French firm. A further development of this penetration would have also hit the other European companies soon, due to starting integration with the European markets. The solution to implicate the other European partners of the Club arrived after the refusal of the French colonial ministry to openly hamper ALCAN's actions in Guinea. The French colonial minister himself, Pierre-Henri Teitgen, suggested finding a private agreement to tame ALCAN, which led to the inclusion of ALCAN in AFRAL.[28] In 1956, also BACO became a member of AFRAL, in order to play the game with the other members of the Club.[29]

In spite of this strategy of inclusion, AFRAL risked losing its leadership in Africa. In 1955, the Belgian electromechanical company Traction Electrique, an affiliate of SGB, announced the creation of Syndicat Belge de l'Aluminium (SBA) to develop aluminium production in Belgium. In 1957, SBA changed its name to Compagnie Belge de l'Aluminium (COBEAL), when the first real programmes about African sources were outlined.[30] After the Second World War Belgium became one of the leading European markets for aluminium and that fact attracted newcomers into this business. SBA settled a programme for the exploitation of the Inga River's hydroelectric capacities in Belgian Congo to achieve this goal and formed an ad hoc study group, called Aluminga. However, SBA did not have the know-how to enter the aluminium business and asked for cooperation from the European firms.[31] It also implicated ALCAN and the US companies from an early stage. In particular, Reynolds became a leading member of this project, which also considered its strategic alliance as a possible way to enter the European markets.[32] In this period, also Olin Mathienson, a new entrant in the US aluminium industry, became a member of AFRAL, after the Europeans refused the inclusion of Kaiser, fearing a too large penetration of American firms in this Eurafrican affair. Olin was mainly interested in becoming a partner only of the alumina side of the project, the Fria alumina refinery in Guinea, which in retrospect we can consider the only achievement of this Eurafrican momentum. Moreover, AFRAL decided to became a member of Aluminga with the twofold prospect of refraining the development of the Belgian concurrent project and to tame the North American producers that were taking leadership of this project.[33]

In spite of this rivalry, the African study groups meant a concrete rapprochement between European and American companies. Before these study groups, meetings between Europeans and North Americans were only very occasional and on a bilateral basis. Since then, the two sides of the aluminium industry had occasion to meet up each six months to debate the long-term development of their industry and about its market structure.[34] The study groups were in a forum in which the global balance between supply and demand was often debated. The presence of three different projects (Konkouré in Giunea, Kouilou in Congo, and

Inga in Belgian-Congo) implied a general coordination to avoid overcapacity and did not exclude a certain competition amongst them. In particular, Pechiney desired to keep control over 'its' African sources and it tried to postpone the Aluminga and Volta River projects, in which the Americans had a too big force. The entrance of the US companies in AFRAL was considered at first by the Europeans as a good opportunity to obtain new funds for the construction of the African affairs, which the French firm could have controlled with much ease. In 1956, Raoul de Vitry also used this fact to negotiate the settlement of a loan for AFRAL with the International Bank for Reconstruction and Development (IBRD), trying at the same time to implicate Pechiney in the strategic policies of the US to take over raw materials abroad in support of Olin and to the new entrants of the US industry.[35]

Thanks to the central position that AFRAL had in the whole development of the African sources, this 'study group' was in position to elaborate a general programme for the evolution of world capacities in the next ten years, when it was forecast that global demand would increase twofold. By 1964, the members of the Club forecast that the evolution of European demand would be able to absorb the output of a first smelter built in Guinea of about 150,000 tons. Pechiney planned to own 50 per cent of this production (about 75,000 tons), while ALCAN would have owned 20 per cent, and Alusuisse, Montecatini, and VAW together the remaining 30 per cent. According to the programme established by Pechiney, at the beginning of the 1960s, the full development of the project in Congo would have been possible, while the development of Inga project was postponed to the period after 1966, when the evolution of European consumption over 900,000 tons would have demanded new capacities. In order to accelerate this development, which would have represented a big opportunity for the expansion of the European firms in the global aluminium industry, the partners of AFRAL also created a new company Aluminium Guinée (ALUGUI) that was in charge of starting the construction of the site and that obtained the support of the French government for a partial funding of the project.[36]

The figures prepared by the European firms were contested by the overcoming of a passing recession in the aluminium market that, as we will see, coincided with a drastic reconfiguration of US strategic policies and with the concomitant explosion of exports from the Soviet countries. In this context, the twofold increase of European demand, foreseen by the Club, appeared too optimistic according to the American studies. The American firms, in particular Reynolds, considered the acceleration that AFRAL aimed to give to French colonial Africa inopportune because 'in short, there are no aluminum customers of power in the foreseeable future'. Reynolds' report continued: 'the state of the world aluminum markets is aggravated by the AFRAL group's decision to bow to the French Government to expand there first in order to protect their extensive bauxite holdings'.[37] In this phase, the African project pushed for the first time that the American firms consider their industry as a true global affair, for which a certain degree of coordination with the Europeans was desirable in order to provide a rational development of the global balance between demand and supply. This cooperation passed through a confrontation about statistical data and forecasts about the future trend of aluminium consumption, which escaped for the first time from a mere national context swiftly to the European and global contexts.

Reynolds tried to review the development of Aluminga to obtain a reduced output. The original scheme foreseen by COBEAL was to develop a programme for a smelter that ten years later would have been able to produce about 500,000 tons per year. In 1958, this programme was reduced to 150,000 tons per year, while the last studies carried out during 1960 reported only 50,000 tons.[38] The independence of the French African colonies in 1958 represented a turning point for these programmes because, cut off from integration with the European markets, their economic interest was heavily reduced and the programmes were not continued. Only the alumina unit of Fria came to production and became an important supplier for the firms that participated in its capital. One year before, in 1957, the independence of Gold Coast (Ghana) from Great Britain had also meant putting the Volta River Scheme on hold, from which BACO was already forced to pull back because of its financial crisis.[39] Only Aluminga continued to be explored as a possibility until 1960, when the independence of the Democratic Republic of Congo from Belgium stopped the negotiations.[40] African decolonisation however changed this path, raising a new political risk behind the process of exploitation of African sources that was instrumental to the reorientation of investment strategies in the national markets.[41]

## Between the two blocs of the Cold War: the quest for a new international governance

At the end of the 1950s, Reynolds' anxieties about the continuation of the African projects were mainly caused by an economic and institutional change that the US aluminium industry was passing through. At the end of 1956, the US government dismissed its former guardianship over its national aluminium industry, ending its control over prices and investments. This change was produced at a time when in the US market there was a short recession partially provoked by the end of military contracts.[42] Also Europeans were worried about the end of the former political control over North American aluminium producers, since they recognised that, in retrospect, this was the cause of a potential unregulated expansion abroad of the US industry.[43] The problem of an idle capacity emerged in the US as a main legacy of post-war strategic policies. These anxieties also reshaped the path of global governance of the aluminium industry: on the one hand, they caused questioning about the proper nature of aluminium as a stable price metal and led some merchant milieux to forecast the creation of a futures market for aluminium for the first time; on the other hand, they pushed the American and European producers to find some ways to coordinate their actions. As Irving Lipkowitz recognised in 1958:

> The free world aluminum industry has full confidence that future markets can and will absorb the capacity output of all facilities now in operation or under construction. But this bright horizon does not lessen the necessity for finding a healthy solution to the more immediate world surplus problems confronting the industry ... Past experience has proven that market growth

must be cultivated at considerable expense by aluminum producers and fabricators. If already developed world markets are burdened with surpluses, prices weaken and profits shrink. The healthiest and most rapid absorption of today's surplus therefore requires more intense and broader marketing efforts, not a surrender to 'commodity trading' on world markets.[44]

More than the difficulties linked to the ongoing end of strategic policies, which assured growth and protection to the US primary producers, many anxieties came from an uprising trend of imports into the US market. At the end of the 1950s, the US market was by far the largest world outlet. It was calculated by AAA that in the US the average per capita consumption of aluminium was about 10 kg, while in Europe this average was 3.5 and in the developing countries was only 0.6. Higher wages and a more consumeristic way of life contributed to this outcome, but the US producers were convinced that this record, which was also impressing European producers,[45] was the aftermath of continuous marketing and R&D activity that was supported by a 'healthy' industry that re-invested its earnings in these activities. As recognised in Lipkowitz's writing, this was possible also thanks to the stable price policy, which granted fair and constantly growing revenues instead of bust–boom speculative cycles. From the end of the 1950s, this virtuous circle has been menaced not only by the end of political protection, but also by an uprising trend of imports that attracted the flow of metal coming from the European producers in the US market.[46]

This flow of metal from Europe, which came in all forms (both as ingots and as semi-finished goods), was essentially caused by the spread that existed between the national prices settled in European countries by political authorities and the US market. While the US market price was 26 ¢/lb, the French official price was 22.67, in Italy it was 29.03, in Germany was 24.07, in Switzerland was 26.53, while in the UK it was equal to ALCAN's export price, which was 22.5. Even if in almost all these countries national production was not sufficient to fulfil domestic demand, the producers were led to export to the US market either to exploit the good prices of this market, or because they were encouraged by their own government for monetary reasons – or for both.[47] The outcome of imports during 1958 was the reduction of the US market price from 26 ¢/lb to 24. The situation worsened at the eve the 1960s, when the effective price on the US market was lowered to 23 ¢/lb and even 22, as was reported on many occasions. In phase of relative trade opening, this market slump was transposed abroad with ease, determining a general depression of market prices. Market pressure was also caused by an ongoing series of trades that, since the mid-1950s, came from the Soviet Union and at the end of the 1950s were becoming more important.[48]

Rather than claiming protection from their national powers, the US producers elaborated a programme that, in retrospect, led to the proposal of a first global cartel with the Europeans of the post-war era. Between 1958 and 1961, the US producers and, in particular, Irving Lipkowitz in his twofold role of AAA's chairman of the Foreign Trade Committee and of Reynolds' chief economic adviser, elaborated a programme to bring back some order to US imports and to consent that the US firms find additional outlets in the export markets. The international vision of Reynolds was given not only for its implication in the African projects and for its progressive penetration of the Belgian market, but also because this American company was becoming a true global firm. In 1958, Reynolds success-fully managed to take control of BACO after a hostile manoeuvre in the City Stock Exchange, which was helped by the 'haut financier' Siegmund Warburg and by the direct implication of an allied British firm, Tube Investments. This operation was one of the first of its kind and was often reported in the press as the 'aluminium battle'. Taking over BACO, Reynolds also inherited the British-Canadian Aluminium Company and other international investments of this firm.[49] As a consequence, when Reynolds elaborated a 'Positive programme for aluminium industry', as it was called in Lipkowitz's report, it was becoming a true global firm with a twofold position of major amongst US producers and leading importer in this country.[50]

Since 1958, AAA agreed with Lipkowitz's action. It was recognised that, while the US market had been fully – or almost fully – 'cultivated' by continuous R&D activity and marketing, the export markets were far from being developed at their maximum possibility.[51] In spite of the global growth of aluminium consumption, in the European countries the average per capita consumption of this metal was far below the US record. This difference between Europeans and Americans was also linked to the difference in the vertical integration of the two sides of the aluminium industry: while in Europe firms were integrated for 50 per cent of their output, in the US the three majors were almost fully vertically integrated. In this phase, only ALCAN was essentially an exporter of ingots with lower market-ward integration. According to Lipkowitz, the settlement of a true global aluminium programme should have, on the one hand, created a global market for aluminium in which the absence of tariffs and other protections could have assured the optimal flow of US production. On the other hand, American firms should have helped cultivation of the market, which would have also worked as a solution for the actual problems of overcapacity in the aluminium industry. This conception of the US's positive role in the expansion of the aluminium industry had two important corollaries: first, it could hamper the USSR's expansion abroad, which was becoming a serious threat at that time; second, it could hamper the construction of new facilities in those countries where there was not a sufficient market to absorb them.[52] This new role was also carried out in a continuous dialogue with political powers, who continued to meet the AAA representatives each semester to follow the situation of this indus-try in order to implement a consistent policy with the industry's needs within a spe-cific industry–government agency, the Aluminum Producers Industry Advisory Committee (APIAC).[53]

In the specific nexus between the US aluminium producers and the American government, a programme was implemented to assist commercial expansion of the US firms abroad during this period of overcapacity, trying to exploit the inter-national agenda and to overcome the policy that, in the meanwhile, the Club was trying to enact to protect the European market.[54] Actually, two main events, par-tially linked, were reshaping this US approach: the creation of the European Common Market, as derived from the Treaty of Rome, and the start of GATT's new negotiations in Geneva. At the beginning, the strategy of the Club towards these events was essentially to slow down the process of market integration in order to keep each national market as 'chasses gardées' for the producers.[55] This did not mean that the Club was contrary to the creation of a European market for aluminium. The rise and fall of the Eurafrican projects and the new situation of the international aluminium industry pushed the Club to coordinate its efforts to support the process of market integration started by the Treaty of Rome. However, the situation of the tariffs in the EEC and the related national prices were too heterogeneous to advance fast in this direction. Beside France and Italy, which benefited from high tariffs, Germany and, above all, Benelux had low protection. The metal that came from the US and USSR (or also that which would pass though the UK) found in these countries a privileged access to the EEC market and, once admitted, it also perturbed the more protectionist markets.[56] As a consequence, the Club tried to impose a Common External Tariff (CET) of 15 per cent and free circulation inside Europe of Six (see Table 11.2).

This strategy was not easy to implement because Benelux's authorities were against a CET of 15 per cent, also after the sunset of the Aluminga project. The Club also tried to offer to the European Wrought Aluminium Association (EWAA), which included many integrated and non-integrated fabricators, a quota of free imports (about 40,000 tons per year), but this level was not judged satisfactory.[57] Due to this turmoil, any strategy of acceleration in the Club was questioned in particular by members that could obtain a great tariff protection from their national powers, such as Montecatini. Behind the tariff problem, there was a too big difference in the Club members' producing costs that, in many cases, was the outcome of different taxations, interest rates, and energy bills. In almost all these countries, prices were settled by political powers according to the recommendations expressed by national producers. The creation of the European market pushed the firms that participated in the Club to debate a harmonisation of prices, which aimed, on the one hand, to lead to the settlement of a 'European price' for aluminium for the Common Market but, on the other, to find common ways to promote an European self-sufficiency and to shield their markets against the progressive penetration of the US firms.[58]

This strategy was formalised in the 'agreement of Zurich' that was concluded by Pechiney, Alusuisse, VAW, and Montecatini in 1959. BACO was not included in this agreement because this firm was not part of the EEC and also because Reynolds now controlled it, but a price agreement was settled with BACO in order to harmonise prices also with the British sister company. The agreement of Zurich foresaw that the aluminium producers would carry out a common action to their respective governments when a common European price for aluminium would be reached. Before this achievement, each producer would have respected national prices not to disturb the business of the Club members. The Club explored the inclusion of aluminium in the 'G list' of goods that were submitted to contingents for importation, in order to prevent the specific situation of Belgium, where no tariff existed.[59] This policy, which may be called 'delayed acceleration' to the European market, ended with losing the battle for the tariff of 15 per cent in the future, but served to shield the European market from dangerous flows of imports in the short term. As other studies showed,

Table 11.2 EEC tariffs: national protection before EEC, Club's proposal, and actual tariffs in 1961, 1968, and 1971 (%)

| | Before EEC | Club's proposal 1959 | | Tariffs 1961 | | Common external tariffs (CET) | |
| | 1958 | Inter-EEC | CET | Inter-EEC | Extra-EEC | 1968 | 1971 |
|---|---|---|---|---|---|---|---|
| France | 21.0 | 0.0 | 15.0 | 14.0 | 17.0 | 9.0 | 7.0 |
| Italy | 24.0 | 0.0 | 15.0 | 17.5 | 20.5 | 9.0 | 7.0 |
| West Germany | 10.0 | 0.0 | 15.0 | 7.0 | 7.5 | 9.0 | 7.0 |
| Benelux | 3.0 | 0.0 | 15.0 | 0.0 | 1.5 | 9.0 | 7.0 |
| Average | 14.5 | 0.0 | 15.0 | 9.6 | 11.6 | 9.0 | 7.0 |

Source: author's elaboration from various files in RPA.

when CET was finally established in 1968 and revised in 1971, its level was far below 15 per cent as forecasted in 1959. According to these studies, the producers were able to coordinate a common front to promote the adoption of a specific European policy neither to EEC, nor to the GATT negotiations of the Kennedy Round. At the same time, political logic prevailed over the producers' visions, pushing these last to reconfigure the ways of their international governance.[60]

At the end of the 1950s, the European market for aluminium was not only hit by progressive penetration of sales from the US, but also by low quotations from deals with the USSR. The problem with controlling this flow of metal was not anodyne because it implied a big risk for the whole price stability policy of the aluminium firms. Passing through Belgium, this metal was afterward re-sold in the European market with very low quotations and with very low tariffs. At the same time, the metal from the Soviet countries also entered the UK, and it was often re-exported to the US market, causing troubles also to US producers. The Europeans already observed in 1955 a first sporadic wave of exports from the East that, once introduced in the UK market at ALCAN's export prices, was systematically underquoted by metal traders in order to find room for this metal.[61] These imports knew a real intensification between 1959 and 1961, which caused many anxieties in the Club's meetings and demanded concerted action both in the field of firms' strategies and political aids.[62]

During 1959, ALCAN also tried to approach the European companies in order to start some negotiations to link the creation of a European Common Tariff with the issues created by the US recession and Russia's commercial dealings. In ALCAN's idea, the European market could have served as an outlet for North American overcapacity and it aimed to negotiate an agreement with the European producers instead of starting a commercial war.[63] This attempt was also reiterated by Reynolds, which had direct contacts with the Club in 1959. Irving Lipkowitz and Richard Reynolds went to Paris during 1959 and debated with the heads of Pechiney the opportunity of creating an 'economic NATO', relying on US exports of metal, that would shield the Western aluminium industry from the imports from Russia. According to Lipkowitz, the 'Soviet dumping' was not led by a commercial strategy, but was the outcome of a deliberate policy that the USSR focused on the destruction of the Western aluminium industry using the commercial weapons of low priced quotations. Lipkowitz aimed to create coordination among the Western aluminium producers in their actions towards their own governments in order to create consistent political protection against this flow of metal from the East. In the meanwhile, the US overcapacity could have occupied all the commercial room preventing Russian sales. As Dupin reported to the Club, Lipkowitz wanted to explore the European endorsement on this project before acting after his own government.[64]

## Managing the relations with the Club: Lipkowitz's report and US international policy

The Club was not convinced about the real intention of ALCAN and Reynolds. Moreover, there was no consensus about the strategy to adopt as regards the imports that came from the US and USSR. On the one hand, the Europeans still believed that the EEC could shield them from the too low quotations from outside, and they also explored on many occasions the possibility of implementing some anti-dumping measures. However, the Europeans were not convinced about this strategy and procrastinated its formal endorsement. They feared also American expansion on the European markets. For instance, at the same time when Reynolds proposed the 'economic NATO' to the European companies, it had just taken over BACO and it also became the owner of the Canadian project that BACO was carrying out. It was also able to take control of the Aluminga project that, before being put on hold by the Democratic Republic of Congo's independence, was still up for discussion and knew a final acceleration. Actually, in the first half of 1960, it succeed in forming Aluminium & Electric International Limited, in which Reynolds was the *chef de file* with COBEAL and ALCOA while Europeans had only marginal positions. In Belgium, Reynolds also ventured the creation of a joint venture with COBEAL, Aluminium-Europe (ALEUROPE), which became a big fabricator that, using primary metal imported from the US, competed with Pechiney and Alusuisse in the field of semi-finished products.[65]

However, the main problem for the European market was that, once the Eurafrican ventures ended, an output deficiency was prospected during the 1960s. Actually, domestic European production was not sufficient to follow the uprising demand trend and put in jeopardy the self-sufficiency strategy of the Club. Even if we consider the inclusion of Norway, UK, and Switzerland in the European situation, the picture is still characterised by a deficiency of supply (see Table 11.3). The continuation of a high tariff policy to shield the European market was also politically risky because the Club feared the possibility of losing the support of the national and European powers in this strategy. For instance, this was particularly true for Germany, a country in which the expansion of demand was great and in which VAW feared that the non-integrated fabricators of aluminium would have soon asked the political powers for a harsh reduction of the tariff in order to fulfil their needs. Even if the European producers recognised that some European common projects should have started in order to increase primary aluminium output and vertical integration of firms in Europe, this strategy was not easy to implement quickly. Furthermore, it would have resulted in general

*Table 11.3* The European Aluminium Market, 1957–1961: the views of US producers vs the Club

| EEC | 1957 | 1958 | 1959 | 1960 | 1961 |
|---|---|---|---|---|---|
| Production | 426,000 | 442,000 | 486,000 | 535,000 | 641,000 |
| Consumption | 497,000 | 487,000 | 390,000 | 757,000 | 725,000 |
| Deficiency | −71,000 | −45,000 | −104,000 | −172,000 | −87,000 |
| With UK, Norway, and Switzerland* | −205,000 | −169,000 | −272,000 | −386,000 | −211,000 |

Source: various files in RPA and VHS.

Note
* Calculated adding production-consumption of these three countries.

overcapacity, which would have worsened the situation. Moreover, the US firms had already started a policy of penetration in Europe, which would have compromised the continuation of the European firms' political strategy.[66]

While the relationships between US producers and the Club were not easy, they were reshaped during 1961 with a last attempt made by Lipkowitz to settle some arrangements with the European firms. The US producers reported to Alusuisse that they were not disposed to enter some price agreements with the Europeans for antitrust reasons, even though they inferred that they aimed to keep prices as stable as possible.[67] However, they were exploring some new fashions to cope with the market recession that was causing a harsh reduction of market prices. During 1961, Lipkowitz elaborated a report that aimed to conjugate the US's will to create a true global market for aluminium with some measures to please the Europeans. This report was the continuation of AAA's opinions expressed above: instead of shielding the US market with high tariffs, AAA asked for a global reduction of tariffs in order to create a global outlet for aluminium. The belief that the global aluminium market should be cultivated by US expansion is expressed in the report. The novelty from what had already been planned in 1958 was the prospect of implementing this path towards the creation of a global aluminium market with some private arrangements embedded into a political understanding. In particular, Lipkowitz clearly proposed in his report the creation of a general agreement according to which US firms would make room in the US market for European exports and to invest. This 'hybridisation' of the American market, along with the concomitant penetration of the US firms in Europe, would have resulted in a generalised 'cultivation' of the aluminium market achieved through the transfer of technology and know-how. As the report clearly claimed, its 'central theme reflects the hope of a healthy industry, not the fears of a sick one'.[68]

In order to fully seize the real reach of Lipkowitz's report, it has to be recalled that this report went along with a huge military and institutional transformation of the US aluminium industry, which mainly motivated the need to find some international cooperation in the new context. Concomitantly with this proposal, the US government announced its will to start a revision of the stockpile, which would be followed by disposal of the excess. This became a real cause for anxiety both in the US and abroad, also alarming the European firms. Behind the decision to interrupt the stockpiling there were two series of considerations. First, from the military standpoint, in the era of transcontinental missiles, military experts reported that a 'future war' would not have lasted more than three years instead of the five years hitherto calculated. Second, the US problem of its balance of payments, which was afflicted by the dollar gap, pushed the Kennedy administration to review the global policy of the stockpile in order to reduce public expenditures: since the beginning of 1961, all the strategic materials reserves had been inspected and it turned out that too much stock had been accumulated, such as in the case of aluminium. The disruption of the global aluminium market would have been derived from a deregulated liquidation of the stockpile.[69]

The US producers aimed to link stockpile disposal to foreign trade expansion. It became vital for them to outline a programme to shift global consumption of aluminium in order to find additional outlets abroad, not only individually through ventures such as ALEUROPE, but also collectively. However, it was recognised that this task was not easy because, if Lipkowitz's ideas provided bright insights about a long-range solution for the excess, it was not implementable in the short run. Faced with the resistance from European producers opposed to trade liberalisation, Lipkowitz aimed to find new ways to manage a 'private' understanding with them in order to help the final achievement of his plan. His report proposed an agreement of five years' duration to share the US market with the Europeans. Lipkowitz was also elaborating some alternatives, in order to find practical solutions to the need of international governance that, in spite of US antitrust legislation, the aluminium industry needed to manage the passage through this delicate phase. In Lipkowitz's idea, some political involvement was the key to settle acceptable agreements. In January 1961, he reported the possibility of creating an 'Aluminium Study Group' under the guardianship of the United Nations, which would have created a forum in which Europe and North America could debate the global demand–supply situation to find harmonisation of their respective strategies.[70] Since this solution was not practicable, because it would end with reducing the real strength of the North American industry through political compromise, Lipkowitz turned his attention to the possibility of creating the Aluminum Export Development Association, under the Webb-Pomerene legislation. The idea to create an 'export cartel' in this way would have been functional to coordinate exports to the European market. However, the Webb legislation did not permit any arrangement with the European producers about their imports in the US market, ending up not resolving the international situation.[71]

Lipkowitz preferred to find political endorsement for his report, in order to be embedded while finding some private arrangements with the Europeans. Initially, he succeed in this goal and, when this report was presented to the European companies at the end of 1961, it was claimed as fully supported by the US Department of Commerce. In order to show goodwill to the Europeans, during 1961 also an international gentlemen's agreement on prices was arranged and, as the Club's documents reported, 'Americans played the game'.[72] As a consequence, the 'Rapport Lipkowitz', as the Europeans called this proposal, was perceived by the members of the Club as a first attempt to recreate a global cartel that, unlike the association that belonged to the pre-war era, had a sort of clear and open political endorsement by the US authorities.[73] However, the US authorities soon expressed some perplexities. The Department of Commerce asked not to present this report as linked to the US administration. In spite of certain lobbying activity by the US majors, its implementation was procrastinated during the end of 1961. In spite of many attempts that were made by the US primary producers to adjust this report and to promote it in the different political milieux, it resulted impossible to be continued. During the last phase of 1961 it provoked many criticisms from the US government for its antitrust implications.[74] Its feasibility was soon questioned and, as a matter of fact, it was given up during 1962, when the US producers told the Europeans that the US Congress rejected it.[75]

The idea to continue with an ongoing mélange of the two sides of the aluminium industry was seriously taken into account by the private strategy of each firm. Not only did Americans invest in Europe, especially in the semi-fabricated field as Reynolds and later also Kaiser and ALCOA did, but also the Europeans started a policy of progressive penetration into the US market as well. The *chefs de file* of this strategy were Pechiney and Alusuisse, which both started a policy of direct investments in 1962 in the US. Pechiney, which was historically present in this market with an important sale agency – ISCO – started the creation of new fabricating facilities in the US.[76] Alusuisse did the same and, at the same time, also started the construction of its own smelter, becoming the first foreign company to invest in the US primary aluminium industry and the seventh producer in the US.[77] In his seminal article about the transformation of the nexus between big aluminium business and public powers in Europe, Zuhayr Mikdashi pointed out that a tendency towards the creation of supra-national interests had been reshaping this international aluminium industry since the 1960s, which would end up overcoming the 'national champions' strategy of governments.[78] These ideas were partially contained also in Lipkowitz's report and, as we will see, were implemented by other means during the 1960s when both the US stockpile and the Russian threat became more pressing.

## The road to an ordered balance between supply and demand during the 1960s

Once the US authorities stopped Lipkowitz's report, new problems came from the relationships between the US producers and their own national government. The problem of stockpile disposal emerged then as one of the main issues for the US producers. The first talks about stockpile disposal were almost concomitant with the end of US guardianship over the domestic aluminium industry in 1957 and were resumed on several occasions until 1960, but they neither became urgent, nor did they result in a clash between companies and governemt until 1962.[79] The expansion programme abroad was also elaborated by the US firms to provide additional outlets for this metal, which in any case was not considered as a serious source of market disorder. However, the situation became more negative at the beginning of the 1960s. While during 1962 the excess for the aluminium industry was calculated as equal to about 800,000 tons, further analysis revealed a more serious situation. The Symington Sub-Committee, which was appointed under the chairmanship of the stockpile's creator, Senator Stewart Symington, to establish the evaluation of excess and to make propositions about its disposal, calculated that in case of a war, the US government would only need 450,000 tons of aluminium. The global reserves of aluminium were calculated at about 2,000,000 tons of aluminium, which meant that about 1.5 millions tons should be released on the market to meet the new military programmes.[80]

This dramatic change in US stockpiling policy was a real watershed for the US producers. Between 1962 and 1965, the US producers and their administration tried to find a compromise to handle stockpile disposal. In 1961 and 1962, the US producers succeed in stopping an attempt that was made by the General

Service Administration to sell a first bulk of about 150,000 tons directly on the market. As a consequence, the three US majors, ALCOA, Reynolds, and Kaiser, managed to elaborate a programme to re-purchase part of the excess and use an important portion of the aluminium stockpile to promote international aid programmes.[81] The changing of military concepts that lay behind the stockpile disposal opened a new situation for the nexus between private firms and the US government. While the US government would have liked to tackle the issue also from a financial point of view (earn as much as possible from the sales), the US producers recognised that the disposal of this huge quantity of metal on the market could have disrupted the domestic industry. Some direct talks were carried out between the Stockpile Committee and the leading US companies, either to work out a programme for the disposal of the surplus in the very long run (20 years) or to elaborate future military purchases.[82] While the US administration rejected the US industry's views, on some occasions the re-sale of stock to an institutional commodity market was also prospected. This decision would have destroyed the price stability of this metal and was extremely opposed by the US producers.[83] The threat represented by this proposal was particularly risky because, since 1963, the COMEX of New York declared at different times its intention to start a futures aluminium market. Even though AAA succeeded in convincing the US government of the undesirability of this kind of operation, its rumours made the proposal of a futures trade for aluminium appealing within the commercial milieux.[84]

At the same time, also the London Metal Exchange released some news about its will to start an aluminium futures market in London and it also explored the possibility of implicating European producers in this strategy. Both the US and European producers refused to adopt a futures market for aluminium, also coordinating their actions. For instance, while BACO and ALCAN put pressure on the British government not to support LME's action,[85] Pechiney volunteered an action of propaganda in the US where the director of ISCO, Victor Besso, convinced the US Aluminum Extruders Council, which gathered independent and non-integrated fabricators that depended on the European and Canadian imports of aluminium, to boycott COMEX's action, declaring that

> A futures market in aluminum is neither needed nor advantageous to the aluminum fabricators or producers. Such an operation is invaluable, particularly to the world's producers of copper, lead, zinc and tin … but aluminum producers and fabricators have long recognised the value of a stable price: their development, marketing and research programs have shown the way to the copper, lead and zinc producers and they have never turned over to the speculators or merchant the job of finding a home for their products. … We have been able to judge our market and its needs, and to accommodate these needs for better than could a Commodity Exchange where values may reflect nothing else than a dock strike or speculative activities. We are interested in seeing that our customers can buy metal at the lowest possible price. But, even more, we are interested in the stability of a market for, without it, no one benefits but speculators.[86]

Even if both US and European producers were sympathetic about hampering these attempts, the situation was still critical. The US producers avoided the risk that part of the stockpile surplus was released on the market through COMEX futures contracts, but it was alleged that COMEX, and in particular the broker firm Bache & Company, aimed to start a trade with some Japanese supplies in any case. Also, a possible supply from Eastern Europe was rumoured. In Europe, LME was concomitantly exploring the possibility of launching an aluminium futures market after firm refusal from the Club of using aluminium from the Soviet countries.[87] This was not the first time that COMEX and LME thought about the possibility of creating an aluminium futures trade; yet in the past no material conditions could have helped the fulfilment of this proposal. According to Lipkowitz, at the beginning of the 1960s, three main conditions served as the background for this renewed interest by the institutional markets. First, the stabilisation of other non-ferrous metal prices reduced the turnover of LME and COMEX, pushing these institutional markets to other materials. Second, 'the weakening of the aluminum price had attracted the traders' attention'. Finally, the existence of some external supplies, such as Russian exports, was a material basis to make this programme happen.[88]

The trade with the Soviets caused anxiety because it presented some political difficulties. This trade was embarrassing for some governments in Europe, in particular West Germany, France, Italy, and the United Kingdom, which were trying to settle cordial economic relationships with Eastern Europe. National political action would have meant imposing either anti-dumping procedures or limitations to trade with licences. European action was not achievable because, before the settlement of European general tariffs, Belgium was against the settlement of high barriers. Moreover, the main target of Russian metal exports was the UK, which was not part of the European Community.[89] According to Club documents, the political powers aimed to avoid this kind of action, also because they were not willing to change the West–East diplomatic situation. Imports from the Soviet countries were also commercially dangerous because, while Americans and Europeans set prices in relation to their production costs, for the Russians national production costs had only a secondary importance. During the beginning of the 1960s, EEC had not defined policies to shield firms from this commercial attack, while the GATT agreement was not able to define these sales as real 'dumping'.[90]

In this context, the producers feared that LME could have used the Russian metal to start futures trading. In the Club, a political approach to this issue prevailed and BACO was delegated to put pressure on the British government to hamper the establishment of a futures market for aluminium.[91] While halting the LME proposal, BACO found also the active cooperation of ALCAN. These firms also discussed with the Board of Trade to find a private way to solve the problem of USSR imports, which helped the producers, as it did for other commodities, to find a private way out of the issue.[92] In particular, a gentlemen's agreement between Western and the Eastern producers was blessed by the Board of Trade. The other producers also involved their own governments in a general endorsement of this 'commercial solution', which was considered the best way to avoid

Table 11.4 Rings of international industrial cooperation: the Club, the Club of Zurich, the Jouven's Club, and EPAA

| The Club (1953–) | The Club of Zurich (1961–) | Jouven's Club (1964–1968) | EPAA (1969–) |
| --- | --- | --- | --- |
| Alusuisse | Alusuisse | Alusuisse | Alusuisse |
| Pechiney (AF) | Pechiney (AF) | Pechiney (AF) | Pechiney (AF) |
| Montecatini | Montecatini | Montecatini | Montecatini |
| VAW | VAW | VAW | VAW |
| BACO | BACO | BACO | BACO |
|  | Årdal (Norway) |  | Årdal |
|  | Elektrokemisk (Norway) |  | Elektrokemisk |
|  | Vereinigte Metallwerke Ranshofen–Berndorf (Austria) |  | Vereinigte Metallwerke Ranshofen–Berndorf |
|  | Svenska Aluminium (Sweden)* |  | Svenska Aluminium |
|  | ENDASA (Spain)* |  | ENDASA |
|  | Delfzil Aluminium (Holland)** |  | Delfzil Aluminium |
|  | ALCAN (UK)*** |  | ALCAN |
|  | Norsk Hydro (Norway)**** |  | Norsk Hydro |
|  | ALNOR**** |  | ALNOR |
|  | MOSAL (Norway)**** |  | MOSAL |
|  |  |  | Giulini |

Source: author's elaboration from various files in RPA.

Note
* Since 1962; ** since 1965; *** since 1966; **** since 1968.

diplomatic issues among powers and disruption of the basic features of the international aluminium market.[93] In the meanwhile, the Club had extended to other
producers, creating a larger ring called the 'Club of Zurich' with the aim of
negotiating price agreements in the tight market situation generated by the
imports from the US and USSR. Also, this larger meeting of producers aimed to
organise the European market and define common prices to fulfil EEC consumption. By 1963, also Spanish (Empresa Naciona del Aluminio – ENDASA), Austrian (Vereinigte Metallwerke Ranshofen-Berndorf – VMR), Norwegian (Årdal,
Elekem and Aluminium Norsk Hydro – ALNORD), and Swedish (Swenka Aluminium – SAKO) producers were implicated in the Club of Zurich, while in
1964 the Canadians took part in some meetings as well. In 1964, the Club of
Zurich agreed to raise the price from 22.5 ¢/lb to 24, following the decision that
the US producers had taken for their price-list. Also ALCAN harmonised its
internal list price to this decision.[94]

The agreement with the Soviets was negotiated as follows. The Club settled
specific agreements with the main Soviet metal exporter, Raznoimport from
1963. This firm was based in London and it was in charge of managing all exports
of aluminium from the USSR and its satellite countries. Russians entered this
agreement because they understood the desirability of a stable outlet, which could
suit their planned economy in a better way. In a specific meeting the European
firms agreed on the quantity of metal and its price, referring to the referral market
price for this metal, i.e. 'ALCAN's export price' that, as we have seen, was settled
in connection with US producers and accepted also by the extra-club Europeans.
Alusuisse and ALCAN were in charge of the actual negotiations that happened
either in Switzerland or in the Soviet Union. Yet, the European producers used a
London-based metal trader, Brandeis Goldschmidt Ltd, to act as their middleman
for the final settlement of the agreements. For that, in the trading press, the
Russian agreements are reported as the 'Brandeis agreements'. Brandeis was part
of the Warburg Group, the leading financial supporter of the British Aluminium
Company that had helped its takeover by Reynolds in 1958, and it was also a
member of the ring of LME. Its implication would have avoided any further
action of LME.[95]

Without entering into the details of these agreements, it was a bilateral
agreement between the agency of Brandeis and Raznoimport. All the other
European producers signed different bilateral agreements with Brandeis, in
order to share the metal that Brandeis agreed to purchase from Raznoimport.
All the European producers agreed to buy out part of the metal flow which
was managed by Brandeis, sharing quotas that were set according to their
respective sales (for quotas, see Table 11.5). Also the Japan Light Metals association decided to take part in the purchase of the metal from the Soviet Union,
even if it acted without the intermediation of Brandeis.[96] The US firms also
agreed to enter these purchases with a quota of 5.5 per cent of the total
because, while no political solutions such as the ones prospected by Lipkowitz,
were workable, the flow of Russian metal was recognised as a main disturbing
factor of US market trends. However, in 1967 ALCAN and ALCOA discussed
with the Europeans a plan to coordinate the purchase of Soviet metal and the

flow of the American stockpile in the European market, claiming for a general harmonisation between these two extra-supplies. In exchange for the continuation of US participation in the purchases of the Eastern metal, the US producers wanted to implicate the European producers in the stockpile disposal, finding room for this metal in the European market.[97] Moreover, the US firms expressed some anxieties about the Eastern contracts, fearing that a diplomatic issue could have derived from the disclosure of information about US participation. In particular, ALCOA claimed that US participation in the purchases from the East should have been 'In a hidden fashion without making appear the participation of the representatives of Americans Producers, neither in the negotiations that may be made either with the Eastern European countries, nor among western producers to set quotas.'[98]

As a consequence, from 1967, the US producers' quotas were included in the metal purchased by the other firms and completely disappeared from the Eastern purchases files: Reynolds' and Kaiser's quotas were included in BACO's share, while ALCOA's quota was included in Elkem's. As we will see, when Kaiser and Reynolds had invested during the 1970s in Europe, they had entered again in the agreement. In turn, Raznoimport was the middleman for other metal traders from Eastern Europe, such as Metalimpex (of Romania), Impexmetals (of Poland), and others.[99] Several agreements were signed between Brandeis and Raznoimport from 1963 to 1976 and the European producers' quotas were settled following the sales of each company in the EEC market during the previous years. Also Nippon Light Metals agreed to enter into the agreement, with a quota of about 5 per cent (see Table 11.5).[100]

*Table 11.5* The shares of the Brandeis agreements, 1963–1969

|  | 1963 | 1964–1965 | 1966 | 1967 | 1968 | 1969 |
|---|---|---|---|---|---|---|
| ALCAN | 3,200 | 6,750 | 7,595 | 10,440 | 11,044 | 13,204 |
| ALCOA** | 300 | 670 | 780 | 1,070 | – | – |
| Kaiser* | 300 | 670 | 770 | 1,060 | – | – |
| Reynolds* | 300 | 670 | 770 | 1,060 | – | – |
| Pechiney | 3,500 | 7,300 | 8,440 | 11,590 | 17,675 | 17,651 |
| Alusuisse | 2,575 | 5,295 | 6,115 | 8,405 | 9,691 | 10,828 |
| Årdal | 665 | 1,385 | 1,605 | 2,220 | 3,712 | 5,649 |
| BACO | 1,500 | 3,100 | 3,590 | 4,920 | 8,409 | 10,054 |
| Elkem | 470 | 985 | 1,140 | 1,570 | 3,563 | 4,260 |
| ENDASA | 350 | 730 | 840 | 1,160 | 1,500 | 1,780 |
| Montecatini | 920 | 1,900 | 2,200 | 3,020 | 3,351 | 4,006 |
| VMR | 840 | 1,750 | 2,025 | 2,780 | 3,060 | 3,659 |
| Svenska-SAKO | 350 | 365 | 420 | 585 | 1,140 | 1,364 |
| VAW | 2,500 | 5,110 | 5,910 | 8,120 | 8,621 | 9,345 |
| Nippon Light Metals | – | 5,000 | 2,500 | 3,000 | 4,000 | 4,450 |
| Total | 17,700 | 41,500 | 44,700 | 61,000 | 76,340 | 86,250 |

Source: author's elaboration from various files in RPA and AEPAA.

Notes
* After 1967, included in BACO's quota; ** after 1967, included in Elkem's quota.

This agreement with the US firms was possible because it appeared as a *do ut des* in regards to the stockpile problem, which finally found a solution in 1965. In this year, COMEX finally failed in starting a futures trade in aluminium. In spite of the refusal that the US primary producers showed to COMEX, the commodity exchange decided to continue its action, which revealed to be a fiasco. Neither the US government nor other suppliers decided to use COMEX to trade in aluminium and, after a ridiculous turnover of tons traded and very small price fluctuation, this channel was considered as not influential at all in the aluminium trade and was closed down.[101] After having avoided its disposal through a merchant channel, the US producers tried to negotiate with the administration a programme to allow the aluminium industry to re-purchase the stockpile excess and to liquidate it in the long run. Even if the US administration and the aluminium producers wrestled about the stockpile disposal during 1964, when budgetary reform under the Lyndon Johnson presidency would have preferred to use this disposal to find some earnings for the US national budget, the US producers succeeded in finding a compromise with the administration. An aspect that delayed this compromise was also the decision to raise prices in 1964 from ¢22.5 to ¢24, which alerted the authorities about a possible combinatory attitude of the US aluminium industry.[102] In 1965 a final agreement was signed between the US aluminium industry and the administration for stockpile disposal. The producers, according to their productive capacity in 1965, committed to buy the excess of 1,400,000 tons from the stockpile between 1966 and 1975 until its depletion. Also ALCAN and the Alusuisse's subsidiary in the US were part of the agreement.[103] As Richard Reynolds wrote to George Donet, the director of the Business Defense and Security Administration, the agency that controlled the stockpile: 'Such a plan would permit the industry and its customers to plan additional facilities with a stockpile in mind and without the resulting dislocation in employment, distribution, and aluminum business in general.'[104]

The Brandeis agreement and stockpile disposal served to bridge together the two sides of the aluminium industry during the mid-1960s. The entry in the European market of metal both from the US and the Soviet Union made it necessary to settle a structure to find a balance between global supply and actual demand. From 1963, Pierre Jouven, who in the meanwhile became the CEO of Pechiney, proposed the creation of a self-regulator committee for the aluminium industry. Lipkowitz's approach (to create a political embedded body for the governance of the aluminium industry) was put aside, since it proved not to be workable. Jouven's idea was that only a less informal association would have been able to provide some order in the aluminium industry that, balancing production with demand constantly and providing some forecast about the future balance, would also bring an effective price stability to the market. In other words, Jouven's idea was to create a '*bourse* for surpluses' that were affecting the aluminium market. Another group was formed, called 'Club Jouven' in which only the five initial firms were members and could debate the creation of an international aluminium association. Jouven's action was initially oriented to create an association that would have included the American firms as well.[105]

During the first half of 1964, the Jouven proposal progressed towards the creation of a global trade association, which could have bridged the two sides of the aluminium industry: the Association Internationale de l'Aluminium Brut (AIAB). AIAB's main goal was to exchange information in order to provide a more harmonised evolution of global capacity.[106] Even if US producers did not accept joining such an association, Irving Lipkowitz, who became a member of the board of the Non-Ferrous Metal Committee of the OECD,[107] obtained in 1964 that the sharing of statistics was allowed on a voluntary basis between the US and the European producers.[108]

Since this decision, a system of statistical sharing was progressively created with the idea not to settle a global association, but to establish a confederation of statistical information with US producers in the future. Club Jouven obtained the consent of all the other European firms that participated in the Zurich Club to share information about production, capacities, sales, and stock. The association that Jouven prospected shifted from the global scale to the European one, in order to allow the European producers to create a reliable corpus of statistical information to be shared with ease with the AAA. Actually, an association such as the one forecasted by Jouven was reformulated on the European level, whose provisional name was Association Européenne de l'Aluminium Brut (EURAL). One of EURAL's main goals was to provide a unique voice to the European producers towards the EEC as regards the settlement of polices towards this industry. In this case, AAA served as the sample that was adopted by the

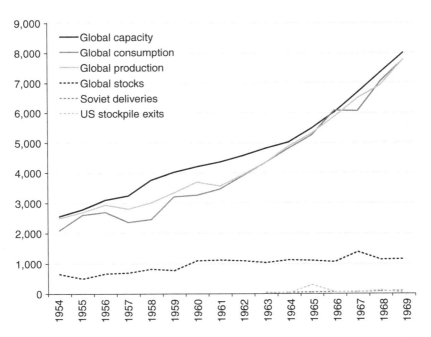

*Figure 11.1* The global aluminium industry from 1953 to 1969: towards a balanced development of output.

Europeans to create their association.[109] According to Jouven, the main problem of the continuation of the strategy of price stability was represented by the fact that some firms overproduced and over-invested because they were not able to actually understand the market situation.[110]

Since the end of 1966, the ideas elaborated in Club Jouven were extended to the Zurich Club and a first collection of statistical data was started. While the provisional secretariat of this statistical office was based in Düsseldorf, at the head-quarters of AZ, the European firms asked an external audit firm to check the information that the firms provided to the central bureau. Like in the past, Price, Waterhouse & Co served this task.[111] At the end of 1967, the European aluminium industry had already been working as general controller over global supply/demand and it had been able to collect data about production, sales, capacities, and stock each month. According to what was established by the Non-Ferrous Metal Committee of OECD, the European producers shared these data with the North Americans every three months. Thanks to the implementation of the USSR's and US's agreements about the supply of their metal, the Club was able to share information to adjust the producers' production rate to the global market situation.[112] The achievement of this goal clearly appears in Figure 11.1, which shows the supply/demand situation during the period 1954–1969. In 1969, this organisation reached its definitive shape, when EPAA was finally created including all the former members of the Club of Zurich plus Giulini, which accepted to enter this official ring.[113]

## Notes

1 About EPAA, see Marco Bertilorenzi, 'Défendre le Marché Européen de l'Aluminium : Pouvoirs Publics, Diplomatie Industrielle et Trade Associations (1953–1975)', in *Formes et Moyens d'Action des Organisations Patronales dans la Sphère Publique*, edited by Danièle Fraboulet, Clotilde Druelle-Korn, and Pierre Vernus. Rennes: Presses Universitaire de Rennes, 2013, 289–303.

2 Louis Galambos, *Competition and Cooperation: The Emergence of a National Trade Association*. Baltimore MD: John Hopkins University Press, 1966.

3 Louis Galambos, 'The American Trade Association Movement Revisited', in *Trade Associations in Business History: Proceedings of the Fuji Conference*, edited by Hiroaki Yamazaki and Matao Miyamoto. Tokyo: Tokyo University Press, 1988. About the debate on institutionalisation, see also Neil Rollings, Matthias Kipping, 'Private Transnational Governance in the Heyday of the Nation-State: The Council of European Industrial Federations (CEIF)', *Economic History Review*, vol. 61, no. 2, 2008, 409–431.

4 About this topic, see Zuhayr Mikdashi, 'Aluminum', in *Big Business and the State: Changing Relations in Western Europe*, edited by Raymond Vernon. Cambridge MA: Harvard University Press, 1974, 170–195. Florence Hachez-Leroy, 'La Construction Européenne et ses Conséquences sur l'Industrie Française de l'Aluminium', in Hachez-Leroy (ed.), *L'Europe de l'Aluminium*.

5 Stuckey, *Vertical Integration*.

6 Harald Rinde, 'The Powerhouse of Europe: The Growth of the Norwegian Aluminium Industry, 1945–1970', in Hachez-Leroy (ed.), *L'Europe de l'Aluminium*, 37–44.

7 Nappi, *L'Aluminium*.

8 RPA, 001-8-20514, Aluminium, Ententes, Compte-Rendu de la Réunion Internationale, 17 July 1953.

9 RPA, 001-8-20514, Aluminium, Ententes, Compte rendu de la réunion des producteurs d'aluminium, 17 June 1954.
10 RPA, 001-8-20514, Aluminium, Ententes, Réunion des producteurs d'aluminium à Cologne, 1 December 1955.
11 RPA, 001-8-20514, Aluminium, Ententes, Réunion des producteurs d'aluminium, 10 December 1953.
12 RPA, 001-8-20514, Aluminium, Ententes, Réunion des producteurs d'aluminium à Paris, 17 June 1954. This investment was the Mosjøen smelter, which started its operations in 1958 and which was sold to ALCOA in 1962, when Alusuisse started another unit in Husnes (Sør-Norge Aluminium SØRAL). Knoepfli, *From Dawn to Dusk*, 48–49.
13 RPA, 001-8-20514, Aluminium, Ententes, Réunion des producteurs d'aluminium à Londres, 9 January 1955. This smelter (Canadian British Aluminium Co.) was one of the main causes of BACO's financial issues that led this company to be taken over by Reynolds. See Perchard, *Aluminiumville*, 58–59.
14 RPA, 001-8-20514, Aluminium, Ententes, Réunion des producteurs d'aluminium à Paris, 7 June 1956.
15 RPA, 001-8-20514, Aluminium, Ententes, Compte-Rendu de la réunion de Zurich, 6 December 1956. About the Thropée, see also Rinde, 'The Powerhouse of Europe', 39.
16 Maurice Laparra, Ivan Grinberg, *Alucam, un Destin Africain: 50 Ans d'Aluminium au Cameroun, 1957–2007*. Aix en Provence: REF.2C, 2007. Edy-Claude Okalla Bana, 'L'Electrification du Cameroun par EDF et Pechiney (1945–1965)', *Cahiers d'Histoire d'Aluminium*, no. 35, 2005–2006, 54–73.
17 RPA, 001-8-20514, Aluminium, Ententes, Réunion des producteurs à Rome, 2 December 1954.
18 See for instance, Bonnie K. Campbell, *Les Enjeux de la Bauxite: La Guinée Face aux Multinationales de l'Aluminium*. Montréal: Presse Universitaire de Montréal, 1983. Ronald Graham, *The Aluminium Industry and the Third World Multinational Corporations and Underdevelopment*. London: Zed Press, 1982.
19 See the contributions on this topic in Robin S. Gendron, Mats Ingulstad, Espen Storli (eds), *Aluminium Ore: The Political Economy of the Global Bauxite Industry*. Toronto: University of British Columbia Press, 2013. About delocalisation strategies, see Lesclous, *Histoire des Sites Producteurs d'Aluminium*, 166–178.
20 RPA, 001-14-20462, Dupin (Pechiney), Mise en valeur des territoires d'Afrique, 1955. RPA, 001-8-20514, Aluminium, Ententes, Réunion des producteurs d'aluminium à Londres, 9 June 1955.
21 About Eurafrica, see (not exhaustive) Marie-Thérèse Bitsch, Gérard Bossuat (eds), *L'Europe Unie et l'Afrique: De l'Idée d'Eurafrique à la Convention de Lomé I*. Brussels: Bruylant, 2005. Guia Migani, *La France et l'Afrique Sub-saharienne, 1957–1963: Histoire d'une Décolonisation entre Idéaux Eurafricains et Politique de Puissance*. Brussels: Peter Lang, 2008, 45–60. Sylvie Lefevre-Dalbin, 'L'Idée d'Eurafrique dans les Années 1950: L'Exemple des Projets Économique Franco-Allemands', in *L'Europe Communautaire au Défi de la Hiérarchie*, edited by Bernard Brunetau and Yousef Cassis. Brussels: Peter Lang, 2007. Yves Montarsolo, *L'Eurafrique, Contrepoint de l'Idée d'Europe: Le Cas Français de la Fin de la Deuxième Guerre Mondiale aux Négociations des Traités de Rome*. Aix en Provence: Publications de l'Université de Provence, 2010. Adekeye Adebayo, Kaye Whiteman (eds), *The EU and Africa: From Eurafrique to Afro-Europe*. London: Hurst, 2012.
22 RPA, 001-8-20514, Aluminium, Ententes, Réunion des producteurs d'aluminium à Londres, 9 June 1955.
23 Archives Historiques de la Commission Européenne, Brussels (hereafter AHCE), BAC 56-1980, no. 194, Rapport du groupe de travail de l'association des territoires d'outre-mer à la Communauté Economique Européenne, 11 August 1958.
24 RPA, 504-2-10-9659, Projet de création d'une industrie européenne de l'aluminium en Afrique, 6 September 1955.

25

Les producteurs d'aluminium européens ne pourront plus accomplir leur mission essentielle qui est d'alimenter leur propre pays en aluminium s'ils ne recourent pas à des sources d'approvisionnement extérieures. L'Afrique Noire Française présente des possibilités exceptionnelles qui peuvent être mises en valeur dans le cadre d'une coopération européenne. Sur le plan industriel comme sur le plan de la politique générale, le moment est venu d'aller de l'avant et de donner une forme concrète à une coopération européenne.

RPA, 504-2-10-9660, Procès-verbal de la réunion des fondateurs de la Société Européenne pour l'Etude de l'Industrie de l'Aluminium en Afrique, 26 July 1955.

26  Etienne Deschamps, 'L'Eurafrique à l'Epreuve des Faits: La Belgique, la France et les Projets de Barrages Hydroélectriques en Afrique (1954–1958)', in Bitsch, Boussuat (eds), *L'Europe Unie et l'Afrique*, 165–184. Jean-Claude Willame, *Zaïre, l'Épopée d'Inga: Chronique d'une Prédation Industrielle*. Paris: l'Harmattan, 1985. About SGB, see Jo Cottenier, *La Société Générale, 1822–1992*. Brussels: EPO, 1989. Hermann Van Der Wee, *La Générale de Banque, 1822–1997: Un Défi Permanent*. Paris: Racine, 1997.

27  About Ghana, see Jon Olav Hove, 'The Volta River Project and Decolonization, 1945–1957: The Rise and Fall of an Integrated Aluminum Project', in Gendron, Ingulstad, Storli (eds), *Aluminum Ore*, 185–209. About Guinea, see Jacques Larrue, *Fria en Guinée: Première usine d'Alumine en Terre d'Afrique*. Paris: Karthala, 1997.

28  RPA, 504-2-10-9659, Projet de création d'une industrie de l'aluminium en Afrique française, 7 October 1955. Conversation avec M. Moussa (directeur des Affaires économiques et du Plan au ministère de la France d'outre-mer), 11 August 1955. RPA, 504-2-10-9660, Procès-verbal d'AFRAL, 27 September 1955.

29  RPA, 001-8-20514, Procès-Verbal de la réunion des producteurs européens, 17 June 1956.

30  Archives Générales du Royaume, siège Joseph Cuvelier (AGR2), Tractionel records, file 5431, Procès Verbal de la Réunion du Comité de Direction du Syndicat Belge de l'Aluminium, 29 April 1957. RPA, 504-2-10-9660, Procès-Verbal du Comité d'AFRAL, 2 July 1956.

31  AGR2, Tractionel records, file 5438, Procès-verbal de la réunion entre le Syndacat Belge de l'Aluminium et le groupement européen, 20 March 1956. Note confidentielle – Aluminga, 6 November 1956.

32  VHS, MSS3, R3395a, Series 4, Papers of Richard Reynolds Jr., box 80, fold. 2814, Memorandum. COBEAL, 11 November 1957.

33  RPA, 504-2-10-9660, Procès-verbal du comité d'AFRAL, 3 August 1956. Procès-Verbal du comité d'AFRAL, 15 March 1957. About strategic policies of the US firms, also as regards to Africa, see Peck, *Competition in Aluminum*. Smith, *From Monopoly to Competition*.

34  VHS, MSS3, R3395a, Series 4, Papers of Richard Reynolds Jr., box 80, fold. 2814, Memorandum Aluminga. Meeting 27 September 1957 in Brussels.

35  RPA, 504-2-10-9659, de Vitry (from New York) to Matter (Pechiney), 9 September 1957. About the history of IBRD, see Michele Alacevich, *The Political Economy of the World Bank: The Early Years*. Stanford CA: Stanford University Press and the World Bank, 2009.

36  RPA, 504-2-10-9664, Procès-Verbal d'ALUGUI, 13 March 1958.

37  VHS, MSS3, R3395a, Series 4, Papers of Richard Reynolds Jr., box 80, fold. 2814, Memorandum on the meeting of Aluminga, 26 November 1956.

38  AGR2, Tractionel records, file 5827, Procès-verbal du comité restreint d'Aluminga, 2 March 1958.

39  RPA, 504-2-10-9664, Procès-verbal d'ALUGUI, 12 May 1959.

40  AGR2, Tractionel records, file 5827, Procès-verbal du comité restreint d'Aluminga, 20 January 1960. See also Willame, *Zaïre, l'épopée d'Inga*.

41  Florence Hachez-Leroy, 'Enjeux et Stratégies Internationaux dans le Secteur de l'Aluminium en Afrique (1960–2010)', in *L'Afrique Indépendante Dans Le Système International*, edited by Emilia Robin-Hivert and Georges-Henri Soutou. Paris: Presses de l'Université Paris-Sorbonne, 2012, 261–281.

42  VHS, MSS3, R3395a, Series 4, Papers of Richard Reynolds Jr., box 78, fold. 2753, Memorandum on the meeting at the executive office of the president of Defence Mobilization, 17 May 1956. Box 80, fold. 2840, Irwing Lipkowitz to Richard Reynolds Jr., 30 January 1957. About the late 1950s in the US market, see also Smith, *From Monopoly to Competition*, 311–312.

43  RPA, 001-1-4-20478. Etats-Unis. Aides d'Etat à la production d'aluminium en Amérique du Nord, 16 November 1964.

44  VHS, MSS3, R3395a, Series 4, Papers of Richard Reynolds Jr., box 84, fold. 2955, Lipkowitz, The World Market for Aluminum. An opportunity for US-Canadian Leadership, Draft, 11 November 1958.

45  RPA, 001-8-20514, Aluminium, Ententes, Réunion des produceurs européens d'aluminium à Cologne, 1 December 1955.

46  VHS, MSS3, R3395a, Series 4, Papers of Richard Reynolds Jr., box 88, fold. 3140, Irving Lipkowitz, Aluminum foreign trade notes, 3 September 1959.

47  RPA, 001-8-20514, Aluminium, Ententes, Compte rendu de la réunion des producteurs européens d'aluminium, 8 May 1958.

48  VHS, MSS3, R3395a, Series 4, Papers of Richard Reynolds Jr., box 92, fold. 3234, Irving Lipkowitz, Imports of aluminum products, statement to the committee for reprocity information, June 1960.

49  About BACO's takeover, see Perchard, *Aluminiumville*. Ludovic Cailluet, 'The British Aluminium Industry, 1945–1980s: Chronicles of a Death Foretold?' *Accounting Business and Financial History*, vol. 11, no. 1, 2001, 79–97. Also the biographies of the banker Siegmund Warburg, who helped this takeover, provided details, see for instance Jacques Attali, *Un Homme d'Influence: Sir Siegmund G-Warburg, 1902–1982.* Paris: Fayard, 1985, 377–378. Niall Fergusson, *High Financer: The Lives and the Time of Siegmund Warburg.* London: Penguin, 2010, 183–199.

50  VHS, MSS3, R3395a, Series 4, Papers of Richard Reynolds Jr., box 86, fold. 3044, Reynolds Metals, the Common Market and the Free Trade Area, 3 November 1958.

51  VHS, MSS3, R3395a, Series 4, Papers of Richard Reynolds Jr., box 87, fold. 3051, World Trade and Aluminum Industry, July 1958 (prepared by Irving Lipkowitz for AAA).

52  VHS, MSS3, R3395a, Series 4, Papers of Richard Reynolds Jr., box 84, fold. 2955, Lipkowitz, The World Market for Aluminum. An opportunity for US-Canadian Leadership, Draft, 11 November 1958. Box 88, fold. 3140, Irving Lipkowitz to Richard Reynolds Jr., 6 July 1959.

53  VHS, MSS3, R3395a, Series 4, Papers of Richard Reynolds Jr., box 83, fold. 2937, Meeting of aluminum industry with Secretary Seaton and Assistant Secretary Hardy, 2 August 1958.

54  VHS, MSS3, R3395a, Series 4, Papers of Richard Reynolds Jr., box 92, fold. 3234, US Department of Commerce special conference with the aluminum industry on the export trade programme, 16 August 1960. Fold. 3235, US Department of Commerce. Export trade promotion conference with the aluminum industry, 16 August 1960.

55  RPA, 001-8-20514, Aluminium, Ententes, Réunion des produceurs européens continentaux à Zurich, 14 February 1959.

56  RPA, 001-8-20514, Aluminium, Ententes, Réunion de travail sur le Marché commun, 23 March 1959.

57  About EWAA, see also Valérie Huré, *Les Organisations Européennes de l'Aluminium: Premiers Contacts avec des Associations à la Recherche de Leur Identité (1953–1984).* Unpublished Master Thesis, Artois University, 1996.

58  RPA, 001-8-20514, Aluminium, Ententes, Compte rendu de la réunion des producteurs du marché commun, 29 October 1959.

59  RPA, 001-8-20514, Aluminium, Ententes, Bruxelles. Réunion des 16 et 17 juin pour la détermination des droits de l'aluminium et du magnésium de la liste G, 19 June 1959.

60  Hachez-Leroy, 'La Construction Européenne'. Mathieu Ly Van Luong, 'L'Aluminium Européen'. Lucia Coppolaro, *The Making of a World Trading Power: The European Economic Community in the GATT Kennedy Round Negotiations (1963–1967)*. Farnham: Ashgate, 2013.

61  RPA, 001-8-20514, Aluminium, Ententes, Réunion des producteurs d'aluminium à Cologne, 1 December 1955.

62  RPA, 001-8-20514, Aluminium, Ententes, Réunion des producteurs à Londres, 8 May 1958. Réunion des producteurs continentaux à Zurich, 14 February 1959. CR réunion des producteurs européens, à Zurich, 6 September 1961.

63  RPA, 001-8-20514, Aluminium, Ententes, Compte-Rendu de la réunion des producteurs d'aluminium à Zurich, 23 March 1959.

64  RPA, 001-8-20514, Aluminium, Ententes, Compte Rendu de la réunion des producteurs d'aluminium à Venise, 8 May 1959.

65  AGR2, Tractionel records, file 3357, Aluminium & Electric International Limited, March 1960. RPA, 001-8-20514, Aluminium, Ententes, Réunion des members de Aluminga, Bruxelles, 22 April 1960. About Aluminium-Europe, see AGR2, Tractionel records, file 5434, Procès-verbal de la réunion du conseil d'administration de COBEAL du 28 Juillet 1961, Prise de participation dans la société Aluminium-Europe SA.

66  RPA, 001-8-20514, Aluminium, Ententes, Visite de M. Pickard des VAW à Bon par MM. Dumas et Sablé, le 5 mai 1960.

67  IHA archives, 982501IHABAZ06/14, Réunions des producteurs, Compte rendu de la réunion des producteurs d'aluminium, à Zurich, 18 April 1961.

68  VHS, MSS3, R3395a, Series 4, Papers of Richard Reynolds Jr., box 96, fold. 3394, Aluminum Association, Increasing Free World Production. An Aluminum Industry Report, 15 August 1961.

69  VHS, MSS3, R3395a, Series 4, Papers of Richard Reynolds Jr., box 109, fold. 3753, The stockpile story, 1964.

70  VHS, MSS3, R3395a, Series 4, Papers of Richard Reynolds Jr., box 99, fold. 3450, Irving Lipkowitz, A program for more aluminum consumption, 17 January 1961. About UN study groups, see UNCTAD, *Intergovernmental Producer–Consumer Cooperation in Commodities in mid 1990s: A Handbook on International Commodity Agreements, Arrangements and Study Groups*. Geneva: United Nations Doc. UNCTAD/ITCD/COM/11, 1998.

71  VHS, MSS3, R3395a, Series 4, Papers of Richard Reynolds Jr., box 107, fold. 3684, Aluminum Export Development Association, 10 September 1961.

72  RPA, 001-8-20514, Aluminium, Ententes, CR de la Conférence intetnationale sur les prix de l'aluminium à Zurich, le 14 June 1961.

73  RPA, 001-0-20516, Etats-Unis, Aluminum-Association, Consommation Croissante d'aluminium dans le monde libre. Un plan de commerce international. Rapport établi pour l'industrie de l'aluminium, 15 aout 1961. Pierre Jouven (Pechiney), Pierre Jouven, Réflexions sur le Rapport Lipkowitz, 29 December 1961. RPA, 00-8-20514, Aluminium, Ententes, Réunion des producteurs européens, 30 November 1961.

74  VHS, MSS3, R3395a, Series 4, Papers of Richard Reynolds Jr., box 96, fold. 3394, Draft letter prepeared by Irvign Lipkowitz, Re: Aluminum foreign trade programme, 14 December 1961. Aluminum Report. List of distribution, 11 December 1961. Richard Reynolds Jr. to Luther M. Holpes (Secretary of Commerce), 2 November 1961. Key facts Re: Foreign Trade Report, 1961.

75  RPA, 00-8-20514, Aluminium, Ententes, Réunion des producteurs européens, 30 November 1961. Réunions de produceurs européens, 15 February 1962.

76 Cauillet, *Stratégies*. See also Michel Beaud, Pierre Danjou, Jean David, *Une Multinationale Française : Pechiney Ugine Kuhlmann*. Paris: Seuil, 1975. Philippe Thaure, *Pechiney?... Vendu!* Paris: Presses des mines, 2007.
77 Knoepli, *From Dawn to Dusk*, 77–78.
78 Mikdashi, 'Aluminum'.
79 VHS, MSS3, R3395a, Series 4, Papers of Richard Reynolds Jr., Box 83, fold. 2914, Irving Lipkowitz, Aluminum stockpile and future military consumption, 8 August 1957. Box 88, fold. 3089, Aluminum Producers Industry Advisory Committee, 27 November 1959. Box. 94, fold. 3303, Government stockpile withdrawals, 22 August 1960.
80 NARA I, Legislative papers, Senate, Report no. 1592, S. Symington, Disposal of certain materials from the national stockpile, Report to Senate, 14 June 1962.
81 VHS, MSS3, R3395a, Series 4, Papers of Richard Reynolds Jr., box 104, fold. 3626, Special industry advisory committee on aluminum stockpile disposal, 8 October 1962. Box 109, fold. 3753, Disposing of excess stockpiling materials, 11 January 1963. Executive Office of the Present. Office of the Emergency Planning, 11 July 1963.
82 NARA I, Legislative papers, RG 46, Records of the Senate, 87th Congress, Subcommittee on the national stockpile, box 637, fold. Aluminum, general, Richmond C. Coburn (Stockpile Subcommittee), Memorandum for the fils. Subj: Aluminum, 29 March 1962. Leon E. Hickman (Stockpile subcommittee) to Robert B. Anderson, 19 August 1962.
83 HHC, MSS #282, ALCOA, box 68, fold. 2, The stockpile incident, 1962. VHS, MSS3, R3395a, Series 4, Papers of Richard Reynolds Jr., box 101, fold. 3532, The Aluminum industry and the trade expansion act. For internal company use only, 21 February 1962. Box 104, fold. 3626, Maxwell M. Caskie (Reynolds Vice-President), The Stockpile and the Aluminum industry, 18 January 1963.
84 VHS, MSS3, R3395a, Series 4, Papers of Richard Reynolds Jr., box 109, fold. 3753, Memorandum meeting with Edward A. McDermott, Office of Emergency Planning, 26 April 1963.
85 European Primary Aluminium Association Archives (hereafter AEPAA), R. Utiger (BACO), The United Kingdom and the Eastern Metal Agreements, 9 November 1978.
86 VHS, MSS3, R3395a, Series 4, Papers of Richard Reynolds Jr., box 107, fold. 3700, Victor Besso (ISCO) to Milton Smith (AEC), 7 February 1963.
87 RPA, 001-8-20154, Aluminium, Ententes, Compte rendu de la réunion européenne, à Zurich – le 15 mars 1963.
88 VHS, MSS3, R3395a, Series 4, Papers of Richard Reynolds Jr., box 107, fold. 3700, Irving Lipkowitz, Aluminum Futures, 18 January 1963.
89 AHCE, BAC 56-1980, no. 194, Reunion du sous-groupe d'experts 'aluminum' du 20 juillet 1962. TNA, BT BT 258/1745, The Import of Soviet Aluminium, note no. 3, 23 August 1967; Note no. 13, The Import of Soviet Aluminium, 19 September 1967.
90 IHA archives, 982501IHABAZ06/14, Réunions des producteurs d'aluminium. Réunion de Milan, 27 October 1961. RPA, 502-1-8-51287, Aluminium, Réunions producteurs, CR de la Réunion des producteurs d'aluminium à Zurich, le 16 Janvier 1964.
91 RPA, 00-8-20514, Aluminium, Ententes, Réunion des producteurs à Zurich, 15 March 1963. Réunion internationale, à Cologne, 15 and 16 May 1963.
92 See for instance, Niklas Jensen-Eriksen, 'The Cold War in Energy Markets: British Efforts to Contain Soviet Oil Exports to Non-communist Countries 1950–1965', in *Le Petrole et la Guerre: Oil and War*, edited by Alain Bertrand. Brussels: Peter Lang, 2012, 191–208.
93 RPA, 201-6-56739, Alugate III, Pechiney, Note sur la protection des industries de l'Aluminium dans le cadre de la CEE, 21 February 1966.

94 RPA, 001-8-20514, Aluminium, Ententes, CR de la réunion des producteurs européens de l'aluminium à Cologne, les 15 et 16 mai 1963. RPA, 201-6-56740, Réunion des producteurs à Zurich, 11 March 1964.
95 RPA, 201-6-56740, Alugate III, Compte Rendu de la réunion des producteurs à Bruxelles, 4 March 1964.
96 RPA, 201-6-56739, Alugate III, Note. Accords Brandeis, 30 October 1967.
97 RPA, 201-6-56739, Alugate III, Pierre Jouven. Conversation avec Monsieur Nathaniel Davis à Londres, 5 July 1967. Olivier Bès de Berc (Pechiney), ALCOA. Visite de M. Harrison, 11 August 1967.
98 'De façon detournée sans que jamais n'apparaissent les representatns des Producteurs Américains, tant dans les négociations, que dans les accords qui pourraient etre faits, soit avec les Pays de l'Est, soit entre producteurs occidentaux pour fixer des quotas.' RPA, 201-6-56739, Alugate III, Bès de Berc. ALCOA. Visite de M. Harrison, 11 August 1967.
99 RPA, 201-6-56739, Alugate III, Pechiney, Protection douanière de l'aluminium dans la CEE. Note à Monsieur Bocquentin de G. Baudart, 25 February 1966.
100 RPA, 201-6-56739, Alugate III, Note. Accords Brandeis, 30 October 1967. RPA, 201-6-56742, Castera (Pechiney), Accords Brandeis, 27 November 1978.
101 VHS, MSS3, R3395a, Series 4, Papers of Richard Reynolds Jr., box 115, fold. 3959, Irving Lipkowitz, Aluminum Futures Trading at Comex, July 29 – August 9, 1965, 10 August 1965. Al. Futures. The first month of trading, 21 June 1965.
102 Cuff, 'Stockpile and Defense Escalation'.
103 VHS, MSS3, R3395a, Series 4, Papers of Richard Reynolds Jr., box 117, fold. 3997, Memorandum of understandings about the aluminum stockpile disposal, 22 November 1965. US Department of Commerce, BDSA Aluminum and Magnesium Division, background information Aluminum Stockpile Disposal, Conference with representations of the aluminum industry on the disposal of aluminum from government stockpile, 10 March 1965.
104 VHS, MSS3, R3395a, Series 4, Papers of Richard Reynolds Jr., box 117, fold. 3997, Richard Reynolds Jr. to George Donet, 20 May 1965.
105 RPA, 00-8-20514, Aluminium, Ententes, Pierre Jouven, Project. Association international pour l'instauration d'une concurrence loyale entre les producteurs d'aluminium, 27 September 1963.
106 RPA, 201-6-56744, Alugate, Divers, Club Jouven, Rapport du groupe de travail reuni à Zurich, le 21 mai 1964. Draft du statut: Association Internationale de l'Aluminium Brut (AIAB).
107 VHS, MSS3, R3395a, Series 4, Papers of Richard Reynolds Jr., box 103, fold. 3581, Irving Lipkowitz to Richard Reynolds Jr., 22 February 1962. OECD took the place of OEEC in 1960, when aside from the 17 European countries that benefited from the Marshall plan, also the United States and Canada were admitted in this body. See, Richard Woodward, *The Organisation for Economic Co-operation and Development (OECD)*. New York: Routledge, 2009.
108 AOCED, NF(M)64/1, Comité special des métaux non ferreux, compte rendu de la 4ème session tenue à Paris les 28 et 29 avril 1964.
109 RPA, 201-6-56744, Alugate, Divers, Messud, Statistiques aluminium brut aux Etats-Unis, 12 January 1967.
110 RPA, 201-6-56744, Alugate, Divers, Pierre Jouven. Memorandum pour la constitution d'une Association européenne des producteurs d'alminium brut, EURAL. 10 December 1964. Rapport d groupe de travail réuni à Zurich, 21 Mai 1964.
111 RPA, 201-6-56744, Alugate, Divers, Reunion des producteurs européens à Paris, 17 November 1966. Réunion des producteurs. Note sur une éventuelle publication des stocks d'aluminium brut, 1 March 1967.
112 RPA, 201-6-56744, Alugate, Divers, Réunion des producteurs, 23 October 1967.
113 AEPAA, Minutes of the Foundation Meeting of the European Primary Aluminium Association (EPAA), held in Düsseldorf, 11 November 1969.

# 12 The 'swan-song' of the aluminium cartel

## The end and the criminalisation of aluminium governance, 1970–1978 (1984)

During the 1970s, a more disordered evolution replaced the balance that the international aluminium industry had reached during the last phase of the 1960s thanks to the new global order established by the producers and their associations. In retrospect, we can argue that the old strategic vision of aluminium producers, which focused on price stability, was questioned by economic and legal issues. The economic conjuncture reshaped the former 'informal regulated cooperation', as we can define – amending Galambos' definition[1] – the governance that was designed during the second half of the 1960s. More robust interventions were necessary to manage the international balance between demand and supply in a critical period for the market, during which also new strategic groups of suppliers were emerging. Two main initiatives were taken during this period: the first was the creation of a world association of primary producers, the International Primary Aluminium Institute (IPAI), which virtually gathered the global output excluding the Soviet countries; the second was the settlement of a new series of agreements that implemented the previous informal international governance.[2] As we will see, not only did these measures show not to be fully consistent with the new economic conjuncture, but they also drew criticism from the European Commission that put aluminium cartelisation to an end.

As a consequence, the 1970s can be described as the 'swan-song' of the international aluminium cartel. At the same time as the aluminium industry came back to cartel-like agreements and succeeded in settling a global device for its governance, it drew the criticism of antitrust authorities that curbed them. The model of international regulation that had governed this industry since the eve of the twentieth century was seriously compromised. It would be anodyne to claim that the European Commission imposed the aluminium futures market to the old majors. Price instability already emerged when LME contracts were designed and aluminium was no longer 'different' as regards the need of the futures markets. However, the EEC action accelerated the transition to a new model of governance, which ended up making aluminium converge to the pricing structure of other – and older – non-ferrous metals. At the same time as LME declared its will to force the majors' resilience to start a futures markets, the antitrust division of the European Commission (DG IV) sent a dossier of over 200 pages to all the European aluminium producers in which it claimed their guilt for the infringement of articles 85 and 86 of the

Treaty of Rome. The European Commission focused the core of its accusation on the Brandeis agreements and on the decennial boycott that the aluminium producers gave to LME.[3] This trial, which is referred as 'Alugate' in the companies' archives – taking inspiration from the almost contemporary 'Watergate' – marked the definitive economic and political criticism of former international governance of the aluminium industry.

Proceeding in order, at the eve of the 1970s, the European producers were aware that their association was still perfectible in three main areas. First, the non-inclusion of European aluminium fabricators in their association appeared a serious lack to reach a full understanding of the market situation. Unlike AAA, EPAA was an assembly of only ingot producers that, even if they were integrated in fabricating utilities, were still far from the integrated structure of the US association. One of the desires that the EPAA members expressed since its foundation meeting was to help the creation of a European Aluminium Federation (EAF), in which also fabricators and secondary producers were members. Second, the statistical organisation of the European producers was considered to be lacking key figures to understand the actual market situation and to forecast the future. Effective international governance would have requested a clear vision, not only about the current supply/demand situation, but also about the future expansion of capacities in order to programme expansion and operating rates. A five-year outlook would have been necessary to provide a general harmonisation of the future balance. Third, it was recognised that it would have been of utmost importance to be able to continue a federation with AAA, in order to arrive at the creation of an Aluminium World Council (AWC).[4]

From its inception in 1969 and until 1972, EPAA tried to deal with these three issues, which required much energy from its members. Its members considered EPAA as a step towards the creation of EAF that would have followed the model of AAA. CIDA suggested an exploratory meeting in 1970 with EPAA, EWAA, OEA (the Organisation Européenne des Affineurs), and AFCO (Aluminium Foils Conference), in order to bridge the primary producers with the associations of the fabricators of finished and semi-finished goods. These associations were born after the Second World War and, differently from EPAA, their membership was very large, due to the relative bigger number but smaller size of their members. However, since many members of EPAA were also members of the other associations through their integrated fabricators, this action was not considered too problematic.[5] In spite of this belief, the creation of EAF was procrastinated by the strong refusal of OEA, by the attitude of AFCO, which expressed its desire to wait before entering the new association, and by CIDA's will to keep its autonomy vis-à-vis the new association in order to keep economic and technical activities separate. As seen, CIDA's semi-official feature, which was derived by its recognition within OECD, was judged essential to settle a dialogue with the US producers. This fact showed a real dilemma: until AWC was not settled, CIDA was necessary to the producers' governance; however, the existence of CIDA was a main threat for the creation of EAF which, in its turn, would have led to the creation of AWC. As a consequence, in spite of the initial opinion of the EPAA members, its creation did not help the 'federation' with fabricated and secondary branches. The idea to create EAF was abandoned, while the economic crisis made the producers concentrate on other issues.[6]

At the beginning of 1970, the producers observed a dramatic change in market conditions. An abrupt slowdown broke the ongoing trend of growth, which pro-voked an uprising tendency of the accumulation of unsold inventories in the hands of the producers. As it was reported in the minutes of an EPAA meeting,

> The economic slowing down taken place in many countries necessitates a caution and reserved attitude ... The aluminium industry, for the time being only in the USA, is forced to production cut-backs which for 1971 have to be taken into consideration for Europe, too.[7]

In order to be more consistent with the changing economic situation, EPAA created an ad hoc statistical committee, which was also in charge of gathering figures on capacities, expansion, and integrated inventories in its studies, focusing on better comprehension of the industry's future evolution. This action was undertaken because the economic crisis completely changed the aluminium industry's situation, having a very bad impact on prices, which was considered 'catastrophic' at the beginning of 1971. During the previous years, aluminium demand grew 9–10 per cent on average – as producers have observed in their meeting since the 1950s; in the early 1970s the situation was more complex and the old method undertaken by the Club to control the balance between demand and supply was no longer effective. Actually, still at the end 1970, EPAA was convinced that during 1971 growth would be reduced to 6–7 per cent; at the beginning of 1971, it became clear that the actual rate growth for 1971 was next to zero. According to the minutes of the meeting held at the beginning of 1971, implementation of the statistic work of the association was of utmost importance for aluminium industrial cooperation. In fact

> Due to the growth rate of 1970 being below the 9% decennial trend and that one of 1971 being probably also below that trend the statistical experts have used two hypotheses for 1972: a) return to the trend in one year (which shows the maximum) and b) to return to the trend in two years (which shows the minimum). It is pointed out that all these figures can only give indications for future decision. [It is] asked to provide the EPAA-Secretariat with the real production and expansion data. It is being suggested to issue the statistics quarterly in order to keep the producers up to date all the time.[8]

The sharing of data that was obtained at the end of the 1960s was not sufficient to implement more consistent cooperation in this market situation because it did not provide an actual understanding of the market situation. Inventories and expansion programmes were recognised as key to understand the market trend, which was no longer easily forecast with the 9–10 per cent growth formula, which characterised the past development of this industry. At the beginning of 1970, there was a kind of 'statistical' war about the forecast of the market trend. It was not only EPAA that tried to understand the actual direction of the market, but also some financial-broker experts, such as Stewart R. Spector of Oppenheimer & Co who started to compile his own forecast about the trend in the early 1970s.[9] This penetration in the forecast debate was perceived as a risk by the producers, which aimed to keep 'figures compiled by the aluminium producers themselves'.[10] The implementation of an in-house forecast activity, however, was not easily achieved. Europeans alone could not understand the actual trend but the US association was not in a position to share data to implement a five-year outlook, because of US antitrust law. As a consequence, AAA was not able to follow its European counterpart in such an operation, even though it already shared past data.[11] The institutional creativity that led to the creation of EPAA proved to be neither useful for immediate implementation of a European association with non-integrated fabricators, nor to serve as a definitive merger with the Americans. While the creation of a new world association was not easily achieved, the producers explored the possibility of carrying out some joint action to tackle the tight economic conjuncture. Some implementations were taken at the end of 1970, when for the first time an alarming market situation was observed.[12]

## Underpinning the balance between supply and demand: new and old agreements

At the eve of the 1970s, the historical producers had the perception that, in spite of the market crisis, aluminium was still far from being an 'old metal' with a stable consumption. Coordination of investments, operation rates, and consumption was indeed still necessary to achieve an ordered development and to keep price stability. As a consequence, transitional actions should be elaborated to cope with the business cycle that was slowing down the decennial progress of global demand for this metal. In spite of the abrupt recession that was observed in 1971 and 1972, when aluminium demand interrupted its decennial growth, the producers believed that from 1973 demand would again reach the former growth of 9–10 per cent per year. In this context, where possible, the producers aimed to put on hold ongoing investments launched at the end of the 1960s. Also, reduction of production was debated: US producers already announced an output reduction of 20 per cent during the crisis and the Europeans in turn judged a reduction as opportune. However, in January 1971, in the board of EPAA the idea to create a specific tool to cope with the tight economic conjuncture was debated. Michel Castera (Pechiney) and John Wonlich (Alusuisse) proposed to the EPAA board to 'freeze' inventory excesses as an alternative to severe reductions. From this insight, some months later a new company called Alufinance was born.[13]

Despite its importance for the European aluminium industry, Alufinance is almost unknown to scholarship. Its existence was quoted only by a few studies, which often labelled it as a mere 'cartel', providing only little information about its history, about the way in which it operated, and about its achievements.[14] In fact, even though Alufinance was theoretically similar to Alliance (acting on inventories to balance demand and supply), this stock scheme had some specific particularities that made it very different from the cartel of the 1930s. Alufinance was created in a more hostile situation for cartels: according to scholarship, the

1970s coincided with the enforcement of European antitrust law and with the first real attempts to regulate the cartelisation of the European economy.[15] Edward Kane also insightfully suggested that regulatory restraints were a central cause of innovation and creation in finance.[16] Even if Alufinance clearly supported this insight, it was not only a smart device to save the producers from antitrust consequences. The idea to 'freeze' inventories was also a key idea to keep output running in a period of market incertitude and an utmost tool to indirectly serve the strategy of price stability. In the post-war era, stock buffering schemes were often recognised as essential tools to govern commodities providing price stability and, consequently, to control inflation.[17] Alufinance can be read also in the mirror of this general governance in commodities.

A further aspect led to a system to control the surplus of stock. In the specific case of aluminium, a huge quantity of inventories could have questioned price stability as a whole again. As we have seen, since the early 1960s, the proposal to set a futures market for aluminium was resumed several times: both the American and European producers opposed a strong refusal to this eventuality. An excess of inventory in 1971 re-opened the door to the eventuality of launching aluminium contracts at LME. As a consequence, Alufinance was essential to hamper any action of LME.[18] During 1971, the producers set in detail the company that initially was drafted as Alustock and then took the name of Alufinance & Trade Limited. The idea expressed in its first draft was to create a collective 'cushion' of stock between production and the market. The control over these inventories had to be carried out with a mechanism of warrants to be financed with bank loans, which the producers aimed to gather collectively. This collective mechanism would have obliged the producers, even the weaker ones, to warrant the excess of stock instead of selling it on the market. The collective action on inventories was crafted to redress the market situation, working positively on price levels without serious cuts of production.[19]

In spite of these theoretical insights, three main issues alarmed the producers as regards the feasibility of this project. The first was represented by the funds required to carry it out. In particular, a single bank was not able to provide the funds required to freeze inventory surpluses, which were evaluated to an extent of 200,000 tons by the European producers in early 1971. The second was represented by European antitrust laws, which did not allow this scheme without significant modifications. According to European antitrust law, producers had not the right to arrange collective action in terms of stock behaviour, production restrictions, and price fixing. Finally, the relative small number of firms involved risked reducing the effectiveness of the scheme. Actually, the production of historical European producers that endorsed Alufinance represented only a little part of global output.[20] Warburg was called to play the key role of drafter, like it did during the settlement of the first Brandeis agreement, when its subsidiary Brandeis Goldschmidt bridged Soviet suppliers with Western producers. In the second half of the 1960s, SG Warburg and Co. (SGW) also became a leading actor in the eurodollar capital market and an innovative institution in the creation of 'flat rate' financial facilities. In this double role of European middleman and financial innovator, SGW was involved in the settlement of the scheme that, according to the original ideas expressed by European producers, should have patched all the troubles outlined above. The implication of SGW was considered essential to transform the idea of cartel outlined by Alufinance into a firm able both to raise the money for its operations and to pledge against anti-trust authorities.[21]

During the first months of 1971, SGW proposed to arrange Alufinance as a mere financial organisation in which some banks were the preferred shareholders that owned its control. Producers appeared only as 'deferred shareholders' and the shares that each producer owned were proportional to the loans provided by Alufinance (see Table 12.1). SGW succeed in involving in the scheme the main financial backers of producers: Crédit Lyonnais, Société Générale, Deutsche Bank, Crédit Suisse, Lloyds, and Commerzbank.[22] SGW's idea was to create a consortium of banks to pool the finance facilities and to offer them to the producers on a bilateral basis.[23] Another intuition provided by SGW was to set Alufinance as a Jersey holding company. The ability to gather capital for SGW was due to the privileged access to the eurodollar market of the City of London. According to SGW, a pool of banks could have obtained up to 100 million eurodollars with ease. British anti-trust laws were considered stricter than the EEC's, and this fact allowed avoidance of the registration of Alufinance in London. The island of Jersey, still being in the sterling area, provided good access to the eurodollar markets and it was also cheap in terms of fees for registration and taxes. Actually, Alufinance was then registered at Saint-Helier, Jersey, in May 1971 by SGW and two other affiliated companies, Nutraco Nominees Co. Limited and Seligman Trust.[24]

From the standpoint of functioning, Alufinance provided financial facilities to its members, according to the decisions taken by the consultative committee and endorsed by its board. It decided to make free the choice about either to warrant or to buy the metal with the obligation to resale after a certain period. The important aspect of Alufinance's mechanism was that it indirectly aimed to fix a price: the selling price to Alufinance or the value of each ton warranted with Alufinance's

Table 12.1 The evolution of 'deferred' shares of Alufinance

|  | 1971 | | 1975 | | 1977 | |
|---|---|---|---|---|---|---|
|  | Shares | % | Shares | % | Shares | % |
| Alusuisse | 149,171 | 33.15 | 161,202 | 35.83 | 234,488 | 39.08 |
| Pechiney | 124,309 | 27.63 | 107,467 | 23.88 | 104,188 | 17.36 |
| VAW | 74,586 | 16.57 | 74,586 | 16.57 | 74,518 | 12.43 |
| BACO | 59,669 | 13.26 | 64,480 | 14.33 | 52,093 | 8.68 |
| Alumetal | 19,889 | 4.42 | 19,889 | 4.42 | 23,440 | 3.90 |
| Giulini | 9,945 | 2.21 | 9,945 | 2.21 | 9,945 | 1.66 |
| VMR | 9,945 | 2.21 | 9,945 | 2.21 | 19,015 | 3.17 |
| Holland Aluminium | 2,486 | 0.55 | 2,486 | 0.55 | 26,047 | 4.34 |
| Årdal og Sundal | – | – | – | – | 38,030 | 6.34 |
| Swenska-Granges | – | – | – | – | 18,236 | 3.04 |
| Total | 450,000 | 100.00 | 450,000 | 100.00 | 600,000 | 100.00 |

Source: author's elaboration from various files in RPA, ACL, and AHCE.

facilities were based on the 'ALCAN export price'. All revolving facilities provided by Alufinance were based on a buying price equal to ALCAN's export list price minus 10 per cent and to be resold at 100 per cent. As a consequence, Alufinance's goal was to stabilise the price around ALCAN's, supporting the effectiveness of producers' list price in the market quotations.[25] SGW suggested introducing some 'viscosity' in the mechanism thanks to the application of a fee to be paid in case of non-use of the facility proposed by Alufinance to its members.[26] However, after its settlement, some anxieties still persisted. In particular, the European producers that had conceived Alufinance also tried to involve some North American producers in their scheme, in particular ALCAN and Kaiser (both members of the EPAA because of the productive units in Europe), some marginal producers in Europe, and also some Japanese companies.[27]

In spite of this specific construction of the scheme, many firms that enquired about participation in Alufinance refused to enter its capital. Actually, the Japanese and some Norwegian companies refused to enter the scheme because their respective governments settled public stockpiling schemes to cope with the economic depression. North Americans, in particular ALCAN, announced not to be willing to enter the scheme for the fear of antitrust persecutions, but it informed European producers to continue its stability in prices and to cut 20 per cent off production during 1971. As a consequence of these refusals, the scheme was launched on a smaller scale than initially expected. Their members were Alusuisse, Pechiney, VAW, BACO, Alumetal (the aluminium subsidiary of Montecatini-Edison), Giulini, VMR, and Holland Aluminium. These last three companies took only a very marginal facility. SGW gathered 100 million eurodollars that, lent on a revolving basis to producers for a duration of three years, were judged as sufficient to control about 90,000 tons. The effects of Alufinance on the European aluminium industry are shown in Figure 12.1: Alufinance drastically reduced the producers' stock during the most dramatic moments of the international conjuncture, reducing the financial burden to handle them.[28] These financial facilities, expiring after three years, were renewed in 1974, 1976, and 1978.

Alufinance was the kernel of the price stability policy of the European producers during the 1970s, but its weak points led the European producers to implement their policies with other action. Two other initiatives were undertaken to save price stability. First, in 1972, the European producers formed an 'open price system' called IFTRA (International Fair Trade Practice Rules Administration for Primary Aluminium). Its shareholders were, apart from the members of Alufinance, also ALCAN, Kaiser Preussag Aluminium GmbH, Metallgesellschaft, which in the meanwhile had re-entered the aluminium business, ALNORD, Årdal og Sundal A/S, Elkem Huset, ENDASA, Riotinto Zinc Pillar LTD (RTZ), which in the meanwhile entered the aluminium industry, and ALSAR Industria dell'Alluminio in Sardinia (Italy). IFTRA was conceived to share information about production costs and set 'private' anti-dumping rules to cope with low prices provoked by the international slowdown of sales. The key idea behind IFTRA was to obtain information about costs and prices from those producers that were not members of Alufinance to prevent sales below their production costs.[29] Second, Pechiney proposed to the other members of EPAA to

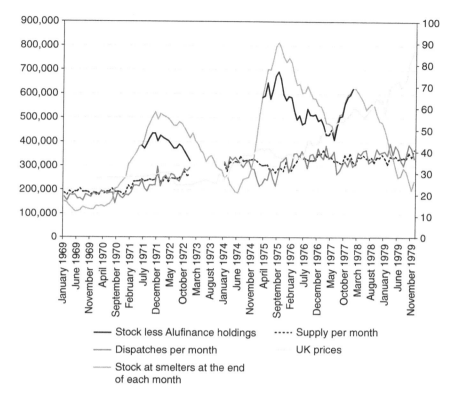

*Figure 12.1* European Primary Aluminium Association, 1969–1979: supply, dispatch, stock
at smelters, and Alufinance's holdings (metric tons and UK prices) (*Metal Bulletin*'s other quotation monthly average £ per ton).

Note
Data are lacking (about Alufinance's stock and European supply and dispatch) for 1973.

create a further organism that would work in tandem with Alufinance to implement global governance of the aluminium industry. The producers recognised
that, in order to harmonise the current global supply/demand balance, a more or
less stable system of swaps should be introduced as well. The main idea was to
create a kind of 'bank of metal' that, owning a reserve of aluminium, would be in
the position to lend and lease metal. During 1972 and 1973 the producers
debated the possibility of creating a new firm, called Aluleasing to handle aluminium swaps among them. This project turned out to be impracticable from an
antitrust standpoint and was never implemented.[30]

The management of the balance between demand and supply also asked a
tough redefinition of the external supplies that were the kernel of governance in
the late 1960s. On the one hand, the European producers defined new clauses in
the Brandeis agreement with the suppliers of the Soviet countries in order to
reduce the entry of Eastern metal in the European market (see Table 12.2 for the

Table 12.2 The evolution of the Brandeis agreements, 1970–1976: quotas of the participants in metric tons

| | 1970 | 1971 | 1972 | 1973 | 1974 | 1975 | 1976* |
|---|---|---|---|---|---|---|---|
| Pechiney | 18,785 | 19,670 | 16,780 | 21,595 | 14,145 | 10,095 | 7,320 |
| ALCAN | 14,385** | 12,810 | 11,650 | 14,260 | 9,325 | 8,815 | 6,330 |
| Alusuisse | 12,700 | 13,800 | 12,514 | 14,530 | 11,280 | 11,090 | 6,600 |
| VAW | 9,180 | 8,870 | 7,665 | 9,385 | 6,420 | 5,685 | 3,970 |
| BACO | 6,695*** | 5,490*** | 5,605*** | 6,080*** | 2,765 | 3,040 | 2,830 |
| Elkem | 5,060**** | 5,440**** | 5,095**** | 4,305**** | 3,505**** | 3,365**** | 2,325 |
| Årdal og Sundal | 4,825 | 6,300 | 5,205 | 7,340 | 4,565 | 4,755 | 3,040 |
| Endasa | 4,210 | 4,110 | 2,570 | 3,320 | 2,415 | 2,270 | 2,025 |
| Alugasa | – | – | 1,738 | 2,240 | 2,005 | 1,880 | 1,475 |
| Alumetal | 3,680 | 3,510 | 3,035 | 4,070 | 5,480 | 2,995 | 1,750 |
| VMR | 3,200 | 3,090 | 2,495 | 3,085 | 2,270 | 2,015 | 1,245 |
| Svenska-Grange | 2,775 | 2,870 | 2,170 | 2,945 | 2,035 | 1,970 | 1,230 |
| Norsk Hydro-ALNOR | 2,385 | 2,190 | 1,813 | 2,485 | 1,795 | 1,675 | 1,260 |
| Holland AL.-ALUMINED | 1,580 | 2,140 | 1,695 | 2,100 | 2,120 | 2,415 | 1,870 |
| Giulini | 1,240 | 600 | 580 | 470 | 710 | 1,135 | 825 |
| Reynolds | | | | | 2,495 | 2,320 | – |
| Metallgesellschaft | – | 1,160 | 725 | 795 | 405 | 1,420 | 685 |
| Kaiser-Preussag | – | 1,540 | 1,813 | 1,540 | 2,035 | 1,880 | 1,220 |
| Nippon Light Metals | 4,800 | 7,100 | 6,260 | 7,565 | 5,735 | 5,180 | 4,000 |
| Total | 95,200 | 100,690 | 89,408 | 108,110 | 81,505 | 74,000 | 50,000 |

Source: author's elaboration from various files in RPA, AHCE, and AEPAA.

Note

* 6 months; ** including Kaiser's quota; *** including Reynolds' quota; **** including ALCOA's quota.

new quotas of the Brandeis agreements during the 1970s, and Table 12.3 later in the chapter, for their impact on global balance). The European producers obtained the inclusion of new Eastern suppliers into the Brandeis agreement, such as Romania, and also included aluminium from scrap in the agreement. Also the specific clause about non-delivery to LME was confirmed, due to the tight market situation that would have resumed the proposal about a futures market.[31] On the other hand, the US producers discussed stockpile disposal again with the government to harmonise the reduction of output with sales from the national stockpile. Since the 1970s, they obtained some important derogations to the memorandum of understanding that was agreed between the US government and producers in 1967. In 1971, it was decided to pause the disposal of the stockpile because, if continued, it would have a 'ripple effect' on the US aluminium industry, which was already affected by overcapacity and cutbacks.[32]

## The political embedment of cooperation: OECD study group and IPAI

In spite of these practical measures, the European producers recognised that the imbalance between demand and supply was the outcome of an institutional lack in the aluminium industry. The impossibility of creating a study group with the North American producers to share present and future key figures about their industry was considered a serious danger that burdened the equilibrate evolution of the aluminium business. Moreover, during the 1970s, many new producing countries came on stream, eroding the historical control that the international oligopoly had over the global aluminium market. In the early 1970s, there was a new bulk of producing countries that were entering the aluminium industry, such as Australia, Argentina, Bahrain, Brazil, Egypt, Ghana, Iran, India, New Zealand, and Turkey. Many studies already showed the deep transformation that, since the 1970s, hit the international aluminium industry, asking for a global restructuring of production also as a consequence of the oil shocks and of the changing patterns of the global situation.[33] Here, it is claimed that, along with this transformation, the primary aluminium producers tried to adapt their governance with new tools that aimed, at least in part, to save the long-run strategy of price stability.

Unlike the 1960s, when the geographical expansion of aluminium producers was controlled by the majors such as in Greece, where Pechiney and Reynolds formed a new integrated unit,[34] and the Netherlands, where a new integrated industry was created to follow the European growth of consumption first by Alusuisse and then by Pechiney,[35] many of the new entrants of the 1970s were non-integrated producers that came from countries that were far from the principal outlets. Only in a few cases, did the historical producers have control over these new entrants; most of them were under the control of national political powers, which aimed to invest in the aluminium industry following balance of payments considerations. Even though the majors often provided the technology, they were not in a position to control these new entrants. As regards these projects, the majors did not offer resistance because, on the one hand, they were not able to block this action and, on the other hand, they preferred to exploit the situation both to increase global production without the burden of financing it and to diversify their earnings through the selling of technology. While these considerations were optimal at the end of the 1960s, when global demand was still increasing at impressive rates, the new slumps of the 1970s seriously questioned them. This trend towards a disordered fulfilment of new capacities was worsened by a series of investments that were made in the old producing countries to reduce imports, such as in Germany and UK, where also new entrants were encouraged (such as Metallgesellschaft, Reynolds, and Kaiser in Germany and Rio Tinto Zinc Pillar and ALCAN in the UK)[36] or to provide a solid basis to national economic development, such as in Norway.[37]

Carmine Nappi has already pointed out that this transformation broke the unity of the strategic group of aluminium producers and it was one of the main long-run causes of the end of price stability. While the historical producers were interested in an ordered development of their industry, the new entrants did not have the same strategic vision of the old producers. Even though the 'big six', as the first six producers were often called in the specialised press (ALCOA, ALCAN, Reynolds, Kaiser, Pechiney, and Alusuisse), strongly controlled about the 73 per cent of the global output in 1972, many marginal producers were starting to erode their market shares during the 1970s.[38] One possible way to manage the new situation would have been the quick settlement of a global association able to gather all the producing countries, and the new entrants of the aluminium industry. While it was impossible to continue with the creation of AWC simply merging the European associations and federating them with AAA, the European producers recognised that more room was necessary on the primary production level to help both the dialogue with the Americans and with the new wave of producers. EPAA aimed to settle a Commission for market analysis to help producers make decisions, even though it was recognised that 'the adaptation of production to consumption requires individual and autonomous decisions of the different producers'.[39] In order to support this action, also some recommendations should have been diffused to the new entrants in order to adjust the balance between demand and supply. Thanks to VAW's official German government démarche, EPAA producers succeeded in summoning a special study group on aluminium at OECD at the end of 1971, which the producers aimed to use to coordinate global reduction of output to balance the demand/supply situation.[40]

This solution, prospected through the special study group at OECD, was conceived as the optimal way to cope with the need of industrial coordination during market difficulty. As was recognised in the board of EPAA:

> Cutbacks alone will not do for the recovery of the industry. Even Alufinance can offer only partial help. All smelters interested in obtaining a reasonable aluminium price in the near future will have to make up their mind whether they should renounce to build any new aluminium smelting plants throughout a three years period and abstain from selling know-how for smelters and refrain from concluding long-term delivery contracts below their list prices.[41]

OECD seemed to the aluminium producers to be the perfect place in which both to find cooperation between the European and American firms and to spread some governance to the countries that were outside the producers' network. In a phase in which new producers, which lay outside the strategic group of the old aluminium firms, entered the aluminium business, this operation was considered necessary to bring back some market order. It was also considered necessary in the long run, when the relative power of the old firms would decrease. Actually, without global coordination of the balance between demand and supply, the cut-backs both that the US producers announced and that the Europeans already explored in support of their stockpiling strategy would not be effective to provide actual governance to the aluminium industry. New non-integrated producers from Asia, the Persian Gulf, and South America risked taking profit from the cut-backs made by the historical producers, which felt 'devoir supporter les effort supplémentaires de réduction de capacité et de stockage nécessaire à l'équilibre du marché'. Actually, new producers, such as the ones from Iran (Barheim) and New Zealand (Comalco), recently formed by Rio Tinto Zinc to exploit Australian bauxite, were considered particularly dangerous, because they showed the desire to 'vendre à tout prix [sell at any price]' to take part in the international market.[42]

OECD could provide some help to find overall governance for this industry. OECD was actually in the phase of a strong enlargement of its membership and it was proving to be a key and reliable tool for international economic govern-ance.[43] Moreover, the aluminium producers wanted to use the political and eco-nomic authority of OECD to make their overall cooperation embedded. At OECD, the special study group on aluminium was set in 1972 and worked until 1978, after being resumed at the end of its first (1973) and second (1975) man-dates. This study group became controlled by the primary producers, which were able to coordinate the action of output restriction at the global level, exchanging information about the global situation.[44] Pechiney also volunteered an activity of coordination among the European producers, in order to provide a consistent argumentation about the general situation of the international aluminium indus-try, which was considered necessary to drive the recommendations of the study group. The so-called 'Comité Poincaré', which took the name from the Pechiney director who organised a reunion with VAW, Montecatini, Alusuisse, and BACO to discuss a common position towards the OECD, agreed to show the actions made within the EPAA, such as Alufinance and a voluntary reduction to 80 per cent of output, as optimal solutions. It also established discussion, within the OECD study group, of the settlement of some anti-dumping measures.[45]

The OECD study group made some aligned with the visions of the producers in order to delay the launch of new capacities, suggesting the reduction of existent output to 80 per cent, following the example of the European and American industries, and also supported the idea that prices below 24 ¢/lb should be con-sidered as dumping. Actually, an official declaration by David Culver, chairman of ALCAN, reported that the production cost of a new smelter was about equal to this price in 1971, while Spector reported that it was about 22 in the most effi-cient units where investments had already been written off. The report of OECD also recommended the adoption of Alufinance as a model to cope with the crisis and save both labour and price stability. In particular, the aluminium study group identified as the main causes of the current market situation the over-investments that resulted from governmental aids and from the too easy sharing of technology of the aluminium multinationals, and suggested refraining from new investments until 1975 and to create, in the meanwhile, a true international cooperation to share information about rate utilisation, prices, and inventories. The OECD aluminium study group also alerted the governments of the producing countries that, instead of national commercial protection, the industry should have again found international balanced development through the achievement of complete trade liberalisation, offering again Lipkowitz's report's ideas.[46] Many of these recommendations, including claims about the benefit of Alufinance and about the negative influence of governments, were also reported in the official publication that came from the OECD's Aluminium Working Party.[47]

One of the main achievements of the study group summoned at OECD was the move forward to the creation of a world association for the aluminium primary producers, which would not operate under the pressure of emergency, but which would manage the evolution of the balance between demand and supply on a regular basis. One of the key ideas of the European producers, while they managed a common front at the OECD study group, was that only a new global study group would be able avoid new imbalances in the future, but that any global cooperation was not feasible because of the different antitrust laws that hampered 'true' cooperation. Also, the opening of trade, derived from the GATT new tariff, which in 1971 lowered the CET, and the prospect that the UK would enter the EEC, proved to the firms that a new transnational board should have replaced the old governance, creating a tool to settle a global 'last-resort' balance. As reported in a memorandum shared by the European producers, 'il faut créer un outil de concertation vraiment mondial, sous l'égide de l'ONU par example, pour éviter de législations anti-entente'.[48]

While in the late 1960s, the informal association of the US and European producers was judged as sufficient, in the new context an organisation as large as possible could have, on the one hand, provided a more effective governance that also included the new entrants to the industry both in the old lands of aluminium producers (such as in UK and Germany) and in the new countries (such as in Asia, Persian Gulf, and Oceania), and on the other hand would provide some 'safe' tool to coordinate action without fear of antitrust persecution. The initiative taken at OECD offered this occasion. Actually, in the OECD meetings, John Wonlich (CEO of Alusuisse) and Irving Lipkowitz (AAA) played a key role in the settlement of the aluminium industry's future governance. While Wonlich claimed the necessity to redress the world situation through the settlement of a permanent committee of aluminium producers, and did not exclude the desirability to settle even some gentlemen's agreements on price to cope with the global crisis and to extend the activity of Alufinance outside the European Community,[49] Lipkowitz clearly pointed out the main problem that lay behind their action:

> The health of the industry, in each country, depends on supply and demand being in reasonable balance both internationally and domestically … In view of the consequences of over-expansion during the late Fifties and during the past few years, both government and industry should take extra precaution against it happening again.[50]

The only way to achieve this goal was to create an institution that was authorised to gather global data about the evolution of the aluminium industry. A few months after the first meeting at OECD, the International Primary Aluminium Institute (IPAI) was announced in London as the direct outcome of the OECD working party.[51] Since the initial meetings held in Paris at OECD, the settlement of such an institution requested thorough statistical work to gather consistent data from all the producers. IPAI's methods were different from the ones of EPAA. While EPAA recreated a statistical committee similar to those of the pre-war cartels (sharing of data about production, sales, stock, and capacity of each firm), this operation was judged not safe from an antitrust standpoint by the American producers. As a consequence, IPAI was created as a 'confederation' of regional trade associations and of their data. A lawyer from the leading global law firm White and Case, who served as legal consultant during the settlement of IPAI, suggested that the works of IPAI should not include the data of each member in order to be legally safe. Instead, 'statistics should be in general form, preferably dealing with the industry as a whole'. He also suggested that these data should be made available to the public generally. Also the idea to include in IPAI's data the future capacity of production was judged as potentially dangerous because 'the case in the US in this area indicate that statistical forecast of future production, especially in concentrated industries, will be subject to vigorous scrutiny'.[52]

Pierre Jouven, the CEO of Pechiney, played a key role in leading the producers to the settlement of IPAI. As recalled, he was the first manager of the 'new guard' who claimed already in 1963 the need to move towards a global association for primary aluminium. During the settlement the OECD aluminium working party, he led the construction of the new world organisation, claiming the necessity to create a working committee on statistics as soon as possible, to work out a practical solution to cope with the misunderstanding of the market situation. This committee was in charge studying the situation in order to cope with both economic and legal issues linked to the creation of a global database of figures for this industry. The practical solution for these issues was the creation of a corpus of data without the figures of each firm, but with only consolidated data for each region: Asia, Europe, North America, etc. Both on the global scale and the regional level, IPAI would provide the information to define currently the supply/demand situation, including the level of stock. In spite of the need also to include forecasts on the future situation of capacities in the activity of IPAI, this aspect was left out of negotiations due to antitrust concerns. The American representatives of IPAI clearly asked that this activity was attributed to a working study of OECD.[53]

This last opinion reshaped the final institutional creation of the new tools for the governance of the international aluminium industry. On the one hand, since 1972, the working group on aluminium continued to forecast future tendencies of this industry. Several meetings were organised during the 1970s, which essentially aimed to explore the future of the aluminium industry and to make recommendations to governments. Until 1978, the OECD aluminium study group continued to represent the official place in which the evolution of future capacities was analysed by the firms' statistical experts.[54] On the other hand, the producers went ahead with the creation of IPAI. The first meeting of IPAI was officially summoned in London in September 1972 and it represented the achievement of a long institutional creation that had lasted for about 20 years. Jouven was named first president of IPAI because of his long-lasting efforts, since the beginnings of 1960s, to establish such an institution, while Peter Martyn (BACO) became the general secretary. Jouven kept this charge until his retirement in 1974 and afterward he was named 'honorary president' of this institution. At the foundation meeting in London, Nathaniel Davis (ALCAN) declared that 'many of today's problems could have been avoided by the availability of better information'. This statement clearly summed up the producers' spirit about their new organisation: they were confident that, thanks to better knowledge on the supply/demand situation, prices would be kept stable and a more rational development of the global aluminium industry would be obtained, providing real governance to this industry at the global level.[55]

In retrospect, we can define the architecture of the new governance of the international aluminium industry as a threefold action. Essentially, three organisations shared the different tasks of this governance: IPAI was the gatherer of liable information (output, stock, and deliveries) about the present situation based on nations and regions; EPAA made forecasts about demand and defined the optimal output rate to adjust supply to demand; while the Aluminium Working Party at OECD shared the forecast outside the old producers' network and was in charge of making recommendations aligned with what was debated in EPAA to governments. This patching architecture maybe did not reflect a deliberate strategy of the historical producers, but it came from a more pragmatic approach to the different economic and institutional issues. Nevertheless, this structure was the outcome of a thorough institutional creativity and adaptation to the new context. Even though its actual organisation was far different from the cartels that had been in charge of the governance of this industry before 1945, it provided optimal solutions to the new context. Practical solutions were adopted to fix legal, political, and economic problems that the governance of a global industry, such as the aluminium one, was facing during a tight recession like the one of the 1970s. The global governance of this industry proved to be reshaped by a tactical vision of the producers that, keeping price stability as a centrepiece of their approach, aimed to create the conditions to apply it on the global scale in a changing economic and institutional environment.

## International governance during the 1970s: the sunset of price stability

In spite of this institutional creativity, aluminium producers only partially achieved their goal during the 1970s and, in particular, during the second half of the decade. In 1972, these actions had still a good outcome on price stability of the global aluminium market, when a redressing of international prices was obtained to a satisfactory level after a period of very low quotations in 1971. This outcome was linked both to the work on balancing demand and supply, which was accomplished in the different fora (EPAA, IPAI, and OECD), but also by the stock cushion established with Alufinance. Most importantly, Alufinance and a kind of gospel about price stability, which was also spread through semi-official publications, succeed in depriving the LME of the material and immaterial basis to launch trade in aluminium. Throughout the 1970s, the European producers claimed on many occasions the need to hamper the creation of an aluminium futures trade at LME. In several EPAA meetings, between 1974 and 1977, they coordinated a common position in response to the pressing request and announcements that LME made to introduce aluminium into its operations.[56] However, the risk of LME was avoided also thanks to the practical solutions that the producers adopted to manage the surpluses that emerged from the balance between demand and the supply. In particular, the European firms negotiated with Soviet suppliers to boycott any initiative of LME, introducing in their contracts a 'spirit of the agreement clause', which made agreements not valid if LME started to trade.[57] Moreover, Alufinance played a key role in this action and its importance proved to be growing when, after the UK's entry into the EEC market in 1973, LME became more 'integrated' with the European metal trade. The functioning of the first revolving facility of Alufinance was used until January 1974, then credits were reimbursed to the consortium of banks at the good outlay expected by SGW. The success of Alufinance pushed its members to ask for its

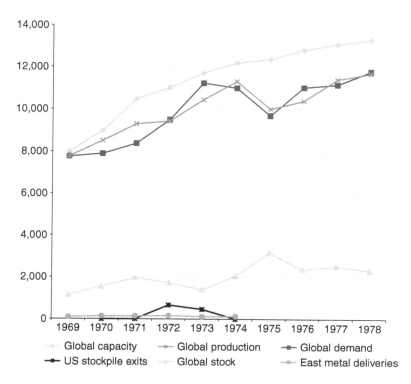

*Figure 12.2* The supply/demand balance of the global aluminium industry during the 1970s (metric tons × 1,000).

continuation after 1974 to manage the difficult situation in the 1970s, characterised by a swinging demand, monetary problems, and the general depression derived from the first oil shock of 1973.[58]

In spite of these initial achievements, during the 1970s the governance of the international aluminium industry appeared not to be as easy as foreseen. The international commodity market was revealed to be deeply affected by general instability that was due to changing energy prices, which reflected the actions of the oil cartel, OPEC, and showed the development of different boom–bust cycles during the decade.[59] These changes were not only the outcome of the changing commodity market: the oil shock also troubled the currencies market putting the stability of the Bretton Woods system to an end.[60] Actually, the 1970s was a period of crisis for commodity markets and reshaping of regulatory tools. For instance, growing preoccupations of exporting countries pushed UNCTAD to formulate a 'Common Fund' to finance stock in order to stabilise incomes. The key feature of these new regulatory schemes was direct involvement of the international financial institutions in the mechanism of stock financing, such as the World Bank and the International Monetary Fund, which were progressively involved in settlement of the Common Fund and in UNCTAD's stabilisation policies.[61] Aluminium again diverged from this trend: on the one hand, Alufinance represented a 'private' mechanism of stock financing; on the other hand, the group of aluminium producers avoided bauxite entering the official commodity governance in the north–south negotiations for a New Economic Order in this period.

Actually, in March 1974, the leading producing countries of bauxite met in Conakry, Guinea, to create the International Bauxite Association (IBA). Conceived as a raw material cartel, this association included representatives of the governments of Australia, Guinea, Guyana, Jamaica, Sierra Leone, Surinam, and Yugoslavia. The objectives announced by IBA included securing of fair and equitable returns from the exploitation of bauxite resources within the member countries and obtaining effective national control over the bauxite industries. In November of the same year, during the first meeting of the IBA held in Guyana, the Dominican Republic, Ghana, and Haiti were also admitted in the Association: the ten country members owned about 75 per cent of the global extractive capacity and 66 per cent of the world reserves of bauxite. The connection between this cartel and OPEC, the oil cartel, was twofold. First, OPEC served as a model in the strategy to impose a so-called 'New Economic Order', characterised by a more equal redistribution of wealth to the exporting countries by means of control over national resources. Second, the rise of the oil-bill, which resulted from raising prices for oil established by OPEC, led the less developed countries to adopt effective ways to improve the balance of payments.[62] In order to reduce the requests of IBA, Pechiney and ALCAN developed together an alternative process for alumina, called H+. Also the US Bureau of Mines, started a season of intense research about alternative ores resuming a technical alliance with the majors of this industry.[63]

Even though neither the firms' nor the US's initiative came to an industrial application of their research, it was recognised by a report, which the consulting agency Charles Rivers Associates compiled for AAA, that 'new techniques that would lower the cost of obtaining alumina from nonbauxitic ores would, of course, reduce the upper limits to which the cartel [IBA] could raise price'.[64] Moreover, the producers aimed not to include bauxite in the works of UNCTAD, preferring to carry out negotiations in a 'government to government relationships, similar to the OECD working party'.[65] No official records are available about the negotiations between the bauxite cartel and the aluminium producers, but primary producers effectively tamed IBA's requests during the 1970s, while UNCTAD claimed that bauxite was not included in the Common Fund's negotiations because producers and consumers found a private means of agreement. In three subsequent meetings held between 1978 and 1980, IBA agreed to link its price to the producers' list price for aluminium ingots (at the level of 2 per cent).[66] This outcome was also due to the fact that one leading member of the cartel, Australia, was not willing to raise the price too much – because it preferred to extend its production, and that the 1980s saw the creation of the largest mining centre in Porto Trombetas in Brazil, which refused to join the cartel. Yet we can formulate the hypothesis that alternative processes served in the long run as a sort of technological diplomacy, which was used to change the given international conditions of this industry as soon as it was shocked by an external factor and which bridged firms' and governments' strategies.[67]

In spite of the political embedment that covered the creation of the new network of governance and the avoidance of IBA's risks, the aluminium industry was not able to keep the former ordered balance during the 1970s. As shown by Figures 12.1 and 12.2, global overcapacity persisted during the decade, while demand was characterised by a succession of boom–bust cycles that replicated in a relative brief lapse of time the coming about of serious inventories accumulations and too fast depletions. After the first slowdown of demand in late 1970, dispatches suddenly decreased again twice during the 1970s, at the end of 1974 and during the second half of 1977. These slowdowns of demand, as in the case of the late 1970s, caused again a quick accumulation of inventories, which was even worse in 1974 and 1977 than the first crisis of 1971. During this period, also ALCAN's export price was revisited more frequently than in the past to be more consistent with rising producing costs linked to the oil shocks, with inflation, and with the actual market situation. While since 1964, international list prices staged at 24 ¢/lb, between 1972 and 1978 it changed about 20 times to adapt to monetary fluctuations, to inflation, and to the change in energy costs. Apart from this list price, other quotations became alternative barometers for this industry. For instance, *Metal Bulletin*'s 'other offers' record became – before aluminium entered the LME in October 1978 – an important barometer for market quotations, which was often considered more consistent with the actual economic situation. As shown in Figure 12.3, the producer list prices lost adherence with the actual situation of the market on many occasions.

This decline in the efficiency of producer governance reflected a double change in the international situation. On the one hand, the end of monetary stability and the swinging value of the US dollar made it more difficult for ALCAN's list price to continue to act as a real barometer for the global industry.

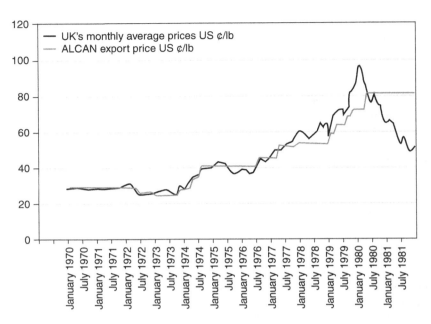

*Figure 12.3* ALCAN's export price and UK monthly average market prices during the 1970s.*

Note
* Since 1979, the UK's monthly average prices is the same as LME's.

On the other hand, periods of crisis were alternated with a great and unexpected upward trend, which many observers considered a 'pipeline' effect provoked by the consumers' need to reform their inventories after the period of crisis. In the case of aluminium, this unexpected uprising trend provoked an abrupt reversing of the situation that happened when key consumers took the decision to recharge their stock after the market slump. When the demand rose again in 1973, the producers found themselves in a critical supply situation, after cutbacks and post-ponement of new investments, they were not ready to supply the market. As a matter of fact, in 1973 and 1974 only quick disposal of the whole US stockpile saved the producers from market failure (see Table 12.3) that, it should be said, was also due to a series of strikes that hit North American production.[68] However, this positive trend was not a definitive recovery of the aluminium market: EPAA recognised that, still in 1975

> The situation is very serious and there is unlikely to be a significant improve-ment before the end of the year. 1976 should see a movement toward balance and in subsequent years a shortage of metal could emerge ... there may within a year be a 'risk' of a sharp increase in demand for aluminium as occurred in 1973, but this time there will be no stockpile to take up part of the burden.[69]

This fact reflects that EPAA was aware that it was progressively losing its capacity to make reliable forecasts about the market trend, because the new market situation was characterised by the loss of its stable rate of growth. From 1974 to 1978, EPAA tried to re-discuss its statistical work several times: a study of 'fluctuations of metal in the pipelines' was started, even though no specific solutions were found on how to handle the balance between demand and supply.[70] In 1976, the statistical committee tried to integrate the data gathered by IPAI in a better way and also debated the option of starting to use Spector's analysis as a basis in order to make better forecasts, sharing with the financial analyst some data on a quarterly basis (while EPAA worked on monthly data). EPAA also renounced continuing its five-year forecast, because it was not recognised as a reliable way to forecast, and tried to set a three-year outlook that, however, proved to be no more useful than the older five-year one. A sort of dilemma existed in the governance of the aluminium industry. While short-term forecasts always showed a critical situation, in the long-run all the forecasts claimed an insufficiency of supply. The five-year outlook was not able to predict the boom–bust cycles that aluminium was facing. In 1977, finally the EPAA statistical committee claimed the necessity to make 'changes in the statistical methods of calculating the supply and demand balance in future'.[71] Even though many attempts were made to make use of better information that had become available and to give a more accurate indication of the prospective balance, no actual solutions were found to cope with the 'pipeline effect', as the short boom of demand that followed each slump was defined.[72] For instance, in 1978, it was recognised that a big incertitude 'was post-poning the optimism from quarter to quarter'.[73]

*Table 12.3* EPAA management of the global balance between demand and supply before the mid-1970s (metric tons × 1,000)

|  | 1970 | 1971 | 1972 | 1973 | 1974 | 1975 |
|---|---|---|---|---|---|---|
| Beginning stock | 259 | 590 | 970 | 830 | 541 | 954 |
| New production | 8,066 | 8,625 | 9,188 | 10,132 | 11,082 | 9,904 |
| Stockpile disposal | 22 | – | 5 | 663 | 463 | 1 |
| Eastern bloc supply* | 140 | 140 | 160 | 120 | 125 | −195**** |
| Total supply | 8,487 | 9,355 | 10,323 | 11,745 | 12,211 | 10,668 |
| Demand | 7,897 | 8,385 | 9,493 | 11,204 | 11,257 | 8,785 |
| Working stock** | 503 | 570 | 672 | 676 | 527 | 636 |
| Closing stock | 590 | 970 | 830 | 541 | 954 | 1,883 |
| Excess | 87 | 400 | 158 | −135 | 427 | 1,247 |
| Mid-year capacity | 8,492 | 9,728 | 10,752 | 11,376 | 11,939 | 12,217 |
| Operation rate %*** | 95.0 | 88.7 | 85.5 | 89.1 | 92.8 | 81.1 |

Source: author's elaboration from various files in RPA and AEPAA.

Notes
* Data indicated as maximum to negotiate within the Brandeis agreement (actual data in Table 12.2); ** normal inventory at smelters is defined as 6% of the following year's demand; *** defined as % of mid-year 97% capacity; **** the data is negative because China imported 350,000 tons in 1975, changing the pattern of the Eastern-metal trade.

In this situation, the actual market situation made it difficult to optimise the former governance, because the market situation passed continually from a state of oversupply to one of shortage. In the board of EPAA, it was recognised that a practical solution to these troubles was the continuation of Alufinance, claiming the idea to turn this company into an ordinary tool of inter-firm cooperation during the swinging market conjuncture. Also the study group at OECD was summoned again in order to provide some recommendations and to coordinate the action of each government to cope with the new aluminium crisis and to spread the general idea that 'self-help solutions' should have been supported to help the aluminium industry find its own governance.[74] In this general market confusion, LME came again to the fore as a possible new way of governance. Since 1974, LME declared its will several times to start a futures market on aluminium. In 1977, as shown in Figure 12.3, a quick rise in stock accelerated this attempt: while the board of LME tried to implicate the UK Aluminium Federation in the definition of a contract, Phillip Brothers and Gerald Metals started to trade with metal coming from Eastern Europe exploiting the end of the Brandeis agreement, as we will see.[75] At the same time, Raynar-Harwill Ltd, a key merchant in LME's ring, started to define a futures contract for aluminium, convincing the board of LME to go ahead with the inclusion of this metal in the ring.[76] Even if EPAA, EWAA, UK Aluminium Federation, and many governments showed their opposition to the LME proposal, the Committee of LME decided to continue its operation and also found, this time, support from the Bank of England and the Board of Trade.[77]

The producers' strong refusal of a futures market did not hamper them to reconsider their governance. The great instability that was emerging was also reflected in the working of Alufinance, whose subsequent credit lines settled in 1974 and 1977 were progressively made without reference to ALCAN's list price, and each firm's production costs had been taken as basis.[78] In the new facilities, also the Swedish firm Granges Aluminium (which took over Svenska) and the Norwegian Årdal og Sundal became deferred stockholders of Alufinance. Also in the Brandeis agreements settled during 1974 and 1975, ALCAN's export price list was abandoned and a more 'flexible' price was considered as a basis for Eastern supply, building an average with the *Metal Bulletin*'s 'other transactions', along with ALCAN's price and a 'mercurial' of the other producers' national prices.[79] Alufinance was reshaped as a mere financial aid, to provide off-balance facilities to firms. In other words, while the first Alufinance was a stock cushion, its new facility became a tool to temporarily remove a portion of inventories out from the balance sheet, which improved the profitability of enterprises and their liquidity at once.[80] The producers became increasingly interested in the financial side of Alufinance, leaving aside the industrial aspects that led to this company being created. A sort of dematerialised financial working was predicted for Alufinance, which would help above all to balance the companies' financial sheets. Also monetary instability served as a changing factor to reshape Alufinance. The first Alufinance's funding were provided in US dollars, while in the second and in the third also other currencies were admitted.[81]

Alufinance still represented a practical tool to be used by the economic cycle when needed, to work out firms' financial troubles. The continuation on a regular basis of Alufinance's facilities also meant that firms progressively escaped from the mere need to regulate the flux of metal. Off-balance loans appeared as a key instrument of market regulation. Firms' profitability became progressively an utmost preoccupation, whose importance overcame the demand/supply position of the industry.[82] In this tendency we can see not only a transformation of the financial behaviour of firms, but also a progressive convergence to some regulatory options that were owned by institutional markets such as LME: providing control over stock and partially working as a stock buffer, LME was also a way to provide financial facilities on stock operations.[83] This idea was shared by many aluminium trade observers during the 1970s, the opinion of whom was that Alufinance was not too far from the tools that LME could have provided to this industry. However, as Trevor Tarring, the editor of *Metal Bulletin* underlined,

> the critical difference between Alufinance and LME warehouse stocks is of course that the industry itself had to find the interest for the financing of the stock in the case of Alufinance, whereas the market mechanism automatically provided contango financing in the case of LME.[84]

We could add that another striking difference was that Alufinance was a stabilisation device, while LME was not. As a matter of fact, LME was not an appealing mechanism for firms and the aluminium industry entered this new governance almost forced by the European Commission, whose action coincided with the start of the aluminium futures market.

## The new legal strategy, the European Commission, and LME

During the 1960s, the producers did not have a legal approach to their agreements. This strategy was thoroughly reconsidered at the beginning of the 1970s. Before periodical renewal of the Brandeis agreements, VAW expressed some perplexities about the fact that, until then, these agreements had not been notified to the EEC Commission, while the German authorities had been informed and had accepted them. The head of VAW saw in this mismatch a critical political issue, which could have damaged the continuation of the agreements. The vision of VAW was that antitrust legislation could have helped the settlement of more stable agreements with the Eastern suppliers instead of working against them in a critical market situation. It is also true that, since the German authorities, who led the legal background of EEC, had already accepted these agreements it was not difficult to expect that the Commission would have accepted them too.[85] To achieve this goal, VAW proposed to rewrite the Brandeis agreements in order to align them with current European antitrust legislation. VAW's legal expert, Dr Alexander Rudell, was in charge of the revision both of the agreement between Brandeis and Raznoimport, and of each agreement between Brandeis and Western producers. He was committed to delete all the 'restrictive clauses' from these agreements, while he suggested moving the kernel of the agreement from Brandeis' agency in London to Switzerland to stop any possible future action from the UK authorities.[86] As we outlined in the previous chapter, this choice was adopted by the producers because the UK authorities accepted this fact as the best way to support the commercial solution to the Soviet import problem.

Alexander Rudell was the designer of the whole legal strategy that was carried out by Western producers during the 1970s. He worked as chief lawyer for VAW and, since its foundation in 1969, for EPAA. He was considered one of most influential specialists in business and antitrust law in Germany, with long experience both in the Kartellamt since the interwar period (Rudell took his PhD in 1935) and at the Gesetz gegen Wettbewerbsbeschränkungen afterward. He was considered the inventor of the Open Price Systems in Europe: aside IFTRA in the aluminium industry, Rudell was also the crafter of a similar tool in the glass industry.[87] Rudell's key idea was that notification of the Brandeis agreements to the Commission would have protected these agreements because, since they were built up as short-lived contracts, they needed legal safety during the frequent renewals and negotiations. While the European firms debated this opportunity, the emergence of the international crisis extended this reflection to the other agreements that were made: Alufinance and IFTRA. Following Rudell's advice, the firms preferred to notify also these agreements because this action would have been concomitant with the OECD's study group, in which also the EEC took part and which was considered as a further guarantee of immunity. A further argument used by Rudell was to claim very good relationships with DG IV's higher officials (in the Division on Concurrence), such as Hermann Schumacher and René Jaume, and also with Ernst Albrecht, the general director in 1970, when the agreements were notified to the Commission.[88]

In the new context of the crisis, the aluminium producers formulated a specific legal strategy not to be concerned by antitrust actions or political control during this tight market context. In the three cases (Alufinance, IFTRA, and Brandeis), the producers made the decision to notify the agreements to the European Commission. According to the rules of the antitrust norms established in 1962, the notification to the Commission provided safety during inspections. In the case of Alufinance, the choice to notify corresponded to the producers' need to launch the facilities as soon as possible, because of the dramatic situation of stock, without risking legal concerns. However, the members of Alufinance also tried to show their scheme to the Commission not only as a mere financial institution, but also as a tool to keep production and, as a consequence, to save employment. For that, some meetings were organised also with the DG III (the Division of European social affairs), to which Alufinance was presented as a method to avoid general firing of aluminium workers during the crisis. The idea to conjugate the self-regulation of producers with social welfare of European countries represented an important aspect of the discourse that surrounded the construction of Alufinance.[89] Also IFTRA and the Brandeis agreements were notified to the European Commission at the same time, following the same legal and political strategy.[90]

According to Rudell, notification was designed to obtain negative clearance (*attestation négative*) that could have either protected the firms during the wait for DG IV's decision, or provided an exemption at the end of the examination. In any case, there was a good chance that it would take many years before a decision was taken, and during this lapse of time the agreements would be safe from the legal point of view. It is interesting to show the general understanding of the legal situation that the European companies believed they were facing. In an internal note that was discussed during a meeting of the producers, the problem of the notification to EEC's DG IV was presented as follows:

> The interest of the notification is twofold: it allows ... to avoid any possibility of a fine until the Commission has made a decision.... If the negative clearance could not be obtained, the use of the application of the exemption provided in paragraph 3, remains possible.... Given these uncertainties, it appears desirable ... that the project can be settled from a recommendation of the OECD. In this case, it is arguable that the European Commission would agree to grant more easily, either a negative clearance or an exemption decision and will monitor the implementation of the agreement less closely.[91]

As a consequence of this change in the legal strategy of the firms, the agreements were notified to the EEC's DG IV, in order to request a negative clearance, as in three different cases: DG IV/26870 (Brandeis agreements, registered in December 1970), DG IV/26919 (Alufinance, registered in April 1971), and DG IV/27000 (IFTRA Rules, registered in March 1972). This strategy was also focused on another issue. In the specific situation of 1970, when Alufinance was still under construction and when the OECD had not yet summoned the study group on aluminium, the legalisation of the agreements could have served to push the Americans to join these schemes. The approaching crisis was stimulating the Europeans to find official recognition of their cooperative policies also in order to involve North American producers in their schemes.[92]

However, since the mid-1970s, the legal strategy of the European producers turned out not to be as safe as Rudell had thought. Instead, it became the Achilles heel of the aluminium producers' market strategy. DG IV put on hold the examination of Alufinance, subordinating the decision on it to IFTRA and the Brandeis agreements.[93] At first, DG IV seemed to be willing to accept the principles of Brandeis as a result of personal links that Rudell had with Jaume and Schumacher.[94] However, since its notification, DG IV showed concern about IFTRA's text. The legal procedure seemed to DG IV unnecessary and this fact caused the European Commission to suspect that, behind the IFTRA, there were some other collusive practices that were hidden behind this organisation. In October 1973, DG IV sent its critical judgement on IFTRA's text and a first trial began in a general context of distrust between DG IV and the aluminium producers. According to the legal position of DG IV, the agreement was too 'right' to be true, and was judged a pretext by the producers to meet to discuss other issues, such as prices, quotas, etc.[95] In December 1973, Albert Borschette, the

EEC Commissar for concurrence,[96] publicly explained the attitude of DG IV to IFTRA and the current status of the competition policies in Europe:

> The experts at Brussels are bound to observe that the businessmen who want to 'collude' are moving away from the practice of written agreements – and fall back on forms of cooperation with general 'neutral' rules, which provided opportunities to set oral agreements. Their attention was drawn to the work of a German lawyer [Rudell], author of a kind of model contract called 'International Fair Trade Practice Rules Administration' (or IFTRA) which lists – as the name suggests – all the 'loyal' arrangements among companies, that is to say, the formulas that are not condemned by the laws, or that in any case are generally accepted. This is a dangerous device.[97]

The distrust in the IFTRA-like organisation and in its crafter, Alexander Rudell, opened a Pandora's box of EEC curiosity. Instead of accepting the opinions of Rudell, DG IV started a big trial against the European aluminium producers that lasted for about ten years. As anticipated, the European producers often referred to this long-lasting legal issue as 'Alugate'. Actually, in the accusations sent to the European producers, DG IV claimed that not only IFTRA would be inspected, but that

> la structure du marché en cause ... Il en résulte que toute restriction de concurrence convenue entre les producteurs, ou pouvant résulter de leurs accords, vient aggraver sensiblement le manque de fluidité propre à un tel marché. Or l'étude des règles IFTRA fait ressortir qu'elles ont pour objet ou pour effet une série de restrictions particulièrement manifestes.[98]

DG IV was not yet aware of the complex architecture of the aluminium cartel and each of the inter-connections of the aluminium firms became suspicious. Rudell also tried to invite DG IV commissioners to take part in the meeting of IFTRA in order to monitor its actions. In spite of Rudell's legal effort to obtain an exception for IFTRA, this request was rejected in 1975. This was only the tip of the iceberg, because at this point the Commission started to investigate the other agreements. In 1975, after inspecting the dossiers, DG IV concluded that Alufinance was only a secondary agreement (actually, the notification of this agreement had never received a reply from the Commission) and concentrated itself on Brandeis, considering these agreements as harmful to the European market for aluminium. The inspection had a bad outcome on the continuation of the Brandeis agreements and they were not renewed after the summer of 1976, opening the door to the first contracts between LME and Russian suppliers.[99] This outcome was also driven by the progressive end of price stability for aluminium as the main aftermath of monetary instability in the 1970s: the producers stated that their control over Soviet imports had became useless and they also decided to stop the agreements in order to assist the termination of their inspection.[100]

While companies decided to provide the European Commission with all the documents about the Brandeis agreements and promptly replied to several inquiries by the Commission, in order to show the 'bonne foi' that led the producers to make such agreements, the European Commission also issued a search warrant for the producers' offices at the end of 1976.[101] After three years of inspections into the companies' archives and of several questions that the producers were asked, about the working of their agreements, DG IV sent to all the European companies a consistent dossier of objections, according to which the firms were accused of infringing articles 85 and 86 of the Treaty of Rome. These accusations arrived in September 1978, a couple of weeks after the official presentation of LME's aluminium contract and a couple of weeks before its actual launch. DG IV's core argument was that the aluminium producers used the Brandeis agreements to collude on prices, to take control over important supplies that voluntarily created a situation of shortage, and, above all, to voluntarily boycott LME, colluding on collective action against it. The defensive strategy of the producers was to try to show the benefit for consumers in having stable prices and the general architecture of their governance, which supported a balanced evolution of output. In turn, DG IV well understood that the only way to impose a market economy in the aluminium industry was to help LME start a contract, ending the market management that had characterised the aluminium business until then. Between 1976 and 1978 the Bank of England and LME had drafted the working of a possible contract on aluminium and also DG IV was implicated in the drafting of these procedures, providing its full endorsement to this proposal.[102]

DG IV's action also reflected a more general political change, which was a consequence of the entry of the UK into the ECC. In the second half of the 1970s, the Board of Trade's attitude towards the political ground of Brandeis became less important than the policy that aimed to bring London back to the centre of the commodity markets. The idea to establish the aluminium contract at LME was concomitant with the idea to open gold, silver, and nickel trade as well, which would have supported the creation of a World Commodity Centre in the City to compete with New York as an international financial centre for trade operations.[103] Actually, the preparation of this project led the Zinc and Lead Study Group, the intergovernmental commission that regulated the trade of these two metals, to move from New York to London.[104] After aluminium, also nickel – another stable priced metal – entered LME in 1979 and attempts were made with silver and gold. We can formulate the hypothesis that LME's proposal for aluminium was a way to 'steal' the aluminium trade from the US dollar's influence and put it within the British – now European – sphere. This was the main reason for the Board of Trade's changing position in this matter and for the Commission's endorsement. DG IV EEC also intervened because, serving as an adviser for LME and the Bank of England during the recasting of commodity futures markets, it seized a unique possibility to intervene in the commodities trade to teach a lesson about how markets should be. In its vision, an institutional market with the key guarantees of transparency and publicity was considered the best way to fight concentration and collusive attitudes that characterised the aluminium industry. This idea is confirmed by the fact that in 1978 DG IV started five other actions, in cocoa, sugar, coffee, rubber, and grain, that ended, as aluminium, in 1985 authorising the works of their respective futures markets.[105]

Even though the Brandeis agreements had already ended when the European Commission started its inspections, DG IV decided to go on with the trial until it had a final judgement about the Eastern metal agreements and, as a consequence, about the whole experience of aluminium cartels. In December 1984, DG IV finally published its decision on the Brandeis case of Eastern metal, which was published at the beginning of 1985. Although it decided not to impose any fines on the producers, DG IV refused negative clearance (after 14 years) and declared the producers, the EPAA, and Brandeis Goldschmidt guilty of infringement of article 85, paragraph 1 of the Treaty of Rome, i.e. to have hampered competition. Amongst the motivations, the most relevant fact was declared 'the arrangements [aimed] not to make any quantity of aluminium available for trading on the London Metal Exchange, made between the foreign trade organizations and the producers, through Brandeis, and between those aluminium producers'.[106] Not only did DG IV express very critical words for the system of agreements that had governed the aluminium industry during the former decades, but the exceptions for the agreements were also refused for the specific reason that the consumers, according to DG IV, had no particular benefit from the policy of stable prices. As a consequence, the negative clearance foreseen in the cases of paragraph 3 of article 85 were not considered applicable.

LME started trading in aluminium in October 1978, but the producers continued to publish their 'price list' during the 1980s and until the publication of the Commission's decision. In particular, ALCAN and then Pechiney continued to oppose to LME their own prices, and the other producers aimed to follow this strategy hoping to discontinue LME contracts.[107] Actually, LME, during its first years, used aluminium from the Arabian region (Bahrain, Iran, and Oman) and also from Eastern Europe. After an uprising trend of prices at LME during 1979 (see Figure 12.3), some European producers started to sell aluminium through LME as well. Three years later, a sudden crisis provoked a trend of failures amongst the producers, for instance Pechiney was nationalised to escape failure while British Aluminium was absorbed by ALCAN, and they also started to sell to LME. In 1984, also ALCOA abandoned the system of list prices and, in 1985, after the publication of DG IV's decision, ALCAN stopped publishing its 'export price', which since the 1950s had served as a barometer for this industry.[108] Consequently, if the opening of the Eastern aluminium case served to support the launching of aluminium contracts, the decision of DG IV worked as a final watershed for the last resilience to LME: it condemned the whole former experience, hampering the resurgence of any 'producer list price' and of any cooperation that aimed to help price stability.

## Notes

1  Galambos, *Competition and Cooperation*.
2  Bertilorenzi, 'Defendre le Marché Européen'.
3  RPA, 201-6-56742, Alugate IV, Le Directeur Générale de la Concurrence de la Commission des Communautés Européennes to Pechiney-Ugine-Kuhlman, Re: Affaire no. IV/26.870, Importations d'aluminium de l'Europe de l'Est. Engagement de la procedure et communictions de griefs, 19 September 1978.

4  AEPAA, Minutes of the Foundation Meeting of the European Primary Aluminium Association (EPAA), held in Düsseldorf on 11 November 1969. VHS, Reynolds Archives, Box 129, fold. 4320, Wilfried F. Wildschutz (EPAA secretary) to S.L. Goldsmith (AAA Secretary), 17 November 1969.
5  RPA, 001-16-70257, CIDA, Comité de Direction, 19 October 1970.
6  AEPAA, Minutes of the EPAA meeting, held in Innsbruck, 11 February 1971. RPA, 001-16-70257, CIDA, Comité de Direction, 20 April 1971.
7  AEPAA, Minutes of the EPAA meeting, held in Düsseldorf, 7 October 1970.
8  AEPAA, Minutes of the EPAA meeting, held in Innsbruck, 11 February 1971.
9  VHS, MSS3, R3395a, Series 4, Papers of Richard Reynolds Jr., box 137, fold. 4522, S.R. Spector (Oppenheimer & Co) to Richard Reynolds Jr., 25 October 1971. EPAA Archives, S.R. Spector to Wonhlich (Alusuisse), 20 March 1970. RPA, 201-6-56739, Alugate II, Spector to Leflon (Pechiney), 22 October 1971.
10  AEPAA, Minutes of the EPAA meeting, held in Innsbruck, 11 February 1971.
11  Wohnlich reported a recent journey to the US, during which he met up with several US producers. AEPAA, Minutes of the EPAA meeting, held in Düsseldorf, 15 October 1971.
12  AEPAA, Minutes of Meeting of EPAA, held in Düsseldorf, 7 October 1970.
13  RPA, 020-1-4-46663, Alufinance, Michel Castera, Note à M. Lefon, 14 January 1971. RZA, Ausschuss Protokolle, Protokoll nr. 566, 5 December 1970.
14  Isaiah A. Litvak, Christopher J. Maule, 'Cartel Strategies in the International Aluminum Industry', *Antitrust Bulletin. Journal of American and Foreign Antitrust and Trade Regulation*, vol. 20, no. 3, 1975, 641–663. Cailluet, 'The British Aluminium Industry'. M.H. I. Dore, 'Mineral Taxation in Jamaica: An Oligopoly Confronts Taxes on Resource Rents and Prevails', *American Journal of Economic and Sociology*, vol. 46, no. 2, April 1987, 179–203. Mikdashi, 'Aluminum'. For an execption, see Marco Bertilorenzi, 'Alufinance & Trade Ltd: Cartelisation and Financial Regulation in the European Aluminium Industry during the 1970s', in Barjot, Bertilorenzi (eds), *Aluminium*, 171–188.
15  About EEC competition policies, see Bussière, 'La Concurrence'. Walrouzet, 'The Rise of European Competition Policy, 1950–1991'. Stine Andersen, *The Enforcement of EU Law: The Role of the European Commission*. New York: Oxford University Press, 2012. Lee McGowan, *The Antitrust Revolution in Europe: Exploring the European Commission's Cartel Policy*. Cheltenham: Edward Elgar, 2010. Kiran Klaus Patel, Heike Schweitzer (eds), *The Historical Foundations of EU Competition Law*. New York: Oxford University Press, 2013.
16  Edward J. Kane, 'Good Intentions and Unintended Evil: The Case Against Selective Credit Allocation', *Journal of Money, Credit and Banking*, vol. 9, no. 1, February 1977, 55–69.
17  See Chapter 10 about the debate on inventory management. About approaches during the 1970s and 1980s, see Maizels, *Commodities in Crisis*. Atsé, *Commodity Futures Trading*. For a theoretical approach, see also Robert S. Pindyck, 'Inventories and the Short-Run Dynamics of Commodity Prices', *RAND Journal of Economics*, vol. 25, no. 1, 1994, 141–159.
18  RPA, 90.1.020.DAF.156, Alufinance, Société internationale de stockage, 25 January 1971. Personal interview with Michel Castera, 20 May 2011.
19  RPA, 90.2.080.DFX.25, Société de stockage Alustock, 19 February 1971.
20  RPA, 90.1.020.DAF.17, Alustock Finance Limited, Formation and Operation, SG Warburg & Co. LTD, s.d., but Febraury 1971; RPA, 90.2.080.DFX.25, Hypothèses de schéma de rapports contractuals entre les Associés et Alustock, 16 February 1971. Alustock. Legal opinion, 16 February 1971.
21  Attali, *Un Homme d'Influence*, 377–378. Cailluet, 'L'Industrie Britannique de l'Aluminium'. Fergusson, *High Financer*, 183–199. Perchard, *Aluminiumville*.
22  ACL, 233 AH 093, Iles Anglo-Normandes, Alufinance And Trade Ltd, Crédit Lyonnais, Déclaration préalable au Ministère de l'économie et des finances, 18 June 1971.

23 RPA, 90.1.020.DAF.156, Alufinance, Réunion de Londres du 29 Janvier, 30 January 1971. Warburg, Aluminium stockpiling, 28 January 1971. RPA, 90.1.020.DAF.17, Structure et financement d'Alufinance & Trade Limited, s.d. but about August 1971. All these issues were debated before the settlement of Alufinance in a meeting held in London at the SGW offices: Minutes of the meeting held in London, 25 and 26 March 1971.
24 Jersey Trust Archive (JTA), D.402.A.4751, Alufinance and Trade Limited, 28 May 1971. RPA, 020-1-4-46663, S.G. Warburg & Co. Ltd., Euro-Dollar Credits and Forward Exchange Operations, s.d. but summer 1971.
25 RPA, 90.1.020.DAF.17, Alufinance – Loan agreement, s.d. but 1971. RPA 020-1-4-46663, Alufinance – Schéma de la vente suivie de rachat, 12 May 1971.
26 RPA, 90.1.020.DAF.17, Alufinance, 3 June 1971. Explanatory Note on Alufinance, 21 May 1971. RPA, 020-1-4-46663, Alufinance, Schéma de la vente suivie du rachat, 12 May 1971.
27 Some meetings with ALCAN and Kaiser were organised during the first half of 1971, see AEPAA, Minutes of the meeting held in Innsbruck, 11 February 1971. Minutes of the meeting held in London, 3 June 1971. Minutes of the meeting held in Düsseldorf, 22 June 1971. RPA, 201-6-56744, Alugate Divers, L.F. Rothschild & Co., Aluminum. Analyst's Comments Based in Part on Conversations with Management Contacts in the Aluminum Industry, 1 July 1971. Market comments, 9 July 1971. Archives IHA, 90-12-SOL-IHA-6, Entretien du 29 octobre 1971. Monsieur Culver (ALCAN), Monsier Bès de Berc, Monsier Bernard (Pechiney), 2 November 1971.
28 RPA, 020-1-4-46663, Alufinance, Castera to Bès de Berc, 31 August 1971; Fax SGW to Pechiney, 29 June 1971. Note de M. Castera. % dans Alufinance, 24 September 1971.
29 RPA, 200-8-31264, Aluminium, IFTRA, Note sur IFTRA, 14 March 1972. CEE. Audiction du 25/9/1974 à Bruxelles. Réponse du Dr. Rudell, 30 September 1974. Alexander Rudell was EPAA's lawyer, formerly legal expert of VAW, and he was charged to follow the dossier of the European producers to the EEC, including Alufinance and IFTRA.
30 RPA, 201-6-56739, Alugate III, La Situation d'Aluleasing au regard du droit européen de la concurrence, 28 September 1972.
31 RPA, 201-6-56740, Alugate III, Compte Rendu d'Entretien, Negociations Brandeis 1970 à Zurich, 15 September 1970.
32 VHS, MSS3, R3395a, Series 4, Papers of Richard Reynolds Jr., box 135, fold. 4462, Harper (ALCOA) to Bob Ron (GSA), Re: Stockpile Disposal, 6 July 1971.
33 Merton Peck (ed.), *The World Aluminum Industry.* Nappi, *L'Aluminium.* UNCTAD, *Etudes sur la Transformation, la Commercalisation et la Distrubution des Produits de Base: La Transformation et la Commercialisation de l'Alumine et de l'Aluminium: Domaines de Coopération Internationale.* New York: United Nations, 1984. Centre des Nations Unies sur les société transnationales, *Les Société Transnationales dans l'Industrie de Production de l'Aluminium à Partir de la Bauxite.* New York: United Nations, 1982. See also, Florence Hachez-Leroy, 'Stratégie et cartels internationaux, 1901–1981', in Grinberg, Hachez-Leroy (eds), *Industrialisation et Sociétés,* 164–174.
34 Ivan Grinberg, Philippe Mioche, *Aluminium de Grèce: L'Usine aux Trois Rivages.* Grenoble: Presses Universitaires de Grenoble, 1996.
35 Rudi Gomperts, 'Le Combat Perdu pour le Prix de l'Énergie: L'Histoire de l'Usine d'Électrolyse Pechiney Nederland (1969–2011)', *Cahiers d'Histoire de l'Aluminium,* no. 51, 2013, 79–95. Knoepli, *From Dawn to Dusk,* 76–77.
36 Knauer, 'A Difficult New Beginning'. Perchard, *Aluminiumville.* Many of these projects were supported by the availability of new nuclear power stations which came on stream. On this point, see also René Lesclous, 'Nuclear Power and the Revival of Primary Aluminium Production in Europe', in Hachez-Leroy (ed.), *L'Europe de l'Aluminium,* 29–35. Perchard, *Aluminiumville,* 69–70, 120–124.

37 Pål Thonstad Sandvik, 'European, Global or Norwegian? The Norwegian Aluminium Companies, 1946–2005', in *The European Enterprise: Historical Investigation into a Future Species*, edited by Harm Schröter. Berlin: Springer, 2008, 241–253.
38 Nappi, *L'Aluminium*. See also, Carmine Nappi, 'L'Industrie Internationale de l'Aluminium, 1980–2006: Changements Structurels et Perspectives', *Cahiers d'Histoire de l'Aluminium*, no. 37, 2006, 27–51, and Camine Nappi, 'L'Industrie Internationale de l'Aluminium: Changements Structurels et Perspectives, 1970–2020', in Barjot, Bertilorenzi (eds), *Aluminium*, 151–170.
39 EPAA Archives, Minutes of the EPAA meeting, held in London, 3 June 1971.
40 RPA 201-6-56738, Alugate II. Jean Poincaré (Pechiney), Note. Entretien avec les producteurs européens de l'aluminium, 8 November 1971.
41 AEPAA, Minutes of the meeting held in Düsseldorf, 15 October 1971.
42 RPA, 201-6-56739, Alugate III, Poincaré (Pechiney), Memo sur la sitation de l'industrie de l'aluminium, 2 November 1971.
43 Woodward, *The Organisation for Economic Co-operation and Development*. Matthias Schmeizer, 'The Crisis before the Crisis: The "Problems of Modern Society" and the OECD, 1968–1974', *European Review of History*, vol. 6, no. 9, 2012, 999–1020. Matthias Schmeizer, 'A Club of the Rich to Help the Poor? The OECD, "Development", and the Hegemony of Donor Countries', in *International Organizations and Development, 1945 to 1990*, edited by Marc Frey, Soenke Kunkel, and Corinna Unger. Basingstoke: Palgrave Macmillan, 2014, 171–195.
44 VHS, MSS3, R3395a, Series 4, Papers of Richard Reynolds Jr., box 140, fold. 4588, Irving Lipkowitz, Summary memorandum Re: OECD aluminium meeting, 27 and 28 January 1972.
45 RPA 201-6-56738, Alugate II, Note. Concertation en vue des réunions de l'industrie de l'aluminium de l'OCED, November 1971. RPA, 201-6-56739, Alugate III, Aluminium Brut, prix de barème – OCED, 23 March 1972.
46 AOECD, AL 72(5), Compte Rendu succinct de la première session du groupe de travail ad hoc sur les problèmes de l'industrie de l'aluminium tenue au siège de l'OCED le 24 et 25 avril 1972, 10 May 1972. AOECD, AL 73(5), Industrie de l'Aluminium. Rapport du groupe de travail ad hoc au comité de l'industrie sur l'execution de son mandat, 30 May 1973.
47 OECD, *Problèmes et Perspectives de l'Industrie de l'Aluminium de Première Fusion*. Paris: OECD, 1973.
48 RPA, 201-6-56939, Alugate III, Aluminium Brut, October 1971.
49 Archives IHA, 051502BIZINFO6, John Wohnlich, Assainissement du marché international de l'aluminium, 7 June 1972.
50 Archives IHA, 051502BIZINFO66, Notes of the American expert (IL) to OECD Aluminium Working Party, 6 September 1972. IL is Irving Lipkowitz.
51 Actually, this meeting was recorded as the 'second' one. The first was at OECD's offices in Paris. See Archives IHA, 051502BIZINFO66 Minutes of the Second Meeting of the Board of Directors held at Norfolk House, St James's Square, London SW1, on Wednesday, 28 September 1972. The first meeting was the one held at OECD. About the creation of the IPAI, see also Bertilorenzi, 'Defendre le Marché Européen de l'Aluminium'.
52 Archives IHA, 051502BIZINFO66, Constitution de l'IPAI, Note de l'expert légal (M. Hurlock), 3 July 1972.
53 Archives IHA, 051502BIZINFO67, Ergas (Pechiney), Note to Michel Castera, Quelques remarques de Charles W. Parry, representant l'ALCOA au comité statistique de l'IPAI, 18 September 1972.
54 AOECD, boxes IND/AL/75 and IND/AL/78.
55 Archives IHA, 051502BIZINFO66 Minutes of the Second Meeting of the Board of Directors held at Norfolk House, St James's Square, London SW1, on Wednesday, 28 September 1972.

56   AEPAA, Minutes of the Meetings of EPAA, 4 November 1974, 30 September 1976, 4 October 1977.
57   RPA, 201-6-56943, Alugate, Divers, Meeting Brandeis. Réunion des 16 et 17 avril 1973 à Zurich.
58   RZA, Alusuisse, Ausschuss – Protokolle, Protokol nr. 596, 3 February 1974. RPA, 90.1.020.DAF.17, Note on Alufinance, 25 September 1973. SGW to Castera (Pechiney), 21 November 1973. RPA, 90.1.020.DAF 18 Alufinance – renouvlement de la facilité – suite à notre note du 5 Février 1974, 15 February 1974.
59   About the commodities conjuncture of mid-1970s, see Kenji Takeuchi, Bension Varon, 'Commodity Shortages and Changes in World Trade', *Annals of the American Academy of Political and Social Science*, vol. 420, 1975, 46–59; Richard N. Cooper, Robert Z. Lawrence, Barry Bosworth, Hendrik S. Houthakker, 'The 1972–75 Commodity Boom', *Brookings Papers on Economic Activity*, vol. 1975, no. 3, 1975, 671–723.
60   Elisabeth Benning, 'The Road to Rambouillet and the Creation of the Group of Five', in *International Summitry and Global Governance: The Rise of the G7 and the European Council, 1947–1991*, edited by Emmanuel Mourlon-Droul and Federico Romero. London: Routledge, 2014, 39–63. Harold James, *International Monetary Cooperation since Bretton Woods*. New York: Oxford University Press, 1996. Harold James, *Rambouillet, 15. November 1975: Die Globalisierung der Wirtschaft*. Munich: Dtv, 1997.
61   Maizels, *Commodities in Crisis*. Thomas George Weiss, *Multilateral Development Diplomacy in UNCTAD: The Lessons of Group Negotiations, 1964–84*. London: Macmillan, 1986. Helen O'Neill, *A Common Interest in a Common Fund: Proposals for New Structures in International Commodity Markets*. Geneva: United Nations, 1977. Gamani Corea, *Taming Commodity Markets: The Integrated Programme and Common Fund in UNCTAD*. Manchester: Manchester University Press, 1992.
62   Bureau of Mines, Annual Report on Bauxite and Alumina (1975), 239. About IBA, see (not exaustive) Isaiah A. Litvak, Christopher J. Maule, 'The International Bauxite Agreement: A Commodity Cartel in Action', *International Affairs*, vol. 56, no. 2, 1980, 296–314. F. Gèze, 'La Bataille des Matières Premières Minérales: Multinationales contre pays Producteurs' *Tiers-Monde*, vol. 66, 1976, 289–306. Norman P. Girvan, 'Transnational Corporations and Non-fuel Primary Commodities in Developing Countries', *World Development*, vol. 15, no. 5, 1987, 713–740. Holloway, *The Aluminium Multinationals*.
63   Marco Bertilorenzi, Philippe Mioche, 'Between Strategy and Diplomacy: History of Alumina Alternative Technologies (1900s–1980s)', *Cahiers d'Histoire de l'Aluminium*, no. 51, 2013, 43–63.
64   D.W. Woods, J.C. Burrow, *The World Aluminium-Bauxite Market: Policy Implications for the United States*. New York: Charles Rivers Associates, 1980.
65   NARA, RG 56 Department of treasury, Office of the raw materials and oceans policy, box 6, Memorandum of Conversation with Kaiser Aluminum, subject Bauxite, IBA, UNCTAD talks and investments, 16 August 1977.
66   Bibliothèque Cujas, Division manuscrits (BCM), Fonds ONU, Sous fonds CNUCED, Produits de base, TD/B/IPC/BAUXITE1, Conseil du Commerce et du développement. Programme intégré pour les produits de base. Réunion préparatoire sur la bauxite, 7 October 1977.
67   Bertilorenzi, Mioche, 'Between Strategy and Diplomacy'. Also Holloway speculated about the eventuality that the IBA and the aluminium multinationals had found a compromise to allign their joint interests, see Holloway, *The Aluminium Multinationals*, 81–82.
68   VHS, MSS3, R3395a, Series 4, Papers of Richard Reynolds Jr., box 148, fold. 4742, Richard Reynolds Jr. The US aluminum industry at the turn of the year. Prepared for the Aluminium Zentrale publication, 26 November 1974. Fold. 4797, Memorandum Aluminum Inventories, 30 October 1974. Memorandum World Primary Aluminum Production, 30 May 1974.
69   AEPAA, Minutes of the EPAA meeting held in Düsseldorf, 18 February 1975.

70 AEPAA, Minutes of the EPAA meeting held in Munich, 31 October 1974.
71 RPA, 502-1-8-51284, EPAA Minutes of the Statistical Committee, Minutes of the EPAA statistical Commitee on 3 and 4 May 1977 in Zurich.
72 AEPAA, Minutes of the EPAA meeting held in London, 30 September 1976.
73 AEPAA, Minutes of the EPAA meeting held in Düsseldorf, 11 May 1978.
74 AEPAA, Minutes of the EPAA meeting held in Düsseldorf, 18 February 1975. VHS, MSS3, R3395a, Series 4, Papers of Richard Reynolds Jr., box 151, fold. 4840, Irving Likpowitz, Re: OECD Aluminum Party. Ad hoc working party of the industry, 28 February 1975.
75 AEPAA, Minutes of the EPAA meeting held in Rottach-Ergen, 10 February 1977. This information is also reported by an insider of LME, Trevor Tarring, *Corner! A Century of Metal Market Manipulation*. London: Metal Bulletin Books, 1997, 111.
76 IHA, Pechiney's document about LME, n.c., David Hargreaves, Aluminium and the London Metal Exchange. A report on the decision of the LME to launch an aluminium contract, October 1977.
77 AEPAA, Minutes of the EPAA meeting held in Düsseldorf, 11 May 1978.
78 UGD/UGA, BACO, 347/1/2/1, Memorandum on Alufinance, 19 July 1974; RPA, 90.1.020.DAF.18, Alufinance, Renouvlement de l'ancienne facilité 1974, 27 July 1976. RHZ, Alusuisse documents, Ausschuss – Protokolle, Protokol nr. 618, 19 October 1977.
79 RPA, 201-6-56742, Alugate, Divers, Castera (Pechiney), Accords Brandeis, 27 November 1978.
80 AEPAA, Minutes of the EPAA meeting held in Megève, 14 March 1974; UGD, BACO, 347/1/2/1, Memorandum on Alufinance, 19 July 1974. London School of Economics Archives (hereafter ALSE), Siegmund G. Warburg documents, 11/153/1975, Note for D. Scholey from S.G. Warburg, 11 March 1975.
81 RPA, 90.1.020.DAF.156, Alufinance, Renouvlement de l'ancienne ligne de crédit Alufinance, 6 May 1976. SGW. New 1978 facility, s.d. but end of 1977. RPA, 020-1-4-46664, Note Alufinance, Aluminium Pechiney Vente, 3 April 1977. Note. Aluminium 1976, 21 January 1977. RPA, 90.1.020.DAF.18, Note. Alufinance – new terms of agreements, 25 January 1978.
82 AOECD, DSTI/IND/AL/78.2, La situation actuelle, les perspectives et les problèmes de l'industrie de l'aluminium de première fusion, 20 October 1978. RPA, 90.1.020.DAF.156, Note. Alufinance 1980, 28 May 1981.
83 About the working of LME, see Rudolf Wolff, *Wolff's Guide to the London Metal Exchange*. London: Metal Bulletin Books, 1980. Robert Gibson-Jarvie, *The London Metal Exchange, a Commodity Market*. New York: Woodhead-Faulkner, 1989. Tarring, *Corner!*
84 Trevor Tarring, 'Mad or Magic?' *Metal Bulletin*, no. 5935, 25 October 1974.
85 About the post-war cartels in Germany see Werner Abelshauser, *Deutsche Wirtschaftsgeschichte seit 1945*. Munich: Beck, 2004, 239–247. About German antitrust and its impact on EEC laws, see Stefan Sorin Mureşan, *Social Market Economy: The Case of Germany*. Berlin: Springer, 2014. David J. Gerber, *Global Competition: Law, Markets, and Globalisation*. New York: Oxford University Press, 2010, 181–183. Hannah L. Buxbaum, 'German Legal Culture and the Globalization of Competition Law: A Historical Perspective on the Expansion of Private Antitrust Enforcement', *Berkeley Journal of International Law*, vol. 23, no. 2, 2005, 474–495. Kronstein. *The Law of International Cartels*, 228–233. Walrouzet, 'The Rise of European Competition Policy'.
86 RPA, 201-6-56739, Alugate III, Note confidentielle. Accords Brandeis, 1 March 1968. Examen des questions par le renouvellement des accords Brandeis, réunion entre Escherich et Rudell (VAW) et Reuter, Matignon, Rey et Rossigneux (AF-Pechiney), 18 March 1968.
87 Ruddel for instance was invited to give the inaugural lecture of the 1972–1973 academic year at the faculty of law at Düsseldorf University, cf. Alexander Rudell, *Die Zulässogkeit Horizontaler Empfehlungen nach Deutschem und EWG-Kartellrecht*. Düsseldorf: Carl Heymanns Verlag KG, 1973.

88 RPA, 201-6-56739, Rudell to Pechiney and Montecatini, 27 May 1969. Rudell to Jaume, re. Importations de l'Est, 17 August 1970. About Jaume, Schumacher and Albrecht, some information can be found in Katja Seidel, *The Process of Politics in Europe: The Rise of European Elites and Supranational Institutions*. London: Tauris, 2010, 164–165. Sigfrido M. Ramirez Pérez, Sebastian van der Scheur, 'The Evolution of the Law on Article 85 and 86 EEC: Ordoliberalism and its Keynesian Challenge', in Patel, Schweitzer (eds), *The Historical Foundations of EU Competition Law*, 19–52.

89 AHCE, BAC 383-1998-795, Alufinance DG IV 26919, Anlage zur Alufinance-Anmeldung bei der EWG-Kommission von 3.6.1971, 14 July 1971. RPA, 90.1.020. DAF.18, Alufinance. Operation relations publiques, 11 June 1971.

90 RPA, 200-8-31264, Aluminium. Note sur IFTRA, 14 March 1972.

91

L'intérêt de la notification est double: elle permet … d'éviter toutes possibilités d'amende jusqu'à ce que la Commission ait pris une décision…. Si l'attestation négative ne pouvait être obtenue, le recours à l'application de l'exemption prévue au paragraphe 3, resterait possible…. Compte tenu de ces incertitudes, il apparait souhaitable … que le projet puisse trouver son fondement dans une recommandation de l'OCDE. Dans cette éventualité, il est permis de penser que la Commission Européenne accepterait d'accorder plus aisément, soit une attestation négative, soit une décision d'exemption, et surveillerait de façon moins étroite l'application de l'accord.

RPA, 201-6-56739, La Situation d'Aluleasing au regard du droit européen de la concurrence, 28 September 1972.

92 Archives IHA, 90-12-SOL-IHA-6, Entretien du 29 Octobre 1971 de Monsieur Culver (ALCAN), Monsieur Bès de Berc, Monsieur Bernanrd (Pechiney). AOCDE, AL 75(2), Compte rendu succinct de la première session du groupe de travail ad hoc sur les problèmes de l'industrie de l'aluminium, tenue au siège de l'OCDE le 24 et 25 avril 1972, 10 May 1972.

93 AHCE, BAC 383/1998 no. 795, 1971–1975. IV-4 26919, Alufinance, Carisi, Note pour Monsieur le Directeur Jaume, 29 June 1971; Jaume, Affaire DG IV 26919, 19 Aug 1972.

94 RPA, 201-6-56739, Alugate III, Wonlich (Alusuisse) to Bès de Berc (Pechiney), 4 November 1970.

95 RPA, 200-8-31264, Aluminium, IFTRA, Note sur IFTRA, 14 March 1972. CEE. Audiction du 25/9/1974 à Bruxelles. Réponse du Dr. Rudell, 30 September 1974.

96 About Borschette, see Mauve Carbonell, *De la Guerre à l'Union de l'Europe: Itinéraires Luxembourgeois*. Berlin: Peter Lang, 2014.

97

Les experts de Bruxelles ne manquent pas d'observer que les industriels qui veulent 's'entendre' sont en train de délaisser la pratique des accords écrits – et se rabattent sur des formules de coopération en général 'neutres', qu'ils doublent de pratiques concertées arrêtées oralement. Leur attention a été attirée par les travaux d'un avocat allemand, auteur d'un sorte de contrat-type, appelé 'International Fair Trade Practice Rules Administration (ou IFTRA) qui recense – comme son nom l'indique – tous les arrangements 'loyaux' entre sociétés, c'est-à-dire les formules qui ne sont pas condamnées par les législations, ou qui en tout cas sont généralement admises. C'est un appareil dangereux.

'La Politique de Concurrence des neuf se raffermit. Une interview de M. Albert Borschette, membre de la Commission des Communautés européennes', *Le Figaro*, Saturday 8 – Sunday 9 December 1973.

98 RPA, 200-8-31264, CEE, Direction général de la concurrence to Pechiney-Ugine-Kuhlman, 17 July 1974.

99 RPA, 200-8-31264, IFTRA Aluminium. Compte-Rendu de l'Audition par la Commission des Communautés Européennes, 25 September 1974. EPAA archives, box 2, Minutes of the meeting held in Düsseldorf, 25 March 1976.

100 AEPAA, Minutes of the EPAA meeting held in London, 30 September 1976. RPA, 201-6-56742, Alugate divers, Castera (Pechiney), Accords Brandeis, 27 November 1978.

101 RPA, 201-6-56739, Alugate III, Commission des Communautés Européennes, Mandat de vérification, 16 November 1976. Note pour les dossiers. Contrat USSR, 23 November 1976.

102 Bank of England Archives (BEA), 10A324/4, Report of the Commodities Co-ordinating Group (Bank of England, LME, DG IV EEC), 4 March 1979.

103 BEA, 10A324/4, Gold. Report by LME, 16 February 1978. CLH, Common sitting, Foreign and Commonwealth Affairs, World Commodities Centre, 26 April 1978, vol. 948, cc. 1361–1363.

104 George Ionescu, *The European Alternatives: An Inquiry into the Policies of the European Community*. London: Sijthoff & Noordhoff, 1979.

105 Decisions 85/563/EEC, 85/564/EEC, 85/565/EEC, 85/566/EEC, and 85/45/EEC.

106 *Official Journal of the European Communities*, No. L 92/1, 30 March 1985, Commission Decision of 19 December 1984 relating to a proceeding under Article 85 of the EEC Treaty, IV/26.870 – Aluminium imports from Eastern Europe, 85/206/EEC.

107 RPA, 001-1-3-62939, Pechiney, Developpement du négoce international, 30 December 1982.

108 Smith, *From Monopoly to Competition*, 416. Campbell, *Global Mission*, vol. III, 256.

# Conclusions

In October 1978, it was not yet taken for granted that LME would succeed in settling firmly established futures contracts for aluminium. During settlement of the contracts, many trade analysts were concomitantly wondering whether LME would continue to propose this kind of trade in the future. Also the material source of supply to LME was uncertain. It is true that LME hoped to rely on Eastern Europe and Persian Gulf suppliers, from which some brokers of the City had already imported since 1976, but the strong refusal of the big producers represented a main risk.[1] In an editorial note in the summer of 1978, a few weeks before the effective launching of the contract, pro-LME *Metals Week* sadly reported that 'at this point, the only group that is roundly supporting the LME aluminium contract is a handful of the LME ring dealers who will trade it'.[2] The abrupt failure of COMEX's tentative introduction of an aluminium futures trade in the mid-1960s was still fresh in the memory of the traders. At that time, a few months after the start of a first futures market, only a ridiculous turnover was registered for aluminium, whose higher and lower price brackets were almost identical. At the end of the 1970s, the strong opposition of the big aluminium business to LME was considered a potential danger that was looming on the good achievement of an aluminium futures market. Since COMEX had failed in becoming the 'price master' of the aluminium industry, LME was not considered have more chances this time.

Still in 1975, Trevor Tarring, the influential editor of *Metal Bulletin* and one of the stronger supporters of an aluminium futures trade, confessed to Victor Besso, the director of Pechiney's sale agency in the US, that 'LME missed the turn'.[3] However, the situation was strongly different from the mid-1960s. Since the mid-1970s, the nature of international trade was changing and general economic and monetary instability, which went along with a progressive dismantling of the Bretton-Woods order, made futures markets emerge in the key commodities again. While the former stabilisation tools were failing in almost all commodities, institutional markets came again to the fore as powerful regulators in trade.[4] Moreover, the aluminium industry was deeply changed, and the domination of the big six on the market was doomed to end. The merchant firm that led the proposal to set an aluminium futures contract at LME, Rayner-Harwill, fully understood that there was space to settle a firm contract at LME. Unlike the past, aluminium majors were losing their power to control the international market.

Apart from the majors, which had integrated production, new strategic groups were emerging and were characterised by the absence of integration and by strong interests in full-scale operation of their output. These producers were not under control of the old-established firms, but the governments in developing regions controlled them. It was predicted that, while in 1977 the majors still controlled 70 per cent of the global primary aluminium output, their portion would decrease to 56 per cent in the mid-1980s. At the same time, aluminium output controlled by governments would increase from 28 to 45 per cent.

We can add to this sketch that aluminium was no longer a little business and that political protection that surrounded post-war expansion was ending as well. Actually, after the US stockpile's dismantling, this metal was also no longer linked to the strategic policies of governments. In this context, Rayner-Harwill seized the opportunity for LME to arrange during the inception of this transition the settlement of an aluminium contract, in order to occupy the position when future developments would definitively achieve the 'commoditisation' of aluminium. The projections about the relative power of the 'big six' in controlling world output were doomed to decrease in the next five to ten years. Even though it had not yet reached its full maturity and new expansions were still foreseen, even though at a lower rate than the 10 per cent per year of the former period, this metal was already the most important amongst the non-ferrous metals and it was obvious that LME aimed to include it to extend its business. Rayner-Harwill bet on the future erosion of the market power of the 'big six' that, in spite of their formal refusal to use LME either as a supplier or as a terminal market, sooner or later would surrender to the new international pricing fashion of LME.[5] Moreover, LME could count on the support of the European antitrust authorities that proved to be supporting the new model of aluminium governance in the most difficult phase of this transition, when LME had to face the opposition of the majors.

Despite the memoirs that were written by LME insiders, the history of this institution is still rather unknown to scholarship and a better understanding of the way in which it operated could reveal new insights about the formation of the present commodity trade and, even broadly, about the process of institutionalisation of trade that lay behind contemporary globalisation. The working of institutional markets should be integrated into business histories that focus on commodities, in order to better understand how market forces really work and how they reshaped the strategies and structures of firms. The switch of aluminium from a model to another was a twofold challenge for the firms that, on the one hand, had to realise whether LME could really provide new advantages in the transaction costs of handling stock or not; on the other they had to understand if their credo on price stability was only a matter of path dependency (or of resilience) or if it was still consistent with the actual nature of their business. As it was reported by George Smith, at first the head of ALCOA was amongst the strongest opponents of LME. However, George Krome, the CEO of ALCOA, changed this attitude in the mid-1980s, when the American giant started to be supplied with LME metal and entered the mechanism of hedging provided by the London metal market.[6]

At the end of the 1970s, Krome was not alone in criticising LME: also in Europe, almost all the main firms reported the undesirability of LME action and about the awkward way in which it was undertaken. This industry and its directors were deeply shocked by the economic and political attack that the joint LME–EEC action represented. The European firms also tried to work some lobbying at the highest level to prevent the introduction of aluminium at LME and to find a compromise with DG IV. In particular Ron Utiger, CEO of BACO and temporary chairman of EPAA when LME started to design the aluminium contract, tried to implicate the Board of Trade in hampering the action of LME, but without success.[7] Moreover, Pechiney aimed to coordinate a strong opposition to LME with the other producers.[8] Pechiney, BACO, and VAW also manoeuvred the representatives of their governments in the EEC, in order to stop the Commission's legal action.[9] After publication of the refusal of North American producers to enter into LME mechanisms, also a possible intervention of IPAI was rumoured.[10] Despite the reduction of the force of ALCAN's list prices, the specific situation of LME action also pushed other producers to publish their list price on the national market, as Pechiney and VAW did during the early 1980s in their respective countries, believing to be able to curb LME. Two aspects, however, should have alerted the majors about the foreseeable failure of their boycott. The first was that, at the beginning of the futures trade, LME negotiated prices for aluminium that were fairly higher than those settled by the firms, as showed in Figure 12.3. Probably, producers did not raise prices because the concomitant EEC action acted as a main deterrent. Nevertheless, this fact proved to the market that self-governance by the producers was failing in programming extensions. Actually, the trade analyst forecasts about a probable future shortage led prices to a higher level than the producers'. The second was the European Commission attitude in this period, which held the balance of power of the global situation.

Actually, in response to the attempts made by the majors to boycott LME, the role of the European Commission was to continue its initial support to LME, also during the whole transition process that accompanied the admission of aluminium at LME in its first five years. In fact, while in 1978 and 1979 the producers continued to publish their price list, as shown in the last chapter, in 1979 DG IV sent two other dossiers of objections, each of about 150 pages, in which it confirmed its will to pursue the case until a decision was reached, alarming aluminium producers about the European Commission's kind of attitude. A strong attitude against the governance of the producers was also confirmed during the two weeks of hearings that the European Commission had with the directors of the aluminium industry at the end of November 1979 in Brussels. The producers settled their defence trying to show that their cooperation was not 'a hole in the corner conspiracy', but 'an attempt to deal in a reasonable way with a very difficult international economic and political problem'. However, the Commission's lawyers clearly pointed out that the main antitrust concern was not only the arrangements with Eastern metal, but also and above all the continuous boycott of LME. The evidence advocated by the aluminium producers was fruitless, in particular that of Castera, who tried to show the 'morality' of a stable priced market linked to production costs, or of Utiger who described with these words the situation that had arisen in October 1978

> The LME prices have been plotted weekly instead of monthly, [they] have for the most of the time been above the ALCAN price and at the end of October about £100 per ton higher ... The trading on the Exchange does lead to excessive price instability. I am told that most of the transactions are only paper transactions of the speculative nature involving very little movement of metal.... It seems therefore, I would say fortunately, that the prices at which aluminium were being traded on the Exchange haven't yet had any appreciable effect on the prices of what I would call genuine aluminium trading. But if the price instability was to spread to the aluminium market generally, then I suggest that the fears of the industry and the consumers would prove to be fully justified.[11]

Despite the fact that the producers were sure the case was terminated because the normal delay allowed in proceeding had passed (the case was notified in 1970), and about hampering of a firm contract at LME at the eve of the 1980s, DG IV wanted to continue the case until a decision was made. Informal talks continued between the German lawyer of the European firms, Alexander Rudell, and the Commission to explore a compromise on this case, but in vain.[12] The final decision finally arrived in December 1984. Even though no fine was applicable, the five years of close survey hampered the continuation of former cooperation in the delicate period when LME was imposing itself on the global scene as the 'price master' for aluminium. In DG IV's final decision, 'the arrangement not to make any quantity of aluminium available for trading on the London Metal Exchange', among other elements that constituted the case, 'constituted infringements of Article 85 (1) of the EEC Treaty'.[13] The Commission made this case as a matter of principle, with which it aimed to lead the global market of aluminium in new directions. In the long document of about 80 pages that explained the decision, the whole international aluminium governance was revisited and it was clearly claimed that all the behaviour of the European primary producers in term of pricing and self-regulation was, on the one hand, harmful to the principles of EEC competition laws and, on the other hand, contrary to the national policies of the members' countries.

Another aspect is very meaningful in the Commission's decision. Also the UK and German governments' implication in the agreements were denied because they were not 'in any sense a party to the Brandeis agreements' and because the support that was given to these agreements 'can[not] properly be described as ratification on the acts of the western producers so that they became acts of State'. These agreements were also claimed as non-indispensable to protect the Western aluminium market because the aluminium producers' 'proper course would have been to make an application entrusted by law with the regulation of trade'.[14] In other words, through its actions, DG IV criticised not only the economics of aluminium cooperation, which relied on price stability, but also its politics, minimising the political endorsement that came with the whole experience of the international aluminium cartel and with its declaimed self-regulatory behaviour. This operation was not without contradictions, as was reported by Pechiney's answer to DG IV

> We cannot support the position taken by the Direction Générale de la Concurrence about the virtuosity of a highly speculative market whose prices necessarily exaggerate upward and downward; whereas, it seems, for many years the policy of the European governments, and of the Commission specifically, was trying to stabilise as much as possible the price of raw materials by making them escape the speculation; that there is a paradox that deserves an explanation from the Commission.[15]

Reading the last phase of the history of the aluminium cartel, we can conclude that this long-lasting history was finally curbed by an outlandish alliance of the European Commission with the British authorities, with the more neoliberal merchant milieux of the City and with the newcomers in the international aluminium industry, also coming from Eastern countries and the Middle East. The European Commission's support to LME finally helped the creation of a marginal attitude to the formation of aluminium prices, curbing the resilience of the aluminium multinationals to continue their old-fashioned pricing method linked to production costs. This strange alliance, however, should not be emphasised, even though it was determinant in changing the actual situation, according to which the start of a futures trade, even amongst the traders, seemed very difficult. As we showed in the last chapter, the fact that the European Commission helped LME in its struggle against the historical aluminium producers to sell aluminium like the other non-ferrous metals should be read, if not as a coincidence, at least as a combination of historical processes that started at the same time, at the end of the 1970s. The governance model of the aluminium producers was already self-ending, due to the incapacity of the producers to make reliable forecasts in a swinging economic situation. In this phase, producers experimented with some tools to enable self-hedging methods, such as the one carried out with Alufinance, which proved to be more costly than the one that LME could provide to the industry because its financial burden was charged to the producers themselves.

Actually, in the new instable phase of the aluminium market, characterised by ups and downs instead of a robust and continuous growth, the old governance was neither useful to obtain information about the market situation, nor to save cost of transactions in handling stock during the boom–bust cycles. We are convinced that in the long run and, in many aspects, the structure of aluminium cartels provided, as epitomised by Jeffrey Fear, firms with some decisive advantages that did not deal with the classic alternative between market and hierarchies.[16] In the long-lasting life of the aluminium cartel, firms did not look for the information that they needed on the market; they always relied on the network of statistical capabilities that the cartel provided them. When the metal was lacking or was abounding, the cartel had always proved to be able to work as a 'bank of surpluses' and rebalance the situation. The cartel represented a valid alternative to Coase's divide between market and hierarchies:[17] in the long run, it proved both to be a reliable source of information and a consistent tool to administrate the producers' supply positions. Maybe, LME became more efficient both in handling stock from a financial point of view and in providing information already before the settlement of contracts. Not only ALCOA, as reported by Smith, but also other European firms were already alerted about the sunset of their governance and were trying to integrate the new futures markets in their daily operations. This was for instance also the position of Alusuisse, which was progressively divesting from primary production to become a more diversified and finance-oriented company.[18] Also Pechiney, in spite of its strong opposition to LME, was highly changing its financial structure at the end of the 1970s, as Dominique Barjot recently revealed, because the power of its financial backers was overcoming its historical self-financing capabilities.[19]

However, if the economic factors of the change were self-evident in the late 1970s, they were not sufficient to drive this industry to new models of governance. The resilience of the producers about a consolidated method of governance, which emerged at the eve of the twentieth century, was a stout path dependency, according to which the producers did not perceive the changes of the 1970s as permanent ones, but only as further complications to their old long-lasting governance. In this situation, the European Commission's action was able to reverse the *régime*, or we would say the paradigm, of this market. It was the final sign for the aluminium producers that the institutional paradigm that supported the long lasting international governance of this industry was changing. While in the long history that we have outlined cartels were a key tool in reducing the risks of the conjuncture, both of economic slumps and of trade expansion, they became a risky tool in the new context. The economic instability that characterised the 1970s showed that models to forecast economic trends were not effective and the measures that were undertaken to help producers in balancing between demand and supply, like Alufinance, were extremely costly if compared with the 'free' LME facilities. Cartels became also a political and legal risk because, differently from the past, firms ended with being endorsed or at least embedded during their cooperation.

The group of European companies, including also the American ones that invested in Europe since the 1960s, were all hit by a long lasting, penetrating, and 'unfriendly' antitrust action. The huge 'Alugate', which lasted for about as long as US v. ALCOA and which had an even more destabilising power over the international cartelisation, finally taught two lessons to aluminium firms. Not only was their cartel no longer endorsed by the political powers, but it was also the source of anxieties and risks. In this new context of the 1970s, LME could offer new valuable services to the industry, such as hedging operations in a time of price volatility and fluctuations, and additional finance for stocks in surplus periods, which were not only effective and 'free', but also 'safe'. Coming back to the literature on cartels, the institutional change represented by the transition to LME should be read from the standpoint both of Barjot's dichotomy of endogenous–exogenous factors and of Levenstein and Suslow's cartel success approach. Also, epitomising Schröter's institutional approach, we can claim that for a long time the cartel was the general rule of the game, which delimited the firms' action in a well defined range of options. When external conditions (political and economic) that supported the centrepiece of cartelisation, i.e. price stability, were over, both the industry and political powers eventually ended up with adapting their action to the new context, and new rules were necessary to administrate this industry. In other words, price stability was no longer a per se value: the end of 'stability' as the main goal both of firms and of governments represented the end of a paradigm that, settled at the eve of the twentieth century and underpinned at the aftermath of the Second World War, did not survive to the 1970s.[20]

As we have seen, the principal goal of the aluminium cartel was not simply to collude, but to provide governance to this global industry, in which producers tried to harmonise – not without difficulties –national levels with the international situation. It proved to be a system shaped by a certain degree of institutional creativity. The formal and 'official' cartels of the pre-1945 period were replaced by trade associations and study groups of the post-1945 phase. Governments often helped this creativity, considering an optimal action if private producers managed to find commercial solutions to the issues that, otherwise, could have raised diplomatic and international polity dangers. The transition during the institutional change from pre-1945 to post-1945 cartelisation is central to our research: the transition from a phase of formal cartelisation to a new institutional industrial cooperation cannot be explained as the mere outcome of the rise of antitrust law. Military, political, financial, and corporate-value considerations affected this change. In this continuous adaptation, cartelisation was never a simple European affair, contradicting the belief according to which cartels are essentially a European phenomenon. This is true even though the Europeans on many occasions led the process of cartelisation: AIAG, then Alusuisse, and AF, then Pechiney, played the role of the *chefs de file* of international cartelisation for a long time. However, the Americans had a huge role in this process as well. They were not passive participants in global governance, but in some cases they also were the architects of the agreements and the leading actors that volunteered their settlement. The case of the Davis brothers in the 1930s, who settled a finance company to hide a powerful stock-buffering scheme, or of Lipkowitz in the 1960s, who tried to find a political consensus to a general agreement with Europeans, are illuminating from this standpoint. Moreover, when the US industry, for a complex nexus of reasons (antitrust, political etc.), did not collaborate with the Europeans, such as in the 1930s, the global governance of this industry passed through maybe one of the worst crises of its history.

The complex nexus of practical solutions that producers and political powers found in the long run knew an abrupt modification in the 1970s. The actual reach of institutional change behind the admission of aluminium at LME was great, because it was the starting point of a huge transformation that led aluminium primary production to disappear from Europe and almost from the US, to be concentrated in low-cost energy countries. At the mid-1980s, when LME prices fell abruptly, many of the European firms passed through severe turmoil, which for instance determined the end of BACO, which was taken over by ALCAN, the nationalisation of Pechiney, and a strong restructuring of VAW and of the other German actors. It also meant a slow downfall of the Italian aluminium industry that, even though it was already nationalised in 1973 – during the first oil shock – became highly anti-remunerative and expensive for the Italian government. Also Alusuisse, as Adrian Knoepfli reported, passed through severe difficulties that menaced its existence. Only the bigger North American companies, with much greater financial strength, could afford the new swinging price situation, fluctuating between big earnings and severe slumps. If we compare the situation of aluminium with the situation of the steel industry, for instance, in which the persistence of government aid, national protection, and cartels procrastinated the displacing of this industry, this impact seems even bigger.[21] In aluminium, the key outcome of the joint LME–EEC action was to help the transition to a new kind of institutional governance for the international aluminium industry because it won the last resistance to this change. The outcome of this action was to make aluminium converge to the methods that characterised the governance other non-ferrous metals. This change could be considered as oneway, from which it would be impossible to come back, because today it would not be possible to forecast a return to a stable price trade in the aluminium industry and because the governance tools that focused on price stability would not be able to cope with the complexity of today's interplay in the aluminium industry.

However, this does not mean that cartels and 'collusion' disappeared from the aluminium industry after the 1980s. In 1994, for instance, as Joseph Stiglitz reported in his *Globalisation and its Discontents*, a new 'cartel' was created to save Western producers from the too harsh fall of international prices due to a big wave of imports from Russia. The US government helped the settlement of a 'Memorandum of Understanding' that would set a voluntary reduction of output in order to make room in the market for reasonable imports from Russia, with the final goal to influence the prices of LME. This Memorandum of Understanding was signed in Brussels and also European producers entered this 'voluntary' agreement with the tacit consent of their own governments and of the European institutions. Like in the past, in the 1990s, a cartel aimed at managing the transition to a more globalised economy, when new economic actors started to access the 'free economy' markets after the fall of the Communist regime. Moreover, governments supported a 'commercial solution' to a tight diplomatic issue. Like in the past, antitrust laws served to conceive and design safe agreements and not as an effective deterrent.[22] However, unlike the past, in the mid-1990s the goal of the aluminium producers was not to keep price stability and to strike a better balance between demand and supply; they just wanted to save profits during a harsh conjuncture.

Acceding to US archives about this case, we know that in the 1990s, governments, especially the US government, cooperated with this action because it was aligned with the political goals to save a strategic industry during a period of potential danger and of powers' confrontation at the end of the Cold War.[23] As a matter of fact, this operation was harmful, not only because, according to Stiglitz, it taught to ex-Soviet producers a 'wrong lesson' about how the market economy works in an important transitional period for Russia.[24] It also hampered the diffusion of aluminium in a new market such as the one of car frames, because, as an acute market analyst recently reported, the rise of prices happened at the very wrong time, when the car constructors were settling cost models to substitute steel with aluminium, which ended with hindering its diffusion in this new application.[25] In other words, this new agreement, which was neither a real cartel such as the ones that lived in the interwar period, nor a continuation of informal cooperation that governed this industry before 1978, was done without any long-run strategic vision about the future of the market and the long-run perspectives of pricing trends. In the 1990s, the transition to LME had already been achieved; firms were no longer 'responsible' for the evolution of their industry or for the balance between demand and supply. The time when chairmen considered 'their' metal not as a mere commodity and, as a matter of fact, wrote Aluminium with a capital 'A' in their own correspondence, was definitively over.

Further research could reveal if the European Commission was aware of the real reach of its action, which can be considered as a deus ex machina of the historical change of 1978. A broader comprehension of the economic role of antitrust action could reveal if the European Commission action, aside the sample of aluminium, coordinated a big convergence towards a model of industrial governance that, in the end, was equal to the one provided by the institutional markets. As anticipated in the last chapter, the decision on the aluminium case was concomitant with other five decisions that blessed the starting of futures markets in other commodities, which in the past had already been affected by private cartels and public study groups. Also John Hillman, in his study about tin, confirms that the curbing of the tin cartel by the British authorities arrived almost in the same year and it acted as a watershed for stabilisation tools as a whole. Moreover, the decision to promote LME as the general regulator of the aluminium industry appears as a decisive and maybe unique case of resilience against cartels. The Commission's action in this case, like few others, provided a unique impact on the way in which a global industry should be governed and regulated. It curbed, we may say forever, not the attitude of firms to collude, but a specific modus operandi of a long lasting cartel, which focused on price stability and which lasted for almost a century. The regulatory structure of the aluminium cartel had been more and more ineffective during the last phase of the 1970s and, if we wonder what could have happened without the European Commission action, probably we could answer that sooner or later aluminium could have entered LME in any case, as the merchant firm Raynar-Harwill predicted when designing the futures contract. However, the action of the European Commission destroyed the last opposition of the majors of the aluminium industry about futures markets and played a unique role in the process of 'commoditisation' of aluminium, which hitherto was perceived more as an industrial material than as a real commodity.

However, this change should not be read only from the standpoint of antitrust action. It reflects a broader transformation of the nexus between politics and business on the one hand, and between business and finance on the other. Actually, the Commission not only stopped a type of economic behaviour, but also a long lasting political and financial justification of this behaviour. The historical relevance of this political entry reveals a far-reaching output for the understanding of the relationships between business and politics. The aluminium cartel was, broadly speaking, an example of industrial self-regulation because firms settled their agreements following mainly private and economic considerations. For instance, it is not surprising that Louis Marlio, one of the strongest 'cartel matadores' of our history, is also accredited to be the inventor of the term 'neo-liberalism'. State intervention in the regulation of this industry was historically very sporadic, and even contrary to its main leitmotif. This was the very nature of this cartel: provide economic tools for governance where and when public powers abdicated from carrying out direct action. One leading thread of the history of the aluminium cartel since its earliest stages has been the complex nexus of relationships that were settled between producers and political powers in the governance of this industry. The entry of political visions into the aluminium industry sometimes disrupted international cartelisation, driving the agreements to an end or destroying the prerequisites on which cartels were based. In almost all these cases, governments did not oppose cartels for antitrust reasons – or at least, this was a secondary motivation of governmental action – but above all for military and political reasons. Also in the case of US policy during and at the end of the Second World War, we showed that antitrust action helped to impose a military-strategic vision that had not followed an abstract competition policy. For a long time, even when questioning the authority of the cartel, political authorities did not support other models of governance. In many cases, governments were also able to fix prices and give guidelines for investments and output, covering other tasks that had previously belonged to cartel regulation.

Since the 1930s, a real mismatch between national goals towards this strategic material and the international scheme of producers has existed: this is one of the main reasons for its collapse after the Second World War and a decisive argument of this book. This mismatch also reshaped the nexus between politics and business in the 1950s and afterwards. In the context of the Cold War, political powers (especially the US) established specific policies towards this industry, but none of them was 'global' in its scope. The existence of national policies, and especially of governmental stockpiles, made the survival of an international cartel superfluous and shaped the interplay of producers. It was only when the role of governments in each national aluminium industry faded that private networks of producers were revitalised, opening the door to new cartel-like organisations. In many cases, political powers endorsed this way to provide governance; we also showed that a specific political attitude often helped the formation of these organisations, even in more hostile situations for cartels characterised by an established antitrust policy. Actually, in the post-1945 period much political action endorsed international self-governance of the aluminium producers. For instance, during the 1950s, industrial cooperation was both supported by OEEC and was made possible by US strategic policies. During the 1960s, the British governments 'blessed' the commercial answer to Eastern metal concerns and helped the producers hamper LME to start a futures market with aluminium. Again in the 1960s and 1970s, OECD represented an international forum to start new phases of international industrial cooperation, providing practical approaches to the current economic difficulties. Until the end of the 1970s, even though the actors and the forms of international governance of this industry changed, the overall modality focused on price stability was kept as the common basis of this industry.

Despite these long lasting relationships that made aluminium's 'credo' part of the statecraft attitude towards this metal, an ambivalent position can be read in the relationships between the aluminium industry and the European authorities at the beginnings of the 1970s. In spite of the studies that proliferate about the anti-cartel activity of the European Commission, which often focused on the detecting methods of the Commission and, more recently, on the leniency programme, i.e. a system that either forecasts the reduction or the exemption from fines for the firms that denounce an agreement to the antitrust authorities,[26] it seems that the history of aluminium cartels is far from the contemporary developments of EEC antitrust action. Aluminium producers had not perceived the action of the European antitrust authorities as a potential danger, but only as a regulatory constraint that, far from fighting cartels, could have helped the settlement of more reliable agreements both with Eastern importers and amongst them. As a matter of fact, the history of the aluminium case is not a history of a secret cartel that was detected by the European authorities. Even though the EEC leniency programme was not yet implemented at that time, this would not have been of any utility, because the producers decided to communicate to the Commission all the material that they had about the working of the Brandeis agreements and the framework of their governance. Producers did not perceive the big institutional transition towards neoliberal approaches to economy and to antitrust policies, while they were still plunged in a classic-industrialist vision of their own industry. Aluminium producers believed they lived in an economic and political paradigm that a fortiori tolerated cartels as practical solutions to complex international problems, while in reality the perception of cartels by the public authorities was already moving to a priori condemnation of any anticompetitive behaviour.

The reshaping of the nexus between business and policy in the international governance of such an important commodity as aluminium seems to have been decisive to impose new governance models. The institutional change that was described led to wonder whether the actors of this change operated in a deliberated way or not. For instance, it was proposed that the US stockpile was used as a substitute for a real international cartel, in spite of the antitrust preoccupation of US authorities, because it served as a manager of the war oversupplies and because it also had an unwanted impact over international trade. Its general buoyancy towards aluminium helped the construction of a positive attitude of the European producers towards both the North Americans and the resettlement of international cooperation after the Second War World. During the 1960s, cartels played the role of 'industrial diplomacy' again, which is often quoted by scholarly studies, because they prevented both the European Community and the UK from settling unfriendly commercial relationships with the Soviet countries. While price stability was not contrary to public welfare, cartels were tolerated also because they represented a practical approach to the serious concerns of international policy. As a consequence, the history of a cartel in such a political commodity as aluminium should be read from the standpoint of the changing relationships between industry and politics, which often showed aligned interests, but sometimes struggled in the way in which international governance should be settled. The transversal alliance between business and politics had begun to be changed when, on the one hand, the general desire for stability was no longer a priority in the political agenda and, on the other hand, new relationships with the financial world emerged. As Charles Maier revealed, stability could be the object of historical research because, like all historical process, it has changing social, political, and economic values over time.[27]

Essentially, the claim that the aluminium cartel ended as a consequence of institutional change may deserve further explanation. This change can be read from the standpoint of the so-called process of 'financiarisation' that hit the international economy during the 1970s and which was concomitant with liberalisation and deregulation.[28] Also, a changing interplay between finance and cartels is not secondary to the history of aluminium. During the history of the aluminium cartel, we argued that finance in many cases helped international cartelisation, often reshaping the actual way in which cartels were settled and administrated, even though in the case of aluminium the direct implication of banks was less consistent than in other industrial branches, as revealed by some scholarly studies.[29] We can argue that a certain alignment between finance and industry existed for the first Aluminium-Association, which was born from the mind of one of the leading financial backers of AIAG, Carl Fürstenberg. This was also the case for Alliance, which adopted financial devices both to make the cartel acceptable from a legal standpoint for North Americans producers and to cope with the specific economic situation of overproduction that the aluminium industry was facing; and for the Brandeis agreements during the 1960s, which were written by an affiliate company of Warburg, and of Alufinance, which was a *chef d'oeuvre* of the financial engineering of Warburg and which shows what kind of complicated financial framework can lie behind the cartels. Before the 1970s, the general perception of the nexus between producers and finance in aluminium firms was that price stability was the only way to generate a virtuous circle for which stable earnings could support a robust investment strategy in a period of big growth of outlets. This was also central to the narrative that Lipkowitz tried to impose, through AAA's voice, in the national and international polity. Afterward, stability became the limit to the earnings that the stockholder could have obtained during the uprising market trends.

As a consequence, the institutional change that determined the end of the aluminium cartel was not only legal and political. It was also a financial one because the financial perception of the firms was completely transformed during the 1970s. As shown, Alufinance opened the door to a first financial perception of the governance of the aluminium industry. Even though it was settled to hamper the start of LME, Alufinance owned many of the characteristics of hedging operations and of financial off-balance controls of inventories that are essential to LME. Also for that it diverged from Alliance, which was essentially an output restriction scheme associated with a stock-buffering device. This study about cartelisation reveals a specific aspect in the history of corporate governance that is often neglected. The progressive sunset of the aluminium cartel could also be read from the standpoint of the changing interplay between managers and stockholders. While in the past and since the Great War, aluminium firms had lived in a certain way as the representatives of the military-industrial complex of the nations, they progressively moved towards other scenarios in the following decades. In the complex continuous confrontation of powers in the international panorama, aluminium firms perfectly represented the key national champions in the international exchequer. In the context of the 1930s, the cartel failed to grasp the political role of aluminium, which did not consent to a too 'international' vision in terms of stock handling and output restrictions. Afterward, the cartel partially abdicated the role of first level planners, becoming more of a controller of 'last resort' for this industry. When economic nationalism faded and trans-national interests were reshaping the aluminium firms into modern multination-als, paraphrasing Walter Benjamin's insight about the angel of history, they were 'looking as though [they are] about to move away from something [they are] fixedly contemplating ... [their] face is turned toward the past'.[30]

While they did not cease immediately to play the political role that they played before the 1970s, aluminium firms started to become something different from the past. While the corporate value of their managers was still the ability to provide an ordinated expansion to their industry and to their metal, the social value of the shareholders and backers had already become the need to pay back larger dividends and extra-bonuses to the stockholder. In the so-called new economy, the place for price stability was very little if not nonexistent. As a con-sequence, the transformation of the perception of cartels from a tool to manage the risk to a risky tool, which we have outlined above, should be seized from the standpoint of new financial understanding. Not only did stability end up being a political value, but it also became a barrier to what could be earned during the periods of expansion. Moreover, investments programmes and their auto-financing became unattractive if compared to the ability to generate extra profits. Some attitudes of the aluminium majors towards LME, such as the changing ideas of ALCOA and Alusuisse, are examples of this fundamental transformation of industrial capitalism as regards finance. Also in the arguments of Ian Forster, when he listed the positive roles that LME would play in aluminium governance after 1978, advocated that LME would free funds from the corporate finance of firms, taking over the burden of financing the inventory accumulation that resulted from the swings of the market. In his words, 'the LME does offer a service by taking excess material off the market'.[31]

In retrospect, we can argue that these changes have been emphasised in the following decades. The creation of big transnational conglomerates, such as Riotinto-ALCAN, did not only virtually merge ALCAN, Pechiney, BACO, and Alusuisse with Riotinto, but also represented a huge diversification business in almost all the non-ferrous metals, could serve as a key sample of this change. Even the emergence, within this industry, of leading profile new-economy man-agers, with new financial and global capabilities, such as Sergio Marchionne who lead Alusuisse in the late 1990s before arriving at FIAT-Chrysler, could serve as another example of this transformation that, incepted at the end of the 1970s, blossomed in the following decades. Also the takeover of LME by leading global financial actors, such as Goldman Sachs or JP Morgan, is meaningful of this change. The change incepted at the end of the 1970s was not only a transforma-tion of international commodity governance towards new models; it was also an internal transformation of firms, which ended up considering themselves as responsible for the growth of their metal, and started to transform them in seeking additional earning opportunities. This meant considering slumps as the other face of the coin of the period of uprising benefits, the desirability of which could no longer be traded with stability. This transformation started at the end of the 1970s and, in the case of aluminium, was possible thanks to a new model of global governance that overcame the old one. Of course, this transformation also affected cartels themselves: ending up serving stability, they became more similar to 'take the money and run' cartels that are often described in contemporary blockbusters.

## Notes

1 Trevor Tarring, 'Shapes and Futures', *Metal Bulletin*, no. 21, October 1977, 25–26; 'Twenty Years On', *Metal Bulletin*, no. 25, August 1978, 1–3; 'The Man from Mars', *Metal Bulletin*, no. 5, September 1978, 1–2.
2 'LME to Trade Aluminium on October 2: Major Western Producers strongly Opposed, fearing Market Instability; Material may come from the East', *Metals Week*, no. 25, August 1978, 1–3.
3 Archives IHA, Pechiney's document about LME, n.c, Victor Besso (PTC Partners – Pechinay sales at the US) to Michel Castera (Pechiney Paris), 22 April 1975.
4 Richard L. Gordon (ed.), *Energy, Markets, and Regulation*. Cambridge: MIT Press, 1987. Philippe Chalmin, *Traders and Merchants: Panorama of International Commodity Trading*. New York: Taylor & Francis, 1987. Yannick Marquet, *Négoce International des Matières Premières*. Paris: Eyrolles, 1992. Maizels, *Commodities in Crisis*. Takamasa Akiyama (ed.), *Commodity Markets Reforms: Lessons of Two Decades*. New York: World Bank Publications, 2001. Thomas Cottier, Panagiotis Delimatsis, *The Prospects of International Trade Regulation: From Fragmentation to Coherence*. London: Cambridge University Press, 2011.
5 Archives IHA, Pechiney's document about LME, n.c, David Hargreaves, Aluminium and the London Metal Exchange. A report on the decision of the LME to launch an aluminium contract, October 1977.
6 Smith, *From Monopoly to Competition*, 416–418.
7 Archives IHA, Pechiney's document about LME, n.c, Ronny Utiger to D.C. Clark (Department of Industry), 25 August 1976. Besso to Castera, 4 May 1978.
8 Archives IHA, Pechiney's document about LME, n.c, L'aluminium sera coté au Londom Metal Exchange à partir du 2 Octobre 1978. Premiers commentaires, Reuters informations, 23 August 1978.
9 RPA, 201-6-56739, Alugate III, Castera to M. Dietrich (Direction des Mines), 15 June 1977. Utiger to Castera, 25 May 1977. Castera, Note. Accords Brandeis vs. Bruxelles, 23 June 1977.
10 Archives IHA, Pechiney's document about LME, n.c, Henri Missonnier to Michel Castera et Charles Guignard, 27 Avril 1978.
11 RPA, 201-6-56743, Alugate IV, Commission of the European Communities, Draft Minutes of the Hearing held in the Manhattan Center, Brussels, on the 12, 13, 14, 15, 16, 19, 20, 21, 22, 23, 26 and 27 November 1979 in Case No. IV/26/870 – Aluminium.
12 RPA, 90-5-55444, Dossier de M. Rudell, Comité exectuvif de l'EPAA, Bruxelles, le 25 Novembre 1981, CR par M. Rudell de sa visite personelle du 4 November 1981 à M. Caspari.
13 *Official Journal of the European Communities*, No. L 92/1, 30 March 1985, Commission Decision of 19 December 1984 relating to a proceeding under Article 85 of the EEC Treaty, IV/26.870 – Aluminium imports from Eastern Europe, 85/206/EEC.

14  *Official Journal of the European Communities*, No. L 92/1, 30 March 1985, Commission Decision of 19 December 1984 relating to a proceeding under Article 85 of the EEC Treaty, IV/26.870 – Aluminium imports from Eastern Europe, 85/206/EEC

15
> On ne peut pas soutenir la position prise par la Direction Générale de la Concurrence sur les vertus d'un marché hautement spéculatif dont les prix exagèrent nécessairement les tendances à la hausse comme à la baisse; alors que, semble-t-il, depuis de nombreuses années la politique des gouvernements européens, et celle plus précisément de la Commission, a été de tenter de stabiliser autant que faire se peut, le prix des matières premières en les faisant échapper à la spéculation; qu'il y a là un paradoxe qui mériterait de la part de la Commission des éclaircissements.

RPA, 201-6-56743, Alugate IV, Jean Loyette, Xavier de Roux, Memoire en reponse de Pechiney Ugine Kuhlmann à la Communication des griefs de la Commission des Communautés Européennes en date du 11 septembre 1978.

16  Fear, 'Cartels'.

17  Ronald H. Coase, 'The Nature of Firm', *Economica*, New Series, vol. 4, no. 16, 1937, 386–405. See also Oliver E. Williamson, 'The Economics of Organization: The Transaction Cost Approach', *American Journal of Sociology*, vol. 87, no. 3, 1981, 548–577.

18  RZA, Emanuel Meyer, Alusuisse at the eve of the 1980s, 1979. See also Knoepfli, *From Dawn to Dusk*.

19  Dominique Barjot, 'Performances, Strategies and Structures: Pechiney (1949–1970). The Lessons of the Accounting Analysis, First Results', in Barjot, Bertilorenzi (eds), *Aluminium*, 221–232.

20  See for instance, Niall Ferguson, Charles Maier, Erez Manela, Daniel J. Sargent (eds), *The Shock of the Global: The 1970s in Perspective*. London: Belknap Press, 2010.

21  Charles Barthel, Ivan Kharaba, Philippe Mioche (eds), *Les Mutations de la Sidérurgie Mondiale du XXe Siècle à nos Jours: The Transformations of the World Steel Industry from the XXth Century to the Present*. Brussels: Peter Lang, 2014.

22  Joseph Stiglitz, *Globalisation and its Discontents*. New York: Norton & Co., 2002, 173–175. Also some information passed through the press: 'Don't Call it a Cartel, But World Aluminum has Forged New Order', *Wall Street Journal*, 9 June 1994, 28–30.

23  NARA, RG 60, General Records of the Department of Justice, box 128, Anne K. Bingaman to the Attorney General, Memorandum, Re: International Aluminum Memorandum of Understanding, 14 June 1994. This archive document was disclosed to me thanks to a FOIA (Freedom of Information Act) procedure.

24  Stiglitz, *Globalisation*, 175.

25  Nnamdi Anyadike, *Aluminium: The Challenges Ahead*. Cambridge: Woodhead, 2002, 1–14.

26  For instance (not exhaustive), Christopher Harding, *Regulating Cartels in Europe: A Study of Legal Control of Corporate Delinquency*. New York: Oxford University Press, 2003. Emmanuel Combe, *Cartels et Ententes*. Paris: Presses Universitaires de France, 2004. Brendan J. Sweeny, *The Internationalisation of Competition Rules*. New York: Routledge, 2009. MacGowan, *Antitrust Revolution in Europe*. Mark S. LeClair, *Cartelization, Antitrust and Globalization in US and Europe*. New York: Routledge, 2010. Gerber, *Global Competition*.

27  Charles S. Maier, *In Search of Stability: Explorations in Political Economy*. Cambridge: Cambridge University Press, 1988.

28  About the 'financiarisation', see (not exhaustive), Michel Aglietta, Antoine Rébérioux, *Dérives du Capitalisme Financier*. Paris: Albin Michel, 2004. Jürgen Bischoff, *Zukunft des Finanzmarkt-Kapitalismus: Strukturen, Widersprüche, Alternativen*. Hamburg: VSA Verlag, 2006. Luciano Gallino, *Finanzcapitalismo: La Civiltà del del Denaro in Crisi*. Torino: Einaudi, 2011. Focused on the reshaping of the nexus between European public powers and private enterprises, see also Bastiaan Von Apeldoom, *Transnational Capitalism and the Struggle over European Integration*. New York: Routledge, 2002.

29 See for instance, Elina Kuorelahti, 'Boom, Depression and Cartelisation: Swedish and Finnish Timber Export Industry 1918–1921', *Scandinavian Economic History Review*, vol. 63, no. 1, 2015, 45–68. Cerretano, 'European Cartels'.

30 With these words, Benjamin described Paul Klee's picture, Angelus Novus, Walter Benjamin, 'Theses about the Philosophy of History', in *Illuminations*, edited by Hannah Arendt. London: Schocken Books, 1969, 259.

31 UGD, 347/10/7/13, American Metal Market Forum, notes by J.S. Bridgeman, 30 October 1978.

# Bibliography

Abelshauser, Werner. *Deutsche Wirtschaftsgeschichte seit 1945*. Munich: Beck, 2004.

Adebayo, Adekeye and Kaye Whiteman (eds). *The EU and Africa: From Eurafrique to Afro-Europe*. London: Hurst, 2012.

Aglietta, Michel and Antoine Rébérioux. *Dérives du Capitalisme Financier*. Paris: Albin Michel, 2004.

AIAG. *Die Anlage der Aluminium-Industrie-Actien-Gesellschaft*. Schaffhausen: Brodtmann'sche Buchdruckerei, 1890.

AIAG. *Geschichte der Aluminium-Industrie-Aktien-Gesellschaft Neuhausen 1888–1938*. Zurich: Gebr. Fretz AG, 1942.

Akiyama, Takamasa (ed.). *Commodity Markets Reforms: Lessons of Two Decades*. New York: World Bank Publications, 2001.

Alacevich, Michele. *The Political Economy of the World Bank: The Early Years*. Stanford CA: Stanford University Press and the World Bank, 2009.

Aldrich, Henry R. and Jacob Schmuckler. *Prices of Ferroalloys, Nonferrous Metals and Rare Metals*. Washington DC: United States War Industries Board, 1919.

Allart, Henri. *Traité des Brevets d'Invention*. Paris: Albert Rousseau, 2 vols, 1885.

Amatori, Franco. 'Italy: The Tormented Rise of Organizational Capabilities between Government and Families', in *Big Business and the Wealth of Nations*, edited by Alfred D. Chandler, Franco Amatori, Takashi Hikino. Cambridge: Cambridge University Press, 1997, 246–276.

Amatori, Franco. 'The Fascist Regime and Big Business: The Fiat and Montecatini Cases', in *Enterprise in the Period of Fascism in Europe*, edited by Harold James, Jakob Tanner. Aldershot: Ashgate, 2002.

Amatori, Franco and Bruno Bezza (eds). *Montecatini, 1888–1966: Capitoli di Storia di una Grande Impresa*. Bologna: Il Mulino, 1990.

Andersen, Stine. *The Enforcement of EU Law: The Role of the European Commission*. Oxford: Oxford University Press, 2012.

Anderson, Robert J. 'Germany's Aluminum Economy', *Iron Age*, 20 June 1940, 40–44.

André, Louis. *Aristide Bergès, une Vie d'Innovateur: De la Papeterie à la Houille Blanche*. Grenoble: Presses Universitaires de Grenoble, 2013.

André, Louis. 'Les stratégies des papeteries des Alpes face à l'aluminium, 1888–1914', in Dominique Barjot, Marco Bertilorenzi (eds), *Aluminium: Du Métal de Luxe au Métal de Masse. From Luxury Metal to Mass Commodity (XIXe–XXe Siècles)*. Paris: Presses de l'Université Paris-Sorbonne, 2014, 63–76.

Anyadike, Nnamdi. *Aluminium: The Challenges Ahead*. Cambridge: Woodhead, 2002.

Arndt, Heinz Wolfgang. *The Economic Lessons of Nineteen-Thirties*. London: Oxford University Press, 1944.

Arnold, Thurman W. *Cartels or Free Enterprise?* Washington DC: Public Affairs Press, 1945.

Atsé, David. *Commodity Futures Trading and International Market Stabilization.* Uppsala: Acta Universitatis Upsaliensis, 1986.

Attali, Jacques. *Un Homme d'Influence: Sir Siegmund G-Warburg, 1902–1982.* Paris: Fayard, 1985, 377–378.

Ball, Simon. 'The German Octopus: The British Metal Corporation and the Next War, 1914–1939', *Enterprise and Society*, vol. 5, no. 3, 2004, 451–489.

Ballande, Laurence. 'Prix de Cartels et prix de Concurrence: Etude Statistique Relative aux Métaux non Ferreux', in *Les Ententes Internationales de Matières Premières*, edited by William Oualid. Paris: Société des Nations, 1938, 13–32.

Barbezat, Daniel. 'Cooperation and Rivalry in the International Steel Cartel, 1926–1933', *Journal of Economic History*, vol. 49, no. 2, June 1989, 435–447.

Barbezat, Daniel. 'A Price for Every Product, Every Place: The International Steel Export Cartel, 1933–39', *Business History*, vol. 33, no. 4, 1991, 70–86.

Barjot, Dominique. 'Introduction', in Dominique Barjot (ed.), *International Cartels Revisited: Vues Nouvelles sur les Cartels Internationaux (1880s–1980s).* Caen: Editions du Lys, 1994, 9–70.

Barjot Dominique (ed.). *International Cartels Revisited: Vues Nouvelles sur les Cartels Internationaux (1880s–1980s).* Caen: Editions du Lys, 1994.

Barjot, Dominique. 'Un Nouveau Champ Pionner pour la Recherche Historique: Les Cartels Internationaux (1880–1970)', *Revue d'Allemagne et des Pays de Langue Allemande*, vol. 30, no. 1, 1998, 31–54.

Barjot, Dominique (ed.). *Catching up with America: Productivity Missions and the Diffusion of American Economic and Technological Influence after the Second World War.* Paris: Presses de l'Université Paris-Sorbonne, 2002.

Barjot, Dominique, Olivier Dard, Jean Garrigues, Didier Musiedlak, and Eric Anceau (eds). *Industrie et Politique en Europe Occidentale et aux Etats-Unis (XIXe–XXe siècles).* Paris: Presses de l'Université Paris-Sorbonne, 2006.

Barjot, Dominique. 'Les Cartels, une Voie vers l'Intégration Européenne? Le Role de Louis Loucheur (1872–1931)', *Revue Economique*, vol. 64, no. 6, 2013, 1043–1066.

Barjot, Dominique. 'Cartels et Cartelisation: Des Instruments Contre les Crises?' *Entreprises et Histoire*, no. 76, 2014, 5–19.

Barjot, Dominique. 'Performances, Strategies and Structures: Pechiney (1949–1970). The Lessons of the Accounting Analysis, First Results', in Dominique Barjot, Marco Bertilorenzi (eds), *Aluminium: Du Métal de Luxe au Métal de Masse. From Luxury Metal to Mass Commodity (XIXe–XXe Siècles).* Paris: Presses de l'Université Paris-Sorbonne, 2014, 221–232.

Barjot, Dominique and Marco Bertilorenzi (eds). *Aluminium: Du Métal de Luxe au Métal de Masse. From Luxury Metal to Mass Commodity (XIXe–XXe Siècles).* Paris: Presses de l'Université Paris-Sorbonne, 2014.

Barjot, Dominique and Harm Schröter. 'General Introduction: Why a Special Edition on Cartels?' *Revue Economique*, vol. 64, no. 6, 2013, 957–972.

Barlow, Colin, Sisira Jayasuriya, and Choo Suan Tan. *The World Rubber Industry.* London: Routledge, 1994.

Barthel, Charles, Ivan Kharaba, and Philippe Mioche (eds). *Les Mutations de la Sidérurgie Mondiale du XXe Siècle à nos Jours. The Transformations of the World Steel Industry from the XXth Century to the Present.* Brussels: Peter Lang, 2014.

Baumol, William J. 'Horizontal Collusion and Innovation', *Economic Journal*, vol. 102, no. 410, 1992, 129–137.

Bayer, Wolfran. 'So Geht es … L'alumine pure de Karl Bayer et son Intégration dans l'Industrie de l'Aluminium', *Cahiers d'Histoire de l'Aluminium*, no. 49, 2013, 21–46.

Beauchamp, Christopher. 'Who Invented the Telephone? Lawyers, Patents and the Judgement of the History', *Technology and Culture*, vol. 51, no. 4, 2010, 854–878.

Beaud, Michel, Pierre Danjou, and Jean David, *Une Multinationale Française: Pechiney Ugine Kuhlmann*. Paris: Seuil, 1975.

Becker, Susan. 'The German Metal Traders', in *The Multinational Traders*, edited by Geoffrey Jones. New York: Routledge, 1998, 66–85.

Becker, Susan. *Multinationalität hat Verschiedene Gesichter: Fromen Internationaler Unternehmenstätighkeit der Société Anonyme des Mines et fonderies de Zinc de la Vielle Montagne und der Metallgesellschaft AG*. Stuttgart: Franz Steiner, 1999.

Beltran, Alain, Sophie Chauveau, and Gabriel Galvez-Behar, *Des Brevets et des Marques: Une Histoire de Propriété Industrielle*. Paris: Fayard, 2001.

Benjamin, Walter. 'Theses about the Philosophy of History', in *Illuminations*, edited by Hannah Arendt. London: Schocken Books, 1969, 253–264.

Bennet, Michael K. *International Commodity Stockpiling as an Economic Stabilizer*. New York: Stanford University Press, 1949.

Benning, Elisabeth. 'The Road to Rambouillet and the Creation of the Group of Five', in *International Summitry and Global Governance: The Rise of the G7 and the European Council, 1947–1991*, edited by Emmanuel Mourlon-Droul and Federico Romero. London: Routledge, 2014, 39–63.

Berend, I. and Gy Ranki, 'Die Deutsche Wirtschafliche Expansion und das Ungarische Wirtschaftleben zur Zeit des Zweiten Weltekriegs', *Acta historica Academiae Scientiarum Hungaricae*, vol. 5, 1958, 313–359.

Berge, Wendell. *Cartels: Challenge to a Free World*. Washington DC: Public Affairs Press, 1946.

Berger, Françoise. *La France, l'Allemagne et l'Acier (1932–1952), De la Stratégie des Cartels à l'Élaboration de la CECA*. Unpublished PhD Thesis, Paris-I Panthéon-Sorbonne University, 2000.

Bertilorenzi, Marco. 'The Italian Aluminium Industry: Cartels, Multinationals and the Autarkic Phase, 1917–1943'. *Cahiers d'Histoire de l'Aluminium*, no. 41, 2008, 43–72.

Bertilorenzi, Marco. *Il controllo della sovrapproduzione. I cartelli internazionali nell'industria dell'alluminio in prospettiva storica (1886–1945). Le contrôle de la surproduction. Les cartels internationaux dans l'industrie de l'aluminium en perspective historique (1886–1945)*. PhD thesis, Università degli Studi di Firenze & Université Paris-Sorbonne, 2010.

Bertilorenzi, Marco. 'L'Alliance Aluminium Compagnie, 1931–1939. Organisation et gestion de la branche international de l'aluminium entre Grande Crise et Guerre Mondiale'. In *Contribution à une histoire des cartels en Suisse*, edited by AlainCortat. Neuchatel: Editions d'Alphil – Presses Universitaires Suisses, 2010, 219–253.

Bertilorenzi, Marco. 'From Patents to Industry: Paul Héroult and International Patents Strategies, 1886–1889', *Cahiers d'Histoire de l'Aluminium*, no. 49, 2012, 46–69.

Bertilorenzi, Marco. 'Défendre le Marché Européen de l'Aluminium: Pouvoirs Publics, Diplomatie Industrielle et Trade Associations (1953–1975)', in *Formes et Moyens d'Action des Organisations Patronales dans la Sphère Publique*, edited by Danièle Fraboulet, Clotilde Druelle-Korn, Pierre Vernus. Rennes: Presses Universitaire de Rennes, 2013, 289–303.

Bertilorenzi, Marco. 'Big Business, Inter-Firm Cooperation and National Governments: The International Aluminium Cartel, 1886–1939', in *Organizing Global Technology Flows: Institutions, Actors, and Processes*, edited by Pierre-Yves Donzé, Shigehiro Nishimura. London, Routledge, 2014, 108–125.

Bertilorenzi, Marco. 'Business, Finance, and Politics: The Rise and Fall of International Aluminium Cartels, 1914–45', *Business History*, vol. 56, no. 2, 2014, 236–269.

Bertilorenzi, Marco. 'Alufinance & Trade Ltd: Cartelisation and Financial Regulation in the European Aluminium Industry during the 1970s', in *Aluminium: Du Métal de Luxe au Métal de Masse. From Luxury Metal to Mass Commodity (XIXe–XXe Siècles)*, edited by Dominique Barjot, Marco Bertilorenzi. Paris: Presses de l'Université Paris-Sorbonne, 2014, 171–188.

Bertilorenzi, Marco. 'Legitimating the International Cartels Movement: League of Nations, International Chamber of Commerce, and the Survey of International Cartels', in *Regulating Competition: Cartel Registers in the Twentieth Century World*, edited by Susanna Fellman, Martin Shahannan. London: Routledge, forthcoming 2015.

Bertilorenzi, Marco and Philippe Mioche. 'Between Strategy and Diplomacy: History of Alumina Alternative Technologies (1900s–1980s)', *Cahiers d'Histoire de l'Aluminium*, no. 51, 2013, 43–63.

Bianchi, Bruna. 'L'Economia di Guerra a Porto Marghera: Produzione, Occupazione, Lavoro, 1935–1945', in *La Resistenza nel Veneziano: La Società Veneziana tra Fascismo, Resistenza, Repubblica*, edited by Giannantonio Paladini and Maurizio Reberschak. Venezia: Istituto veneto per la storia della resistenza, 1985, 167–169.

Bischoff, Jürgen. *Zukunft des Finanzmarkt-Kapitalismus: Strkturen, Widersprüche, Alternativen.* Hamburg: VSA Verlag, 2006.

Bitsch, Marie-Thérèse and Gérard Bossuat (eds). *L'Europe Unie et l'Afrique: De l'Idée d'Eurafrique à la Convention de Lomé I.* Brussels: Bruylant, 2005.

Board of Trade. *Safeguarding of Industries, Report of the Committee on Aluminium Hollow-Ware.* London, HMSO, 1925.

Board of Trade. *Survey of International Cartels and Internal Cartels*, 2 vols. London: Board of Trade, 1944–1946.

Bocquentin, Jacques. 'La Fabrication de l'Aluminium par l'Électrolyse', in, *Histoire de la Technique de la Production d'Aluminium*, edited by Paul Morel. Grenoble: Presses Universitaires de Grenoble, 1991, 21–130.

Bonfils, René. 'Pechiney au Pays des Soviets: Le Contrat Russe de 1930', *Cahiers d'Histoire de l'Aluminium*, no. 23, 1998, 29–41

Bonfils, René. 'Pechiney au Pays des Vikings, 1912–1958', *Cahiers d'Histoire de l'Aluminium*, no. 27, 2000/2001, 18–42.

Bonfils, René. 'Pechiney en Espagne, 1925–1985', *Cahiers d'Histoire de l'Aluminium*, no. 38–39, 2007, 77–101.

Borkin, Joseph. 'The Aluminum Battle', in *Germany's Master Plan: The Story of Industrial Offensive*, edited by Joseph Borkin, Charles A. Welsh. New York: Sloan Long, 1943, 203–222.

Borkin, Joseph and Charles A. Welsh. *Germany's Master Plan: The Story of Industrial Offensive.* New York: Sloan Long, 1943.

Born, Karl Erich. *International Banking in the 19th and 20th Century.* New York: Leamington, 1983.

Born, Karl Erich. *Internationale Kartellierung einer Neuen Industrie: Die Aluminium-Association 1901–1915.* Munich: Berg, 1994.

Brault, Thierry. 'L'Introduction de l'Aluminium au London Metal Exchange (1978): Cause ou Effet de la Transformation du Marché Mondial?' *Cahiers d'Histoire de l'Aluminium*, no. 40, 2008, 31–43.

Broder, Albert. 'L'Expansion Internationale de l'Industrie Allemande dans le Dernier Tiers du XIXe Siècle: Le Cas de l'Industrie Électrique', *Relations Internationales*, no. 29, 1982, 65–87.

Brodley, Joseph F. 'Joint Ventures and Antitrust Policy', *Harvard Law Review*, vol. 95, no. 7, 1982, 1521–1590.

Brusse, Wendy Asbeck and Richard T. Griffiths, 'L'European Recovery Program e i Cartelli: Una Indagine Preliminare', *Studi Storici*, vol 37, no. 1, 1999, 41–67.

Bryan, Ford R. *Henry's Lieutenants*. Detroit: Great Lakes Books, 1993.

Burhop, Carsten and Thorsten Lubbers. 'The Design of Licensing Contracts: Chemicals, Pharmaceuticals, and Electrical Engineering in Imperial Germany', *Business History*, vol. 54, no. 4, 2012, 574–593.

Bussière, Eric. 'La SDN, les Cartels et l'Organisation Économique de l'Europe entre les Deux Guerres', in Dominique Barjot (ed.), *International Cartels Revisited: Vues Nouvelles sur les Cartels Internationaux (1880s–1980s)*. Caen: Editions du Lys, 1994, 273–283.

Bussière, Eric. 'La Concurrence', in *La Commission Européenne. Mémoires d'une institution*, edited by the European Commission. Brussels: Commission Européenne, 2007, 315–329.

Buxbaum, Hannah L. 'German Legal Culture and the Globalization of Competition Law: A Historical Perspective on the Expansion of Private Antitrust Enforcement', *Berkeley Journal of International Law*, vol. 23, no. 2, 2005, 474–495.

Cailluet, Ludovic. *Stratégies, Structures d'Organisation et Pratique de Gestion de Pechiney des Années 1880 à 1971*. Unpublished PhD Thesis, Lyon III University, 1995.

Cailluet, Ludovic. *Chedde: Un Siècle d'Industrie au Pays du Mont-Blanc*. Grenoble: Presses Universitaires de Grenoble, 1997, 27–28.

Cailluet, Ludovic. 'L'Impact de la Première Guerre Mondiale et le Rôle de l'Etat dans l'Organisation de la Branche et des Entreprises', in *Industrialisation et Sociétés en Europe Occidentale de la Fin du XIXe Siècle à nos Jours: L'Âge de l'Aluminium*, edited by Ivan Grinberg, Florence Hachez-Leroy. Paris: Armand Colin, 1997, 95–105.

Cailluet, Ludovic. 'The British Aluminiun Industry, 1945–1980s: Chronicles of a Death Foretold?' *Accounting Business and Financial History*, vol. 11, no. 1, 2001, 79–97.

Cailluet, Ludovic and Matthias Kipping. 'Ménage à Trois: Alcan in Spain, 1950s to 1980s', *Cahiers d'Histoire de l'Aluminium*, no. 44–45, 2010, 79–106.

Cameron, Rondo and B.I. Bovykin, *International Banking 1870–1914*. Oxford: Oxford University Press, 1991.

Campbell, Bonnie K. *Les Enjeux de la Bauxite: La Guinée Face aux Multinationales de l'Aluminium*. Montréal: Presse Universitaire de Montréal, 1983.

Campbell, Duncan C. *Global Mission: The History of Alcan*, 3 vols. Don Mills: Ontario Publishing, 1985–1992.

Cannadine, David. *Mellon: An American Life*. London: Allen Lane, 2006.

Carbonell, Mauve. *De la Guerre à l'Union de l'Europe: Itinéraires Luxembourgeois*. Berlin: Peter Lang, 2014.

Caron, François. *Les Brevets: Leur Utilisation en Histoire des Techniques et de l'Économie*. Paris: IHMC-CNRS, 1985.

Caron, François. *La Dynamique de l'Invention: Changement Technique et Changement Social (XVIe–XXe Siècle)*. Paris: Gallimard, 2010.

Carr, Charles. *Alcoa: An American Enterprise*. New York: Rinehart, 1952.

Casson, Mark. 'Multinational Monopolies and International Cartels', in *The Economic Theory of the Multinational Enterprise*, edited by Mark Casson, Peter J. Buckley. London: Macmillan, 1985, 61–97.

Casson, Mark (ed.). *Multinationals and World Trade: Vertical Integration and the Division of Labour in World Industries*. New York: Routledge, 2011.

Centre des Nations Unies sur les société transnationales. *Les Société Transnationales dans l'Industrie de Production de l'Aluminium à Partir de la Bauxite*. New York: United Nations, 1982.

Cerretano, Valerio. 'European Cartels and Technology Transfer: The Experience of the Rayon Industry, 1920 to 1940', *Zeitschrift für Unternehmensgeschichte*, vol. 56, no. 2, 2011, 206–224.

Cerretano, Valerio. 'European Cartels, European Multinationals and Economic De-globalisation: Insights from the Rayon Industry, c. 1900–1939', *Business History*, vol. 54, no. 4, 2012, 594–622.

Chadeau, Emmanuel. *De Bériolt à Dassault: Histoire de l'Industrie Aéronautique en France, 1900–1950*. Paris: Fayard, 1987.

Chalmin, Philippe. *Traders and Merchants: Panorama of International Commodity Trading*. New York: Taylor & Francis, 1987.

Chamberlin, Edward. *The Theory of Monopolistic Competition: A Re-orientation of the Theory of Value*. London: Harvard University Press 1933.

Chandler, Alfred Dupont. *Scale and Scope: The Dynamics of Industrial Capitalism*. Cambridge MA: Belknap Press, 1994.

Chickering, Roger. *Imperial Germany and the Great War, 1914–1918*. London: Cambridge University Press, 2004.

Clavert, Frédéric. *Hjalmar Schacht, Financier et Diplomate (1930–1950)*. Brussels: Peter Lang, 2009.

Coase, Ronald H. 'The Nature of Firm', *Economica*, New Series, vol. 4, no. 16, 1937, 386–405

Coates, Austin. *The Commerce in Rubber: The First 250 years*. Oxford: Oxford University Press, 1987.

Cohen, Jerome B. *Japan's Economy in War and Reconstruction*. Minneapolis MN: University of Minnesota Press, 1949.

Collier, James E. 'Aluminium Industry of Europe', *Economic Geography*, vol. 22, no. 2, 1946, 75–108.

Combe, Emmanuel. *Cartels et Ententes*. Paris: Presses Universitaires de France, 2004.

Cooper, Richard N., Robert Z. Lawrence, Barry Bosworth, and Hendrik S. Houthakker, 'The 1972–75 Commodity Boom', *Brookings Papers on Economic Activity*, vol. 1975, no. 3, 1975, pp. 671–723.

Coppolaro, Lucia. *The Making of a World Trading Power: The European Economic Community in the GATT Kennedy Round Negotiations (1963–1967)*. Farnham: Ashgate, 2013.

Corea, Gamani. *Taming Commodity Markets: The Integrated Programme and Common Fund in UNCTAD*. Manchester: Manchester University Press, 1992.

Cortat, Alain. *Un Cartel Parfait. Réseaux, R&D et Profits dans l'Industrie Suisse des Cables*. Neuchatel: Éditions Alphil – Presses Universitaires Suisses, 2009.

Cottenier, Jo. *La Société Générale, 1822–1992*. Brussels: EPO, 1989.

Cottier, Thomas. Panagiotis Delimatsis, *The Prospects of International Trade Regulation: From Fragmentation to Coherence*. London: Cambridge University Press, 2011.

Cowles, Alfred. *The True Story of Aluminum Industry*. Chicago IL: Henry Regnery Co., 1958.

Cuff, Robert D. *The War Industries Board: Business–Government Relations during World War I*. Baltimore MD: Johns Hopkins University Press, 1973.

Cuff, Robert D. 'Stockpiles and Defense Escalation, 1965–1968', *Public Historian*, vol. 9, no. 4, 1987, 44–64.

Däbritz, Walther. *Fünfzig Jahre Metallgesellschaft, 1881–1931*, Frankfurt am Main: Metallgesellschaft, 1931.

Darling, Alan S. 'The Light Metals, Aluminium and Magnesium', in *An Encyclopedia of the History of Technology*, edited by Ian McNeil. London: Routledge, 2002, 102–120.

Davis, Joseph S. 'Experience under Intergovernmental Commodity Agreements, 1902–45', *Journal of Political Economy*, vol. 54, no. 3, 1946, 193–220.

De Luigi, Guido, Edgar Meyer, and Andrea Saba. 'Industrie, Pollution et Politique: La "Zone Noire" de la Società Italiana dell'Alluminio dans la Province de Trente

(1928–1938)', in *Industrialisation et Sociétés en Europe Occidentale de la Fin du XIXe Siècle à nos Jours: L'Âge de l'Aluminium*, edited by Ivan Grinberg, Florence Hachez-Leroy. Paris: Armand Colin, 1997, 314–323.

De Rousiers, Paul. *Syndicats Industriels des Producteurs en France et à l'Étranger: Trust – Cartells – Comptoirs*. Paris: Armand Colin, 1901.

De Syon, Guilleaume. *Zeppelin! Germany and the Airship, 1900–1939*. Baltimore MD: Johns Hopkins University Press, 2002.

De Vries, Benjamin W. *Of Mettle and Metal: From Court Jews to World-wide Industrialists*. Amsterdam: Neha, 2000.

Deschamps, Etienne. 'L'Eurafrique à l'Épreuve des Faits: La Belgique, la France et les Projets de Barrages Hydroélectriques en Afrique (1954–1958)', in *L'Europe Unie et l'Afrique: De l'Idée d'Eurafrique à la Convention de Lomé I*, edited by Marie-Thérèse Bitsch, Gérard Bossuat. Brussels: Bruylant, 2005, 165–184.

Dore, M.H.I. 'Mineral Taxation in Jamaica: An Oligopoly Confronts Taxes on Resource Rents and Prevails', *American Journal of Economic and Sociology*, vol. 46, no. 2, April 1987, 179–203.

Dux, Carl. *Die Aluminium-Industrie-Aktiengesellschaft Neuhausen und ihre Konkurrenz-Gesellschaften*. Luzern: Albins, 1911.

Eddy, Arthur Jerome. *New Competition: An Examination of the Conditions underlying the Radical Change that is taking Place in the Commercial and Industrial World – The Change from a Competitive to a Cooperative Basis*. New York: Appleton & Co., 1912.

Edgerton, David. *Warfare State: Britain 1920–1970*. Cambridge: Cambridge University Press, 2006.

Edwards, Corwin D. *Economic and Political Aspects of International Cartels: A Study made for the Subcommittee on War Mobilization of the Committee on Military Affairs of United States Senate*. Washington DC: Government Printing Office, 1944.

Edwards, Corwin D., Theodore J. Kreps, Ben W. Lewis, Frits Machlup, and Robert P. Terill, *A Cartel Policy for the United Nations*. New York: Columbia University Press, 1945.

Edwards, Junius. *The Immortal Woodshed: The Story of the Inventor who Brought Aluminum to America*. New York: Dodd Mead, 1955.

Edwards, Junius D., Francis C. Frary, and Zay Jeffries. *The Aluminum Industry*, 2 vols. New York: McGraw-Hill, 1930.

Engle, Nathaniel H., Homer E. Gregory, and Robert Mosse, *Aluminum: An Industrial Marketing Survey*. Chicago IL: Irwin, 1945.

Escard, Jean. *L'Aluminium dans les Industries: Métal pur et Alliages*. Paris: Dunod et Pinat, 1918.

Evenett, Simon J., Margaret C. Levenstein, and Valerie Suslow, 'International Cartel Enforcement: Lessons from the 1990s', *World Economy*, vol. 24, no. 9, 2001, 1221–1245.

Falck, Oliver, Christian Gollier, and Ludger Woessmann (eds). *Industrial Policy for National Champions*. Cambridge MA, London: MIT Press, 2011.

Fear, Jeffrey. 'Cartels and Competition: Neither Markets nor Hierarchies', *Harvard Business School Discussion Paper*, no. 07-011, 2006.

Fear, Jeffrey. 'Cartels', in *The Oxford Handbook of Business History*, edited by Geoffrey Jones, Jonathan Zeitlin. London: Oxford University Press, 2008, 268–292.

Ferguson, Niall. *High Financer: The Lives and the Time of Siegmund Warburg*. London: Penguin, 2010.

Ferguson, Niall, Charles Maier, Erez Manela, and Daniel J. Sargent (eds). *The Shock of the Global: The 1970s in Perspective*. London: Belknap Press, 2010.

Ferrand, Louis. 'Le Problème des Prix dans la Métallurgie de l'Aluminiun', *Revue d'Économie Politique*, vol. 51, March/April 1937, 299–332.

Ferrand, Louis. *Histoire de la Science et des Techniques de l'Aluminium et ses Développements Industriels*, 2 vols. Paris: Unpublished Manuscript, 1960.

Figuerola, F.I. and C.L. Gilbert. 'Price Volatility and Marketing Methods in the Non-ferrous Metal Iindustry', *Journal of Financial Economy*, vol. 27, no. 3, 2001, 169–177.

Figuerola, F.I. and C.L. Gilbert. 'Price Discovery in the Aluminium Market', *Journal of Future Markets*, vol. 25, no. 10, 2005, 967–988.

Fletcher, W. Miles III. 'Japanese Banks and National Economic Policy, 1920–1936', in *The Role of Banks in the Interwar Economy*, edited by Harold James, Hakan Lindgren, Alice Teichova. New York: Cambridge University Press, 1991, 25–71.

Fligstein, Niel. *The Transformation of Corporate Control*. London: Harvard University Press, 1990.

Freyer, Tony A. *Antitrust and Global Capitalism*. London: Cambridge University Press, 2005.

Friedel, Robert. 'A New Metal! Aluminum in its 19th-Century Context'. In *Aluminum by Design*, edited by Sarah Nichols, Elisabeth Agro, Elizabeth Teller. Pittsburgh PA: Carnegie Museum of Art, 2000.

Friedman, Milton. 'Commodity-Reserve Currency', *Journal of Political Economy*, vol. 59, no. 3, 1951, 203–232.

Frøland, Hans Otto and Jan Thomas Kobberrød. 'The Norwegian Contribution to Göring's Megalomania: Norway's Aluminium Industry during World War II', *Cahiers d'Histoire de l'Aluminium*, no. 42–3, 2009, 131–149.

Frøland, Hans Otto. 'Nazi Planing and Aluminium Industry', in *Alan S. Milward and a Century of Eurpean Change*, edited by Fernando Guirao, Frances M.B. Lynch, Sigfrido Ramirez Pérez. London: Routledge, 2012, 168–188.

Frøland, Hans Otto and Mats Ingulstad (eds). *From Warfare to Welfare: Business–Government Relations in the Aluminium Industry*. Trondheim: Akademika, 2012.

Fumian, Carlo. 'Commodity Trading', in *The Palgrave Dictionary of Transnational History*, edited by Akira Iriye, Pierre-Yves Saunier. New York: Palgrave Macmillan, 2009, *ad vocem*.

Gagliardi, Alessio. *L'Impossibile Autarchia: La Politica Economica del Fascismo e il Ministero Scambi e Valute*. Milan: Rubattino, 2006.

Galambos, Louis. *Competition and Cooperation: The Emergence of a National Trade Association*. Baltimore MD: Johns Hopkins University Press, 1966.

Galambos, Louis. 'The American Trade Association Movement revisited', in *Trade Associations in Business History: Proceedings of the Fuji Conference*, edited by Hiroaki Yamazaki, Matao Miyamoto. Tokyo: Tokyo University Press, 1988, 121–135.

Gallino, Luciano. *Finanzcapitalismo: La Civiltà del Denaro in Crisi*. Torino: Einaudi, 2011.

Galvez-Behar, Gabriel. *La République des Inventeurs: Propriété et Organisation de l'Innovation en France (1791–1922)*. Rennes: Presses Universitaires de Rennes, 2008.

Geiger, Till and Dennis Kennedy. *Regional Trade Blocs, Multilateralism, and the GATT: Complementary Paths to Free Trade?* London: Pinter, 1996.

Gendron, Robin S., Mats Ingulstad, and Espen Storli (eds), *Aluminium Ore: The Political Economy of the Global Bauxite Industry*. Toronto: University of British Culumbia Press, 2013.

Gerber, David J. *Global Competition: Law, Markets, and Globalisation*. New York: Oxford University Press, 2010.

Gèze, F. 'La Bataille des Matières Premières Minérales: Multinationales contre Pays Producteurs', *Tiers-Monde*, vol. 66, 1976, 289–306.

Gibson-Jarvie, Robert. *The London Metal Exchange, a Commodity Market*. New York: Woodhead-Faulkner, 1989.

Gignoux, Claude Joseph. *Histoire d'une Entreprise Française*. Paris: Hachette, 1955.

Gilbert, Christopher L. 'Modelling Market Fundamentals: A Model of the Aluminium Market', *Journal of Applied Econometrics*, vol. 10, no. 4, 1995, 385–410.

Gillingham, John. *Coal, Steel, and the Rebirth of Europe, 1945–1955: The Germans and French from Ruhr Conflict to Economic Community*. Cambridge: Cambridge University Press, 1991.

Girvan, Norman P. 'Transnational Corporations and Non-fuel Primary Commodities in Developing Countries', *World Development*, vol. 15, no. 5, 1987, 713–740.

Godfrey, John F. *Capitalism at War: Industrial Policy and Bureaucracy in France, 1914–1918*. Leamington: Berg, 1987.

Golzio, Silvio. *L'Industria dei Metalli in Italia*. Torino: Einaudi, 1942.

Gomperts, Rudi. 'Le Combat Perdu pour le Prix de l'Énergie: L'Histoire de l'Usine d'Électrolyse Pechiney Nederland (1969–2011)'. *Cahiers d'Histoire de l'Aluminium*, no. 51, 2013, 79–95.

Gordon, Richard L. (ed.), *Energy, Markets, and Regulation*. Cambridge: MIT Press, 1987.

Gourvish, Terry (ed.). *Business and Politics in Europe, 1900–1970: Essays in Honour of Alice Teichova*. Cambridge: Cambridge University Press, 2003.

Graham, Benjamin. *Storage and Stability: A Modern ever Normal Granary*. New York: McGraw-Hill, 1937.

Graham, Margaret. 'Aluminum and the Third Industrial Revolution', in *The Third Industrial Revolution in Global Business*, edited by Giovanni Dosi, Louis Galambos. Cambridge: Cambridge University Press, 2013, 220–228.

Graham, Margaret B.W. 'R&D and Competition in England and the United States: The Case of the Aluminum Dirigible', *Business History Review*, vol. 62, no. 2. 1988, 261–285.

Graham, Margaret B.W. and Bettye H. Pruitt. *R&D for Industry: A Century of Technical Innovation at Alcoa*. Cambridge MA: Harvard University Press, 1990.

Graham, Ronald. *The Aluminium Industry and the Third World Multinational Corporations and Underdevelopment*. London: Zed Press, 1982.

Grard, Charles. *Aluminium and its Alloys: Their Properties, Thermal, Treatment and Industrial Application*. London: Constable, 1921.

Grinberg, Ivan. *Aluminium: Light at Heart*. Paris, Gallimard, 2009.

Grinberg, Ivan and Florence Hachez-Leroy (eds). *Industrialisation et Sociétés en Europe Occidentale de la Fin du XIXe Siècle à nos Jours: L'Âge de l'Aluminium*. Paris: Armand Colin, 1997.

Grinberg, Ivan and Philippe Mioche. *Aluminium de Grèce: L'Usine aux Trois Rivages*. Grenoble: Presses Universitaires de Grenoble, 1996.

Gross, Martin. 'A Semi Strong Test of the Efficiency of the Aluminium and Copper Markets at the LME', *Journal of Futures Markets*, vol. 8 no. 1, 1988, 67–77.

Guarneri, Felice. *Battaglie Economiche fra le due Guerre*. Milano: Garzanti, 1953.

Guillet, Léon. 'Un Nouvel Alliage d'Aluminium: L'Alpax', *Le Génie Civil*, 1923, 32–37.

Guillet, Léon. 'Les Progrès et les Avantages de la Construction Métallique en Aviation', *Revue de l'Aluminium*, no. 1, 1924.

Gupta, Bishnupriya. 'Why did Collusion Fail? The Indian Jute Industry in the Inter-War Years', *Business History*, vol. 47, no. 4, 2005, 532–552.

Hachez-Leroy, Florence. 'Le Cartel International de l'Aluminium du Point de Vue des Sociétés Françaises, 1901–1940', in Dominique Barjot (ed.), *International Cartels Revisited: Vues Nouvelles sur les Cartels Internationaux (1880s–1980s)*. Caen: Editions du Lys, 1994, 153–162.

Hachez-Leroy, Florence. 'Stratégie et Cartels Internationaux, 1901–1981', in *Industrialisation et Sociétés en Europe Occidentale de la Fin du XIXe Siècle à nos Jours: L'Âge de l'Aluminium*, edited by Ivan Grinberg, Florence Hachez-Leroy. Paris: Armand Colin, 1997, 164–174.

Hachez-Leroy, Florence. *L'Aluminium français: La Création d'un Marché, 1911–1981*. Paris: CNRS Editions, 1999.

Hachez-Leroy, Florence. *L'Europe de l'Aluminium (1945–1975)*. Special Issue no. 1, *Cahiers d'Histoire de l'Aluminium*, 2003.

Hachez-Leroy, Florence. 'La Construction Européenne et ses Conséquences sur l'Industrie Française de l'Aluminium', in Florence Hachez-Leroy (ed.), *L'Europe de l'Aluminium (1945–1975)*. Special Issue no. 1, *Cahiers d'Histoire de l'Aluminium*, 2003, 22–34.

Hachez-Leroy, Florence. 'Enjeux et Stratégies Internationaux dans le Secteur de l'Aluminium en Afrique (1960–2010)', in *L'Afrique Indépendante Dans Le Système International*, edited by Emilia Robin-Hivert, Georges-Henri Soutou. Paris: Presses de l'Université Paris-Sorbonne, 2012, 261–281.

Hall, Peter and David Soskice (eds). *Varieties of Capitalism: The Institutional Foundations of Comparative Advantage*. Oxford: Oxford University Press, 2001.

Hamon, Claude. *Le Groupe Mitsubishi (1870–1990): Du Zaibatsu au Keiretsu*. Paris: Harmattan, 1995.

Hannah, Leslie. *The Rise of Corporate Economy: The British Experience*. London: Johns Hopkins University Press, 1976.

Hara, Terushi. 'La Conférence Économique Internationale de 1927 et ses Effets sur la Formation des Cartels Internationaux', in Dominique Barjot (ed.), *International Cartels Revisited: Vues Nouvelles sur les Cartels Internationaux (1880s–1980s)*. Caen: Editions du Lys, 1994, 265–272.

Harding, Christopher. *Regulating Cartels in Europe: A Study of Legal Control of Corporate Delinquency*. New York: Oxford University Press, 2003.

Hardouin Duparc, Olivier. 'Alfred Wilm et les Débuts du Duralumin', *Cahiers d'Histoire de l'Aluminium*, no. 34, 2005, 63–76.

Hart, Albert G., Nicholas Kaldor, Jan Tinbergen, *The Case for an International Commodity Reserve Currency*. Geneva: UNCTAD, 1963.

Hausman, William, Peter Hertner, and Mira Wilkins. *Global Electrification: Multinational Enterprise and International Finance in the History of Light and Power, 1878–2007*. Cambridge MA: Cambridge University Press, 2008.

Hayes, Peter. *Industry and Ideology: IG Farben in the Nazi Era*, Cambridge: Cambridge University Press, 1987.

Herfindahl, Orris C. *Copper Costs and Prices: 1870–1957*. Baltimore MD: Johns Hopkins University Press, 1957.

Héroult, Paul. *L'Aluminium à Bon Marché*. Saint-Etienne: Théollier & Thomas, 1900.

Hexner, Ervin. *The International Steel Cartel*. Chapel Hill NC: North Carolina University Press, 1943.

Hillman, John. *The International Tin Cartel*. London: Routledge, 2010.

Holloway, Steven K. *The Aluminium Multinationals and the Bauxite Cartel*. London: Macmillan, 1988.

Homze, Edward L. *Arming the Luftwaffe: The Reich Air Ministry and the German Aircraft Industry 1919–39*. London: University of Nebraska Press, 1976.

Hove, Jon Olav. 'The Volta River Project and Decolonization, 1945–1957: The Rise and Fall of an Integrated Aluminum Project', in *Aluminium Ore: The Political Economy of the Global Bauxite Industry*, edited by Robin S. Gendron, Mats Ingulstad, Espen Storli. Toronto: University of British Columbia Press, 2013, 185–209.

Hughes, Justin. 'A Short History of "Intellectual Property" in Relation to Copyright', *Cardozo Law Review*, vol. 33, no. 4, 2012, 1293–1340.

Hughes, Thomas Parke. *Networks of Powers: Electrification in Western Society, 1880–1930*. Baltimore MD: Johns Hopkins University Press, 1993.

Huré, Valérie. *Les Organisations Européennes de l'Aluminium: Premiers Contacts avec des Associations à la Recherche de leur Identité (1953–1984)*, Unpublished Master Thesis, Artois University, 1996.

Husson, Édouard. 'Idéee Européenne, Europe Allemande, ordre Nouveau Nazi', in *Penser et Construire l'Europe (1919–1992)*, edited by Dominique Barjot. Paris: Editions Sedes, 2007, 109–125.

Ingulstad, Mats. 'Cold War and Hot Metal: American Strategic Materials Policy, the Marshall Plan and the Loan to the Sunndal Smelter', *Cahiers d'Histoire de l'Aluminium*, Special Issue no. 2, 2007, 125–145.

Ingulstad, Mats. 'We want Aluminium not Excuses! Antitrust and Business–Government Partnership in the American Aluminium Industry, 1917–1957', in *From Warfare to Welfare: Business–Government Relations in the Aluminium Industry*, edited by Hans Otto Frøland, Mats Ingulstad. Trondheim: Akademika, 2012, 33–68.

Ingulstad, Mats. 'National Security Business? The United States and the Creation of the Jamaican Bauxite Industry', in *Aluminium Ore: The Political Economy of the Global Bauxite Industry*, edited by Robin S. Gendron, Mats Ingulstad, Espen Storli. Toronto: University of British Columbia Press, 2013, 107–137.

Ionescu, George. *The European Alternatives: An Inquiry into the Policies of the European Community*. London. Sijthoff & Noordhoff, 1979.

Jabara, Carley Michael. 'Five Kopecks for Five Kopecks: Franco-Soviet Trade Negotiations, 1928–1939', *Cahiers du Monde Russe et Soviétique*, vol. 33, no. 1, 1992, 23–57.

James, Harold. *International Monetary Cooperation since Bretton Woods*. New York: Oxford University Press, 1996.

James, Harold. *Rambouillet, 15. November 1975: Die Globalisierung der Wirtschaft*. Munich: Dtv, 1997.

James, Harold. *The End of Globalisation: Lessons from the Great Depression*. London: Harvard University Press, 2001.

James, Harold. *The Nazi Dictatorship and the Deutsche Bank*. Cambridge: Cambridge University Press, 2004.

James, Harold and Jakob Tanner (eds). *Enterprise in the Period of Fascism in Europe*. Aldershot: Ashgate & Turner: 2002.

James, Harold, Hakan Lindgren, and Alice Teichova (eds). *The Role of Banks in the Interwar Economy*. New York: Cambridge University Press, 1991.

Jensen-Eriksen, Niklas. 'The Cold War in Energy Markets: British Efforts to Contain Soviet Oil Exports to Non-communist Countries 1950–1965', in *Le Petrole et la Guerre: Oil and War*, edited by Alain Bertrand. Brussels: Peter Lang, 2012, 191–208.

Johnson, Chalmers. *Miti and the Japanse Miracle: The Growth of Industrial Policy, 1925–1975*. Stanford CA: Stanford University Press, 1985.

Kalecki, Michal. 'The World Production of Aluminium', originally published in 1928, now in *Collected Works of Michal Kalecki: Volume VI, Studies in Applied Economics 1927–1941*, edited by Jerzy Osiatynski. Oxford: Clarendon Press, 1996, 8–10.

Kane, Edward J. 'Good Intentions and Unintended Evil: The Case Against Selective Credit Allocation', *Journal of Money, Credit and Banking*, vol. 9, no. 1, February 1977, 55–69.

Kanji, Ishii. 'Japan', in *International Banking 1870–1914*, edited by Rondo Cameron, B.I. Bovykin. Oxford: Oxford University Press, 214–232.

Kelly, T.D. and Matos, G.R., Aluminum, Copper, Tin, and Zinc Statistics, *Historical Statistics for Mineral and Material Commodities in the United States*, U.S. Geological Survey Data Series 140, available online at http://pubs.usgs.gov/ds/2005/140/ (accessed 4 December 2013).

Keynes, John Maynard. 'The Policy of Government Storage of Food-Stuffs and Raw Materials', *Economic Journal*, vol. 48, no. 191, 1938, 449–460.

Kindleberger, Charles Poor. *The World in Depression, 1929–1939*. London: Penguin, 1973.

Kipping, Matthias and Ove Bjarnar (eds). *The Americanisation of European Business: The Marshall Plan and the Transfer of US Management Models*. New York: Routledge, 1998.

Kipping, Matthias. 'The Changing Nature of the Business–Government Relationship in Western Europe after 1945', *European Yearbook of Business History*, no. 2, 1999, 35–51.

Kipping, Matthias. *La France et les Origines de l'Union Européenne: Intégration Économique et Compétitivité Internationale*. Paris: Cheff, 2002.

Kipping, Matthias and Ludovic Cailluet. 'Mintzberg's Emergent and Deliberate Strategies: Tracking Alcan's Activities in Europe, 1928–2007', *Business History Review*, no. 84, 2010, 79–104.

Knauer, Manfred. 'A Difficult New Beginning : The Race of the German Aluminium Industry to Catch up with the Competition in the 1950s and 1960s', *Cahiers d'Histoire de l'Aluminium*, no. 51, 2013, 65–77.

Knauer, Manfred. 'Les "Trente Glorieuses" de l'Industrie Européenne de l'Aluminium dans le Boom Économique de l'Après-guerre', in Florence Hachez-Leroy (ed.), *L'Europe de l'Aluminium (1945–1975)*. Special Issue no. 1, *Cahiers d'Histoire de l'Aluminium*, 2003, 13–23.

Knetsch, Stefanie. *Das Konzerneigene Bankinstitut der Metallgesellschaft im Zeitraum von 1906 bis 1928: Programmatischer Anspruch und Realisierung*. Munich: Franz Steiger Verlag, 1998.

Knoepfli, Adrian. *From Dawn to Dusk: Alusuisse, Swiss Aluminium Pioneer from 1930 to 2010*. Zurich: Jetz, 2010.

Kobrak, Christian and Paul Hansen (eds). *European Business, Dictatorship, and Political Risk, 1920–1945*. New York: Berghahn, 2004.

Koskoff, David E. *The Mellons: Chronicle of America's Richest Family*. New York: Crowell, 1978.

Kossmann, Wilfried. *Über die Wirtschaftliche Entwicklung der Aluminiumindustrie*. Strasbourg: Straßburger Druckerei, 1911.

Köster, Roman. 'Zeppelin, Carl Berg and the Development of Aluminium Alloys for German Aviation (1890–1930)', *Cahiers d'Histoire de l'Aluminium*, no. 50, 2014, 72–87.

Köster, Roman. 'Aluminium for the Airship: Zeppelin and the Adaptation of a "New" Construction Material', in *Aluminium: Du Métal de Luxe au Métal de Masse. From Luxury Metal to Mass Commodity (XIXe–XXe Siècles)*, edited by Dominique Barjot, Marco Berti-lorenzi. Paris: Presses de l'Université Paris-Sorbonne, 2014, 77–97.

Kreps, Theodore J. 'Cartels, a Phase of Business Haute Politique', *American Economic Review*, vol. 35, no. 2, 1945, 297–311.

Kronstein, Heinrich. *The Law of International Cartels*. London: Cornell University Press, 1973.

Krug, John A. and James Boyd. *The Japanese Aluminum Industry: Prepared for the Department of Interior*. Washington DC: Department of Interior, 1949.

Kudo, Akira, and Terushi Hara (eds), *International Cartels in Business History*. Tokyo: Tokyo University Press, 1993.

Kudo, Akira and Terushi Hara. 'Introduction', in *International Cartels in Business History*, edited by Akira Kudo, Terushi Hara. Tokyo: Tokyo University Press, 1993, 1–24.

Kuorelahti, Elina. 'Boom, Depression and Cartelisation: Swedish and Finnish Timber Export Industry 1918–1921', *Scandinavian Economic History Review*, vol. 63, no. 1, 2015, 45–68.

Lammers, Clemens (ed.). *Ententes Internationales, Proceedings of the Congress of Berlin of the International Chamber of Commerce.* Paris: International Chamber of Commerce, 1937.

Lamoreux, Noemi R., Kenneth L. Solokoff, and Dhanoos Sutthiphisal, 'Patent Alchemy: The Market for Technology in the US History', *Business History Review,* vol. 87, no. 1, 2013, 3–38.

Lanthier, Pierre. 'ALCAN de 1945 à 1975: Les Voies Incertaines de la Maturation', in Florence Hachez-Leroy (ed.), *L'Europe de l'Aluminium (1945–1975).* Special Issue no. 1, *Cahiers d'Histoire de l'Aluminium,* 2003, 63–84.

Laparra, Maurice. 'The Aluminium False Twins: Charles Martin Hall and Paul Héroult's First Experiments and Technological Options', *Cahiers d'Histoire de l'Aluminium,* no. 48, 2012, 84–105.

Laparra, Maurice and Ivan Grinberg, *Alucam, un Destin Africain: 50 Ans d'Aluminium au Cameroun, 1957–2007.* Aix en Provence: REF.2C, 2007.

Larrue, Jacques. *Fria en Guinée: Première usine d'Alumine en Terre d'Afrique.* Paris: Karthala, 1997.

Laur, Francis. *De l'Accaparement: Essai Doctrinal.* Paris: Publications scientifiques et industrielles, 1900.

Le Roux, Muriel. *L'Entreprise et la Recherche: Un Siècle de Recherche Industrielle à Pechiney.* Paris: Editions Rive Droite, 1998.

LeClair, Mark S. *Cartelization, Antitrust and Globalization in US and Europe.* New York: Routledge, 2010.

Lefevre-Dalbin, Sylvie. 'L'idée d'Eurafrique dans les Années 1950: L'Exemple des Projets Économique Franco-allemands'. In *L'Europe Communautaire au Défi de la Hiérarchie,* edited by Bernard Brunetau, Yousef Cassis. Brussels: Peter Lang, 2007, 81–96.

Lejeal, Adolphe. *L'Aluminium le Manganèse, le Baryum, le Strontium, le Calcium et le Magnésium.* Paris: Baillière 1894.

Lesclous, René. 'Nuclear Power and the Revival of Primary Aluminium Production in Europe', in Florence Hachez-Leroy (ed.), *L'Europe de l'Aluminium (1945–1975).* Special Issue no. 1, *Cahiers d'Histoire de l'Aluminium,* 2003, 29–35.

Lesclous, René. *Histoire des Sites Producteurs d'Aluminium: Les Choix Stratégiques de Pechiney, 1892–1992.* Paris: Presses des Mines, 2004.

Leslie, Christopher L. 'Trust, Distrust and Antitrust', *Texas Law Review,* vol. 82, no. 3, 2004, 571–580.

Levenstein, Margaret. 'Price Wars and the Stability of Collusion: A Study of the Pre-World War I Bromine Industry', *Journal of Industrial Economics,* vol. 45, no. 2, 1997, 117–137.

Levenstein, Margaret and Valerie Suslow, 'What Determines Cartel Success?' *Journal of Economic Literature,* vol. 46, 2006, 43–95.

Levenstein, Margaret and Valerie Suslow, 'Breaking Up is Hard to Do: Determinants of Cartel Duration', *Journal of Law and Economics,* vol. 54, no. 2, 2011, 455–494.

Liefmann, Robert. *Schutzzoll und Kartelle,* Jena: Fischer, 1903.

Liefmann, Robert. *Cartels, Concerns and Trusts.* London: Europa, 1932.

Liepmann, Heinrich. *Tariff Levels and the Economic Unity of Europe: An Examination of Tariff Policy, Export Movements and the Economic Integration of Europe, 1913–1931.* London: Allen & Unwin, 1938.

Lindner, Stephan H. *Inside IG Farben: Hoechst during the Third Reich.* New York: Cambridge University Press, 2008.

Litvak, Isaiah A. and Christopher J. Maule, 'Cartel Strategies in the International Aluminum Industry', *Antitrust Bulletin. Journal of American and Foreign Antitrust and Trade Regulation,* vol. 20, no. 3, 1975, 641–663.

Litvak, Isaiah A. and Christopher J. Maule, 'The International Bauxite Agreement: A Commodity Cartel in Action', *International Affairs*, vol. 56, no. 2, 1980, 296–314.

Litvak, Isaiah A. and Christopher J. Maule, 'Assessing Industry Concentration: The Case of Aluminium', *Journal of International Business Studies*, vol. 15, no. 1, 1984, 97–104.

Love, Philiph H. *Andrew W. Mellon, His Life and His Work*. Baltimore MD: Heath Cogging, 1929.

McGowan, Lee. *The Antitrust Revolution in Europe: Exploring the European Commission's Cartel Policy*. Cheltenham: Edward Elgar, 2010.

Maier, Charles S. *In Search of Stability: Explorations in Political Economy*. Cambridge: Cambridge University Press, 1988.

Maizels, Alfred. *Commodity in Crisis: The Commodity Crisis of the 1980s and the Political Economy of International Commodity Policies*. Oxford: Clarendon Press, 1992.

Marlio, Louis. *A Short War through American Industrial Superiority*, Washington DC: Brookings Institution, 1941 (Brookings Pamphlets no. 28).

Marlio, Louis. *Will Electric Power be a Bottleneck?* Washington DC: Brookings Institutition, 1942.

Marlio, Louis. *Le Liberalisme Social*. Paris: Fortin, 1946.

Marlio, Louis. *The Aluminum Cartel*. Washington DC: Brookings Institution, 1947.

Marquet, Yannick. *Négoce International des Matières Premières*. Paris: Eyrolles, 1992.

Marshall, Luitgard. *Aluminium: Metal der Moderne*. Munich: Oekom, 2008.

Mason, Edward S. *Controlling World Trade: Cartels and Commodity Agreements*. New York: McGraw-Hill, 1946, 262–268.

Massell, David. *Amasing Power: J.B. Duke at Saguenay River, 1897–1927*. Quebec City: McGill-Queen's University Press, 2000, 176–177.

Michels, Rudolf K. *Cartels, Combines and Trusts in Post-war Germany*. New York: Columbia University Press, 1928.

Migani, Guia. *La France et l'Afrique Sub-saharienne, 1957–1963: Histoire d'une Décolonisation entre Idéaux Eurafricains et Politique de Puissance*. Brussels: Peter Lang, 2008.

Mikdashi, Zuhayr. 'Aluminum', in *Big Business and the State: Changing Relations in Western Europe*, edited by Raymond Vernon. Cambridge: Harvard University Press, 1974, 170–195.

Milward, Alan S. *The Fascist Economy in Norway*. Oxford: Clarendon Press, 1972, 171.

Milward, Alan S. *The European Rescue of the Nation-state*. London: Routledge, 2000.

Minet, Adolphe. *L'Aluminium: Fabrication, Emploi, Alliages*. Paris: Tignol, 1890.

Minniti, Fortunato. 'La Realtà di un Mito: L'Industria Aeronautica durante il Fascismo', in *L'Aeronautica Italiana: Una Storia del Novecento*, edited by Paolo Ferrari. Milano: Franco Angeli, 2004, 43–67.

Mioche, Philippe. *Le Plan Monnet: Génèse et Élaboration, 1941–1947*. Paris: Presses de l'Université Paris-Sorbonne, 1987.

Mioche, Philippe. *L'Alumine à Gardanne de 1893 à nos Jours : Une Traversée Industrielle en Provence*. Grenoble: Presses Universitaires de Grenoble, 1994.

Mioche, Philippe. 'La Vitalité des Ententes Sidérurgiques en France et en Europe de l'Eentre-deux-guerres à nos Jours', in *International Cartels Revisited: Vues Nouvelles sur les Cartels Internationaux (1880s–1980s)*, edited by Dominique Barjot. Caen: Editions du Lys, 1994, 119–128.

Mioche, Philippe. *Les Cinquantes Années de l'Europe du Charbon et de l'Acier*. Luxembourg: Commission Européenne, 2004.

Mioche, Philippe. 'Contribution à l'Histoire du Procédé Bayer: Le Procédé à Gardanne, 1893–2012', in *Aluminium: Du Métal de Luxe au Métal de Masse. From Luxury Metal to Mass Commodity (XIXe–XXe Siècles)*, edited by Dominique Barjot, Marco Bertilorenzi. Paris: Presses de l'Université Paris-Sorbonne, 2014, 27–62.

Montarsolo, Yves. *L'Eurafrique, Contrepoint de l'Idée d'Europe: Le Cas Français de la Fin de la Deuxième Guerre Mondiale aux Négociations des Traités de Rome.* Aix en Provence: Publications de l'Université de Provence, 2010.

Morel, Paul (ed.). *Histoire Technique de la Production d'Aluminium: Les Apport Français au Développement International d'une Industrie.* Grenoble, Presses Universitaires de Grenoble, 1991.

Morel-Lopez, Miguel and José M. O'Kean. 'Rothschilds' Strategies in International Non-ferrous Metals Markets, 1830–1940', *Economic History Review*, vol. 67, no. 3, 2014, 720–749.

Mori, Giogio. 'Le Guerre Parallele: L'Industria Elettrica in Italia nel Periodo Della Grande Guerra (1914–1919)', *Studi Storici*, vol. 14, 1973, 292–372.

Morsel, Henri. 'Contribution à l'Histoire des Ententes Industrielles (à Partir d'un Example, l'Industrie des Cclorates)', *Revue d'Histoire Économique et Sociale*, vol. 54, no. 1, 1976, 118–129.

Morsel, Henri. 'Pechiney et le Plan Marshall', in *Le Plan Marshall et le Relèvement Économique de l'Europe*, edited by René Girault, Maurice Lévy-Leboyer. Paris: Comité pour l'Histoire économique et financière de la France, 1991, 291–298.

Morsel, Henri. 'Louis Marlio, Position Idéologique et Comportement Politique d'un Dirigeant d'une Grande Entreprise dans la Première Moitié du XX$^e$s', in *Industrialisation et Sociétés en Europe Occidentale de la Fin du XIXe Siècle à nos Jours: L'Âge de l'Aluminium*, edited by Ivan Grinberg, Florence Hachez-Leroy. Paris: Armand Colin, 1997, 106–122.

Mouak, Prosper. *Le Marché de l'Aluminium: Structuration et Analyse du Comportement des Prix au Comptant et à Terme au London Metal Exchange.* Unpublished PhD Thesis: Université d'Orléans, 2010.

Moulton, Harold G. and Louis Marlio, *The Control of Germany and Japan.* Washington DC: Brookings Institution, 1944.

Muller, Charlotte. *Light Metals Monopoly.* New York: Columbia University Press, 1946.

Müller, Christian. *Arbeiterbewegung und Unternehmerpolitik in der Aufstrebenden Industriestadt: Baden nach der Gründung der Firma Brown Boveri 1891–1914.* Zurich: Buchdruckerei Wanner, 1974.

Mureşan, Stefan Sorin. *Social Market Economy: The Case of Germany.* Berlin: Springer, 2014.

Nappi, Carmine. *Commodity Market Controls: A Historical Review.* Toronto: Lexington, 1978.

Nappi, Carmine. *L'Aluminium.* Paris: Economica, 1994.

Nappi, Carmine. 'L'Industrie Internationale de l'Aluminium, 1980–2006: Changements Structurels et Perspectives', *Cahiers d'Histoire de l'Aluminium*, no. 37, 2006, 27–51.

Nappi, Carmine. 'L'Industrie Internationale de l'Aluminium: Changements Structurels et Perspectives, 1970–2020', in *Aluminium: Du Métal de Luxe au Métal de Masse. From Luxury Metal to Mass Commodity (XIXe–XXe Siècles)*, edited by Dominique Barjot, Marco Bertilorenzi. Paris: Presses de l'Université Paris-Sorbonne, 2014, 151–170.

Neher, Frederich L. *Kupfer, Zinn, Aluminium.* Leipzig: Wilhem Goldmann Verlag, 1940.

Nocentini, Sara. 'Building the Network: Raw Materials Shortages and the Western Bloc at the Beginning of the Cold War, 1948–1951', *Business History On-line*, vol. 2, 2004.

North, Douglass C. *Institutions, Institutional Change and Economic Performance.* Cambridge: Cambridge University Press, 1990.

Notz, William. 'Export Trade Problems and an American Foreign Trade Policy', *Journal of Political Economy*, vol. 26, no. 2, 1918, 105–124.

Nussbaum, Helga. 'International Cartels and Multinational Enterprises', in, *Multinational Enterprise in Historical Perspective*, edited by Maurice Levy-Léboyer, Helga Nussbaum, Alice Teichova. Cambridge: Cambridge University Press, 1980, 131–144.

O'Neill, Helen. *A Common Interest in a Common Fund: Proposals for New Structures in International Commodity Markets.* United Nations: Geneva, 1977.

Okalla Bana, Edy-Claude. 'L'Électrification du Cameroun par EDF et Pechiney (1945–1965)', *Cahiers d'Histoire d'Aluminium*, no. 35, 2005–2006, 54–73.

Olson, Mancur. *The Logic of Collective Action: Public Goods and the Theory of Group.* Cambridge MA: Harvard University Press, 1965.

Overy, Richard. *War and Economy in the Third Reich.* Oxford: Clarendon Press, 1994.

Overy, Richard. *The Air War, 1939–1945.* Dulles: Potomac Press, 2005.

Paquier, Serge. *Histoire de l'Électricité en Suisse: La Dynamique d'un Petit Pays Européenne, 1876–1939.* Geneva: Passé et Présent, 1998.

Pascaud, Claude. 'Le Développement du Procédé Hall-Héroult et son Accompagnement par la Propriété Industrielle (1886–1994)', *Cahiers d'Histoire de l'Aluminium*, no. 20, 1997, 61–86.

Peck, Merton. *The World Aluminum Industry in a Changing Energy Era.* Washington DC: Resources for the Future, 1988.

Penrose, Edith. *The Economic of International Patent System*, Baltimore MD: Johns Hopkins University Press, 1951.

Perchard, Andrew. *Aluminiumville: Government, Global Business and the Scottish Highlands.* Lancaster: Crucible Books, 2012.

Perron, Regine. *Histoire du Multilateralisme: L'Utopie du Siècle Américain de 1918 à nos Jours.* Paris: Presses de l'Université Paris-Sorbonne, 2014.

Perugini, Mario. *Il Farsi di una Grande Impresa: La Montecatini tra le due Guerre Mondiali.* Milan: Franco Angeli, 2014.

Peterson. S. Warren and Ronald E. Miller (eds), *Hall-Héroult Centennial: First Century of Aluminum Process Technology 1886–1986.* Warrendale: Metallurgical Society, 1986.

Petri, Rolf. 'Acqua Contro Carbone : Elettrochimica e Indipendenza Energetica Italiana degli anni Trenta', *Italia Contemporanea*, no. 168, 1987, 63–96.

Petri, Rolf. 'L'Industrie Italienne de l'Aluminium à la Veille de la Seconde Guerre Mondiale', in *Industrialisation et Sociétés en Europe Occidentale de la Fin du XIXe Siècle à nos Jours: L'Âge de l'Aluminium*, edited by Ivan Grinberg, Florence Hachez-Leroy. Paris: Armand Colin, 1997, 143–152.

Petrick, Fritz. *Der 'Leichtmerallausbau Norwegen' 1940–1945: Eine Studie zur deutschen Expansions – Un Okkupationspolitik in Nordeuropa.* Frankfurt am Main: Peter Lang, 1992.

Pezet, Anne. *La Décision d'Investissement Industriel: Le Cas de l'Aluminium*, Paris: Economica, 2000.

Pindyck, Robert S. 'Inventories and the Short-Run Dynamics of Commodity Prices', *RAND Journal of Economics*, vol. 25, no. 1, 1994, 141–159.

Pitaval, Robert. 'Les Ententes dans l'Industrie Mondiale de l'Aluminum', *Journal du Four Électrique*, vol. 46, no. 3, 1937, 83–85.

Pitaval, Robert. *Histoire de l'Aluminium: Metal de la Victoire.* Paris: Publications minières et métallurgiques, 1946.

Plumpe, Gottfried. *Die I.G. Farbenindustrie AG. Wirtschaft, Technik und Politik, 1904–1945.* Berlin: Duncker & Humblot, 1990.

Pohl, Hans. 'Die Wiederaufnahme des Metallhandels durch die Metallgesellschaft nach dem zweiten Weltkrieg', in *Wirtschaft, Unternehmen, Kreditwesen, Soziale Probleme: Ausgewählte Aufsätze*, edited by Hans Pohl. Munich: Franz Steiner Verlag, 2005.

Pohl, Manfred. *VIAG Aktiengesellschaft 1923–1998: Vom Staatsunternehmen zum Internationalen Konzern.* Munich: Piper, 1998.

Polanyi, Karl. *The Great Transformation.* New York: Ferrar & Rinehart, 1944.

Pollard, Robert A. *Economic Security and the Origins of the Cold War, 1945–1950.* New York: Columbia University Press, 1985.

Political and Economic Planning. *Report on International Trade: A Survey of Problems affecting the Expansion of International Trade, with Proposal for the Development of British Commercial Policy and Export Mechanism.* London: PEP, 1937.

Pope, Franklin L. and Walter T. Barnard, *Aluminium and its Alloys: A Report.* New York, 1888.

Porter, Cathrine. 'Mineral Deficiency versus Self-Sufficiency in Japan', *Far Eastern Survey*, vol. 5, no. 2, January 1936, 9–14.

Porter, Michael. *Competitive Strategy: Techniques for Analyzing Industries and Competitors.* New York, Free Press.

Pose, Alfred. *Notice sur la Vie et les Travaux de Louis Marlio (1878–1952).* Paris: Firmin-Didot, 1955.

Pribram, Karl. *Cartel Problems: An Analysis of Collective Monopolies in Europe with American Application.* New York: Brookings Institution, 1935.

Py, Gaëtan. *Progrès de la Métallurgie et leur Influence sur l'Aéronautique.* Paris: Mémoires de la Société des ingénieurs civils de France, 1928, 19–21.

Raffalovich, Arthut. *Trusts, Cartels & Syndicats*, Paris: Librairie Guillaumin, 1903.

Ramirez Pérez, Sigfrido M. and Sebastian van der Scheur, 'The Evolution of the Law on Article 85 and 86 EEC: Ordoliberalism and its Keynesian challenge', in *The Historical Foundations of EU Competition Law*, edited by Kiran Klaus Patel, Heike Schweitzer. New York: Oxford University Press, 2013, 19–52.

Rauch, Ernst. *Internationale Kartellierung einer neuen Industrie: Die Aluminium-Association 1901–1915.* Munich: Berg, 1994.

Rauh, Cornelia. *Schweizer Aluminium für Hitlers Krieg? Zur Geschichte der Alusuisse 1918–1950.* Munich: Beck, 2009.

Richards, Joseph William. *Aluminium: Its History, Occurrence, Properties, Metallurgy and Applications, including its Alloys.* London: Martson & Co., 1896.

Rinde, Harald. 'The Powerhouse of Europe: The Growth of the Norwegian Aluminium Industry, 1945–1970', in Florence Hachez-Leroy (ed.), *L'Europe de l'Aluminium (1945–1975).* Special Issue no. 1, *Cahiers d'Histoire de l'Aluminium*, 2003, 37–44.

Ritchie, Sebastian. *Industry and Air Power: The Expansion of British Aircraft Production, 1935–1941.* London: Frank Cass, 1997.

Robert-Hauglustaine, Anne-Catherine. 'Le Carbure de Calcium et l'Acétylène, de Nouveaux Produits pour de Nouvelles Industries, 1885–1914', in *Des Barrages, des Usines et des Hommes: L'Industrialisation des Alpes du Nord entre Ressources Locales et Apports Extérieurs*, edited by Hervé Joly, Alexandre Giandou, Muriel Le Roux, Ludovic Cauilluet. Grenoble: Presses Universitaires de Grenoble, 2002, 101–116.

Roberts, John G. *Mitsui: Three Centuries of Japanese Business.* New York: Cambridge University Press, 1973.

Rollings, Neil and Matthias Kipping. 'Private Transnational Governance in the Heyday of the Nation-State: The Council of European Industrial Federations (CEIF)', *Economic History Review*, vol. 61, no. 2, 2008, 409–431.

Rousseau, Joseph. *Applications de l'Electricité à la Métallurgie: Fabrication de l'Aluminium.* Paris: Berger-Levrault, 1893.

Ruch, Dominic. *Une Route Ardue pour un si Léger Métal: 100 Ans d'Aluminium Martigny AS.* Zurich: Orell Fussli, 2009, 35–37.

Rudell, Alexander. *Die Zulässogkeit Horizontaler Empfehlungen nach Deutschem und EWG-Kartellrecht.* Düsseldorf: Carl Heymanns Verlag KG, 1973.

Rumbold, Walter G. *Bauxite and Aluminium: Monographs on Mineral Resources with Special Reference to the British Empire.* London: Imperial Institute, 1925.

Saito, Hiroshi. 'Japan's Foreign Trade', *Annals of American Academy of Political and Social Science*, vol. 186, July 1936, 178–182.

Sandvik, Pål Thonstad. 'European, Global or Norwegian? The Norwegian Aluminium Companies, 1946–2005', in *The European Enterprise: Historical Investigation into a Future Species*, edited by Harm Schröter. Berlin: Springer, 2008, 241–253.

Schatzberg, Eric. *Wings of Wood, Wings of Metal: Culture and Technical Choice in American Airplane Materials 1914–1945.* Princeton NJ: Princetown University Press, 1999.

Schatzberg, Eric. 'Symbolic Culture and Technological Change: The Cultural History of Aluminum as an Industrial Material', *Enterprise and Society*, vol. 4, no. 2, 2003, 226–271.

Schmeizer, Matthias. 'The Crisis before the Crisis: The "Problems of Modern Society" and the OECD, 1968–1974', *European Review of History*, no. 9, vol. 6, 2012, 999–1020.

Schmeizer, Matthias. 'A Club of the Rich to Help the Poor? The OECD, "Development", and the Hegemony of Donor Countries', in *International Organizations and Development, 1945 to 1990*, edited by Marc Frey, Soenke Kunkel, Corinna Unger. Basingstoke: Palgrave Macmillan, 2014, 171–195.

Schmookler, Jacob. *Invention and Economic growth*, Cambridge MA: Harvard University Press, 1966.

Schröter, Harm. 'Cartels as a Form of Concentration in Industry: The Example of the International Dyestuffs Cartel from 1927 to 1939', in *German Yearbook on Business History*, edited by Hans Pohl, Rudolf Bernd. Berlin: Springer, 1988, 113–144.

Schröter, Harm. 'The International Potash Syndicate', in *International Cartels Revisited: Vues Nouvelles sur les Cartels Internationaux (1880s–1980s)*, edited by Dominique Barjot. Caen: Editions du Lys, 1994, 75–92.

Schröter, Harm. 'Cartelisation and Decartelisation in Europe, 1870–1995: Rise and Decline of an Economic Institution', *Journal of European Economic History*, vol. 25, no. 1, 1996, 129–153.

Schröter, Harm. *Americanization of the European Economy: A Compact Survey of American Economic Influence in Europe since the 1800s.* Berlin: Springer, 2005.

Schröter, Harm. 'Das Kartellverbot und Andere Ungereimtheiten: Neue Ansätze in der Internationales Kartellforschung', in *Regulierte Markte: Zünfte und Kartelle. Marchés Régulés. Corporations et Cartels*, edited by Margrit Muller, Heinrich R. Schmidt, Laurent Tissot. Zurich: Chronos, 2011, 199–212.

Schröter, Harm. 'Cartels Revisited: An Overview on Fresh Questions, New Methods, and Surprising Results', *Revue Économique*. vol. 64, no. 6, 2013, 989–1010.

Schwob, Claude. 'Keynes, Meade, Robbins et l'Organisation Internationale du Commerce', *L'Actualité Économique*, vol. 83, no. 2, 2007, 255–283.

Segreto, Luciano. 'Elettricità ed Economia in Europa', in *Storia dell'Industria Elettrica in Italia: Vol. 1, Le Origini, 1882–1914*, edited by Giorgio Mori. Rome-Bari: Laterza, 1990, 697–750.

Segreto, Luciano and Ben Wubs, 'Resistance of the Defeated: German and Italian Big Business and the American Antitrust Policy, 1945–1957', *Enterprise and Society*, vol. 15, no. 2, 2014, 307–336.

Seidel, Katja. *The Process of Politics in Europe: The Rise of European Elites and Supranational Institutions.* London: Tauris, 2010.

Sheller, Mimi. *Aluminum Dreams: The Making of Light Modernity.* Cambridge: MIT Press, 2014.

Smith, George David. *From Monopoly to Competition: The Transformation of Alcoa, 1888–1986.* Cambridge MA: Cambridge University Press, 1988.

Smith, Robert J. *The Bouchayers of Grenoble and French Industrial Entrerprise, 1850–1970.* Baltimore MD: Johns Hopkins University Press, 2001.

Soudain, Paul. *Historique Technique et Économique de la Fabrication de l'Alumine*, Paris: Compagnie Pechiney, May 1970, 13–15.

Spar, Debora. *The Cooperative Edge: The International Politics of International Cartels*. London: Cornell University Press, 1994.

Spaventa, Luigi and Franco Cotula (eds). *La Politica Monetaria tra le due Guerre, 1919–1935*. Rome-Bari: Laterza, 1993.

Stigler, George. 'A Theory of Oligopoly', *Journal of Political Economy*, no. 72, 1964, 44–61.

Stiglitz, Joseph. *Globalisation and its Discontents*. New York: Norton & Co., 2002.

Stocking, George W. and Myron W. Watkins, *Cartels or Competition? The Economics of International Controls by Business and Government*. Washington DC: Twentieth Century Fund, 1948.

Stokes, Raymond G. *Opting for Oil: The Political Economy of Technological Change in the West German Chemical Industry 1945–1961*. Cambridge: Cambridge University Press, 1994.

Stokes, Raymond G. 'From the IG Farben Fusion to the Establishment of BASF AG (1925–1952)', in *German Industry and Global Enterprise. BASF: The History of a Company*, edited by Werner Abelshauser, Wolfgang von Hippel, Jeffrey Allan Johnson, Raymond G. Stokes. New York: Cambridge University Press, 2004, 206–301.

Storli, Espen. 'The Norwegian Aluminium Industry, 1908–1940: Swing Producers in the Hands of the International Oligopoly?' *Cahiers d'Histoire de l'Aluminium*, Special Issue 2, 2007, 11–26.

Storli, Espen, 'Trade and Politics: The Western Aluminium Industry and the Soviet Union in the Intewar Period', in *From Warfare to Welfare: Business–Government Relations in the Aluminium Industry*, edited by Hans Otto Frøland, Mats Ingulstad. Trondheim: Akademika, 2012, 69–99.

Storli, Espen. 'Cartel Theory and Cartel Practice: The Case of International Aluminium Cartels, 1901–1940', *Business History Review*, vol. 88, no. 3, 2014, 445–467.

Storli, Espen and David Brégaint, 'The Ups and Downs of a Family Life: Det Norske Nitridaktienselskap, 1912–1976', *Enterprise and Society*, vol. 10, no. 4, 2009, 763–790.

Stuckey, John A. *Vertical Integration and Joint Ventures in the Aluminum Industry*. London: Harvard University Press, 1983.

Suslow, Valerie. 'Cartel Contract Duration: Empirical Evidence from Inter-war Period', *Industrial and Corporate Change*, vol. 14, no. 5, 2005, 705–744.

Suslow, Valerie and Margaret Levenstein. 'What Determines Cartel Success?' *Journal of Economic Literature*, vol. 44, no. 1, 2006, 43–95.

Svennilson, Ingvar. *Growth and Stagnation, in the European Economy*. Geneva: United Nations Economic Commission for Europe, 1954.

Sweeny, Brendan J. *The Internationalisation of Competition Rules*. New York: Routledge, 2009.

Takeuchi, Kenji and Bension Varon, 'Commodity Shortages and Changes in World Trade', *Annals of the American Academy of Political and Social Science*, vol. 420, 1975, 46–59.

Tarring, Trevor. *Corner! A Century of Metal Market Manipulation*. London: Metal Bulletin Books, 1997.

Taylor, Graham D. 'Debate in the United States over the Control of International Cartels, 1942–1950', *International History Review*, vol. 3, no. 3, 1981, 385–398.

Teichova, Alice. *An Economic Background to Munich: International Business and Czechoslovakia, 1918–1938*. London: Cambridge University Press, 1974.

Telesca, Giuseppe. *Il Mercante di Varsavia: Giuseppe Toeplitz: Un Cosmopolita alla Guida della Banca Commerciale Italiana*. Unpublished PhD thesis, Università degli studi di Firenze, 2010.

Thaure, Philippe. *Pechiney? . . . Vendu!* Paris: Presses des mines, 2007.

Tooley, Hunt T. 'The Hindenburg Program of 1916: A Central Experiment in Wartime Planning', *Quarterly Journal of Austrian Economics*, vol. 2, no. 2, 1999, 51–62.

Trebilcock, Clive. '"Spin-Offs" in British Economic History: Armaments and Industry, 1760–1914', *Economic History Review*, vol. 22, no. 3, 1969, 474–490.

Tschierschky, Sigfried. *Etude sur le Nouveau Régime Juridique des Ententes Économiques (Cartels etc.) en Allemagne et en Hongrie, Préparé pour le Comité Économique de la Société des Nations*. Geneva: League of Nations, Doc. E. 529, 1932.

Turnock, David. *The Economy of East Central Europe, 1815–1989: Stages of Transformation in a Peripheral Region*. New York: Routledge, 2006.

Tyson, Jocelyn Pierson. *Grosvenor Porter Lowrey: Thomas Alva Edison's Lawyer*. New York: Topp-Litho, 1978.

UNCTAD, *Etudes sur la Transformation, la Commercalisation et la Distrubution des Produits de Base: La Transformation et la Commercialisation de l'Alumine et de l'Aluminium: Domaines de Coopération Internationale*. New York: United Nations, 1984.

Van Der Wee, Hermann. *La Générale de Banque, 1822–1997: Un Défi Permanent*. Paris: Racine, 1997.

Van Luong, Matthieu Ly. 'L'Aluminium Européen dans les Négociations Commerciales du Kennedy Round', *Cahiers d'Histoire de l'Aluminium*, no. 28, 2001, 43–59.

Von Apeldoom, Bastiaan. *Transnational Capitalism and the Struggle over European Integration*. New York: Routledge, 2002.

Von Steiger, Anne. 'A "German" Firm in France, AIAG during World War One', unpublished working paper, EBHA annual conference, Geneva, 2007.

Wallace, Donald Horace. *Market Control in Aluminum Industry*. Cambridge MA: Cambridge University Press, 1937.

Waller, Spencer Weber. 'The Story of Alcoa: The Enduring Questions of Market Power, Conduct, and Remedy in Monopolization Cases', in *Antitrust Stories*, edited by Eleanor M. Fox, Daniel A. Crane. New York: Foundation Press, 2007, 121–143.

Walrouzet, Laurent. 'The Rise of European Competition Policy, 1950–1991: A Cross-Disciplinary Survey of a Contested Policy Sphere', European University Institute Working Papers, RSCAS 2010/80.

Watkins, Myron W. 'The Aluminum Alliance', in *Cartels in Action: Cases Studies in International Business Diplomacy*, edited by George W. Stocking, Myron W. Watkins. New York: Twentieth Century Fund, 1946, 216–273.

Weiss, Thomas George. *Multilateral Development Diplomacy in UNCTAD: The Lessons of Group Negotiations, 1964–84*. London: Macmillan, 1986.

Wells, Wyatt. *Antitrust and the Formation of the Postwar World*. New York: Columbia University Press, 2002.

Wilkins, Mira. *The History of Foreign Investment in United States to 1914*. Cambridge: Harvard University Press, 1989.

Wilkins, Mira. *The History of Foreign Investment in United States, 1914–1945*. Cambridge: Harvard University Press, 2004.

Willame, Jean-Claude. *Zaïre, l'Épopée d'Inga: Chronique d'une Prédation Industrielle*. Paris: l'Harmattan, 1985.

Williams, Andrew J. *Trading with the Bolsheviks: The Politics of East-West Trade, 1920–39*. Manchester: Manchester University Press, 1992.

Williamson, Oliver E. 'The Economics of Organization: The Transaction Cost Approach', *American Journal of Sociology*, vol. 87, no. 3, 1981, 548–577.

Wolff, Rudolf. *Wolff's Guide to the London Metal Exchange*. London: Metal Bulletin Books, 1980.

Woods, D.W. and J.C. Burrow. *The World Aluminium–Bauxite Market: Policy Implications for the United States.* New York: Charles Rivers Associates, 1980.

Woodward, Richard. *The Organisation for Economic Co-operation and Development (OECD).* New York: Routledge, 2009.

Wurm, Clemens. *Business, Politics and International Relations: Steel, Cotton and International Cartels in British Politics, 1924–1939.* London: Cambridge University Press, 1988, 36–42.

Yergin, Daniel. *The Prize: The Epic Quest for Oil, Money, and Power.* New York: Free Press, 2009.

Zeitlin, Jonathan and Gary Herriger (eds). *Americanization and its Limits: Reworking US Technology and Management in Post-war Europe and Japan.* New York: Oxford University Press, 2000.

# Index

Page numbers in *italics* denote tables, those in **bold** denote figures.